For
Angela, Francesca, Camilla,
and the memory of
Jack, Ellen, and Marisa

Acknowledgements

The book was originally a PhD thesis prepared for the University of Keele under the supervision of the late Professor Michael Akehurst. I valued his assistance enormously. His close reading of the text, critical comments and suggestions for improvement did much to sustain my interest in the subject of minority rights and move my efforts towards a positive conclusion. I very much regret that he is not with us to witness publication. So also my parents, Jack and Ellen Thornberry, and my wife's mother, Marisa Cozzolino, saw the beginning of the work, but not the final product.

I would also like to thank the librarians at Liverpool Public Library, Nick Spalton and Ken Graham of Liverpool Polytechnic, Derek Way of Liverpool University and Patricia Farquhar of the United Nations Centre in London for patient responses to many queries. Thanks are also due to Ben Whitaker, Alan Phillips and Kaye Stearman at Minority Rights Group for valuable background material from their archives. Rodolfo Stavenhagen of The College of Mexico encouraged a broadening of my studies.

My wife and children endured the preparation of the book with patience and encouragement; its completion would have been impossible without them.

P.T.

Contents

PART IV. The Right to Identity

PART V. The Right Not to be Discriminated Against

Abbreviations

AFDI	Annuaire Français de Droit International
AJIL	American Journal of International Law
BYIL	British Year Book of International Law
CERD	International Convention on the Elimination of All Forms of Racial Discrimination
CCPR	International Convenant on Civil and Political Rights
CLP	Current Legal Problems
DR	Decisions and Reports of the European Commission of Human Rights
ECOSOCOR	UN Economic and Social Council Official Records
GAOR	UN General Assembly Official Records
ICJ	International Court of Justice
ICLQ	International and Comparative Law Quarterly
ILM	International Legal Materials
ILO	International Labour Organization
ILR	International Law Reports
LNTS	League of Nations Treaty Series
LQR	Law Quarterly Review
MLR	Modern Law Review
MRG	Minority Rights Group
OAS	Organization of American States
OAU	Organization of African Unity
PCIJ	Permanent Court of International Justice
Procs. ASIL	Proceedings of the American Society of International Law
RDH	Revue des Droits de l'Homme
Recueil des Cours	Recueil des Cours de l'Académie de Droit International
Rev. ICJ	The Review of the International Commission of Jurists
RIAA	Reports of International Arbitral Awards
SCOR	UN Security Council Official Records
UNCIO	United Nations Conference on International Organization
UNTS	United Nations Treaty Series
YBECHR	Year Book of the European Convention on Human Rights
YBILC	Year Book of the International Law Commission
YBUN	Year Book of the United Nations
ZAÖR	Zeitschrift für ausländisches und öffentliches Recht und Völkerrecht

Citations of United Nations documents are taken from these documents, and follow the rules set out in *United Nations Documentation, UN DocOC. ST/LIB/34/Rev.1* (New York, 1981).

1. Introductory Reflections and Scope of the Present Work

The protection of ethnic, religious, and linguistic groups is one of the oldest concerns of international law.[1] The rise of the State system in the sixteenth and seventeenth centuries and the emergence of an international law reflecting that system, necessitated concentration on minority groups. The ideals of national unity, manifested by a centralization of power, a common language, culture, and religion, fundamental to the self-identification of the States, tended to express themselves in intolerant attitudes, and repression of those who were perceived as 'others'. Unity in this context seems to correlate with exclusiveness and there was a natural necessity to regulate some of its consequences. For pragmatic as well as humanitarian reasons, international law has been a protective instrument, because the minorities question has never contained itself entirely within national boundaries. Minorities in some States were majorities in others, and the latter States might assert interest in their co-nationals or co-religionists. Pragmatic wisdom required that this transnational effect did not produce international conflict, hence the instigation of treaty protection among interested Powers. In so far as not all minorities relate to kin States, the mainsprings of international action have also been humanitarian. That the pragmatic and the humanitarian coexist can be seen in the Universal Declaration of Human Rights,[2] the standard-bearer of rights in the present age; the Declaration recites in its preamble that 'it is essential . . . if man is not to be compelled to have recourse, as a last resort, to rebellion against tyranny and oppression, that human rights should be protected by the rule of law.' This is a sensible and practical proposition.

The minorities also concern international law in the second half of the twentieth century. A cursory glance at the spectrum of internal and international disputes reveals that a minority of one kind or another is frequently the focus, which justifies the need for a continuing corpus of rules. One needs only to recall the names of such groups as the Baha'i of Iran, the

---

[1] Useful introductions to the history of protection of minorities include Fouques-Duparc, *La Protection des Minorités de Race, de Langue et de Religion* (Paris: Librarie Dalloz, 1922); Macartney, *National States and National Minorities* (London: OUP, 1934); Modeen, *The International Protection of National Minorities in Europe* (Åbo: Åbo Akademi, 1969); Wintgens, *Der völkerrechtliche Schutz der nationalem, sprachlichen und religiösen Minderheiten* (Stuttgart: Kohlhammer, 1930); Robinson, *Das minoritäten Problem und seine Literatur* (Berlin: W. de Gruyter and Co., 1928); Baron, *Ethnic Minority Rights: Some Older and Newer Trends* (Oxford: OUP, 1985).

[2] UNGA Res. 217A(III), 1948.

Biharis of Bangladesh, the Catholics of Northern Ireland, the Hungarians of Romania, the Kurds in Iraq, Iran, Turkey and Syria, the Miskito Indians of Nicaragua, the Philippine Moslems, the Québécois of Canada, the Tamils of Sri Lanka, and the Sikhs of India, to make the point.[3]

Ethnic, religious, and linguistic differences within States may be of startling complexity: religions divide into sects and denominations, languages branch into dialects, cultures flourish in diverse forms. To describe diversity in terms of a tapestry, or a hundred banners, or a coat of many colours, does inadequate justice to its richness. On closer examination most historical communities turn out to be *complex* communities. The Italy achieved through the efforts of Mazzini, Garibaldi and Cavour on the basis of 'Italianità' reveals major linguistic divisions: besides Italian, French, German and Slovenian are spoken and written languages, as are Albanian, Greek and Ladino. Languages with a closer relationship to Italian include Friulano and Sard, to say nothing of others which may be classified as languages or dialects, and sub-dialects. Besides religions brought by recent immigrants, long established communities of Waldensians, Orthodox and Jews are found in Italy in addition to Roman Catholics. Groups of Roma are scattered throughout Italy, as they are throughout Europe.[4] Smaller and apparently more homogeneous States also reveal complexity. The main ethnic groups in Finland, besides the Finns, are the Swedes and the Lapps. The latter form part of the circumpolar peoples of Eurasia and North America. Within the states bordering the Arctic, a study identified seventy-one different 'circumpolar peoples'.[5]

According to the *Instituto Nacional de Estadistica* of Bolivia, there are five principal ethnic groups among its aboriginal population; Quechua, Aymara, Chiquitano, Chiriguano, and Moxo. Thirty languages are known among these groups but other estimates would assert a higher figure.[6] Italy is a medium sized State; Finland and Bolivia are much smaller in terms of population. While it is not axiomatic that the larger the population, the

---

[3] Concise accounts of these and other minority related disputes may be found in the various reports issued by the Minority Rights Group, London. A number of such reports are referred to in the present work. See also Caratini, *La Force des Faibles* (Paris: Larousse, 1986); Heinz, *Indigenous Populations, Ethnic Minorities and Human Rights* (Berlin: Quorum Verlag, 1988); Sigler, *Minority Rights. A Comparative Analysis* (Westport, Conn. and London: Greenwood Press, 1983); Van Dyke, *Human Rights, Ethnicity, and Discrimination* (Westport, Conn. and London: Greenwood Press, 1985); Wirsing, *Protection of Minorities, Comparative Perspectives* (New York: Pergamon Press, 1981). The present author has compiled 'profiles' of minority situations in some 60 States for the UN University.

[4] Thornberry, *Minorities and Human Rights Law*, Minority Rights Group Report No. 73, Minority Rights Group, London 1987; Monograph 23 prepared by Special Rapporteur Capotorti towards his *Study on the Rights of Persons belonging to Ethnic, Religious and Linguistic Minorities* for the UN Sub-Commission on Prevention of Discrimination and Protection of Minorities, UN Doc E/CN.4/Sub.2/384/Add.1–7, UN Sales No. E.78. XIV.I.

[5] Siuruainen and Aikio, *The Lapps in Finland* (Helsinki: Society for the Promotion of Lapp Culture, 1977).

[6] Capotorti, Monograph 51, see n. 4 above.

more complex the taxonomy, the differentiation in such large population centres as the USSR, India, China, or Indonesia, is on an even more considerable scale, although large States such as Japan may be relatively homogeneous.[7]

In his study of the rights of minorities for the United Nations Sub-Commission on Prevention of Discrimination and Protection of Minorities, Special Rapporteur Capotorti prepared seventy-six country monographs, which describe highly differentiated patterns of ethnicity, language and religion in the States. Another Special Rapporteur for the Sub-Commission, M. Martinez-Cobo, studied the aboriginal populations of thirty-seven States.[8] It may be asserted with confidence that while any and every State in the world may not contain minority groups—ethnic, religious, and linguistic—almost all States do. Many States deny the relevance of the term 'minorities' to their own populations.[9] They do not share the perspective offered to them by the United Nations Secretary-General:

Many nations possess a common language, a common origin, a common culture, a common religion or common folk-ways and traditions. On the other hand, many other nations include substantial numbers of individuals and groups of diverse languages, origins, cultures, religions, or folk-ways and traditions. The fact that a nation belongs to the latter category does not alter its status, for it is what its constituent individuals and groups have in common, rather than what they have alike, that engenders the sense of belonging together, the sentiment of sharing a common destiny and the striving to fulfil a common task, that are the basic ingredients of the nation.[10]

The Secretary-General's memorandum described ways in which minorities originated; this is not a complete taxonomy but serves to indicate that groups may demand different relationships with their host-State. The minority may formerly have (*a*) constituted an independent nation with its own State (or a more or less independent tribal organisation); (*b*) been part of a nation living under its own State, which was segregated from this jurisdiction and annexed to another State; or (*c*) been or may still be, a regional or scattered group which, though bound to the predominant group by certain feelings of solidarity, has not reached even a minimum degree of assimilation with the predominant group.[11] Clearly, groups of type (*a*) may desire a broader range of powers within the State than groups of type (*c*):

[7] Capotorti, Monographs 69, 36, and 57 (USSR, India, Indonesia), see n. 4 above. For China, see *World Minorities in the Eighties* (Minority Rights Group, 1980), 18.

[8] *Study of the Problem of Discrimination against Indigenous Populations*: a detailed study prepared at the UN over a decade by Martinez-Cobo and Willemsen Diaz of the UN Centre for Human Rights. The final volume is available as a UN publication, UN Sales No. E.86.XIV.3. References in the present work are to individual volumes by their UN documentation numbers.

[9] This viewpoint is particularly associated with Latin American States. Many expressions of their view are recounted in the present text, particularly in relation to the interpretation of Article 27 of the UN Covenant on Civil and Political Rights.

[10] *Definition and Classification of Minorities*, UN Doc E/CN.4/Sub.2/85, para. 24.

[11] Ibid. para. 38.

terms such as autonomy or self-government naturally suggest themselves. Type (*b*) suggests the classic issue of irredentism. A minority of type (*c*) may require a lesser share of power, perhaps only enough to acknowledge its existence in the wider community.

This variety of demands is matched by the variety of policies of the State. 'Assimilation' and 'integration' are terms that figure in the present text. A subtle account of the spectrum of State policies was outlined in a United Nations study on Racial Discrimination in the Political, Economic, Social, and Cultural Spheres.[12] Assimilation is described as being based on the idea of the superiority of the dominant culture, (aiming) to produce a homogeneous society by getting groups to discard their culture in favour of the dominant one. There is a willingness on the part of the dominant group to accept members of other groups, but this is contingent, as a *conditio sine qua non*, upon their accepting its culture.[13] On the other hand, integration, which from the point of view of groups the subject of this work, is a more 'benign' policy, is described as 'a process by which diverse elements are combined into a unity while retaining their basic identity. There is no insistence upon uniformity or elimination of all differences, other than the difference of each component group which would *disturb or inhibit the total unity*.'[14] The report notes that integration can easily become assimilation, and the words in italics indicate that it may generate its own restrictive characteristics for groups wishing to retain their identity. Integration seeks '(i) to eliminate all purely ethnic lines of cleavage; (ii) to guarantee the same rights, opportunities and responsibilities to all citizens, whatever their group membership.' Such an official State policy might be intolerant of individuated laws for particular minorities in the State. Assimilation needs to be distinguished from fusion whereby two or more cultures combine to produce another which is different from the parent cultures. Fusion reflects the equality of cultures as a process and a result.[15] The concept of pluralism has a similarly egalitarian face; it is a policy 'which aims at uniting different ethnic groups in a relationship of mutual interdependence, respect and equality, while permitting them to maintain and cultivate their distinctive ways'.[16] In multiethnic societies, such a policy symbolizes diversity and unity or diversity within unity. The element of separateness in pluralism needs to be distinguished from a policy of *segregation*. Segregation may be defined as a policy 'based on the belief in the superiority of the dominant culture (which) aims at keeping certain ethnic groups separate, unmixed, and ranked in a hierarchical position.[17] It is imposed by a dominant majority (or, in the case of South Africa, a dominant minority) rather than chosen by the groups subjected to it.

In the context of indigenous groups a newer concept has been elaborated.

---

[12] UN Sales No. 71.XIV.2.
[13] Ibid. para. 370.
[14] Ibid. paras. 373–7.
[15] Ibid. para. 380.
[16] Ibid. para. 379.
[17] Ibid. paras. 366–7.

Thus, it is affirmed that '*ethnodevelopment* is an inalienable right of Indian groups', which means 'strengthening and consolidating a culturally distinct society's own culture by increasing its independent decision making capacity to govern its own development'.[18] In practice this has been more an indigenous group demand than a State policy.[19] This range of policies does not exhaust all the nuances of State attitudes towards minorities. Regrettably, crude attempts at physical destruction of groups are still made by States, even if not admitted to be such:[20] no State proclaims genocide as a policy. The response of international law to this fact forms the subject-matter of the section on the 'right to existence'.

In summary, the issue for international and municipal law is to assist in the achievement of justice and order faced with widely different factual situations, demands, attitudes, policies, and possibilities for regulation. For much of the period after the Second World War, the minorities issue was elbowed aside by the international community[21] because it appeared to raise too many problems, the response to which did not command international consensus. The issue is a complex one. The study of minority rights provides an immediate introduction to contradictions or antinomies in international law, political theory, and practice.[22] Analysis of the effort of law to deal with the existence of ethnic, religious, and linguistic groups implies reflection on individual and collective rights and duties; the rights and duties of the State and those of the group; on whether minorities are to be eliminated or encouraged, or, introducing two further terms into the dichotomy, repressed or tolerated; on the separation of groups or their integration into the State; on rights to equality against special privileges for groups; on the uniformity among citizens of a State or the acceptance of cultural and religious differences; on universal rules of international law or the acceptance of regional laws or principles dealing with minorities on a non-uniform pattern. When 'indigenous groups' or 'aboriginal populations' are imported into the argument, further antinomies become apparent in addition to, or in intense versions of, the above. Should their traditions be preserved or allowed to undergo processes of natural change? What are the respective roles of the State, the international community, and the groups

---

[18] Martinez-Cobo, UN Doc E/CN.4/Sub.2/1982/2/Add.1, n. 8 above. See also the definition cited by Stavenhagen, in 'Indigenous Peoples, the State, and the UN System', paper presented to the Workshop *Minorities and Indigenous Peoples in the United Nations System*, Oxford 1989, p. 40. The Draft Universal Declaration on Indigenous Rights (below, ch. 41) refers to this concept in its preamble, UN Doc E/CN.4/Sub.2/1988/24.

[19] The matter is further discussed in the chapters of the present work on indigenous peoples, chs. 38 ff.

[20] Whitaker, *Revised and Updated Report on the Question of the Prevention and Punishment of Genocide*, UN Doc E/CN.4/Sub.2/1985/6, para. 24; Kuper, *The Prevention of Genocide* (New Haven: Yale UP, 1985).

[21] Thornberry, 'Is There a Phoenix in the Ashes: International Law and Minority Rights', *Texas International Law Journal*, 15 (1980), 421.

[22] Van Dyke (*supra*, n. 3); Thornberry (*supra*, n. 4); Moskowitz, *The Politics and Dynamics of Human Rights* (Dobbs Ferry, New York: Oceana Publications, 1968).

themselves? Should norms and standards be directed primarily to economic improvement or respect for the uniqueness and irreplaceability of indigenous cultures?

A synchronic picture of international law related to minorities requires supplementation by a consideration of epochs of legal change, of considerations *de lege ferenda*. There are fashions in international law which may illuminate its present state and signify its future in terms of trends, patterns, and probabilities. This is the case with minority rights, as Kunz observed in 1954: 'At the end of the First World War international protection of minorities was the great fashion: treaties in abundance, conferences, League of Nations activities, an enormous literature. Recently, this fashion has become nearly obsolete. Today, the well dressed international lawyer wears "human rights".'[23] One may quarrel with this statement now, when minority rights have become at least a minority fashion amongst international lawyers, but the point is taken about change and the paradigms of an era. The question is now to what extent one of the historic issues of international law is integrated into the present paradigm of that law, the humanitarian aspect of which presents itself as an international law of human rights. In the present work, the historical international law of minorities is dealt with as a subordinate concern, as an introduction to the modern law, but indications of a *lex ferenda* are integrated into the body of the discussion. The historical context demonstrates a movement from the protection of particular groups to rules applied to all human beings on a universal basis. The present study also indicates responses to the question: are minorities subjects of international law?

It is necessary to outline a preliminary definition of 'minority'. More detailed discussion of this is found in the analysis of Article 27 of the UN Covenant on Civil and Political Rights. The most widely accepted definition of minority appears to be that proposed by Capotorti[24] that a minority is a 'group numerically inferior to the rest of the population of a State, in a non-dominant position, whose members—being nationals of the State—possess ethnic, religious or linguistic characteristics differing from those of the rest of the population and show, if only implicitly, a sense of solidarity, directed towards preserving their culture, traditions, religion or language'.[25] The definition has been widely cited in the recent legal literature.

While utilization of the Capotorti definition implies a measure of 'conventionalism': taking a standard usage of a term in the selection of an object of study, it would appear to the present author to represent a realistic approach. Broader and more restrictive approaches are discussed in the text.

---

[23] Kunz, 'The Present Status of the International Law for the Protection of Minorities', *AJIL*, 48 (1954). For a review of the extensive inter-war literature, consult Ermacora, 'The Protection of Minorities before the United Nations', *Rec. des Cours*, 182 (1983), 247.

[24] *Supra*, n. 4.

[25] Ibid. The definition was drawn up with particular reference to Article 27 of the Covenant but can serve a more general purpose.

A refinement of this definition has been proposed by Deschênes: a minority is

A group of citizens of a State, constituting a numerical minority and in a non-dominant position in that State, endowed with ethnic, religious or linguistic characteristics which differ from those of the majority of the population, having a sense of solidarity with one another, motivated, if only implicitly, by a collective will to survive and whose aim is to achieve equality with the majority in fact and in law.[26]

The Deschênes definition differs from Capotorti's in minor respects. One improvement is the replacement of 'numerically inferior to the rest of the population of a State' by 'constituting a numerical minority'. This is more than *elegantia juris*: the term 'inferior' is avoided, even though in Capotorti it clearly refers to a number and is not a cultural value-judgement. Deschênes prefers 'citizens' to 'nationals' (of a State), dispelling potential criticism on the vagueness of the Capotorti term. 'Equality in fact and in law' is explicit in Deschênes, but only implicit in Capotorti. Both formulae perhaps carry an incorrect implication through contrasting 'the rest of the population' (Capotorti) and 'the majority' (Deschênes) with minorities, as if the majority were a monolithic cultural block in opposition to the minority, which is not the case in many States. An earlier refinement of Capotorti proposed by Canada had contrasted 'others of the population' with the minority, which can be reconciled with a general cultural heterogeneity in the State. There is not much to choose between the definitions and the present work adopts Capotorti as the longer established of the two. It is doubtful if any international instrument of the future attempting a definition will depart greatly from this line of approach.

Some consequences of adopting this formula may be considered. In the first place, the issue of the human rights of aliens is not a subject of the present study. Capotorti refers to nationals of a State. As he explained, his definition:

excludes foreigners residing in a country. The Special Rapporteur is not unaware of the problems encountered nowadays as a result of phenomena such as the migration

---

[26] *Proposal concerning a Definition of the term 'Minority'* by Mr Jules Deschênes, a Canadian member of the UN Sub-Commission on Prevention of Discrimination and Protection of Minorities, UN Doc E/CN.4/Sub.2/1985/31/, para. 181. The Sub-Commission considered the definition at its thirty-eighth session, and adopted Res. 1985/6, by which it decided to transmit to the Human Rights Commission the Deschênes report, together with the summary records of the discussion thereon, UN Doc E/CN.4/Sub.2/1985/SR.13–16. At its 1986 session, the Commission's Working Group on the Rights of Persons Belonging to National, Ethnic, Religious, and Linguistic Minorities agreed to postpone the consideration of the question of a definition to be included in a Declaration on the rights of persons belonging to minorities, UN Doc E/CN.4/1986/43, para. 12. A compilation of proposals concerning the definition of the term 'minority' has been prepared by the Secretariat, UN Doc E/CN.4/1987/WG.5/WP.1. Thus, the definition of minority has still not been 'finalized' at the UN. The earlier definition proposed by Canada is in UN Doc E/CN.4/1984/42.Add.2. Some responses of States to proposed definitions are considered in the section (*infra*, chs. 15 ff) on Article 27 of the Covenant on Civil and Political Rights.

of workers and the establishment of sometimes quite substantial groups of foreign workers in certain industrialised countries. The case of foreigners is different, however, from that of persons who possess the nationality of the country in which they live. As long as a person retains his status as a foreigner, he has the right to benefit from the protection granted by customary international law to persons who are in a country other than their own, as well as from any other special rights which may be conferred upon him by treaties or other special agreements.[27]

His conclusion is that the minorities provision in the UN Covenant on Civil and Political Rights, Article 27, should be given a restricted interpretation. Although the present study is wider than that of the Special Rapporteur whose brief related to Article 27, his general line of demarcation is followed. Absolute rigour is not possible. For example, the Convention on the Prevention and Punishment of the Crime of Genocide 1948 is discussed; its prohibition and definition of genocide refer to destruction of 'a national, ethnical, racial or religious group, as such.'[28] Clearly it is an absurdity to distinguish between nationals and non-nationals: the prohibition transcends the category. Similarly, in view of the promise of modern international law to protect human rights on a universal basis, the national and non-national distinction is frequently of little relevance. The rights of aliens, therefore, are occasionally comprehended by this study, but they are not its focus.

Besides aliens, the narrower categories of migrant workers, refugees and stateless persons are also excluded from the Capotorti formula. In relation to the first of these categories, a seminar on the human rights of minorities at Ohrid, Yugoslavia in 1974 saw a division of opinion: whereas some participants believed that migrant workers should not be considered minorities because they did not usually acquire the citizenship of the State where they temporarily established themselves, and thus did not enjoy the political rights of citizens, others regarded them as a special category of minority, a social minority, and considered that, in human rights, emphasis should not be placed on citizenship.[29] However, a study of minorities will encompass such groups both in terms of international human rights law, and in view of the fact that in many cases immigrants are permanent rather than transient members of the social community of their host States, may settle down and acquire its citizenship, forming new minorities in the narrow definitional sense. These comments apply, *mutatis mutandis*, to other groups mentioned above.

A second comment on the Capotorti definition is that it excludes dominant groups like the white minority in South Africa, and does not

---

[27] *Supra*, n. 4, Add.1, para. 57. For a contemporary summary of Human Rights law affecting aliens, see Elles, *International Provisions Protecting the Human Rights of Non-Citizens*, UN Sales No. E.80.XIV.2; also, Lillich, *The Human Rights of Aliens in Contemporary International Law* (Manchester: Manchester University Press, 1984).

[28] *Infra*, ch. 6.

[29] Capotorti. Add.1. para. 50.

include the dominated majority in that State because of the numerical requirement. The black majority in South Africa may be described as a 'reversed' minority.[30] A commentator refers to the special measures recommended by the United Nations in the case of apartheid: 'these contain requests for self-determination and respect for human rights in their entirety. All these recommendations form a complex of anti-apartheid measures which demand from the . . . government positive action to guarantee political, civilian and social equality, but this Government should also refrain from its apartheid actions. This complex of measures . . . is, in its complexity, . . . different from all protective measures provided for minorities.'[31] The author also uses the term 'racial-political minority'[32] to describe the South African majority. The present study incorporates sections which deal directly or indirectly with the issue of apartheid. However, as Ermacora indicates, apartheid is very much a *sui generis* issue in international law with its own corpus of legal and political analysis. The problem of apartheid is ultimately that of self-rule or self-determination for a *people*, rather than protection of a minority. The South African black majority might consider it rather surprising to be considered as a minority, and would regard their right to complete self-rule as axiomatic: this is also the United Nations view. The South African issue requires discussion nevertheless in that the policy of racial separation practised there has misguided States into a certain hostility to differential treatment of minority groups; as noted above, distinctions have to be made between apartheid and measures to protect minority cultures.[33]

The Capotorti definition is also restrictive in that while it refers to what one writer has termed 'minorities by will' (voluntary minorities) it does not

[30] Ermacora (*supra*, n. 23, 284).
[31] Ibid. 319.
[32] Ibid.
[33] Thornberry, *supra*, n. 21; Dugard, 'The Influence of Apartheid on the Development of the Law Governing the Protection of Minorities', paper presented to the workshop *Minorities and Indigenous Peoples in the United Nations System*, Oxford, 1989; Tanaka, Dissenting Opinion in *The South West Africa Cases, Second Phase, ICJ Reports, 1966, Infra*, ch. 36. On the majority and minority distinction in South Africa, Dugard writes (p. 5): 'The National Party Government, which came to power in 1948 on the platform of Apartheid, sees South Africa as a plural society, in which the largest ethnic group is the Zulu group and in which there is therefore no majority group. For it, language and culture, as much as race, determine the parameters of an ethnic group. Hence it refuses to see black Africans as comprising one group, as a majority group, in South African society'. See also *South Africa 1986, Official Yearbook of the Republic of South Africa* (Pretoria: Bureau for Information, for Department of Foreign Affairs, 1986), 12th edn. (Pretoria, 1986), chs. 2 (population data), 4 (the peoples of South Africa), and 11 (the national states). The UN view of South Africa evolved from a willingness to consider a political order in South Africa which took account of the diverse ethnic composition of South African society, through condemning apartheid (Report of the Commission on the Racial Situation in South Africa, UN Doc A/2719 (1954)) to the General Assembly's statement in 1984 that 'only the total eradication of Apartheid and the establishment of a non-racial democratic society based on majority rule through the full and free exercise of adult suffrage by all the people in South Africa can lead to a just and lasting solution to the explosive situation in South Africa.' (UNGA Res. 39/50A, 13 Dec. 1984).

refer to 'minorities by force' (involuntary minorities).[34] The former wish to maintain their distinctive cultures, languages or religions; the latter require only a guarantee of non-discrimination so that their integration into the wider national society can be expedited. This leads to a distinction between 'prevention of discrimination' and 'protection of minorities', reflected in the title of the relevant UN body.[35] Adopting the Capotorti definition would appear to imply exclusion of any reference to the prevention of discrimination because it does not clearly imply the preservation of specific characteristics. Capotorti none the less makes copious references to prevention of discrimination and regards it as an essential prerequisite for measures tending to help minority groups to remain distinctive. 'Classical' protection of minorities through specific treaties almost invariably included measures of non-discrimination as a preliminary to differential rules.[36] Anti-discrimination provisions are included in a compilation by the UN of 'Special Protective Measures of an International Character for Ethnic, Religious or Linguistic Groups'.[37] That this approach is more than conventionalism is indicated by the UN Sub-Commission:

1. Prevention of discrimination is the prevention of any action which denies to individuals or groups of peoples equality of treatment which they may wish.

2. Protection of minorities is the protection of non-dominant groups which, while wishing in general for equality of treatment with the majority, wish for a measure of differential treatment in order to preserve basic characteristics . . .[38]

This suggests a logical as well as practical link between the concepts which requires comment—otherwise the result would be a rather impoverished and needlessly stringent analytical strategy, concentrating on one to the exclusion of the other. The broader approach is taken here, though it is postulated that there also exists a tension between the two concepts. The roots of the tension lie in the contrast between the terms 'equality' and 'differential treatment'; the problem arises from the desire expressed by some States that the goal of non-discrimination is in effect the disappearance of minority consciousness.[39]

The present work is not structured on what may be termed the rights of a group or collective human rights. Dinstein makes the correct point that:

International human rights are not monolithic, and a cardinal distinction must be drawn between individual and collective rights granted directly to human beings [as opposed to rights of, for example, the State]. Individual human rights (for example,

---

[34] Laponce, *The Protection of Minorities* 5–22 (Berkeley and Los Angeles: University of California Press, 1960).

[35] *Infra*, ch. 12.

[36] *Infra*, chs. 2 and 3.

[37] UN Doc E/CN.4/Sub.2/214/Rev.1; UN Doc E/CN.4/Sub.2/221/Rev.1, UN Sales No. 67.XIV.3.

[38] UN Doc E/CN.4/52, Section V.

[39] *Infra*, Parts 4 and 5.

freedom of expression or freedom of religion) are bestowed upon every single human being personally. Collective human rights are afforded to human beings communally, that is to say, in conjunction with one another or as a group—a people or a minority. It must be stressed that collective human rights retain their character as direct human rights . . . [which] . . . shall be exercised jointly rather than severally.[40]

Dinstein finds only two rights in international law which pertain to a minority: the right to physical existence (prohibition of genocide), and the right to preservation of a separate identity (Article 27 of the Covenant on Civil and Political Rights). This does not give a complete picture of the provisions for protection of minorities in international law—though perhaps it is not intended to do so. Whilst taking only 'collective human rights' results in a sharp focus for a particular study, it leaves out of account one of the most interesting tensions present in efforts to protect minorities. Van Dyke points out: 'Since the time of Hobbes and Locke, Liberal political theorists have made it their primary purpose to explore relationships between the individual and the State. The truths that Thomas Jefferson held to be self-evident are truths concerning the individual and the State: all men have inalienable rights, and Governments derive their just powers from the consent of the governed.'[41] The modern contractarian, John Rawls, also assumes that the parties in the 'original position' who work out principles of justice for themselves are individuals, and the justice they seek is justice for individuals.[42] Hobbes spoke of 'a multitude of men'[43] making a covenant, and Locke of 'any number of men'.[44] Reflecting this tradition, the Universal Declaration of Human Rights describes rights which apply to 'everyone, without distinction of any kind . . .'.[45] Human rights instruments generally follow language which is universalist and individualist and does not accept a group dimension of rights without some strain.[46] The reality elided by this

[40] Dinstein, 'Collective Human Rights of Peoples and Minorities' *ICLQ*, 25 (1976), 102 at 102–3. The preference of draftsmen of contemporary international instruments is for clear reference to the rights of 'members of minorities', rather than 'rights of minorities'. Deschênes, UN Doc E/CN.4/Sub.2/1985/31/, paras. 51 and 56, offers an opinion for preliminary reflection: 'Affording protection to a minority as a group suggests the possibility of privilege, perhaps even secession, and endangers a nation's unity . . . Every minority undoubtedly constitutes a group, but where it is a question of determining its rights, it is on the individual as a member of the minority that the emphasis should be placed.'

[41] 'The Individual, the State, and Ethnic Communities in Political Theory', *World Politics* 23 (1976–7), 343.

[42] Rawls, *A Theory of Justice* (Cambridge, Mass.: Harvard University Press, 1971).

[43] Hobbes, *Leviathan* (Oxford OUP: 1909), ch. XVIII, 133.

[44] Barker (ed.), *Social Contract: Essays by Locke, Hume, and Rousseau*, 3, 42 (Oxford: OUP, 1951). For a less individualistic theory, stressing association as the art of politics, and describing a series of social contracts by which various social groups come into being, consult Althusius, in Friedrich (ed.), *Politica Methodice Digesta* (Cambridge, Mass.: Harvard University Press, 1932). See the discussion in Van Dyke, *supra*, n. 3, 200.

[45] Article 2.

[46] Moskowitz, *supra*, n. 22, 167–70, comments: 'The individual whose Human Rights and fundamental freedoms the United Nations seeks to proclaim and defend is man in his national, cultural and spiritual environment. Stripped of his . . . characteristics, spiritually adrift from his

concentration on the individual as legal subject is that of the group. Individuals do not exist shorn of cultural, linguistic or religious peculiarities; they do not exist *in abstracto*. States are much more complex than philosophies of the State. Thus, an interesting aspect of the contemporary law of minorities is the attempt to grapple with the group dimension within the individualist framework of human rights law. One may, therefore, expect to find individual human rights and collective rights in any living scheme for the protection of rights: this may be doctrinally impure but it respects practicality and complexity. It seems insufficient to the present writer to concentrate on either group rights or individual rights. Fawcett describes the main political axioms to protect minorities: there is an 'instrumental approach' where the collective identity of the group is secured by some form of self-determination; and there is a 'social approach' which culminates in the principle of non-discrimination on the other side.[47] One solution is separation, the other is integration: this may be taken as a 'reductionist' version of the policy range outlined above. In strict Kelsenian terms, the ultimate decision of 'what kind of law' involves political choices, but it is a relevant focus for enquiry to reveal the choices made in the leading international instruments, and to indicate in which direction international law is moving. The present study therefore deals both with 'collective human rights' (Dinstein) as well as individual human rights—principally in terms of its architectural principle of equality, and non-discrimination.[48] The work also concerns itself with indigenous groups. This is sometimes discussed in works dealing with the rights of minorities,[49] and the United Nations compilation of minorities instruments includes the Indigenous and Tribal Populations Convention prepared by the International Labour Organization.[50] Reciprocally, the 'Study of the Problem of Discrimination against Indigenous Populations' includes many references to rules which deal with minorities.[51] The more inclusive approach is adopted without

past and loosed from his traditional moorings, man loses his essential humanity . . . the United Nations . . . must redress the distortions . . . which have tended to separate the . . . individual from his immediate environment.' Also Thornberry, *supra*, n. 4.

[47] Fawcett, *The International Protection of Minorities*. Minority Rights Group Report No. 41, Minority Rights Group, London 1979.

[48] Consult McKean, *Equality and Discrimination under International Law* for a comprehensive review of equality as a legal principle (Oxford: OUP, 1983); also Vierdag, *The Concept of Discrimination in International Law—with Special Reference to Human Rights* (The Hague: M. Nijhoff, 1973); Greenberg, 'Race, Sex, and Religious Discrimination in International Law', in Meron (ed.), *Human Rights in International Law: Legal and Policy Issues* (Oxford: OUP, 1984), ch. 8.

[49] Ermacora, 'The Protection of Minorities before the United Nations'.

[50] *Supra*, n. 37, 10. The Convention in question is ILO Con. No. 107, *UNTS* 328, 248.

[51] Deschênes, *Proposal concerning a Definition of the term 'Minority'*, UN Doc E/CN.4/ Sub.2/1985/31/, para. 32, writes that some indigenous populations, 'and by no means the least representative, strenuously oppose the idea of being identified as minorities'. He quotes a representative of the International Indian Treaty Council: 'The ultimate goal of their colonizers would be achieved by referring to indigenous peoples as minorities.' (para. 33). From such evidence he concludes (para. 38) that 'the definition [of "minority"] which we seek should not

suggesting a complete identity between the two; the United Nations, it may be said, recognizes them as separate but related. In conceptual terms, the minorities instruments comprehend indigenous populations because they are usually a numerical minority in States, and they are always non-dominant. Some intense deprivations of human rights are found among indigenous groups;[52] the deprivations are inflicted on the groups precisely because of their 'minority quality' as weak and defenceless groups, obstacles on the path to progress as envisioned by States. The indigenous issue is separable from minorities in general principally because of the enormous cultural gulf between them and ruling groups in States. In some cases the only desire of the groups may be to have as little contact as possible with the institutions of the twentieth century. Most of these groups are now in contact with majority cultures to which they have often been introduced by force. Representatives of such peoples[53] attempt to use international law as a stimulus to more positive attitudes on the part of States. This is an important area of international law with great potential for development. International law has developed a relationship with the groups which hitherto has insufficiently incorporated the attitudes of the groups themselves. There are clear signs of change in this field.

Self-Determination

A number of references are made in this work to the concept of self-determination.[54] It is not, however, a major focus of enquiry. Self-determination is usually described as a right of peoples,[55] not minorities. But self-determination and minority rights are locked in a relationship which is part of the architecture of the nation State, since whenever a State is forged, the result is the creation of minorities. This applies in the twentieth century

attempt to deal with the question of indigenous populations.' But the attempt by indigenous groups to appropriate to themselves the term 'peoples' as more powerful than 'minority' should not lead to the conclusion that the rights of minorities may not be applied to them. The rights of minorities function as a necessary minimum standard in the treatment of indigenous groups. A more expansive, functioning international environment to benefit indigenous groups has yet to be achieved (*infra*, ch. 41).

[52] Independent Commission on International Humanitarian Issues, *Indigenous Peoples, a Global Quest for Justice* (London and New Jersey: Zed Books, 1987).

[53] The present text uses 'peoples', 'populations' and 'groups' to describe the indigenous merely to achieve some variety of terminology. The theoretical and practical issues behind particular terminological choices are dealt with in later discussions devoted to this question.

[54] In particular, in chapters on the UN Covenant on Civil and Political Rights, and on indigenous populations.

[55] *Infra*, references to the UN Charter, the UN Covenants on Human Rights, the African Charter on Human and Peoples' Rights, the Helsinki Final Act, UN General Assembly Declaration on the Granting of Independence to Colonial Countries and Peoples, the Declaration on Principles of International Law concerning Friendly Relations among Nations, the Universal Declaration of the Rights of Peoples (the Algiers Declaration). See also, Crawford (ed.), *The Rights of Peoples* (Oxford: OUP, 1988).

as it did in the nineteenth; indeed the many contemporary exercises in nation building have produced many new minorities; the boundaries of the new States are not based on any concept of ethnic homogeneity.[56] While secession from Western Empires has resulted in the creation of States, these same States deny the possibility of further secession by disaffected groups, which are required to accept the dogma of the territorial integrity of States.[57] Self-determination is now an accepted principle of international law, possibly *jus cogens*,[58] but a restricted principle for minorities; a work of *lex lata* on minority rights could plausibly omit reference to it. This would not, however, be entirely justified. In the first place, there is a slipperiness in the concept of a 'people' which makes for uncertain attribution of rights. Some brief account of the interpretation of this term in international instruments and its relation to minorities is instructive.[59] Secondly, whether States like it or not, minorities and indigenous groups have often appropriated the term 'self-determination' to express the essence of their political claims;[60] in the case of indigenous groups, the description of them as 'peoples' is current usage,[61] and this requires elucidation. Thirdly, while 'external' manifestations of self-determination may be denied to minorities (prohibition of secession from States), the concept of 'internal' self-determination, which promises to say something about the internal organization of States is of relevance, however unformed it may be at

[56] Crawford, *The Creation of States in International Law* (Oxford: OUP, 1979); Day (ed.), *Border and Territorial Disputes* (Harlow: Longmans, 1982); Johnson, *Self-Determination Within the Community of Nations*; Pomerance, *Self-Determination in Law and Practice* (The Hague; M. Nijhoff, 1982); Rigo-Sureda, *The Evolution of the Right of Self-Determination* (Leiden: Sijthoff, 1973). The nineteenth and twentieth century treaties on minorities were, in some cases, a substitute for self-determination; see *infra*, chs. 2 and 3.

[57] The territorial integrity rule is forcibly summed up in the Declaration on the Granting of Independence to Colonial Countries and Peoples, UNGA Res. 1514(XV), *infra*, text following n. 25.

[58] Gros-Espiell, Special Rapporteur, *Implementation of United Nations Resolutions relating to the Right of Peoples under Colonial and Alien Domination to Self-Determination*, UN Doc E/CN.4/Sub.2/40, 5 June 1978, *passim*.

[59] See particularly the chapter on self-determination in the UN Covenants.

[60] The secession of Bangladesh from Pakistan is an example of a 'successful' post-colonial self-determination; the attempt of Biafra to secede from Nigeria was unsuccessful; see on Bangladesh, Crawford, *The Creation of States in International Law*; Nanda, 'Self-Determination in International Law: The Tragic Tale of Two Cities', *AJIL*, 66 (1972), 321; International Commission of Jurists, *The Events in East Pakistan 1971* (Geneva: International Commission of Jurists, 1972). On Biafra, Panter-Brick, 'The Right to Self-Determination, Its Application to Nigeria', *International Affairs*, 44 (1968), 254; also Akehurst, *A Modern Introduction to International Law*, 6th edn. (London, 1987), ch. 5 (London: George Allen and Unwin, 1987).

[61] *Analytical Compilation of Existing Legal Instruments and Proposed Draft Standards relating to Indigenous Rights*, prepared by the UN Secretary-General in accordance with Sub-Commission Res. 1985/22, UN Doc M/HR/86/36. In the Revision of ILO Convention 107 on Indigenous and Tribal Populations, the term 'peoples' has gradually supplanted 'populations': International Labour Conference 76th Session, 1989, Report IV (2B), *Partial Revision of the Indigenous and Tribal Populations Convention, 1957 (No. 107)* (Geneva International Labour Office, 1989), text of proposed Convention concerning Indigenous and Tribal Peoples in Independent Countries; *Draft Universal Declaration on Indigenous Rights*, UN Doc E/CN.4/Sub.2/1988/25.

present. What follows is a brief explanatory account of the appearance of self-determination in the UN Charter and relevant General Assembly resolutions. Questions of external and internal self-determination (principally the latter) are taken up later in chapters on the UN Covenant on Civil and Political Rights, and on indigenous peoples.

The United Nations Charter

Despite its invocation in the inter-war years, self-determination was not part of positive international law. The 'principle' is expressly mentioned in the UN Charter, in Articles 1(2) and 55. Article 1(2) places the principle among the purposes of the United Nations. Article 55 provides: 'With a view to the creation of conditions of stability and well-being which are necessary for peaceful and friendly relations among nations based on respect for the principle of equal rights and self-determination of peoples, the United Nations shall promote . . .' and there follows a list of important social, and economic goals.[62]

Self-determination in the Charter attaches to 'peoples'. The meaning of 'peoples' occasioned inconclusive discussion at the San Francisco Conference. The terms 'State', 'nation', and 'people' are all used in the Charter. The UN Secretariat examined the terms: 'The word "nation" is broad . . . enough to include colonies, mandates, protectorates and quasi-States as well as States . . . "nations" is used in the sense of all political entities, States and non-States, whereas "peoples" refers to groups of human beings who may, or may not, comprise States or nations.'[63] The broad interpretation provoked a French delegate to say that the Charter appeared to sanction secession; others disagreed.[64]

The references to self-determination in Articles 1(2) and 55 are complemented by Chapters XI and XII on Non-Self-Governing Territories, and the International Trusteeship System. Bowett states that it is permissible 'to regard the entirety of Chapters XI and XII of the . . . Charter as reflections on the basic idea of self-determination.'[65] Neither Chapter contains an express reference to self-determination, but the principle is established indirectly. Article 73 in Chapter XI describes the development of self-government in non-self-governing territories as a 'sacred trust'. Article 76

---

[62] Including: '(c) universal respect for, and observance of, human rights and fundamental freedoms for all without distinction as to race, sex, language, or religion'.

[63] *UNCIO Docs.* 18, 657–8.

[64] *UNCIO Docs.* 17, 142; Cassese, in Buergenthal and Hall (eds.), *Human Rights, International Law and the Helsinki Accord*, 95 ff. (New York: Allanheld, 1977); Russell and Muther, *A History of the United Nations Charter. The Role of the United States 1940–45* (Washington: Brookings Institution, 1958).

[65] 'Problems of Self-Determination and Political Rights in the Developing Countries', *Procs. ASIL 1966*, 129 at 134.

on the International Trusteeship System refers to progressive development in the Trust Territories towards 'self-government or independence'. A key issue was the distinction between 'self-government' and 'independence'. The colonial Powers were unhappy about referring to 'independence' in the generally applicable Article 73. In the view of the United States, however, 'self-government' did not rule out 'independence' in appropriate cases.[66] The Philippines interpreted Article 73 to imply eventual independence for dependent territories.[67]

Chapter XI of the Charter gave a tremendous impetus to the development of self-determination with a real possibility of implementation. Subsequent practice has hardened the meaning of Charter terms, but the result has been unfavourable to minorities. Chapter XI is a declaration on 'Non-Self-Governing Territories'. The territorial aspect is vital: the Chapter refers to '*territories* whose peoples have not attained a full measure of self-government . . .' and the sacred trust is to promote 'the well-being of the inhabitants of these *territories*'. A territorial concept of self-determination appears to rule out minorities without a specific territorial base. Further, concentration on territory, in the light of the reality of mixed and inextricable populations, languages, and religions, weighs heavily towards taking political demarcations as they stand, and making these the focal point of political change.

The Belgian Thesis

Article 73 of the Charter was utilised by the General Assembly in the promotion of self-determination through the requirement of reports on the progress made by States administering territories towards the objectives set by the Article. The main thrust of the Assembly's effort was in the direction of the colonial Empires. The Belgian representatives pointed out that the Charter does not single out 'colonialism', but non-self-governing territories.[68] Belgium stated that

a number of States were administering within their own frontiers territories which were not governed by the ordinary law; territories with well-defined limits, inhabited by homogeneous peoples differing from the rest of the population in race, language and culture. These populations were disenfranchised; they took no part in national life; they did not enjoy self-government in any sense of the word.

[66] Russell and Muther, *A History of the United Nations Charter. The Role of the United States 1940–45*, 813 ff.

[67] Ibid.

[68] Van Langenhove, 'Le Problème de la Protection des Populations Aborigènes aux Nations Unies', *Rec. des Cours*, 89 (1956), 321, and *The Question of Aborigines Before the United Nations: The Belgian Thesis* (Brussels: Royal Colonial Institute, 1954); Toussaint, 'The Colonial Controversy in the United Nations' *Year Book of World Affairs*, 177 (1956); Bennett, *Aboriginal Rights in International Law*, Occasional Paper of the Royal Anthropological Institute of Great Britain and Ireland (London, 1978); UN Doc A/AC.67/2, 3–31.

It was not clear how such groups were excluded from the terms of Chapter XI.[69] Groups in respect of which Chapter XI applied would include Indian tribes of Venezuela, the Nagas of India, indigenous African tribes in Liberia, Somalis in Ethiopia, tribals of the Philippines, Dyaks of Borneo, etc. The generality of the Belgian concerns was expressed in the delegate's remark that 'Similar problems [to colonialism] existed wherever there were under-developed groups.'[70] The thesis radicalizes self-determination by insisting that it can apply to indigenous groups and minorities.

The thesis did not prevail. Latin American States and their allies did not agree that their situation could be assimilated to that of the colonies. The problems of the indigenous groups were economic rather than colonial.[71] In the view of Iraq, the Belgian argument was based on 'anger at the criticism directed against conditions in the non-self-governing territories by less advanced States'.[72] One of the authors of the thesis, Dr Van Langenhove, effectively admitted to the thesis as a Belgian tactic.[73]

The United Nations built a consensus on self-determination in response to the Belgian thesis to bring order to the inevitable historical movement of decolonization. The delegate of Iraq to the Fourth Committee of the General Assembly offered the opinion that: 'In the long run, colonialism must give way to self-government . . .'[74] The thesis was rejected in favour of the theory of 'salt-water' colonialism, summed up in *General Assembly Resolution 1541 (XV)*.[75] Principle IV states that: 'Prima facie there is an obligation . . . to transmit information in respect of a territory which is geographically separate and is distinct ethnically and/or culturally from the country administering it.'[76] The coupling of geography and the ethnic factor is important; without geography, the designation of non-colonial territories as entitled to self-determination was a possibility, though even with this factor, the definition is not perfect if the intention is to exclude all minority groups.[77]

The restrictive view of the non-applicability of self-determination to minority groups is strengthened by a consideration of General Assembly

---

[69] UN Doc A/C.4/SR. 429, para. 61.

[70] UN Doc A/C.4/SR. 419, paras. 14 ff. The delegate also noted that the indigenous were still recognized as having problems akin to colonialism by the ILO: see *infra* on ILO Convention 107.

[71] Delegate of Peru to the Fourth Committee, UN Doc A/C.4/SR. 420, para. 40.

[72] UN Doc A/C.4/SR. 257, para. 11.

[73] Van Langenhove, 'The Question of Aborigines Before the United Nations' (*supra*, n. 68), 83–4.

[74] UN Doc A/C.4/SR. 257, paras. 11–14. The reference is to Chapter XI; this need not be taken to rule out a post colonial future for self-determination as such.

[75] GAOR 15th Session, Supplement 16, 29.

[76] Ibid.

[77] For some points on the application of the definition to indigenous peoples, see Bennett *Supra*, n. 16, 13. The physical separation of East and West Pakistan and the consequences of this for self-determination are discussed by the International Commission of Jurists in *The Events in East Pakistan*, 1971, *supra*, n. 60.

Resolution 1514, the Colonial declaration, passed on the day before Resolution 1541.[78] The holder of the right of self-determination is, once more, declared to be the people. The meaning of the term 'people' is conditioned by repeated references to colonialism. Paragraph 6 of the resolution states that 'Any attempt aimed at the partial or total disruption of the national unity and the territorial integrity of a country is incompatible with the Purposes and Principles of the Charter of the United Nations.' The effect is that colonial boundaries function as the boundaries of the emerging States. Minorities, therefore, may not secede from States, at least, international law gives them no *right* to do so.[79] The logic of the resolution is relatively simple: peoples hold the right of self-determination; a people is the whole people of a territory; a people exercises its right through the achievement of independence.

General Assembly Resolution 2625(XXV) and Minorities

Resolution 2625(XXV) appears, on one reading, to construct a link between self-determination and minorities.[80] The text deals with the most important principles of international law,[81] each principle to be construed in the light of the others.[82] Three preambular paragraphs of the Declaration

[78] GAOR 15th Session, Supplement 16, 66; for reviews of the Declaration, see Pomerance, *Self-Determination in Law and Practice*, Rigo-Sureda, *The Evolution of the Right of Self-Determination*, Whiteman, *Digest of International Law*, vol. V. (Washington: Dept. of State, 1963–65); Castañeda, *The Legal Effects of United Nations Resolutions* (New York: Columbia UP, 1969).

[79] The emergence of Bangladesh furnishes an example. The international community adjusted to the situation through recognition of the new State. Some authorities hold that Bangladesh was a unit to which self-determination applied: Crawford, *The Creation of States in International Law*; Nanda, 'Self-Determination in International Law: The Tragic Tale of Two Cities', *AJIL*, 66 (1972), 321; International Commission of Jurists, *The Events in East Pakistan 1971* (Geneva, 1972). The response of the United Nations was muted, making it difficult to draw firm conclusions: Salzberg, 'UN Prevention of Human Rights Violations—The Bangladesh Case', *International Organization*, 27 (1973), 115.

[80] Rosenstock, 'The Declaration of Principles of International Law Concerning Friendly Relations: a Survey', *AJIL*, 65 (1971), 713.

[81] See Arangio-Ruiz. 'The Normative Role of the General Assembly of the United Nations and the Declaration of Principles on Friendly Relations', *Rec. des Cours*, 137 (1972), 528.

[82] The Declaration states: 'In their interpretation and application the above principles are interrelated and each principle should be construed in the context of the other principles . . . Nothing in this Declaration shall be construed as prejudicing in any manner the provisions of the Charter or the rights and duties of Member States under the Charter or the rights of peoples under the Charter taking into account the elaboration of these rights in this Declaration.' This means that the self-determination principle must fit consistently with such principles as that of non-intervention in the domestic affairs of other States, the principle of the sovereign equality of States, and the principle of the non-use of force. The text of the Declaration contains a number of references to territorial integrity and political independence of States. Under the heading of 'The Principle of Sovereign Equality of States', we may note: '(d) The territorial integrity and political independence of the State are inviolable'; (e) Each State has the right freely to choose and develop its political, social, economic and cultural systems.' These principles clearly impinge on self-determination. The last would be just as appropriate in the

refer to self-determination, the third reference reiterates the prohibition on disruption of the national unity and territorial integrity of a country. The principle is set out at some length in the operative part of the Declaration. There is not the same emphasis on colonialism as is Resolution 1514(XV). The preferred modes of implementing self-determination reflect more flexible options set out in Resolution 1541(XV): independence, free association, integration with an independent State, 'or the emergence into any other political status freely determined by a people'.

Writers have given attention[83] to the penultimate paragraph on self-determination:

Nothing in the foregoing paragraphs shall be construed as authorizing or encouraging any action which would dismember or impair, totally or in part, the territorial integrity or political unity of sovereign and independent States conducting themselves in compliance with the principle of [self-determination] and thus possessed of a government representing the whole people belonging to the territory without distinction as to race, creed or colour.

This is followed by the obligatory clause on territorial integrity.[84] The reference to representative government has been picked out as innovative by Rosenstock: 'a close examination of its text will reward the reader with an affirmation of the applicability of the principle to peoples within existing States and the necessity for governments to represent the governed.'[85] Thus, if 'peoples within existing States' are treated in a grossly discriminatory fashion by an unrepresentative government, they can claim self-determination and not be defeated by arguments about territorial integrity. The guarantee of integrity is contingent upon the existence of representative government. There are, however, reasons to caution against this kind of claim, and Cassese doubts if the Declaration can be pressed too far.[86] In his view, the paragraph would apply to peoples living under racist regimes. He emphasizes the negative wording as forbidding self-determination where there is representative government and where this government is non-racist. Pomerance supports Cassese's view.[87]

context of the paragraphs on self-determination in that it states an important aspect of that concept. It may also, by implication, hint at the effective transformation of the right holder into the State itself?

[83] Rosenstock, *supra*, n. 80; Cassese, *supra*, n. 64.

[84] As in Res. 1514(XV). India expressed satisfaction that Res. 2625(XXV) retained this element, UN Doc A/8018.

[85] 'The Declaration on Principles of International Law, etc.', *AJIL*, 65 (1971), 732.

[86] *Supra*, n. 64, 88–92.

[87] *Self-Determination in Law and Practice*, p. 39. In a recent paper, Cassese develops his views on Res. 2625, arguing that the Declaration must be read literally to refer to racial and religious minorities suffering oppression (denied equal access to the political decision-making process), but not, for example, to a linguistic, national, or political group. He also makes it clear that this kind of minority (racial or religious) is entitled to self-determination in the situation contemplated by the paragraph under discussion: Cassese, *The Right of Self-Determination and Non-State Peoples*, prepared for the workshop 'Minorities and Indigenous Peoples in the United Nations System', Oxford, March 1989.

The drafts support the more cautious views. A proposal of the United States made the 'internal' aspects of self-determination much clearer: 'The existence of a sovereign and independent State possessing a representative government, effectively functioning as such to all distinct peoples within its territory, is presumed to satisfy the principle of equal rights and self-determination as regards those people.'[88] A text proposed by Czechoslovakia and others made a similar point.[89] The crucial difference between the United States draft and the final version is that, in the former, the key phrase is 'all distinct peoples', whereas the final wording is 'the whole people'. The gaze of the international community is deflected from detailed 'internal' scrutiny of most States and the conduct of Governments towards the 'peoples' within their territories: only pariah States like South Africa which oppresses its majority on racial grounds are likely to be affected.[90] Whether one discusses 'internal' or 'external' self-determination, the point is that 'whole' territories or peoples are the focus of rights, rather than ethnic groups. Cassese's analyses of 'internal' self-determination[91] should not be taken to fragment the meaning of 'people'.

The development of international law on this issue does not cease with the proclamation of Resolution 2625(XXV). The resolution is, however, a strong contender for customary law status.[92]

More recent international instruments do not advance any contrary view on the applicability of self-determination to minority groups. The African Charter on Human and Peoples' Rights offers little to minorities; this is inherently unsurprising, and reflects the views of many African States that the minorities 'problem' is essentially European.[93] The 'peoples' of the Charter are undefined, but they have important rights. Article 19 reads: 'All peoples shall be equal; they shall enjoy the same respect and shall have the

---

[88] UN Doc A/AC.125/L.32.

[89] UN Doc A/AC.125/L.74.

[90] Cassese (*supra*, n. 64). South Africa exhibits a singular combination of racism and minority rule.

[91] It seems that Cassese did not originally intend such a fragmentation. He regarded self-determination as, *inter alia*, an anti-racist postulate, and writes: ' "internal" self-determination amounts to the right of an ethnic, racial or religious segment of the population in a sovereign country not to be oppressed by a discriminatory government'. 'Segment' might be taken as an equivalent to 'minority', but Cassese noted also that 'Self-determination . . . has not been accepted as a principle protecting national or ethnic groups . . . State sovereignty . . . has shielded States from the demands of ethnic minorities . . .' *International Law in a Divided World*, 134 (Oxford: OUP, 1986). However, the 1989 paper by Cassese, *supra*, n. 34, appears to admit secession as a possibility for the groups contemplated by Res. 2625(XXV).

[92] Cassese (*supra*, n. 64). The resolution is not as partial a statement of self-determination as Res. 1514(XV), and appeals to a wider constituency of States.

[93] OAU DOC CAB/LEG/67/3/Rev.5, reprinted in *Report of the Secretary-General of the OAU on the Draft African Charter on Human and Peoples' Rights*, OAU DOC CM/1149 (XXXVII), Annex II; *ILM*, 21 (1982), 58; *EHRR*, 4 (1982), 417. For reviews, see Gittleman, 'The African Charter on Human and Peoples' Rights: A Legal Analysis' *Virginia Journal of International Law*, 22 (1982), 667; Umozurike, 'The African Charter on Human and Peoples' Rights', *AJIL*, 77 (1983), 902. Also Kiwanuka, 'The Meaning of "People" in the African Charter on Human and Peoples' Rights', *AJIL*, 82 (1988), 80.

same rights. Nothing shall justify the domination of a people by another.'
Article 20(1) reads: 'All peoples shall have the right to existence. They shall
have the unquestionable and inalienable right to self-determination . . .'.
The rights of peoples are buttressed by the duties of individuals, which
include the duty 'to preserve and strengthen the national independence and
the territorial integrity of . . . [their] . . . country'.[94] There is no explicit
reference to minorities, though Article 2 and the preamble refer to discrimination based on 'ethnic group', as well as 'race, colour, . . . language,
religion . . . national or social origin'. The Charter lays tremendous stress on
its 'African' character throughout.[95] This includes the African view of self-
determination which stresses the territorial integrity of the State, even in
cases of severe oppression of minorities.[96] There is little to suggest that
'peoples' means anything other than the whole peoples of the States, and not
ethnic or other groups. This conclusion is strongly supported by discussions
at the Nairobi Conference convened by the International Commission of
Jurists in December 1985, and is likely to represent the future practice of the
implementing organ of the Charter, the African Commission on Human and
Peoples' Rights.[97] The people and minority distinction is also clear in the
Final Act of the Helsinki Conference, and the remarks on the African
Charter apply, *mutatis mutandis*, to this instrument of European space.[98]
Instruments advancing a view more favourable to the association of minor-
ities with self-determination tend to be 'unofficial', that is, without the clear
support of States.[99]

[94] Article 29(5).

[95] The tone is set by the Preamble, which makes 3 specific references to the OAU, recalls the
Charter of that organization, and refers to the virtues of the historical tradition and the values
of African civilization which should inspire and characterize the States Parties' reflections on
the concept of Human and Peoples' Rights. See also Articles 21(4), 23, 29(7), 29(8), 56, 60.
Article 61 on the role of the African Commission on Human and Peoples' Rights provides: 'The
Commission shall . . . take into consideration, as subsidiary measures to determine the
principles of law . . . general international conventions, laying down rules expressly recognised
by Member States of the Organisation of African Unity, African practices consistent with
international norms on human and peoples' rights, customs generally accepted as law, general
principles of law recognised by African States . . .'

[96] It is doubtful if the Commission will deviate from current OAU notions of sovereignty
and threats to it from secessionist movements: works cited, *supra*, n. 7 and 40; Kamanu,
'Secession and Self-Determination: An OAU Dilemma'; Shaw, *Title to Territory in Africa*.

[97] *Human and Peoples' Rights and the African Charter* (Geneva International Commission
of Jurists, 1986).   [98] *Infra*, ch. 29.

[99] The Universal Declaration of the Rights of Peoples, Algiers, 4 July 1976, (text in Cassese,
(ed), *UN Law. Fundamental Rights* (Alphen aan den Rijn: Sijthoff and Noordhoff, 1979),
219–223) an unofficial declaration of scholars and publicists is a case in point. According to
Article 19, when a 'people' constitutes a minority within a State, it has a right to respect for its
identity, traditions, language, and cultural heritage. Article 21 provides that, in the exercise of
these rights, the legitimate interests of the whole country must be respected, and no disruption
of the territorial integrity and political unity of the State is justified, as long as the State
conducts itself in conformity with the principles of the Declaration. This would widen enormously the 'gap' suggested by some to have been opened by Res. 2625. See also Sacerdoti,
'New Developments in Group Consciousness and the International Protection of the Rights of
Minorities', *Israel Yearbook On Human Rights*, 13 (1983), 116.

PART I

Concept and History of the Protection of Minorities

2. Historical Background: International Law Moves from Protection of Particular Groups to Norms of a Universal Character

Throughout the history of international law[1] there are examples of protective treaties concluded for the benefit of specific groups; the treaty is the paradigmatic instrument recognizing the right of minorities to fair treatment. The treaties produce a wilderness of single instances rather than any comprehensive scheme. There is, however, a certain similarity in the occasions and circumstances resulting in a treaty, even though the occasions and circumstances did not produce this result in all cases. Occasions for instituting a protective treaty were similar to those relating to the protection of aliens; a bond between protecting Power and protected minority, whether of religion, nationality, or culture. The minority could, indeed, consist of former nationals of the protecting Power on ceded territory. Hence the association of minority rights with cession of territory. An early example is the Treaty of Oliva of 1660,[2] by which Poland and the Great Elector ceded Pomerania and Livonia to Sweden, guaranteeing the inhabitants of the ceded territories the enjoyment of their existing religious liberties. Article 2(3) of the treaty provides that the 'cities of Royal Prussia, which, as a consequence of this war, have become the property of . . . (Sweden), will maintain all the rights, liberties and privileges which they have enjoyed . . . in the ecclesiastical or the lay domain.' A later example is the multilateral Convention of 1881 for the Settlement of the Frontier between Greece and Turkey.[3] Article III provides that 'The lives, property, honour, religion, and customs of those of the inhabitants of the localities ceded to Greece who shall remain under the Hellenic administration will be scrupulously respected. They will enjoy exactly the same civil and political rights as Hellenic subjects of origin.' Article VIII complements this in providing:

Freedom of religion and of public worship is secured to Mussulmans in the territories ceded to Greece. No interference shall take place with the autonomy or

[1] Works cited, *supra*, ch. 1, n. 1.
[2] Fouques-Duparc, *La Protection des Minorités de Race, de Langue et de Religion.* 75–6.
[3] Hurst, *Key Treaties of the Great Powers*, vol. 2 (Newton Abbot: David & Charles, 1972) 592.

hierarchical organisation of Mussulman religious bodies now existing, or which may hereafter be formed; nor with the management of the funds and real property belonging to them. No obstacle shall be placed in the way of the relations of these bodies with their spiritual heads in matters of religion.

The convention also provides for the retention of property[4] titles to religious and educational institutions, and the autonomy of local religious courts.[5]

The Convention of Constantinople, 1879, between Austria-Hungary and Turkey[6] respecting the occupation by the former of the Provinces of Bosnia and Herzegovina is another example of a wide-ranging guarantee of religious liberty on a cession of territory. The guarantee is not confined to Mussulmans; Article II provides: 'the freedom and outward exercise of all existing religions shall be assured to persons residing or sojourning in Bosnia and the Herzegovina. Especially, entire freedom is assured to Mussulmans in their relations with their spiritual chiefs.' The Austro-Hungarian authorities promised that they would protect the honour, customs, freedom of religion, personal security, and property of Mussulmans. Further, all aggression against them, their property or religion, would be severely punished.[7]

It may be seen that the protection of such 'new' minorities could be generous in spirit. The identification of beneficiaries was in terms of religious affiliation, but the guarantee extended beyond the religious aspects of the minorities' existence to customs, property, educational institutions, and law. No distinction is made between religious belief and outward exercise of religion; the latter issue has been troublesome in recent times when States purport to accept freedom of religious belief, but curtail its exercise in terms of public order, etc. The rights in the conventions described are not limited in this fashion; they are simply declared.

Aspects of the treaties are emblematic of earlier, less disciplined societies despite the privations undoubtedly suffered by minorities; Article IV of the last convention provides that 'The Ottoman currency shall continue to have free circulation in Bosnia and the Herzegovina.' The stringency and discipline of modern societies provide an added element of threat to minorities which may produce similar culture disintegrating effects to the cruder methods of earlier times. The centralizing, homogenizing, and organizing tendencies of modern States are as great and perhaps greater than in earlier epochs. The Convention of Constantinople provides that the minorities are under the sovereignty of Austria-Hungary; they are not apparently compelled, as minorities are in many modern States, to subscribe to a national (or international) ideology as a condition of their continued existence.

Of course, not all treaties were so generous on their face and the condition of minorities was perilous over continents and centuries. Relations

---

[4] Article IV.   [5] Article VIII.
[6] Hurst, *supra*, n. 3, p. 583.   [7] Article II.

between Christian and Islamic powers were frequently strained and gave rise to early instances of protection. An example which belongs to the protection of minorities rather than the protection of aliens is the promise by St Louis of France in 1250 to protect the Maronites as if they were French subjects.[8] The promise was contained in a letter to the Emir, Patriarch, and Bishop; it was renewed in 1649 by Louis XIV in a communication to the Maronite Patriarch of Antioch and the Maronite nation, and by Louis XV in 1737.[9] These were unilateral acts; the earliest treaty in this context appears to be the Austro-Ottoman Treaty of 1615, article 7 of which reads:

Ceux qui professent être le peuple de Jésus – Christ et qui obéissent au Pape, de quelque dénomination que le soit, écclesiastiques, moines, ou Jésuites, auront le droit de construire les églises dans les Etats du sérénissime Empire des Turcs où ils pourront d'après leur usage, conformément au statut de leur ordre et d'après l'antique rite, lire l'évangile, se réunir en assemblées et vaquer ou service divin; ils seront traités avec bienveillance par le sérénissime empereur des Turcs et par ceux qui dépendent de lui . . .[10]

Many treaties followed the one of 1615, as the status of France as a Christian protector was rivalled by Austria and Russia in relations with the Sublime Porte. The Treaty of Carlowitz, 1699, provided a method of implementing guarantees in article 7:

les religieux catholiques româins, partout où ils ont leurs églises, pourront, sans empêchement, exercer leurs fonctions et vivre en toute sécurité, conformément aux ordres émanés de la Sublime Porte, et il sera permis à l'ambassadeur de Pologne près de la Sublime Porte d'exposer devant le trône impérial toutes les demandes qu'il aura ordre de faire au sujet de la réligion.[11]

In the Treaties of Koutchouk-Kainardji, 1774,[12] and Adrianople, 1829,[13] Russia obtained the right to make representations on behalf of Orthodox Christians.

If these instances were a melancholy reflection of relations between Christian and Moslem powers, the Reformation gave rise to the pressing need of protecting one Christian sect from another when religious wars and spontaneous changes resulted in the partisans of one faith finding themselves within the territory of a prince belonging to a different confession. Therefore, several treaties dealt with the rights of Protestants in Catholic

---

[8] A brief analysis of pre-Westphalia instruments protecting minorities is provided by Wintgens, *Der völkerrechtliche Schutz der nationalem, sprachlichen und religiösen Minderheiten*. See also Heyking, 'The International Protection of Minorities—the Achilles Heel of the League of Nations', *Transactions of the Grotius Society*, XII (1937), 31; Rosting, 'Protection of Minorities by the League of Nations', *AJIL*, 17 (1923), 641.

[9] Fouques-Duparc, *La Protection des Minorités de Race, de Langue et de Religion*, 79.

[10] Ibid.

[11] Fouques-Duparc, 79

[12] *Parrys Treaty Series*, 45, 349.

[13] Hurst, *supra*, n. 5, vol. i, 188.

territory, and vice versa. The Treaty of Oliva may be cited as one example. Others include the Treaty of Vienna, 1607, signed by the King of Hungary and the Prince of Transylvania, granting to the Protestant minority in the latter region the free exercise of their religion.[14] The Peace of Westphalia, 1648,[15] between France, the Holy Roman Empire, and respective allies, while confirming the rule of *cuius regio, eius religio* set out in the Religious Peace of Augsburg, 1555,[16] provided safeguards for minorities, though the protection was applied incompletely. Thus, Protestant worship was excluded in the Dominions of the House of Austria as a whole. The Treaty of Nijmegen, 1678, between France and Holland, is another example of an inter-Christian treaty;[17] this guaranteed freedom of worship to the Roman Catholic minority living in the territories ceded by France to Holland. To similar effect is the Treaty of Ryswick, 1697,[18] concluded between the same parties. The emphasis in early treaties is on freedom of conscience and worship, though sometimes even these freedoms were subject to restrictions in favour of public order. Article 14 of the Treaty of Peace between France and Great Britain, 1713, by which France gave Hudson Bay and Acadia to Great Britain is one example:

it has been expressly agreed that in all the territory and colonies which by virtue of this treaty must be ceded or returned by [the King of France], the subjects of the said King will have the liberty of leaving within a year with all their movable properties. Those who, nevertheless, would choose to stay and remain under the domination of Great Britain, must be able to enjoy the exercise of the Roman Catholic religion, *in so far as the laws of England permit it.*[19]

Similarly, the Treaty of Paris, 1763, provides in Article 4 that the King of Great Britain 'agrees to grant to the inhabitants of Canada the freedom of the Catholic religion: consequently [he] will give the most precise and most effectual order, that his new Roman Catholic subjects may profess the worship of religion according to the rites of the Romish church, *as far as the laws of Great Britain permit*'.[20] By contrast, other treaties, for example, those of Oliva and Nijmegen, provided more precise guarantees in that they simply reaffirmed the status quo. An extreme example is provided by the Treaty of Dresden, 1745,[21] between the King of Prussia and the Elector of Saxony: Article 8 stipulated that the Protestant religion would be main-

---

[14] Balogh, *La Protection Internationale des Minorités*, 23 (Paris: Les editions internationales, 1930).
[15] *Parrys Treaty Series*, 1, 119, 271.
[16] Wintgens, *Der völkerrechtliche Schutz der nationalem, sprachlichen und religiösen Minderheiten*, 62–3.
[17] Ibid. 72.
[18] Israel, *Major Peace Treaties of Modern History 1648–1967*, 152 (New York: Chelsea House, 1967).
[19] *Parrys Treaty Series*, 27, 475.
[20] *Parrys Treaty Series*, 42, 320..
[21] Toscano, *Le Minoranza di Razza, di Lingua e di Religione nel Diritto Internazionale*, 16.

tained in the territories of the two parties, in accordance with the Treaty of Westphalia, without it ever being possible to introduce the slightest innovation.

After the Congress of Vienna, treaty clauses for protection of minorities become more detailed and there is a shift from protection of religious minorities to protection of national minorities. At no time would it appear that any doctrinal 'purity' was maintained in treaty practice in conferring rights on individuals or collectivities: churches, religious courts, those who profess to be the people of Jesus Christ, inhabitants of ceded territories, were all mentioned in texts as objects of protection. One writer surmises that there is a difference between inter-Christian instruments and the Christian and Turkish treaties in that the former tended to confine protection to ceded territories and the latter were more wide-ranging, applying throughout the Ottoman Empire. One reason for this may be that minority clauses were in contradiction to the spirit of the law in European states, whereas in Turkey the traditional *Millet*[22] system granted religious freedom to minorities throughout the Empire.[23] From the end of the fifteenth century to the 1920s each religious community (*Millet*) in the Empire enjoyed wide-ranging autonomy in civil and religious matters: *Millets* controlled education, records of birth and death, marriage, and wills. *Millets* could tax members, subject to paying a tribute to the Sultan. The origins of the system in the fall of Constantinople may have been inglorious for minorities in that it derived from the Moslems' contempt for Christians, whom they thought unworthy of the community of the faithful.[24] It was none the less a beneficial autochthonous system, not imposed by treaty.

The new era in Europe, building upon the French and American Revolutions, developed treaty protection in a more secular style: the French revolution of 1789 established in France the principle of freedom of religion and public worship; the First Amendment of the Constitution of the United States of America provided that Congress could 'make no law respecting an establishment of religion or prohibiting the free exercise thereof'. The emergence of nationality as a principle for nation building and identifying 'alien' minority elements within nation States did not mean that religious differences were of no account is the institution of treaty regimes. The religious distinction was always an element in the Turkish treaties, and national and religious differences between majority and minority coexisted:

---

[22] Capotorti, 'Study on the Rights of Persons belonging to Ethnic, Religious and Linguistic Minorities', UN Doc E/CN.4/Sub. 2/384, Add. 1–7, Intro., para. 6.

[23] Laponce, *The Protection of Minorities*, 84–5.

[24] Ibid. 84. Thus, the Sultan gave the Orthodox Patriarch, the Armenian Patriarch, and the Great Rabbi extensive jurisdiction over their respective religious communities (Millets). Members of the Millet did not have direct relations with the Turkish administration, but were required to act through the Community, which had legal personality. Compare the Kahal system, by which mediaeval kings of Poland allowed Jews to organize their own local government, the Kahal: see Laponce, *The Protection of Minorities*, 91.

the conflict in Northern Ireland is a striking contemporary example of such coexistence; it is at once a religious, an ethnic, and a political conflict. The Congress of Vienna, 1815,[25] provided for various categories of minority. Article 77 provided that the inhabitants of the Bishopric of Basle and those of Berne, united to the Cantons of Berne and Basle, should 'enjoy, in every respect, without any distinction of religion . . . the same political and civil rights which are enjoyed, or may be enjoyed by the inhabitants of the ancient parts of the said Cantons'.[26] Act XIV, annexed to the Treaty, on cessions made by the Kingdom of Sardinia to the Canton of Geneva, regulated the rights of populations in ceded territory, in case the Protestant tradition of the Canton might result in oppression of the Catholic minority. Article 3 provides:

Sa Majesté [the King of Sardinia] ne pouvant se résoudre a consentir qu'une partie de son territoire soit réunie a un Etat, où la religion dominante est diffŕehte, sans procurer aux habitants du pays qu'elle cède, la certitude qu'ils jouiront du libre exercise de leur religion, qu'ils continueront à avoir les moyens de fournir aux frais de leur culte, et à jouir eux-mêmes de la plénitude des droits de citoyens.[27]

Protection of the Poles was on the basis of nationality. Article 1 of the Treaty, reflecting the dismemberment of the Polish State, makes provision for the Polish nation so that Polish nationality could be preserved: 'The Poles, who are . . . subjects of Russia, Austria and Prussia, shall obtain a Representation and National Institutions, regulated according to the degree of political consideration, that each of the Governments to which they belong shall judge expedient and proper to grant them.'[28] Annex X to the main treaty, concluded between Austria and the Netherlands, proclaiming the unification of Belgium and Holland, contained guarantees for the Belgian Catholic minority.

The tradition of protecting minorities by treaty continued throughout the nineteenth century. A tendency to devise multilateral instruments is evident throughout the century. The practice also demonstrates distinctions between States, since obligations were imposed on some States, indicating a second-class citizenship. The gravitational centre of the 'minorities question' moved eastwards: it was perceived as a predominantly Central and East European problem. An example of these tendencies is the Treaty of Berlin, 1878:[29] Bulgaria[30] and Eastern Roumelia[31] were recognized as autonomous principality and province, respectively, under the Sultan, provision being made, in both cases, for religious liberty. Article XXVI recognized the independence of Montenegro. Article XXVII relates that the 'High Contracting Parties agree on the following *conditions*' and there follows provision for non-discrimination on religious grounds and freedom of religious

---

[25] Hurst, *Key Treaties of the Great Powers*, vol. i, 76.
[26] Ibid.   [27] *Parrys Treaty Series*, 64, 318.
[28] Hurst, vol. i, 45.   [29] Ibid. vol. ii, 551.
[30] Article I.   [31] Article XIII.

worship. The independence of Serbia is also recognized by Article XXXIV 'subject to the *conditions* set forth'. Clauses on non-discrimination and freedom of worship similar to those for Montenegro are set out.[32] A more extensive array of conditions is provided for Romania, which is recognized as independent. Article XLIV provides: 'In Romania, the difference of religious creeds and confessions shall not be alleged against any person as a ground for exclusion or incapacity in matters relating to the enjoyment of civil and political rights, admission to public employments, functions and honours, or the exercise of the various professions and industries in any locality whatsoever.' The second paragraph provides that 'freedom and outward exercise of all forms of worship shall be assured to all persons belonging to the Romanian State, as well as to foreigners, and no hindrance shall be offered either to the hierarchical organisation of the different communions, or to their relations with their spiritual chiefs'. The final paragraph is headed 'Equal Treatment of Foreigners' and stipulates that subjects and citizens of all the Powers shall be treated in Romania, without distinction of creed, on a footing of perfect equality.

This comprehensive clause encompasses civil and political rights, freedom and outward exercise of worship, and equal treatment of foreigners. It reflected rights in 'all persons' and in religious communities. Article XLIII repeats the conditional recognition formula. The freedoms are absolute in that there is no public order requirement. The 'conditions' related to religious minorities; elsewhere in the treaty, national minorities are the object of protection. Article IV provides in relation to Bulgaria that 'In the districts where Bulgarians are intermixed with Turkish, Romanian, Greek or other populations, the rights and interests of these populations shall be taken into consideration as regards the elections and the drawing up of the Organic Law of the Principality.' The 'populations' may be added to the list of right holders described in the treaty. The document describes itself as a treaty 'for the Settlement of the Affairs of the East'. Thus the Sublime Porte promised to guarantee the security of the Armenians against attacks by Circassians and Kurds,[33] and it made a 'spontaneous declaration'[34] in favour of the principle of religious liberty, as a preamble to an extensive article on this subject.

It has been mentioned that the *locus* of the minorities question was essentially East European through the nineteenth century. The treaties provided models for regulation in other continents where European Powers were involved. The Treaty of Tientsin, 1858,[35] between Great Britain and China, made provision for religious toleration in China. Article VIII stated that

The Christian religion, as professed by Protestants or Roman Catholics, inculcates

---

[32] Article XXXV.   [33] Article LXI.
[34] Article LXII.   [35] Hurst, vol. i, 343.

the practice of virtue, and teaches man to do as he would be done by. Persons teaching or professing it, therefore, shall alike be entitled to the protection of the Chinese authorities, nor shall any such, peaceably pursuing their calling, and not offending against the law, be persecuted or interfered with.

It may be noted that this treaty protected only *Christian* sects.

The development of treaty protection of minorities exhibits organized, and unorganized features. It was more than a wilderness of single instances in that it tended to become localized (mainly Eastern Europe), and the occasions for guarantees displayed certain similarities. Analytically, there was a movement to broaden guarantees beyond freedom of worship to encompass the range of civil and political rights. The treaties reflect a movement to extend to Eastern Europe what had become accepted in the West. The terms were in the main not generous to minorities, and in some cases were extremely vague, such as the reference to Polish nationality in the Treaty of Vienna. The texts occasionally recognized existing privileges of groups, but did not create them: they reveal little attempt to compensate for the numerical inferiority of the minorities in the States. The tone of the instruments is one of tolerance rather than encouragement. Despite this, the existence of so many examples of treaty protection of groups makes it possible to describe a tradition of minority protection in international law. The tradition replenished itself whenever the factum of international power was presented with a suitable opportunity for regulation. The treaties were a symbol of international concern. They were forward-looking rather than retrogressive. The twentieth century has accepted the continuance of the tradition of protecting particular communities, while elaborating a much more ambitious 'universal' scheme.

The principal failing was implementation; this negative 'tradition' has maintained itself in the twentieth century in the difficulties with full international implementation of human rights, whatever the successes of regional and bilateral systems. Claude offers damning criticism of the early period: 'The system of minority protection based upon special treaties guaranteed by the great powers was condemned to failure by the inadequacy of its scope, the vagueness of its substantive provisions, the rudimentary nature of its machinery and organization, and the uncertainty, ineffectiveness and susceptibility to abuse of its sanctions.'[36] In terms of efficaciousness of procedures, the criticism is realistic. It is not necessary to outline the history of atrocities against minority groups to make the point. One merely needs to recall the well-known episodes[37]—the religious wars of Western Europe, the persecution of Romanian Jews and the *pogroms* against them in Russia, the Ottoman massacres (genocide) of the Armenians. All are matters of histori-

---

[36] Claude, *National Minorities: An International Problem* (Cambridge, Mass.: Harvard UP, 1955).

[37] Franck and Rodley, 'After Bangladesh: the Law of Humanitarian Intervention by Military Force', *AJIL*, 67 (1973), 271, 271.

cal record. Effective intervention on behalf of threatened groups was occasional and sporadic, outmatched by cases of non-intervention. Many scholars postulate none the less that there existed a customary law right of humanitarian intervention at least in the nineteenth century.[38] If this is so, it would substantially supplement the treaty tradition.

The right of intervention given by treaty was often rather limited. The Treaty of Koutchouk-Kainardji, 1774,[39] provided for ministers of the Imperial Court of Russia to make representations in favour of the Orthodox religion. Article IX(I) of the Treaty of Paris, 1856, takes note of the proclamation by the Sultan of a Firman 'recording his generous intentions towards the Christian populations of the Empire'[40] and Article IX(II) recites that

The Contracting Powers recognise the high value of this communication. It is clearly understood that it cannot, in any case, give to the said Powers (Great Britain, Austria, France, Prussia, Russia and Sardinia) the right to interfere, either collectively or separately, in the relations of His Majesty the Sultan with his subjects, nor in the Internal Administration of his Empire.

The function of the conditional recognition clause,[41] on the other hand, may have been to grant a right of intervention.[42] Specific clauses in treaties could sometimes give grounds for intervention more forceful than a right to 'make representations'. The London Protocol of 1830 guaranteeing Greek independence contained a declaration by France, Great Britain, and Russia that each power 'would consider it its duty to interpose its influence with the Porte, so as to ensure to the inhabitants [of Crete and Samos] protection against "oppressive and arbitrary acts" '.[43] Apart from treaty-right, a number of interventions (defined by Oppenheim as 'the dictatorial interference by a State or group of States in the affairs of another State for the purposes of maintaining or altering the actual condition' of things therein[44]) point towards a right not limited by the terms of the treaty or limited to the parties to it. Examples are the intervention[45] by France, Great Britain, and Russia in Greece in 1827, consequent upon numerous massacres perpetrated by Turkey. In so far as States not parties to the Treaty of Koutchouk-Kainardji

---

[38] The development of the literature on intervention is surveyed by Fonteyne, 'The Customary International Law Doctrine of Humanitarian Intervention: its Current Validity under the UN Charter', *California Western International Law Journal*, 4 (1974), 203.

[39] *Supra*, n. 12.

[40] Hurst, vol. i, 320.

[41] *Supra*, text following n. 31.

[42] Lauterpacht, *Recognition in International Law*, 357 (London: Cambridge UP, 1948); Moore, *A Digest of International Law*, vol. i, paras. 27, 72–4 (Washington: Govt. Printing Office, 1906); Hackworth *Digest of International Law*, para. 34 (Washington: Govt. Printing Office, 1940–44).

[43] XVII *British and Foreign State Papers* (1827–30), 203.

[44] *International Law: A Treatise*, 305.

[45] Fonteyne, 203; Franck and Rodley, 271.

took part (that treaty only concerned Turkey and Russia), that action could not be based on the treaty. Further, the implementation provisions were weak. The Powers indicated that humanitarian and pragmatic motives[46] justified intervention. Another example is said to be the mandate given by the Powers for France to intervene on behalf of Christians in the Levant in 1860, again following massacres. However, this is a weak example in that the official grounds for justification were a Protocol of 1860[47] signed by France, Great Britain, Prussia, Russia, and Turkey; and the Treaty of Paris, 1856,[48] though the latter, for reasons described (the provision in Article IX(II)) is hardly sustainable as a treaty justification.

Other cases cited as instances of the doctrine display features which confirm rather than dispel doubts on its generality of application. Fonteyne cites the intervention in Bosnia, Herzegovina and Bulgaria from 1876 to 1878.[49] But this involved a formal declaration of war by Serbia and Montenegro against the Porte in 1876, and a subsequent declaration of war by Russia. Fonteyne writes that:

the declarations of war by Serbia and Montenegro were officially justified by humanitarian solidarity with the oppressed populations in the neighbouring countries. On the other hand, the demands of the European Powers [six Powers indicated in a Protocol of 1877 their determination to watch over the fulfilment of the promises in the Treaty of Paris, 1856] as well as the war waged by Russia were formally based upon an invocation of Article IX of the Treaty of Paris.[50]

Doubtful interventions could always be legalized by a declaration of war given the general *laissez-faire* attitude to war in the nineteenth century so that this may not constitute a precedent. Further, despite its restrictive quality, Article IX of the Treaty of Paris is still invoked. Ganji provides a less restrictive interpretation of Article IX(II) of the treaty: 'The principle of non-intervention in the second paragraph of Article IX was embodied for the sole purpose of providing that, as long as the Sultan was acting in good faith in implementing the *Firman*, the European Powers were to abstain from intervening.'[51] Such an interpretation gives treaty-right a broader scope.

While it is not a case of intervention to protect minorities, the intervention of the United States in Cuba in 1898 is sometimes cited as a clear precedent to advance the general doctrine.[52] President McKinley's message

[46] Fonteyne, 208.
[47] Ibid. See also the Convention of 1861 Prolonging the Occupation of Syria, Hurst, vol. i, 408.
[48] Fonteyne, 317.
[49] Fonteyne, 211–12.
[50] Ibid.
[51] Ganji, *International Protection of Human Rights*, 30–1 (Geneva: Librairie E. Droz, 1962).
[52] Behuniak, 'The Law of Unilateral Humanitarian Intervention by Military Force: A Legal Survey', *Military Law Review*, 17 (1978), 157.

to Congress stated that the United States was intervening 'in the cause of humanity and to put an end to barbarities, bloodshed, starvation, and horrible miseries'.[53] Even commentators generally sceptical about the doctrine admit this as a possible exception.[54] However, humanitarian concern was simply one ground for intervention; the most important ground appears to have been protection of American citizens and their property in Cuba, rather than protection of Cubans.[55] One commentator cites the 'powerful influence of endangered investments and trade'.[56] The point is not the hidden motives, but the public justifications for intervention. If humanitarian justifications are sufficient ground in themselves, it is supererogatory to cite a cluster of reinforcing reasons.

Further evidence of lack of confidence in a justifying principle is provided by the Powers' reticence in the face of persecutions of the Jews. Responses to persecutions were mainly verbal, sometimes harsh, but often couched in extremely courteous terms. Fairly typical is the instruction from the US Secretary of State to the United States Consul in Bucharest: 'You will not be backward in joining any . . . protest, or other measure which the foreign representatives there may deem advisable, with a view to avert or mitigate further harshness towards the Israelites.'[57] The Department of State, more cautiously, instructed its Minister in St Petersburg that 'it would . . . be inadmissible for the Government of the United States to approach the Government of Russia in criticism of its laws and regulations, except so far as such laws and regulations may injuriously affect *citizens of this country*'.[58] Clearly the United States Government was inclined to intervene when protection of US citizens was the issue and not for Russian citizens persecuted by their own Government.[59] In connection with massacres of Armenians by the Turks, the United States Ambassador in Constantinople wrote to the Department of State: 'It is difficult for me to restrain myself from doing something to stop this attempt to exterminate a race, but I realise that I am here as Ambassador and must abide by the principles of non-interference.'[60]

Jurists were not unanimous on the doctrine; more significantly, it is

[53] Franck and Rodley, 285.

[54] Ibid.

[55] President McKinley in his message to Congress, 28 March 1898, listed four grounds for the intervention: humanity; protection of United States citizens in Cuba; injury to American commerce; the constant menace to peace from the feebleness of Spanish rule in Cuba: Moore, *A Digest of International Law*, vol. vi, 219; Brownlie, *International Law and the Use of Force by States* (Oxford: OUP, 1963), 340.

[56] Fitzgibbon, *Cuba and the United States 1900–1935* (Menasha, Wis., 1935, reprint New York: Russell, 1964), 25.

[57] Moore, *A Digest of International Law*, vol. vi, 360.

[58] *Foreign Relations of the United States, Diplomatic Papers, 1880* (Washington, 1861–), 873.

[59] *Foreign Relations, 1882*, 451; Stowell, *Intervention in International Law* (Washington: Byrne, 1921), 76–8.

[60] Stowell, 295.

difficult to find a broad consensus which would include most of them. There
are hints of a supporting doctrine in Grotius,[61] but Vattel wrote that 'if the
Sovereign buries his subjects under taxes, if he treats them harshly, it is the
Nation's business; no one else is called upon to admonish him, to force him
to apply wider and more equitable principles'.[62] These sentiments were
developed in an age when national sovereignty had not reached the sacred
status which it acquired later. In the nineteenth century there are clearly two
schools of thought. The non-intervention school includes Mamiani, Car-
nazza-Amari, Pradier-Foderé, Pereira, and Halleck.[63] Italian and Latin
American scholars were generally non-interventionists. Pereira describes a
typical position: 'Internal oppression, however odious and violent it may be,
does not affect, either directly or indirectly, external relations and does not
endanger the existence of other States. Accordingly, it cannot be used as a
legal basis for use of force and violent means.'[64] The interventionist school
included Creasy, de Martens, Wheaton, Woolsey, and Arntz.[65] Creasy
declares a principle with direct application to minorities; 'we intervene on
behalf of a grievously oppressed people, which has never amalgamated with
its oppressors as one nation, and which its oppressors have systematically
treated as an alien race, subject to the same Imperial authority, but in other
respects distinct.'[66] De Martens, however, introduces what today is
regarded as an unacceptable distinction and which was not delineated by all
writers: 'vis-à-vis non-civilised nations . . . intervention by the civilised
Powers is in principle legitimate, when the Christian population of those
countries is exposed to persecutions or massacres . . . [this is] not applicable
to the relations between civilised Powers.'[67]

In all this, it is difficult to discover an *opinio juris*. The strongest advocates of the doctrine came from 'strong' States such as the USA; the jurists of
the 'weak' States developed principles from their often negative experience
of intervention. This is still true today, the loudest advocates of humanitarian intervention are to be found in the USA.[68] It seems that there is a gulf
here which cannot be bridged. Treaty-right remained the surest ground for

---

[61] *De Jure Belli ac Pacis*, 2, 'Grotius on the Rights of War and Peace', tr. W. Whewell,
Cambridge: CUP, 1853, ch. xxv, 438.
[62] *Le Droit des Gens*, 2, cited by Fonteyne, *supra*, n. 38, 215.
[63] Fonteyne, 215 ff.
[64] Fonteyne, 217.
[65] Fonteyne, 216.
[66] Creasy, Sir E., *First Platform of International Law* (London: John van Voorst, 1876),
303–5.
[67] De Martens, *Traité de Droit International*, cited Fonteyne, 219.
[68] Lillich, 'Forcible Self-Help by States to Protect Human Rights', *Iowa Law Review*, 53
(1967), 325; Lillich (ed.), *Humanitarian Intervention and the United Nations*; Behuniak, 'The
Law of Unilateral Humanitarian Intervention by Military Force: A Legal Survey'; Moore, *Law
and Civil War in the Modern World* (Baltimore: Johns Hopkins, 1971)—compare the articles
by Brownlie, 'Humanitarian Intervention', p. 217, and Lillich, 'Humanitarian Intervention—A
Reply to Dr Brownlie and a Plea for Constructive Alternatives', p. 229; McDougal, Lasswell
and Chen, *Human Rights and World Public Order* (New Haven: Yale UP, 1980).

intervention, and collective action was preferable to unilateral action. In the context of minority protection, whatever position is taken on the legal status of humanitarian intervention, it is clearly a defective approach to the resolution of minorities issues. Humanitarian intervention by individual States could hardly serve as a model for the future. It is something of a blind alley, dangerously destabilizing to international society and ultimately counter-productive for its intended beneficiaries. International law could hardly afford such a doctrine in the age of advanced technological wars.[69]

[69] Perhaps the best overall review of the twentieth century doctrine is Ronzitti, *Rescuing Nationals Abroad through Military Coercion and Intervention on Grounds of Humanity* (Dordrecht: M. Nijhoff, 1985). The doctrine of humanitarian intervention is hardly supported at all by post Charter State practice. It could not be otherwise in view of the prohibitions in the UN Charter (Article 2(4): 'All members shall refrain . . . from the threat or use of force against the territorial integrity or political independence of any State, or in any other manner inconsistent with the Purposes of the United Nations') and the development of the principle of non-intervention. Interventions in support of co-nationals do not escape the general censure. When the Sixth Committee of the General Assembly was debating the definition of aggression in 1954, Greece and The Netherlands argued in favour of a right of humanitarian intervention in cases where there were ethnic ties between the intervening State and the minority suffering persecution, Israel contradicted this view in clear terms: 'It seemed advisable to refrain from any action that might be construed as authorizing military intervention of a co-national minority. Humanitarian intervention had frequently been invoked to justify intervention, although the true motives had been very different. In the period between the two world wars, certain minorities had also been used for subversion against the States of which they were citizens. Since the second World War . . . the problem of minorities had been greatly reduced. Consequently, neither the realities of modern life, nor the accepted concept of legal and illegal use of force, nor the teachings of history, could justify the use of force in such a hypothesis'. Panama added that 'The representative of Greece had spoken of the hypothetical case of armed intervention by a State to halt the extermination by another State of part of the former's population on racial, religious or other grounds. Such intervention would certainly conflict with the principles of the Charter'. *GAOR* 9, Sixth Committee, 412th meeting, para. 35; *GAOR*, 9, Sixth Committee, 418th meeting, para. 13. Greece and The Netherlands appear to have taken a different view of the legitimacy of intervention in subsequent cases: Akehurst, 'Humanitarian Intervention', in Bull (ed.), *Intervention in World Politics* (Oxford: OUP, 1984). Some of the argument bases itself on the proposition that the international law on human rights has failed to make sufficient progress and that unilateral action by States in the service of human rights may be the only method of rectifying abuses. In view of the newness of the concept of universal rights in international law, (*infra*, Part III) and the painstaking efforts of the international community to make the rights a reality, this view cannot be accepted. A forthright condemnation of 'humanitarian intervention' was issued in *The Nicaragua Case* (Merits), *ICJ Reports 1986* at para. 268: 'In any event, while the United States might form its own appraisal of the situation as to respect for human rights in Nicaragua, the use of force could not be the appropriate method to monitor or ensure such respect'. See Rodley, 'Human Rights and Humanitarian intervention: The Case Law of the World Court', *ICLQ*, 38 (1989), 321.

3. The Protection of Minorities by the League of Nations

The victorious Powers in the Great War did not entirely reject previous approaches to minority protection, though they sought revisions and improvements. The reconstruction of Europe and the attempt by the Powers to apply the principle of self-determination involved the further reduction of Turkish dominions, dismemberment of the Austro-Hungarian Empire, the creation of new States and substantial additions of territory to others. The nineteenth-century precedents were relevant on account of changes which, although they might diminish the minorities problem in extent, would not cure it. President Woodrow Wilson was active in pressing for international protection of 'racial and national minorities' and was conscious of the international repercussions which might arise from their ill-treatment. His second draft of the League of Nations Covenant contained the following article:

The League of Nations shall require all new States to bind themselves as a condition precedent to their recognition as independent or autonomous States, to accord to all racial or national minorities within their several jurisdictions exactly the same treatment and security, both in law and in fact, that is accorded to the racial or national majority of their people.[1]

D. H. Miller, Wilson's legal adviser, made the following comment:

The purpose of this Article is beneficent, but it is submitted that general treatment is impossible. Doubtless equal religious and cultural privileges should be accorded in all cases, but it is impossible to suppose that all racial minorities can be entitled, for example, to have their languages used in official records. In the case of several small minorities in one country this would be impracticable even locally.

While no change in the Article is suggested, the thought is that it should be followed by additional and more specific provisions varying according to the conditions not only in New States, but in some of the older ones, of which Bulgaria is an example.[2]

In the third draft, this advice is ignored and the article widened. In addition to obligations on new States in the above article, Wilson proposed that the League Council should extract similar promises from 'all States seeking admission to the League of Nations'.[3] The whole article was followed by

---

[1] Miller, *The Drafting of the Covenant*, vol. ii, 91 (New York: G. B. Putnam and Sons, 1928).
[2] Ibid.
[3] Ibid. 105.

another which made particular reference to religion, tying in freedom of religion with the maintenance of international peace:

Recognising religious persecution and intolerance as fertile sources of war, the Powers signatory hereto agree, and the League of Nations shall exact from all new States and all States seeking admission to it the promise, that they will make no law prohibiting or interfering with the free exercise of religion, and that they will in no way discriminate, either in law or in fact, against those who practise any particular creed, religion, or belief whose practices are not inconsistent with public order or public morals.[4]

These two articles were retained substantially unchanged in Wilson's fourth draft,[5] but do not appear in the Covenant of the League. A variant was later tried, but without success:

The High Contracting Parties agree that they will not prohibit or interfere with the free exercise of any creed, religion or belief whose principles are not inconsistent with public order or public morals and that no person within their respective jurisdictions shall be molested in life, liberty or pursuit of happiness by reason of his adherence to any creed, religion or belief.[6]

All attempts to widen the traditional practice of protection of groups by treaty were repulsed. The Wilson clauses were more than rules against discrimination—they would have required the relevant States to act in a positive manner towards their 'racial or national' minorities. They included collective rights. As a general formula, this approach, interposing minorities as collectivities with special claims on the State, provoked general resistance. Even under modern conditions of universal individual human rights, attempts to describe collective rights additional to those of the individual, are rejected by many States as a general principle, whatever its validity in specific, treaty defined instances.[7]

The 'religious' article has become a standard article in modern law; the right holders are those who practise religion, that is, individuals. The burdens placed on the State by this article are fewer than in the case of the minorities article. It is negative in character, requiring of the State only that it does not interfere with a freedom and does not discriminate against practitioners of a creed. The character of the Wilsonian article, linking peace with religious tolerance, might have made it attractive as a rationalization of the interventionist policies over the previous century. The fact that it was not accepted, in particular by some of the Powers, made their humanitarian claims *vis-à-vis* the interventions for Christians in Turkey retrospectively suspect.[8] The standard objection to the proposed articles

---

[4] Ibid. [5] Ibid. 153–4.
[6] Ibid. 307. [7] *Infra*, Part IV.
[8] Franck and Rodley, 'After Bangladesh: The Law of Humanitarian Intervention by Military Force', *AJIL*, 67 (1973), 275.

was that they encroached on the sovereignty of League members. However, as such encroachments had been practised by the Powers on weaker States for a prolonged period in history, a deeper reason may have been that any generalization of such provisions would have affected the Powers themselves.[9] Despite the promise of a new order of equality of States, the concept of a Concert of Europe had not lost its sway. Further evidence is provided by the inability of the delegate of Japan to insert provisions in the Covenant intended to recognize equality of nations and peoples.[10] Racialism itself was not as uncongenial a notion to the Statesmen in the post-World War I period as it might be today. The concept of inferior and superior nations, peoples, and races is present to some extent in Covenant provisions on Mandates, coexisting with their forward-looking character.[11] The Wilson drafts of the Covenant were confronted with the British drafts. The British view was that the 'controversial' minority section was better dealt with in the territorial treaties to settle post-war boundaries.[12] Pressure from Australia and New Zealand, fearful of League scrutiny of their treatment of aboriginal and Maori populations, hardened British views. The religious question was considered too delicate for international regulation. Wilson himself, despite speeches on the equality of nations and races, declared that his interest was 'to quiet discussion that raises national differences and racial prejudices', accepting deletion in order to avoid 'embarrassments'.[13]

Thus, international law hesitated to enter the age of human rights. Instead it entered the age of minority rights, in that, although there was no general system, the League's minority regime was the most extensive developed by the international community. Clemenceau compared the League system with what had gone before in a letter to Paderewsky:

Under the older system, the guarantee of the execution of similar provisions was vested in the Great Powers. Experience has shown that this was in practice ineffective, and it was also open to the critics in that it might give to the Great Powers, either individually or in combination, a right to interfere with the internal constitutions of the States affected which could be used for political purposes. Under the new system the guarantee is entrusted to the League of Nations.[14]

The other policy-setting address was by President Wilson:

Nothing, I venture to say, is more likely to disturb the peace of the world than the

---

[9] Robinson, *Were the Minorities Treaties a Failure?*, 10 (New York: Institute of Jewish Affairs, 1943); for Wilson's views on the equality of States, see Robinson, 14.

[10] McKean, *Equality and Discrimination under International Law*, 16–19; Robinson, 13.

[11] '. . . peoples which are not yet able to stand by themselves under the strenuous conditions of the modern world . . .' (Article 22 of the Covenant of the League of Nations). The Mandate system required that 'the tutelage of such peoples should be entrusted to advanced nations . . .'.

[12] Robinson (*supra*, n. 9), 10.

[13] Ibid. 15.

[14] Miller, *My Diary at the Peace Conference of Paris* (New York: Appeal Print Co., 1924–8); Ermacora, 'The Protection of Minorities Before the United Nations', 260.

treatment which might, in certain circumstances be meted out to the minorities . . . If this Conference is going to recognise these various Powers as new sovereignties within definite territories, the chief guarantors are entitled to be satisfied that their territorial settlements are of a character to be permanent, and that the guarantees given are to insure the peace of the world. It is not therefore, the intervention of those who would interfere, but the action of those who would help.[15]

The thrust of arguments advanced by statesmen representing the dominant Powers was that they were seeking to maintain a tradition, in radically improved form, without overtones of second-class citizenship *vis-à-vis* contracting States. They emphasized the benefits to these States in terms of reconciliation of different races, because the minorities of different race and language would understand that the international community would guarantee them against injustice and oppression.

The League of Nations system included the following instruments:[16]

Minorities in Poland: Treaty between the Principal Allied and Associated Powers and Poland, Versailles, June 1919;

Minorities in Austria: Treaty of Peace between the Allied and Associated Powers and Austria, Saint-Germain-en-Laye, September 1919;

Minorities in the Serb-Croat-Slovene State: Treaty between the aforementioned Powers and the Serb-Croat-Slovene State, Saint-Germain-en-Laye, September 1919;

Minorities in Czechoslovakia: Treaty between the Powers and Czechoslovakia, Saint-Germain-en-Laye, September 1919;

Minorities in Bulgaria: Treaty between the Powers and Bulgaria, Neuilly-sur-Seine, November 1919;

Minorities in Romania: Treaty between the Powers and Romania, Paris, December 1919;

Minorities in Hungary: Treaty of Peace between the Powers and Hungary, Trianon, June 1920;

Minorities in Greece: Treaty concerning the Protection of Minorities in Greece, Sèvres, August 1920;

Minorities in the Free City of Danzig: Convention between Poland and Danzig, Paris, November 1920;

Preservation of Swedish Traditions in the Aaland Islands: Agreement between Sweden and Finland placed on record and approved by a resolution of the Council of the League of Nations, June 1921;

Minorities in Albania, Lithuania, Latvia, Estonia and Iraq: Declarations made to the League of Nations in October 1921 (Albania), May 1922

---

[15] Robinson, (*supra*, n. 9), 21.

[16] A list of instruments is contained in United Nations, Protection of Minorities, *supra*, ch. 1, n. 37. For texts to 1927 see *Protection of Linguistic, Racial and Religious Minorities by the League of Nations, Provisions Contained in the Various International Instruments At Present In Force* (Geneva, August 1927), League of Nations Publications IB Minorité 1927. IB 2.

(Lithuania), July 1923 (Latvia), September 1923 (Estonia), and May
   1932 (Iraq);
Upper Silesia: German-Polish Convention relating to Upper Silesia, Geneva,
   May 1922;
Minorities in Turkey and Greece: Treaty of Peace between the British
   Empire, France, Italy, Japan, Greece, Romania, the Serb-Croat Slovene
   State, and Turkey regarding the protection of minorities in Turkey and
   Greece, Lausanne, July 1923;
Minorities in the Territory of Memel: Convention concerning the Territory
   of Memel, Paris, May 1934.

The wording of the instruments was schematic, though there are some
exceptions. The Polish Treaty served as a model for others, since it
preceded them chronologically. The treaties contain provisions on the
protection of members of groups resident or born in the States concerned
against loss of nationality resulting from the post-war territorial settlement.
For example, by Article 3 of the Treaty with Poland, Poland recognized as
nationals those of German, Austrian, etc., nationality habitually resident
in what had become Polish territory or whose parents were habitually
resident in the territory. This was made subject to a right in the above individuals to opt for any other nationality which was open to them. Those
who exercised the right of option were obliged to transfer to the State of
option.

   The States were obliged to grant to all inhabitants full and complete
protection of life and liberty, and to recognize that they were entitled to free
exercise of any creed, religion, or belief whose practices were not inconsistent with public order or morals. The treaties distinguished between
inhabitants and nationals in that nationals were accorded equality before
the law and equal enjoyment of civil and political rights. Additionally there
were provisions for minorities. Nationals belonging to racial, religious, or
linguistic minorities were to enjoy the same treatment in law and fact as
other nationals. In particular, they had an equal right to establish schools
and charitable, religious, and social institutions at their own expense; they
could use their own language and freely exercise their own religion. The
States agreed to grant adequate facilities to enable nationals whose mother
tongue was not the official language to use their own language, orally or in
writing, before the courts.

   Further, in towns and districts with a considerable proportion of nationals whose mother tongue was not the official language, adequate facilities
were to be provided to ensure that in the primary schools, instruction would
be given to the children of such nationals through their own language,
though the official language could still be made an obligatory part of the
curriculum. Finally, the treaties provided that in those towns and districts,
the minorities would be assured of an equitable share in the enjoyment and

application of sums provided out of public funds under State, municipal, or other budgets for educational, religious, or charitable purposes.

The first two classes of rights above, dealing with the rights of all inhabitants and nationals, reflect the preoccupations of Western statesmen, who were convinced that whatever rights minorities should have would be served best in a Liberal setting. The rights included in special minorities provisions, from the viewpoint of minorities, constituted the *raison d'être* of the system, providing, in some cases, compensation for inability to achieve full self-determination. The purpose of the system as characterized by the Permanent Court of International Justice was to

secure for certain elements incorporated in a State, the population of which differs from them in race, language or religion, the possibility of living peaceably alongside that population and co-operating amicably with it, while at the same time preserving the characteristics which distinguish them from the majority, and satisfying the ensuing special needs.

In order to attain this object, two things were regarded as particularly necessary . . . The first is to ensure that nationals belonging to racial, religious or linguistic minorities shall be placed in every respect on a footing of perfect equality with the other nationals of the State.

The second is to ensure for the minority elements suitable means for the preservation of their racial peculiarities, their traditions and their national characteristics. These two requirements are indeed closely interlocked, for there would be no true equality between a majority and a minority if the latter were deprived of its own institutions and were consequently compelled to renounce that which constitutes the very essence of its being as a minority.[17]

The reference to 'peaceful living' and 'co-operating amicably' suggested that minorities should be loyal to their host States. This duty is also implied in the rights of citizenship rather than expressed in the treaties. Opponents of the system none the less pointed out the superficial imbalance in the respective duties of minorities and States. The loyalty question has continued to be prominent in post World War II debates on minorities.[18]

The above scheme is a summary of the general provisions. Some instruments went further. In the Romanian treaty, the Szeklers and Saxons of Transylvania were to be granted autonomy in religious and educational matters, as were the Vlachs of the Pindus (Greece).[19] The Ruthenes of the Carpathians were to have the greatest degree of autonomy compatible with the unity of the Czechoslovak State.[20] Special provisions were also made in favour of the Jewish minority in Greece, Poland and Romania, for example, Article 7 of the Romanian treaty obliged Romania to recognize as Romanian nationals 'without the requirement of any formality'[21] Jews inhabiting

---

[17] *Minority Schools in Albania* (1935), PCIJ Ser. A/B, No. 64, 17.
[18] *Infra*, ch. 17.
[19] Fouques-Duparc, *La Protection des Minorités de Race, de Langue et de Religion*, 260.
[20] Ibid. 265.
[21] Ibid. 98–112.

Romanian territory. The Moslem communities in Albania, Greece and the Serb-Croat-Slovene State were also singled out for special protection. The monastic communities of Mount Athos were guaranteed their traditional rights (Greece). The Aaland Islanders of Finland were another specific group to be granted wide-ranging rights. Measures of autonomy were favoured by geographical concentration.

The League Guarantee

The League of Nations guarantee for the protection of minority rights was both internal and external. Internally, the obligated state undertook that the treaty provisions were to be regarded as fundamental laws invalidating all laws, regulations, or official action in conflict with them, whether relating to minorities or the population as a whole. Externally, the guarantee was more limited, applying to the various rights only 'so far as they affect persons belonging to racial, religious or linguistic minorities'.[22] In that case they constituted 'obligations of international concern'.[23] It is correct to describe the League regime as a minorities regime despite the mixing of rights for all inhabitants with minority rights. For such a scheme to work, it was imperative that individuals should not be arbitrarily excluded from the minority, an issue on which every kind of chicanery was possible and practised.[24]

The term 'guarantee' implied the following: (*a*) the provisions were inviolable, they could not be modified without the approval of a majority of the League Council, and the League had responsibility for their enforcement; (*b*) the League Council and Permanent Court were the twin pillars, political and judicial, of the guarantee; (*c*) the Council was to take action in the event of any infraction of minorities obligations; (*d*) Council members had a right and duty to call attention to actual or threatened infractions; and (*e*) the right of Council members did not preclude minorities or states not represented on the Council from calling the League's attention to infractions, but such acts had to remain in the nature of a petition because they could not have the legal effect of putting the matter before the Council.[25]

The procedural steps within the League for addressing minorities ques-

---

[22] Article 12 of the Polish treaty.   [23] Ibid.

[24] Jones, 'National Minorities: A Case Study in International Protection', *Law and Contemporary Problems*, 14 (1949), 599 at 610–24.

[25] For the petition procedure, see generally, *Protection of Linguistic, Racial or Religious Minorities by the League of Nations*, League of Nations Publications, IB Minorités, 1931 IB 1 (C.8.M.5. 1931. 1.); de Azcárate, *The League of Nations and National Minorities* (Washington: Carnegie Endowment for International Peace, 1945); Capotorti, *Study on the Rights of Persons Belonging to Ethnic, Religious and Linguistic Minorities*, UN Doc E/CN.4/Sub.2/384/Add.1–7, UN Sales No. E.78.XIV.I; Roucek, *The Working of the Minorities System under the League of Nations* (Prague: Orbis, 1929); Sohn and Buergenthal, *Interna-*

tions gegan with examination of the petition by the League Secretariat for receivability. If accepted, it passed to a committee of the Council,[26] which, together with the minorities section of the Secretariat, would conduct an intensive investigation and ascertain the response of the accused State. If this proved unsatisfactory, the matter was placed on the Council agenda by formal recommendation and the case was handled by the Council as one brought before it by a member. The petition procedure was important, since it was an attempt to ensure some means of defence to the minority whose rights were threatened. However, it was also designed, by withholding from the minority any *locus standi* before the Council or the Permanent Court, to reduce the incidence of controversial public debates between minority and host State. Such debates were thought to reduce the possibility of improving relations between majority and minority. The question of publicity was considered an extremely delicate one; the sensibilities of the minorities States were constantly considered as the petition procedure underwent a series of mutations.

The role of the Permanent Court of International Justice[27] may also be noted. To cite the Polish Treaty, it was provided that any differences of opinion on questions of law or fact arising out of the Treaty articles between Poland and the other parties or a member of the Council of the League of Nations was to be regarded as a dispute of an international character under

tional Protection of Human Rights, 213–335 (Indianapolis: The Bobbs-Merrill Co., 1973); Robinson, *Were the Minorities Treaties a Failure?* For a comparison of the procedure with other petition systems, consult Nørgaard, *The Position of the Individual in International Law* (Copenhagen: Munksgaard, 1962) (Copenhagen: Munksgaard, 1962).

[26] Committees of Three (members of the League Council) were formed partly to avoid the 'thankless and invidious' task of individual Council members having to serve as the accuser of a State: de Azcárate, *The League of Nations and National Minorities*, 182–4. The rules for the composition of the Committees were designed to secure as much objectivity as possible: e.g., the President of the Council, in appointing two colleagues to the Committee, could not appoint either the representative of the host State of the minority, nor of a neighbouring State, nor 'the representative of a State a majority of whose population belong from the ethnical point of view to the same people as the persons [petitioners] in question'; *Protection of Linguistic, Racial or Religious Minorities by the League of Nations* (*supra*, n. 25), 10. State sensitivity (host States of the minorities) is reflected in conditions for the receivability of petitions defined by the League Council in 1923, one of which was that the petition must not be submitted '. . . in the form of a request for the severance of political relations between the minority . . . and the State of which it forms a part'. The other conditions for receivability were: the petition must have in view the protection of minorities in accordance with the treaties; it could not be anonymous or emanate from an unauthenticated source; it could not be couched in violent language; and it must not be, in essence, a repeat of a previous complaint. The rule requiring the exhaustion of domestic remedies before embarking on an international procedure was not included.

[27] Feinberg, *La Juridiction de la Cour Permanente de Justice dans le Système de la Protection Internationale des Minorités* (Paris: Rousseau, 1931). The Court produced advisory opinions on *German Settlers in Poland* (*PCIJ*, Ser.B. No.6); on the *Acquisition of Polish Nationality* (Ser.B, No.7); on the *Exchange of Greek and Turkish Populations* (Ser.B. No.10); on the *Interpretation of the Greek and Turkish Agreement of 1 December 1926* (Ser.B. No.16); on the *Greco-Bulgarian Communities* (Ser.B. No.17); on *Access to German Minority Schools in Upper Silesia* (Ser.A–B. No.40); and on *Minority Schools in Albania* (Ser.A–B. No.64). See also Fachiri, *The Permanent Court of International Justice* (Oxford: OUP, 1925).

Article 14 of the Covenant of the League of Nations. Article 14 of the Covenant set up the Permanent Court of International Justice to hear and determine disputes referred to it by the Assembly or Council of the League. Thus the political competence of the League Council was supplemented by the jurisdictional and advisory competence of the Court.

The peak years for petitions received were 1930 to 1931 and 1931 to 1932, when 305 petitions were received of which 153 were declared admissible.[28] The subject matter of the petitions varies enormously—from suppression of private schools,[29] use of biased historical textbooks,[30] restrictions on minority languages,[31] agrarian reform to the detriment of minority landholders,[32] discriminatory policies in job placement,[33] denial of pension rights,[34] denial of citizenship, etc.,[35] to many acts of violence, repression, and terror on the part of the authorities.[36] Germans and Hungarians were the most assiduous petitioners; Jewish petitions were extremely rare. This indicates something about the fate of the system, used progressively by 'strong' minorities conscious of belonging to a wider community and unhappy at their subjection to 'inferior' peoples.[37] The system coped with everyday frictions, but failed to solve wider problems. The League was not, of course, a supreme State organization, but merely an international body. Ultimately, what could not be achieved by persuasion and mediation could not be achieved at all.

Failure of the League System

In 1939 there were four petitions, three of which were rejected; this indicates that the system had virtually ceased to function. The winding down

---

[28] Robinson, *Were the Minorities Treaties a Failure?*, 128, sets out a table of petitions.

[29] *Minority Schools in Albania* (*supra*, n. 27).

[30] For example, letter from members of the Minorities Committees which examined the petition from the Hungarian Party of Romania, concerning the situation of the educational institutions of the Hungarian minority and, in particular, the setting up of a cultural zone by the Romanian Government in Transylvania and the observations of that government thereon, *LNOJ*, 14 (1932), 157–82; letter from the Representatives of France, Norway, and Spain, members of the Minorities Committee which examined the petition from M. de Balogh and M. Gabor concerning the textbooks used in Romanian schools and the observations of the Government, *LNOJ*, 13 (1932), 1109–10; also, again concerning the Hungarians in Romania, *LNOJ*, 14 (1933), 429–66.

[31] *LNOJ*, 14 (1933), 437–8.

[32] This reflects the class background of some petitions. Minority members who were landowners attempted to use the system to serve their social class rather than minority group interests. In general, the Council refused to sustain complaints if legislation was part of a genuine national economic policy: de Azcárate, *The League of Nations and National Minorities*, 61–6.

[33] *LNOJ*, 13 (1932), 184.

[34] *LNOJ*, 16 (1935), 453–4; *LNOJ*, 18 (1937), 314–17.

[35] *LNOJ*, 13 (1932), 183.

[36] De Azcárate, *The League of Nations and National Minorities*, 66–73.

[37] Robinson, *Were the Minorities Treaties a Failure?* 255–60.

had been evident for some time, certainly since the Polish denunciation of its Minority Treaty in 1934, which went largely unchallenged.

There had been considerable difficulties from the start which made for a certain precariousness in operation. The attitudes of the main participants: minority States, minorities, and kin-States, were fundamental. For the minority States, the system denied the reality of their right to sovereign equality, stamping them as second-class citizens of the international community.[38] New or reconstituted States also expressed the view that, in perpetuating separateness, the League posed a threat to their internal stability. They demanded generalization of the system or its abolition, preferably the latter.

There were double standards implicit in confining the system to the 'fault-line'; the 'insult' was keenly felt and resulted in unco-operative attitudes, and restrictive minorities legislation, although national 'performance' in this respect was rather uneven. The jurist Robinson and his collaborators noted two groups of States with liberal minorities legislation: the Central European trio of Austria, Czechoslovakia, and Hungary; and the Baltic Republics.[39] Mid way between the two in conduct was Poland. Four States were regarded as having less generous provisions: Yugoslavia, Bulgaria, Romania, and Greece. 'Peripheral' States such as Turkey, Iraq, and Albania almost entirely neglected the minorities. But even in the 'liberal' States the record was patchy with regard to different kinds of rights.

In the Baltic States, the tendency was to restrict rather than expand the use of minority languages. On the other hand, Estonia followed a more generous policy than any of the minorities States and founded a system of complete cultural autonomy which went beyond international requirements. Perhaps it is true to say that there was a strong connection between the general level of democracy in a State and the fate of minorities. The minorities themselves, beneficiaries of the system, were also its keen critics. They demanded, *inter alia*, liberalization of the petition procedures which had such regard for the sensitivities of States, and assurances that the system was not a stepping stone to assimilation and greater autonomy. They were not as monolithically opposed to the system as were the States, though the 'strong' minorities articulated and characterized opposition to the League.

Finally, and especially after Hitler's *Machtergreifung*, the more destructive minority sentiments were inflamed by propaganda emanating from kin States such as Germany, Austria, Hungary, and Bulgaria, all committed to a fundamental revision of the Versailles settlement.[40] It is not surprising that

---

[38] See the observations submitted by the Governments of Czechoslovakia, Greece, Poland, Romania, and the Serb-Croat-Slovene State to the Committee appointed by the League Council in 1929 to examine proposals on the system submitted by Canada and Germany, *LNOJ Special Supplement No.73* (1929), 70–4.

[39] Ibid. 151–4.

[40] Fischer, *Nazi Germany and International Law* (PhD Dissertation, University of Washing-

the system foundered under the pressure of this attack: it seemed to please no one who participated in its functioning. Sober and constructive analysis of the strong and weak points of this limited system was ultimately impossible in the face of unwillingness to make it work. The failure was ultimately a political failure on the highest level, in company with the League itself and of democracy. The connection between the collapse of the system and the general malaise is vividly made by Bagley:

> It is unjust to view the failure of the minority system of the League . . . independently of the general international conditions of its time. The minorities protection system was but a part of the world structure established at Paris. Inevitably [it] depended on the general state of international order and relations, and inevitably when that order disintegrated the system collapsed with it, like one floor of a toppling building. The between-war world was witness to an appalling phenomenon of retrogression, a backsliding of morals and politics. Dictatorships replaced democracies, hate and intolerance flourished, power over-rode reason, and passionate nationalism crushed the growing bloom of international co-operation. That minorities should suffer in such a climate was inevitable.[41]

Evaluation of the League System

In terms of international law and the themes of the present work, it may be recalled that the treaties and declarations were not principally group centred, but ascribed rights to individuals: nationals, inhabitants, and persons belonging to racial, religious, or linguistic minorities. Robinson and collaborators noted that: 'In some instances, the articles are almost verbatim extracts from the classical documents of individual and national emancipation, such as the English Bill of Rights, the American Declaration of Independence, the Preamble and Amendments 1, 4, 5, 14 . . . and 15 of the United States Constitution, and the Declaration of the Rights of Man of the French Revolution.'[42] The difference between them is, of course, that the League documents are not couched in universal terms; it is not so much a case of 'all men' as all 'inhabitants (or nationals) of Poland', etc. The documents also describe communities and the rights of communities: 'minorities' are to be afforded an equitable share of funds for educational, religious or charitable purposes (Article 9 of the Treaty with Poland). The Treaty with Romania provided rights for the communities of Szeklers and Saxons; in the Greek Treaty it is the 'Communities' of the Vlachs of the Pindus (Article 12).[43] The Treaty with Poland also refers to 'Jewish Com-

ton, 1973); Bischoff, *Nazi Conquest through German Culture* (Cambridge, Mass.: Harvard UP, 1942).

[41] *General Principles and Problems in the Protection of Minorities*, 126 (Geneva: Imprimeries Populaires, 1950).

[42] Ibid. 39.   [43] Capotorti Report, Add. 2, 13.

munities' (Article 10). Petitions could emanate from individuals or associations, these did not have to belong to the minority concerned or even to the country referred to in the petition.[44]

The instruments are eclectic in nature, the language of equality is pervasive, but it applied indifferently to individuals and groups—the Permanent Court (above) describes equality for 'nationals', 'minority elements', and between 'majority and minority'. The League scheme was not an exercise in theory but practical and humanitarian, recognizing the group dimension of human existence.

There was a good deal of debate on the ultimate purposes of the system. M. de Mello-Franco (Brazil) believed that those who conceived the system wished the members of the minority to enjoy legal protection of the inviolability of the person; this would prepare the way for conditions necessary to establish a complete national unity.[45] Sir Austen Chamberlain spoke of minorities being merged in the national community to which they belonged, but without losing their specific characteristics.[46] In line with the distinctions set out above,[47] this would appear to mean integration rather than assimilation. On the other hand, M. de Mello-Franco appears to describe assimilation as an ideal; this reflects much of official Latin American thinking.[48] The Latin American view was studied in the inter-war period by Yepes: 'En Amérique—spécialement en Amérique Latine—il n'existe pas d'antagonisme de race, de langue ou de religion. Les pays-là n'ont pas à supporter le poids d'une tradition de haines et de luttes séculaires. C'est pourquoi les problèmes de minorités—casse-tête des hommes d'État en Europe—ne se posent pas en Amérique.'[49] Latin American States have continued to present this ideal to the world as a justification for assimilationist policies.

The League's concept of the purpose of the system remains best explicated by the Statement of the Permanent Court, and, with suitable modifications of vocabulary, by the French statesman Aristide Briand. He described the 'problem of minorities' as:

while ensuring that the minorities shall preserve their language, culture, religion and traditions, to keep them (the minorities) as a kind of small family within the larger family, . . . with the object of harmonising all its constituent elements with those of the country as a whole. The process at which we aim is not the disappearance of the minorities but a kind of assimilation which will tend to the greatness of the nation

[44] *Protection of Linguistic, Racial or Religious Minorities by the League of Nations* (*supra*, n. 25), 176; Robinson, *Were the Minorities Treaties a Failure?* pp. 85 ff.

[45] *Protection of Minorities by the League of Nations*, ibid. 41–7.

[46] Ibid. 87–92, 96, 101.

[47] *Supra*, ch. 1, text to n. 12 ff.

[48] *Infra*, chs.14 ff. on the interpretation of Article 27 of the Covenant on Civil and Political Rights.

[49] Yepes, 'Les Problèmes Fondamentaux du Droit des Gens en Amérique', *Rec. des Cours*, 47 (1934), I, 5, at p. 14.

as a whole without in any way diminishing the importance of the smaller family. That is how I understand the problem of minorities.[50]

Again, as with Sir Austen Chamberlain, 'assimilation' appears to equate with 'integration', though more liberal meanings are not excluded. Briand uses 'assimilation' after his own fashion.

Consistent with this recognition of the value of the 'small family' within the 'larger family', the instruments went beyond tolerance of minorities; minorities had a claim on public funds in the interests of equality between dominant and non-dominant groups in society. This positive aspect has proved difficult to reproduce in post World War II conditions, but an interpretation is offered of the leading treaty article on minorities which promotes such a view.[51] Rights of autonomy went even further than this in cases such as the Ruthenes. In many cases the minorities arrangements were a substitute for self-determination, since the map of Europe was redrawn in the Versailles settlement; autonomy naturally suggests itself as compensation for inability to achieve full political self-determination culminating in independence. Its appeal in this respect is undiminished for statesmen as a device for dealing with particular minorities situations.[52]

The League system was not intended for general application—the authors of the treaties did not attempt to set out principles of government of universal application.[53] It reflected European history and experience. It coexisted with the colonial system, and the Mandates under League supervision. In certain respects the system was an improvement over what had gone before: minorities in a broad belt of States had the benefit of a collective guarantee by the international community. International law gained much experience in dealing with violations of human rights. Individuals were enabled to claim against injustices caused by their own States and thus continued the gradual erosion of the concept of domestic jurisdiction; the internationalization of the treaties in so far as they affected members of minorities represented the extreme limit of State concessions.

Such treaties and declarations could never exhaust the substance of minority rights. International law did not then exhibit a general and fundamental commitment to human liberty and equality. The substance of the law did not reflect the range and gravity of threats to non-dominant

---

[50] *Protection of Minorities by the League of Nations*, (*supra*, n. 25) 101–2.

[51] *Infra*, Part IV.

[52] Examples of autonomy are outlined in United Nations, Protection of Minorities, *supra*, ch. 1, n. 37. For contemporary reviews of autonomy, see Dinstein (ed.), *Models of Autonomy* (New Brunswick and London: Transaction Books, 1981); Hannum and Lillich, 'The Concept of Autonomy in International Law', *AJIL*, 74 (1980), 858; Lapidoth, 'Some Reflections on Autonomy'; Sohn, 'The Concept of Autonomy in International Law and the Practice of the United Nations', *Israel Law Review*, 15 (1980), 180. For a discussion relating autonomy to self-determination, see Brownlie, 'The Rights of Peoples in Modern International Law' in Crawford (ed.), *The Rights of Peoples* (Oxford: OUP, 1988), 1.

[53] *Infra*, ch. 9.

groups. The protective nature of the League treaties does not imply that treaties in general were protective. A notorious inter-war example of a treaty exhibiting the reverse tendency is the Convention concerning the Exchange of Greek and Turkish Populations, signed at Lausanne, January 1923.[54] Article 1 provides that:

As from the 1st May, 1923, there shall take place a compulsory exchange of Turkish nationals of the Greek Orthodox religion established in Turkish territory, and of Greek nationals of the Moslem religion established in Greek territory. These persons shall not return to live in Turkey or Greece respectively without the authorisation of the Turkish Government or of the Greek Government respectively.

Article 6 provides: 'No obstacle may be placed for any reason whatever in the way of the departure of a person belonging to the populations which are to be exchanged.' The only 'rights' of individuals allowed in the Convention are such as 'the right to take away freely or to arrange for the transport of . . . movable property . . .', that is, rights which are incidental to the exchange but do not frustrate it. The transfer, which involved appalling human misery, was initiated by a treaty which represents the crudest expression of State power over individuals and groups.

The phrase 'the rights of minorities' was destined to acquire new meanings. That there was still a need for the concept of collective human rights may be deduced from the scale and motivations of Nazi attacks on Jews and other twentieth century genocides.[55] The censure of such acts appropriate to international law required concepts which were not present in the League's instruments; concepts reflecting the highest degree of international opprobrium of the denial of the right of existence to human groups. The League treaties were designed to protect the right to an identity of the minorities concerned. Despite the low regard in which the system was eventually held, the heterogeneous nature of States in ethnic and religious terms, and the fact that dominant majorities could not be relied upon to treat minority cultures with respect, made it a natural necessity that the right would continue in some form.[56] The 'new' theme

---

[54] *AJIL*, 18 (1924), Supplement, 84; *Protection of Linguistic, Racial and Religious Minorities* (*supra*, n. 16), 106. Séfériàdes, 'L'Échange des Populations', *Rec. des Cours*, 24 (1928(IV)), 311; de Zayas, 'International Law and Mass Population Transfers'; and *Nemesis at Potsdam: The Anglo-Americans and the Expulsion of the Germans* (London: Routledge and Kegan Paul, 1979).

[55] *Infra*, ch. 5, and, generally, Kuper, *Genocide: Its Political Use in the Twentieth Century* (London: Penguin Books, 1981). See also, Porter (ed.), *Genocide and Human Rights: A Global Anthology* (Washington: University Press of America, 1982).

[56] The present study does not deal with the Mandates operated by the League contemporaneously with the system for minorities. The basis of the system was Article 22 of the Covenant (*supra*, n. 11), and it was designed to advance the autonomy of peoples formerly subject to the colonial control of Germany and Turkey. This represented a compromise between immediate self-determination and respect for colonialism, at that time practised extensively by the Allied Powers victorious in the Great War. Different classes of Mandates were created with varying degrees of control and guarantees, but the approach to supervision

which appeared in the post World War II era is the theme of human rights.

was similar in some respects to that of minorities, despite the fact that the minorities were not handled within the Covenant itself. In the case of Mandates, petitions came to the League Council through the Permanent Mandates Commission, and abusive petitions were screened. The League organs were active in preventing excesses in a number of instances in Mandates. For example, the Mandates Commission criticized The Union of South Africa for air bombings of the Bondelzwarts tribe in South West Africa, the conduct of France in Syria (the bombing of Damascus in 1925), and the British for their attitude to slavery and forced labour in Tanganyika. The experience of Mandates favoured the emergence of the right of self-determination after the Second World War, and gave the international community further experience in dealing with grievances on humanitarian grounds. For colonies not under Mandate, Article 23(b) of the Covenant required that the inhabitants be treated 'justly', but no international machinery was set up to supervise their treatment. Consult Nørgaard, *The Position of the Individual in International Law*; Walters, *A History of the League of Nations* (London: OUP, 1952); Kelly, 'National Minorities in International Law' *Journal of International Law and Policy*, 3 (1973), 253; Webster and Herbert, *The League of Nations in Theory and Practice* (London: Allen and Unwin, 1933); Margalith, *The International Mandates* (Baltimore and London: Johns Hopkins and OUP, 1930); Millot, *Les Mandats Internationaux* (Paris: Larose, 1924).

4. Postscript to the League System

It is now primarily of historical interest to recall the conclusions of a study by the United Nations Secretariat in 1950[1] that the engagements entered into by States after World War I on the treatment of minorities had ceased to exist. The authors of the study examined ordinary causes of extinction of the treaties and declarations: the effects of war, the dissolution of the League of Nations, the implicit abrogation of the minorities undertakings upon the coming into force of the United Nations Charter, the implicit abrogation of the treaties by the stipulations concerning human rights and fundamental freedoms in the Peace Treaties of 1947 with ex-enemy States, and population movements in consequence of World War II. In relation to ordinary causes of extinction, an assessment of validity was made on a case by case basis. The line taken by the Secretariat on the effects of war was that it did not entail the extinction of obligations; the obligations arose out of multilateral agreements to which belligerent or neutral States were parties or out of declarations made before the Council of the League which represented an international community; further, the minorities obligations were regarded as 'undertakings of general interest', entered into 'in the interest of good understanding, international order and peace'.

On the dissolution of the League, the obligations under the treaties were considered not to be affected; in the case of the declarations, they were suspended pending a decision by the United Nations to take over the powers and functions of the League. As regards the United Nations Charter, the study concluded that there was no implicit abrogation by the Charter of the minorities undertakings, since the concepts of protection of minorities, and the concept of universal human rights were not identical. Further, the Peace Treaties of 1947 did not implicitly abrogate earlier treaties, because the latter had been deprived of validity by the force of events. Finally, population movements did not in themselves terminate the treaties, unless all minority elements in a State had disappeared. The study was none the less able to conclude that:

If the problem is regarded as a whole, there can be no doubt that the whole minorities protection regime was in 1919 an integral part of the system established to regulate the outcome of the First World War and create an international organization, the League of Nations. One principle of that system was that certain States and

---

[1] *Study of the Legal Validity of the Undertakings Concerning Minorities*, UN Doc E/CN.4/367.

certain States only (chiefly States that had been newly reconstituted or considerably enlarged) should be subject to obligations and international control in the matter of minorities. But this whole system was overthrown by the Second World War. All the international decisions reached since 1944 have been inspired by a different philosophy. The idea of a general and universal protection of human rights and fundamental freedoms is emerging. It is therefore no longer only the minorities in certain countries which receive protection, but all human beings in all countries who receive a certain measure of international protection.

Thus, 'Reviewing the situation as a whole, . . . one is led to conclude that between 1939 and 1947 circumstances as a whole changed to such an extent that, generally speaking, the system should be considered as having ceased to exist.'

The assumption in effect was that the ordinary causes of extinction had no function to play because the undertakings on minorities were already extinct due to a radical (fundamental) change of circumstances: the so called *clausula rebus sic stantibus* could be invoked. The authors of the study clearly believed that a new age had been ushered in by the United Nations Charter, the Potsdam decision on population transfer and subsequently, the Universal Declaration of Human Rights. The philosophy proclaimed in the Universal Declaration was the new philosophy, and not the support of the rights of particular groups. It is not proposed to dispute the validity of the Secretariat's conclusions, but rather to point to its description of a new legal, philosophical, and spiritual *moment* in human affairs.[2]

[2] Analyses of the Secretariat's document are made by Bruegel, 'A Neglected Field: The Protection of Minorities', *RDH*, 4 (1971), 413; Feinberg, 'The Legal Validity of the Undertakings Concerning Minorities and the Clausula Rebus Sic Stantibus', *Studies in Law, Scripta Hierosolymitana*, 5 (1958), 95; Modeen, 'The International Protection of the National Identity of the Aaland Islands' *Scandinavian Studies in Law*, (1973), 177. See also, for discussions of the question written before the publication of the UN Study, Bagley (n. 41, ch. 3); Renouf, 'The Present Force of the Minorities Treaties', *1950 Canadian Bar Review*, 804; Robinson, 'From Protection of Minorities to Promotion of Human Rights' *Jewish Year Book of International Law* (1948), 115. Greece and Turkey have proceeded on the basis that the minority provisions of the Treaty of Lausanne continue to apply to them, Sohn and Buergenthal, *International Protection of Human Rights*, 304. Monographs on Greece and Turkey compiled by Capotorti for his UN Study, *Study on the Rights of Persons Belonging to Ethnic, Religious and Linguistic Minorities*, UN Doc E/CN.4/Sub.2/384/Add.1–7, UN Sales No.E.78. XIV.I., make reference to the Treaty of Lausanne. Modeen concludes ('The International Protection of the National Identity of the Aaland Islands', 210) in relation to the Islands: 'Finland's obligation towards Sweden still exists. The obligation undertaken by Finland towards the Council of the League of Nations as representative of the international community is suspended until such time as an express decision has been taken by the United Nations to put it back into force.'

Part II

The Right to Existence

5. Introduction: Existence

In any consideration of the rights of minorities under contemporary international law, the right of existence must be a necessary prerequisite for other rights. 'Existence' is a notion which has a special sense for a collectivity. An individual 'exists' or he does not; his non-existence is individual death. A collectivity such as a minority group exists in the individual lives of its members; the physical death of some members does not destroy the 'existence' of the group, though it may impair its health. There is, however, another existence for a minority through the shared consciousness of its members, manifested perhaps through language, culture, or religion, a shared sense of history, a common destiny. Without this 'existence' it is possible to say that individuals live but the group does not: it has been replaced by something other than itself, perhaps a new group, larger or smaller.

The most basic sense of existence is existence through the lives of members, or 'physical existence'.[1] Physical extermination of groups renders law and rights redundant. The rights of individuals *qua* individuals are best thought of as subject to protection by human rights law. The destruction of groups through the extermination of their members is the province of international criminal law. Not all international criminal law is relevant to the protection of groups. The specific focus of this discussion is the Convention on the Prevention and Punishment of the Crime of Genocide, 1948.[2] International criminal law deals with a heterogenous mass of crimes such as piracy, drug trafficking, terrorism, torture, etc., which are not specifically concerned with group destruction.[3] The concept of international criminal law seems to lack a certain cohesion, partly because of the non-existence of an international criminal jurisdiction, but also because of the piecemeal approach,[4] directed towards the criminalization of specific acts seemingly

---

[1] Dinstein, 'Collective Human Rights of Peoples and Minorities' *supra*, ch. 1, n. 40.

[2] *UNTS*, 77, 277; HMSO, Misc. No. 2 (1966), *Cmnd. 2904*. The law on genocide has been the subject of recent study at the United Nations. In Res. 1420(XLVI) of June 1969, the Economic and Social Council approved the decision adopted by the Sub-Commission on Prevention of Discrimination and Protection of Minorities in its Res. 8(XX) to undertake a study of the question of the prevention and punishment of the crime of genocide. The Council authorized the designation of a Special Rapporteur, and the Sub-Commission duly appointed M. Ruhashyankiko of Rwanda. The Study was presented to the Sub-Commission in 1978: UN D E/CN.4/Sub.2/416. A revised and updated version of the Study was prepared by Special Rapporteur Whitaker of the UK: UN Doc E/CN.4/Sub.2/1985/6.

[3] Some writers define the scope of international criminal law with remarkable freedom. See, for example, Glaser, *Droit International Pénal Conventionnel*, vols. i and ii (Brussels: Emile Bruylant, 1970 and 1978). Glaser is reviewed in *AJIL*, 74 (1980), 458.

[4] Lillich and Newman (eds.), *International Human Rights: Problems of Law and Policy*, 752 (Boston and Toronto: Little, Brown and Co., 1979).

unconnected with a general theme. Defining international criminal law as 'the set of legal rules recognised in international relations which are aimed at protecting the international legal or social order'[5] seems to do justice to some aspects of the law better than others. Schwarzenberger has doubted whether the existence of an international criminal law can be affirmed in the absence of treaties.[6]

The core of international criminal law for the post-war world is undoubtedly the Nuremberg Principles under which the process of punishing individuals for participating in the Nazi war effort was undertaken in a variety of legal contexts. As Pella noted, the idea of punishment for acts committed either by States or by individuals 'was often regarded as manifestation of a dangerous revolutionary sentiment . . . It was not until the Second World War, with its tragic lessons, that the rulers of States finally decided to cast off the old armour of prejudice which had led them to declare any international penal justice impossible.'[7] As a legal notion, genocide emerges from these principles with its specific focus on the group. The general topic of war crimes is discussed below only to the extent that it illuminates some features of genocide. Crimes against humanity are discussed in more detail because that category of crime is the parent of genocide and relates to the theme of this work in that the original inspiration for punishing crimes against humanity was protection of a population from its own government, not from foreign governments. Glaser writes that the same act may be described as either a crime against humanity or an act of genocide, depending on the motives of the person committing it: 'if his aim is to eliminate the victim because of the latter's race, religion or political beliefs, with no other interest, his act constitutes a crime against humanity, whereas if committed with intent to destroy, in whole or in part, a national, ethnic, racial or religious group, it will be qualified as genocide.'[8]

There is little mention in the texts of international criminal law of 'rights'; the law is directed to the condemnation or 'criminalization' of acts which violate standards of civilization. None the less the context of the criminal prohibition makes it clear that the reason why this particular conduct is regarded as criminal is precisely because it violates a fundamental right.

---

[5] Glaser, *Droit International Pénal Conventionnel*, vol. i, 165.

[6] Schwarzenberger, 'The Problem of an International Criminal Law', *CLP*, 3 (1950), 263. This proposition is tested below through discussion of the customary law on genocide and crimes against humanity.

[7] Pella, *La Guerre-Crime et les Criminels de Guerre* (Geneva/Paris, 1946), 16, cited in 'Study Concerning the Question of Apartheid from the point of view of International Law', UN Doc E/CN.4/1075, 14.

[8] Glaser, vol. i, 109.

6. The Convention on Genocide and the Protection of Minorities

Introduction

The Convention on the Prevention and Punishment of the Crime of Genocide, 1948[1] is notable as the first of the post World War II general conventions which has any bearing on minority protection. It has been discussed in this context by writers[2] and is listed in the compilation by the United Nations Secretariat of the texts of those international instruments and similar measures of an international character which provide special protective measures for ethnic, religious, or linguistic groups.[3] It is also significant in that it is part of international criminal law[4] and underlines a profound concern of modern international law with at least some aspects of the welfare of minorities. This truth is not affected by the fact that minorities 'as such' are not mentioned in the Covention,[5] because they are clearly comprehended by it as the natural victims of genocidal measures.

None the less, the Genocide Convention is a product of its time. The immediate post-war years, as has been pointed out, were not remarkable for public expressions of concern for minorities; the plight of 'the individual' rather than 'the group' was brought to the forefront of international consciousness.[6] The question therefore arises as to what extent the Genocide

---

[1] *Supra*, ch. 5, n. 2.

[2] Claude (*supra*, ch. 3, n. 36); Laponce (*supra*, ch. 1, n. 34); Modeen (*supra*, ch. 1, n. 1). Also Bruegel, 'A Neglected Field: The Protection of Minorities'. There is an especially useful account by Daes: 'Protection of Minorities under the International Bill of Rights and the Genocide Convention' in *Festschrift für Pan J. Zepos*, II (Athens, 1973), 35. See also the Capotorti Report, *supra*, ch. 1. n. 4.

[3] *Supra*, ch. 1, n. 37.

[4] Works cited *supra*, ch. 5, n. 3; also Bassiouni and Nanda (eds.), *A Treatise on International Criminal Law* (Illinos: Charles C. Thomas, 1973); Mueller and Wise (eds.), *International Criminal Law* (London: Stevens and Sons, 1965. The International Convention on the Suppression and Punishment of the Crime of Apartheid, 1973 might also be regarded as a convention of international criminal law relevant to minorities: text in Brownlie, *Basic Documents in Human Rights* (Oxford: OUP, 1981), 164. The crime of apartheid is in theory not confined to South Africa and applies to various inhuman acts 'committed for the purpose of establishing and maintaining domination by one racial group over any other racial group . . .' (Article II). The Convention is also not confined to domination *by* a minority. See the remark by the representative of Australia in the Third Committee of the General Assembly, UN Doc A/C.3/SR. 2004, para. 4. The Convention is not considered in the Capotorti Report.

[5] *Infra*, text following n. 42.

[6] *Supra*, ch. 1.

Convention is evidence of a more positive attitude. The issue requires careful examination and it is convenient to begin with an account of the background to the Convention before proceeding to an analysis of its provisions and their significance for minority protection.

The Term 'Genocide'

'The fact of genocide is as old as humanity. To this day there has been no society protected by its structure from committing that crime. Every case of genocide is a product of history and bears the stamp of the society which has given birth to it.' (J. P. Sartre)[7] The Preamble to the Genocide Convention recites the contracting parties' recognition that at all periods of history genocide has inflicted 'great losses on humanity', as well as their conviction that international co-operation is required to liberate mankind from 'such an odious scourge'. While acts of genocide in antiquity may be recognized for what they are, the term itself is modern. The jurist Lemkin[8] is credited with having coined the word from the Greek 'genos' meaning race, nation, or tribe, and the Latin verb 'caedere' meaning to kill; it thus corresponds in its formation with tyrannicide, homicide and patricide.[9] Some of the premises of this concept were expounded by Lemkin as early as 1933 in a special report to the Fifth International Conference on Penal Law. He proposed that certain acts aimed at destroying a racial, religious, or social group should be declared *delicta juris gentium*, distinguishing two separate

---

[7] Cited in Falk, Kolko and Lifton (eds.), *Crimes of War* (New York: Vintage Books, 1971), 534.

[8] Lemkin, *Axis Rule in Occupied Europe* (Washington: Carnegie Endowment for International Peace, 1944), listed examples of ancient wars of extermination: the destruction of Carthage, 146 BC; the destruction of Jerusalem by Titus, 72 AD; the Holy Wars of Islam; the Crusades; the persecution of the Albigensians and the Waldensians; the siege of Magdeburg in the Thirty Years War; the wars of Genghis Khan and Tamerlane. Lemkin formulated his views on genocide over a period. The massacres of the Armenians were the initial stimulus. Some 45 members of his own family were exterminated by the Nazis. Shorter accounts of his views are: 'Le Crime de Génocide', *Revue de Droit International de Sciences Diplomatiques, Politiques et Sociales*, 24 (1946), 13; Le Crime de Génocide, *Revue Internationale de Droit Pénal* (1946), No. 10. Whitaker, B., Revised and Updated Report on the Question of the Prevention and Punishment of the Crime of Genocide, UN Doc E/CN.4/Sub.2/1985/6, para. 20, writes: 'Throughout human history, war has been the predominant cause or pretext for massacres of national, ethnic, racial or religious groups. Wars in ancient and classical eras frequently aimed to exterminate if not enslave other peoples. Religious intolerance could also be a predisposing factor: in religious wars of the Middle Ages as well as in places in the Old Testament, some genocide was sanctioned by Holy Writ. The twentieth century equally has seen examples of "total wars" involving the destruction of civilian populations and which the development of nuclear weapons makes an almost inevitable matrix for future major conflicts. In the nuclear era, indeed the logical conclusion of this may be "omnicide".'

[9] Lemkin noted that another term could be used for the same idea as genocide: 'ethnocide', from the Greek *ethnos* (nation), *Axis Rule in Occupied Europe*, 79. However, 'ethnocide' has come to refer to what is essentially 'cultural' genocide, particularly in connection with indigenous peoples—see *infra*, chs. 38 ff.

crimes: 'barbarity', which would consist of attacks against the laws or economic existence of the members of the group; and 'vandalism', visualized as an attack against the cultural values of a group, including (*a*) transfer of children to another human group; (*b*) forced and systematic removal of elements representing the culture of a group; (*c*) prohibition of the use of the national language; and (*d*) systematic destruction of books in the national language and other cultural artefacts.

In his detailed study of 'Axis Rule in Occupied Europe', he repeated the proposals in modified form using the term 'genocide' to describe and condemn Nazi practices during World War II when all aspects of the nationhood of certain groups were systematically attacked. He defined genocide as signifying

a co-ordinated plan of different actions aiming at the destruction of essential foundations of the life of national groups, with the aim of annihilating the groups themselves. The objective of such a plan would be disintegration of the political and social institutions of culture, language, national feelings, religion, and the economic existence of national groups and the destruction of the personal security, liberty, health, dignity and even the lives of the individuals belonging to such groups. Genocide is directed against the national group as an entity, and the actions involved are directed against individuals, not in their individual capacity, but as members of the national group.[10]

Consistently with this, Lemkin identified forms of genocide, taking examples from Nazi practice.[11] Thus 'political genocide' implied the complete destruction of national government and the imposition of Nazi administration down to street level. 'Social genocide' involved attempts to weaken national spiritual resources, especially by attacking the intelligentsia. 'Cultural genocide' included prohibiting use of local languages, compulsory education in the spirit of National Socialism, and rigid control of culture generally, including such crude manifestations of this policy as burning libraries. 'Economic genocide' meant the destruction of the foundations of a nation's economic life. 'Biological genocide' signified various measures to favour a lower birth rate in non-German populations and a higher rate in German groups—measures such as forcibly separating male from female, deliberate undernourishment of parents in order, *inter alia*, to lower the survival capacity of children born to weakened adults, and conversely, the payment of benefits to children fathered by German troops. 'Physical genocide' meant at worst mass killings of certain groups as well as racial discrimination in feeding populations (Germans first). 'Religious genocide' meant simply the elimination of religion and its replacement with the teachings

---

[10] *Axis Rule in Occupied Europe*, 79.
[11] Ibid. ch. IX, part II: 'Techniques of Genocide in Various Fields'. Also, Wormser-Migot, 'Les Phases du Pré-Génocide Nazi', *Études Internationales de Psycho-Sociologie Criminelle*, No. 11/12/13 (1967), 3.

of National Socialism. Finally, 'moral genocide' represented an attempt
to debase particular groups, perhaps in order to render them more deserving
of elimination, by such methods as encouraging the consumption of alcohol
and the spread of pornography! Taken as a whole, genocide had two
phases; the destruction of the national pattern of the oppressed group, and
the imposition of the national pattern of the oppressor. A term such as 'mass
murder' was inadequate for this purpose, because it did not carry with it any
sense of the motives for such acts.[12] On the other hand, 'denationalization'
was inadequate because: '(1) It does not connote the destruction of the
biological structure; (2) in connoting the destruction of one national pattern
it does not connote the imposition of the national pattern of the oppressed;
and (3) 'denationalization' is used by some authors to mean only deprivation of citizenship.'[13] Further, terms such as 'Germanization', 'Italianiza-
tion', told only part of the story—as he asked rather caustically, 'Pourrions-
nous trouver un sujet plus ridicule que celui de traiter de la "Germanisa-
tion" des Polonais en Pologne Occidentale, alors que les Allemands
désiraient leur extermination totale?'[14]

It was therefore proper that international law, in an age marked by
doctrines of total war, and racist and nationalist ideologies, should employ
the term genocide. Previous legal approaches, including the Minorities
Treaties,[15] had proved ineffective in controlling the totalitarian threat,
though he noted that the progressive development of international law had
'brought about a considerable interest in national groups as distinguished
from States and individuals'.[16] The explanation given for the failure of the
Minorities Treaties was that not every European country had a sufficient
judicial machinery for the enforcement of its constitution. On the other
hand, enforcement of criminal law was efficient, hence, amongst other
reasons, the need to include genocide within criminal law and procedure.
This is by no means acceptable as a synoptic explanation of the alleged
failure of the treaties, and was not perhaps intended as such; it represents,
rather, one element in the complex history of the League of Nations system
of protection which gave weight and point to his criminalization proposals.
It may be noted finally that Lemkin was clear about the international
implications of genocidal policies against minorities apart from the particular example of the Nazis. Thus, even in peacetime and, in his view, especially in Europe, certain groups were obliged to live as minorities within the
boundaries of other States. If these groups were not adequately protected,
such lack of protection would result in international disturbance. His pro-

---

[12] Le Crime de Génocide, 213–14.
[13] Axis Rule in Occupied Europe, 80.
[14] Le Crime de Génocide, 214.
[15] See also his discussion of the lacunae in the contemporary humanitarian law, Axis Rule in
Occupied Europe, 92–3.
[16] Ibid. 90.

posed multilateral treaty aimed at 'protecting minority groups from oppression because of their nationhood, religion or race'.[17]

Genocide as an International Crime

The term 'genocide' has passed into international law, as well as ordinary usage in a number of languages.[18] The process of indicating the criminality of genocide began with the Charter of the International Military Tribunal at Nuremberg. Although it did not refer to genocide as such, the definition of 'crimes against humanity' in Article 6(c) was wide enough to include it. The article referred to 'murder, extermination, enslavement, deportation, and other inhumane acts committed against any civilian population, before or during the war, or persecution on political, racial or religious grounds in execution of or in connection with any crime within the jursidiction of the Tribunal, whether or not in violation of the domestic law of the country where perpetrated'.[19] The word 'genocide' was used in the indictment of 8 October 1945, against major German war criminals. It stated that they had 'conducted deliberate and systematic genocide, viz., the extermination of racial and national groups, against the civilian population of certain occupied territories in order to destroy particular races and classes of people and national, racial or religious groups, particularly Jews, Poles and Gypsies, and others'.[20] However, although the International Military Tribunal delivered a lengthy judgment on the substance of acts of genocide, it did not use the term.[21]

The term reappears in the trials of Nazi war criminals by national tribunals of the Allies.[22] The usage varies from the identification of genocide in a physical sense to a wider conception which stressed economic, social, and cultural implications. Thus, the second count of the indictment in the trial of *Ulrich Greifelt et al.* by the United States Military Tribunal at Nuremberg referred to 'a systematic programme of genocide, aimed at the destruction of foreign nations and ethnic groups, in part by murderous extermination, and in part by the elimination and suppression of national characteristics', itemizing various acts to substantiate this charge.[23] A broad notion is also reflected in the judgment of the Supreme National Tribunal of

---

[17] Ibid. 93.

[18] Ruhashyankiko (*supra*, ch. 5, n. 2), 1.

[19] Texts of the Agreement for the Establishment of an International Military Tribunal and Annexed Charter, *UNTS*, 5, 251; *AJIL*, 39 (1945), Supplement, 257.

[20] *Trial of the Major War Criminals before the International Military Tribunal, Nuremberg, November 14 1945–October 1 1946*, vol. I, 406–6.

[21] But see, for example, the concluding speeches of the British and French prosecutors, ibid., vol. XIX, vol. XX, 1.

[22] *Law Reports of Trials of War Criminals* (London: HMSO, 1947–9), VI, 48; VII, 7–9, and 24–6; XIII, 2, 3, 6, 112, and 114; XIV, 122–3.

[23] Ibid, XIII, 1, at 2–3.

Poland in the *Greiser* case, which enumerated, *inter alia*, the following acts of genocide: 'Repression, genocidal in character, of the religion of the local population by . . . restriction of religious practices . . . and by destruction of churches, cemeteries and the property of the Church' and 'genocidal attacks on Polish culture and learning'.[24] The Tribunal's condemnation of 'physical and spiritual' genocide was explicit.[25]

The legal condemnation of 'genocide' prompted United Nations interest in the concept, culminating in the Genocide Convention, 1948. The Convention reflects a more restricted concept of the crime than that originally outlined by Lemkin. Beyond an immediate reaction to Nazi excesses, States were not prepared to give their assent to an unduly broad notion of genocide which might fetter aspects of State policy. The trimming of genocide has important consequences for the protection offered to minorities.

Preparation of the Genocide Convention

The first session of the United Nations General Assembly included on its agenda the item entitled 'Resolution on the Crime of Genocide' and adopted, on 11 December 1946, Resolution 96(I),[26] the basis of subsequent United Nations action. The resolution, adopted unanimously and without debate, defines genocide as 'a denial of the right of existence of entire human groups, as homicide is the denial of the right to live of individual human beings'. Such denial 'shocks the conscience of mankind [and] results in great losses to humanity in the form of cultural and other contributions represented by these groups, and is contrary to moral law and to the spirit and aims of the United Nations'. Without naming them, the resolution records that instances of genocide have occurred 'when racial, religious, political and other groups have been destroyed, entirely or in part'.[27] The punishment of

---

[24] *Law Reports of Trials of War Criminals*, XIII, 112.

[25] Ibid. 113–14.

[26] *YBUN*, 1946–7, 255.

[27] Official UN bodies have been very reluctant about 'naming names'. For examples and comment, see Kuper, *Genocide. Its Political use in the Twentieth Century*. Contemporary examples of genocide (some are referred to in the present text) are 'named' by Whitaker, *supra*, n. 8, para. 24 and accompanying footnotes. In this context, the extraordinary case of the reference to the Armenian genocide in the Ruhashyankiko report may be noted. Para. 30 of an earlier version of the report (UN Doc E/CN.4/Sub.2/L.583) contained the sentence: 'Passing to the modern era, one may note the existence of relatively full documentation dealing with the massacres of Armenians, which have been described as the first case of genocide in the twentieth century.' Following discussion and representations by Turkey in the Human Rights Commission, the implied reference to Turkey (the Ottoman Empire) is absent from the final report despite protests from members of the Sub-Commission. See also for 'allegations' at various points along the spectrum of objectivity: Jaulin, *L'Ethnocide à travers les Amériques*; (Paris: Librairie Arthème Fayard, 1972); Report of the Fourth Russell Tribunal, *The Rights of the Indians in the Americas* (Amsterdam: Workgroup Indian Project, 1980); Kennedy, 'Biafra, Bengal and Beyond: International Responsibilities and Genocidal Conflict', *Procs. ASIL 1972*,

genocide is 'a matter of international concern'. In positive terms, the General Assembly affirmed that 'genocide is a crime under international law which the civilised world condemns' and that those who commit it 'whether private individuals, public officials or statesmen are punishable'. The resolution recommended national legislation and international co-operation to prevent and punish genocide and requested the Economic and Social Council to undertake studies with a view to drawing up a convention. The crime outlined in the resolution is independent of crimes against peace or war crimes. Article 6(c) of the Nuremberg Charter had provided that 'crimes against humanity' could only be committed 'in execution of or in connection with any crime within the jurisdiction of the (International Military) Tribunal', that is, crimes against peace or war crimes. No such limitation was to apply to genocide. Many points in this resolution are taken up in drafts and in the final version of the Convention. The notion of the right of existence of human groups and of the group as victim is present, as well as the international nature of the crime. Individual and international action to combat genocide are envisaged. The strong language of the resolution and its unanimous adoption underlined the determination of the United Nations to prevent the recurrence of the kind of criminal acts perpetrated by the Nazis. The resolution represented an optimistic beginning to United Nations efforts.[28] The subsequent processing of genocide involved a number of United Nations organs. Thus, at its fourth session, the Economic and Social Council, by Resolution 48(IV) adopted on 28 March 1947,[29] instructed the Secretary-General to undertake with the assistance of experts in the field of international and criminal law the necessary studies with a view to drawing up a draft convention in accordance with the Resolution of the General Assembly. The draft was to be submitted to the next session of the Economic and Social Council after consultation with the Committee on the Development and Codification of International Law and, if feasible, the International Commission on Human Rights, and after reference to all member governments for comments. The Secretariat's Division of Human Rights consulted three experts, Professors Lemkin, Pella, and Donnedieu de

89; International Commission of Jurists, *The Events in East Pakistan 1971: A Legal Study*; Lemarchand and Martin, *Selective Genocide in Burundi* (London: Minority Rights Group, 1974); Arens (ed.), *Genocide in Paraguay* (Philadelphia: Temple University Press, 1976); Bedau, 'Genocide in Vietnam', *Boston University Law Review*, 53 (1973), 574; *Israel in Lebanon, The Report of the International Commission* (London: Ithaca Press, 1983); *Study Concerning the Question of Apartheid from the Point of View of International Penal Law*, Report of the Ad Hoc Working Group of Experts under Commission Res. 8(XXVII), 15 February, 1972, UN Doc E/CN.4/1075 (elements of genocide in the practice of apartheid).

[28] The early drafts are discussed by Robinson, *The Genocide Convention. A Commentary* (New York: Institute of Jewish Affairs, 1960), Part I; and Drost, *The Crime of State*, vol. ii, ch. II (Leiden: Sijthoff, 1959); also, Claude, *National Minorities: An International Problem*, 154–7.

[29] *Resolutions adopted by the Economic and Social Council*, 4th Session, UN Doc E/437 (March, 1948), 33.

Vabres for assistance in drafting.[30] Consultation with the Commission on Human Rights did not prove possible, and the Committee on the Development and Codification of International Law was unable to express any opinion.[31] By Resolution 77(V) of 6 August 1947, the Economic and Social Council requested the Secretary-General to transmit the draft and comments by member governments to the General Assembly.[32]

At its second session, the General Assembly adopted Resolution 180 (II) of 21 November 1947,[33] which requested the Economic and Social Council to continue with its work of study and elaboration of a Convention.[34] The Economic and Social Council at its sixth session established, by Resolution 117 (VI) of 3 March 1948, an Ad Hoc Committee composed of the following Council members: China, France, Lebanon, Poland, the USSR, the USA, and Venezuela. The Ad Hoc Committee was instructed (*a*) to prepare the draft Convention and submit it, together with the recommendation of the Commission on Human Rights, to the Economic and Social Council; and (*b*) to take into consideration the draft prepared by the Secretariat and any comments on it by member governments and on other drafts prepared by any member of the United Nations.[35] The Ad Hoc Committee's draft convention is the second draft United Nations convention on genocide.[36]

The Commission on Human Rights was unable to consider the draft thoroughly, though it expressed the opinion that it represented 'an appropriate basis for urgent consideration and decisive action by the Economic and Social Council and by the General Assembly'.[37] Thus, it cannot be said that the Commission on Human Rights participated fully in deliberations leading to the Convention, and the same is true of its Sub-

[30] Described here as the Secretariat Draft Convention, the Secretary-General's preliminary draft as supplemented by the comments of the three experts consulted, UN Doc E/447. The draft, and comments on it by States, is reproduced as UN Doc A/362, in *GAOR, 2nd Session*, 6th Committee, Summary Records, 16 September–26 November 1947, Annex 3, and Annex 3a (comments). There is a useful article by article comparison of drafts in Robinson (*supra*, n. 28), Appendices II and IV.

[31] Drost, *The Crime of State*, ii, ch. 1. The Committee justified this on the grounds that no government responses to the draft had been received at that stage, E/447, Part III. The Human Rights Commission did not meet between the 4th and 5th Sessions of the Economic and Social Council.

[32] UN Doc E/573, 21.

[33] Djonovich, *United Nations Resolutions* (New York, 1972), Ser. I, vol. i, 320; Robinson (*supra*, n. 28), Appendix III.

[34] The resolution noted that 'a large majority of the Governments of Members of the United Nations have not yet submitted their observations on the draft Convention . . .'. It also reaffirmed Res. 96(I), and declared that genocide is an international crime entailing 'national and international responsibility on the part of individuals and States'.

[35] UN Doc E/734.

[36] The Ad Hoc Committee met at Lake Success from 5 April to 10 May 1948 and prepared a report containing a Draft Convention on genocide: *ECOSOC OR*, 7th Session, Supplement 6, and Annex. The text is Appendix IV to Robinson (*supra*, n. 28); also Drost, *The Crime of State*, ch. III.

[37] *ECOSOC OR*, 7th Session, Supplement 2, para. 24.

Commission on the Prevention of Discrimination and Protection of Minorities.[38]

By Resolution 153 (VII) of 26 August 1948, the Economic and Social Council decided to transmit the Ad Hoc Committee's draft and report to the General Assembly together with records of the Council's proceedings at its seventh session.[39] The draft was comprehensively examined by the Sixth (Legal) Committee of the General Assembly on an article by article basis together with amendments.[40] The revised draft and certain amendments not accepted by the Sixth Committee were considered by the General Assembly.[41] In Resolution 260 (III) of 9 December 1948, the General Assembly approved the Convention on the Prevention and Punishment of the Crime of Genocide which was annexed to the Resolution, proposing it for signature, ratification, or accession in accordance with Article XI. The Resolution was passed by 55 votes to none with no abstentions. Immediately after approval by the General Assembly, twenty Governments signed.[42]

Substantive Law of the Convention: Principal Aspects in Relation to Protection of Minorities

(a) The groups protected

Article II of the Genocide Convention defines the object of protection as the whole or part of 'a national, ethnical, racial or religious group, as such'. There is no definition of terms. General Assembly Resolution 96 (I) did not mention national or ethnic groups.[43] It did mention political as well as 'other' groups. The Secretariat draft referred to racial, national, linguistic, religious, and political groups but not ethnic groups, which were first mentioned in the text prepared by the Ad Hoc Committee.

The groups in the final text were regarded as sharing certain features. The descriptions commonly employed in debates in the Sixth Committee were 'distinct', 'permanent', 'stable', 'sharing a common origin', or having 'characteristic features in common'; membership was not 'optional' but 'inevitable': they could be identified by 'objective criteria'.[44] The assumption was that the groups were stable communities indentifiable through possession of distinct characteristics. The concept of genocide related to groups

---

[38] *Infra*, ch. 12.   [39] UN Doc E/1065; UN Doc E/1049.

[40] *GAOR*, 3rd Session, Part I, Sixth Committee and Annexes (1948–9), 63rd–69th meetings, 71st–81st meetings, 91st–110th meetings, and 128th–134th meetings.

[41] 178th and 179th meetings.

[42] The text of the Convention is in *UNTS*, 78, 277; HMSO, Misc. No. 2 (1966), *Cmnd. 2904*. Also Brownlie, *Basic Documents on Human Rights*, 31; Robinson (*supra*, n. 28), Appendix IX. Cosa Rica, The Union of South Africa and El Salvador did not participate in the vote. Costa Rica and El Salvador but not South Africa are parties to the Convention.

[43] *Supra*, text following n. 26.

[44] Meetings, *supra*, n. 40.

which were 'the product of circumstances beyond the control of their members'.[45] Doubts were expressed on the advisability of including religious groups (the members of which were as 'free to leave as they were to join')[46] in the list in Article II, but this was a minority view.[47]

It may be remarked that if stability is a key for inclusion of a group, the omission of linguistic groups is surprising, because such groups could claim to be as 'stable' and 'permanent', as, for example, national or religious groups.

Linguistic groups had been included in the Secretariat's Draft.[48] However, comments by Governments on that draft were unfavourable on their inclusion; they claimed that genocide would not be committed because of language as distinct from race, nationality, or religion.[49] This objection was sustained by the Ad Hoc Committee and the General Assembly followed suit. Drost, in expressing his agreement with this omission, comments that: 'Difference of language as the distinctive . . . characteristic of the persecuted minority does not seem likely to occur apart from disparity of religious tenets and practices, diversity of national character and aspirations or dissimilarity of racial features and colour of the skin. In fact, language is nearly always an element of national, collective identity.'[50]

The question of whether or not to include political groups was very contentious and much debated. The proposal to include economic groups also provoked discussion. In debates in the Sixth Committee,[51] considerations supporting inclusion of political groups in the Convention were principally advanced by the United States, and principally opposed by the Soviet Union. In favour of including these groups it was argued that they should be considered similar to religious groups, a distinguishing mark of both groups being the common ideal uniting their members. The Representative of the United States cited examples of Nazi identification of Communists as a group to be persecuted, and Allied identification of Nazi party members to be prosecuted, the point being that political groups were identifiable as easily as other groups.[52]

---

[45] 75th meeting (Poland).   [46] 69th meeting (UK).

[47] Only a limited degree of attention was paid to distinctions between the listed groups; much more attention was focused on whether the range of groups was sufficiently broad. In relation to distinguishing the groups, the distinction between 'ethnic' and 'racial' occasioned discussion. Some held the terms to be identical. Others held that the addition of 'ethnic' widened the Convention: *GAOR*, 3rd Session, 74th and 75th meetings. The representative of the USSR regarded the ethnic group as a sub-group of a national group, a smaller collectivity than the nation. All of this echoes debates on minorities as such. See *infra*, chs. 14 ff.

[48] Article I(I) of the Secretariat Draft stated that 'The purpose of this Convention is to prevent the destruction of racial, national, linguistic, religious or political groups of human beings.'

[49] The comment of the United States was that the inclusion of linguistic groups was superfluous. Repression was due to racial characteristics, *GAOR* (*supra*, n. 30), Annex 3a, 326.

[50] *The Crime of State*, 23.

[51] *GAOR*, 3rd Session, Part I, 6th Committee, 69th, 74th, 75th, and 128th meetings.

[52] Ibid., 74th meeting, 102. The Representative of Ecuador pointed to one danger of omit-

It was recalled that General Assembly Resolution 96 (I) mentioned political groups. The main conceptual argument against inclusion was that a political group had no stable characteristics; it was an 'optional' rather than an 'inevitable' grouping, based on the will of its members and not on factors independent of that will.[53] There were also a number of practical points, principally that the text of the Genocide Convention should be such as to secure the widest possible acceptance. It was further contended that including political groups would hamper the efforts of legally established governments in preventive action against subversive elements. The majority view was that protection of political and other groups was better ensured through national legislation and the Universal Declaration of Human Rights. A United States proposal to include 'economic groups' was also not adopted.[54] It does not appear to have been clearly defined and some delegates professed themselves unable to understand it.[55] The United States withdrew the suggestion.[56]

The range of groups subject to the Genocide Convention is similar to the other international instruments dealing with protection of minorities, though the omission of the linguistic group is a departure. Apart from such racial characteristics as are externally visible manifestations of differences between individuals, the possession of a distinct language may be an important and permanent symbol of identity for groups susceptible to persecution, and the most significant pointer to the existence of these groups. The 'national' group, by contrast, is a vague entity, and might perhaps be rendered 'invisible' more easily by governments or others determined to achieve their objectives by genocidal means.[57] The omission of the linguistic group represents a weakening of the Convention, and an unnecessary weakening, as the question of linguistic groups did not give rise to the same intensity of discussion and polarization of opinion as that of political groups.

The discussion of this issue throws light on the objectives of the Convention and on the minorities problem. The object is to deal with the persecu-

ting reference to political groups, namely, that Governments might 'use the pretext of the political opinions of a racial or religious group to persecute or destroy it, without becoming liable to international sanctions'. The point is a valid one. US critics of the Convention continued to be critical of the omission and proposed an appropriate amendment. See Leblanc, 'The United Nations Genocide and Political Groups: Should the United States Propose an Amendment?', *Yale Journal of International Law*, 13 (1988), 268.

[53] The inclusion of such groups would be 'entirely out of place in a scientific definition of genocide', ibid., 64th meeting, 14.

[54] UN Doc A/C. b/214.

[55] Ibid., 69th meeting (Representatives of Egypt and Venezuela).

[56] Ibid., 75th meeting.

[57] In the sense that 'national' is ambiguous and contains at least two opposed meanings: the 'cultural' or 'sociological' nation, and the 'political' or 'politico-legal' nation. Rival meanings have plagued the law on self-determination (territorial v. ethnic criteria), and difficulties are not necessarily set at rest by adopting 'peoples' as a substitute description of the right holder in that case.

tion of more or less permanent groups of individuals, the qualities of which groups are visible and intractable, and not with fleeting and evanescent groupings such as political movements or associations. This is not to maintain that the latter are undeserving of protection, the Representatives of States disclaimed any intention of refusing protection to political groups, though as the collective element in these cases is rather more transient than with protected groups, it was appropriate that their protection by international law should be secured under individualistic norms of human rights. Critics of the Convention have pointed out[58] that the omission of the political group can work against the Convention as a whole in that it can furnish a cover for repression of other groups. This is an important practical point which has relevance in the application of the Convention. However, in the context of the exigencies of securing the passage of the Convention, it was a necessary price to pay. It also, more positively, prevented the Convention from becoming submerged by Cold War politics.

(b) Acts constituting genocide

Article II provides that genocide consists of 'any of the following acts committed with intent to destroy in whole or in part' the listed groups:

(*a*) Killing members of the group;
(*b*) Causing serious bodily or mental harm to members of the group;
(*c*) Deliberately inflicting on the group conditions of life calculated to bring about its physical destruction in whole or in part;
(*d*) Imposing measures intended to prevent births within the group;
(*e*) Forcibly transferring children of the group to another group.

The trimming of the concept of genocide is evidenced by this definition. The categories in the Article are exhaustive, not merely illustrative of genocide,[59] and are a substitute for a general formula such as that in General Assembly Resolution 96 (1) which declared that genocide 'is a denial of the right of existence of entire human groups'. One alleged disadvantage of a broad definition was that it might allow States to decide for themselves what constituted genocide. On the other hand, the preference for an exhaustive enumeration of acts of genocide rested in part on the principle of *mulla poene sine lege*, and in part on securing consistency in the application of the Convention.[60]

---

[58] *Supra*, n. 52.

[59] Two amendments before the Sixth Committee aimed at the adoption of an illustrative definition, but were rejected: UN Doc A/C.6/232/Rev.1; UN Doc A/C.6/223 and Corr. 1. The precedent urged in favour of this approach was to be found in the Nuremberg Charter, Article 6(b), which defined war crimes as violations of the laws and customs of war including but not limited to the listed acts. Article 6(c), which defines 'crimes against humanity', is also illustrative rather than exhaustive.

[60] GAOR (*supra*, n. 51), 69th, 71st, and 72nd meetings. On the distinction between the

Categories (*a*) to (*c*) are usually described as 'physical genocide', and category (*d*) as 'biological genocide'. Category (*e*) was included in the draft prepared by the Secretariat as an aspect of 'cultural genocide', the comment on the text stating that: 'The separation of children from their parents results in forcing upon the former at an impressionable and receptive age a culture and mentality different from their parents. This process tends to bring about the disappearance of the group as a cultural unit in a relatively short time.'[61] The debates in the Sixth Committee, however, stressed the physical and biological effects of forced transfer of children, so that the provision could be regarded as in keeping with the rest of the article.[62] There were misgivings on this point; it was argued that the inclusion of such transfers would go far beyond the other provisions of Article II, which did not deal with cultural genocide. Doubts have been expressed by writers on including this category of acts in the Convention, they are not true cases of genocide.[63] But this depends on the concept of genocide employed by the critic.

The whole question of 'cultural genocide' raised in the Convention drafts indicates some aspects of the relationship between 'genocide' and 'protection of minorities'. Article I of the Secretariat's Draft Convention classified as 'cultural genocide' the following:

Destroying the specific characteristics of the group by (a) forced transfer of children to another human group; or (b) forced and systematic exile of individuals representing the culture of a group; or (c) prohibition of the use of the national language even in private intercourse; or (d) systematic destruction of books printed in the national language or of religious works or prohibition of new publications; or (e) systematic destruction of historical or religious monuments or their diversion to alien uses, destruction or dispersal of documents and objects of historical, artistic or religious value and of objects used in religious worship.[64]

The accompanying comment is instructive: it notes the argument that cultural genocide represents an extension of the concept of genocide amounting to a reconstitution of the protection of minorities under the cover of the new term. It goes on to say that the preservation of a group's spiritual and moral unity should be protected against drastic measures aimed at the rapid and complete disappearance of the cultural, moral, and religious life of the group. The comments of governments, however, indicate

various types of definition, see Bridge, 'The Case for an International Court of Criminal Justice and the Formulation of International Criminal Law', *ICLQ*, 13 (1964), 1255, at 1262–3.

[61] *Supra*, n. 30.

[62] GAOR (*supra*, n. 51), 82nd meeting.

[63] Thus, it has been argued that forcible transferring of children is a crime against human or minority rights or against humanity. However, since the aim of the transfer is not the actual destruction of the generation, it cannot be a 'true' case of genocide: Graven, 'Les Crimes contre l'Humanité', *Rec. des Cours* 76 (1950)(I), 490 at 501–2.

[64] *Supra*, n. 30.

the unease with which they regarded cultural genocide. Thus, the Government of the United States of America considered that cultural genocide should be dealt with in connection with protection of minorities,[65] as did the Government of France.[66] In view of the latter, the inclusion of cultural genocide invited 'the risk of political interference in the domestic affairs of States'. The United States had a specific objection to the reference in paragraph (b) of the definition relating to forced exile: this 'might be interpreted as embracing forced transfers of minority groups such as have already been carried out by members of the United Nations'.[67]

The Ad Hoc Committee decided to retain cultural genocide. During the debate,[68] the Committee was asked to consider whether the General Assembly had intended only physical genocide in its Resolution 96(I). The answer was that cultural genocide should be included because this resolution mentioned it ('denial of the right of existence' of groups 'results in great losses to humanity in the form of cultural and other contributions represented by these groups . . .'). The Ad Hoc Committee devoted the separate Article III of their draft convention to cultural genocide:

In this Convention genocide also means any deliberate act committed with the intent to destroy the language, religion or culture of a national, racial or religious group on grounds of the national or racial origin or religious belief of its members such as:
1 Prohibiting the use of the language of the group in daily intercourse or in schools or the printing and circulation of publications in the language of the group:
2 Destroying or preventing the use of libraries, museums, schools, historical institutions and objects of the group.

The question of cultural genocide was extensively debated in the Sixth Committee.[69] The discussions revealed wide differences of opinion. In favour of including cultural genocide, it was stressed that it was intrinsically linked to other forms in so far as loss of the specific characteristics of a group could lead to its disappearance without any attempt on the life of its members; further, if acts of cultural genocide went unpunished, this would facilitate physical genocide, in which such acts normally culminated, as acts of cultural genocide were always inspired by the same motives as those of physical genocide. It was argued that it was not enough to set prohibitions on acts constituting cultural genocide in national legislation or in international instruments dealing with human rights or minority rights—national

---

[65] Ibid., Annex 3a, 237.
[66] Ibid. 245.
[67] *Infra*, ch. 9.
[68] UN Doc E/A.C. 25. SR. 1–28, summarized in Drost, *The Crime of State*, ii, ch. III.
[69] Two amendments to delete the Ad Hoc Committee's article were deferred: UN Doc A/C.6/216; A/C.6/218. The first of these amendments said that the attention of the Third Committee should be drawn to the need for the protection of language, religion, and culture within the framework of an international declaration on human rights. Another proposed a restricted text on cultural genocide because the Committee's draft was too broadly worded, UN Doc A/C.6/229. *GAOR*, 3rd Session, Part I, 6th Committee, 83rd meeting.

legislation had been demonstrably ineffective historically, and human rights
and minority rights instruments lacked the international penal character of
the Genocide Convention. In the minds of many representatives cultural
genocide was no less serious an offence than other manifestations of the
crime.[70]

The above arguments did not prevail. Those opposed to including
cultural genocide complained of the vagueness of the concept; it was not
amenable to the precision of definition necessary for inclusion, and would
be open to abuse, reducing the value of the Convention by transforming it
into an instrument suitable for exploitation by political propaganda. From
the practical point of view, international or national tribunals would experience grave difficulties of interpretation and judgment; governments would
be required to determine the concrete elements of a group's religion and
culture, with which they could not interfere, and also to what extent
assimilation resulting from 'civilizing action' would constitute genocide.
The adoption of the article on cultural genocide would make it difficult for
some countries to ratify the Convention. As well as this, it was claimed, as in
previous debates, that cultural genocide was better suited to human rights
and minorities instruments.[71] The Sixth Committee decided not to include a
provision on cultural genocide in the Convention by twenty-five votes to
sixteen with four abstentions.[72]

Taking an overall view of the discussions, the majority opinion seems to
have been that genocide is *sui generis*, and must be differentiated from
questions of human and minority rights. It is narrower than either and
represents an easily identifiable evil, at least in its recent historical
manifestations. The general and rapid international condemnation of genocide, in so far as it was narrowed to essentially physical acts, illustrates the
view that it is easier to secure agreement on what amounts to an evil than on
what is for the good of mankind.[73] Hence the need to avoid diluting the
definition of genocide by including acts which involved questionable
assumptions about the standing of minority cultures.

(c) Intention in genocide: a note

Apart from its *actus reus*, genocide also has a *mens rea*, the 'intent to
destroy, in whole or in part, a . . . group'. It was pointed out in the Sixth
Committee that the intention to destroy the group was what distinguished
genocide from murder. Genocide was characterized by the factor of particu-

---

[70] Ibid.
[71] Ibid.
[72] Thirteen delegates were absent during the vote, ibid., 206.
[73] The point is generalized for philosophical purposes by Popper, *The Open Society and its Enemies* (London: Routledge and Kegan Paul, 1966). For a cluster of practical and logical reasons it is better to devote efforts to 'minimizing unhappiness', than to 'maximizing happi-ness' as the Utilitarian formula would have it.

lar intent, *dolus specialis*, to destroy a group. In the absence of this factor, whatever the degree of atrocity of an act and however much it resembled acts described in the Convention, that act could not be called genocide.[74] Thus, measures which effectively result in the partial or total destruction of a group, but without that intention, do not amount to genocide and, conversely, acts which do not accomplish this objective are punishable under the Convention if they are intended to cause total or partial destruction of the group. A proposal in the Sixth Committee to replace this subjective element with a more objective characterization of the offence was not accepted. The proposal would have replaced 'intent to destroy' the group with 'aimed at the physical destruction of' groups. It was explained that the suggestion stemmed from the fact that the perpetrators of genocide would in certain cases claim that they were not guilty of genocide, having had no intent to destroy a particular group, in whole or in part.[75] The purpose of the amendment was to guard against the possibility that the reference to 'intent' might be used as a pretext for pleading 'not guilty' on the grounds of absence of intent.[76]

The original conception of *mens rea* presented in the Secretariat's Draft Convention was wider than the final formulation. Article I defined genocide as a criminal act directed against one of the protected groups with the purpose of destroying it in whole or in part, or 'of preventing its preservation or development'. The first part of the definition is the obvious progenitor of the present Article II, but the second part is not reflected therein. The Ad Hoc Committee's Draft Convention similarly makes no mention of any alternative form of *mens rea*, either in its Article II (physical and biological genocide) or Article III (cultural genocide). The omission from the later drafts may be taken as another indication of limited nature of the concept of genocide in the Convention. Thus, only acts committed 'with intent to destroy' groups are prohibited by the Convention, and not acts committed 'with intent to prevent the preservation' or 'with intent to prevent the development' of national, ethnic, racial, or religious groups. The strictness of the requirement of *mens rea* reflects a negative rather than a positive view of the 'right of existence' outlined in General Assembly Resolution 96(I). As developed in the Genocide Convention, 'existence' is a constricted notion which does not imply the right of a group to develop and flourish.

In conclusion, it seems that the Convention does not require proof of further reasons or 'motives' for genocidal actions, although the words 'as such' were inserted by the Venezuelan Representative in the Sixth Committee[77] in substitution for 'on grounds of the national or racial origin, religious

---

[74] A/C.6/SR.69, 72.   [75] Robinson (*supra*, n. 28), 59.

[76] For a criticism of the subjective definition, see Jacob, 'À Propos de la Définition Juridique du Génocide', *Études Internationales de Psycho-Sociologie Criminelle*, No. 16–17 (1969), 56.

[77] A/C. 6/231.

belief or political opinion of its [the group] members' in the Ad Hoc Committee's Draft. A difference of opinion ensued in the Sixth Committee on the precise effect of the substitution. In view of this, a statement was included in the report of the Sixth Committee that the Committee, in taking a decision on any proposal, did not necessarily adopt the interpretation of its author.[78] Thus, according to Drost:

In the absence of any words to the contrary, the text offers no pretext to presume the presence of an unwritten, additional element in the definition of the crime. Whatever the ultimate purpose of the deed, whatever the reasons for the perpetration of the crime, whatever the open or secret motives for the acts or measures directed against the life of the protected group, wherever the destruction of human life of members of the group as such takes place, the crime of genocide is fully committed.[79]

(d) Individual responsibility

Article IV of the Convention lays down the principle of individual criminal responsibility: 'Persons committing genocide or any of the other acts enumerated in Article III shall be punished, whether they are constitutionally responsible rulers, public officials or private individuals.' An attempt was made in the Sixth Committee to introduce the idea of State responsibility through an amendment calling for the addition of the following to the Convention: 'Criminal responsibility for any act of genocide . . . shall extend not only to all private persons or associations, but also to States, Governments or organs or authorities of the State or Government, by whom such acts are committed. Such acts committed by or on behalf of States or Governments constitute a breach of the Convention.'[80] The sponsor of this amendment did not envisage punishment of offending States or governments, but merely that an international court could order the cessation of genocidal acts, thereby expressing the preventive as well as the punitive aspects of the Convention.[81] It was also asserted that State responsibility would emphasize the close relationship between genocide and the maintenance of peace, which might be jeopardized by the genocidal actions of States.[82] The essence of the proposal was that as genocide was always committed on a large scale, it was proper to implicate the whole State system, and not merely individuals.

The amendment was rejected by twenty-four votes to twenty-two,[83] in part because of doubts about the need to implicate States if there was no question of punishment, and because it would make evasions of individual responsibility possible by shifting responsibility to the State. The precedent

[78] *GAOR*, 3rd Series, Pt 1, 6th Committee, 77th meeting.
[79] Ibid. 84.
[80] UN Doc A/C.6/236 and Corr. I, *GAOR*, 3rd Session, Part I, 6th Committee, Annexes, 24.
[81] Ibid., 6th Committee, 93rd meeting, 314–15, and 96th meeting, 353.
[82] Ibid., 92nd meeting, 302.
[83] Ibid., 96th meeting, 355.

of Nuremberg was evoked; only individual criminals were convicted and not the German State.[84] Thus, the Genocide Convention affirms general international practice since World War II in relation to international crimes, the principles of which were given eloquent expression by the International Military Tribunal of Nuremberg: 'Crimes against international law are committed by men, not by abstract entities, and only by punishing individuals who commit such crimes can the provisions of international law be enforced.'[85]

The Convention does not deal with the related issue of superior orders. Article 8 of the Nuremberg Charter provided: 'The fact that the Defendant acted pursuant to order of his Government or of a superior shall not free him from responsibility, but may be considered in mitigation of punishment.'[86] In its judgment, the Tribunal declared:

That a soldier was ordered to kill or torture in violation of the international law of war has never been recognised as a defence to such acts of brutality, though, as the Charter here provides, the order may be urged in mitigation of the punishment. The true test, which is found in varying degrees in the criminal law of most nations, is not the existence of the order, but whether moral choice was in fact possible.[87]

None of the drafts of the Convention expressly incorporated this principle, although an amendment to Article IV of the Convention, which was not accepted, proposed an addition which read: 'Command of the law or superior orders shall not justify genocide.'[88] The arguments against the proposed amendment in the Sixth Committee of the General Assembly[89] were mainly centred around the proposition that the Convention had to contain only general provisions, and that it should be left to national legislation to determine application. The argument as to the necessity of securing the widest possible participation in the Convention was again prominent. Drost regards the exclusion of any reference to *respondeat superior* as 'a serious failure' of the Convention.[90] Other writers such as Robinson[91] stress

---

[84] *GAOR*, 3rd Session, Part I, 95th meeting, 345–6.

[85] International Military Tribunal, *supra*, n. 20 vol. 27. For further discussion of the concept of criminal responsibility of States, see the proposals of the International Law Commission, *YBILC* 1976, II, part 2, 95–122. This section also contains a very full reference to the academic literature and other sources. Also Whiteman, *Digest of International Law*, vols. i and vii. The concept of state criminal responsibility receives its most vigorous criticism in Tunkin, *Theory of International Law* (London: George Allen and Unwin, 1974), 396–404.

[86] *AJIL*, 39 (Supp. 1945, Official Documents).

[87] *Supra*, n. 20.

[88] UN Doc A/C.6/215/Rev.1.   [89] UN Doc A/C.6/SR.92.

[90] Vol. ii, 26.

[91] *Supra*, n. 28, 72–3. Robinson disagrees with Jacoby (*Schweitzerische Zeitschrift für Strafrecht*, 1949, fasc. 4), who contended that the plea of superior orders is excluded under Article IV, even though such pleas are permissible under the domestic law of the country, and contends instead: 'The non-inclusion of a proviso relating to superior orders . . . leaves the tribunals applying the Convention the freedom of interpreting it in accordance with the domestic legislation and the circumstances of the case.' He distinguishes 'command of law' i.e., domestic law could not be invoked as a defence to non-fulfilment of an international obligation.

instead the freedom of tribunals applying the Convention to interpret it in accordance with domestic legislation and the circumstances of the case. Furthermore, it seems to be widely accepted that the test of 'was a moral choice possible' to a subordinate ordered to commit a war crime or act of genocide, is a general principle of law in the sense of Article 38(1)(c) of the Statute of the International Court of Justice which finds expression in many municipal legal systems as well as the documents of international penal law.[92] In practice, therefore, the Genocide Convention is likely to be interpreted consistently with the main corpus of law on this topic. The *travaux préparatoires* of the Convention do not appear to contradict this proposition.

Implementation of the Genocide Convention

(a) Domestic law

The implementation measures in the Convention have national and international aspects. This is normal with regard to international human rights legislation.[93] The parties to the Genocide Convention, in virtue of Article V, 'undertake to enact, in accordance with their respective constitutions, the necessary legislation to give effect to the provisions of the present Convention and, in particular, to provide effective penalties' for those guilty of genocide. States parties are given considerable freedom to implement the Convention nationally. The categories of punishable acts will be interpreted and judged differently by the courts of the signatory States in accordance with their criminal law: uniform legislation is not demanded by the Convention. There is considerable variation in the national laws of States parties.[94] Many States considered that their existing legislation was adequate to deal with genocide and sufficient to fulfil their obligations under the Convention even though in some cases no specific crime of genocide was delineated by their legal systems. The majority of States have defined genocide domestically in similar or identical terms to the Convention.

---

[92] Dinstein, *The Defence of 'Obedience to Superior Orders' in International Law* (Leyden: Sitjhoff, 1965); Bassiouni (ed.), *International Criminal Law*, vol. iii, 72–88; Green, *Superior Orders in National and International Law* (Leyden: Sitjhoff, 1976); Wilner, 'Superior Orders as a Defence to Violations of International Criminal Law', *MLR*, 26 (1966), 127.

[93] Among a voluminous literature, see Hannum, *Guide to International Human Rights Practice* (London, Macmillan, 1984); Humphrey, 'The Implementation of International Human Rights Law' *New York Law School Law Review*, 24 (1978), 31; Sohn, 'Human Rights: Their Implementation and Supervision by the United Nations', in Meron (ed.), *Human Rights in International Law* (Oxford: 1984), 369. The present text contains many references to implementation of particular treaties.

[94] Ruhashyankiko (*supra*, ch. 5, n. 2), provides summaries of national legislation on genocide with many text quotations.

(b) The competent courts

Article VI provides: 'Persons charged with genocide . . . shall be tried by a competent tribunal of the State in the territory of which the act was committed or by such international penal tribunal as may have jurisdiction with respect to those Contracting Parties which shall have accepted its jurisdiction.'

The first alternative is territorial jurisdiction, namely that of the *forum loci delicti commissi*. The Secretariat preferred the notion of universal punishment or competence, whereby States parties would 'pledge themselves to punish any offender under this Convention within any territory under their jurisdiction, irrespective of the nationality of the offender or of the place where the offence has been committed'.[95]

The universal principle was voted down in the Ad Hoc Committee whose text became, with minor drafting alterations, the present Article VI.[96] The essential argument against the universal approach[97] was that, since genocide generally implied the responsibility of the State in the territory of which it was committed, the principle of universal repression would lead national courts to judge the acts of foreign Governments thereby creating a risk of international tension. Genocide was perceived as different from other offences subject to universal jurisdiction such as trafficking in drugs and counterfeiting currency: it has clearer political implications. The sensibilities of States were to the forefront of deliberations in the Ad Hoc Committee and the Sixth Committee.[98] States have entered reservations to the Convention in case Article VI should be interpreted as conferring jurisdiction on foreign tribunals.[99] Although there are now further examples of international conventions applying liberal principles of jurisdiction,[100] States still express doubts on applying such principles to the punishment of genocide, though this negative sentiment is not unanimous.[101]

---

[95] UN Doc E/447, 8 and 38.

[96] By four votes to two, with one abstention. France, the USA, and the USSR were among those voting against the proposal.

[97] UN Doc E/794 summarizes the discussions in the Ad Hoc Committee.

[98] UN Doc A/C.6/SR. 97–8, 100, 129–134.

[99] Burma, Morocco, the Philippines, and Venezuela have all made reservations on this point. The text of the Moroccan reservation reads: 'With reference to Article VI, the Government of His Majesty the King considers that Moroccan courts and tribunals alone have jurisdiction with respect to acts of genocide committed within the territory of Morocco'. See Robinson (*supra*, n. 28), Appendix VI.

[100] Compare, for example, Article V of the International Convention on the Suppression and Punishment of the Crime of Apartheid which provides that persons charged with acts constituting this crime may be tried 'by a competent tribunal of any State Party to the Convention which may acquire jurisdiction . . .' over the person of the accused. Text in *ILM*, 13 (1974), 50. See also Convention for the Suppression of Unlawful Seizure of Aircraft 1970, *ILM*, 10 (1971), 133; Convention for the Suppression of Unlawful Acts against the Safety of Civil Aviation 1971, *ILM*, 10 (1971), 1151; Convention on the Prevention and Punishment of Crimes against Internationally Protected Persons, including Diplomatic Agents, *AJIL*, 68 (1975), 383.

[101] See communications from the Governments of Bulgaria, Finland, The Netherlands,

The second alternative of an 'international penal tribunal' was retained despite efforts to delete it from Article VI.[102] It was felt that, although it was logical that an international crime should be punished at the international level, logic and theory must be subordinated to practical considerations. Questions of State sovereignty and prestige were again prominent in the arguments against international jurisdiction.[103] The reference in the Ad Hoc Committee's draft to a 'competent international tribunal' was deleted by the Sixth Committee at its 98th meeting, but restored at its 131st meeting in an altered form.

A special 'international penal tribunal' has still not been constituted. There was some initial enthusiasm for such a body at the United Nations. The General Assembly, in Resolution 260B(III) of 9 December 1948, considered that 'in the course of development of the international community, there will be an increasing need of an international judicial organ for the trial of certain crimes under international law'. It invited the International Law Commission 'to study the desirability and possibility of establishing an international judicial organ for the trial of persons charged with genocide or other crimes over which jurisdiction will be conferred upon that organ by international conventions' and, in carrying out that task, 'to pay attention to the possibility of establishing a criminal chamber of the International Court of Justice'. The International Law Commission favoured the idea of 'an international judicial organ' but did not recommend the establishment of the criminal chamber.[104]

The General Assembly subsequently established a Committee on International Criminal Jurisdiction[105] which prepared a draft statute for an international criminal court.[106] This was revised by a later committee composed of Representatives of seventeen Member States.[107] However, by its Resolution 898(IX) adopted on 14 December 1954,[108] the General Assembly, noting the connection between the problem of the Court, the Draft Code of Offences against the Peace and Security of Mankind, and the question of defining aggression, decided to postpone the question of the international criminal court. This position was reaffirmed by later resolutions by which progress on the Draft Code and an international criminal court was made to depend on progress in defining aggression.[109]

The General Assembly adopted the Definition of Aggression on 14

Romania, Ecuador, and Italy to Special Rapporteur Ruhashyankiko for positive views on a broader assumption of jurisdiction (*supra*, ch. 6, n. 2), 52–5.

[102] A/C.6/215/Rev.1; A/C.6/217; A/C.6/218.

[103] *GAOR*, 3rd Session, Part I, 6th Committee, Summary Records of meetings, 366 ff.

[104] *GAOR*, 5th Session, Supplement No. 12, paras. 128–45.

[105] UNGA Res. 489(V), 12 December 1950.

[106] *GAOR*, 7th Session, Supplement No. 11.

[107] *GAOR*, 9th Session, Supplement No. 12.

[108] Djonovich, 'United Nations Resolutions—Series 1, General Assembly, vols. i–xiii (Oceana, Dobbs Ferry, 1973–6), vol. v, 166.

[109] UNGA Res. 1186(XII), and 1187(XII), Djonovich, ibid., vol. vi, 243–4.

December 1974, by Resolution 3314(XXIX).[110] The question of the international criminal court has since received some attention, much of it
unfavourable, from the Sub-Commission on Prevention of Discrimination
and Protection of Minorities.[111] Sub-Commission members proposed as an
alternative the setting up of an international investigatory body to act not
only on the basis of majority decisions by political organs of the United
Nations, but also on its own initiative, in cases where there was evidence
that genocide was being or was about to be committed.[112] There seems to be
little support at the United Nations or elsewhere for the idea of an international criminal court to try individuals accused of genocide. The lack of a
tribunal means that allegations of genocide, which have been fairly common
since the term became part of the vocabulary of international law, have for
the most part not been the subject of impartial judicial determination.[113]

The jurisdictional provisions of Article VI are supplemented by Article
VII which provides that: 'Genocide and the other acts enumerated in Article
III shall not be considered as political crimes for the purpose of extradition.
The Contracting Parties pledge themselves in such cases to grant extradition
in accordance with their laws and treaties in force.'

(c) The right to call upon the competent organs of the United Nations

According to Article VIII, parties may call upon the competent organs of the
United Nations to take such action under the Charter of the United Nations
as they consider appropriate for the prevention and suppression of acts of
genocide or the other acts enumerated in Article III. This is superficially a
very important article for the functioning of the Convention machinery. The
Convention is described as a convention for 'the prevention and punishment' of the crime of genocide, but Article VIII is the only article dealing
with the preventive aspect; other articles concentrate on the question of

---

[110] *GAOR*, 29th Session, Supplement No. 19; *AJIL*, 69 (1976), 480.

[111] UN Doc E/CN.4/Sub.2/L.565, L.583, L.623, Reports of Special Rapporteur
Ruhashyankiko examined at the 25th, 26th, and 28th Sessions of the Sub-Commission on
Prevention of Discrimination and Protection of Minorities.

[112] Ruhashyankiko, *Study*, 135–9, UN Doc E/CN.4/Sub.2/SR.658, 63; SR.736, 203. The
idea of an investigatory body was favourably regarded by the Governments of The Netherlands, Congo, Ecuador, the United Kingdom (desirable in principle, difficult in practice),
Finland, Rwanda, and Oman. Also, Whitaker, Revised and Updated Report on the Question
of the Prevention and Punishment of the Crime of Genocide, UN Doc E/CN.4/Sub.2/1985/6,
paras. 85 ff. The Baha'i International communicated to Whitaker: 'We believe that, at the
present time, the most effective means of preventing and controlling genocide is through the
establishment by the United Nations of a new international body dealing exclusively with
genocide and charged with responsibility for considering allegations . . . Since secrecy is the
greatest ally of any Government that seeks to engage in genocide, and international publicity
and condemnation the greatest enemy, it might be expected that . . . opprobrium . . . would
attach to any Government which was identified as a violator of the Convention by a
high-level international body of known competence and impartiality . . .' UN Doc
E/CN.4/Sub.2/1984/NGO/9.

[113] *Infra*, ch. 8.

punishment. Article VIII also envisages United Nations intervention to prevent and suppress genocide. The draft prepared by the Secretary-General made it clearer that what was envisaged was a partnership or sharing of responsibility between contracting Parties and the United Nations; the parties would 'do everything in their power to give full effect to the intervention of the United Nations'.[114]

The parties are accorded a right to bring a case to the United Nations though this is not coupled with any duty to exercise it. The question of imposing a duty was discussed and rejected. Article VIII was deleted at one stage by the Sixth Committee on the grounds of redundancy as States members of the United Nations were already entitled to appeal to the United Nations in case of need.[115] The right of appeal was raised again in connection with Article IX of the Convention on the function of the International Court of Justice and was reinstated with minor alterations in order, principally, to avoid the impression that the International Court was the only United Nations organ competent in this respect.[116]

It is not entirely clear that Article VIII adds anything substantial to the Genocide Convention. It does not strengthen the powers of the United Nations organs in relation to the measures in cases of genocide—action is to be taken 'under the Charter of the United Nations'. A number of commentators affirm the article's lack of legal significance because what it refers to is a right already existing under the Charter.[117] However, according to Planzer:

An appeal to the organs of the United Nations in cases of genocide is nevertheless of some psychological importance. It is a new form of intervention on humanitarian grounds by the world community. In the absence of an international court, an appeal to the United Nations would not be pointless, for it would bring the matter before world public opinion, which might induce a State to renounce any such acts.[118]

(d) Role of the International Court of Justice

Article IX of the Convention provides: 'Disputes between the contracting Parties relating to the interpretation, application or fulfilment of the . . . Convention, including those relating to the responsibility of a State for genocide or any of the other acts enumerated in Article III, shall be submitted to the International Court of Justice at the request of any of the parties to the dispute.' As evidenced by the *travaux préparatoires* and reservations

---

[114] UN Doc E/447, 45.
[115] The article was deleted at the 101st meeting of the 6th Committee: the voting was 21 to 18, with one abstention. *GAOR*, 3rd Session, Part I, 6th Committee, 101st meeting, 417; UN DOC, A/C.6/SR.101.
[116] Ibid., SR.105, by 29 votes to 4, with 5 abstentions.
[117] Drost refers to the article's 'lack of significance and consequence', *The Crime of State*, 109.
[118] Planzer, *Le Crime de Génocide* (thesis: St. Gallen, 1956), 155.

to the Convention, this has been one of the most contentious articles in the Convention, because it threatens States with a judgment of their conduct by a forum not susceptible to political influences and pressure to the same extent as other organs of the United Nations. Accordingly, there have been a number of reservations to this article, the most common of which concedes jurisdiction to the International Court only upon the agreement of all parties to a dispute. The whole of the Soviet bloc has made reservations.[119] Clearly, the non-consensual nature of the reference to the International Court is irksome to many States.

The Convention itself contains no reference to reservations. The Draft prepared by the Secretariat included the title 'Article XVII (reservations)' but no text was proposed. The comments under that title are illuminating none the less; they clearly regard reservations as inappropriate: 'reservations of a general scope have no place in a Convention of this kind which does not deal with the private interests of a State, but with the preservation of an element of international order . . . It is unthinkable that . . . the scope of the Convention should vary according to the reservations possibly accompanying accession by certain States.'[120] The Ad Hoc Committee on Genocide decided that there was no need for reservations,[121] and no proposal was put forward in the Sixth Committee of the General Assembly for the inclusion of an article on reservations.

None the less reservations made by a number of States when signing the Convention,[122] or introduced by States in their instruments of ratification and accession to the Convention, together with objections to the substance of the reservations, very soon created a problem for the Secretary-General of the United Nations with respect to performance of depository functions under Article XIII of the Convention.[123] The practice of the Secretary-General in the absence of specific provision in the Convention had been to follow the rule that reservations were permissible only with the consent of

---

[119] ST/HR/5, 178 ff. Some 22 States have made reservations which include a reference to Article IX; 10 States have objected.

[120] UN Doc E/447, 55.

[121] The Ad Hoc Committee instructed a sub-committee to deal with that problem, and in adopting the sub-committee's conclusions decided that there was no need for any reservations, UN Doc E/A.C.25/10, 5–7.

[122] After the final text was accepted in the 6th Committee, several delegations reserved the position of their Governments with respect to the draft convention. This can be seen as part of the continuing process of retraction from the idealism which inspired the earliest stages of promotion of the Convention: UN Doc A/C.6/SR.132–3.

[123] Article XIII reads: 'On the day when the first twenty instruments of ratification or accession have been deposited, the Secretary-General shall draw up a procès-verbal and transmit a copy thereof to each Member of the United Nations and to each of the non-Member States contemplated in Article XI. The present Convention shall come into force on the ninetieth day following the date of deposit of the twentieth instrument of ratification or accession. Any ratification or accession effected subsequent to the latter date shall become effective on the ninetieth day following the deposit of the instrument of ratification or accession.'

all parties. To what extent, therefore, could States making reservations which were subject to objections be counted among the parties to the Convention for the purpose of deciding when it entered into force? The question was the subject of an Advisory Opinion by the International Court of Justice[124] which effectively permitted a greater liberty to States in the matter of reservations than the traditional rule, though the Opinion is framed with the special characteristics of the Genocide Convention in mind: the Convention was based on principles which are recognized by States even without any conventional obligation;[125] it had a universal character; it was manifestly adopted for a purely humanitarian or civilizing purpose. One could not speak therefore of 'individual advantages or disadvantages to States, or of the maintenance of a perfect contractual balance between rights and duties'.[126] With these principles in mind, the court attempted to find a *via media* between the goal of 'universalism' in relation to the Convention, and the integrity of the document, which implied that its objectives could not be sacrificed to the 'vain desire to secure as many participants as possible'.[127] It followed that it was 'the compatibility of a reservation with the *object and purpose* of the Convention that must furnish the criterion'[128] for the reserving and objecting States. The subjective quality of this criterion means that States will disagree as to the compatibility with the Convention of reservations made by other States and therefore as to whether these States are properly regarded as parties. The reservations referred to above are of considerable significance and cannot be described as minor reservations of a technical nature; they relate to a crucial aspect of the implementation procedures. This view has been expressed by a number of States parties.[129] The argument against such reservations was incisively formulated by Counsel for Pakistan in the *Case Concerning Trial of Pakistani Prisoners of War (Pakistan v. India)*[130] in relation to the Indian reservation to Article IX. In his view, no reservation was possible because the ultimate test of the validity of a reservation is recourse to this selfsame article. Article IX 'must rank as a fundamental provision on which the very future and fulfilment of the Convention depends'.[131]

It may be noted that this was not the only controversial aspect of Article IX: the reference to 'the responsibility of a State for genocide' provoked

---

[124] Reservations to the Convention on the Prevention and Punishment of the Crime of Genocide, Advisory Opinion, *ICJ Reports 1951*, 15.

[125] Ibid. 23.   [126] Ibid.   [127] Ibid. 362.   [128] Ibid. 24.

[129] Observations submitted by the Governments of The Netherlands and the United Kingdom to Ruhashyankiko, *Study on the Question of the Prevention and Punishment of the Crime of Genocide*, UN Doc E/CN.4/Sub.2/416, 101–02.

[130] *Trial of Pakistani Prisoners of War, International Court of Justice Reports 1973*, 347. The case was entered on the Court's General List on 11 May 1973, and was discontinued by order of the Court on 15 December 1973. See Paust and Blaustein, 'War Crimes Jurisdiction and Due Process: The Bangladesh Experience', *Vanderbilt Journal of Transnational Law*, 11 (1978), 1.

[131] Trial of Pakistani Prisoners, ibid.

divergences of opinion in the Sixth Committee, reminiscent of the debates on Article IV.[132] The reference raised the twin spectres of State criminal responsibility and of States being responsible for injuries to their own nationals. These aspects are reflected in the reservation maintained by the Philippines which 'does not consider [the] said article to extend the concept of State responsibility beyond that recognised by the generally accepted principles of international law'.[133]

The responsibility issue was discussed in a number of meetings devoted to it by the Sixth Committee of the General Assembly.[134] The debates are not a model of clarity. The reference to international responsibility is the product of an amendment submitted by the United Kingdom and Belgium,[135] the deletion of which was rejected narrowly by nineteen votes to seventeen, with eight abstentions. The Representative of the United Kingdom maintained that 'the Convention would be incomplete if no mention were made of the responsibility of States'.[136] and that 'all speakers had recognised that the responsibility of the State was almost always involved in acts of genocide'.[137] The Representative of France expressed his agreement with the UK and Belgian amendment 'as long as it was a matter of civil and not criminal responsibility'.[138] Other States agreed with this.[139] The Philippines expressed doubts which led ultimately to the above reservation. The Representative stated that 'the joint amendment did not specifically state that criminal responsibility was involved, but from the very nature of the Convention, the purpose of which was the punishment of genocide, that idea could be inferred.'[140] Thus, the Philippines 'could not accept the idea that a whole State should be stigmatised for acts for which only its rulers or its officials were responsible'.[141] The gist of the objections (and the meaning of the reference in the reservation to 'generally accepted principles of international law') appears to be directed to the criminal and civil responsibility aspect of the amendment, and perhaps goes no further than that.

Greece raised a different objection. If State responsibility were accepted, 'the State responsible for genocide would have to indemnify its own nationals. But in international law the real holder of a right was the State and not private persons. The State would thus be indemnifying itself.'[142] It is presumably this kind of reasoning that encouraged UN Special Rapporteur Ruhashyankiko to deny that there is civil responsibility of a State for injuries to its own nationals.[143] However, Greece voted for the amendment and later stated only that States in the Convention undertook to prevent and punish genocide, but did not undertake obligations as to 'the nature and

---

[132] UN Doc A/C.6/SR.103–4.
[133] UN Doc ST/HR/5, 183–4.
[134] See especially meetings 103 and 104, *GAOR*, 3rd Session, Part I, 6th Committee (1948).
[135] Ibid. 447, UN Doc A/C.6/258.
[136] Ibid. 430.   [137] Ibid. 430.   [138] Ibid. 431.
[139] Remarks of representatives of Egypt, ibid. 431, and Greece, 432–3.
[140] Ibid. 433.   [141] Ibid. 433.   [142] Ibid. 433.   [143] Para. 329.

extent of the reparations',[144] which apparently leaves untouched the *principle* of responsibility, including responsibility to one's own nationals. Other States, however, were not greatly disturbed by the implication of responsibility to the State's own nationals. Haiti declared its acceptance of civil responsibility, and 'the same principle applied if a State committed the crime of genocide against its own nationals'.[145] Egypt simply approved the general principle of the article—it was important in view of 'the absence of a general organisation for international punishment'.[146] Other delegations did not so much object to responsibility to one's own nationals as, in view of its apparent novelty, to question the modalities of its application.[147] The present author prefers the interprepation advanced by Robinson:

The fact that a special provision relating to the civil responsibility of the States, despite the general rule of international law that a violation of an international treaty establishes the obligation of the violating State to repair the resulting damage and that every State is authorised to pursue cases, was discussed, may well indicate that Article IX, in dealing with the problem of civil responsibility of the States, goes beyond the generally accepted rules of international law.[148]

It seems clear that it is civil rather than criminal responsibility that was under discussion. Most delegations agreed on this; the Representative of The Netherlands described the reaction of the Philippines as 'exaggerated', because it was clear that only civil responsibility was intended.[149] The Convention to that extent maintains the fiction of the virtuous State' and the 'wicked individual', or between the 'delinquent or tortfeasor State' and the 'criminal individual'.

---

[144] *GAOR*, 3rd Session, Part I, 6th Committee, 445.
[145] Ibid. 436.
[146] Ibid. 431.
[147] See the remarks of the Representative of Peru, ibid. 434. This appears to be the substance of the Greek comments, *supra*, n. 139.
[148] *The Genocide Convention. A Commentary*, 104.
[149] 103rd meeting of the 6th Committee, 435.

7. Does the Prohibition of Genocide Bind All States?

Introduction

In view of the limited participation by States in the Genocide Convention,[1] the question of its relationship to customary international law retains considerable significance for many minority groups. Those States which are not parties[2] are quite as ethnically heterogeneous as the States Parties and do not present themselves as a group of particular, outstanding political stability. Their minorities are exposed to the same physical and cultural

[1] By 1 September 1988 there were ninety-seven States parties to the Genocide Convention. Four States had signed but not ratified the Convention: Bolivia, Dominican Republic, Paraguay, and the US. For States parties, see *Human Rights, Status of International Instruments*, ST/HR/5. For the current position of the United States, see Leblanc, 'The United Nations Genocide Convention and Political Groups: Should the United States Propose an Amendment?', *Yale Journal of International Law*, 13 (1988), 268. The United States Senate resolved to ratify the Convention in February 1986. However, the resolution stated that the President 'will not deposit the instrument of ratification until after . . . implementing legislation has been enacted'. The USA is now a Party to the Convention. The history of US hesitations in relation to the Convention is documented in Sohn and Buergenthal, *International Protection of Human Rights*, 913 ff., and McFarland, *The United States and the United Nations Convention on the Prevention and Punishment of the Crime of Genocide* (PhD thesis: American University, 1971).

[2] Non-parties include States against which allegations of genocide have been made, such as Burundi, Equatorial Guinea (under the dictator Macias Nguema), Paraguay, and South Africa. On the other hand, Democratic Kampuchea is a party—this State has been the subject of allegations: see Whitaker (*supra*, ch. 5, n. 2), n. 17: 'It is estimated that at least two million people were killed by Pol Pot's Khmer Rouge Government of Democratic Kampuchea out of a total population of 7 million. Even under the most restricted definition, this constituted genocide, since the victims included target groups such as the Chams (an Islamic minority) and the Buddhist monks.' On the other hand, Leblanc (*supra*, n. 1), 290, writes: 'the atrocities committed in Kampuchea . . . may not constitute genocide under the terms of the Convention. Hundreds of thousands died but it could be argued that the slaughter was not directed at specific groups on the grounds of their national, ethnic, racial, or religious identity.' Leblanc's argument is in the course of a general discussion of politically motivated killings in relation to the Convention. However, whatever the general direction of Kampuchean policy, it seems unarguable that it at least included acts of genocide. See Can, *Kampuchea Dossier: the Dark Years* (Hanoi: Vietnam Courier, 1979); Hawk, *The Cambodia Documentation Commission* (New York: Columbia University Press, 1983); Kuper, *International Action against Genocide*. The number of Parties to the Convention is disappointing, given the length of time since it was promulgated. There is no resource problem for poorer States in implementing the Convention: it does not oblige States to establish minority schools, nor to establish local autonomy, nor to minimize disparities of income between different ethnic, racial, or social groups. The Convention only threatens those who would commit an unmitigated evil, not, on the face of it, a serious burden for any State, rich or poor. Special Rapporteur Ruhashyankiko has admitted to a lack of precise information on why so many States have not become Parties to such a basic treaty (Ruhashyankiko, N., *Study on the Question of the Prevention of the Crime of Genocide*, UN Doc E/CN.4/Sub.2/416, at 167–71).

insecurities as minorities in any modern State, so that the benefits, such as they are, of an international convention seeking to provide a fundamental guarantee of their right to exist, are hardly less desirable.

The discussion of the universal status of the prohibition of genocide may be approached in a number of ways. The developments associated with the United Nations are clearly of primary importance. None the less, by way of preliminary clarification, the relationship between genocide and the customary law of crimes against humanity requires consideration.

Crimes Against Humanity

The Charter of the International Military Tribunal at Nuremberg[3] articulated three categories of offence: (*a*) crimes against peace; (*b*) war crimes; and (*c*) crimes against humanity. The first and third of these can best be described as embryonic categories of international crimes which were given explicit definition by the Charter; the category of war crimes approximated more to prevailing international law.[4] The first application of the concept of 'crimes against humanity' was in the context of the laws of war. Thus, the Fourth Hague Convention of 1907, concerning the Laws and Customs of War on Land, stated that the inhabitants and the belligerents remain under the protection of and subject to the principles of the law of nations, as established by the usages prevailing among civilised peoples by the *laws of humanity*, and the dictates of the public conscience.[5] But these 'laws of humanity' were not defined by the Hague Convention, and neither did the accompanying Regulations on land warfare describe any specific violations as crimes against humanity.[6] These crimes were first distinguished from war crimes in the declaration made on 28 May 1915, by the governments of France, Great Britain, and Russia with reference to the massacres of Armenians in Turkey, denouncing the 'crimes against humanity and civilisation for which all members of the Turkish Government will be held responsible together with its agents implicated in the massacres'.[7] In January 1919

[3] *Supra*, ch. 6.　　　　　　　　　　　　　　　　　　[4] *Supra*, ch. 6.

[5] Bassiouni, 'International Law and the Holocaust', *California Western International Law Journal*, 9 (1978), 202; Ehard, 'The Nuremberg Trial and International Law', *AJIL*, 43 (1949), 223; Garner, 'The Punishment of Offenders against the Laws and Customs of War', *AJIL*, 14 (1920), 70; Lauterpacht, 'The Law of Nations and the Punishment of War Crimes', *BYIL*, 21 (1944), 58; Schwelb, 'Crimes against Humanity' *BYIL*, 21 (1946), 178.

[6] The Convention and Regulations are not expressly based on a premise of individual responsibility for crimes. Article 3 of the Convention states: 'A belligerent party which violates the provisions of the said regulations shall, if the case demands, be liable to pay compensation. It shall be responsible for all acts committed by persons forming part of its armed forces.' In practice, breach of the Convention and its Regulations has been treated as creating individual criminal responsibility. For texts, see Roberts and Guelff, (eds.), *Documents on the Laws of War* (Oxford, OUP, 1987) ch. 5.

[7] 'History of the United Nations War Crimes Commission and the Development of the Laws of War' (HMSO for the UNWCC, London, 1948), 35.

the Preliminary Peace Conference of Paris decided to convene a Committee of Fifteen which would, *inter alia*, find facts relating to violation of the laws and customs of war committed by the German Empire and its Allies. The report of the Committee found that breaches of the laws of war and the laws of humanity had occurred, concluding that 'all persons belonging to enemy countries . . . who have been guilty of offences against the laws and customs of war or the laws of humanity, are liable to . . . prosecution.'[8] The latter category did not find its way into any of the ratified peace treaties after the war.[9] The unratified Treaty of Sèvres provided for such crimes[10] but was replaced by the Treaty of Lausanne which did not, and which in addition granted amnesty to all those who committed massacres during the period 1914–22. It is clear, therefore, that the concept of crimes against humanity had not emerged in 1923 in either conventional or customary law.[11] This meant, *inter alia*, that the commission of offences by a government against its own nationals was not within any accepted category of international crime.

The purpose of Article 6(c) of the Nuremberg Charter was to enable the prosecution of those whose crimes were not restricted to violation of the laws and customs of war perpetrated on Allied territory or against Allied nationals, but were committed on Axis territory against persons of other than Allied nationality. The crimes against humanity, however, had to be committed 'in execution of or in connection with any crime within the jurisdiction of the Tribunal', that is, in connection with war crimes or crimes against peace. It is clear, as a matter of construction, that this phrase was intended to govern all forms which the offence might take. The scope for prosecution under this head was much reduced and the Tribunal found few acts to be crimes against humanity if they were committed before 1 September 1939.[12] The provision served only to reach those crimes of a war criminal committed in an area not governed by the Hague Rules of Land Warfare, for example, occupied territory in which all domestic resistance has ceased.[13] The situation under the Nuremberg Charter is summarized by Schwelb:

---

[8] Schwelb (*supra*, n. 5), 180.

[9] The two American members of the Committee of Fifteen objected to the inclusion of a reference to violation of the laws of humanity in the Versailles Peace Treaty. Their view was that war by its very nature was inhumane and, therefore, that acts consistent with the laws of war, though inhumane, were not punishable, Bassiouni (*supra*, n. 5), 211. The Treaty of Versailles did, however, establish the punishability of war criminals and also ordered, *inter alia*, the prosecution of Kaiser Wilhelm II by an international tribunal for an offence against 'international morality and the sanctity of treaties'. The Netherlands refused to extradite him because he was charged with a political offence: Wright, 'The Legal Liability of the Kaiser', *American Political Science Review*, 13 (1919), 120.

[10] Article 230 of the former treaty stated as an offence 'the massacres committed during the continuance of the state of war on territory which formed part of the Turkish Empire . . .'.

[11] Bassiouni (*supra*, n. 5), 211.

[12] Schwelb (*supra*, n. 5). See for example, the 'Judgment against defendant Von Neurath', 1 *Trial of the Major War Criminals at Nuremberg*, Judgment, 302, 304, 334.

[13] The Hague Rules on Belligerent Occupation would apply here: Roberts and Guelff, *Documents on the Laws of War* (Oxford: OUP, 1982).

The crime against humanity, as defined in the London Charter, is not, therefore, the corner-stone of a system of international criminal law equally applicable in times of war and peace, protecting the human rights . . . 'of any civilian population', against anybody, including their own States and Governments. As interpreted in the Nuremberg judgment, the term has a considerably narrower connotation. It is . . . a kind of by-product of war . . . destined primarily, if not exclusively, to protect the inhabitants of foreign countries against crimes committed, in connection with an aggressive war, by the authorities and organs of the aggressor State . . . It denotes a particular type of war crime . . . 'accompanying' or 'accessory' to either crimes against peace or violations of the laws and customs of war.[14]

The Nuremberg Charter represented an advance, though a cautious one, in the development of international criminal law. The restriction of crimes against humanity to acts in connection with war was omitted from the definition of such crimes by Control Council Law No.10, issued by the Control Council for Germany on 20 December 1945. On the other hand, under the terms of its Preamble, Law No.10 was enacted in order to give effect to the Nuremberg Charter; and by Article I of the Law 'the Moscow Declaration . . . and the London Agreement of August 8th, 1945 . . . are made integral parts of this Law.' This link may be thought to give the definition of crimes against humanity in Law No.10 the same connotation as in the Nuremberg Charter.[15]

However, even if the Control Council Law is considered to have widened the scope of this crime, it appears that it does so as a municipal statute enacted by the sovereign Power in post-war Germany and not as an international legal instrument.[16] Given this difference, the caution exhibited in the Charter in examining the internal affairs of a State and applying international law is understandable—the doctrine of domestic jurisdiction restricted the scope of the tribunal. The scope of crimes against humanity as a general category of international law continued to be viewed in a narrow fashion; this is evidenced from General Assembly Resolution 95(I), adopted unanimously on 11 December 1946. The Resolution 'affirmed' the 'principles of international law recognised by the Charter of the Nuremberg Tribunal and in the judgment of the Tribunal' also directing that these principles recognized in this Charter were to be formulated in the context of 'a general codification of offences against the peace and security of mankind'.[17] Resolution 95(I) did not break the link between crimes against humanity and war crimes; crimes against humanity were still a subsidiary category of offence.

---

[14] Schwelb (*supra*, n. 5), 206.
[15] Ibid. 217 ff. Also *War Crimes Trials*, vol. XIII, 41 (Notes on the Greifelt Trial).
[16] Schwelb, 218.
[17] Gross, 'Some Observations on the Draft Code of Offences Against the Peace and Security of Mankind', *Israel Yearbook on Human Rights*, 13 (1983), 9.

Emergence of Genocide as a Separate Concept

The term 'genocide' was used in the Nuremberg indictments and in trials of less highly placed criminals. It is at this point that the lineaments of a separate criminal concept of genocide begin to emerge from the existing customary law, though there was no dramatic break—the dominant concepts were still crimes against humanity and war crimes, as reflected in the Nuremberg Charter and Control Council Law No.10. Thus, for example, in the *Greifelt Case*[18] Count I of the indictment charged, in paragraph 1, crimes against humanity, which, according to paragraph 2 were carried out as part of 'a systematic programme of genocide'; a programme 'aimed at the destruction of foreign nations and ethnic groups, in part by murderous extermination, and in part by elimination and suppression of national characteristics'. Thus, genocide was treated within the circumstances of the case, as an offence perpetrated in time of war and committed through a series of individual acts constituting crimes against humanity. It remained within the sphere of the laws of war and fell within the jurisdiction of the tribunal which tried the accused. The emerging crime of genocide received detailed discussion in the so-called *Justice Trial (Josef Altostötter and Others)*[19] before the United States Military Tribunal at Nuremberg. All the accused had been judges, law officers, and officials in the Ministry of Justice in the Nazi Government. All were accused of having commited war crimes and crimes against humanity. These were outlined in the indictment:

Between September, 1939 and April, 1945, all of the defendants herein unlawfully, wilfully, and knowingly committed crimes against humanity as defined by Control Council Law No.10, in that they were principals in, accessories to, ordered, abetted, took a consenting part in, and were connected with plans and enterprises involving the commission of atrocities and offences, including but not limited to murder, extermination, enslavement, deportation, illegal imprisonment, torture, persecution on political, racial or religious grounds, and ill-treatment of, and other inhumane acts against German civilians and nationals of occupied countries.[20]

The judgment reveals that genocide was regarded as a crime against humanity which can be committed by a government either against its nationals or against those of another State. The relationship between genocide and crimes against humanity was outlined: 'As the prime illustration of a crime against humanity under Control Council Law No. 10, which by reason of its magnitude and its international repercussions has been recognised as a violation of common international law, we cite "genocide" . . . '.[21] In relation to the defendant Lautz, the tribunal concluded that he was 'criminally implicated in enforcing the law against Poles and Jews which we

---

[18] Ch. 6, n. 23.   [19] *War Crimes Trials*, vol. VI.
[20] Ibid. 48.   [21] Ibid.

deem to be a part of the established governmental plan for the extermination of those races. He was an accessory to and took a consenting part in the crime of genocide.'[22] In relation to defendant Rothaug, it was said that: 'It is of the essence of the charges against him that he participated in the national programme of racial persecution. It is of the essence of the proof that he identified himself with this national programme and gave himself utterly to its accomplishment. He participated in the crime of genocide.'[23] While distinctions can be made between the two categories, the post-war case-law on crimes against humanity provided a reasonable customary basis for the developing concept of genocide, though the restricted definition given to these crimes was inadequate to express the range of its potential applications; limiting genocide to a relationship with war would have marked hardly any advance over the existing law. It is instructive that in the *Justice Trial*, an external point of reference was adopted to point the way. In its remarks on the recognition of genocide in international law, the tribunal cited General Assembly Resolution 96 (I), declaring that: 'We approve and adopt its conclusions.'[24]

Resolution 96(I)

The crime of genocide outlined in this resolution[25] is entirely independent of any connection with aggressive war and war crimes. The resolution 'affirmed' that genocide is a crime under international law. Other operative paragraphs invite States to enact the necessary legislation to punish this crime and recommend them to cooperate to facilitate its speedy prevention and punishment—as well as requesting the Economic and Social Council to undertake the necessary preliminary studies for the Draft Convention. The scheme of these paragraphs implies that the crime of genocide exists already, but that the necessary procedures and institutions to secure its repression have yet to be devised. The clear language of the operative paragraphs must be taken to override the rather tentative, in legal terms, preambular claims that genocide 'is contrary to *moral law* and to the *spirit* and *aims* of the United Nations'. Similarly, at its second session, the General Assembly, in requesting the Economic and Social Council to continue its work on the Convention, again declared that 'genocide is an international crime entailing national and international responsibility on the part of individuals and States': Resolution 180(II), 21 November 1947.[26]

Resolution 96(I) has since been quoted by many commentators to support the view that genocide was condemned by customary international law

---

[22] Ibid. 75.   [23] Ibid. 99.
[24] Ibid. 48.   [25] *Supra*, ch. 7.
[26] Djonovich, *United Nations Resolutions*, vol. I, 320. The resolution was passed by 38 votes to 0, with 14 abstentions.

independently of the Genocide Convention.[27] This is reflected in Article I of the Convention, wherein the parties '*confirm* that genocide, whether committed in time of peace or in time of war, is a crime under international law which they undertake to prevent and punish'. General Assembly resolutions normally have recommendatory force only. However, they can represent the best possible statement of customary international law provided that certain conditions are fulfilled. The resolution deals clearly with a legal question and purports to be declaratory of existing law rather than an exhortation to create it;[28] the hortatory part of the resolution relates instead to creating machinery to suppress genocide. The resolution is a persuasive piece of evidence for the existence of a rule which is accepted as law. As noted above, the United States Military Tribunal in the *Justice (Altostötter) Trial* was impressed by it, observing that: 'The General Assembly is not an international legislature, but it is the most authoritative organ in existence for the interpretation of world opinion. Its recognition of genocide as an international crime is persuasive evidence of the fact.'[29]

During the drafting of the Convention, many references were made to Resolution 96(I) and to the Nuremberg Charter. Some delegates in the Sixth Committee of the General Assembly held the view that as a result of the resolution, or the resolution and the Charter taken together, genocide was already illegal under international law. The United Kingdom regarded physical genocide as already a crime, so that the proposed convention would make no significant contribution to international law.[30] The Representative of Poland referred to Resolution 96(I) as having recognized that genocide was a crime under international law and gave instances of Polish implementation through legislation of its provisions.[31] The Representative of Belgium considered that Resolution 96(I) was of 'a declaratory character; it specified what the General Assembly considered to be the law, but it did not create law'.[32] He argued that it was a mistaken assumption that a convention was necessary in order to act, by passing implementating legislation, and he cautioned against simply repeating the terms of Resolution 96(I) in the Convention as this would imply doubt as to the declaratory force of the resolution.[33] His view was supported by the Representative of Czechoslovakia who said that 'While it was true that the General Assembly could not by a resolution adopt new rules of law, its resolution could reaffirm the already existing law and as such they would be

---

[27] See the citation in Oppenheim, *International Law: A Treatise*, 8th edn., Lauterpacht (ed.), vol. i, 749–51. Note, however, the negative opinion of Kunz, based in part on the view that Res. 96(I) had merely the force of a recommendation; Kunz, 'The United Nations Convention on Genocide', *AJIL*, 43 (1949), 738.

[28] Akehurst, 'Custom as a Source of International Law', *BYIL*, 47 (1974–75), 1.

[29] *VI Law Reports of trials of War Criminals*, 48.

[30] *GAOR*, 3rd Session, Part I, 6th Committee, 64th meeting.

[31] Ibid. 18.

[32] Ibid. 22.

[33] Ibid., 67th meeting, 44.

binding on the members, particularly if they were unanimously adopted.'[34] Not all agreed with these views. Thus the Representative of Egypt remarked that the General Assembly resolution was only a recommendation whereas the convention would be binding on the parties.[35]

The position taken by the United States of America was that some doubt existed as to the criminality of genocide under international law. One Representative noted that the Nuremberg Charter only condemned genocide in time of war.[36] Another depicted four stages in the criminalization of genocide, taking as his standpoint the advice which a lawyer would give on the question. These were: 1, before Nuremberg, when the lawyer would find if difficult to prove in court that genocide was a crime; 2, after Nuremberg, when he would have a better chance, but still experience difficulty; 3, after the General Assembly resolution, when his chances would have improved, though the resolutions were not mandatory; 4, on the conclusion of the Convention which represents the final stage in his search for the law.[37]

While the majority of States felt that genocide was at this stage proscribed by international law, some expressed doubts. The main reason was the hesitation in accepting that General Assembly resolutions could have obligatory force. The doubters did not directly address the question as to whether a principle of customary law could none the less have been created. One of the Representatives of the United States reminded the Sixth Committee that the principle of outlawing genocide had been unanimously accepted by the United Nations.[38] Article I of the Genocide Convention which declared genocide to be a crime under international law, was one of the least contentious articles and passed through various drafting stages with relatively little comment. It is submitted that the *travaux préparatoires* reveal much support for and weak dissent from the view that genocide was contrary to international law.

Case-Law

Further reflections on the law before the Convention were outlined in the *Reservations to the Genocide Convention Case*,[39] where the International Court of Justice quoted liberally from Resolution 96(I):

The origins of the Convention show that it was the intention of the United Nations to condemn and punish genocide as 'a crime under international law' involving a denial of the right of existence of entire human groups, a denial which shocks the conscience of mankind, etc. (Resolution 96(I) of the General Assembly, December 11th, 1946). The first consequence arising from this conception is that the principles underlying the Convention are principles which are recognised by civilised nations as

---

[34] Ibid., 68th meeting 47.
[35] Ibid., 67th meeting 39.
[36] Ibid., 63rd meeting, 4.
[37] Ibid., 68th meeting, 50.
[38] Ibid., 63rd meeting, 4.
[39] *The Reservations Case, ICJ Reports*, 1951, 15.

binding on States, even without any conventional obligation. A second consequence is the universal character both of the condemnation of genocide and of the co-operation required 'in order to liberate mankind from such an odious scourge' . . . The Genocide Convention was therefore intended by the General Assembly and by the Contracting Parties to be definitely universal in scope.[40]

The views expressed by the International Court, apart from strengthening the claims of Resolution 96(I), represent in themselves an authoritative statement of the universal status of the prohibition of genocide.

These observations are substantiated by the *Eichmann Case*[41] where the District Court of Jerusalem stated in its judgment, which was confirmed by the Supreme Court of Israel, that 'the crime against the Jewish people' had been defined in the relevant Israeli law in the same terms as in the Genocide Convention because it was not a crime under that law alone but also an offence against the law of nations. Further, the Court declared that, in view of the repeated statements to that effect in General Assembly Resolution 96(I), the Genocide Convention, and the *Reservations Case*, 'there is no doubt that genocide has been recognised as a crime under international law in the full meaning of this term *ex tunc*, that is to say, the crimes of genocide committed against the Jewish people and other peoples during the period of the Hitler regime were crimes under international law.'

A later case of the International Court adds strength to the view that genocide is contrary to customary law. Furthermore, it represents this principle as being more deeply grounded than other principles of customary law. The Court in the *Barcelona Traction, Light and Power Co. Case*[42] distinguished between:

the obligation of a State towards the international community as a whole and those arising vis-à-vis another State in the field of diplomatic protection. By their very nature the former are the concern of all States. In view of the importance of the rights involved, all States can be held to have a legal interest in their protection; they are obligations *erga omnes*.[43]

These latter obligations were specified as deriving, for example:

in contemporary international law, from the outlawing of acts of aggression, and of genocide, as also from the principles and rules concerning the basic rights of the human person, including protection from slavery and racial discrimination. Some of the corresponding rights of protection have entered into the body of general interna-tional law (*Reservations to the Convention on the Prevention and Punishment of the*

---

[40] *The Reservations Case*, 23.

[41] *Attorney-General of the Government of Israel v. Eichmann* (1961), *International Law Reports*, 36, 5. See the commentaries on the case by Fawcett, *BYIL*, 38 (1962), 181; Green, *MLR*, 23 (1960), 507; Lador-Lederer, 'The Eichmann Case Revisited', *Israel Yearbook on Human Rights*, 14 (1984), 54; Lasok; Schwarzenberger, *Current Legal Problems*, 15 (1962), 248.

[42] *Barcelona Traction, Light and Power Co. Case* (*Belgium v. Spain*), *International Court of Justice Reports 1970*, 3.

[43] Ibid., para. 33.

Crime of Genocide); others are conferred by international instruments of a universal or quasi-universal character.[44]

There are, in the Court's opinion, a small number of obligations in whose fulfilment all States have a legal interest. The prohibition of genocide is one. The prohibition of genocide is fundamental to international law; its illegality is beyond question.

Jus Cogens

The Court's reference to the special nature of genocide prompts consideration of the related point of *jus cogens*. The doctrine in its present form is reflected in Articles 53 and 64 of the Vienna Convention on the Law of Treaties, 1969.[45] Article 53 states that:

A treaty is void if, at the time of its conclusion, it conflicts with a peremptory norm of general international law. For the purposes of the present Convention, a peremptory norm of general international law is a norm accepted and recognised by the international community of States as a whole as a norm from which no derogation is permitted and which can be modified only by a subsequent norm of general international law having the same character.

Article 64 provides that: 'If a new peremptory norm of general international law emerges, any existing treaty which is in conflict with that norm becomes void and terminates.' There is no specification of these norms. None the less, the commentary of the International Law Commission mentioned that 'a treaty contemplating or conniving at the commission of acts, such as trade in slaves, piracy or *genocide*[46] had been suggested by some Commission members as an illustration of an arrangement contrary to "obvious and best settled" rules of *jus cogens*.' Cases were not listed in the Convention in order to avoid possible misunderstandings of unlisted cases, and because a detailed study of principles of *jus cogens* would have been outside the scope of the Commission's project.

Earlier drafts were not so reticent. Thus, in relation to treaties void for

---

[44] Ibid., para. 34. The language of the *Reservations Case* is again taken up in a statement by the Government of Cyprus in reply to questions posed by Special Rapporteur Ruhashyankiko, *Study on the Question of the Prevention and Punishment of the Crime of Genocide*, UN Doc E/CN.4/Sub.2/416, 47: 'although Cyprus is not a party to the Genocide Convention . . . the Government of Cyprus believes that the principles underlying the Convention are principles which are recognised by civilized nations as binding on States even without conventional obligation.' The statement is important in itself as 'evidence' of the customary status of the prohibition of genocide. To similar effect is a statement by the Government of the Philippines (ibid. 144) explaining the relationship between the Constitution and genocide: the Philippine Constitutions of 1935 and 1973 are 'not bereft of provisions which are broad enough to declare the policies of the country which absorb the "generally accepted principles of International Law" and therefore, that of the Convention'.

[45] Misc. 19 (1971), *Cmnd.* 4818; *AJIL*, 63 (1969), 875.

[46] *YBILC 1966*, vol. ii, 247–8.

illegality, the fourth Special Rapporteur, Sir Humphrey Waldock, noted that 'the development—however tentative—of international criminal law presupposes the existence of an international public order containing rules having the character of *jus cogens*.'[47] His proposed description of *jus cogens* included any 'act or omission in the suppression or punishment of which every State is required by international law to co-operate'.[48] This was explained as implying a reference to the slave trade, piracy, or genocide.[49] His suggestion is supported by commentators' reflections on the Vienna Conference on the Law of Treaties as well as in their personal views. Thus, Capotorti writes: 'J'ajoute que les quelques exemples de normes internationales impératives sur lesquelles il y a eu une large convergence à Vienne concernent des règles impregnées certainement de valeurs morales comme les normes interdisant la traite des esclaves, le génocide, ou la piraterie.'[50] Beyond these cases, examples varied 'selon la philosophie politique et les intérêts de chaque État'.[51] This point is outlined further in relation to the statements made at the Conference by the State delegates.[52] Virally mentions 'activités considerées comme criminelles par le droit international'.[53] Verdross cites, *inter alia*, as *jus cogens* 'all rules of international law created for a humanitarian purpose',[54] and regards the *Reservations Case* as demonstrating that these are not created in the interests of individual States but in the higher interest of humanity as a whole. Schwelb is more specific; apropos the Genocide Convention he notes that; 'The case for attributing to its provisions (whether it restates pre-existing law or creates new law) the character of peremptory norms is particularly strong.'[55] Further, the *Reservations Case*, in his opinion, permits the interpretation that not only are the principles of the Convention universal customary law, but also *jus cogens*.[56]

There is considerable support for Brownlie's position: 'Certain portions of *jus cogens* are the subject of general agreement, including the rules relating to the use of force by States, self-determination and *genocide*.'[57] The

---

[47] Second Report on the Law of Treaties, UN Doc A/CN.4/156, and Add. 1–3. *YBILC* (*supra*, n. 46), 52.

[48] Ibid.   [49] Ibid. 53.

[50] Capotorti, 'L'Extinction et la Suspension des Traités', *Rec. des Cours, 1971*, III, 417, at 522.

[51] Ibid.   [52] *Infra*, text following n. 57.

[53] Virally, 'Réflections sur le "Jus Cogens" ', *AFDI*, 12 (1966), 5 at 28.

[54] Verdross, 'Jus Dispositivum and Jus Cogens in International Law', *AJIL*, 60 (1966), 55 at 59.

[55] Schwelb, 'Some Aspects of International Jus Cogens', *AJIL*, 61 (1967), 946 at 954.

[56] Ibid. 955.

[57] Brownlie, *Principles of Public International Law* (Oxford: OUP, 1979), 515. For extensive references, see *The Concept of Jus Cogens in International Law*, Conference on International Law at Lagonissi, Greece (Geneva: CEIP, 1967), esp. pp. 26 ff.: 'In general, the same examples [of jus cogens] are cited: the principle of the prohibition of the use of force . . . humanitarian principles; prohibition of slavery, of traffic in women and children and of genocide . . .' Ibid. 49.

point is that the prohibition of genocide *per se* or as part of international criminal law seems to figure in practically every listing of principles of *jus cogens*.

At the Vienna Conference on the Law of Treaties most of those who ventured to identify rules of *jus cogens* mentioned genocide. The Representative of Ghana mentioned 'the principles of self-determination and the sovereign equality of States . . . the prohibition of genocide and slavery and its bastard son, racial discrimination'.[58] The Representative of Poland listed 'The freedom of the high seas, the prohibition of slavery and genocide and . . . the rules of land warfare . . .'.[59] The Representative of Czechoslovakia stated his opinion that 'a State could not conclude a valid treaty designed to exterminate a nation or ethnic group, or to destroy the territorial sovereignty and political independence of a State, or to promote the slave trade or piracy.'[60] The 'treaty designed to exterminate a nation or ethnic group' is clearly a treaty about genocide. A more oblique reference was made by the Representative of Ceylon who mentioned treaties 'to promote the slave trade, *decimate populations* or commit aggression'.[61] The triumvirate of genocide, slave trade, and use of force was also adverted to by the Representatives of Tanzania,[62] and the Philippines.[63] The Representative of Canada adopted a similar formula and asked that while these were generally agreed to be examples of *jus cogens* rules, 'was it possible to go further?'[64] An extended list was set out by the Representative of Italy; it does not specifically mention genocide, but the concept is clearly included:

Rules of *jus cogens* were to be found essentially in the following three major categories: first, the rules intended to safeguard the fundamental rights of the human person; secondly, the rules concerning the prevention of the use of force and the maintenance of peace—a treaty whereby two or more states agreed to wage war could constitute a crime against peace; thirdly, the rules for the protection of the independence of States—a treaty on the lines of the eighteenth century agreements for the partition of Poland would now constitute a violation of a peremptory norm of international law.[65]

The criteria for a norm of *jus cogens* set out in the Vienna Convention may be recalled. The peremptory norm must be both a 'norm of general international law' and a 'norm accepted and recognized by the international community of States as a whole' as a norm from which derogation is not

---

[58] *United Nations Conference on the Law of Treaties, 1st Session, Official Records*, UN Doc A/CONF.39/11, 53rd meeting of the Committee of the Whole, para. 15.

[59] Ibid., para. 35. Also, *Conference, 2nd Session*, UN Doc A/CONF.39/11/Add.1, 19th meeting, para. 71.

[60] *Conference*, 1st Session, 55th meeting, para. 25.

[61] Ibid., para. 38. [62] Ibid., 56th meeting, para. 2.

[63] Ibid., para. 20. [64] Ibid., para. 22.

[65] *Conference*, 2nd Session, Plenary Meetings, 20th meeting, para. 29, UN Doc A/CONF.39/11/Add.1.

permitted. This formulation has a strongly consensual character in that it is general recognition by the international community that is decisive. Oppenheim wrote that 'immoral obligations cannot be the object of an international treaty'.[66] Lord McNair in the *Oscar Chinn Case* declared that 'In every civilised community there are some rules of law and some principles of morality which individuals are not permitted by law to ignore or modify by their agreements.'[67] Raising this principle to the level of international law, he offered the opinion that a treaty in which allies agreed to wage a war by methods which violated the customary rules of warfare was invalid.[68] But whatever the moral, humanitarian, or natural law inspirations of the concept of *jus cogens*, the Vienna Convention is clear that if a particular moral or humanitarian rule (or any other rule, for example, outlawing international aggression) is to have this status the imprimatur of international acceptance must be achieved.

What is lacking in the Vienna Convention formula is any more explicit test for verification or 'processing' of a rule which is claimed to be *jus cogens*. In relation to 'general international law' this means at least that both treaties of universal or quasi-universal character and customary international law can contribute to *jus cogens* as a source. Because treaties and customary law are the main vehicles for change in international law, they must both be included as sources of *jus cogens*.[69] This view is supported by reports of the International Law Commission.[70] The International Law Commission went further and referred to the content of the rules of *jus cogens* being worked out in State practice and the jurisprudence of international tribunals.[71] This cannot, logically speaking, count as an exclusive 'list' of sources, coupling together as it does a 'principal' source of international law (custom) and a 'subsidiary' source (judicial decisions), though it may only mean that international tribunals will assist in the elucidation of rules of *jus cogens*.[72] Any other interpretation of this coupling of sources would be rebuttable by reference to the terms 'acceptance' and 'recognition' by the community of States. Rules emanating from international tribunals or other sources of law must pass the test of acceptance and recognition, so that they will enter international law through treaty and custom. Similar

---

[66] *International Law: A Treatise*, vol. i, 896–7.

[67] *PCIJ* Ser. A/B No. 63, 213–4.

[68] Ibid. 214–5.

[69] Rozakis, *The Concept of Jus Cogens in the Law of Treaties* (Amsterdam and: North Holland, 1976); Scheuner, 'Conflict of Treaty Provisions with a "Peremptory" Norm of International Law', ZAÖR, 29 (1969), 288; Van Hoof, *Rethinking the Sources of International Law* 151 ff. (Deventer: Kluwer, 1983); Akehurst, 'The Hierarchy of the Sources of International Law', ZAÖR, 47 (1974–75), 273.

[70] *AJIL*, 58 (1964), 265–6; *AJIL*, 61 (1967), 411.

[71] See the opinions expressed by the delegates of Cuba, Chile, Poland, Malaysia, and Cyprus, Conference (*supra*, n. 60), 297, 298, 302, 326, 387.

[72] Akehurst, (*supra*, n. 69), 283, states that this formula means that the jurisprudence of international tribunals is probably intended to serve as evidence of existing rules of Jus Cogens, not to create new ones.

remarks may be applied to 'general principles of law recognised by civilised nations'. The most explicit reference to this source was contained in a proposal by the United States at the Vienna Conference that recognition in common by 'the national and regional legal systems of the world'[73] was required for a rule to be *jus cogens*. This proposal was heavily defeated though it did attract some support at the Vienna Conference.[74] Poland criticized the formula because it appeared to elevate the national over the international legal system.[75] In any case, the Soviet Union does not at present accept general principles of law as a source of law, except in the narrow sense of technical 'lawyer's' rules such as *lex posterior derogat priori*, so that their use is very limited.[76]

The second aspect of *jus cogens* rules is that they must be accepted by the community of States as a whole as norms of *jus cogens*. The phrase 'as a whole' would seem to imply universal acceptance and recognition. The phrase was inserted into the text on the initiative of the Drafting Committee, the Chairman of which explained that these words were meant to indicate that:

there was no question of requiring a rule to be accepted and recognised as peremptory by all States. It would be enough if a very large majority did so; that would mean that, if one State in violation refused to accept the peremptory character of a rule, or if that State was supported by a very small number of States, the acceptance and recognition of the peremptory character of the rule by the international community as a whole would not be affected.[77]

One writer comments that this means that 'no individual State should have the right of veto in the determination of a rule as a *jus cogens* norm.'[78] None the less a number of States at the Vienna Conference argued that rules of *jus cogens* must be accepted by all States; others regarded it as sufficient if they were recognized by an overwhelming majority of States.[79] Another writer argues that two questions must be distinguished: that of the alleged peremptory norm as law, and that of the alleged peremptory norm as

---

[73] UN Doc A/CONF.39/C.1/1.302.

[74] The proposal of the US was rejected by 57 votes to 24, with 7 abstentions, at the 57th meeting.

[75] UN Doc A/CONF.39/C.1/SR.53. The representative of Cuba considered that the proposal of the US would allow a State, by invoking its domestic legislation, to thwart any peremptory rule of international law: A/CONF.39/C.1/SR.52. See also the remarks of the representative of Tanzania, ibid., SR.56; and Tunkin, *Theory of International Law*, 147 ff.

[76] Tunkin, ibid. 190 ff.: 'in our view, "general principles of law" are those non-normative provisions common to national legal systems and to International Law which . . . have significance for applying norms of prevailing law . . . [they] . . . enter International Law through treaty or custom' (p. 202). See however the views of Levin and Lukin cited by Tunkin, 196–7, which propose a different view. Soviet scholars are not monolithically opposed to normative general principles, nor are scholars in East European Communist States, see Tunkin, 197.

[77] Rozakis, (*supra*, n. 69), 77.

[78] Ibid.

[79] Citations in Akehurst (*supra*, n. 69), 284–5.

peremptory *jus cogens*. He submits that most of the delegates who argued at the Vienna Conference in favour of the view that all States must recognize the norms were addressing themselves to the norms as law; and that most of the States arguing only that an overwhelming majority must accept the rule were referring to the case of the rule as one of *jus cogens*. Thus the conclusion is that for a rule to be *jus cogens* all States must accept the putative rule as law; and.an overwhelming majority must accept it as *jus cogens*.[80] Yet another formulation is that all the major components of the international community must concur in the acceptance of a rule as *jus cogens*.[81]

In the light of the above assessment of *jus cogens*, it is easy to see why the prohibition of genocide is, apparently, relatively uncontroversial. It is doubtful if a realistic case for inclusion as *jus cogens* can be made for rules which favour preponderantly the interests of the Third World, Western, or Communist States. Certain 'structural' or 'organizational' principles of international society, such as the principle of *pacta sunt servanda*, may be favoured by the concept, as may also such vital requirements for the continuance of the human species in a technologically advanced world as the prohibition of aggression.[82] The post-war world, the new *ordo rerum*, began with documents and institutions enshrining human rights and freedoms and criminalizing their gross violation—the United Nations Charter, the Law of Nuremberg, the twin pillars of the new order as the protection of human rights and the promotion of international peace. The criminalization of the deliberate destruction of races, genocide, is part of the self-perception of the age; the crime is the most fundamental denial of human dignity and equality, and its prohibition is fittingly *jus cogens*.[83]

---

[80] Ibid. 285.

[81] This formulation has been suggested by the International Law Commission.

[82] Van Hoof (*supra*, n. 69), for examples and comments; Brownlie (*supra*, n. 57), 515.

[83] Some observations on the position of the US on the customary status of the prohibition of genocide are in order. The US appears to have vacillated on this, as it has on much else in relation to genocide. In a summary of the provisions prepared by the Department of State in 1954, (*XXX Department of State Bulletin*, No. 780, 7 June 1954) it was noted that the US was not a party, and that, therefore, 'its provisions in no way bind the United States or its citizens'. Further, the Governments 'which have signed the Genocide Convention but have failed to ratify it are under no legal duty to execute its provisions or carry out in any way the obligations created by it'. On one reading, this would mean that the US is outside the scope of customary as well as conventional obligations. On the other hand, in a report to the US Congress in 1947, President Truman declared that genocide was established as a crime under international law on a plane with piracy even though no treaty had been signed to that effect (cited by Lemkin, 'Genocide as a Crime under International Law', *AJIL*, 41 (1947), 145, at 150, text of speech in the New York Times, 6 Feb. 1947). The usefulness of the treaty lay in facilitating the prevention and punishment of the crime and apprehension of criminals. The US representative to the UN also used the charge of genocide to belabour Communist China during the Tibet crisis in 1959, though neither China nor the US were parties (Whiteman, *Digest of International Law*, 11 (1968), 872). The present position on customary status appears to be an unequivocal affirmation of this fact (see *infra* on the Restatement of the Foreign Relations Law of the US, ch. 26).

8. Content of the Customary Law

The Meaning of Genocide in Customary International Law

It was noted in the previous chapter that in two of the decisions before War Crimes Tribunals, the *Greifelt Case*[1] and the *Greiser Case*,[2] a broader notion of genocide was expounded in contrast to the narrower version present in the Genocide Convention itself. In the former case, the first count of the indictment, in referring to the crimes against humanity which were part of *'a systematic programme of genocide'*, further alleged that: 'The object of this programme was to strengthen the German nation and the so-called "Aryan" race at the expense of . . . other nations and groups by imposing Nazi and German characteristics upon individuals selected therefrom (such imposition being hereinafter called "Germanization") and by the extermination of "undesirable" racial elements.' The indictment further specifies the means by which the programme of genocide was to be implemented:

(a) Kidnapping the children of foreign nationals in order to select for Germanization those who were considered of 'racial value';

(b) Encouraging and compelling abortions on Eastern workers for the purpose of preserving their working capacity as slave labour and weakening Eastern nations;

(c) Taking away, for the purpose of exterminating or Germanization, infants born to Eastern workers in Germany;

(d) Executing, imprisoning in concentration camps, or Germanizing Eastern workers and prisoners of war who had had sexual intercourse with Germans, and imprisoning the Germans involved;

(e) Preventing marriages and hampering reproduction of enemy nationals;

(f) Evacuating enemy populations from their native lands by force and resettling so-called 'ethnic Germans' (Volksdeutsche) on such lands;

(g) Compelling nationals of other countries to perform work in Germany, to become members of the German community, to accept German citizenship and to join the German armed forces . . .;

(h) Plundering public and private property in Germany and in the incorporated and occupied territories, eg., taking church property, real estate . . . etc.;

(i) Participating in the persecution and extermination of Jews.[3]

The conception of genocide as expounded by the United States Prosecutor

---

[1] *Supra*, text following ch. 6, n. 22.
[2] Ibid.
[3] *Law Reports of Trials of War Criminals*, vol. XIII, 2–3.

in the case is wide. It includes genocide in the physical and biological sense, cultural genocide, denationalization, forced evacuations, forced labour and invasion of religious rights. This broad version of the crime is not reflected in the judgment of the United States Military Tribunal which did not mention genocide, though the Tribunal stated that the entire programme carried out by the accused had the twofold objective of weakening and eventually destroying other nations while at the same time strengthening Germany, territorially and biologically, at the expense of conquered nations.[4] Similarly, in the trial of Hauptstürmfuhrer Amon Goeth,[5] before the Supreme National Tribunal of Poland, the prosecution drew attention not only to the physical and biological aspects of genocide, but also to the economic, social, and cultural implications. The judgment, however, makes only brief mention of genocide and in a seemingly restrictive fashion. Thus, it was noted that 'The wholesale extermination of Jews and . . . Poles had all the characteristics of genocide in the biological meaning of this term, and embraced in addition the destruction of the cultural life of these nations.'[6] This appears to distinguish between 'genocide' and 'destruction of cultural life' within the context of a programme of wholesale extermination and does not represent a commitment to 'genocide' in the wider sense as including 'cultural genocide'. The *Greiser Case* before the same Supreme Tribunal reflects a greater congruence of approach between the crimes alleged and the crimes proved. The wording of the judgment, summarised above[7] in relation to 'spiritual' and 'cultural' genocide, referred also to 'the general totalitarian genocidal attack on the rights of the small and medium nations to exist, and to have an *identity and culture* of their own'.[8]

It needs to be recalled, in attempting to assess the significance of these cases for the content of the customary law prohibition of genocide, that the concept of genocide was barely formed at the time and had not been categorized as such in the Nuremberg Charter. The ensemble of distinctions between these categories of crime and genocide were matters of suggestion and discussion rather than sharply drawn lines. The cases reflect a certain hesitancy about the exact scope of genocide rather than a clear affirmation that genocide is an international crime of the widest connotation. Even the Polish cases, in a nation profoundly shocked by the horrors of war and the scale of the Nazi attack on all aspects of Polish life, do not reveal great consistency of approach in this respect. Reasoned statements about the nature of genocide are absent; the references made are generalized, with attention naturally focused on the established customary and conventional law. Genocide is not so much a specific offence as a background to specific

---

[4] Ibid. 28–36.
[5] 27 August–5 September 1946, *Law Reports of Trials of War Criminals*, VII.
[6] Ibid. 9.
[7] Ch. 6, text following n. 23.
[8] *Law Reports of Trials of War Criminals*, vol. XIII, 114.

crimes against humanity and war crimes. As regards defining the offence as well as asserting its separate existence, the best case remains the *Altstötter Case* which drew its inspiration from the General Assembly of the United Nations, including Resolution 96(I).

The resolution's description of genocide has been noted above,[9] it is a denial of the 'right of existence' of entire human groups, as homicide is the denial of the individual's right to live. Any actions undermining the existence of groups are capable of constituting genocide, thus opening up a broad prospectus for the crime. The 'life' of individuals is contrasted with the 'existence' of groups'; this 'existence', as Lemkin argued, involves not only the physical existence of the members, but also its biological continuity through procreation as well as its spiritual or cultural expression, without which it would be meaningless to speak of a group at all. The logic of this classification implies that genocide can be physical, biological, or cultural (spiritual). 'Right of existence' would appear to encompass a broader notion of genocidal threats than Article II of the Genocide Convention. The description in the resolution of the protected groups as 'racial, religious, political and other groups' is also different from the definition in the Convention. It is submitted that the omission of 'national' and 'ethnical' groups from the resolution does not appreciably narrow its scope when compared to the Convention's formula—in any case the reference to 'other groups' compensates for any narrowing of scope, as well as indicating that the definition in the resolution is not exhaustive. The inclusion of political groups in the resolution is more significant. The resolution reflects a more generous protection than the Convention. Some jurists consider that genocide should protect all human groups and Resolution 96(I) does not preclude this interpretation. The operative part of the resolution sees genocide as a crime committed on religious, racial, political, or any other grounds.[10]

Travaux Préparatoires of the Convention: Views of States

While the *travaux préparatoires* of the Genocide Convention do not detract from the customary law status of genocide, they throw serious doubts on any claims that the customary law reflects a broader conception of genocide than the Convention.[11] A treaty or its *travaux préparatoires* can also be evidence of customary law if the requirements of *opinio juris* are met and the treaty or *travaux* contain claims that the treaty declares existing law.[12]

---

[9] Text following ch. 6, n. 26.
[10] For the distinction between 'political groups' as victims of genocide, and 'political grounds' as motives, *supra*, text following ch. 6, n. 42.
[11] *Supra*, ch. 6.
[12] *Supra*, ch. 7.

The reference to existing law in Article I of the Convention as 'confirmed' by the treaty is evidence of customary rules, but is it then the case that the definition in the treaty is exhaustive? It would seem plausible to argue thus, though it is equally not implausible that the Convention only defines a part of the concept. In cases like this, consultation of the *travaux préparatoires* can be of assistance. The Convention is ambiguous here, for example, the definition of genocide in Article II is prefaced by the words 'In this Convention'. Does this point to a prohibition of genocide in wider terms existing outside the Convention?

It was noted in the previous chapter that 'political' groups and 'cultural' genocide were the focus of intense dispute.[13] The references to political groups and political grounds in Resolution 96(I) were a natural starting point for discussion. The references were not conclusive on the content of genocide for many States, even those who clearly supported the customary law status of the genocide prohibition. Thus, the Representative of Poland in the Sixth Committee of the General Assembly who argued that Resolution 96(I) was declaratory of international law was none the less against the inclusion of political groups in the Convention. This was 'not genocide proper'; genocide needed a 'proper definition'.[14] He said later that the operative part of Resolution 96(I) did not mention political groups but referred only to the grounds on which genocide could be committed. The question of protected groups and motives for committing genocide should be distinguished. In his view, Resolution 96(I) only gave a general indication of the attitude of the United Nations; genocide had not yet been defined.[15]

Similarly the Representative of Venezuela said that political groups were mentioned as an example; the delegation had not contemplated the protection of political groups by a Convention. Resolution 96(I) was only a guide; it was a mistake to take its provisions literally.[16] The Representative of Belgium also referred to the resolution as only a condemnation in general terms.[17] None of these delegations regarded themselves as in any way bound or estopped by this particular detail of resolution 96(I), although they were criticized by the United States for 'completely ignoring'[18] it. The dominant view of the majority of States opposed to including political groups seems to have been that there was a central 'core' to genocide associated with Nazi practice which had been condemned as a crime. Beyond that core practice, the United Nations resolution merely indicated the possibilities open to the drafters of any eventual convention.

There is even less support from the *travaux* in favour of regarding cultural genocide as prohibited by customary law. The Representative of Brazil advised strict adherence to the definition in Resolution 96(I) which made an

---

[13] See n. 10.
[14] *GAOR*, 3rd Session, Part I, 6th Committee and Annexes, 64th meeting, 19.
[15] Ibid., 75th meeting, 110–11.
[16] Ibid. 112–13.   [17] Ibid., 74th meeting.   [18] Ibid., 75th meeting, 112–13.

analogy between genocide and homicide. This meant that cultural genocide was not a form of genocide. The plea for strict adherence to the resolution did not prevent this delegate from expressing himself against regarding political groups as victims of genocide.[19] The Representative of India also noted that cultural genocide went beyond Resolution 96(I).[20] Those opposed to regarding cultural genocide as equivalent to genocide proper sometimes stated their opinions in a highly abstract fashion; their remarks are applicable to genocide *per se*, and not simply genocide for the purposes of a convention. Their views implied that, reprehensible though cultural genocide may be, it was something essentially different from physical genocide and was more appropriate to the sphere of human rights.

One implication of the above arguments is that while customary law does not appear, on a close evaluation of the evidence, to provide a conception of genocide wider than that outlined in the Genocide Convention, there is commitment to the definition in the Convention as an acceptable minimum. This is largely borne out by considering the reservations to the Convention. The reservations almost exclusively relate to the procedural aspects of the Convention, not to the definition of the crime. There are no reservations against the first three articles to the Convention which form an undisputed 'core' of genocide. The distinction between the two kinds of article is reflected in the judgment of the International Court of Justice in the *North Sea Continental Shelf Cases*:

Speaking generally it is a characteristic of purely conventional rules and obligations that . . . some faculty of making unilateral reservations may . . . be admitted;— whereas this cannot be so in the case of general or customary law rules and obligations which, by their very nature, must have equal force for all members of the international community, and cannot therefore be the subject of any right of unilateral exclusion exercisable at will by any one of them in its own favour.[21]

---

[19] Ibid., 63rd meeting, 5–7.

[20] Ibid., 64th meeting, 15–16. Matters do not appear to have advanced greatly since the Convention in the matter of cultural genocide. International law could still provide an expanded definition of genocide through, for example, the Draft Code of Offences Against the Peace and Security of Mankind in preparation by the International Law Commission. At its 33rd session, the General Assembly adopted Res. 33/97, recalling that the International Law Commission had submitted a draft Code in 1954 and requesting the Secretary-General to invite States and intergovernmental organizations to submit observations on this question. In general, States did not quarrel with the definition of genocide in the Convention, and Norway appeared to express disapproval of moving beyond it. UNESCO proposed a widening of the definition to include cultural genocide: UN Doc A/35/210, 11 June 1980. The ILC text inserted 'including' before the forms of genocide set out in Article II of the Convention, implying a more open-ended definition not limited to enumerated acts, but made no reference to cultural genocide: *Yearbook of the International Law Commission 1986*, Vol. ii, Part 2, 43. See Ferencz, 'The Draft Code of Offences Against the Peace and Security of Mankind', *AJIL*, 75 (1981), 674; Gross, 'Some Observations on the Draft Code of Offences Against the Peace and Security of Mankind', *Israel Yearbook on Human Rights*, 13 (1983), 9. See also Ruhashyankiko, *supra*, ch. 5, n. 2, 124: most governments regarded cultural genocide as at best *lex ferenda*.

[21] *ICJ Reports* 1969, 38–9. The Court concluded that, consequently, where customary law

This distinction was also mentioned by Israel in argument before the International Court in the *Reservations Case*: even if reservations were inadmissible in relation to the 'normative' rules, it did not necessarily follow that they are inadmissible against the 'contractual' rules.[22] If a rule of law in a Convention is superimposed on a rule of customary law, the reservations will not necessarily affect the customary rule, at least if the rule is well established and a significant number of States do not dissent from it.

In the *Reservations Case*, Israel gave early notice, later to be translated into action in the *Eichmann Case*,[23] that it took a broad view of what counted as normative or customary in the Convention. Thus it regarded the core articles as normative, but also Articles IV and VI on responsibility and jurisdiction.[24] The notion of individual responsibility is surely part of the customary law on genocide since there can be no crime without a criminal and the concept of State responsibility for genocide cannot be said to be securely established. Again, by a process of negative inference, it can be pointed out that Article IV is subject to a reservation which does not greatly affect the substance of the principle of individual responsibility.[25] Individual responsibility for genocide and related acts is accepted by the Nuremberg Tribunal,[26] by the Charter of the International Military Tribunal for the Far East,[27] by Article I of the Draft Code of Offences Against the Peace and Security of Mankind adopted by the International Law Commission in 1954.[28] and by Article III of the International Convention on the Suppression and Punishment of the Crime of Apartheid.[29] It is also accepted by writers on international law.[30]

The Israeli argument favouring Article VI (the first part) as customary

figures in a Convention, it will generally be among the provisions where the right of unilateral reservation is not conferred, or is excluded.

[22] *ICJ Reports 1951*, Pleadings, Oral Arguments, Documents, 339.

[23] *Supra*, ch. 7, n. 41.

[24] Pleadings (*supra*, n. 22), 337: 'Neither the definition of acts of genocide and the description of its characteristics, nor the class of persons who may commit it or be tried and punished for it, is limited in any way to the contracting parties, persons under their jurisdiction.' The second part of Article VI referring to an international penal tribunal was, of course, clearly accepted as *lex ferenda*, not *lex lata*.

[25] The reservation is maintained by the Philippines and objected to by a number of States: the Government of the Philippines 'cannot sanction any situation which would subject the Head of State, who is not a Ruler, to conditions less favourable than those accorded other Heads of State, whether constitutionally responsible rulers or not. The Philippine Government does not consider the said article, therefore, as overriding the existing immunities from judicial processes guaranteed certain public officials by the Constitution of the Philippines': ST/HR/5, 183–4.

[26] *Trial of the Major War Criminals supra*, ch. 6, n. 85.

[27] *Trial of Japanese War Criminals*, Documents, (Washington: US Government Printing Office, 1946), 40.

[28] Report of the International Law Commission covering the work of its 6th session, 3 June– 28 July 1954, UN Doc A/2693/11.

[29] Brownlie, *Basic Documents on Human Rights*, 164.

[30] See citations in Bassiouni, *International Criminal Law: A Draft International Criminal Code* (Alphen aan den Rijn: Sitjhoff and Noordhoff, 1980).

law, was broadened in the *Eichmann Case*[31] to an assertion that international law recognized universal jurisdiction in cases of genocide. This cannot so easily be accepted. In the *Eichmann Case*, the Jerusalem District Court's positive findings on the condemnation of genocide as a crime under general international law were accompanied by the ruling that 'in accordance with accepted principles of international law' the jurisdiction to try genocide was 'universal'. The Court none the less noted a possible objection to this view based on the provisions of Article VI of the Genocide Convention conferring jursidiction in genocide on the courts of the State in which offences were committed or on an international penal tribunal. This was overcome by drawing a distinction between those articles of the Convention which confirmed the customary law and applied to past crimes, and articles, including Article VI, which were merely conventional and which were thus 'intended for cases of genocide which will occur in the future after the ratification of the treaty or the adherence thereto by the States concerned'. Article VI was thus 'a special provision undertaken by the contracting parties with regard to the trial of crimes that may be committed in the future'.[32] It may be noted that this appears to represent a rather different view from that advanced by Israel in the *Reservations Case*. There, Article VI (first part) was described as a 'normative provision'. This term was defined in the written statement by Israel in that case: 'The normative articles of the Convention purport to state and do state international criminal norms. These norms are uniformly binding on all States, whether or not they are parties to the [Genocide] Convention.'[33] The District Court examined the *travaux préparatoires* of the Genocide Convention in order to show that the narrow jurisdiction mentioned therein was not exhaustive. In particular, it referred to the Report of the Sixth Committee of the General Assembly where it was stated that 'The first part of Article 6 contemplates the obligation of the State in whose territory the act of genocide has been committed. In particular, it does not affect the right of any State to bring to trial before its own tribunals any of its nationals for acts committed outside the State.'[34] The Chairman of the Sixth Committee declared that this statement only represented the views of the majority of the Committee and could not be binding on delegations which opposed it.[35] Nevertheless, the District Court took the view that Article VI of the Convention may have only provided for 'a compulsory minimum'[36] of jurisdiction. But, in any case, the claim to universality of jurisdiction here did not ultimately depend on a wider interpretation of the Convention or the Israeli law derived from it, but derived 'from the basic nature of the crime of genocide as a crime of the

---

[31] *A–G of the Government of Israel* v. *Adolf Eichmann, International Law Reports*, 36, 18 (District Court), and, ibid. 277 (Supreme Court of Israel).
[32] Ibid. 36. [33] *Reservations Case* (*supra*, n. 22), 202.
[34] UN Doc A/C.6/SR.134, 5. [35] UN Doc A/C.6/SR.132, 10.
[36] Para. 25 of District Court judgment.

utmost gravity under international law'.[37] In other words, customary international law recognized a universal jursidiction for genocide, even though the conventional law was (probably) more restrictive. Leaving aside the question of universality of jurisdiction over genocide when it also amounts to a war crime, it is worth recalling that when the question was discussed during the passage of the Genocide Convention, it was not only discussed with the provision of the future Convention in mind, but also in a more general sense, incorporating reflections on customary law. Apart from surmising that incorporating the universality principle in the Convention would make it very difficult for some States to become parties, some Representatives emphasized that the principle was not yet universally accepted, and was contrary to the tenets of traditional international law. These included respect for the principle of territoriality and the principle of State sovereignty. According to the Representative of the USSR in the Sixth Committee, 'the principle of universal punishment was even more incompatible with the sovereignty of States than international punishment'[38] (that is, by an international tribunal). Even some of those who proposed universal jursidiction expressed themselves in terms which suggested that it was a *desideratum* rather than an established principle. A number of Representatives drew distinctions between genocide and such cases as piracy, the punishment of which would fail in the absence of a universal jurisdiction.[39] The *travaux préparatoires* throw doubt on the claim in the *Eichmann Case* that customary law accepted universal jurisdiction in relation to this new crime. The doubts are substantiated rather than dissolved by examining reservations to the Convention. It has already been noted that Article VI of the Convention has been subjected to reservations by States unwilling to allow acts of genocide on their own territory to be tried elsewhere than in their own courts. Apart from these, a number of governments in their responses to the United Nations Sub-Commission on Prevention of Discrimination and Protection of Minorities have indicated that they take a restricted view of competence to try genocide. Some statements favourable to universal jurisdiction recommend an additional protocol to the Convention in such a manner as to suggest that the matter is not clearly covered by customary law.[40]

The implicit justification of the doubts on the part of many States is that, while genocide has been 'formally' constituted as a crime of individuals, i.e. individual responsibility, in may cases it will be committed by governments

[37] *International Law Reports*, 39.

[38] *GAOR*, 3rd Session, 6th Committee, 100th meeting, 403.

[39] Representatives of Egypt, ibid. 398; USSR, 403; United Kingdom, 402; Uruguay, 398. Also Brazil, 97th meeting, 371; Belgium, 98th meeting, 374–5.

[40] The Government of Oman responded to Ruhashyankiko, *Genocide*, 55, that there may be 'a possibility of preparing an additional protocol to the . . . Convention to grant competence to the courts to try the crime of genocide committed in a country other than theirs, but it is unlikely to be favoured by a majority of States and, moreover, it is feared that it may be a source of aggravating the conflict on an international level'.

who will not allow their acts to be judged elsewhere. Other efforts at enshrining the principle of universal jurisdiction in modern international law do not meet with this objection to the same extent. While there is a certain attractive logic in coupling universal jurisdiction to international crimes in general, this logic is not acceptable to an overwhelming majority of States, so that a customary law consensus cannot be said to have been clearly established. The 'collective' views of jurists expressed through the International Commission of Jurists and the International Association of Penal Law have also reflected a negative opinion.[41] The restrictive view would not apply to genocide considered as a war crime,[42] or when aspects of genocide can be qualified as constituting the crime of apartheid.[43]

The customary law outlined so far accepts a minimum definition of the conduct to count as genocide, coupled with a principle of individual responsibility for the crime and, it seems, a competence on the part of courts on the territory where genocide was committed to try the offence. In relation to any duty on the part of States recognizing genocide as an international crime to adopt laws to punish it as a specific offence, this again seems problematical. Certain of the responses to Special Rapporteur Ruhashyankiko by States which were not parties to the Genocide Convention cast doubt on any asserted 'duty' of States to adopt laws defining and punishing genocide.[44] But in this respect, the performance of the non-parties is little different from the parties to the Genocide Convention: many parties deemed the legislation in force prior to their becoming parties to the Convention to be sufficient to ensure the prevention and punishment of genocide, even though genocide as such was not punishable.[45] Thus, the customary law has, as it were, symbolic significance for minorities rather than practical effect in virtue of its existence as customary law, though this appears largely true also in relation to many States parties to the Convention.

[41] Ibid.

[42] Carnegie, 'Jurisdiction over Violations of the Laws and Customs of War', *BYIL*, 39 (1963), 402.

[43] UN Doc E/CN.4/1075, *Study Concerning the Question of Apartheid From the Point of View of International Penal Law*, Report of the Ad Hoc Working Group of Experts under Commission Res. 8(XXVII), 15 February 1972. See also the International Convention on the Suppression and Punishment of the Crime of Apartheid, adopted by UNGA Res. 3068(XXVIII) of 30 November 1973, text in Brownlie, *Basic Documents on Human Rights*, 164. Article V of the Convention provides that persons charged with the crime of apartheid 'may be tried by a competent tribunal of any State Party to the Convention which may acquire jurisdiction over the person of the accused or by an international penal tribunal with respect to those States Parties which shall have accepted its jurisdiction'.

[44] UN Doc E/CN.4/Sub.2/416, 151 ff. Information was supplied by the Governments of Cyprus, Malawi, Kuwait, Congo, and Oman. Malawi stated that despite the fact that it was not a party to the Convention and had thus not adopted any laws referring specifically to genocide, a large number of acts referred to in Article II of the Convention constituted grave crimes under the country's existing law, ibid. 152.

[45] Ibid. 140. The States mentioned are Belgium, Egypt, Ecuador, Finland, France, Greece, India, Iraq, Pakistan, Poland, Turkey, the Ukrainian SSR, and the USSR.

Part III

Identity and Non-Discrimination

9. Post-War Attitudes and Reflections on the Significance of the League System in General International Law

The common opinion is that the Minority Treaties under the League of Nations did not create customary law. In the light of the conclusions of the United Nations Study on the League treaties and declarations, this leads to the conclusion that the post-war world started, as it were, with a *tabula rasa* in the matter of tolerance and encouragement of minorities. States could act as they pleased in relation to their populations if they were not inhibited by a relevant treaty. In some respects, this appears too simplistic (the constraints imposed by the Nuremberg principles must be borne in mind), but there is evidence on the limited scope of the League system of treaties in its practice and intentions. As noted, the League system was political and humanitarian in its purposes. The States were effectively obliged to participate in it as a result of wartime defeat, or as a condition of receiving additions of territory or recognition of their independence. There was no intent to establish a universally applicable minorities system, least of all one applicable to the Powers: 'The minorities treaties were created to deal with a special problem existing in a given area for a given time.'[1] The Assembly of the League merely expressed the hope that States which were not bound by treaties or declarations would observe in the treatment of their own minorities at least as high a standard as was required by the treaties and the regular action of the Council.[2] Proposals to extend the system by a General International Convention on minorities were rebuffed.[3]

The consciousness on the part of States within the system that it was *not* regarded as of general applicability contributed to their dissatisfaction and the system's downfall.[4] Some other members of the League recognized this but were unable to achieve reforms.[5] From the point of view of minorities,

[1] *LNOJ*, 130, Sp. Supp., 60 (Anthony Eden).
[2] *LNOJ*, 120, Sp. Supp., Annex 6, 72.
[3] Robinson *supra*, ch. 3, n. 25).
[4] *Supra*, ch. 3.
[5] See, for example, the resolution sponsored by Haiti, which regarded the principle of the international protection of the rights of man solemnly affirmed in the Minorities Treaties as being in harmony with the 'legal sentiments of the world today'. Thus, it was 'highly desirable' that this principle should be generalized: League of Nations, 14th Assembly, *LNOJ*, 115, Sp. Supp. (1933), 51 and 57.

threatened groups such as the Jews in Germany, were outside the scope of League protection—to say nothing of the treatment of ethnic and racial groups outside Europe.[6] Bilateral treaties were resorted to sometimes, in order to deal with cases outside the purview of the League.[7]

The freedom of States to deal with their minorities as they pleased is evidenced by the post-war transfers of minorities, especially German groups. It may be argued that if the League experience had generated principles of customary international law, such transfers would at least have taken place in a more inhibited fashion. Indeed, these transfers promised a bleak future for minority rights, and not only in the limited sense of the principles of Article 27 of the UN Covenant on Civil and Political Rights; the transfers appear to deny basic rights to existence, *a fortiori* they deny rights to minority identity.

Thus, various population transfer treaties were concluded at the end of World War II, including those between Czechoslovakia and Hungary (February 1946) providing for a compulsory transfer of 200,000 Magyars out of Czechoslovakia into Hungary, and 200,000 Slovaks out of Hungary into Czechoslovakia; Hungary and Yugoslavia (September 1946), exchanging 40,000 Magyars for an equal number of Serbs and Croats; Poland and the Soviet Union (July 1945); and Czechoslovakia and the Soviet Union (July 1946).[8] In addition to individual treaties, some fifteen million Germans were simply expelled from various parts of Europe between 1944 and 1949. There was widespread Western support for the transfer principle, especially in relation to Germans. In some cases, there was a 'knock on effect'—as the Soviet Union kept part of Poland, requiring the expulsion of three million Poles, Poland had to be compensated by the expulsion of some nine million Germans from the old Eastern German Provinces.[9] Allied 'authorization' of transfer in relation to German populations may be found in Article XIII of the Potsdam Protocol which reads, in part: 'The three Governments, having considered the question in all its aspects, recognize that the transfer of German populations, or elements thereof, remaining in Poland, Czechoslovakia and Hungary, will have to be undertaken. They agree that any transfers that take place should be effected in an orderly and humane manner.'[10] The expulsions began before the Potsdam Conference

---

[6] League of Nations, 3rd Assembly, 6th Committee (1922), 27 (reference to Indians in South Africa). Also Sørensen, 'The Quest for Equality'.

[7] Robinson, 'International Protection of Minorities: A Global View' *Israel Year Book on Human Rights*, 1 (1971), 61, 73–5.

[8] UN, *Protection of Minorities*, Special Protective Measures of an International Character for Ethnic, Religious or Linguistic Groups (UN, New York, 1967) UN Sales No: 67.XIV.3., 2; De Zayas, 'International Law and Mass Population Transfers' Harvard International Law Journal, 16 (1975), 207.

[9] De Zayas, ibid. 234, citing Churchill, *Triumph and Tragedy* (London: Cassell and Co., 1950–4, vol. 6).

[10] *AJIL*, 39 (1945), Supp., 245 at 256 (Great Britain, the USA, and the USSR).

(July to August 1945). Jurists such as Luza[11] and Gelberg[12] claim that the Protocol retroactively justified the early expulsions[13] and prospectively justified those of 1946 and 1947. Regrettably, many of the transfers were neither 'orderly' nor 'humane' and loss of life attributable to flight and expulsion may have been over two million. Later expulsions appear to have decreased in savagery as the passions of war subsided.[14] In relation to the general issue of minorities, one commentator noted that:

> It does not appear that the agreement to support the mass transfer of German minorities was regarded as a particularly momentous decision by the assembled statesmen . . . (The) real significance of the Potsdam Protocol for the problem of national minorities lay not in the restricted nature of its endorsement of the transfer principle, but in the fact that it contained the first formal, public indication that the statesmen who were in a position to dominate the postwar settlement were prepared to accept the transfer of populations as a respectable and usual device for the solution of minority problems.[15]

He also notes, however, that at the subsequent Paris Peace Conference[16] there was greater opposition to transfer, so that the transfer principle did not function as 'the basic element in the solution of the problem of national minorities'.[17]

It is difficult to see how these principles could be 'justified' at all in the law of the post-war period. German defendants at the Nuremberg War Crimes Tribunal were accused of precisely this operation against, for example, the Polish people.[18] There it was a crime against humanity in terms of Article 6(c) of the Charter of the Tribunal.[19] Huber regarded the Potsdam expulsions as a political event which lawyers were not entitled to condemn.[20] De Visscher and Verdross regarded the expulsions as contrary to international law.[21] De Zayas takes the view that they constituted a political rather than a legal precedent.[22] The present author inclines to accept the view of De

[11] Luza, *The Transfer of the Sudeten Germans* (New York: NYUP, 1964).

[12] 'Poland's Western Border and Transfer of German Populations', *AJIL*, 59 (1965), 590, in rebuttal of Von Braun, 'Germany's Eastern Border and Mass Expulsions', *AJIL*, 58 (1964), 747.

[13] See ICRC, *Report of the International Committee of the Red Cross on its Activities During the Second World War* (Geneva: International Committee of the Red Cross, 1948), vol. i.

[14] De Zayas (*supra*, n. 8), 237.

[15] Claude (*supra*, ch. 2, n. 36), 116.

[16] Ibid. 125 ff.

[17] Ibid. 123.

[18] The expulsions sanctioned at Potsdam were raised at the trial of Hans Frank, accused of mass deportation of Poles, as a *tu quoque* defence. However, the Court sustained the objections of the Chief Prosecutor for the Soviet Union who argued that the expulsions had no bearing on the case, 18, *Trial of the Major War Criminals*, (*supra*, ch. 6, n. 20), 149 ff.

[19] Texts in *AJIL*, 41 (1974), 172.

[20] 44/2 *Annuaire de l'Institut de Droit International* (1952), 168.

[21] Ibid. 168, 186.

[22] De Zayas, (*supra*, n. 8), at 242; see also his *Nemesis at Potsdam* (London: Routledge and Kegan Paul, 1979).

Visscher and Verdross in the light of previous discussion of crimes against humanity.[23] The absence of judgment (if not condemnation) may be explained by the historical circumstances. The Potsdam decision was insufficiently condemned by public opinion and by international law, which, to all intents and purposes, lacked a suitable enforcing tribunal. It was exceptional and did not stand for the future. It cannot be used to deny conclusively the proposition that principles concerning respect for minorities were in existence, though it clearly does nothing to confirm it. In a broader sense, it is emblematic of a climate of opinion relative to minorities which subsequent international efforts have endeavoured to overcome.

The study prepared by the United Nations Secretariat on the 'Legal Validity of the Undertakings Concerning Minorities'[24] does not deal directly with the question of the general status of the League's laws on minorities. However, it seems clear that if general law had been created, it would have meant that certain aspects of the treaties would have survived the fate of the documents themselves (and of the League of Nations); those aspects which represented general international law. The need for the study was explained by M. Nissot of Belgium—the competent organs of the United Nations 'cannot pursue their activity in this domain [prevention of discrimination and protection of minorities] without concerning themselves as to what remains at the time of the international rights and obligations resulting from these [the League's] declarations and treaties'.[25] This formulation is surely wide enough to encompass any claim that the treaties generated customary law. The manner in which the study's conclusions are formulated suggests a similar view: 'Reviewing the situation as a whole, therefore, one is led to conclude that between 1939 and 1947 circumstances as a whole changed to such an extent that generally speaking *the system* should be considered as having ceased to exist.'[26] The term 'the system' seems wide enough to include the treaties and declarations was well as any accompanying general law, if it existed. This view is reinforced by the reference in the study to the different 'philosophy' prevailing in the post-war world: the 'idea of a general and universal protection of human rights'.[27] This is a 'new' conception for a new age; minority rights were a thing of the past. J. L. Kunz's remarks on fashions in neckties and in international law will be recalled.[28] His viewpoint was stated more aggressively by the United States Secretary of State: 'in the kind of world for which we fight, there must cease to exist any need for the use of that accursed term "racial or religious minority" '.[29]

It is submitted that the differences between the despised 'old' system of minority rights and the idealized 'new' system of human rights were exag-

---

[23] *Supra*, chs. 6–8.   [24] UN Doc E/CN.4/367.
[25] UN Doc E/CN.4/52, 15.   [26] Study, ibid. 70–1.
[27] The Study none the less endorsed the Potsdam decisions as part of the 'New Conception', of Human Rights.
[28] *AJIL*, 48 (1954), 282 (*supra*, ch. 1, n. 23).
[29] *US Department of State Bulletin*, 5 June 1943, 482.

gerated. Some did perhaps recognize this in the immediate post-war years: Fitzmaurice, in his Hague lectures in 1948, remarked that the human rights clauses in the Peace Treaties of 1947[30] 'serve as a kind of minorities provision, and replace the elaborate clauses on the treatment of minorities which figures in the Peace Treaties after the War of 1914–1918'.[31] Some of the criticism of the League system in the post 1945 literature has now itself an archaic ring.

The UN study noted that the new dispensation of human rights 'to a large extent coincides with the idea of protection of minorities'[32] but that the two were not identical. It said further that the protection of minorities was the broader concept—it aimed at securing wider rights than equality and non-discrimination such as 'the right to enjoy special privileges (for example, the right to use the minority language in the courts and in official documents) and to maintain special institutions (schools, etc.) . . . in order to enable the minority group to retain its individual characteristics'.[33] These are the concepts that inform Article 27 of the Covenant on Civil and Political Rights[34] which bears the main burden in international law on protection of minority identity. In so far as these concepts still are integral to modern international law and were worked at constantly in the early years of the United Nations, there is apparently a good deal of confusion as to what exactly was being rejected in condemnation of the League experiment—though some of this confusion only becomes apparent using a degree of hindsight. Perhaps what was rejected was the League system as symbol and spectre: its lack of generalization, its misuse by powerful States, its failed political purpose, its limited humanitarian concern. But in rejecting its structure and practice, there need not be an equal rejection of its norms. Even if it may not have generated customary law, the norms may none the less form part of a consistent pattern of international law. Not all its rules have been discarded —the frequent citation of major judgments of the Permanent Court of International Justice on minorities and equality in international law are evidence of this. It is incorrect to set up an antithetical relationship between human rights and minority rights as was done in the post-war years.

---

[30] *Infra*, ch. 10.
[31] *Rec. des Cours*, 73, 1948, II, 302.
[32] UN Doc E/CN.4/52, 15.
[33] Ibid.   [34] *Infra*, chs. 16 ff.

10. *The United Nations Charter and the Treaties of Peace: The Issue of Minorities*

The United Nations Charter makes no specific mention of minorities. Instead the emphasis is on individual human rights.[1] At the San Francisco Conference, the high level of interest in human rights did not provoke proposals for the protection of minorities, though the Covenant of the League did not mention them either. Whereas the League supplemented its founding text with a series of minorities agreements, this did not occur at the United Nations where a different psychology prevailed.[2] References to minorities at San Francisco were few and scattered, and included a remark by the representative of France that international intervention to prevent abuse of minorities might sometimes be necessary to maintain the peace.[3] It may be that the minorities issue was subsumed under the general thrust for a new regime of human rights. In a later discussion, the representative of Belgium said of the Economic and Social Council that 'minority questions fall properly within its province, but under another name and, though on a wider territorial basis, without the special guarantees which in this connection would result from the system of the league of Nations.'[4] On the other hand, one commentator writes that 'the United Nations Charter was formulated without consideration of the questions of principle which are presented by the existence of national minorities in a world dominated by the concept of the national State as the . . . unit of political organisation. It was drafted without recognition of the minority problem as a significant item on the agenda of international relations.'[5] The author states that in effect the United Nations Charter has no viewpoint on minorities, though he considers that the Charter 'did not *preclude*, even though it did not promise, the subsequent construction of an international framework within which those problems might be systematically solved'.[6] The interpretation advanced by

---

[1] Russell and Muther, *A History of the United Nations Charter.*
[2] Consult, among the authors who discuss the era, Capotorti (*supra*, ch. 1, n. 4), Add. 3; Claude (*supra*, ch. 3, n. 36); Huston, 'Human Rights Enforcement Issues of the United Nations Conference on International Organisation' Iowa Law Review 53 (1967), 272; Kunz, 'The Future of International Law for the Protection of Minorities', *AJIL*, 39 (1945), 89; and Kunz, 'The Present Status of International Law for the Protection of Minorities', *AJIL*, 48 (1954), 282; McKean, *Equality and Discrimination in International Law*, 47 ff.; Werck, 'The Minority Problem and Modern International Law', *World Justice*, 7 (1965), 7.
[3] VI UNCIO Docs., 498.   [4] ECOSOC OR, *First Session*, 9.
[5] Claude, *National Minorities*, 113.   [6] Ibid.; and McKean, *supra*, n. 2, 52 ff.

the representative of Belgium on the ambit of the new system is to be preferred to the above view: the Charter *does* have a view on minorities to be read by necessary implication, that the issue is now part of human rights. Minority rights were not spelled out at San Francisco, but neither were any other human rights, the elaboration being reserved to the principle of non-discrimination as a general formula to guide new developments.[7] Within the new conception of rights it was never inherently improbable that some more specialized notion would arise regarding identity as a human right.

The post-war treaties of peace share in the general style of the Charter. The Treaties of Peace with Bulgaria, Finland, Hungary, Italy, and Romania of 10 February 1947[8] contain general provisions by which those countries are obliged to take all measures necessary to secure to persons under their respective jurisdictions, without distinction as to race, sex, language, or religion, the enjoyment of human rights, and of fundamental freedoms. The Treaties of Peace with Hungary and Romania[9] contain, in addition, provisions prohibiting those States from discriminating between their nationals, particularly in relation to their property, business, professional or financial interests, status, political or civil rights. The Preamble to the Peace Treaty with Japan of 8 September 1951,[10] contains a general provision relating to the realization of the objectives of the Universal Declaration of Human Rights in Japan. Hungary sought to secure regulation for minorities at the Paris Peace Conference, but was unsuccessful. Further, Hungarian demands for frontier revisions with Czechoslovakia and Romania in order to reunite Magyars with their mother State were also unsuccessful.[11] Modeen comments that the treaties 'grant to no minority any rights comparable with those prevailing under the post-First World War agreements. There are no . . . rights for the education of minority groups in their own language, or for the use of their own tongue in the courts or other public institutions.'[12]

However, some account needs to be taken of the later Austrian State Treaty.[13] Article 6 begins with the standard human rights clause corresponding to those in the Peace Treaties of 1947, ensuring that all persons under Austrian jurisdiction should be entitled to human rights without distinction as to race, sex, language, or religion. Article 6(2) provides that

---

[7] *Infra*, ch. 11.

[8] Article 2 of the Treaty with Belgium (*UNTS*, 41, 21); Article 6 of the Treaty with Finland (*UNTS*, 41, 203); Article 2(1) of the Treaty with Hungary (*UNTS*, 41, 135); Article 15 of the Treaty with Italy (*UNTS*, 49, 3); and Article 3(1) of the Treaty with Romania (*UNTS*, 42, 3); and, generally, The Interpretation of the Peace Treaties Case, *ICJ Reports 1950*, 227.

[9] Article 2(2); and 3(2), respectively.

[10] *UNTS*, 136, 45.

[11] Claude, *National Minorities*, 120 ff.; Modeen, *The International Protection of National Minorities in Europe*, 76 ff.

[12] 79–80.

[13] *UNTS*, 217, 229: the full title is 'The Austrian State Treaty for the Re-Establishment of an Independent and Democratic Austria', Vienna, 15 May 1955. Relevant extracts may be found in UN, Protection of Minorities, *supra*, ch. 1, n. 37.

Austrian laws shall not, in content or application, discriminate or entail any discrimination between Austrian citizens on the prohibited grounds. However, Article 7 of the State Treaty displays a radically different approach to minorities from the earlier Peace Treaties. Article 7(1) provides that 'Austrian nationals of the Slovene and Croat Minorities in Carinthia, Burgenland and Styria shall enjoy the same rights on equal terms as all other Austrian nationals, including the right to their own organizations, meetings and press in their own language'. Article 7(2) provides that members of these groups 'are entitled to elementary instruction in the Slovene or Croat language and to a proportional number of their own secondary schools. . .'. Article 7(3) provides for the acceptance in designated districts of Slovene or Croat as official languages in addition to German. Article 7(4) provides that members of the Slovene and Croat Minorities in Carinthia, Burgenland, and Styria 'shall participate in the cultural, administrative and judicial systems in these territories on equal terms with other Austrian nationals'. Article 7(5) is an interesting provision prohibiting organizations 'whose aim is to deprive the Croat or Slovene population of their minority character or rights.'[14] Austrian citizens are affected by Article 7, but not aliens. The minorities rules apply to Carinthia, Burgenland, and Styria, and not to Austrian territory as a whole. Schwelb notes that the Czech minority in Vienna is not affected by the Treaty.[15] The provisions of the Treaty have been supplemented by legislation, in particular the Ethnic Groups Act of 1976.[16] However, the point of the Austrian example is not to endeavour to expound the law of Austria, but to note that the Peace Treaties with Axis States do not entirely neglect the minorities issue. The State Treaty of 1955 compares favourably with the Treaty of St Germain-en-Laye of 1919.[17]

---

[14] Schwelb, 'The Austrian State Treaty and Human Rights', *ICLQ*, 5 (1956), 265.
[15] Ibid. 269.
[16] Federal Act of 7 July 1956 on the Legal Status of Ethnic Groups in Austria, Federal Law Gazette No. 396/1976, text in *The Legal Status of Ethnic Groups in Austria. A Documentation* (Vienna: Federal Chancellery, 1977).
[17] *Supra*, ch. 4.

11. The United Nations Charter: Provisions on Non-Discrimination

The United Nations Charter set the pattern for development of the principle of non-discrimination. The Preamble refers to the determination of the peoples of the United Nations 'to reaffirm faith in fundamental human rights, in the dignity and worth of the human person, in the equal rights of men and women...'. Article 1(3) on the Purposes of the United Nations includes among them the promotion and encouragement of respect for human rights and fundamental freedoms for all 'without distinction as to race, sex, language, or religion'. The latter phrase, coupled with references to human rights, is repeated in Article 13 on the functions of the General Assembly in assisting the realization of human rights; in Article 55 on international economic and social cooperation; and in Article 76 on the objectives of the trusteeship system. The achievement of human rights on a non-discriminatory basis is one of the principal aims of the United Nations Organization as the multiple references demonstrate.

These references to non-discrimination and human rights were inserted at San Francisco. The Dumbarton Oaks 'Proposals for the Establishment of a General International Organization' mentioned only the 'solution of international economic, social and humanitarian problems' as a purpose of the organization, and the promotion of 'respect for human rights and fundamental freedoms' in relation to Chapter IX on 'Arrangements for International Economic and Social Co-Operation'.[1] The purposes and principles in the Dumbarton Oaks text dealt more with international peace and security than with a general commitment to humanitarian standards. During the drafting at San Francisco a different emphasis emerged. What appears as the standard formula—'without distinction as to race, sex, language, or religion' crystallized from a wealth of proposals dealing with human rights. A joint four Power amendment[2] to the Dumbarton Oaks proposals included among the purposes of the United Nations the 'promotion and encouragement of respect for human rights and fundamental freedom for all without distinction as to race, language, religion or sex. . . .'[3] A proposal emanating from Latin American States described one of the purposes of the organization as: 'To ensure respect for human rights and

[1] Russell and Muther, *A History of the United Nations Charter*, Appendix 1.
[2] USA, UK, USSR, China.
[3] 5 UNCIO Docs., 555.

fundamental freedoms, without discrimination against race, sex, condition, or creed.'[4] Latin American States were active in promoting non-discrimination at San Francisco. In the proposal by Brazil, the Dominican Republic, and Mexico, reference was made to the Final Act of the Latin-American Conference on Problems of War and Peace, of the Organization of American States, held at Chapultepec in February and March 1945; the Conference proclaimed, among other *desiderata*, the abolition of discrimination based on sex, race, or religion.[5]

No amendments favouring the protection of minorities were submitted at San Francisco. The Charter refers rather to the equal enjoyment of human rights by all human beings, coupled with the non-discrimination principle. In the present context it is important to note that the States promoting the change from a limited minorities regime to a regime of human rights perceived qualitative differences between the concepts of 'prevention of discrimination', and 'protection of minorities' by implication if not expressly. It is not without significance that the momentum in favour of replacing 'protection of minorities' with 'prevention of discrimination' on the international agenda was generated by the 'countries of immigration', principally the United States and Latin American States. The universalization of any system such as the League of Nations minorities regime would have proved a threat, as they believed it, to their political and legal structures. The Latin American States in particular figure elsewhere in this work as obstacles to the recognition of the existence and identity of minorities. It is not surprising, therefore, that, to the extent that they influenced the drafting of the Charter, the inherently vaguer concept of human rights for all on a non-discriminatory basis should have been preferred to the concrete commitment to protect particular vulnerable groups—even if such groups were to be listed as an addition to, and not as a substitute for, the more general protection.[6] There is nothing in the text of the United Nations Charter to elucidate any distinction between the two concepts, but the performance of the delegates in stressing prevention of discrimination and ignoring minority rights, even in the 'mildest' form of individual as opposed to group rights, declares that a distinction between the concepts was generally understood and operated upon in the drafting of the Charter.[7] It is the general principle of non-discrimination that receives the *imprimatur* of the drafters of the United Nations Charter and this has been a powerful indication to the drafters of subsequent treaties that the principle is held in high esteem.

The lack of specific reference to minorities in the Charter did not prevent United Nations action on the question, and it seems inconsistent that the

---

[4] *3 UNCIO Docs.*, 602.
[5] Russell and Muther (*supra*, n. 1) 567–9.
[6] Sørensen, 'The Quest for Equality'; Claude, *supra*, ch. 3, n. 36.
[7] Claude, ibid. 144 ff.

name of the UN Sub-Commission, Prevention of Discrimination and Protection of Minorities, includes 'minorities' in its title while that term was ignored at San Francisco. Under transitional arrangements at San Francisco, a preparatory commission was established to make provisional arrangements for United Nations organs.[8] The Executive Committee recommended a number of Commissions including the Commission on Human Rights, the work of which was to be directed to, *inter alia*, protection of minorities, and prevention of discrimination on grounds of race, sex, language, or religion. This recommendation was surprising in view of the lack of attention paid to minority issues at the conference, but it indicates that, in some sections of the United Nations, it was perceived that minority protection was different from prevention of discrimination but meritorious on any objective view. None the less, the lack of an explicit reference in the text of the Charter to minorities has weakened the impetus towards protection and hindered the perception that their needs and interests are not fully catered for by norms of non-discrimination.

---

[8] See Report by the Executive Committee to the Preparatory Commission of the UN, UN Doc PC/EX/113/Rev.1 (November 1946); and Report of the Preparatory Commission, UN Doc PC/20; also Salzberg, *The United Nations Sub-Commission on Prevention of Discrimination and Protection of Minorities.*

12. The United Nations Sub-Commission on Prevention of Discrimination and Protection of Minorities

The United Nations Sub-Commission on the Prevention of Discrimination and the Protection of Minorities is a subordinate body of the United Nations Commission on Human Rights. The Sub-Commission consists of twenty-six independent experts selected by the Commission on Human Rights from nominations by member States of the United Nations. Places on the Sub-Commission are reserved on a geographical basis: twelve to Afro-Asian States, six to Western Europe and other States, five to Latin American States, and three to Eastern European States.[1] Membership has expanded from an original allocation of twelve. The terms of reference of the Commission on Human Rights include protection of minorities and prevention of discrimination; as approved by the Economic and Social Council, these are:

The Work of the Commission shall be directed towards submitting proposals, recommendations and reports to the [Economic and Social] Council regarding: (a) an international bill of rights; (b) international declarations or conventions on civil liberties, the status of women, freedom of information and similar matters; (c) the protection of minorities; (d) the prevention of discrimination on grounds of race, sex, language or religion; (e) any other matter concerning human rights . . .[2]

The Commission was authorized to establish separate sub-commissions on protection of minorities and prevention of discrimination, but decided at its first session in 1947 to establish only one. The Sub-Commission's terms of reference, as extended in 1949, are: (a) to undertake studies, particularly in the light of the Universal Declaration of Human Rights, and to make recommendations to the Commission on Human Rights concerning the prevention of discrimination of any kind relating to human rights, fundamental freedoms and the protection of racial, national, religious, and linguistic minorities; and (b) to perform any other functions which may be entrusted

---

[1] Salzberg (*supra*, ch. 11, n. 8), 222; Haver, 'The United Nations Sub-Commission on the Prevention of Discrimination and the Protection of Minorities', *Columbia Journal of Transnational Law*, 21 (1982), 103; Humphrey, 'The UN Sub-Commission on Prevention of Discrimination and Protection of Minorities', *AJIL*, 62 (1968), 869; ECOSOC Res. 1334(XLIV), UN Doc E/4548 (1968).

[2] UN Doc A/CONF.32/6, para. 79.

to it by the Economic and Social Council or the Commission on Human Rights.[3]

At its first session in 1947, the Sub-Commission discussed the meaning of 'prevention of discrimination' and 'protection of minorities'. The clarification was designed to assist the Commission on Human Rights in drafting articles for the Universal Declaration. One writer comments that the Sub-Commission did not attempt a general *legal* definition of this distinction.[4] None the less, while not framed in concise terms, the formula devised by the Sub-Commission is succinct and skilfully drawn. The Sub-Commission suggested that the final drafting of articles on prevention of discrimination and protection of minorities might be facilitated by the following considerations:

1. Prevention of discrimination is the prevention of any action which denies to individuals or groups of people equality of treatment which they may wish.
2. Protection of minorities is the protection of non-dominant groups which, while wishing in general for equality of treatment with the majority, wish for a measure of differential treatment in order to preserve basic characteristics which they possess and which distinguish them from the majority of the population. The protection belongs equally to individuals belonging to such groups and wishing the same protection. It follows that differential treatment of such groups or individuals belonging to such groups is justified when it is exercised in the interest of their contentment and the welfare of the community as a whole . . .

If a minority wishes for assimilation and is debarred, the question is one of discrimination and should be treated as such.[5]

The Sub-Commission's formula was commented upon in a memorandum of the Secretary-General of the United Nations entitled 'The Main Types and Causes of Discrimination'.[6] The text indicated that by discrimination was meant any act or conduct which denied to certain individuals equality of treatment with other individuals because they belonged to particular groups in society. To prevent discrimination, therefore, some means had to be found to suppress or eliminate inequality of treatment which may have harmful results, aiming to prevent any act or conduct which implies that an unfavourable distinction is made between individuals solely because they belong to certain categories or groups in society. The aim was to prevent any act which might imply inequality of treatment on grounds of race, colour, sex, language, religious, political, or other opinion, national or social origin, property, birth or other status. Thus, 'the prevention of discrimination [meant] the suppression or prevention of any conduct which denies or restricts a person's right to equality'.[7] The protection of minorities, on the other hand, although inspired by the 'principle of equality of

---

[3] UN Doc A/CONF.32/6, paras. 114, 115.
[4] McKean (*supra*, ch. 10, n. 2), 82.
[5] UN Doc E/CN.4/52, Section V (Sub-Commission, 1st Session, 1947).
[6] UN Sales No. 49.XIV.3, paras. 6 and 7.　　[7] Ibid.

treatment of all peoples' required positive action: concrete service is rendered to the minority group, such as establishment of schools in which education is given in the native tongue of the members of the group. The guiding principle is equality—'if a child receives its education in a language which is not its mother tongue, this might imply that the child is not treated on an equal basis with those children who . . . receive their education in their mother tongue.' Thus the protection of minorities requires positive action, provided that those concerned wished to maintain differences of language and culture.[8]

The essence of the distinction expressed by the Sub-Commission and the memorandum appears to be that anti-discrimination provisions promote equality by a negative, prohibitory mode through the suppression of manifestations of unequal treatment. A limited view of the power of law is expressed in this description; laws do not address themselves to the direct promotion of change in a positive way, they suppress manifestations of inequality rather than promote equality directly. A regime for the protection of minorities confronts its problem in a more direct way. It requires the establishment of educational and cultural institutions for weaker groups; at its most 'positive', from the viewpoint of a State interested in the welfare of such groups, financial as well as moral and legal support would be forthcoming.[9] It may also be deduced from the Sub-Commission's opinion that anti-discrimination measures have only a temporary character, to last as long as the discrimination is manifested in law and society; discrimination against ethnic and racial groups is like a disease to be cured. Once the goal of equal treatment is reached, the social organism is deemed to be healthy. The protection of minorities, on the other hand, would seem to imply a permanent set of arrangements to protect the culture, language, and religion of the minority.[10] The establishment of institutions through 'positive' measures also implies their maintenance. Unless the composition of a population changes, or the balance of political power, the minority will remain a minority in the sense defined elsewhere in this work of a non-dominant group with distinctive characteristics. If equality is to be maintained in the long term, the necessary institutions must also be maintained. The protection of minorities implies whatever is necessary for the maintenance of a distinct identity, a necessity which will be shaped differently in different societies.

Special Rapporteur Capotorti stresses that non-discrimination is an absolute prerequisite of special measures for minorities:

---

[8] See also the Memorandum submitted by the Division of Human Rights of the UN Secretariat to the Sub-Commission 'Definition of the Expressions "Prevention of Discrimination" and "Protection of Minorities" ', UN Doc E/CN.4/Sub.2/8 (October 1947).

[9] See *infra*, chs. 18 ff.

[10] Capotorti, 'The Protection of Minorities under Multilateral Agreements on Human Rights' *Italian Year Book of International Law*, 2, (1976), 3.

It is generally recognised that the effective implementation of the right of persons belonging to ethnic, religious and linguistic minorities to enjoy their own culture, to profess and practise their own religion and to use their own language requires, as an absolute pre-condition, that the principles of equality and non-discrimination be firmly established in the society in which those persons live.[11]

He urges that States should ratify the International Convention on the Elimination of All Forms of Racial Discrimination. In his view, the prevention of discrimination and the implementation of special measures to protect minorities 'are merely two aspects of the same problem: that of fully ensuring equal rights to all persons'.[12] The guiding principle is that no individual should be placed at a disadvantage because he is a member of a particular ethnic, religious, or linguistic group.[13] McKean expresses a similar view; he regards the Memorandum of the Secretary-General as a 'milestone in the progress of understanding the juridical meaning of equality and its related concepts, prevention of discrimination and protection of minorities'. Thus it 'reaffirmed that these two concepts are not unrelated or contradictory, but are complementary methods of attaining equality of treatment for all persons'.[14] Vierdag, on the other hand, criticizes this perception of the distinction and doubts the necessity for any specific regime for minorities. In his view, minority protection can be realized 'through the granting of human rights in combination with the non-discrimination principle . . . while no references to protection of minorities needs to be made. This final element is important because the latter institution enjoys a poor reputation in the United Nations'.[15] He quotes Professor Humphrey to support this last assertion: 'In the higher bodies of the United Nations, at least, there has never been any serious intention of doing anything about minorities.'[16] Vierdag's views depend on a generous assessment of the scope of the anti-discrimination principle together with an ungenerous assessment of the benefits of singling out minorities as beneficiaries of international legal provisions. Part of his argument relates to the political unacceptability of distinct rules on minorities. His writing dates from 1973, and the quotation from Professor Humphrey is taken from an article published in 1968. Interest in minorities had lapsed in the 1950s and 1960s at the United Nations, although in 1967 the Sub-Commission adopted a Resolution in which it decided to initiate a study on 'the implementation of the principles set out in Article 27 of the International Covenant on Civil and Political Rights',[17] which matured into the Capotorti Report—a preliminary report was made by the Special Rapporteur as early as June 1972.[18] Subsequent developments have reduced the force of Vierdag's argument in that it is at

---

[11] *Supra*, ch. 1, n. 4, Add. 5, para. 24.
[12] Ibid., para. 27.   [13] Ibid., para. 28.   [14] McKean, 86.
[15] Vierdag, *The Concept of Discrimination in International Law*, 158.
[16] Humphrey (*supra*, n. 1), 872.   [17] Res. 9(XX).
[18] UN Doc E/CN.4/Sub.2/SR.43 and 44.

least acceptable to confront minorities issues at the United Nations even if they are not enthusiastically received and many States remain sceptical about developing rules to supplement the framework of the International Covenant on Civil and Political Rights.[19]

There is much to be said against deleting proposals for the 'protection of minorities' and subsuming the proposals under 'prevention of discrimination'. Apart from the point of logical difference discussed above, it is important that international law should recognize the validity of diverse languages, cultures, and religions in a positive and direct way rather than to expect this as an implication from an imaginatively interpreted standard or rule of non-discrimination. A direct confrontation of the minorities issue is a more honest and clearer approach than any alternative. The 'unpopular' issue is argued and discussed and, even if progress is limited, it is the case that a relatively clear but limited rule is better than a sweeping but vague and indirect rule; in the former case, there is a clear if limited obligation on States, in the latter case, there may effectively be no obligation at all. Rules relating to the protection of minorities notify the international community of the existence of these groups and express a set of values affirming the contribution of diversity to humankind. They also recognize the individual in cultural context and not merely as a citizen of a State with rights equal to all other citizens. None of this is intended to decry the value of interpreting anti-discrimination rules generously but, by themselves, they fail to do full justice to minorities.

The history of the UN Sub-Commission bears out the above arguments, although the history is often too easily assumed to demonstrate the contrary. The point is that in the early days of the United Nations, and later, it was possible for States to be at once enthusiastic sponsors of rules against discrimination and opponents of discussion or action on minorities questions. States were aware of the differences between the two questions and this includes many States taking an extremely unfavourable view of progress to benefit their minorities. This suggests that from the point of view of valuing the identity of minorities there may be a certain tension between 'prevention of discrimination' and 'protection of minorities'.

Depending on the legal regime in a State, 'prevention of discrimination' alone may be seen as a means of flattening out differences between cultural and religious groups and promoting assimilation, no doubt in the interests of the dominant culture. The situation envisaged by Klineberg may easily arise: an 'undertaking to abolish discrimination against an individual if he becomes similar to the majority is obviously unsatisfactory in the case of those who do not seek to become completely like the majority'.[20] Many States with a culturally heterogenous population have adopted this legal expedient with

---

[19] *Infra*, Part IV.

[20] Klineberg, *Background Paper for the Seminar on the Multinational Society* (Ljubljana, 1965).

negative consequences for the conservation of group identity. The error was in supposing that a regime of non-discrimination is all that is needed was committed by the Soviet expert in the Sub-Commission's consideration of the Secretary-General's memorandum: strictly applied, legislation to combat discrimination could, he suggested, eliminate the discrimination 'thus ensuring the protection of minority rights'.[21] This is not, however, a position generally taken by the Soviet Union which has been progressive in its sponsorship of minority rights in international legal instruments.

It is notable that while the Sub-Commission made considerable progress on the issue of discrimination to be combated by international legal instruments, it made little progress on protection of minorities. It initially conceived its role in the protection of minorities as an extremely important one and sought actively to fulfil this aspect of its mandate. The Sub-Commission's efforts to include an article on minorities in the Universal Declaration of Human Rights were unavailing in the face of rejection by the Commission on Human Rights.[22] Following this, the General Assembly requested the Commission and Sub-Commission to make a thorough study of the problem of minorities.[23] The Sub-Commission prepared a draft resolution for the Commission recommending that Member Governments provide minority groups with educational and judicial institutions using the groups' languages.[24] It also proposed that a provision on minority rights be inserted into the UN Covenant on Civil and Political Rights—a successful proposal.[25] Pending completion of the Covenant, it recommended that the Commission adopt a proposal for interim measures to be taken by States for the protection of minorities.[26]

This activity on behalf of minorities was not welcome to the Commission. The Commission is a body of different character from the Sub-Commission, being composed of the representatives of Member States. It provides a more authentic expression of the limitations of action on behalf of minorities from the viewpoint of States. The arguments marshalled against the Sub-Commission's activism reflect similar arguments discussed in another section of this work.[27] Latin American States claimed that the Sub-Commission had paid little attention to the needs of the countries of immigration; especially in the Western hemisphere, early immigrants had determined the character of the States and later immigrants must assimilate. Assimilation was necessary both for nation building and for the security of the States.

[21] UN Doc E.CN.4/Sub.2/SR.43 and 44.
[22] *Infra*, ch. 13.
[23] UNGA Res. 217(III), *GAOR*, 3rd Session, Part 1 (1948).
[24] UN Doc E/CN.4/357; E/CN.4/Sub.2/78, annex.
[25] *Infra*, ch. 15.
[26] UN Doc E/CN.4/Sub.2/117; also, Salzberg, *The United Nations Sub-Commission: A Functional Analysis* (Michigan: University Microfilms International), 142 ff.
[27] Generally, Sørensen, 'The Quest for Equality' *International Conciliation*, 507 (1956), 291; for examples, Salzberg, ibid.

In later sessions of the Commission on Human Rights and the parent body, the Economic and Social Council, the efforts of the Sub-Commission to make progress on the minorities issue and, *inter alia*, work towards a generally acceptable international law definition of minority met with no success. Proposals by the Sub-Commission were invariably sent back for further study.[28] At length, the Sub-Commission decided to concentrate on the prevention of discrimination, and to 'defer work on a further study of the whole problem of the special protection of minorities, including the definition of the term "minority" pending the issuing by the Commission on Human Rights of a specific directive on the subject'.[29] When the Sub-Commission report was considered by the Commission, no comment was made on the decision to shelve the item.[30] The Sub-Commission's efforts relating to minorities were discontinued until the developments leading to the Capotorti Report were initiated. Its undue concentration on this issue had led to the temporary liquidation of the Sub-Commission by the Economic and Social Council;[31] the Sub-Commission was reinstated through pressure exerted on the Economic and Social Council by the General Assembly.[32] Part of the price for its resuscitation was that it should concentrate efforts on the prevention of discrimination.

Accordingly, at the fifth session (1953) the Sub-Commission proposed a series of discrimination studies. The first of these was its study of discrimination in education.[33] There follow studies relating to discrimination in occupation and employment,[34] political rights, religious rights, residence and movement, and immigration and travel. Later, the Sub-Commission studied discrimination against persons born out of wedlock,[35] equality in the administration of justice, and racial discrimination in political, economic, social, and cultural fields. Besides the programme of studies, the Sub-Commission devoted considerable efforts to the drafting of conventions and

---

[28] Sørensen, *passim*. The main complaint was that the Sub-Commission was too active in its efforts to focus attention on minorities. At its 1950 session, the Commission criticized this active role, indicating that the Sub-Commission should concentrate upon studies rather than implementation, e.g., the Sub-Commission had proposed in 1947 that, pending the establishment of implementation machinery under the proposed Covenant on Human Rights, the Sub-Commission should be given authority to deal with urgent cases within its mandate: Haver (*supra*, n. 1), 107–8.

[29] UN Doc E/CN.4/711 (Feb. 1955).

[30] Sørensen, 'The Quest for Equality'.

[31] UN Commission on Human Rights, UN Doc E/CN.4/Sub.2/SR.86 (1952); also *ECOSOC OR, 13th Sessions*, Annex, UN Doc E/1995 (1951).

[32] UNGA Res. 532B(VI) (1952). At this stage, it was the Western States which opposed a continuing role for the Sub-Commission; other States, including the USSR, favoured its continuing existence.

[33] UN Doc E/CN.4/Sub.2/181/rev. 1 (1956).

[34] This was carried out by the International Labour Organization, and led to ILO Convention No. 111, concerning Discrimination in Respect of Employment and Occupation, *UNTS*, 362, 31. See also the UNESCO Convention against Discrimination in Education, discussed *infra*, ch. 33.

[35] Haver (*supra*, n. 1), 112–13; Salzberg (*supra*, ch. 11, n. 8), 176–226.

declarations relating to discrimination. The movement to the preparation of legal instruments from the educational and information bearing studies coincided with the arrival of new nations at the United Nations; the same nations which gave impetus to the development of self-determination were also concerned about racial questions.[36] Thus, the Sub-Commission prepared early drafts of the Declaration and the Convention on the Elimination of All Forms of Racial Discrimination[37] and parallel documents on religious intolerance. In the midst of all this, it was proposed in 1965 that the name of the Sub-Commission should be changed to the 'Permanent Committee of Experts of the Commission on Human Rights',[38] but no action was taken on the proposal. This is not the only occasion on which a suggestion was made which would have removed any reference to protection of minorities.[39]

The Sub-Commission remains active in the field of prevention of discrimination. At its twenty-third session, the Human Rights Commission expanded the authority of the Sub-Commission to deal with discrimination. Resolution 8(XXIII) required the Sub-Commission to bring the Commission's attention to those situations which revealed a consistent pattern of violations of human rights, including specific discriminatory practices.[40] The Sub-Commission was also requested to consider on a regular basis the question of slavery 'including the slave-like practices of Apartheid and colonialism'.[41] The programme of studies of discrimination continues with increasing emphasis on enforcement.[42]

There are other general human rights aspects of the Sub-Commission's work, the details of which do not directly concern the present argument. The Sub-Commission's work has gradually extended its jurisdictional scope despite efforts to curb this development. In particular it has developed procedures under Economic and Social Council Resolution 1235(XLII) and Economic and Social Council Resolution 1503(LXVIII) for dealing with mass violations of human rights.[43] The element of discrimination still exerts an influence on these procedures. Thus, ECOSOC Resolution 1235(XLII) authorized the Human Rights Commission and the Sub-Commission 'to examine information relevant to gross violations of human rights and fundamental freedoms, as exemplified by the policy of *Apartheid* as practised in the Republic of South Africa . . . and racial discrimination as practised

[36] Citations, *supra*, ch. 1.

[37] *Infra*, ch. 29; McKean, *Equality and Discrimination under International Law*, 79 ff.

[38] *ECOSOC OR*, 41st Session, Supp. No. 8, 119; Salzberg (*supra*, ch. 11, n. 8), 38–9.

[39] In 1979 the Sub-Commission recommended that its name be changed to the Sub-Commission on Human Rights, Sub-Commission Res. 9A(XXXII), UN Doc E/CN.4/Sub.2/435.

[40] Humphrey (*supra*, n. 1), 887.

[41] Human Rights Commission Res. 13(XXXIII), *ECOSOC OR*, 42nd Session, Supp. No. 6, 136.

[42] Haver (*supra*, n. 1).

[43] See Brownlie, *Basic Documents on Human Rights* 15–20; Ermacora, 'The Protection of Minorities before the United Nations', 334.

notably in Southern Rhodesia'. Ermacora interpreted the language of this Resolution to mean that: 'Not any violation of human rights is . . . covered by the ECOSOC Resolutions, but only violations of the type of *Apartheid*'.[44] The reference to apartheid means that persons or groups of persons 'are deprived of their elementary human rights because of their race, sex, language, religion . . .'. This view has, however, been rejected by the Sub-Commission which continues to address *general* violations of human rights.[45] Similarly, under the confidential ECOSOC Resolution 1503(LXVIII) procedure, communications alleging violations of human rights are declared admissible by the Sub-Commission if 'there are reasonable grounds to believe that they may reveal a consistent pattern of gross and reliably attested violations of human rights and fundamental freedoms, including policies of racial discrimination and segregation and of *Apartheid*, in any country, including colonial and other dependent countries and peoples'.[46] The racial discrimination aspect of the communication is an important element in the type of situation to be reviewed and investigated, and its continuing importance as a motif in the Sub-Commission's general work is doubtless assured.

The eclipse of the Sub-Commission's interest in minorities proved ultimately to be partial, not total.[47] The early success in inserting a minorities article into the Covenant on Civil and Political Rights became a focus for subsequent developments. The article in the Covenant, Article 27, carries a great burden in international law and deserves intensive study. International law now recognizes two broad avenues to minority protection besides protection of the right to existence. It is proposed to describe the first right arising from this bifurcation as the right to identity, and the second as the right not to be discriminated against. Both rights function in a 'universal' framework.

---

[44] Ermacora, 'Procedure to Deal with Human Rights Violations', *RDH*, 7 (1974), 670 at 679.

[45] A continuing review of these developments is undertaken in the Review of the International Commission of Jurists (Geneva).

[46] Brownlie (*supra*, n. 43), 18–19.

[47] Many cases discussed within the ambit of procedures under Commission Res. 8(XXIII), and ECOSOC Res. 1503(XLVIII) relate to minorities. The agenda items are not focused on minorities as such but on grave violations of human rights such as torture, disappearances, violations of rights in conflicts not of an international character, etc. According to an assessment made by an NGO source during the 40th Session of the Sub-Commission, violations of the rights of minorities accounted for two-thirds of the total cases discussed: E/CN.4/Sub.2/1988/SR.17. The underlying minority question is often not addressed. Perhaps some refocusing will result from the adoption of a resolution by the Sub-Commission at its 40th Session entrusting one of its members to prepare a working paper 'on possible ways and means to facilitate the peaceful and constructive resolution of situations involving racial, national, religious and linguistic minorities': E/CN.4/Sub.2/1988/L.62.

13. The Omission of a 'Minorities Article' from the Universal Declaration of Human Rights

After the UN Charter, the Universal Declaration of Human Rights is perhaps the most significant document in the field of human rights. The Declaration was adopted by the General Assembly of the United Nations on 10 December 1948, by forty-eight votes to none, with eight abstentions.[1] It contains civil, political, economic, social, and cultural rights. It does not make any references to 'minorities', though it does refer to the principle of non-discrimination or 'non-distinction': 'Everyone is entitled to the rights and freedoms set forth in this Declaration without distinction of any kind, such as race, colour, sex, language, religion, political or other opinion, national or social origin, property, birth or other status' (Article 2). There is also the promise of equality: 'All are equal before the law and are entitled without any discrimination to equal protection of the law. All are entitled to equal protection against any discrimination in violation of this Declaration and against any incitement to such discrimination' (Article 7). Article 16 on the right to marry declares that this should be 'without any limitation due to race, nationality or religion'. Article 23(2) refers to the right to equal pay for equal work 'without any discrimination'.

Apart from the above, the Declaration lists rights and freedoms particularly pertinent to minority identity: the right to freedom of thought, conscience and religion (Article 18), the right to freedom of opinion and expression (Article 19), the right of peaceful assembly and association (Article 20), the right to education (Article 26)—which shall 'promote understanding, tolerance and friendship among all nations, racial or religious groups . . .', and the right freely to participate in the cultural life of the community (Article 27).

The *travaux préparatoires* reveal that attempts were made to include an article on minorities. In a draft drawn up by the Division on Human Rights, it was proposed that:

In all countries inhabited by a substantial number of persons of a race, language or religion other than those of the majority of the population, persons belonging to such ethnic, linguistic or religious minorities shall have the right to establish and

---

[1] UNGA Res. 217A(III)., *GAOR*, 3rd Session, *Part 1, Resolutions*, 71.

maintain, out of an equitable proportion of public funds available for the purpose, their schools and cultural institutions, and to use their language before the courts and other authorities and organs of the State, and in the press and public assembly.[2]

The reference to public funds was deleted from the draft prepared for the Drafting Committee by M. Cassin (France) because, according to a later explanation, France does not make such funds available for private education.[3] The Sub-Commission on Prevention of Discrimination and Protection of Minorities reviewed the text of the article and submitted a revised text to the Human Rights Commission. The Sub-Commission's draft read:

In States inhabited by well defined ethnic, linguistic or religious groups which are clearly distinguished from the rest of the population and which want to be accorded differential treatment, persons belonging to such groups shall have the right as far as is compatible with public order and security to establish and maintain their schools and cultural or religious institutions, and to use their own language and script in the press, in public assembly, and before the courts and other authorities of the States, if they so choose.[4]

This less than enthusiastic provision to benefit minorities was voted down by the Commission which sent the draft declaration to the General Assembly without any minorities article.[5] The Sub-Commission's article was weaker than that prepared by the Division on Human Rights. The rights contained in it were only available in the case of groups which were both 'well defined', and 'clearly distinguished' from the rest of the population. The groups were those who wanted to be accorded differential treatment; the individuals had to choose to utilize the rights. The requirement that the exercise of the rights had to be consistent with 'public order and security' was the most limiting requirement—and is always perhaps a limitation which can be more easily invoked and justified in the case of groups as opposed to individuals because of the greater magnitude of the threat perceived by the State.

When the Third Committee of the General Assembly considered the draft, Denmark, Yugoslavia, and the USSR proposed articles on minorities. The proposal of the USSR was the most detailed, referring to the minorities' right to their own ethnic or national culture, to establish their own schools, to receive teaching in their native tongue, to use that tongue in the press, at public meetings, in the courts, and in other official premises. The Danish proposal dealt essentially with the right to education, whereas the Yugoslav

---

[2] UN Doc E/CN.4/AC.1/3/Add.1, 409.

[3] M. Spanier (France), UN Doc E/CN.4/Sub.2/SR.11 at 20, cited in Verdoodt, 'Ethnic and Linguistic Minorities and the United Nations', 68. On the Declaration and the question of minority rights see also Bruegel, 'A Neglected Field: The Protection of Minorities' *RDH*, 4 (1971), 413, 430; Capotorti, 'The Protection of Minorities under Multilateral Agreements on Human Rights, *Ital. Yr. Bk. Int. L.*, 2 (1976), 3; Capotorti Report, Add. 2, paras. 57–8; McKean (*supra*, ch. 12, n. 37), 62.

[4] UN Doc E/CN.4/SR.52, 9.

[5] UN Doc E/CN.4/SR.74, 5 (by 10 votes to 6).

proposal asserted the individual's right to nationality and the rights of nations which exist within States to equality in national, political, and social rights and to the full development of their own ethnical culture and language.[6]

The minorities issue was given an airing in the Third Committee, though most of the arguments advanced were essentially the same as those in contemporary debates on, for example, the Genocide Convention and the Covenant on Civil and Political Rights.[7] Introducing the draft article submitted by the USSR, its Representative declared that the use of the native language and the right of a population to develop its own culture were fundamental human rights.[8] In effect, the Representative attempted to secure acceptance for the model of the Soviet State as an ideal international standard; he referred to the 'voluntary alliance'[9] of its peoples, the right of these peoples and nationalities to cultural and national autonomy, etc. The Soviet Union also rejected assimilation of peoples as a technique for promoting harmony between groups. The Representative of Yugoslavia laid emphasis on collective as well as individual rights.[10] The Yugoslav Representative stated the following order of priorities:

In order to secure the protection of individuals who formed a community, that community must first of all be recognised and protected. Thus the principle of the recognition and protection of national minorities as communities must appear in the Declaration of Human Rights. The cultural and ethnical rights of all persons belonging to a national minority . . . depended upon the recognition of the minority itself as an ethnical group.[11]

These statements were coupled with the assertion that 'Individual human rights were dependent on the position which the community enjoyed in the State in which it lived.'[12] Members of minorities were bound together by a national bond and were thus in a special situation with regard to the State.

The proposals were heavily criticized in a debate with a strong 'cold war' flavour—though this is not a complete explanation of their ultimate failure. The Representative of Mexico drew the Committee's attention to the fact that there 'was not the same problem of minorities on the American continent as in Europe or in other parts of the world'. Furthermore, foreigners entering America were not affected by discriminatory measures; they had

[6] For texts, see *GAOR*, 3rd Session, Part 1, 3rd Committee, Annexes, UN Doc A/C.3/307/Rev.2, 45–6.

[7] *Supra*, ch. 7, and *infra*, chs. 16 ff. For the 3rd Committee's discussion of the Universal Declaration, consult *GAOR*, 3rd Session, Part 1, 3rd Committee, 161st, 162nd, and 163rd meetings, UN Doc A/C/3/SR.161–3, 717–40.

[8] UN Doc A/C.3/SR.161, 719.

[9] Ibid.

[10] See *infra*, chs. 16 ff. on the Yugoslav Draft Declaration on the Rights of Minorities and the response of the UN.

[11] UN Doc A/C.3/SR.161, 720.

[12] Ibid.

'the advantage of a very generously conceived naturalisation, with the result that the various legislative bodies had not needed to consider the question of the protection of minorities'.[13] However, he recognized that the problem existed elsewhere and did not in principle oppose a suitable article in the Universal Declaration. The Representative of Brazil rehearsed familiar arguments about national unity,[14] and the need for assimilation.[15] To similar effect were the arguments of the Representatives of Chile,[16] France,[17] Haiti,[18] and Australia.[19] The Representative of the United States (Mrs Roosevelt) declared rather forcefully that there should be no minorities article in the Declaration, and criticized Mexico: it was 'impossible to adopt a neutral attitude on the insertion in the Declaration of a right which was not of universal significance'.[20] In her opinion, 'the best solution of the problem of minorities was to encourage respect for human rights'.[21] This is a clear expression of the view that minority rights are somehow different from human rights in general and represent an historically limited conception which would have no validity in the modern era.[22]

The States of Eastern Europe expressed general support for the minorities proposals. They were joined by the Representatives of Belgium,[23] India,[24] and, with qualification, Turkey.[25] The support of the Eastern bloc States enabled them to mount appropriate attacks on Western States. Thus, the Representative of the Byelorussian Soviet Socialist Republic reprimanded Australia for carrying out a policy of forceful elimination of its aboriginal group, and noted that the American Indian 'had almost ceased to exist in the United States'.[26] He criticized colonial policy, remarking that in colonial territories there were no signs that indigenous culture was being developed and encouraged, while the Representatives of 'metropolitan powers'[27] made constant references to the spread of civilization: 'the development of culture and the colonial yoke [are] mutually exclusive.'[28] The Representative of the Soviet Union tried to effect a division between the 'Colonial Powers'[29] and the Latin American countries, by asserting that the former would, being colonialist, support the suppression of minority languages as a matter of course, while he was surprised at this attitude in the non-colonial Latin American States. This attempt to separate their respective positions did not succeed. It did not introduce any majority in favour of a minorities article; in many States it may, on the contrary, have had the effect of hardening their resolve, particularly in view of the Soviet claim that it had successfully 'solved' the minorities problem and its implied invitation to other States to follow the Soviet course. In addition to the 'traditional' threat of 'Balkanization' through allowing ethnic groups full rein, there was added the threat of

---

[13] UN Doc A/C.3/SR.161, 721.   [14] Ibid.   [15] Ibid.   [16] Ibid. 722.
[17] Ibid. 723.   [18] Ibid. 724.   [19] Ibid. 725.   [20] Ibid. 726.
[21] Ibid.   [22] *Supra*, ch. 9.   [23] UN Doc A/C.3/SR.161, 724–5.
[24] UN Doc A/C.3/SR.162, 727–8.   [25] Ibid. 729–30.   [26] Ibid.
[27] Ibid.   [28] Ibid.   [29] Ibid.

'Sovietization'. It is not surprising that, to a majority of States, individualistic human rights without any special concession to particular groups in society seemed a sensible, modern, and democratic programme, altogether worthy of support. The General Assembly ultimately referred the problem of minorities to the Sub-Commission for further study and adopted a separate resolution on minorities. Resolution 217C(III) is no substitute for omitting the article from the Declaration, but it indicated that, at least, the minorities issue was not likely to be exhausted by the debates on the Declaration.

The supporters of minority rights, it may be noted, tended to argue that they were fundamental. The Representative of Yugoslavia described the rights of minority groups as 'a condition for the enjoyment of human rights'.[30] They were simply 'fundamental human rights'[31] for the Representative of the USSR: the proposals of the USSR 'could be accepted there and then', they constituted a 'modest declaration'[32]—this demonstrates that, in the Soviet view, there was nothing exceptional about them. The Representative of Poland regarded the USSR draft as stating the 'essential rights' of minorities; they were the 'positive aspect'[33] of non-discrimination, implying a logical connection between the admitted concept (non-discrimination) and the unadmitted (protection of minorities).

[30] UN Doc A/C.3/SR.163, 740.
[31] UN Doc A/C.3/SR.161, 719.
[32] Ibid. 720.   [33] Ibid. 724.

PART IV

The Right to Identity

14. The Covenant on Civil and Political Rights

Introduction

The argument of a previous chapter was that while the 'right to existence' of minorities was underwritten by international criminal law, the notion of existence is restricted to the 'physical' existence of member of minority groups and did not embrace the notion of 'Cultural Genocide': the oppressive destruction of the 'cultural' existence or identity of minorities. The right to a distinct identity is, however, the subject of international protection. The conventional and customary law recognising this right is considered below with the primary focus on the right as set out in Article 27 of the United Nations Covenant on Civil and Political Rights.

The right to an identity must remain a key element in any overall system to protect minorities. While crude threats to the physical existence of groups have provided a melancholy backdrop to contemporary developments in protecting the rights of man and will continue to do so, minorities may be faced with more subtle threats. The effort to assimilate minorities into society may be as effective in eliminating a group as attacks upon the lives of members; if successful, the result is the death of a culture: the carriers of culture are spared, but they pass on a different culture to succeeding generations—not improbably, the culture of the oppressors.

Cultural change and assimilation are, of course, inevitable processes in human history. It is not necessary to list examples of vanished cultures to understand this fact. International law, like municipal law, cannot attempt, Canute-like, to roll back the tide of cultural development. Nor can it attempt to isolate cultures from processes of peaceful change and preserve them, like museum pieces, for eternity. But it can attempt to locate processes of change in the general context of human rights, so that members of groups can play a part in the development of their heritage and choose the basis on which their culture can adapt to the world. Insofar as minorities, being minorities, may not always have the degree of political; control over their destiny necessary to protect the status of their participation in the world's multiethnic States, it remains a legitimate task of international law to assist them in making cultural contributions to the States on terms which do not unduly privilege the majority populations in those States. Granting minorities a right to defend their special identity, their unique characteristics that distinguish them from other members of the human family is an important task for human rights. Article 27 of the United Nations Covenant on Civil and Political Rights is an inevitable focus for this aspect of minority rights. It is the only expression of the right to an identity in modern human rights conventions intended for universal application. It is, in fact, the first real attempt in the history of international law to provide such a universal right; as such it bears a considerable burden. An extended exegesis of its meaning, in the context of the United Nations Covenant, and of the means for its implementation, is therefore crucial for an appreciation of the extent to which international law accepts the claim of minorities to protect their cultural destiny.

The Drafting of the Covenant

The UN Covenant on Civil and Political Rights, and its 'twin' Covenant on Economic, Social and Cultural Rights[1] are significant modern exercises in human rights law making. They are intended for universal application, in consideration of the 'obligations of States under the Charter of the United Nations to promote universal respect for, and observance of, human rights and freedoms'.[2] In the early days of the United Nations, the Economic and Social Council and its Commission on Human Rights decided that the International Bill of Human Rights should consist of a general Declaration, a separate Covenant, and measures of implementation.[3] With the proclamation of the Universal Declaration by the General Assembly on 10 December 1948, attention switched to the proposed treaty. The drafting took the best part of six sessions of the Human Rights Commission, beginning with consideration of a preliminary draft which included detailed formulation of most of the civil and political rights set out in the Declaration.[4]

The decision to adopt two covenants instead of one was made by the eighth session of the Commission.[5] The idea that economic and social rights were equally part of human rights along with the 'classic' civil and political rights was present in the Universal Declaration of Human Rights. Article 22 of the Declaration introduced Articles 23 to 27, in which economic, social, and cultural rights, the rights to which everyone is entitled as a member of society, are set out. They are indispensable for human dignity and are to be realized through national effort and international cooperation; the Declara-

---

[1] International Covenant on Civil and Political Rights, UNGA Res. 2200A(XXI), *GAOR*, 21st Session, Supp. No. 16, 52 (1966); International Covenant on Economic, Social and Cultural Rights, ibid., 49. The former Covenant entered into force on 23 March 1976; the latter on 3 January 1976.

[2] Preamble to both Covenants. On 1 September 1988, the Covenant on Civil and Political Rights had 87 parties, and the Covenant on Economic, Social and Cultural Rights, 97: ST/HR/5(November 1988), 12.

[3] See generally, Pechota, 'The Development of the Covenant on Civil and Political Rights', in Henkin (ed.), *The International Bill of Rights* (New York Columbia U.P., 1981), 32 ff.

[4] *ECOSOC OR*, 9th Session, Supp. No. 10, UN Doc E/1371, E/CN.4/350, Annexes I and II.

[5] Pechota (*supra*, n. 3), 39.

tion thus recognizes the right to social security,[6] the right to work,[7] the right to equal pay for equal work,[8] the right to rest and leisure,[9] the right to a standard of living adequate for health and well-being,[10] the right to education,[11] and the right to participate in the cultural life of the community.[12] In general terms it may be said that Western States preferred separate covenants despite the juxtaposition of rights in the Declaration.[13] The United States declared that it would find it difficult to accept a treaty containing economic, social, and cultural rights because they went beyond those guaranteed by the Constitution and were, therefore, not enforceable by the courts.[14] Canada expressed a preference that such rights be guaranteed by a declaration rather than a convention.[15] The Resolution of the General Assembly approving two covenants instead of one, none the less emphasized the interdependent nature of the two sets of rights and the unity of purpose of the covenants.[16]

Accordingly, the Commission on Human Rights produced a Draft Covenant[17] that elaborated the civil and political rights set out in the Universal Declaration: the right to life; freedom from inhumane treatment; prohibition of slavery and related practices; liberty and security of the person, humane treatment of those deprived of liberty; prohibition of imprisonment on grounds of inability to fulfil a contractual obligation; freedom of movement; freedom of aliens from arbitrary expulsion; the right to a fair trial; prohibition of retroactive application of criminal law; the right to privacy, honour, and reputation; freedom of thought, conscience, and religion; freedom of opinion and expression; prohibition of advocacy of national, racial, or religious hatred; the right of peaceful assembly; freedom of association; the right to marry and found a family; the right to take part in public affairs; equality before the law; the rights of members of ethnic, religious, and linguistic minorities. The right to property set out in Article 17 of the Universal Declaration is not repeated in the list of proposed Covenant rights. The rights of minorities were additions to the Declaration rights. Another addition was the right of self-determination,[18] the inclusion of which derived from an initiative of the General Assembly, as did a provision on sexual equality in the enjoyment of civil and political rights.

---

[6] Article 22.   [7] Article 23.   [8] Ibid.
[9] Article 24.   [10] Article 25.   [11] Article 26.
[12] Article 27.   [13] Pechota (*supra*, n. 3).   [14] Ibid. 42.   [15] Ibid.
[16] UNGA Res. 543(VI), GAOR, 6th Session, Supp. No. 20, UN Doc A/2119, 36.
[17] The drafting was complete by the 10th Session of the Commission in 1954, *ECOSOC OR*, 18th Session, Supp. No. 7.
[18] In 1950 the General Assembly instructed the Economic and Social Council to request the Commission on Human Rights to 'study ways and means which would ensure the rights of peoples and nations to self-determination, and to prepare recommendations for consideration by the General Assembly at its sixth session'. The Commission did not have time to take up the question, and the Assembly itself decided that the Covenant should include an article stating 'All peoples shall have the right of self-determination': *GAOR*, 6th Session, Supp. No. 20, UN Doc A/2119, 36.

Besides listing the rights, the Draft obliged States to adopt measures to give effect to the rights and to ensure effective remedies for their violation. Rights were not, however, considered as absolute; both general and specific limitation clauses were inserted. The Draft Covenant also contained provisions dealing with international implementation. The key element in the proposals was the Human Rights Committee. A reporting system was envisaged, as well as an inter-State complaints system. The notion of international methods of implementation met with typical Eastern bloc resistance on the grounds that it violated the principle of domestic jurisdiction.[19] The Commission did not favour the right of individual petition for violations of human rights.[20]

The Draft Covenant was subjected to an intense scrutiny and assessment by the Third Committee of the General Assembly. Many substantive changes were made in the draft, but the provision on minorities was broadly accepted as satisfactory. It is outside the scope of the present discussion to detail these changes, though it may be noted that a new article was adopted prohibiting any propaganda for war,[21] as well as an article on the rights of the child.[22]

Implementation of the Covenant on Civil and Political Rights

As a first point the Covenant requires implementation at the national level, which is logical given that the protection of human rights deals with relationships between States and individuals.[23] For many States, it is only this kind of implementation which is fully acceptable, as human rights instruments do not, in this view, provide the individual with direct rights under international law, but create mutual obligations of States to respect human rights at the domestic level.[24] Thus, each State party, by Article 2(1), undertakes 'to respect and to ensure to all individuals within its territory and subject to its jurisdiction the rights recognised in the Covenant' on a non-discriminatory basis. The remainder of the article charges the State to take

---

[19] *GAOR*, 5th Session, Plenary Meeting, 317, UN Doc A/PV.317, at 554. The implementation articles, in the view of the Soviet delegate, should have been deleted, because their inclusion would have constituted an intervention in the domestic affairs of States. Communist States have been reluctant to accept either the inter-State or the individual complaints procedure under the Optional Protocol to the Convention. In September 1988 Hungary became the first Eastern Bloc State to accept the Optional Protocol, its acceptance entering into force in December 1988, *Interights Bulletin 1988* (3), 31.

[20] See the remarks made by the delegate of the USA to the Commission, UN Doc E/CN.4/SR.105 (1949).

[21] Now Article 20 of the Covenant.

[22] Ibid. Article 24.

[23] See generally, Robertson, 'The Implementation System: International Measures' in Henkin (*supra*, n. 3), 332; and Schachter, 'The Obligation to Implement the Convention in Domestic Law', ibid. 311.

[24] See Tunkin, *Theory of International Law*, 79–83.

the necessary steps to give effect to the rights, including the provision of effective remedies for violations of rights, determined by 'competent authorities'. One writer comments that, in the Covenant on Civil and Political Rights, the time allowed to the State to conform its legislation to the international standard is not unlimited,[25] though proposals to fix time limits on the process were rejected during the drafting stages.[26] It was widely accepted that Article 2 of the Covenant on Civil and Political Rights does not incorporate the notion of progressive development in view of the different character of the rights in the two Covenants. The rights are expected to be implemented without undue delay.[27] However, as noted below, not all of the rights in the Covenant on Civil and Political Rights are of the classic, immediately applicable kind.[28] It does not appear to be a Covenant requirement that the Covenant itself be incorporated into domestic law.[29]

The provisions for international implementation are contained in Articles 28 to 45 which provide for a Human Rights Committee consisting of eighteen individual members elected by the States parties to act in their personal capacity.[30] The Committee has basically two functions: to consider reports from the States parties,[31] and to deal with complaints, 'communications', that the obligations assumed by them under the Covenant are not being fulfilled.[32] The Optional Protocol to the Covenant provides for communications from individuals who claim to be victims of human rights violations by a State party.

By Article 40(1) of the Covenant, the reports are to cover measures adopted to give effect to the Covenant rights and to describe 'the progress made in the enjoyment of those rights'. On studying the reports, the Committee will transmit its own reports and 'such general comments as it may consider appropriate'[33] to the States parties; the States' reports, together with the Committee's comments may also be sent to the Economic and Social Council.[34] The reporting procedure is the only procedure of international implementation in the Covenant on Economic, Social, and Cultural Rights where the whole emphasis is on progressive implementation.[35] The reason for its inclusion in the Covenant on Civil and Political Rights appears to be that at the time when proposals for an individual right of petition were rejected by the Commission on Human Rights, leaving only an inter State

---

[25] Humphrey, 'The Implementation of International Human Rights Law', 31 at 39.
[26] UN Doc E/CN.4/SR.327–9.   [27] Schachter (*supra*, n. 23), 323.
[28] *Infra*, ch. 18.   [29] Schachter (*supra*, n. 23), 312–3.   [30] Article 28.
[31] Article 40.   [32] Articles 41 ff.   [33] Article 40(4).   [34] Ibid.
[35] The 'tone' of this Covenant is set by Article 2(1): the States parties undertake 'to take steps, individually and through international assistance and co-operation, especially economic and technical, to the maximum of . . . available resources, with a view to achieving progressively the full realization of the rights recognized in the present Covenant by all appropriate means . . .'. State reports have been transmitted by the Secretary-General to ECOSOC, which referred them to the Sessional Working Group of Governmental Experts. The UN Committee on Economic, Social and Cultural Rights will now review the reports. The first meeting of this 18-member Committee took place in 1987: UN Doc E/C.12/SR.1.

complaints system, certain delegates felt that it would be appropriate for the Committee to exercise some form of supervision over the performance of States, in case the inter State system did not function effectively.[36] The existence of parallel systems does, none the less, emphasize the similarity in the objectives of the two conventions despite differences of style and content.

The second function of the Committee is to 'receive and consider communications to the effect that a State Party claims that another State Party is not fulfilling its obligations under the . . . Covenant'.[37] The Human Rights Committee can consider complaints only if they come from a State party which has made a declaration recognizing in regard to itself the competence of the Committee. No communication shall be received by the Committee if it concerns a State party which has not made such a declaration.[38] This is, in effect, an 'optional clause' which according to Article 41(2) requires ten declarations to bring it into operation. If the disputants and the Committee fail to settle the dispute, the Covenant provides that, with the consent of the parties, a communication may come before a Conciliation Commission of five persons appointed by the Human Rights Committee who are 'acceptable to the States Parties concerned'[39] and who will lend their good offices towards a friendly settlement. If none is reached, the Commission reports its findings of fact to the parties and its views on the possibility of an amicable solution. There is no power to make a judicial determination of the issues.

The Optional Protocol deals with communications from individuals. Article 1 of the Protocol provides that: 'No communication shall be received by the [Human Rights] Committee if it concerns a State party to the Covenant which is not a party to the present Protocol.' The communication procedure is open to individuals claiming to be victims of human rights violations 'who have exhausted all available domestic remedies'.[40] The communication must not be anonymous, nor be 'an abuse of the right of submission' or 'incompatible with the provisions of the Covenant'.[41] The exhaustion of domestic remedies rule is not applied 'where the application of the remedies is unreasonably prolonged'.[42] Communications from individuals are brought to the attention of the 'accused' State party, which has six months to clarify the matter and indicate the remedy, if any, which has been applied. The Committee holds closed meetings; it then 'forwards its views'[43] to the State party and the individual concerned. A summary of its activities under the Optional Protocol is included in the Committee's

---

[36] Humphrey (*supra*, n. 25), 40.

[37] Article 41(1). So far, 23 States have accepted the competence of the Committee under Article 41, *Human Rights, Status of International Instruments*, ST/HR/5; *Interights Bulletin*, 3 (1988), 31.

[38] Article 41 (1).   [39] Article 42(1)(b).

[40] Article 2. On 7 September 1988, Hungary became the 43rd State to accept the right of individual petition.

[41] Article 3.   [42] Article 5(2)(b).   [43] Article 5(4).

annual report to the General Assembly of the United Nations through the Economic and Social Council (Article 45 of the Covenant).

It may be noted that the Protocol gives a right of petition to 'individuals'; under the Convention on the Elimination of All Forms of Racial Discrimination, 'individuals or groups' may petition (Article 14(1)) and this is also the case under the American Convention on Human Rights (Article 44) and the European Convention on Human Rights (Article 25). On the other hand, these three conventions do not contain a 'minorities' article like Article 27 of the Covenant on Civil and Political Rights.[44]

Functioning of the Human Rights Committee

All three systems of implementation in the Covenant are in force, and rules of procedure have been adopted for the Human Rights Committee, the first meetings of which dealt with organizational matters.[45] The reporting procedure remains the most important in practice, though increasingly, the annual reports of the Committee deal at some length with the progress of cases under the Optional Protocol. The consideration of States' reports by the Committee is conceived as a 'constructive dialogue' between the Committee and the State concerned. Thus, Rule 68 of the Rules of Procedure provides that States parties may appoint a Representative to be present who 'should be able to answer questions which may be put to him by the Committee and make statements on reports already submitted by his State and may also request additional information from his State'. The 'dialogue' aspect of the proceedings and the power to request additional information are important developments in view of the often rather bland and self-satisfied reports submitted by States which give a misleading impression of the actual state of human rights within their jurisdiction. There are limits, however, on the extent to which the members of the Committee can challenge the information contained in the reports by reference to outside sources.[46] There are limits also on the nature of the Committee's comments and on recommendations for action. The Committee is authorized to make 'general comments'; this means that reference to individual cases is impermissible.

The 'constructive dialogue' initiated by the Committee is useful in elucidating the content of the rights recognized in the Covenant, even if remedially deficient. Questions are asked on the whole range of rights as

[44] See Ghandhi, 'The Human Rights Committee and the Right of Individual Communication', *BYIL*, 57 (1986), 201. The Human Rights Committee has declared that an organisation as such cannot submit a communication: *A Group of Associations for the Defence of the Rights of Disabled and Handicapped Persons in Italy, etc.*, v. *Italy*, GAOR, 39th Session, Supp. No. 40, 198. See also *JRT and the WG Party of Canada* v. *Canada*, GAOR, 38th Session, Supp. No. 40, 263.

[45] Robertson (*supra*, n. 23), *passim*.

[46] Ibid. 348–9.

their implementation is described in the reports. Questions are regularly asked under Article 27. The dialogue is capable of throwing considerable light on the interpretation of the Covenant, and it is in this spirit that the questions and answers are discussed in this section.[47]

In relation to the inter State complaints system, little can be said, except that it has not produced any such complaints in the first years of its existence. If the experience with the European Convention on Human Rights is any guide, it will prove of limited usefulness in protecting human rights. Complaints are tempting to some States for political rather than purely humanitarian reasons and, even if this is not the case, may only result in increased tensions between nations with little improvement in human rights.[48] This is perhaps particularly the case with regard to minorities; a complaint by a kin State of the minority may be regarded as provocative and interfering by the host State and worsen the minority's situation.

The Optional Protocol had attracted thirty-six parties by 1 January 1986. The Committee's first report recorded the appointment of working groups to consider the admissibility of communications.[49] Members of the Committee may also request that 'a summary of their views shall be appended to the views of the Committee when they are communicated to the individual and to the State Party concerned.'[50] This in effect allows for dissenting opinions and in the words of one writer strengthens the 'quasi-judicial character'[51] of the Committee acting under the Protocol. In 1981 a case was heard for the first time with Article 27 as its focus, though other articles of the Covenant were also discussed. The case is outlined below.[52] The limitations of this procedure as far as Article 27 is concerned is presently a practical one: the small number of parties to the Protocol. The situation improves very slowly, but for the time being, members of most of the world's minorities are outside this procedure.

---

[47] *Infra*, chs. 16 ff.

[48] Consider in this context *Ireland* v. *United Kingdom*, European Court of Human Rights, Judgment, January 1978.

[49] UN Doc A/32/44, 37.

[50] Para. 3, rule 94 of Rules of Procedure, UN Doc A/32/44, Annex I.

[51] Robertson (*supra*, n. 23), 363.

[52] *Infra*, ch. 24; also the *Kitok Case*, ibid. (*infra*, ch. 23).

15. History of Article 27

In General Assembly Resolution 217c(III), entitled 'Fate of Minorities',[1] it was stated that the United Nations could not remain indifferent to the fate of minorities, but that it was difficult to adopt a uniform solution of this complex and delicate question. The General Assembly requested the Economic and Social Council to ask the Commission on Human Rights and the Sub-Commission on Prevention of Discrimination and Protection of Minorities 'to make a thorough study of the problem of minorities, in order that the United Nations may be able to take effective measures for the protection of racial, national, religious or linguistic minorities'. The Sub-Commission discussed the resolution at its third session.[2] Draft resolutions were submitted by members of the Sub-Commission containing positive proposals for the protection of minorities. One proposal[3] suggested a draft protocol to be attached to the International Covenant on Human Rights for the protection of the ethnic, religious and linguistic traditions and characteristics of minorities. Another[4] noted that the teaching of minority languages and their use before the courts were not covered either by the Universal Declaration or by the draft International Covenant on Human Rights, and called upon the Sub-Commission to study the best means of protecting these rights.

Neither proposal proved satisfactory to the Sub-Commission and a new resolution was prepared by a drafting committee taking criticism and suggestions into account.[5] This draft visualized a minorities article in the International Covenant in the following form: 'Ethnic, religious and linguistic minorities shall not be denied the right to enjoy their own culture, to profess and practise their own religion, or to use their own language.' The Sub-Commission preferred that 'persons belonging to minorities' should replace 'minorities' because minorities were not subjects of law and 'persons belonging to minorities' could easily be defined in legal terms. On the other hand, it was decided to include 'in community with the other members of their group' after 'shall not be denied' in order to recognize group identity in some form. The amended draft resolution, therefore, proposed an article for inclusion in the Covenant: 'Persons belonging to ethnic, religious or linguistic minorities shall not be denied the right, in community with the other

---

[1] 10 December 1948.

[2] Report of the Sub-Commission on Prevention of Discrimination and Protection of Minorities, UN Doc E/CN.4/358, paras. 39–48.

[3] UN Doc E/CN.4/Sub.2/108.

[4] UN Doc E/CN.4/Sub.2/106/Rev.1.

[5] UN Doc E/CN.4/Sub.2/112.

members of their group, to enjoy their own culture, to profess and practise their own religion, or to use their own language.'[6]

At its ninth session, the Commission on Human Rights had various articles submitted to it besides the draft prepared by the Sub-Commission. Thus, the Representative of the Soviet Union proposed the following article: 'The State shall ensure to national minorities the right to use their native tongue and to possess their national schools, libraries, museums and other cultural and educational institutions.'[7] Yugoslavia proposed a draft article but later withdrew it in favour of an amendment to the Sub-Commission's draft to be inserted after the text quoted above: 'without being subject on that account to any discrimination whatever, and particularly such discrimination as might deprive them of the rights enjoyed by other citizens of the same State.'[8] Other additions to the Sub-Commission's text were submitted by Chile and Uruguay reflecting very clearly the preoccupations of the 'States of immigration'. The Chilean proposal, which features in the final text of Article 27, added the following to the beginning of the Sub-Commission's text: 'In those States in which ethnic, religious or linguistic minorities exist.'[9] A proposed second paragraph to the Sub-Commission's text was recommended by Uruguay: 'Such rights may not be interpreted as entitling any group settled in the territory of a State, particularly under the terms of its immigration laws, to form within that State separate communities which might impair its national unity or its security.'[10] This amendment was rejected, along with those of the Soviet Union and Yugoslavia.[11] The discussions in the Commission on the amendments indicate general agreement on at least one point: the rights set out in the draft article are in addition to and not in substitution for the other rights in the Covenant. There was less agreement on which minorities should be covered—a division of opinion between those who favoured 'ethnic, religious or linguistic groups' and those who would have preferred the term 'national minorities' and a similar division on the degree to which minorities should be 'established' before they could be the object of protection. The 'integrationists' or 'assimilationists' supported the view that the minorities comprehended by the draft should be only those which were clearly defined and had long existed in a State; otherwise the emergence of 'new' minorities would be encouraged and national integration delayed or frustrated.[12]

[6] Sub-Commission Res. E(III).

[7] ECOSOC OR, 16th Session, Supp. No. 8 (UN Doc E/2447), paras. 51–6; UN Doc E/CN.4/SR.368–71; Capotorti Report, Add. 2, paras. 91 ff.

[8] UN Doc E/2447.

[9] Commission on Human Rights, 9th Session, Capotorti Report, Add. 2, para. 95.

[10] Ibid., para. 96.

[11] The proposal of the Soviet Union was rejected by 8 votes to 4 with 4 abstentions; the Yugoslav amendment was rejected by 5 to 3 with 8 abstentions; the Chilean amendment was adopted by 5 to 1 with 10 abstentions; the Uruguayan amendment was rejected by 7 to 5 with 4 abstentions.

[12] Capotorti Report, Add. 2, 65 ff.

No amendments were submitted to the Third Committee of the General Assembly when it considered the Commission's text.[13] The text was broadly regarded as satisfactory by the Committee, though again the predilections of the countries of immigration were apparent from the discussions, when similar views to those put forward before the Commission on Human Rights were expressed. These are further considered below.[14] It was also noted by some delegations that parts of Africa were dominated by privileged minorities and the article was not intended to protect such dominators; it could not derogate from the principle of majority rule.[15] It was also decided not to subject the article to any such limitation clause as was present in other articles—limiting, for example, freedom to manifest one's religion or belief to an extent 'necessary to protect public safety, order, health or morals or the fundamental rights and freedoms of others' (Article 18(3)). Such clauses as already existed were of a general nature and applied to majorities and minorities alike.[16] The Committee adopted, by eighty votes to none, with one abstention, the text as drafted by the Commission.[17] The International Covenant was adopted by General Assembly Resolution 2200A(XXI) and the draft article became Article 27 of the final text. The Human Rights Committee commenced its functions in 1977 and members have regularly posed questions to States regarding the implementation of Article 27. The questions and responses of States in so far as they throw light on the interpretation of the article are considered below.

Subsequent Developments

At its twentieth session in 1967, the Sub-Commission adopted Resolution 9(XX) relating to the protection of minorities. It decided, *inter alia*, to 'initiate as soon as possible a study of the implementation of the principles set out in Article 27 . . . with special reference to analysing the concept of minority taking into account ethnic, religious and linguistic factors and considering the position of ethnic, religious and linguistic groups in the multinational society'.[18] Further to the recommendations of the Commission on Human Rights, the Economic and Social Council approved the Sub-Commission's decision and authorized it to designate a Special Rapporteur from amongst its members.[19] The Sub-Commission appointed Professor

---

[13] *GAOR*, 16th Session, Annexes; Capotorti Report, Add. 2, paras. 105 ff.
[14] *Infra*, ch. 16.
[15] *GAOR*, 16th Session, 3rd Committee, 1103rd meeting, para. 53 (Guinea); 1104th meeting, para. 8 (Iraq), para. 12 (USSR), para. 21 (Italy), para. 38 (Libya).
[16] Ibid., 1103rd meeting, para. 17 (Netherlands), para. 24 (China), para. 40 (India), para. 47 (Belgium).
[17] Ibid., 1104th meeting, para. 52.
[18] Capotorti Report, Add. 6, para. 1.
[19] Res. 1418(XLVI).

F. Capotorti as Special Rapporteur at its twenty-fourth session in 1971.[20] The study is an extremely valuable contribution to the debate on minorities and opened up discussion on this issue after years of neglect.[21] Apart from the merits of the author's research and analysis, it is a valuable compendium of comments by States on the minorities issue. The final report was presented to the Sub-Commission at its thirtieth session in June 1977[22] having been preceded by a number of interim reports.[23]

In the final report, the Special Rapporteur suggested, among further measures to be taken at the international level, the possibility of a United Nations declaration on the rights of members of minority groups. The essential requirement would be 'to throw light on the various implications of Article 27 and to specify the measures needed for the observance of the rights recognised in the Article'.[24] Adopting the conclusions of the Special Rapporteur, the Sub-Commission recommended the Commission to draw up a declaration within the framework of the principles in Article 27.[25] Shortly after this, Yugoslavia presented a draft declaration entitled 'Rights of Persons belonging to National, Ethnic, Religious and Linguistic Minorities'[26] to the thirty-fourth session of the Commission. A working group was established to consider this draft. By Resolution 14A(XXXIV)[27] of March 1978, the Commission for Human Rights, *inter alia*, requested the Secretary-General of the United Nations to transmit the relevant documents[28] of the thirtieth session of the Sub-Commission and of the thirty-fourth session of the Commission on Human Rights relating to minorities to Governments of the Member States for their comments. Although only a small number of governments responded to this invitation, their comments,[29] besides outlining certain *desiderata* for the international law on minorities, also reflect on the interpretation of Article 27 and are here used primarily for that purpose. At each subsequent session of the Commission, an open-ended working group has been established to continue work on the Declaration. Following Commission Resolution 37(XXXVI) of 12 March

---

[20] Res. 6(XXIV).
[21] *Supra*, ch. 12.
[22] *Supra*, ch. 1, n. 4.
[23] UN Doc E/CN.4/Sub.2/L.564; E/CN.4/Sub.2/L.582; E/CN.4/Sub.2/L.595, E/CN.4/Sub. 2/L.621.
[24] Capotorti Report, Add. 5, para. 59.
[25] Res. 5(XXX), August 1977.
[26] UN Doc E/CN.4/L.1367/Rev.1, March 1978.
[27] UN Doc E/1978/34, 73–4.
[28] The documents in question were the above mentioned Yugoslav Draft Declaration; Chapter XVIII of the Report of the Human Rights Commission on its 34th Session, UN Doc E/CN.4/1291; the Report of the Informal Working Group on the agenda item at the 34th Session of the Commission; and Chapter XIV of the report of the Sub-Commission on its 30th Session, UN Doc E/CN.4/1261.
[29] Replies were received from some twenty-six governments, some of which merely announced that they had no comment to make or simply described their internal constitutional and legal provisions dealing with minorities.

1980, a revised and consolidated text was placed before the Commission in 1981. Work on substantive articles continues, the question of definition of 'minority' having been postponed.[30]

---

[30] *Supra*, ch. 1, n. 26. The latest version of the text on which preliminary agreement has been reached is contained in UN Doc E/CN.4/1988/36, *Report of the Working Group on the Rights of Persons Belonging to National, Ethnic, Religious and Linguistic Minorities*, Commission on Human Rights, 44th Session. The report also outlines various amendments and proposals by States and NGOs.

16. 'In Those States in Which Ethnic, Religious or Linguistic Minorities Exist'

Some Restrictive Interpretations

As noted above,[1] this phrase was introduced by Chile at the ninth session of the Commission on Human Rights. It reflects the widely held view among 'countries of immigration', particularly in the Americas, that the classic 'minorities question', as applied mainly to Europe, has no relevance to their contemporary situation. Comments were made in this connection during General Assembly debates on the draft Universal Declaration of Human Rights.[2] Similar views were expressed in the Third Committee of the General Assembly during debates on Article 27 (draft Article 25). Thus, the Representative of Brazil, after describing briefly the history of the minorities treaties and the League of Nations system, stressed the need for careful definition of the term 'minority'. He argued that the 'mere coexistence of different groups in a territory under the jurisdiction of a single State did not make them minorities in the legal sense. A minority resulted from conflicts of some length between nations, or from the transfer of a territory from the jurisdiction of one State to that of another.' Further, for a minority to exist:

a group of people must have been transferred 'en bloc', without a chance to express their will freely, to a State with a population most of whom differed from them in race, language or religion. Thus, groups which had been gradually and deliberately formed by immigrants within a country could not be considered minorities, or claim the international protection accorded to minorities.

Therefore, Brazil and the other American States 'did not recognize the existence of minorities on the American continent'.[3] Subject to such explanation, Brazil was willing to vote for the draft article. In effect, the Brazilian delegate said that the article, which he approved as a piece of draftmanship[4] and supported for inclusion in the Covenant, bound other States but not Brazil.

A concurring speech was made by the Representative of Chile. The problem of minorities 'which arose in some European and Asian countries did not arise in the American States, particularly those of Latin America'. The

---

[1] *Supra*, ch. 15, n. 9.
[2] *Supra*, ch. 13.
[3] *GAOR*, 16th Session, 3rd Committee, 1103rd meeting, paras. 8–14.
[4] Ibid., para. 10.

Latin American countries understood the problems raised by minorities in some European and Asian countries, and hoped that the latter countries also appreciated Latin American problems. The 'formation' of minority groups in Latin America would seriously impede the efforts of the States to strengthen their national unity. He noted, as an example of dangerous activity by minorities, the activities of the German colony in the South of Chile before World War II 'under the influence of Nazi propaganda'.[5] Similarly, the Representative of Venezuela[6] noted curtly that 'Article 25 did not raise any difficulty for the delegation of Venezuela because the minority problem did not arise there.' The Representative of Panama[7] took the view that Article 25 was not a problem for his country as it 'did not, strictly speaking, concern Panama, which was a melting-pot of numerous races'. The views expressed by Ecuador, Peru, and Nicaragua were to similar effect.[8] Of the Latin American countries speaking before the Third Committee, only Mexico departed from this restrictive line, arguing that the second paragraph of the Article could profitably have gone further and said that efforts should be made to raise the economic and social level of minorities without prejudice to their specific cultural heritage. Such a paragraph, it was claimed, 'would have contributed in no small measure towards national integration, not only in Latin America, but also in many other countries represented in the Committee'.[9] The statement did not, however, clearly admit the presence of minorities in Mexico; it was apparently interpreted by the Representative of Chile as implying the presence of minorities in Mexico, and by the Representative of Nicaragua as concurring with the positions taken by Peru and Chile, which denied their existence.

The Chilean denial of the relevance of the draft Article 25 represents perhaps the clearest negative view of that article, which was 'neither general in scope nor universal in application . . . and pertained only to certain regions of the world'.[10] That other States besides Latin American States would accept this view is clear from the views expressed by the Representatives of Australia, Spain, Liberia, Guinea, Mali, Ghana, and Upper Volta, either because there were no minorities on their territory or because there was no minority 'problem'.[11] Other States did not directly endorse these views, though it was noted that the minorities question assumed different characteristics in various continents. Criticism of the 'restrictive' approach

[5] Ibid., paras. 18–23.
[6] Ibid., paras. 27–8.
[7] Ibid., para. 42.
[8] Ibid., paras. 43–5 (Ecuador); ibid., 1104th meeting, paras. 4–5 (Peru), paras. 35–7 (Nicaragua).
[9] Ibid., 1104th meeting, paras. 2–3.
[10] Ibid., 1104th meeting, para. 23.
[11] In the case of Liberia, for example, the protection of minorities 'was not a problem. At one time there had been a demarcation line between the indigenous population and the descendants of immigrants, but because of a unification programme carried out by the present Government that line had disappeared', 1103rd meeting, para. 49.

did, however, figure in the contribution of the Representative of India who was concerned in case the drafting of the Article 'might encourage dictatorial States to refuse to recognise the rights of minorities living in their territory, simply by denying their existence'.[12]

The principal groups excluded from the purview of the article in the eyes of the restrictionist States were (a) new immigrants, and/or (b) indigenous groups. Thus, in relation to these new nation States reflecting the culture of one time colonisers and their descendants, neither the descendants of the original (indigenous) inhabitants, nor more recent arrivals, could set themselves apart as minorities with distinctive claims. In relation to Australia, it was explained that it 'was doing its best to encourage new immigrants not to set up separatist minority groups, but to merge completely with the Australian community and enrich it . . .'. Besides these, Australia 'had a small group of aborigines whose way of life was still very primitive, but who could not be considered a "minority" . . .' The policy of the Australian Government was to encourage their progressive assimilation into the normal life of the nation.'[13] In Brazil, the indigenous inhabitants could only be called minorities 'in a loose social sense; technically the term was not correct'.[14] The above type of claim is illustrated by the internal legislation of some 'restrictionist' States which does not generally recognize the legal existence of minorities, or special rights of individuals belonging to minorities. France responded to Capotorti that France 'cannot recognise the existence of ethnic groups, whether minorities or not'.[15] Niger declared that 'it is not possible to distinguish within the country a numerically inferior group having cultural characteristics different from those of the remainder of the population'.[16] The Government of the Philippines commented that a single category of 'minorities', national cultural minorities, benefited from legal recognition. These consisted of the indigenous population; groups other than these did not have any legal standing.[17] In fact, the situation relating to indigenous groups in internal law in the 'restrictionist' States differs from that relating to 'new' immigrants in that legal regimes exist that differentiate the interests of these groups from the rest of the States' populations. This is the case of the Indians in Latin America, the United States of America, Canada, and Guyana; the Lapps in Finland, Norway and Sweden; and indigenous groups in Australia, New Zealand, Malaysia and Japan.[18] Such groups may or may not be described in State legislation as 'minorities'.[19] It may be noted that those States which legally recognize the existence and aspirations of minority groups do not necessarily use that term. In Eastern European States, for example, the term 'nationality' is

---

[12] Ibid., para. 37.   [13] Ibid., paras. 25–6.
[14] Ibid., 1104th meeting, para. 19.
[15] Capotorti Report, Add. 1, para. 47.
[16] Ibid., Add. 1, para. 55.   [17] Ibid.   [18] Ibid.
[19] The problem of indigenous groups is discussed, *infra*, chs. 38 ff.

preferred.[20] The question of whether internal law 'recognizes' or does not 'recognize' the existence of minorities cannot determine the extent of the obligations undertaken by becoming a party to the treaty. It is a principle of international law that 'Every State has the duty to carry out in good faith its obligations arising from treaties and other sources of international law, and it may not invoke provisions in its constitution or its laws as an excuse for failure to perform this duty.'[21] And, further, 'a State which has contracted valid international obligations is bound to make in its legislation such modifications as may be necessary to ensure the fulfilment of the obligations undertaken.'[22]

In the context of Article 27, the Special Rapporteur on Minorities emphasizes the fact 'that international protection of minorities does not depend on official recognition of their existence'.[23] It clearly cannot do so, or else the protection afforded by Article 27 would be nullified by simple legislative inaction on the part of States. While this is correct, it may be acknowledged that 'in practice, the recognition of a minority by the State in which it lives improves [its] situation, facilitates the application of the principles enunciated in Article 27 . . . and gives the members of the minority a solid basis for effective protection of the rights guaranteed them at the international level.'[24] Further, it would seem that in States where minorities exist, the Covenant requirements on States to 'respect and ensure' the rights set out in the Covenant, and, where necessary, to adopt 'legislative or other measures' to give effect to those rights, would require explicit or implicit 'recognition' of the existence of relevant groups.[25]

If, however, the absence of 'recognition' by the State does not determine that groups relevant to Article 27 do not exist on State territory, what factors are decisive? In line with the 'ordinary meaning' of terms[26] one may agree with Capotorti that 'the presence of sufficient elements to indicate that a minority exists is sufficient to make applicable the pertinent international rules.'[27] This raises the question of what are 'sufficient elements' to indicate the existence of a minority. The 'existence' of a minority is contingent upon the definition of the term 'minority' itself.

Subsequent practice in the application of the treaty has not so far revealed any great deviation from positions taken up in the preparatory stages with reference to the 'existence' of minorities. Responding to questions by the

---

[20] Capotorti Report, Add. 1, para. 54.

[21] Article 13, Draft Declaration on the Rights and Duties of States 1949, *Year Book of the International Law Commission 1949*, 286.

[22] Exchange of Greek and Turkish Populations, *PCIJ Reports*, Ser. B. No. 10, 20 (1925).

[23] Capotorti Report, Add. 1, para. 41.

[24] Ibid., para. 42.

[25] Article 2 of the Covenant. Consider, e.g., the statement of Romania to the Human Rights Committee: 'The Roman Catholic church is not a recognised church in Romania, since it was not prepared to accept Romanian law . . .', CCPR/C/SR.743, para.14.

[26] Article 31 of the Vienna Convention on the Law of Treaties, *AJIL*, 63 (1979), 875.

[27] Capotorti Report, Add. 1, para. 41.

Human Rights Committee in relation to its report to that Committee, the Chilean view was again that there were no ethnic, religious, or other minorities, within the meaning of Article 27, in Chile. This 'reflected the desire to integrate all ethnic groups into the national community'. It was also pointed out that in the opinion of the Government of Chile, 'the existence of different standards of treatment would be tantamount to discrimination.'[28]

A restrictive view of a different nature appeared in the report of the German Democratic Republic which claimed that there were no religious minorities in that State. Asked whether that meant that there were no religious groups, the Representative replied that there 'was no State religion in the Republic and consequently, there were no religious minorities. Church and State were separate and religious communities . . . managed their own affairs without State interference.'[29] This seems to indicate that something like an established church is necessary in a State before a religious minority can be said to exist. It also implies that there are religious 'communities', but not 'minorities', and these are managing their affairs freely. Their 'freedom to manage their affairs' seems, on the other hand, to imply a reference to Article 27, suggesting that the article is, after all, applicable, unless this freedom accorded to the religious communities refers only to Article 18 of the Covenant which protects freedom to manifest religion or belief 'in worship, observance, practice and teaching'.[30] Some of the disclaimers on the existence of minorities in a State reveal rather tortuous and evasive reasoning. Perhaps the continuing work of the Committee will produce plainer interpretations of the consequences of factual situations for treaty obligations.

Ethnic, Religious, Linguistic

In the fields of anti-discrimination, genocide, and minorities there is a profusion of terms, listed differently in different instruments. The Universal Declaration of Human Rights lists, inter alia, as impermissible grounds of distinction in the entitlement to human rights 'race, colour . . . language,

[28] *GAOR*, 34th Session, Special Supp. No. 40, UN Doc A/34/40, para. 106.
[29] *GAOR*, 33rd Session, Special Supp. No. 40, UN Doc A/33/40, para. 177. Compare the statement of Bulgaria to the Special Rapporteur on the implementation of the Declaration on Religious Intolerance, admitting the presence of a religious group but denying ethnic characteristics: 'Islam is professed by Bulgarian Muslims who are an integral part of the Bulgarian people and are neither ethnically nor nationally related to the Turks. There are no "ethnical Turks" or "Turkish minority" [in Bulgaria] . . .', UN Doc E/CN.4/1988/45, para. 17. Turkey also maintains that it has only religious minorities: 'The concept of minorities in Turkey is defined by the Treaty of Lausanne dated 23 July 1923 . . . The treaty confirms that there are only religious minorities in Turkey, identifying them as "non-Muslim minorities" . . . The members of these minorities are Turkish citizens . . . [who] enjoy the same rights as any other Turkish citizens . . .', ibid., para. 18. Rather inconsistently, the Turkish statement goes on to describe provisions for teaching in minority languages.
[30] Article 18(1).

religion, . . . national or social origin',[31] all of which terms share a certain kinship with those employed in Article 27. The Genocide Convention prefers 'national, ethnical, racial or religious' groups.[32] In the International Convention on the Elimination of All Forms of Racial Discrimination, discrimination on the grounds of 'race, colour, descent, or national or ethnic origin'[33] in the recognition, enjoyment, or exercise of human rights is forbidden. Elsewhere in the Covenant on Civil and Political Rights, the grounds of discrimination are listed in a fashion similar to the Universal Declaration of Human Rights.[34] In the field of minorities, it will be recalled that race, language, and religion were the identification marks of groups protected by the League of Nations.[35]

Up to 1950, the term 'racial minorities' and not to 'ethnic minorities' was generally used in the United Nations. General Assembly Resolution 217c(III) referred to 'racial' and 'national' but not 'ethnic' minorities.[36] The etymological root of 'ethnic' is the Greek *ethnos* or 'nation'. The *Concise Oxford English Dictionary* defines 'ethnic' as 'pertaining to race'. These roots and definitions do not result in any ability to distinguish between 'race', 'ethnic group', and 'nation'—the suggestion is rather that they are synonymous. Some have attempted to give substance to distinctions; thus, one writer defines ethnic groups as 'peoples who conceive of themselves as one kind by virtue of their common ancestry (real or imagined), who are united by emotional bonds, a common culture, and by concern with preservation of their group'.[37] Another writes that 'ethnic group' refers to 'categories of the population . . . who distinguish themselves or are distinguished by the . . . majority groups as differing from each other and the latter in acquired behavioural characteristics or culture, regardless of whether or not they differ in inherited or racial characteristics'.[38] There is, according to these two definitions, some possibility of achieving a distinction between a 'racial' and an 'ethnic' group. A UNESCO Committee of experts on race problems found the following definition of 'race'; it 'designates a group or population characterised by some concentration, relative as to the frequency and distribution, of hereditary particles (genes) . . . which appear, fluctuate, and often disappear in the course of time by reason of geographic and/or cultural isolation'.[39] This highly abstract,

---

[31] Article 2. [32] Article II. [33] Article 1(i).
[34] Article 2. [35] *Supra*, ch. 3. [36] *Supra*, ch. 15.
[37] Burkey, 'Discrimination and Race Relations', *Report on the International Research Conference on Race Relations* (Aspen, Colorado, 1970), 2.
[38] Moore, *Thailand, its People, its Society, its Culture*, (New Haven: Yale University Press, 1974), 64.
[39] *UNESCO Statement on Race* (1950), para. 4. A comment by UNESCO to the UN Sub-Commission is provocative: 'One problem of the academic study of racial relations is that it has been dominated by scholars from the English-speaking world, and particularly by social scientists who have either grown up in the United States or have unconsciously taken over assumptions originating there . . . the economic and mass media power of the United States has permitted that country's folk definitions on race to be transmitted to other regions and

genetically based definition may be supplemeted by referring to the common usage of the term 'race' to denote physical differences between peoples, particularly their colour. The ethnic group, by contrast, refers to a 'cultural' entity with or without distinct 'physical' characteristics.

There was some discussion in the Commission on Human Rights on the desirability of including the term 'national' to supplement or replace the list of minorities in the draft. When the Representative of the Soviet Union proposed the draft article relating to national minorities[40] to the Commission at its ninth session, a 'national minority' was defined as 'an historically formed community of people characterised by a common language, a common territory, a common economic life and a common psychological structure manifesting itself in a common culture'.[41] The Commission's report noted that those who were in favour of 'national' minorities emphasized the right of such groups to use their language and possess national schools, libraries, museums, and other cultural and educational institutions.[42] The Commission preferred not to adopt the term 'national', though, as one writer comments, it 'is not clear, however, that in adopting that formulation the Commission decided that minorities are not entitled to possess "national" schools, libraries, museums, and other cultural and educational instititions'.[43] The net effect, therefore, of preferring the formula in the final text is that many groups are to be protected before they become 'national groups', irrespective of whether they could ever 'develop' in this fashion. Thus, the terms chosen are wider in their context than the suggested alternatives.

In this and other respects 'ethnic' seems to be the broadest term available. It is broader than either 'racial' or 'national'. It is true that, as noted above, the International Convention on the Elimination of All Forms of Racial Discrimination takes 'racial discrimination' to include discrimination based on 'race, colour, descent, or national or ethnic origin'. But this is a stipulative definition rather than one flowing from the usual meaning of 'race' and is perhaps best considered as a definition for the purpose of that Convention. The *travaux préparatoires* of the Covenant on Civil and Political Rights confirm that 'ethnic' is the broadest term available.[44] 'Racial' and

represented as universal categories.' UN Doc E/CN.4/Sub.2/1987/5, 4 (Review of Further Developments in which the Sub-Commission has been Concerned, Report submitted by UNESCO).

[40] *Supra*, ch. 15.
[41] UN Doc E/CN.4/SR.369, para. 16.
[42] UN Doc E/2447, para. 53.
[43] Sohn, 'The Rights of Minorities', in Henkin (ed.), *The International Bill of Rights. The Covenant on Civil and Political Rights* (New York: Columbia University Press, 1981), 281. Note that the UN Working Group on Minorities includes 'national' minorities in its title: supra, ch. 15, n. 30. Despite this, the word 'national' in the latest text continues to be placed in square brackets, indicating the provisional nature of the description of relevant minorities.
[44] UN Doc E/CN.4/Sub.2/SR.48; E/CN.4/Sub.2/119, para. 31; Capotorti Report, Add. 2, para. 120. For a distinction between 'ethnic' and 'cultural' in a specific context, see the

'national' minorities are to be included in 'ethnic' minority. The association of 'ethnic' with 'culture' is borne out by the syntax of Article 27 which literally relates enjoyment of 'culture' to the ethnic group, though the fact that religion and language are also part of 'culture' makes it inappropriate to insist that only 'ethnic' minorities enjoy 'cultural' rights in.the broad sense.

The question of the specifically religious group or minority is to some extent *sui generis* in United Nations law making efforts. Some important aspects of this separate treatment are elaborated elsewhere.[45] Religion is, *inter alia*, mentioned in a number of articles in the Covenant,[46] including Article 18 which protects 'freedom of thought, conscience and religion'; this freedom includes the freedom to have or to adopt a religion or belief of choice, and freedom to manifest religion or belief. That freedom is not simply a matter of an individual's private relationship with the Deity: the freedom to manifest religion or belief 'in worship, observance, practice and teaching' also caters for the external, communal, and public aspects of religious freedom. There is an overlap with Article 27 which is directed essentially to the communal aspects of religious observance. However, the freedom to manifest one's religion described by Article 18 is a limited freedom: it 'may be subject only to such limitations as are prescribed by law and are necessary to protect public safety, order, health, or morals or the fundamental rights and freedoms of others'.[47] No such limitation is prescribed for the religious minority in Article 27. On the other hand, Article 18 is described in the Covenant as an article from which no derogation is permitted;[48] the same is not true of Article 27. The relationship between the two articles is dealt with further below.[49]

In the context of 'religion' in Article 27, the definition of religion is generally not a contentious matter, though the 'existence' of a religious group can be contentious.[50] The problem is rather one of the meaning to be attributed to the right of members of a minority 'to profess and practise their own religion'. 'Religion' itself was given a broad definition in Article 1(a) of the Draft Convention on the Elimination of all Forms of Religious Intolerance, 1967: 'religion or belief' includes theistic, non-theistic and atheistic beliefs.[51] In the context of a minority community, it is difficult,

comments by Sub-Commission member Whitaker, UN Doc E/CN.4/Sub.2/1985/SR.14, para. 20.

[45] *Infra*, ch. 20.
[46] Article 2 (non-discrimination); Article 4 (non-discrimination in taking measures of derogation); Article 18; Article 20 (prohibition of advocacy of national, racial, or religious hatred); Article 24 (rights of children); Article 26 (equality before the law).
[47] Article 18(4).   [48] Article 4(2).   [49] *Infra*, ch. 22.
[50] *Supra*, ch. 15: but see *infra*, n. 52.
[51] *Year Book of the United Nations 1967*, 488–90; Brownlie, *Basic Documents on Human Rights*, 111–15. The UN Declaration on the Elimination of all Forms of Intolerance based on Religion or Belief does not provide a definition of 'religion'. In her Study of the Current Dimensions of the Problems of Intolerance and of Discrimination on Grounds of Religion or

though not perhaps impossible, to imagine members of a community of atheists invoking Article 27. It may, however, be conceded that attacks on 'religious' minorities are as likely to be made in religiously based or 'theocratic' States as anywhere else. The persecution of religious minorities in the contemporary world ranges from the oppression practised against the practitioners of deistic religions in the Communist States, to that practised by the present regime in Iran against communities of believers in religions disfavoured by Shi'ite doctrine.[52] In between there is much evidence of oppression by States placed at various points along the religious and secular spectrum, from the persecution of Jehovah's Witnesses in Africa to the destruction of indigenous religions in Latin America.[53] It is to be predicted that many States will try to evade Article 27 by denying that its terms fit their situation. In the context of Article 18, the view expressed by Cyprus was that freedom of religion does not apply to creeds that kept their doctrine secret.[54] This view is unfounded on any literal reading of Article 18 and Article 27. Neither do the *travaux préparatoires* bear out any such reading. Syria distinguished between 'religion on the one hand and political movements and racist ideologies on the other'.[55] The intention was to distinguish between 'Jews' and 'Zionists'. This overlap between the religious and the political recalls similar controversies in the interpretation of the Genocide Convention—the fear was expressed then that genocide can be disguised by claims that a government is acting against its political enemies,

---

Belief, Special Rapporteur Odio Benito offered the following working definition of 'religion', UN Doc E/CN.4/Sub.2/1987/26, para. 19: ' "religion" can be described as "an explanation of the meaning of life and how to live accordingly". Every religion has at least a creed, a code of action and a cult'. For national views of the meaning of 'belief', see UN Doc E/CN.4/1986/37, 22; ibid. 37; A/C.3/SR.2012, 12.

[52] See, *inter alia*, *Religious Minorities in the Soviet Union*, Minority Rights Group Report No. 1, and *The Bahá'ís in Iran*, Minority Rights Group Report No. 51. In the Commission on Human Rights, the Observer for the Islamic Republic of Iran stated 'the Bahá'ís were not considered to be a religion in his own or in any other Islamic country . . . he did not believe that anyone shrewd enough to put together a few ideas and pose as a prophet should be said to have created a religion . . . the Bahá'ís were not a religion but a political group created in the mid-nineteenth century by the then colonial Powers . . . the group had committed numerous crimes against the Islamic Republic of Iran and other Islamic countries.' UN Doc E/CN.4/1988/SR.28/Add.1, paras. 72 and 75. See also UN Doc E/CN.4/Sub.2/1985/SR.18, para. 17, where an Egyptian representative characterized Bahá'ísm as a 'faith or opinion' and not a religion, since the Bahá'ís were Iranian by race and by culture.

[53] Minority Rights Group Report No. 29, *Jehovah's Witnesses in Central Africa*, and Report No. 15, *What Future for the Amerindians of South America?* Human Rights Commission Special Rapporteur Vidal D'Almeida Ribeiro, Report on Implementation of the Declaration on the Elimination of all Forms of Intolerance and of Discrimination based on Religion or Belief, UN Doc E/CN.4/1988/45, para. 6, refers to 'the nearly universal nature of the problem of intolerance and discrimination based on religion or belief' *Infra*, ch. 20: n. 21.

[54] Report of Cyprus to the Human Rights Committee, UN Doc CCPR/C1/Add.28 (1977), 12. Perhaps there is also room for future dispute as to differences between 'sects' or 'denominations' and religions. Since Article 27 also deals with 'minorities' and 'community' a reasonable answer to such disputes might be found in an examination of these terms.

[55] UN Doc CCPR/C/SR.26, para. 61 (1977).

not against a national, ethnical, racial or religious group, as such.[56] As with genocide, so also with regard to assaults on the cultural and religious identity of groups protected by Article 27.

There will, in most cases, be the closest identification between the 'linguistic' and the 'ethnic' minority. If 'ethnic' is to be defined in terms of culture instead of race, the fact that a distinct language is normally one of the main indicia of cultural unity will require that the ethnic group will enjoy 'linguistic' rights and vice versa. Most minorities would fall into this category. The relationship between language and culture drew the following comment from Lador-Lederer: 'The culture of a group depends on the reality and appropriateness of its language. Suffocation of language has always been part of policies of domination and the struggle for its maintenance was always a pre-condition for any political movement of liberation, whenever it might become possible.'[57] In some cases of minority protection, language has been seen as an important but secondary characteristic of a group rather than an independent characteristic. Vierdag's comment on the League of Nations regime is that: 'Few people were thought of as linguistic minorities without first of all being national minorities. Language was rather one of the main factors on the basis of which it was to be ascertained whether or not an individual belonged to, or a group of individuals constituted, a national minority.'[58] As with religion, the definition of language is not an important issue in the interpretation of Article 27, though some discrimination between 'dialects' and 'languages' may be required in order to apply the Covenant in a reasonable manner. But, given that a distinction is made in that case, the application of Article 27 is capable of giving rise to considerable problems in States where many indigenous languages are used. This was recognized in debates in the Sub-Commission and the Commission on Human Rights,[59] though it relates to the interpretation of the right of linguistic minorities to use their own language, rather than the question of what constitutes a linguistic minority.

[56] *Supra*, ch. 6. For other examples of blurring lines between religion and politics, characterizing activities of religious groups as impermissible political action, see Vidal D'Almeida Ribeiro, UN Doc E/CN.4/1988/45, 22–3. In the discussions on the UN Declaration on the Elimination of Religious Intolerance and Discrimination, Australia stated that the Declaration did not give individuals or groups the right to participate in political activities against the interests of the State, UN Doc A/C.3/36/SR.32, 13.

[57] Lador-Lederer, *International Group Protection, Aims and Methods in Human Rights* (Leiden: Sijthoff, 1968), 25.

[58] Vierdag, *The Concept of Discrimination in International Law with Special Reference to Human Rights*, 92–3.

[59] Capotorti Report, Add. 2.

Minorities

As to what constitutes a minority, there seems only to be general agreement
that there is no generally agreed definition.[60] None is offered by Article 27.
The lack of a 'universal' definition does not, however, prevent a description
of what is and has been understood by the terms, including contradictory
understandings and possible future interpretations. It may be possible to
distinguish a 'core' meaning together with a range of 'penumbral' applications, the appropriateness of which will depend upon subsequent practice in
the application of the Covenant. The Sub-Commission has been trying,
from its first session in 1947, to clarify the concept of 'minority'. A
memorandum prepared by the Secretary-General in 1950 offered the following opinion: 'the term "minority" cannot for practical purposes be
defined simply by interpreting the word in its literal sense. If this were the
case, nearly all the communities existing within a State would be styled
minorities, including families, social classes, cultural groups, speakers of
dialects, etc. Such a definition would be useless.'[61] The implied 'definition'
criticized by the Secretary-General is not wholly applicable to Article 27,
which qualifies the term 'minority(ies)' with 'ethnic, religious and linguistic',
but it does warn against defining the term in a manner which would reduce
it to an absurdity. The memorandum notes that 'minority' is 'frequently
used at present in a more restricted sense; it has come to refer mainly to a
particular kind of community, and especially to a national or similar community, which differs from the predominant group in the State'.[62] This
description contains two important elements of a definition: the notion of
community and the notion of difference from a predominant group. The
notion of community raises further questions in any definition, as the
memorandum itself recognized. But the communities in question were well
described by the Permanent Court of International Justice:

By tradition . . . the 'community' is a group of persons living in a given country or

[60] For a selection of views of States, see Capotorti Report, Add. 1. Recalling debate in the
UN Sub-Commission, the Canadian expert Deschênes (his definition is set out in the Introduction to this work) describes a chorus of negative reaction which may be borne in mind by those
who attempt definitions: 'Widely differing views had been expressed as to the advisability,
usefulness and need for a definition . . . Mr Khalifa . . . had expressed reservations . . . in his
view, it was an almost impossible task. Mr Mazilu saw no need to have a definition . . . Mr
Yimer, to paraphrase his words, thought that the game was not worth the candle . . . Mr Joinet
. . . had endorsed Mr Yimer's view . . . Mr Bossuyt had made a statement which . . . questioned
whether it was possible to arrive at a definition. Mr Bhandare did not think it was possible to
find a complete definition. Mrs Gu Yigie . . . considered that a definition was unnecessary and
Mr Dahak felt that it was preferable not to have one. Mr Al Khasawneh was sceptical . . . Mr
George took the view that it was an academic exerise . . . Mr Martínez Báez considered that, in
law, all definitions were dangerous.' UN Doc E/CN.4/Sub.2/1985/SR.16, para. 31.

[61] *Definition and Classification of Minorities*, Memorandum submitted by the Secretary-
General, UN Doc E/CN.4/Sub.2/85, 27 December 1949, para. 37.

[62] Ibid., para. 39.

locality, having a race, religion, language and tradition of their own and united by this identity of race, religion, language and tradition in a sentiment of solidarity, with a view to preserving their traditions, maintaining their form of worship, ensuring the instruction and upbringing of their children in accordance with the spirit and tradition of their race and rendering mutual assistance to each other.

The court went on to say: 'The existence of communities is a question of fact; it is not a question of law.'[63]

Although the Court is perhaps describing an idealized rather than a real community, it does point to an 'objective' definition of a minority based on the existence of facts. The Advisory Opinion also describes a 'subjective' factor, the 'sentiment of solidarity'. If there is no 'sentiment' directed towards preservation of identity, the provisions of Article 27 are irrelevant to the needs of group members. The group may 'exist' according to 'objective' criteria, but its members either do not see themselves as different from other inhabitants or citizens of the State, despite the 'objective' existence of such differences, or do not wish for these differences to be maintained or have legal recognition. In either case, the Human Rights associated with non-discrimination would seem to be more relevant to individuals concerned than differentiating rights, that is rights that specify (expressly or implicitly) the group as different from others. It is plausible to argue further: can a group which has no consciousness of itself as a group or community be said to 'exist' at all, despite the presence of 'objective' characteristics marking it off from other elements in a State's population? On this view, the 'subjective' aspect of group identity is fundamental to the existence of groups, irrespective of the rights claimed on behalf of members under Article 27 or otherwise. In his summary of the Sub-Commission's work on the definition of minority, Capotorti discerns three main elements: 'the difference between ethnic, religious and linguistic characteristics and traditions of the minority group and those of the rest of the population of the country, the "non dominant" position of the group in relation to the population as a whole, and the group's wish to preserve its special characteristics and remain true to its traditions'.[64] He regards the second and third elements as more contentious than the first which 'is not open to question'.[65]

At its fifth session, the Sub-Commission proposed the following definition of 'minority' to the Commission on Human Rights:

(i) the term minority includes only those non dominant groups in a population which possess and wish to preserve stable ethnic, religious or linguistic traditions or characteristics markedly different from those of the rest of the population; (ii) such minorities should properly include a number of persons sufficient by themselves to

---

[63] *PCIJ*, Ser. B. No. 17, 19, 21, 22 and 33 (Greco-Bulgarian Communities Case).
[64] Capotorti, 'The Protection of Minorities under Multilateral Agreements on Human Rights', 14.
[65] Ibid. 14–15.

preserve such traditions or characteristics; (iii) such minorities must be loyal to the State of which they are nationals.[66]

In relation to (iii), this is hardly a definitional characteristic of a minority in the sense of (i) and (ii); it is rather a statement of the attitude that should be displayed by a minority, but it depends upon the existence of a minority in the first place. The loyalty question has been prominent in United Nations debates on minorities; it is partly a survival of the perception of disloyal minorities operating to undermine their host States under Nazi inspiration. The reference to loyalty stems from a listing of various 'factors' by the Sub-Commission to be taken into account in establishing a definition—including '(d) The risk of taking measures that might lend themselves to misuse amongst a minority whose members' spontaneous desires might be disturbed by parties interested in fomenting among them a disloyalty to the State in which they live.' Whatever the justifications, making 'loyalty' a definitional characteristic of 'minority' means, paradoxically, that there is no such thing as a disloyal minority: a disloyal minority is not a minority at all! Thus, for the application of Article 27, a State might easily deny that minorities exist in its territories because their loyalty is not proven. The applicability of Article 27 would be a reward for good behaviour. The application of the Article can hardly be qualified in a way which subordinates it to announcements of political suspicion by State authorities. Irrespective of strict implications for a definition, insistence on proven loyalty means that minority groups wishing to invoke the Article to preserve their identity would, in effect, be placed under a duty to prove a higher sense of loyalty than the majority of citizens whose human rights are not qualified in this way. Bruegel remarks that 'Only someone who looks upon provisions for the protection of minorities as something reluctantly granted and conceded, as a kind of charity . . . would think of demanding a higher degree of loyalty from members of a minority.'[67] Perceptions of this nature have, despite his criticisms, been widespread.[68] The loyalty question is a genuine question to be confronted in the international protection of minority rights; unless some assurances are given, States will be reluctant to 'concede' more rights or implement existing ones. But in relation to a definition incorporating loyalty as a requirement, the statement by the Representative of the Philippines in the Third Committee of the General Assembly offers a convincing argument against it: loyalty is 'a political matter and a reference to it in a definition based upon ethnic, religious or linguistic traditions would, therefore, be out of place'. A State is entitled to protect itself against overt acts of treason, sedition, or rebellion 'but those were acts which anyone could commit

---

[66] Capotorti Report, Add. 1, paras. 3–4.

[67] Bruegel, 'A Neglected Field: The Protection of Minorities', *Revue des Droits de L'Homme/Human Rights Journal*, 4 (1971), 413, at 440.

[68] See citations, ibid. 439 ff.

irrespective of membership of an ethnic, religious or linguistic group'.[69] Better perhaps to recall the League of Nations' view in 1930: 'majorities must be just and generous and minorities must be loyal.'[70]

The Sub-Commission's definition also attempted some expansion of the notion of minority with references to 'non-dominance' and a vague numerical factor in points (i) and (ii) of the definition. 'Subjective' and 'objective' characteristics in the sense of feelings of solidarity and ethnic differences do not define minority exhaustively; the factor they omit and which the definition tries to grasp is some sense of how the differentiated self-conscious group relates to the remainder of the population. A minority must in some sense or other be 'less than' a majority. The Special Rapporteur on Minorities presented States with a provisional interpretation of minority, inviting their comments: 'an ethnic, religious or linguistic minority is a group numerically smaller than the rest of the population of the State to which it belongs and possesses cultural, physical and historical characteristics, a religion or a language different from those of the rest of the population'.[71] The final definition of minority (see also the Introduction to this work: Capotorti's definition is specific to Article 27) is: 'A group numerically inferior to the rest of the population of a State, in a non-dominant position, whose members—being nationals of the State—possess ethnic, religious or linguistic characteristics differing from those of the rest of the population and show, if only implicitly, a sense of solidarity, directed towards preserving their culture, traditions, religion or language'.[72]

While some States reiterated that there was no generally accepted definition, others expressed their approval of the provisional definition as a broad formula. Some disliked the term 'minority', preferring the terminology of their own constitutional law.[73] Article 27 does, however, use the term minority, and it is this which must be interpreted. There was a measure of agreement on 'objective' differences between a minority and other population elements. Some States insisted on a stronger version of this fact. Thus the Greek Government required that 'the characteristic features should be sufficiently distinctive for the group concerned to be clearly distinguishable as separate from the majority'.[74] Greece declared that Article 27 covered only persons belonging to 'separate or distinct groups, well defined and long established on the territory of a State'.[75] The emphasis placed by the Government of The Netherlands on sufficient distinctiveness was designed to exclude 'all sorts of gradual transitions and minor gradations', since

---

[69] UN Doc A/C.3/SR.401.
[70] Document of the League of Nations, 66, 1930, I, cited by Bruegel, 441.
[71] Capotorti Report, Add. 1, para. 9.
[72] Ibid., Add. 5, para. 10, taking account of many comments by States.
[73] See responses of the Governments of the Philippines, Romania, and Yugoslavia, Capotorti Report, Add. 1, para. 14.
[74] Ibid., para. 12.
[75] Ibid.

otherwise 'every country would be composed of minorities within the meaning of Article 27'.[76]

According to replies received from several governments, the subjective factor was an essential element of any definition. The factor of self-awareness was considered in some cases as important in conjunction with the attitude of other elements in a population: the Greek Government stated that the extent to which 'a minority actually feels itself to be a separate section of the community or is felt to be and *is perhaps treated as such* by others should also be taken into consideration for any interpretation of the term "minority" '.[77] Yugoslavia expressed doubts on placing too great an emphasis on subjective factors, although the manner in which the argument was phrased suggested a means by which the subjective factor could in some cases cheat minorities of their rights under Article 27:

> it would be inappropriate to ascribe too much importance to the need of a declaration of desire by the members of a minority in order to preserve their own national, ethnic, cultural and other features and to manifest their awareness of . . . affiliations to a particular minority, especially in the case of a minority which has for decades been subjected to the pressures of systematic assimilation and denationalisation.'[78]

This last part of Yugoslavia's argument, in so far as it suggests that Article 27 could be invoked in order to reverse a process, perhaps almost 'completed', of assimilation, will be unwelcome to those States committed to assimilation as national policy. Many States expressed doubts on Article 27 precisely on this point—it should not become part of, as it were, a consciousness raising exercise and either create new minorities or awaken others, like Lazarus, from the dead.

As to a minority being 'less than' a majority in whatever sense, Governments commented that the numerical factor was not important in a definition. The Netherlands took a logical approach: 'The definition of the term "minority" . . . rightly states that it should refer only to a group numerically smaller than the rest of the population of the State to which it belongs. . . . a bottom limit can also be assumed in the sense that there would have to be a group, so that an individual could not constitute a minority . . .'.[79] Some took a relative rather than an 'absolute' logical view; according to Yugoslavia 'the minority concept is relative, since in some localities, the population termed a minority can be greater in number than the rest of the population. Important on the whole is the fact that the number of people belonging to a particular minority group is not taken as the basic criterion

[76] Capotorti Report, Add. 1, para. 12.
[77] Ibid., para. 16.
[78] Ibid., para. 17.
[79] Ibid., para. 18. The question of a minimum number to constitute a minority was adverted to by Capotorti and Deschênes, the latter agreeing with the former that 'account must be taken of a reasonable proportionality between the efforts involved and the benefits to be derived therefrom'. UN Doc E/CN.4/Sub.2/1985/SR.13, para. 41.

for establishing their rights.'[80] All governments responding on the point considered that Article 27 was applicable to members of ethnic, religious, and linguistic groups in multinational societies—meaning that the Article goes beyond the 'classic' situation of a beleaguered minority faced with a dominating majority culture, that is in a 'nation State'; Article 27 applies even if various groups are formally equal in a State—where it could none the less occur that one of the groups, even if not numerically superior, achieved a predominant position with a tendency to oppress others and make them conform to itself. Alternatively, bearing in mind that 'non-dominant' does not necessarily mean subordinate, it can happen that in a multinational society none of the groups of which the nation is composed is in a position to dominate—Article 27 would still apply here to all groups wishing to preserve their distinctive character.

Although references to the dominant and non-dominant criterion are fairly sparse in the *travaux préparatoires*, they do not contradict the above assumptions that some criterion is needed. A number of references were made to African countries with dominant minorities.[81] These, it was argued, did not need the guarantees provided by the article. There was little suggestion in the discussion that 'dominant' minorities are not to be classed as minorities. But it is clear that they do not require the guarantees of Article 27; presumably if they lost their dominant position they could invoke Article 27. A number of delegates took the opportunity to denounce colonialism in describing dominant minorities.[82] One delegate made the point that the provisions should not be used by minorities to gain a position of dominance: the 'principle of majority rule was basic to democracy and a State in which the majority was ruled by a small imperialist minority could be nothing but a mockery of democracy'.[83] While this is correct if obvious, it seems only remotely connected with Article 27 and hardly a necessary consequence of utilizing or invoking its meagre ration of rights.

The Special Rapporteur's final definition describes minorities as nationals

---

[80] Para. 20. However, on the numerical factor, the fact that the number of persons belonging to a minority varies in relation to other groups in particular localities is not decisive of 'minority' status: the question is, rather, are they a minority in the State as a whole?

[81] See the remarks of the representatives of Tunisia, Guinea, Iraq, USSR, Mali, Libya, and the UAR, UN Doc A/C.3/SR.1103, paras. 48 and 53, A/C.3/SR.1104, paras. 8, 12, 21, 38 and 51. Deschênes (*supra*, n. 79), para. 42, makes a rather startling claim in his explanation of his proposed definition (*supra*, Introduction): 'Etymologically speaking, the minority should always constitute less than 50 per cent of the population of a State. It was argued . . . that the question was one not of etymology . . . and that a dominated group, even though it might be numerically larger than the dominant group, was in a minority situation and that the definition should therefore be sufficiently flexible to cover an oppressed majority. If that argument were accepted, however, the definition could be taken to cover virtually all minorities throughout the world, since most countries were living under minority rule . . . an oppressed majority needed not protection but liberation.' Deschênes, however, appears to be describing rule by unrepresentative political elites rather than rule by ethnic minorities.

[82] UN Doc A/C.3/SR.1104, paras. 31 and 34 (Venezuela and Saudi Arabia).

[83] Ibid., para. 21 (Mali).

of the State in which they reside. In the purely etymological sense, the term 'minority' makes no distinction between nationals and non-nationals. A 'distinctive', 'long established' community in the territory of a State, in a 'non-dominant' position, whose members wish to preserve distinctive characteristics, could as easily describe communities of foreigners as nationals. The 'protection of minorities' as an institution of international law was, however, regarded as separate from 'protection of aliens'. The latter acquired a developed customary law content; the former rested on treaty law as a primary protective apparatus. Under the League of Nations system, it was noted that whereas the 'human rights' elements in the treaties were secured to 'all inhabitants' of a State, the 'minority rights' element related to 'nationals belonging to minorities'. These provisions were supplemented by others facilitating and defining conditions for the acquisition and loss of nationality. The question as to what extent these distinctions are imported into Article 27 is not elucidated by the text of the Article.

Faithful to the traditions of human rights, the Covenant on Civil and Political Rights recognizes the universality of its listed rights—they apply to 'every human being', 'everyone', 'all persons'. A suggestion to replace 'persons' in Article 2(1) with 'nationals' or 'citizens' was not presssed.[84] The Covenant does not, however, set itself entirely against distinctions between aliens and nationals. Thus, Article 25 requires that 'every *citizen* shall have the right and the opportunity' to take part in public affairs, to vote, and to have equal access to public service 'in *his* country'. Articles 12 and 13 also reflect distinctions between aliens and nationals in relation to entry into a State and expulsion therefrom: 'no one shall be arbitrarily deprived of the right to enter *his own country*' and 'an *alien* lawfully in the territory of a State Party . . . may be expelled therefrom . . .' subject to certain conditions being satisfied. One writer concludes that 'a distinction between aliens and citizens is permitted only where explicitly provided' by the Covenant. Thus the equality of aliens and nationals generally recognized by the Covenant is not absolute.[85]

---

[84] UN Doc A.C.3/SR.1103, para. 38 (India).

[85] Ramcharan 'Equality and Non-Discrimination', in Henkin (ed.), *The International Bill of Rights. The Covenant on Civil and Political Rights*, 263. See, however, the views prepared by the Working Group on formulation of a 'comment' on Article 27 under Article 40 of the Covenant: 'The quality of a community as a minority under Article 27 does not necessarily depend on a formal bond of citizenship of its members with the host State. The text employs the word "persons" and does not speak of "citizens" as it does, for instance, in Article 25.' CCPR/C/SR.590, 2. No comment has yet been finalized by the Human Rights Committee on Article 27. However, the comment by the Committee on the position of aliens states: 'In those cases where aliens constitute a minority within the meaning of Article 27, they shall not be denied the right, in community with other members of their group, to enjoy their own culture, to profess and practise their own religion and to use their own language.' CCPR/C/21/Add. 5, 3 (9 April 1986). The Committee's formula is not helpful, since it refers back to the meaning of minority under Article 27. The reference to Article 25 is also not particularly helpful, since it deals with political rights where specific reference to citizens is reasonable; reference to 'persons' is equally reasonable in Article 25, even given an underlying concept of citizenship (or

If Article 27 does not exclude aliens from its purview explicitly, does it do so implicitly? The answer seems to be that aliens are *prima facie* excluded, for a number of reasons, some more convincing than others. Capotorti argues that aliens are excluded because Article 27 applies to groups settled down in the territory of a State. While this seems to be close to accepting Latin American arguments that minorities should be 'long established' on the territory of the State, it does stress the 'community' aspect of minorities and thus is not a negligible factor. But such a description does not dispose of the matter because there are examples of groups in various States capable of satisfying these requirements, the members of which are not nationals of their host State. A notable case relates to Uganda where many residents were allowed to retain their UK citizenship, notwithstanding the transition to independence of Uganda. There are other cases of this type which have been produced by the decolonization process. Any objective factors such as the above can only assist in the resolution of some, but not all, of the cases to which the article may apply. But if an appeal to etymology is inconclusive, an appeal to 'ordinary meaning' may not be. The historical tradition of distinguishing between 'aliens' and 'national minorities' has contributed to this restricted meaning of minority which still prevails among States. This assumption of a restrictive view is normally unspoken but is fundamental. Many States are unwilling to accept voluntary immigrants taking the State's nationality as being 'minorities'; *a fortiori* they are even less well disposed to accept the notion that *foreigners* are recipients of 'minority rights'. When coupled with the possible demands upon the State which may be made (*infra*, ch. 18) in consequence of an invocation of Article 27, the etymological approach reduces to absurdity. States can hardly be expected to promote foreign culture at their own expense; this obligation, if one exists in any legal sphere, would naturally devolve upon the home State of the group.

Thus, aliens under the Covenant are entitled to all human rights contained therein on the basis of non-discrimination in the enjoyment of such rights, but they do not have the 'identity' right proclaimed by Article 27; aliens may have rights associated with the 'prevention of discrimination' mandate of the Sub-Commission, but not rights for 'protection of minorities'. None of this reflects upon the customary law rights of aliens—or more accurately, of their national States.

Such assistance as can be given by the *travaux préparatoires* confirms the exclusion of aliens. At one stage Yugoslavia proposed the addition of a clause to Article 27 'without being on that account deprived of the rights

nationality). On the other hand, Deschênes has identified the question of aliens as a 'non-problem', that is, as not coming within the purview of a general definition of minorities, suitable for a declaration or convention. If these two lines of development proceed unaltered, the rules in the Covenant on aliens may differ from that in comparable (projected) international instruments. Deschênes comments: 'It would be most regrettable for an open conflict of interpretation to arise between the Human Rights Committee . . . and the Commission on Human Rights . . .', UN Doc E/CN.4/Sub.2/1985/31, para. 47.

enjoyed by other *citizens* of the same State',[86] clearly implying that the rights already covered were applied to 'citizens'. The intention was to spell out the fact that minorities were not to be discriminated against, in addition to the rights contemplated under the draft Article. The suggestion was not pressed by Yugoslavia; *inter alia*, its delegate appeared to recognize that 'non-discrimination' was already covered by Article 2 of the Covenant. Some delegates were more explicit. The view of Iraq before the Third Committee was that 'the obligations of a State within its own territory could only be towards its own citizens'.[87] It was in that sense that she understood the word 'persons' used in the Article. References to minorities contrasted with 'other citizens' were commonly made in debates on the Article. The Representative of Pakistan in the Third Committee considered that members of minorities were as much 'loyal citizens' as members of the majority of the community.[88] The need for minority members to be 'loyal citizens' was stressed by other delegations.[89] Thus, the, rarely explicit, view emerging from the *travaux* is that foreigners are not minorities, or not minorities for the purposes of Article 27. This also implies that, *inter alia*, stateless persons and, in many cases, migrant workers are not within Article 27. The former category is touched upon in Article 24(3) of the Covenant: 'Every child has the right to acquire a nationality' and is elsewhere dealt with by specific treaty provisions. As with nationals of other States, the generality of human rights provisions in international instruments apply to stateless persons. Migrant workers are outside Article 27 if they have not acquired the nationality of their host State, though again they may have the benefit of other international or municipal legal provisions. On acquiring nationality, they may be regarded as 'voluntary immigrants'—as it has already been noted, this is a controversial category of minority in the view of some States.[90]

---

[86] UN Doc A/C.3/SR.1103, para. 54.

[87] UN Doc A/C.3/SR.1104, para. 7. See also the view of Deschênes, (*supra*, n. 85), para. 44: 'when it comes to defining the rights of minorities, the first duty of a State is to its own citizens. To the others, it owes only courtesy . . .'. Elles agrees, *International Provisions Protecting the Human Rights of Non-Citizens*, UN Doc E/CN.4/Sub.2/392/Rev.1, para. 177 at para. 180.

[88] UN Doc A/C.3/SR.1104, para. 17.

[89] Meetings 1103 and 1104 of the 3rd Committee.

[90] For reflections on the definition of minorities and apartheid, see the Introduction to the present work.

17. 'Persons Belonging to Such Minorities . . . in Community with The Other Members of Their Group . . .'

The reference to 'persons belonging to' minorities was inserted at the third session of the United Nations Sub-Commission to replace 'minorities' *simpliciter*.[1] In the opinion of the Sub-Commission member proposing the change, minorities as such were not subjects of the law, whereas persons belonging to minorities could be defined in legal terms. To maintain the idea of a group, the words 'in community with the other members of their group' were inserted after 'shall not be denied the right'.

Thus, whereas 'rights of minorities' is normally used in legal discourse, in the context of Article 27 the preferred phrase should be 'rights of persons belonging to minorities'. The reduction of 'minorities' to 'persons belonging to minorities' assimilates the rights to the other human rights recognized in the Covenant which are the rights of individuals and not groups.[2] The major exception in the Covenant on Civil and Political Rights and its 'twin' Covenant on Economic, Social, and Cultural Rights is self-determination which is described as a collective right belonging to 'all peoples'.[3] The rights in Article 27, however, are a hybrid between individual and collective rights because of the 'community' requirement: the right of a member of a minority is not exercised alone; enjoyment of culture, practice of religion, and use of language presupposes a community of individuals endowed with similar rights. The rights may, therefore, be described as benefiting individuals but requiring collective exercise.[4] There is a similar 'community' aspect to the freedom to manifest religion or belief which applies 'either individually

---

[1] Report of the Sub-Commission, UN Doc E/CN.4/358, paras. 39–48.

[2] Applying to 'every human being', 'everyone', 'all persons', etc. The UN Working Group on Minorities deals with the rights of persons belonging to minorities, and the text of a declaration on minorities agreed so far is, similarly, a text on the rights of persons. However, in the substantive articles, 'persons belonging to' remains in square brackets: UN Doc E/CN.4/1988/36.

[3] Common Article 1 of the UN Covenants on Human Rights.

[4] Dinstein, 'Collective Human Rights of Peoples and Minorities'; Robinson, 'International Protection of Minorities. A Global View', 61. Crawford writes that Article 27 'hovers between being a mere extrapolation from the individual rights of members of a minority group, and being a genuinely "collective" right': 'The Rights of Peoples: "Peoples" or "Governments" ' ', in Crawford (ed.), *The Rights of Peoples*, 55 at 60.

or in community with others'. This does not apply only to minorities, but to all individuals and groups. However this freedom is subject to certain limitations;[5] Article 27 is not so limited, so that, *ex facie*, the religious practices of minorities are endowed with a greater degree of autonomy by the Covenant. The difference may, however, in certain circumstances be illusory, as Article 18 is a 'non-derogable'[6] right according to Article 4(2) of the Covenant, whereas Article 27, as noted previously, is not entrenched. Thus, in neither case is the community right supreme in the 'hierarchy' of human rights.[7]

A purported reason behind the introduction of the words 'persons belonging to' was to avoid giving minorities an 'international personality' sufficient, for example, to allow them to vindicate their rights before the Human Rights Committee. The reporting and 'communications' (complaints) procedures are premised on reports and complaints by States Parties to the Covenant.[8] The Optional Protocol to the Covenant provides for communications to the Committee from individuals who claim to be victims of violations of human rights.[9] The implementation procedures reflect that antinomy of State and individual which dominates the substantive aspects of the Covenant. 'Communities' as such, whether in respect of Articles 18 or 27, are devoid of *locus standi* in the Covenant structure.

The Special Rapporteur adduces historical reasons, *inter alia*, for the concern about the 'international personality' of minorities,[10] noting that the theory of an international personality of minorities developed consequent on the establishment of the League of Nations system 'mainly owing to the fact that the right of petition was granted not only to members of minority groups but also to the groups themselves'.[11] However, the language of the treaties of 1919 to 1920 was consistent with the desire to regard the individual members of minorities, not the groups themselves, as the focus of protection.[12] Too much need not have been read into the petition procedure

---

[5] *Infra*, ch. 22.

[6] According to Article 4, derogations from the obligations undertaken by States Parties are possible in time of a proclaimed public emergency threatening the life of the nation to the extent strictly required by the exigencies of the situation, provided that the measures of derogation are not inconsistent with other obligations under International Law and do not 'involve discrimination solely on the ground of race, colour, sex, language, religion or social origin'.

[7] While human rights are premised on a basic concept of equality, there is a practical hierarchy of rights in the various instruments based on non-derogability.

[8] See generally, Part IV of the Covenant.

[9] See the Preamble and Article 1 of the Optional Protocol for reference to 'victims' of Human Rights violations. The procedures are comprehensively described in Ghandhi, 'The Human Rights Committee and the Right of Individual Communication', *supra*, ch. 14, n. 44.

[10] Capotorti Report, Add. 2, paras. 125 ff.

[11] Ibid., para. 126; also, Monaco, 'Minorités Nationales et la Protection Internationale des Droits de l'Homme', *in Réne Cassin Amicorum Discipulorumque Liber*, vol. I (Paris: Editions A. Pedone, 1969), 175.

[12] *Supra*, ch. 3.

in any case. Strictly speaking, the petitions were regarded as 'sources of information' only and did not have the status of a claim with the correlative capacity in the petitioner to be regarded as party to a case against a respondent State.[13] Furthermore, petitions did not even have to emanate from a minority. As the 1929 Reports of the Committee of Three on Protection of Minorities by the League of Nations noted, petitions 'in order to be accepted . . . need not necessarily emanate from the minority concerned. Petitions from persons or organisations which not only did not belong to the minority concerned, but did not even belong to the country referred to in the petition have often been declared acceptable, provided the source was not anonymous or unauthenticated.'[14] The liberality of this procedure could hardly in itself have the effect of investing all and sundry with 'international personality'.

The notion of 'belonging to a minority' also raises some important issues for the style and balance of post-war minorities law: how is membership of a minority to be determined, and can such membership be renounced? In relation to the first, there are a number of possibilities which flow from the definition of minority. Membership of a group may be defined by law but this cannot, for reasons described above,[15] be regarded as disposing of the matter for purposes of international law. States adopt a variety of methods to make such determinations. Some prefer a purely subjective criterion. The Government of Romania's reply to Special Rapporteur Capotorti stated that: 'Each citizen establishes by his free consent his membership of a nationality, his mother tongue and his religion. This decision is not subject to any administrative control.'[16] The courts in Austria use both 'objective' and 'subjective' criteria but give preference to 'subjective' factors in case of doubt.[17] On the other hand, many countries prefer 'objective' criteria. Thus, for example, in Venezuela, the national census classifies a person as indigenous if he habitually speaks a native language of his own or if his way of life is so obviously aboriginal that he could not be classified with the peasant population.[18] It seems logical to premise membership of a minority on the definition of minority, incorporating subjective and objective criteria. While

---

[13] Report of the Committee of Three, 6 June 1929 on the Protection of Minorities by the League of Nations, *LNOJ Sp. Supp. No. 73* (1929): 'The authors of the treaties deliberately rejected any proposal which would give countenance to the conception of any minority forming a separate corporation within the State. If the [League] Council decided that a petition relating to the treatment of minorities [should] be communicated to its members, it made it clear that it regarded these petitions solely as sources of information, and that the only parties to action which might arise therefrom would be the Government concerned and the Governments of individual Members of the Council or the Council itself'. See also Nørgaard, *The Position of the Individual in International Law*, ch. ix.

[14] *Report of the Committee of Three*, Part II, IV(*a*).

[15] *Supra*, ch. 16.

[16] Capotorti Report, Add. 1, para. 59.

[17] Ibid., para. 60.

[18] Ibid., para. 61.

some States take a generous view of membership, allowing it to be determined by subjective preference uncontrolled by objective criteria, this cannot be said to be demanded by Article 27. In so far as the rights set out in Article 27 are rights for only some of a State's nationals in many cases, it can hardly, in logic and in fairness to the State, be regarded as a right of individuals to be included in a special category with which they have no obvious connection. If States permit this, they are exceeding their obligations. This does not mean that, apart from any subjective preference, unanimity of 'objective' factors will be readily discovered in practice. Criteria such as the language used by an individual, or his name or 'origin', can be difficult to apply in such a manner as to assign him with certainty to any particular group. The mother tongue of an individual may be that of the people among whom he lives, not of the group to which he 'feels' himself to belong. The name of an individual could merely be an indicator of the historical affinity of his ancestors with a particular ethnic group. In cases where objective factors do not give a clear picture of affiliation, the subjective factors will assume increased relevance, and vice versa. In many cases, the combination of approaches will give a clear answer, so that to deny membership of a group will violate the Article—as would denial of the existence of the group itself.

It is submitted that, conversely, the renunciation of the rights accorded by the Article is itself a right of individuals; in the nature of things, this can only be an act of personal choice. An individual cannot be compelled to embrace membership of a minority. If individuals wish to renounce identity as a member of the group, they are free to do so. To prevent this, and coerce into group membership, would violate a cluster of rights recognized as fundamental by the Covenant. Article 18, for example, includes 'freedom to have or to adopt a religion or belief of his choice'. Article 18(2) provides 'No one shall be subject to coercion which would impair his freedom to have or to adopt a religion or belief of his choice.' Freedom of expression and freedom of association are also relevant. Article 26 provides for equality before the law, and all persons 'are entitled without any discrimination to the equal protection of the law'. Compelling an individual to be associated with a minority culture would be discrimination against that individual.

The balance between 'minority rights' and 'individual rights' is an aspect of a larger question,[19] but it is resolved in the Covenant in favour of individual rights. The minority's 'claim' on individuals, even in the case of a minority in difficulties of self-preservation, has only a secondary or subordinate importance. The minority does not mediate between the individual and the State; it has no rights as such to preserve its identity. The

[19] In broadest terms, it is the question of the place of 'communities' other than the State in modern international law. See the introductory section of this work, and Van Dyke, *Human Rights, Ethnicity, and Discrimination*.

individualistic and libertarian focus of human rights law is evident here: to adopt Maine's terms, 'contract' is preferred to 'status' in relations between the individual and the minority.[20]

---

[20] Maine, *Ancient Law* Pollock edn. (London, 1930), 181. The tension between purely 'individual' and 'collective' approaches to minority protection has created difficulties for the Human Rights Commission's Working Group on the rights of minorities: 'the fundamental question of whether to follow an individual or collective rights approach remains unresolved': UN Doc E/CN.4/1988/36, para. 16.

18. 'Shall not be Denied the Right . . . to Enjoy Their Own Culture, to Profess and Practise Their Own Religion, or to Use Their Own Language'

The above phrases describe the State's obligations to its minorities. The phrase 'shall not be denied the right' contrasts with the language used elsewhere in the Covenant. The language of the other Articles is more positive in tone: everyone 'shall have the right' or 'has the right' is normal usage throughout the Covenant as in 'Everyone shall have the right to freedom of thought, conscience and religion' (Article 18(1)) or 'Every child has the right to acquire a nationality' (Article 24(3)). Express prohibitions of governmental or state activity are equally strongly phrased as in 'No one shall be subjected to torture or to cruel, inhuman or degrading treatment or punishment . . .' (Article 7). The 'stronger' phraseology applies to collective as well as individual rights: thus, all peoples 'have the right' of self-determination according to Article 1 of the Covenant. The significance of this difference of language is not clear, and different conclusions have been drawn from it. Robinson comments on Article 27, the tone of which is substantially determined by its negative phrasing, that it represents 'a classic example of restrictive toleration of minorities'.[1] Modeen's comment is that Article 27 represents no real advance in the international protection of minorities, *inter alia*, the minority States 'are not required to enter into any commitment to protect their minorities, beyond avoiding hindrances on the minority group employing their own language and developing their own culture'.[2] Verdoodt comments that 'the assimilationist countries of America are still on their guard, and they have been reinforced by the massive influx of African and Asian delegates [to the United Nations] representing countries largely poly-ethnic and . . . multi-lingual, who are far more concerned with mobilising their energies around a common pole than with giving positive help to the development of each linguistic group.' In his view, this fact 'explains the negative wording of Article 27'.[3] On such interpreta-

---

[1] Robinson, 'International Protection of Minorities: A Global View', 89.
[2] Modeen, *The International Protection of National Minorities in Europe*, 108.
[3] Verdoodt, 'Ethnic and Linguistic Minorities and the United Nations', 70–1.

tions States need only allow minorities to exercise their rights in freedom, there is no obligation to do anything to act positively to protect minority cultures; in a 'contest' between a majority and a minority culture, the State is a mere spectator, maintaining its distance, not obliged to render assistance to the weaker party in an unequal struggle.

The suggestion of a limitation on the State's obligations towards minorities is borne out to a large extent by the *travaux préparatoires*. In the Third Committee of the General Assembly, the delegate of Mexico argued that it should be drafted 'in a positive, and not, as at present, in a negative way'. Thus, it 'was not sufficient that minorities should merely "not be denied" certain rights; they should be given special protection since they often needed it'.[4] This criticism of the draft Article implies that the delegate accepted that the negative interpretation was the prevailing one. This is reflected in the favourable reception accorded to the draft Article by the Representative of the USSR, whose interpretation appears to have been that it allowed minority groups to preserve their own culture,[5] again implying that the approach was substantially one of *laissez faire*. The feeling among the majority of delegates to the Third Committee was that the draft Article provided represented a minimum rather than a maximum of rights for minorities,[6] a situation which a number of States apparently found acceptable.[7]

The total drafting record of the Covenant reveals that suggestions and amendments more demanding of State action to support minorities were rejected. For example, in discussions in the Commission on Human Rights,[8] the negative phrasing was criticized on the grounds that the phrase 'shall not be denied' was devoid of meaning and would probably have no effect. It was suggested, therefore, that the article should oblige the State to adopt special legislative measures to guarantee the enjoyment of certain rights. This was rejected by other speakers who pointed out that in relation to States which have accepted a duty of non-discrimination against minorities, the only new duty represented by Article 27 was that of tolerance. It was widely assumed that the text submitted by the Sub-Commission would not place States and Governments under the obligation, for example, of providing special schools for persons belonging to linguistic minorities. The rejected draft Article of the Soviet Union has already been quoted.[9] To similar effect was the, later withdrawn, draft Article submitted by Yugoslavia, part of which proposed that

Every person shall have the right to show freely his membership of an ethnic or

---

[4] *ECOSOC OR*, 16th Session, Supp. No. 8, UN Doc E/2447, para. 55.
[5] Ibid.
[6] For opinions of jurists, see *infra*, ch. 25.
[7] See the remarks of the Austrian delegate, E/2447, para. 39.
[8] UN Doc E/CN.4/SR.368.
[9] *Supra*, ch. 15.

linguistic group, to use without hindrance the name of his group, to learn the language of this group and to use it in public or private life, to be taught in this language, as well as the right to cultural development together with other members of this group . . .[10]

The references to use of the language in public life, to being taught in the language of the group, as well as the reference to cultural development, manifest a different appreciation of the respective rights and duties of minority and State than is revealed in Article 27, and would have necessitated legislative action on the part of States and perhaps also financial support for the teaching of languages and the 'development' of minority culture.[11]

The Special Rapporteur on Minorities, however, disagrees with the restrictive interpretation and presents a more positive view. From the standpoint of the effective, practical exercise of rights, he argues that neither 'the non-prohibition of the exercise of . . . [such rights] . . . by persons belonging to minority groups, nor the constitutional guarantees of freedom of expression and association are sufficient for the effective implementation of the right of members of minority groups to preserve and develop their own culture'.[12] Adequate cultural development requires considerable human and financial resources, and minorities will rarely possess them. Similar remarks apply to community languages and religions with undiminished force. The implementation of the rights, to have anything but a purely theoretical significance, will thus call for 'active and substantial intervention by States', and a 'passive attitude on the part of the latter would render such rights inoperative'.[13]

The relationship between the rights in the Covenant also suggests the positive view. The point here is that, unless Article 27 is given a more forceful content, it adds nothing to the Covenant. Freedom of thought, conscience, and religion is already protected by Article 18, and there is also, for example, as far as language and culture are concerned, the provision on freedom of expression in Article 19.[14] To have any significance at all in the spectrum of rights provided by the Covenant, Article 27 must again be invested with more than a merely passive significance. A related point is that the right set out in Article 27 bears some resemblance to 'economic and social' rights, even though it is set out in a covenant on 'civil and political' rights. The conventional distinction made between the two categories of

[10] *ECOSOC OR*, 16th Session, Supp. No. 8, UN Doc E/2447, para. 55.
[11] *Supra*, ch. 15.
[12] Capotorti Report, Add. 2, para. 132.
[13] Ibid., para. 136.
[14] This includes the right to hold opinions without interference (Article 19(1)), and the freedom to seek, receive, and impart information and ideas of all kinds (Article 19(2)). The exercise of the right is deemed to be subject to special duties and responsibilities and may be restricted by operation of law to respect the rights or reputations of others, or to protect national security, public order, (ordre public), public health, or morals (Article 19(3)).

rights is that whereas civil and political rights require the State to refrain from certain types of action against individuals, an expression of the *status negativus libertatis*,[15] economic, social, and cultural rights require the State to act positively on behalf of the right holders. Besides the question of normative content, the two kinds of rights are usually complemented by different mechanisms: civil and political rights are 'secured', perhaps through judicial means; economic and social rights are 'achieved' or 'promoted' through incremental modifications to domestic law and practice, in a manner not so obviously susceptible to judicial process.[16] The resemblance to this second kind of right is clearest, Capotorti suggests, in the field of culture, thus, the 'right of members of minorities to enjoy their own culture in community with the other members of their group seems to be involved not merely with freedom of expression, but with the right to education and the right to take part in cultural life, which are provided for under the Covenant on Economic, Social and Cultural Rights'[17] (Articles 13 to 15). The conclusion is that 'at least in the field of culture, the States are under a duty to adopt specific measures to implement Article 27 in the same way as they are in the case of the provision on cultural rights under the Covenant guaranteeing them.'[18] Article 27, therefore, contains a programmatic element, a goal to be achieved. Thus, from the standpoints of the principle of effectiveness, the logic of the Covenant structure, and the nature of the rights themselves, the Special Rapporteur concludes that Article 27 constitutes a positive and not a negative obligation for States Parties.

This logical and literal reading of Article 27 is persuasive. By comparison, most other writers have given the full implications of the article scant attention.[19] It may be remarked in the first place that the siting of a particular human rights norm in a 'civil and political rights' context does not completely determine the character of the obligation generated by it. The distinction between the two kinds of rights referred to above describes theoretical models of rights rather than the contents of existing treaties. Many instruments contain a mixture of both types of rights and the Covenant on Civil and Political Rights is no exception.[20] While the generality of rights confirms to the model and requires the State to abstain

---

[15] Nedjati, *Human Rights under the European Convention* (Amsterdam: North Holland, 1978), 12–13, 237–8; Thornberry, 'Poverty, Litigation and Fundamental Rights—A European Perspective', *ICLQ*, 29 (1980), 250.

[16] Thornberry, ibid., 257–8; Schwelb, in *International Protection of Human Rights: Nobel Symposium 7* (1968), 103.

[17] Capotorti, 'The Protection of Minorities under Multilateral Agreements on Human Rights', 22.

[18] Ibid.

[19] Compare, for example, the works cited in nn. 1, 2 and 3 above.

[20] The Universal Declaration of Human Rights is 'mixed' in this sense, though it is not described as a declaration of 'civil and political rights', or 'economic, social, and cultural rights'. The European Convention on Human Rights *ex facie* contains rights that would normally be described as 'economic, social and cultural' such as the right to education (First Protocol to the Convention).

from certain kinds of infringement on individual freedom, others would appear to require action by States. Thus, whereas the right of the individual to be free from torture[21] requires that, essentially, the State's officials refrain from this activity, such rights as 'recognition everywhere as a person before the law'[22] or 'the right to form and join trade unions',[23] or 'the right to acquire a nationality'[24] will require, even though this is not specified, more than mere inaction on the part of States if they are to be effective. The 'promotional' or 'positive' requirement is perhaps most marked in the case of the right of self-determination, which finds a home in both the Covenant on Civil and Political Rights and its 'twin' Covenant on Economic, Social, and Cultural Rights. In the text, whereas by Article 1(1) and 1(2), peoples 'freely determine their political status' and 'freely dispose of their natural wealth and resources', by Article 1(3), States have the duty, *inter alia*, 'to *promote* the realisation of the right of self-determination', which involves positive action by States, albeit of an unspecified nature.[25]

The distinction between the two kinds of right is not watertight in living conventions. This has been jurisprudentially demonstrated by the European Court of Human Rights in the *Johanna Airey Case*.[26] The European Convention on Human Rights is basically a charter of civil and political rights, but in this case such a basic civil right as access to a court was interpreted as having 'social and economic' implications. The prohibitive cost of access in the particular circumstances of the application violated Article 6(1) of the Convention which reads: 'In the determination of his civil rights and obligations or of any criminal charge against him, everyone is entitled to a fair and public hearing within a reasonable time by an independent and impartial tribunal established by law . . .'. Accordingly, the court indicated that positive action by the Republic of Ireland was required in this case to meet the Convention requirement of effective and not simply theoretical access to the courts, though it left the State a free choice of the means towards this end. In a paragraph which could apply equally to the United Nations Covenant, the European Court stated that whilst the Convention

sets forth what are essentially civil and political rights, many of them have implications of a social or economic nature . . . the mere fact that an interpretation of the Convention may extend into the sphere of social and economic rights should not be a decisive factor against such an interpretation; there is no water-tight division separating that sphere from the field covered by the Convention.[27]

[21] See Article 7 of the Covenant.
[22] Article 16.
[23] Article 22(1).
[24] Article 24(3).
[25] With specific reference to the meaning of self-determination in the UN Covenants, see Cassese, 'The Self-Determination of Peoples', in Henkin (ed.), *The International Bill of Rights*, 92.
[26] European Court of Human Rights, Judgment, 9 October 1979.
[27] *Airey Case*, Judgment, para. 16.

Whether such an interpretation is correct in relation to a particular right is a practical question to be answered by examination of the right itself and not one for abstract theory. These remarks apply particularly well to Article 27. Thus it would seem possible to derive a 'positive' element in relation to minority rights from the provision of the Covenant on Civil and Political Rights, without invoking, as the Special Rapporteur has done, the Covenant on Economic, Social and Cultural Rights, though the latter may legitimately assist the argument.[28] The whole point of inserting a 'minorities' article in both past and present treaties on the subject is to secure for members of groups a real and not fictitious equality with members of the majority in a State; equality in fact as well as equality in law. If no adaptations are made by the State to cater for minorities, the 'non-dominant' groups will ultimately be required against their will to surrender to dominant groups. While this is not a displeasing prospect to many States, particularly those involved in contemporary exercises in 'nation building', it ignores the claims of minorities to their individuality. The provisions of Article 27 may be limited in effect, but they do have the purpose of assisting the groups to maintain their identity, unless the members of minorities wish to surrender that identity into a larger grouping.[29]

The United Nations Covenant contains both a prohibition against discrimination and a minorities article. A memorandum prepared by the United Nations Secretary-General explained the difference between the two concepts as follows:

discrimination implies any act or conduct which denies to certain individuals equality of treatment with other individuals because they belong to particular groups in society. To prevent discrimination, therefore, some means must be found to suppress or eliminate inequality of treatment . . . aiming at the prevention of any act or conduct which implies that an unfavourable distinction is made between individuals solely because they belong to certain categories or groups of society . . . The protection of minorities, on the other hand . . . requires positive action: concrete service is rendered to the minority group, such as the establishment of schools in which education is given in the native tongue of the members of the group. Such measures are . . . also inspired by the principle of equality.[30]

The memorandum illustrates the points made with the example of a child receiving its education in a language which is not its mother tongue, as in

---

[28] The Covenant on Economic, Social, and Cultural Rights shares much of the history of the Covenant on Civil and Political Rights and the two may be regarded as treaties *in pari materia* for purposes of interpretation. Pechota, in Henkin (ed.), *International Bill of Rights*, at p. 43, writes that the 'common ground and the identity of purpose, as well as the similarity of many provisions in the final drafts, make the Covenants complementary and mutually reinforcing. The two Covenants . . . form a single body of new international law on human rights'.

[29] The requirements of true equality between minority and majority were summed up by the Permanent Court of International Justice in the *Case of Minority Schools in Albania, supra*, ch. 3, n. 17.

[30] *The Main Types and Causes of Discrimination*, UN Sales No. 49.XIV.3, paras. 6 and 7.

the case with children of many minority groups across the world. In one sense of equality, formal equality, the child is like all the children of the State, educated through the dominant language. But on the alternative interpretation of equality, equality in fact, the child's equal rights are being violated by such treatment. The latter concept of equality is the relevant one in the case of minority rights.[31] The Sub-Commission on Prevention of Discrimination has advanced a similar distinction between the two notions;[32] in fact, as noted elsewhere,[33] it conceives the two aspects of its mandate 'prevention of discrimination' and 'protection of minorities' in precisely these terms. The provisions of Article 27 do not simply duplicate the anti-discrimination provisions of the Covenant; they have a more extensive significance in that in the interests of true equality between members of minority groups and other citizens, they are measures specially directed at a particular population group or groups in order to assist them to maintain their identity. It follows that the rights in Article 27 are additional to, and not a substitute for, guarantees of non-discrimination. The Covenant prohibits distinction on the ground of 'race, colour, sex, language, religion, political or other opinion, national or social origin, property, birth or other status'[34] and these are applicable *ipso facto* to members of minority groups to the same extent as to other sections of the population. The distinction between the two concepts is indicative of differing normative requirements.

The events subsequent to the publication of the Capotorti Report do not throw much light on what reading is to be given to these provisions of Article 27. There is no unanimity of approach, though the particular point has not figured largely in discussions in the Human Rights Committee or elsewhere. The major contentious point remains that of the existence or non-existence of minorities. States denying their existence are hardly likely to press for a 'positive' interpretation of Article 27, although of course they may do so provided it is accepted that the article applies only to other States. Some States, however, that basically deny the existence of any minorities on their territory occasionally report apparently very favourable measures on behalf of groups which go beyond non-discrimination, though no general pattern emerges. Thus in relation to indigenous groups, the Government of Ecuador responded to the Human Rights Committee that efforts were being made to maintain and preserve their cultural values. It was declared to be government policy to 'promote the culture and language of the indigenous communities and their participation in society'.[35]

Responses to Article 3 of the first Yugoslav Draft Declaration which dealt with this point have also been mixed; Article 3 read:

---

[31] Ibid.
[32] UN Doc E/CN.4/52, Section V.
[33] *Supra*, ch. 12.   [34] Article 2(1).
[35] *GAOR*, 33rd Session, Supp. No. 4, UN Doc A/33/40, para. 572.

For the purpose of realising the conditions of full equality and all-round development of minorities, as collectivities, and members of minorities, it is essential to
undertake measures which will enable them freely to express their characteristics,
develop their culture, education, language, traditions and customs and to participate
on an equitable basis in the cultural, social, economic and political life of the country
in which they live.

This article was received favourably by some governments. Thus, it was
approved by Finland which in its response mentioned its acceptance of the
Capotorti interpretation of Article 27 on this point.[36] However, Greece did
not accept the Capotorti interpretation of Article 27, preferring a restrictive
interpretation and declaring itself sceptical of the usefulness of any Declaration.[37] The United Kingdom in its comments on another article of the draft
also expressed a limited view of the duties of the State.[38] The differences in
interpretation of Article 27, as implying positive or negative duties, do not
exhaust the difficulties of the phraseology under discussion. Whether or not
one accepts the Capotorti interpretation, the meaning of the right of members of minorities 'to enjoy their own culture', to 'profess and practise' their
own religion, and 'to use their own language' may call for elucidation in
specific contexts. These are not phrases of the utmost precision, and would
appear to open up wide areas of discretion even among States accepting a
positive obligation to support minority rights. This is, of course, a problem
with the article as a whole which has a 'generic' or 'framework' character
deriving from its attempt, however limited, to deal with a question which
manifests itself in different ways in different continents and nations.[39] Supporters of a 'positive' view of the article concede that its letter is in some
senses 'ambiguous'.[40]

It is submitted that the positive view expressed by the Special Rapporteur
is the correct one. This entails two consequences: (1) the State should not
interfere with whatever action a minority takes on its own initiative to
preserve and strengthen its culture, religion, and language—this consequence is of necessity admitted even by those who take the restrictive view;
and (2) the State should, in the spirit of true equality between majority and

---

[36] UN Doc E/CN.4/1298, 6: 'Although the formulation of Article 27 . . . seems to imply that
a purely permissive attitude on the part of the State would be sufficient in respect of the rights
envisaged in that article, the wider interpretation presented by the Special Rapporteur to the
effect that it requires active and sustained measures from the States, is justified.'

[37] The words 'shall not be denied the right' seemed to imply that 'the obligations of States
would be limited to permitting the free exercise of the rights of persons belonging to . . .
minorities', UN Doc E/CN.4/1298, 11(g). Article 392) of the revised draft declaration provides
that: 'All States [which have not yet done so] shall [take measures to create favourable
conditions to enable [persons belonging to] minorities to freely] . . . express their characteristics
. . .': the unresolved nature of this is evident: UN Doc E/CN.4/1988/36.

[38] UN Doc E/(N.4/1298,) 17, para. 3.

[39] Generally, Thornberry, 'Is There a Phoenix in the Ashes? International Law and Minority
Rights'.

[40] Capotorti, *supra*, n. 17.

minority, take such measures as are necessary in order to assist the minority to preserve its values. The specific result of these two requirements will vary in different situations; the more a minority is able to fulfil the task of retaining its essential identity through its own resources, the less onerous will be the duties devolving upon the State party. The standard of obligation is necessarily a relative one, sufficient perhaps to criticize or support the general direction of States' efforts, though insufficient to provide a ready answer to many questions of detail. Uniform conduct is not required; legislation which follows a pattern developed in other States may not be sufficient to meet a State's obligations; alternatively, it may exceed them.

19. Enjoyment of Culture

Contemporary indications from legal instruments as to what cultural rights entail are found in Articles 13 to 15 of the Covenant on Economic, Social, and Cultural Rights. By Article 13 the States parties 'recognize the right of everyone to education', which 'shall be directed to the full development of the human personality and the sense of its dignity, and shall strengthen the respect for human rights and fundamental freedoms', as well as, *inter alia*, promoting 'tolerance and friendship among all nations and all racial, ethnic or religious groups'. The States parties also agree to respect the liberty of parents 'to ensure the religious and moral education of their children in conformity with their own convictions'. Article 13(4) provides that the article is not to be construed 'so as to interfere with the liberty of individuals and bodies to establish and direct educational institutions' conforming to minimum standards set down by the State. Article 15 provides for the right of everyone 'to take part in cultural life', and 'to enjoy the benefits of scientific progress and its applications'.[1] Furthermore, Article 15(2) provides that steps are to be taken by States to promote 'the development and thediffusion of science and culture'. The latter Article may be compared with Article 27(1) of the Universal Declaration of Human Rights: 'Everyone has the right freely to participate in the cultural life of the community, to enjoy the arts and to share in scientific advancement and its benefits.' The Universal Declaration also lists the right to education as a fundamental human right, a 'cultural' right. Contemporary legal instruments do not define 'culture' but list cultural rights.[2] They are of limited assistance in elucidating the meaning of 'culture' in the present context, though they point to the importance of education as a prerequisite of any 'culture'. The right to participate in cultural life, which is a general human right applicable to members of minorities equally with others, is certainly not confined to culture in any 'elitist' sense of access to and knowledge of the arts and sciences. As the UNESCO General Conference expressed it, 'culture is not merely an accumulation of works and knowledge which an elite produces, collects and conserves.'[3] Similarly, it is submitted that the right to enjoy culture in Article 27 means all aspects of that culture; what is at stake is the ability of ethnic minorities to preserve their cultural identity and their cultural inheritance, *their own culture.*

[1] See generally Niec, 'Human Right to Culture', YB AAA, 44 (1974), 109; *Cultural Rights as Human Rights* (UNESCO, 1970).

[2] Robertson, 'The Right to Education and Culture and its International Implementation', in Resumé des Cours, Institut International des Droits de l'Homme, 9th Session, 1978.

[3] Cited by Robertson, ibid.

In this broad sense, 'culture' is susceptible to various descriptions of varying usefulness. Tylor defined it as: 'That complex whole which includes knowledge, belief, art, morals, law, custom and other capabilities and habits acquired by man as a member of society.'[4] Others have referred to additional components such as language, literature, philosophy, religion, science, and technology. Culture can be constituted by social organization and technology as well as 'ideological systems' (knowledge, beliefs, values, etc.).[5] Cohen refers more concisely to cultural rights as 'the privilege that a group enjoys vis-à-vis others to maintain its style and strategy of living'.[6] According to Leiris:

culture . . . comprehends all that is inherited or transmitted through society . . . its individual elements are . . . diverse. They include not only beliefs, knowledge, sentiments and literature . . . but the language or other system of symbols which are their vehicles. Other elements are the rules of kinship, methods of education, forms of government and all the fashions followed in social relations . . .'[7]

The 'culture' of a group is, therefore, a concept with complex ramifications; a definition or list of 'cultural' attributes could illustrate, though hardly exhaust the possibilities. The rejected drafts of Article 27 made rather selective attempts to capture the main forms of cultural existence and the means for its preservation and development. References to the use of a minority language in public affairs are frequent, and education through the medium of the minority language. The drafts constantly mention schools, libraries, museums, and other institutional aspects of culture. An early draft prepared by the United Nations Secretariat recalls, in its enumeration of cultural characteristics and its reference to public funds, typical phrases from League of Nations instruments: persons belonging to a minority 'shall have the right to establish and maintain, out of an equitable proportion of any public funds available for the purpose, their schools and cultural and religious institutions, and to use their own languages before the courts and other authorities and organs of the State and in the press and in public assembly'.[8] A similar clause was suggested by Lauterpacht in his *An International Bill of the Rights of Man*.[9] From the negative aspect of what amounts to destroying a culture, the United Nations Secretariat's draft article on cultural genocide included such acts as prohibiting the use of a language in schools and publications, destroying libraries, museums, schools, historical monuments and places of worship, etc.[10]

---

[4] Tylor, *Primitive Culture*, vol. i, 1 (London: Murray, 1871).

[5] See, for example, Taylor, 'Culture: Whence, Whither and Why?', in Alcock (ed.), *The Future of Cultural Minorities* (London: Macmillan, 1979), 9.

[6] Cohen, 'From National State to International Community', in *Cultural Rights as Human Rights* (UNESCO, 1970), at p. 77.

[7] Leiris, *Race and Culture* (UNESCO, 1958), 20–1.

[8] UN Doc E/CN.4/21 at 23 (1947).

[9] (1945), 151.

[10] *Supra*, chs. 6 and 7.

The rejection of the drafts does not necessarily imply a rejection of the aspects of 'culture' contained therein. Other questions such as the existence or non-existence of minorities and the nature of the State's duties towards them occupied the centre of the stage. There are also technical reasons militating against listing as many aspects of culture as can be fitted into a comprehensible draft. The maxim *expressio unius, est exclusio alterius* is relevant here: if a draft mentions the right to have minority schools, does this exclude universities? Despite earlier caveats about ambiguity there is virtue in adopting a general standard, and perhaps some necessity, in a document which devotes only one article to the question. More detailed treatment would require a declaration or convention specifically devoted to the minorities issue. It cannot be concluded, therefore, that the rejection of these drafts represented a rejection of necessary institutional support for assisting members of a minority to maintain their traditions.

The *travaux préparatoires* of the Covenant demonstrate what factors may be involved in supporting a minority group. Questions have subsequently been directed to States by the Human Rights Committee on the use of minority languages in the press, in schools, on radio, and television, etc. This implies that these are typical measures of a State's fulfilment of its obligations under Article 27 even though they are not specified. Besides these, many States responded to Special Rapporteur Capotorti noting typical modifications to their legal systems to cater for minorities. Family law, property law, and criminal law have been modified in many cases to ensure the preservation of customary social institutions and laws. This does not exhaust the possible issues.[11]

It is inevitable that in measurement of a State's performance by Article 27, the *institutional* aspects will continue to be stressed. The reference in the article to 'in community with the other members of their group' makes this unavoidable. A State cannot in good faith claim that as it permits the use of a minority language in the home, the community aspect of the right is satisfied. The test is always likely to be the test of the public forum: are members of a minority group allowed (negative), or encouraged (positive) to band together in various kinds of cultural institutions, including schools, to ensure their survival as a cultural entity? Despite the 'individualist' phrasing of the right as a right belonging to 'persons', it is the *community* aspects

---

[11] Capotorti Report, Add. 4. Prott states the following caveat: 'Culture is not a static concept: cultures change all the time, and even the most enthusiastic supporter of cultural preservation would no doubt find elements in the culture under consideration which no special effort should be made to preserve. Likewise the proponents of cultural development are not urging total change: the degree of development and change of a culture which is desirable may be a subject of keenest debate between members of that cultural group. Assertions of the right to develop and preserve a culture . . . conceal some of the most difficult areas of cultural policy-making': 'Cultural Rights as Peoples' Rights', in Crawford (ed.), *The Rights of Peoples*, 93 at 95.

of this right that pose the sharpest challenge to many States; minority rights are inevitably harder to accept than the rights of individuals because of their communitarian and institutional focus. Hence, the tendency of States to resist their full implications.

20. Profession and Practice of Religion

These last remarks apply with some force to the question of religion. Some conception of what amounts to a religion was outlined above.[1] No doubt States will continue to deny the status of a religion to certain practices in order to evade obligations. But the major problem is not the definition of practices and creeds as religious or non-religious, but the challenges posed by recognized and organized religions to the fabric of States. The issue is not confined to States committed to a rejection of traditional religions, but finds equal expression in States manifesting an attachment to a particular religion in laws or through State policy.[2] Even the formal, constitutional separation of Church and State does not ensure substantive equality between religious faiths, as appears from the following extract from an early Sub-Commission study prepared by Special Rapporteur Krishnaswami: 'Within the framework of [the] principle of separation . . . *de facto* pre-eminence is sometimes achieved by a particular religion and the law of the country—although equally applicable to everyone—reflects in certain important matters the concepts of the predominant group.' He refers to laws governing marriage and its dissolution, holidays and days of rest as examples. Alternatively, the State 'even when applying the principle of separation, may accord a special status to religious organizations, distinct from that accorded to other kinds of associations. But such a status may be granted only on condition that the religious group satisfies certain specified conditions—a possibility for some but not for others.' Also, even if a State 'maintains strict neutrality as between various faiths, inequality of treatment is not necessarily excluded. The demands of various religions are different, and a law prohibiting certain acts, or enjoining the performance of others, may prevent one religious group from performing an essential rite or . . . following a basic observance . . .'[3]

---

[1] *Supra*, ch, 16.

[2] Iran is one example of such a State. See *Report on the Human Rights Situation in the Islamic Republic of Iran* by the Special Representative of the UN Human Rights Commission, Mr Reynaldo Galindo Pohl, UN Doc E/CN.4/1988/24. The separation of Church and State is not a universal feature of societies. For a categorization of types of relationship, see Odio Benito, *Study of the Current Dimensions of the Problems of Intolerance and of Discrimination on the Grounds of Religious Belief*, UN Doc E/CN.4/Sub. 2/1987/26, paras. 83 ff. The genesis of the Odio Benito report is outlined, n. 21, *infra*.

[3] Krishnaswami, *Study of Discrimination in the Matter of Religious Rights and Practices*, UN Sales No. 60.XIV.2, 47–8. The strain in relationships between religious communities and States is hinted at rather delicately by Capotorti: 'By the very nature of religions and religious communities, the exercise of freedom of religion has many implications not only at the

Article 27 addresses itself essentially to the community aspects of religious observance. The right to espouse privately a particular system of beliefs is catered for elsewhere in the Convention, though, as was noted, the reference in Article 18 to the right to manifest religion or belief in 'worship, observance, practice and teaching' itself implies community rather than purely individual aspects. Article 18 is of considerable importance to minorities. Apart from the freedoms quoted, the States Parties, by Article 18(4), 'undertake to have respect for the liberty of parents and, when applicable, legal guardians to ensure the religious and moral education of their children in conformity with their own convictions'.[4] The limitation clause relating to Article 18(3) (manifestation of religion or belief) is so broadly defined, however, as to merit its description by one commentator as 'astonishing',[5] but it does not, despite this, go so far as to legitimate, for example, in an atheist State, the complete suppression of any manifestation of religion or belief: its references to 'public safety, order, health or morals', though broad, are not unlimited. They do not amount to a limitation in terms of '*ordre public*'.[6] No reservations have been entered so far in relation to Article 18, though negatively, some States have sought to extend the restriction on manifestations of religion to other aspects of the guaranteed freedom,[7] as well as providing questionable interpretations of Article 18(3) itself.[8] Some extraordinary situations in relation to Article 18 have been revealed in the Human Rights Committee which do not augur well for parallel interpretations of Article 27. One example is the reported situation in Byelorussia and the Ukraine, where religious instruction in the schools is prohibited and the religious communities are not entitled to maintain their

individual level, but also at the collective level, as witness the extremely complex nature of the relations between States and the various religions', Capotorti Report, Add. 4, para. 60. Also, Odio Benito (*supra*, n. 2), paras 84–8 for a critical discussion of, *inter alia*, the consequences of establishing a religion as a State religion.

[4] The equivalent right in the European Convention on Human Rights has attracted a large number of reservations: see Council of Europe, European Convention on Human Rights, Collected Texts, 11th edn. (1976), 605–11.

[5] Partsch, 'Freedom of Conscience and Expression, and Political Freedom', in Henkin (ed.), *The International Bill of Rights*, 212. Consider the range of limitations on manifestations of religious belief canvassed by Odio Benito, (*supra*, n. 2), paras. 117, 118, from national legislation: 'public safety', 'order', 'health', 'morals', 'respect for the rights and freedoms of others', 'security', 'defence', 'incitement of citizens to refuse social activity or performance of civic duties', 'performance of acts which may be inconsistent with the life, physical integrity or dignity of persons', 'interests of traffic', 'tranquillity or salubrity'. See *infra*, n. 8. Colombia and Panama allow freedom to practise any religion which is not contrary to 'Christian morality', UN Doc E/CN.4/1988/43, 10–11; E/CN.4/1987/37, 13.

[6] The French text speaks of 'la protection de l'ordre' rather than 'ordre public'.

[7] UN Doc A/33/40, paras. 280 and 444; UN Doc CCPR/C/1/Add.33 at 21–5, and, ibid., Add.36.

[8] Such as including 'public indignation' among reasons to restrict religious manifestations (Sweden), UN Doc A/33/40, para. 79, CCPR/C/1/Add.9 and Corr.1. Mongolia has characterized the mere holding of religious services as a form of religious propaganda, CCPR/C/SR.202, 7. Article 86 of the Mongolian People's Republic allows (asymmetrically) for freedom of religious belief, and anti-religious propaganda.

own educational institutions.[9] On the other hand, Swedish law provides for compulsory religious education in schools.[10] The Byelorussian reply to questions by the Human Rights Committee claimed that, not withstanding the restriction on religious teaching, the legislation did not prohibit religious teaching by parents, nor did it prohibit attendance at religious services. Despite these qualifications, it is doubtful if such legislation conforms to the letter or the spirit of Article 18; religious instruction permitted solely to parents and not to ministers of religion is insufficient to satisfy the article's requirements, there is no public permitted religious teaching so that the phrase 'in public or private' is not allowed to take effect.[11] Article 27 has no special limitation clause and might, therefore, be comparatively immune from extravagant assertions by States destined effectively to remove a particular freedom. It is, however, subject to general clauses in the Covenant, considered below.[12] The effectiveness of the article in relation to religion depends firstly on an interpretation of Article 18 which does greater justice to religious groups. Article 27 must take it for granted that the provisions of Article 18 are first adhered to on a basis of non-discrimination. In conformity with the argument above,[13] Article 27 must oblige the State to provide something more than is provided by Article 18; otherwise Article 27 is redundant. Accordingly, it should be interpreted to promote the material equality of religious communities. Because the article gives no precise guidance to States, it becomes a question of interpreting the specific problems raised for religious communities in the light of the above considerations.

The nature of these problems is explicated by the provisions of the Declaration on the Elimination of All Forms of Intolerance and of Discrimination Based on Religion or Belief, which was adopted without a vote by the General Assembly in November 1981.[14] The International Covenants on Human Rights are referred to in the Preamble, as are the United Nations Charter and the Universal Declaration of Human Rights. The Articles of the Declaration delineate the right to freedom of thought, conscience, and religion on a non-discriminatory basis and States are urged to 'take effective

[9] For Byelorussia, see A/33/40, paras. 521–54, CCPR/C/1/Add.27; for Ukraine, A/34/40, paras. 248–85, CCPR/C/1/Add.34. The reply of the USSR to the Human Rights Commission Special Rapporteur on the Implementation of the Declaration on Religious Intolerance, Vidal D'Almeida Ribeiro (*infra*, n. 21) stated that: 'If the parents or guardians so desire, a child may receive religious instruction within the family and, when he has attained his majority, he may enter an ecclesiastical institution of his faith. Thus, in matters of education, the child's interests come first; any action which may impair the health or physical, intellectual and moral development of the child is prohibited and is punishable.' UN Doc E/CN.4/1988/45, para. 19.

[10] *Supra*, n. 8.

[11] Partsch, (*supra*, n. 5), 215–16.

[12] *Infra*, ch. 22.

[13] *Supra*, ch. 18.

[14] UNGA Res. 36/55, GAOR, 36, Supp. No. 51, 171; UN Doc A/36/51 (1981). See generally, Sullivan, 'Advancing the Freedom of Religion or Belief through the UN Declaration on the Elimination of Religious Intolerance and Discrimination', *AJIL*, 82 (1988), 487.

measures to prevent and eliminate discrimination on the grounds of religion or belief in the recognition, exercise and enjoyment of human rights and fundamental freedoms'.[15] Article 5(1) sets out the rights of parents and guardians 'to organise the life within the family in accordance with their religion or belief and bearing in mind the moral education in which they believe the child should be brought up'. Article 5(2) describes a more stringent standard of rights to religious education than is apparently the case with Article 18 of the Covenant on Civil and Political Rights. It reads:

Every child shall enjoy the right to have access to education in the matter of religion or belief in accordance with the wishes of his parents or, as the case may be, legal guardians, and shall not be compelled to receive teaching or religion or belief against the wishes of his parents or legal guardians, the best interests of the child being the guiding principle.[16]

Access to religious education in accordance with parental wishes implies a duty on the State to remove any obstacles to this, as well as, on a reasonable reading of the paragraph, to provide facilities for such education if the right of access is to be an effective right. In relation to minority religious communities, Article 6 of the Declaration is crucial, as it sets out in detail what can properly be regarded as the most common implications for the communities of the broad phrasing of Article 27. Article 6 interprets freedom of thought, conscience, religion or belief as including, *inter alia*, the following freedoms:

(a) To worship or assemble in connexion with a religion or belief, and to establish and maintain places for these purposes;
(b) To establish and maintain appropriate charitable or humanitarian institutions;
(c) To make, acquire, and use to an adequate extent the necessary articles and materials related to the rites or customs of a religion or belief;
(d) To write, issue, and disseminate relevant publications in these areas;
(e) To teach a religion or belief in places suitable for these purposes;
(f) To solicit and receive voluntary financial and other contributions from individuals and institutions;
(g) To train, appoint, elect, or designate by succession appropriate leaders called for by the requirements and standards of any religion or belief;
(h) To observe days of rest and to celebrate holidays and ceremonies in accordance with the precepts of one's religion or belief;
(i) To establish and maintain communications with individuals and com-

---

[15] Article 4(1). It may be noted that the Declaration does not attempt a definition of 'religion', unlike the Draft Convention on the Elimination of All Forms of Religious Intolerance, which defined it to include 'theistic, non-theistic and atheistic beliefs'. *Supra*, ch. 16, n. 51.

[16] The duty in this respect is more explicit than in the case of the above Draft Convention, Article IV of which spoke of States parties undertaking to 'respect the right of parents . . . to bring up in the religion or belief of their choice their children . . .' (Article IV(a)).

munities in matters of religion and belief at the national and international levels.

It is not clear that Article 27 of the Covenant on Civil and Political Rights requires States to address themselves immediately to all of the above freedoms in relation to religious minorities. But implementation of the article will typically involve such issues. The right 'to profess and practise' religion is almost inconceivable without a right to assemble for worship, to prepare materials for religious rituals, to appoint ministers of religion, and to observe religious holy days. The requirement that profession and practice be 'in community with' other members of the group implies, besides the above, which may be conceived of in a community context, the freedom to teach and be taught, including the establishment of training schools for the faithful and their ministers of religion, and the freedom to publish religious matter. The continuance of the religion depends upon all of these, as it does upon the ability to finance religious activities through the creation of institutions and the soliciting of necessary funds.

It may be noted that this newer instrument does not go so far as committing States to expenditure in support of religious activities and that this throws doubt on the radical 'positive' interpretation of Article 27 advocated here.[17] On the other hand, Article 7 of the Declaration provides that 'the rights and freedoms set forth in the present Declaration shall be accorded in national legislation in such a manner that everyone shall be able to avail himself of such rights and freedoms *in practice*.' Thus, as was argued in relation to Article 27, the merely theoretical grant of such rights is not sufficient; practical, effective implementation is required. In the case of the Declaration and Article 27, while they do not clearly demand financing of religious activities, an obligation to provide such assistance cannot be ruled out in all circumstances.[18] Apart from finance, both Article 7 of the Declaration and the typical application of Article 27 will require modification of national legislation as may be necessary to remove obstacles to religious observance. An instance of this will be the position of a religious minority in relation to its holy days; States develop patterns of legislation in this respect with conscious or unconscious reference to the traditions of a particular dominant religion, and the days of rest or religious observance of majority and minority may not coincide.[19] Article 27 does not provide a ready

---

[17] *Supra*, ch. 18.

[18] In Capotorti's view, 'the more a religious community lacks resources, the more the State is bound to take steps to ensure its survival'. *Italian Yearbook of International Law*, 2 (1976), 3 at 23.

[19] A number of States responding to Capotorti's questions and to the Draft Declaration on Minorities instanced legal provisions to deal with the problem. Malaysia reported to Capotorti that the Schedule to the Holiday Ordinance lists eleven public holidays which included the religious celebrations of the main ethnic and religious groups of the country; Sri Lanka stated that the religious festivals of the four major religions professed in the country are celebrated as national holidays; Pakistan reported eighteen holidays: four national, eight Muslim, four

solution to such clashes of interest as it does not to the question of whether the marriage ceremony of minority religions should have the same legal effect as those of majority religions, or whether religious laws should prevail over secular legislation, or whether the objections of members of a minority religion to military service should be recognized, or whether instruction in the majority religion or secular atheism is to be given to members of minority religious groups, etc.[20] As noted before, no standard pattern of conduct is required by the Covenant; but Article 27 is inspired by the notion of preservation of minority religious values; the demands of the religious group and the responses of States are to be tested by that criterion.[21]

Hindu, and two Christian, UN Doc E/CN.4/Sub.2/384, para. 80. See also the list of measures taken by Pakistan to promote the welfare of minorities, submitted to the Human Rights Commission, UN Doc E/CN.4/1298/Add.3. Also, Odio Benito Report, para. 134.

[20] The Capotorti Report contains a compendium of measures adopted by States, ibid., Add. 4. The record reveals considerable variations of approach.

[21] References are made in nn. 2 and 9 above to two reports on the Declaration on Religious Intolerance, by D'Almeida Ribeiro, and Odio Benito. These reports furnish useful information on the implementation of the Declaration. In 1986, the Commission on Human Rights entrusted D'Almeida Riberio with the task of examining incidents of religious intolerance, compliance with norms and recommending remedial measures: Commission on Human Rights, Res. 1986/20, UN Doc E/CN.4/1986/65, 66. The first report was presented in 1987, and demonstrated widespread violations of religious freedom: UN Doc E/CN.4/1987/35. The Special Rapporteur's mandate was extended, and a second report was submitted in 1988, UN Doc E/CN.4/1988/45. Special Rapporteur Odio Benito was appointed by the UN Sub-Commission to report on the causes and current dimensions of religious intolerance and discrimination and to recommend remedial measures: Sub-Commission Res. 1983/31, UN Doc E/CN. 4/Sub.2/1983/43, 98. The final report of Odio Benito is UN Doc E/CN.4/Sub.2/1987/26; an interim report was issued as UN Doc E/CN.4/Sub.2/1985/28.

21. 'To Use Their Own Language'

Article 27 is concise on the question of language, and other provisions of the Covenant are not especially helpful on how this aspect of rights is to be implemented. The protection of culture includes that of its linguistic medium, and discussion of culture necessarily includes a discussion of linguistic aspects. A number of points have already been discussed in the present connection.[1] Rights such as those set out in Article 13(3) of the Covenant on Economic, Social, and Cultural Rights laying down that parents are free to choose schools for their children other than those established by the authorities, and the freedom to seek, receive, and impart ideas 'either orally, in writing or in print . . .' (Article 19(2) of the Covenant on Civil and Political Rights) are clearly relevant to the needs of minorities and form a base for the elucidation of Article 17. Like religion, race, etc., language is an impermissible ground of discrimination in a range of international instruments, including the Covenant on Civil and Political Rights,[2] so in accordance with the interpretation above, the function of Article 27 is to go beyond a guarantee of non-discrimination towards a more positive notion of conservation of linguistic identity. Thus, whereas prevention of members of minorities from acquiring knowledge of a national or official language would constitute discrimination, failure to allow minority languages to be taught in schools or universities when a minority desires this would, *prima facie*, be a breach of Article 27.

As with religion, States adopt a variety of approaches to minority languages. One writer remarks that 'every country that has a language problem tries to solve it its own way' and summarizes that there 'are no universal rules, except perhaps that language rights must be respected if you wish to have domestic peace'.[3] Apart from policies of linguistic suppression, minority languages may be disadvantaged in various ways. Great controversies are caused by such questions as the official status of languages and, in consequence, their use in administration and before the courts, in public educational institutions, and in the mass media. Ostrower finds 'six general

---

[1] *Supra*, ch. 19.

[2] See documents cited *infra*, Part V. Also, McDougal, Lasswell and Chen, 'Freedom from Discrimination in Choice of Language and International Human Rights', *Southern Illinois University Law Journal* 1976, No.1, 151; Reeber, Linguistic Minorities and the Right to an Effective Education *California Western International Law Journal*, 3 (1972), 112.

[3] Scott, 'Language Rights and Language Policy in Canada', *Manitoba Law Journal*, 4 (1971), 243 at 247–8.

patterns'[4] in the responses of States to linguistic diversity, each of which has a slightly different implication for minority languages:

1. Legal equality of national languages for all practical and official purposes;[5]
2. Legal equality of all national languages, some of which are designated as 'official';[6]
3. Formal equality of national languages conditioned upon doctrinal considerations and changing official policies;[7]
4. Supremacy of the language of the dominant national grouping, considered as the official State language, within a system of constitutional protection of linguistic minorities;[8]
5. Recognition of a foreign language as an auxiliary official State language;[9]
6. Designation of one or more native tongues as the official form of State expression.[10]

This list may be supplemented by remarking that in some States, the languages of some groups have been given an official status at the regional but not at national level.[11] A national language has been defined as 'the language of a political, social and cultural entity', an official language as 'a language used in the business of government—legislative, executive and judicial', and a regional language as 'a language which is used as a medium

---

[4] Ostrower, *Language, Law and Diplomacy* (Philadelphia: University of Pennsylvania Press, 1965), 597.

[5] Canada, Ostrower, ibid. 597–605. In Finland, Swedish has been designated a national language in addition to Finnish by Article 14 of the Constitution. The language of the Lapps, however, has not been so designated. See also Paradis, 'Language Rights in Multicultural States: A Comparative Study', *Canadian Bar Review*, 48 (1970), 651.

[6] This is the position in Switzerland, where 75% of the population belong to the German linguistic group, with French accounting for 20% of speakers, Italian 4%, and Romanche under 1%, respectively. All four languages are national languages, but only the first three are official languages. Capotorti Report, Add. 4, para. 106.

[7] As in the USSR, Ostrower (*supra*, n. 4), 609–23. For the formal position in the USSR, see the Constitution (Fundamental Law) of the USSR (Moscow, 1977), Articles 34, 36, 45, and 46. For an account of Soviet policy, see Institute of Marxism-Leninism, *Leninism and the National Question* (Moscow: Progress Publishers, 1977).

[8] Yugoslavia, Romania, and China: Ostrower (*supra*, n. 4), 623–30.

[9] This is the case in the Republic of Ireland (with reservations as to what extent English may be regarded as a 'foreign' idiom following centuries of practical use and its present-day position as mother-tongue to the great majority of the population), the Philippines, and many newly independent States in Asia and Africa.

[10] In many countries of South and South-East Asia, Ostrower (*supra*, n. 4), 632–64.

[11] Austria is an example: Article 8 of the Federal Constitution declares German the official language without prejudice to linguistic rights by Federal law or international treaty. Under the State Treaty of 1955, the Slovene and Croat languages are recognized as official languages in addition to German in those districts of Carinthia, Burgenland, and Styria where the population is Slovene, Croat, or mixed. See *Protection of Minorities: Special Protective Measures of an International Character for Ethnic, Religious or Linguistic Groups* (New York: United Nations, 1967), UN Sales No. 67.XIV.3.

of communication between peoples living within a certain area who have different mother tongues'.[12]

From the point of view of a State which represents a multilinguistic society, the development of a language policy raises practical problems; and even States which are well disposed to the continued flourishing of the languages of its heterogeneous cultural mix, may find it difficult to provide a fair balance of opportunities for different groups. Selection of one language as a national or official language may represent a politically contentious step, especially within States where the other linguistic groups constitute sizeable proportions of the population. On the other hand, it may not be practicable in terms of efficiency and cost to designate a plurality of languages as 'official' in States where many languages are spoken and resources are very limited.[13] This aspect of minority rights is always of the highest relevance whether one is dealing with cultural, religious, or linguistic groups: resources are never limitless and the demands placed upon signatories of the Covenant by Article 27 need to be looked at realistically. On any interpretation of the article, its implementation should not impair the exercise of fundamental rights by those citizens or inhabitants of a State who do not belong to minority groups. Some kind of balance will need to be struck therefore between the minorities' interests and those of the nation as a whole.[14] In the linguistic context, it must not be forgotten that in States struggling to build a national identity from heterogeneous elements, the selection of an official language may be an important symbol and a practical necessity. The issue here is addressed primarily to developing countries, many of which, irrespective of economic problems, may not have forged an identity to sustain their nationhood in the post-colonial era. Paradoxically, continued use of the language of the former colonial power may prove less divisive than the designation of one of the main indigenous languages as the national or official language. In the latter case, if a language 'is not characterised by political neutrality, it is too often regarded merely as a tool by which a particular language group seeks to extend its domination. Quite naturally, this is a cause for alarm among other language communities.'[15] From the point of view of the minority, however, the selection of a particular language as official may place members of the minority at a disadvant-

---

[12] *The Use of Vernacular Languages in Education* (Paris: UNESCO, 1953), 46.

[13] In this and other contexts, the resource problem is an acute one for many States and represents genuine difficulty in terms of respect for Human Rights. On Article 27, the analogy between it and economic, social, and cultural rights is helpful: whereas most rights in the Covenant require immediate implementation (State poverty is no excuse for torture or denial of fair trial for those accused of crime), the rights in Article 27 may be seen as a goal to be achieved. This, of course, implies a 'positive' interpretation on the lines set out above. On the other hand, if a State interprets the article as implying only a 'duty to tolerate' minorities, it has no excuse for failing to tolerate them. See also Article 22 of the Universal Declaration of Human Rights, and Article 2 of the Covenant on Economic, Social, and Cultural Rights.

[14] See comment by the Government of Finland on the Draft Declaration, E/CN.4/1298, 6.

[15] Capotorti Report, Add. 2, para. 151.

age; it would seem incumbent upon the State to ensure that this disadvantage is, as far as possible, eliminated. One would expect, therefore, that in dealings with the authorities or in judicial matters, a system of translation should at least be provided. This is partly dealt with by Article 14(3) of the Covenant which provides that 'everyone shall be entitled . . . in full equality . . . to have the free assistance of an interpreter if he cannot understand or speak the language used in court.' Article 27 would seem to indicate that such a system should go beyond criminal proceedings into other areas of official dealings in order to produce a practical or material equality between speakers of minority and majority languages. Similar remarks apply to other areas where speakers may be placed at a disadvantage, whether it be in law, administration, in the schools and publicly controlled news media, etc. Article 27 is unspecific in these matters, so that it is only possible to indicate the main areas in which the duties of the State in catering for the desire of members of minorities to preserve their linguistic identity may lie, and to assert that the State should strive to promote an equality in fact between members of the various linguistic communities.

Regrettably, neither the *travaux préparatoires* of the Covenant, nor subsequent exercises in interpretation, throw much light on the *extent* of the States' duties in relation to this aspect of Article 27. The Yugoslav Draft Declaration does not specify the point further, and accordingly the comments of States on the Draft do not take up the issue in any specific way that would aid further interpretations of the article. One writer concludes that 'general principles of law' which are partly shaped by the requirements of Article 27 establish the 'right of minorities to the use of their own language in private and public life, in business relations, before courts of law and other State agencies, in religious rites, in the media of public information, at public gatherings and cultural events, etc., . . .', as well as the right of minorities 'to schools of all levels with instruction in the languages of minorities'.[16] It is not clear, however, how much of this is attributable to any interpretation of Article 27 as opposed to all other developments in international law relating to minorities.

But if the limits of the States' responsibilities are unclear, the questioning of States by the Human Rights Committee at least sufficiently indicates where the responsibilities lie. Questions have been consistently directed at States on a fairly standard range of matters which bear out many of the suggested implications of the article: What is the situation of minority-language instruction in schools? Can the minorities publish and does the State assist in the publication of books and newspapers in that language? Is the minority language accepted as an official language? In what language are court proceedings conducted when members of minorities are parties to cases? Are there radio and television programmes in minority languages? An

[16] Vukas, 'General International Law and the Protection of Minorities', RDH, VIII–I (1975), 41 at 47–8.

interesting recurring question has been whether the Covenant itself has been translated and made accessible in minority languages in a State.[17] The replies made by States have been sometimes brief and sometimes full,[18] but no State, it appears, has doubted the legitimacy of such questions—though some have been, perhaps pointedly, left unanswered.[19]

[17] UN Doc A/34/40, para. 114, Bulgaria. The initial Bulgarian report is in UN Doc CCPR/C/1/Add.3. The Bulgarian reply indicated that it had been translated. Also Tanzania, UN Doc A/38/40, para. 218. The Tanzanian reply did not directly address the question, ibid., para. 225. The original Tanzanian report is UN Doc CCPR/C/1/Add. 48.

[18] See, for example, the responses of Poland, UN Doc A/35/40, para. 75. The original Polish report is UN Doc CCPR/C/4/Add.2; also Ukraine, A/34/40, para. 285, CCPR/C/1/Add.34.

[19] UN Doc A/33/40, paras. 521–54, UN Doc CCPR/C/1/Add.27 (Byelorussia); UN Doc A/36/40, paras. 227–52, UN Doc CCPR/C/1/Add.49 (Mali); ibid., paras. 202–26, UN Doc CCPR/C/1/Add.48 (Tanzania); ibid., paras. 104–07, UN Doc CCPR/C/1/Add.4 (Italy).

22. Limitations on Article 27

Apart from the question of the 'existence' or 'non-existence' of a minority which may be used to limit rights in the interpretation of some States, are there other limitations on the exercise of minority rights contained either in the remaining phrases of the Article, at least by implication as there is no express limitation, or by virtue of other provisions of the Covenant?[1] The existence of certain limitations was strongly suggested by a number of States Representatives in the drafting stages of the Covenant. Thus, the Representative of The Netherlands in the Third Committee of the General Assembly declared that he voted for Article 27 on the understanding that it contained similar limitations to those set out in Article 18; accordingly, the article 'could not be held to exempt the rights of minorities from the limitations laid down by law to protect public safety, order, health or morals, or the fundamental freedoms of others'.[2] The Representative of China expressed the same point,[3] as did those of Belgium[4] and Turkey.[5] Other Representatives expressed different kinds of limitation. Thus, while denying that the article had any relevance to his own State, the Representative of Venezuela argued that 'the provisions relating to the rights of minorities should not be so applied as to encourage the emergence of new minority groups, or to thwart the process of assimilation and so threaten the unity of the State'.[6] Similar remarks were voiced by the Representatives of Spain,[7] India,[8] Panama,[9] Ecuador,[10] Cameroon,[11] Peru,[12] Iraq,[13] Brazil,[14] and Nicaragua.[15] The fears expressed by States on the question of 'loyalty' of minorities will be recalled, including the suggestion that 'loyalty' was an element in the definition of 'minority'.[16] These sentiments have been echoed by States' responses to the Yugoslav Draft Declaration on minorities, both in relation

---

[1] Generally, Kiss, 'Permissible Limitations on Rights', in Henkin (ed.), *The International Bill of Rights*, 290.

[2] GAOR, 16 Session, 3rd Committee, 1103rd meeting, para. 17.

[3] Ibid., para. 24.

[4] Ibid., para. 47: the limitation 'in Article 18, para. 3 applied to all acts by which persons belonging to minorities might manifest their opinions or religious beliefs'.

[5] Ibid., 1104th meeting, para. 20.

[6] Ibid., 1103rd meeting, para. 28.

[7] Ibid., para. 24.

[8] Ibid., para. 36.

[9] Ibid., para, 42: the provisions of the article should not 'be invoked to justify breaches of the national integrity of any country'.

[10] Ibid., para. 44: the article 'could in no way thwart the process of their assimilation'.

[11] Ibid., para. 52.

[12] Ibid., 1104th meeting, para. 5: the article was intended to encourage 'the integration of existing variations into one human whole'.

[13] Ibid., para. 6.

[14] Ibid., para. 18.

[15] Ibid., para. 36.

[16] *Supra*, ch. 16.

to any such declaration and as views on Article 27. Thus, Greece noted that the provisions of Article 27 'should not be applied in such a manner as to encourage the creation of new minorities, or to obstruct the process of voluntary integration'.[17]

States visualize various restrictions on the rights set out in the article, some of which appear reasonable; others would destroy the substance of these rights. Apart from inherent limitations specific to Article 27, a reading of the Covenant as a whole discloses that the human rights are not absolute. Although the Covenant sets out rights rather than duties of man, the Preamble recites that 'the individual, having duties to other individuals and to the community to which he belongs, is under a responsibility to strive for the promotion and observance of the rights recognised in the present Covenant.' This recalls Article 29 of the Universal Declaration of Human Rights: '(1) Everyone has duties to the community in which alone the free and full development of his personality is possible'. In the operative sections of the Covenant, Article 5(1) provides that 'Nothing in the present Covenant may be interpreted as implying for any State, group or person the right to engage in any activity or perform any act aimed at the destruction of any of the rights and freedoms recognised herein or at their limitation to a greater extent than is provided for in the present Covenant.' The power to derogate from the provisions of the Covenant has already been mentioned;[18] Article 27 is not listed as a right from which no derogation is permitted, derogations are, however, permitted only in the case of a proclaimed public emergency threatening the life of the nation and then only 'to the extent strictly required by the exigencies of the situation', and provided the measures taken by the State Party are not inconsistent with 'other obligations under international law, and do not involve discrimination solely on the ground of race, colour, sex, language, religion or social origin'.[19] Apart from these general limitations on the Covenant rights as a whole, many Articles are expressly declared to be subject to particular limitations. Thus, the Covenant conforms to a standard pattern developed in international human rights instruments and seeks to find a fair balance between State and individual.

It is possible to derive some indication from the above provisions as to the permitted limits within which the rights of members of minorities are to be

[17] UN Doc E/CN.4/1298, 10. For expressions of the general undesirability of any declaration or convention encouraging separation or threatening national unity, etc., see UN Doc E/CN.4/1298, 5 (Chile), 18 (UK), E/CN.4/1298/Add.4 (Morocco), E/CN.4/1298/Add.7, 2 (Egypt). Article 4 of the first draft of the declaration on minorities provided: '1. In ensuring and promoting the rights of minorities strict respect for sovereignty, territorial integrity, political independence and non-interference in the internal affairs of countries where minorities live, should be observed.' This was not, however, to prevent fulfilment of international obligations towards minorities.

[18] *Supra*, ch. 17.

[19] Article 4(1). Article 4(3) provides that the derogating party shall notify the other States parties of the articles subject to derogation and the reasons.

exercised. A more detailed instrument might have spelled out a reference to the duty of loyalty owed by citizens to their State. There is no such reference in the Yugoslav Draft Declaration 'inspired by the principles of Article 27',[20] but this is not conclusive evidence that no such duty is implied in the Covenant.[21] It is arguable that 'this duty is implicit in the status of citizen; even though there is no reference to it in the Covenant on Civil and Political Rights'.[22] A similar point has been made in relation to the League of Nations minorities treaties.[23] The duty may also be implied from the preambular paragraph quoted above, stressing the obligations of the individual to other individuals and *to the community to which he belongs*, 'community' in this sense being taken as the wider national (State) community rather than simply the 'community' of the ethnic, religious, or linguistic group.

The key provision in the Covenant, designed to prevent abuse of human rights at the expense of others, is Article 5(1); it prohibits freedom-destroying 'activities' or 'acts' by 'any State, group or person', thus implying duties upon individuals as well as States and, in the present context, ethnic, religious, and linguistic groups.[24] The closest domestic law analogue to this principle is the doctrine of *détournement de pouvoir*.[25] The Article 'stipulates, in effect, that rights and powers conferred for one purpose may not be used for another, illegitimate purpose'.[26] Determination of the nature of an 'activity' or 'act' under the Article may involve subjective factors such as motives and purposes whereas, for example, the validity of derogation under Article 4 is premised primarily upon objective factors. In relation to individuals, Article 5(1) prevents them from relying on the rights guaranteed in the Covenant to promote activities aimed at the destruction of these rights. The provision, many of the implications of which have been worked out in relation to the almost identically worded Article 17 of the European Convention of Human Rights,[27] does not authorize the State to deprive these individuals of their rights when they engage in other activities. Further, when they engage in activities aimed at the destruction of the rights

[20] ECOSOC OR (1981) Supp. No.5, 171.

[21] The omission of such a reference has attracted unfavourable comment: Capotorti, 'I Diritti dei Membri di Minoranze: Verso una Dichiarazione delle Nazione Unite?', *LXVI Rivista di Diritto Internazionale* (1981), 30 at 39: 'E singolare ... che del dovere degli individui appartenenti a minoranze di comportarsi in modo leale e fedele verso lo Stato di appartenenza il progetto abbia preferito di non occuparsi; mentre ciò rappresenta un necessario elemento di equilibrio, rispetto ai diritti spettanti a quegli individui.'

[22] Capotorti, 'The Protection of Minorities under Multilateral Agreements on Human Rights', *Italian Yearbook of International Law*, 2, at 25.

[23] Robinson, 'International Protection of Minorities. A Global View', 70; Vukas, 'General International Law and the Protection of Minorities', 48.

[24] See Kiss, in Henkin (ed.), *The International Bill of Rights*, and Buergenthal, 'State Obligations and Permissible Derogations', ibid., 72 at 86 ff.

[25] Buergenthal, ibid., 87, n. 59.

[26] Ibid.

[27] See Jacobs, 'The Restrictions on the Exercise of the Rights and Freedoms Guaranteed by the European Convention: Their Evolution from 1950 to 1975', Fourth International Colloquy on the European Convention, *H.Coll.* 75(5), Strasbourg, 1975.

guaranteed in the Covenant, they only lose the rights that directly promote the destructive activities.[28]

Thus, members of an ethnic, religious, or linguistic group cannot use Article 27 as a base for 'activities' or 'acts' which would aim at the destruction of any of the rights recognized in the Covenant; while it is not entirely accurate to describe the rights therein as a privilege, they are at least 'special measures' not accorded to all citizens or inhabitants of a State, and should not result in intolerable restrictions on the rights of others. Thus, for example, where a minority forms a majority within a particular territory, its establishment of schools or use of language in public affairs should not interfere with the rights of those who do not share in the minority culture or language to safeguard their educational and linguistic preferences. Another aspect is that respect for minority rights should not permit cultural determinism by which an individual, preferring the wider national culture to the minority culture into which he was born, would be denied the right to embrace that culture in all its aspects. As noted above,[29] the Covenant, by investing individuals with rights rather than groups, prefers individual self-determination to group determinism. The broad aspect of this argument was put forward in rather lurid terms by Conor Cruise O'Brien: 'When we are told to respect the cultures of groups we are being told to respect things which may include, for example, the Hindu Caste system, the treatment of women in Islam and a number of other cultures, female circumcision in certain cultures, ostracism of twins . . . and so on.'[30] With the important reservations that these 'regressive' practices are not peculiar to minorities, but may, as the quotation itself suggests, extend to very large cultural and religious groups, the Covenant's answer is that no individual against his or her will can be coerced into acceptance or adoption of such practices in the interests of group solidarity and continuity.

Article 5(1) provides at least part justification to those States[31] who would interpret Article 27 as subject to limitations in favour of preserving public safety, order, etc., and the fundamental freedoms of others. The lack of a particular limitations clause may, however, indicate that there is little threat to the State in the exercise of rights under Article 27; on the contrary, by assuaging the legitimate demands of minorities, they contribute to public order. In fact, Article 27 represents, apart from the right of minority group members to exist physically, a relatively modest demand on States; read together with the limitations on Article 18 and 19, for example, it would

---

[28] *Lawless Case, European Court of Human Rights, Ser. A, vol. 3* (1961).

[29] *Supra*, ch. 17.

[30] 'What Rights should Minorities Have?', *World Minorities*, vol. i (London: Minority Rights Group, 1977), x at xvii. Cf. the comments of Lallah, discussing a draft comment on Article 27 by the Human Rights Committee: 'If it was the custom of a particular minority not to treat men and women equally or to punish certain acts in a cruel and degrading manner, to what extent could specific meaning be given to Article 27 . . .', CCPR/C/SR/590, para. 12.

[31] *Supra*, ch. 17.

appear that the States' fears are already adequately catered for. Any further restrictions would merely enlarge the already wide discretion given to States in the matter of limitations.[32]

The national unity and assimilation argument set out by Venezuela cannot, however, be accepted as a restriction on Article 27, unless some considerable qualifications are made. The basic argument appears to be that the very existence of 'unassimilated' minorities is a threat to national unity. The *raison d'être* of Article 27, on the other hand, is that it is not only perfectly legitimate for members of minorities to remain unassimilated but is also their right, and this is not conceived of as incompatible with the rights of the State. The Venezuelan stance, then, is incompatible with the article and cannot be accepted as an 'interpretation'.[33] On the other hand, Article 27 is ultimately no barrier to assimilation *per se* but only assimilation contrary to the wishes of members of the minority. The article has nothing to say about encouragement of new minorities; it deals only with such groups as 'exist'. A group, it may be argued, 'exists' or it does not, but attempting to stifle cultural development in groups essentially in a state of being born, *in statu nascendi*, would clearly involve the violation of many other rights in the Covenant,[34] so that within the Covenant's terms, it is not an option available to States in most circumstances, irrespective of Article 27.

---

[32] See generally Kiss (*supra*, n. 1). In the *Kitok Case* (*infra*, ch. 23), Sweden submitted to the Human Rights Committee: 'Article 27 guarantees the right of persons belonging to minority groups the right to enjoy their own culture. However, although not explicitly provided for in the text itself, such restrictions on the exercise of the right . . . must be considered justified to the extent that they are necessary in a democratic society in view of public interests of vital importance or for the protection of the rights and freedoms of others.' CCPR/C/D/197/1985, para. 4.3.

[33] It may be noted that no State in the Latin American group has entered a reservation to Article 27.

[34] For example, Articles 18 and 19.

23. Article 27 and the Optional Protocol

The first 'case' under the Protocol with Article 27 as its focal point appears in the Human Rights Committee's report for 1981.[1] Cases such as *Lovelace* v. *Canada*[2] contribute to the interpretation of the Covenant and provide contemporary illustrations of the practical difficulties in implementing any general principle of minority protection. The original 'communication' from Sandra Lovelace who was born and registered as a 'Maliseet Indian' is dated 29 December 1977. The substance of the complaint was that she lost her status and rights as an Indian in accordance with the Indian Act of Canada[3] by marrying a non-Indian in 1970. Pointing out that an Indian man who marries a non-Indian woman does not lose his status, she claimed that the Act is discriminatory on grounds of sex and contrary to Articles 2(1), 3, 23(1), 23(4), 26[4] and 27 of the Covenant. As to the admissibility of the communication, she contended that she was not required to exhaust local remedies since the Supreme Court of Canada in 1974[5] had declared that the relevant section 12(1)(b) of the Indian Act was fully operative, irrespective of its inconsistency with the Canadian Bill of Rights, and of sex discrimination. The communication was declared admissible in August 1979.

In its submission on the merits, Canada recognized that many provisions of the Indian Act were in need of reform and that the government intended to put a reform bill before the Canadian Parliament.[6] None the less, it was stressed that the Act was necessary to protect the Indian minority within Article 27 of the Covenant. A definition of the Indian was inevitable in view of the special privileges granted to the Indian communities, especially their right to occupy reserve lands. Traditionally patriarchal relationships were taken into account in determining legal claims; in the farming societies of the nineteenth century, reserve land was felt to be more threatened by

---

[1] Report of the Human Rights Committee, *GAOR*. 36th Session, Supp. No. 40, UN Doc A/36/40; also, Human Rights Committee, *Selected Decisions under the Optional Protocol (2nd to 16th Sessions)*, UN Doc CCPR/C/OP/1 (New York:, 1985), 10 (admissibility), 37 (interlocutory decision), 83 (views of the Human Rights Committee).

[2] A/36/40, 166.

[3] S.12(1)(b); *Can. Rev. Stat., C.1–6.* For a general review of the history and policy of the Indian Act, see Bartlett, 'The Indian Act of Canada' *Buffalo Law Review*, 27 (1978), 581.

[4] These articles set out the principles of non-discrimination in the enjoyment of rights, the equal rights of men and women, the protection of the family and the equality of rights of spouses, and equality before the law, respectively.

[5] *A–G of Canada* v. *Jeanette Lavelle, Richard Isaac et al* v. *Yvonne Bedard* (1974), SCR 1349.

[6] A/36/40, 167, para. 5.

non-Indian men than by non-Indian women. These reasons were still valid, and the Indians were themselves divided on the issue of legal rights. Reform was accordingly difficult and could not be precipitate. The author of the communication in turn[7] disputed that legal relationships with families were traditionally patriarchal in nature.

The Human Rights Committee gave an Interim Decision in July 1980.[8] This decision hinted at a certain tension between articles of the Covenant. The Committee noted that the legal restrictions in the Indian Act raised the question of protection of family life under Article 23; while not legally restricting the right to marry under Article 23(2), they might cause the complainant to live with her fiancé in an unmarried relationship. There was also the discrimination point under Articles 2 and 3. On the other hand, Article 27 required States Parties to accord protection to minorities and the Committee had to give due weight to that obligation. The Committee requested additional information in order to form an opinion.[9] In particular, as Mrs Lovelace was married before the Covenant entered into force in respect of Canada,[10] the question as to whether the deprivation of status had continuing effects was important. Questions of fact were accordingly directed to the parties.

The Canadian legislation envisaged a loss of certain privileges for Indians who ceased to be members of an Indian band; in particular they were not entitled to reside by right on a reserve though they could do so if their presence was tolerated by other band members. Mrs Lovelace, by marrying a non-Indian, had ceased to be a member of the Tobique band, in addition to the general loss of Indian status mentioned above. It was agreed by both parties[11] that prior to her marriage, Mrs Lovelace's abode was in the Tobique reserve in the home of her parents; since her marriage and loss of Indian status she had, following a subsequent divorce, returned to her parents on the reserve, but could not establish a permanent residence there in her own right. Additionally, she lost access to federal government programmes for Indian people in terms of education, housing, and social assistance. Canada emphasized, however, that Mrs Lovelace enjoyed all benefits under Canadian legislation other than special benefits for Indians.

Mrs Lovelace itemized the detailed consequences of loss of Indian status, stating that 'All the consequences of loss of Indian status persist in that they are permanent and continue to deny the complainant rights she was born with.'[12] The final consequence of such loss was alleged to be the loss of

---

[7] Ibid., para. 6.
[8] Ibid., para. 8.
[9] Ibid., (a)–(f) for the full text of the question.
[10] The Covenant entered into force for Canada on 19 August 1976.
[11] UN Doc A/36/40, 170, para. 9.6.
[12] Ibid., para. 9.9.

cultural benefits of living in an Indian community, the emotional ties to home, family, friends and neighbours, and the loss of identity.[13]

The Committee decided that the essence of the complaint was the continuing effect of the Indian Act in denying Sandra Lovelace Indian status and the right to live on a reserve. Most of the effects listed by the complainant[14] did not, in the Committee's view, affect adversely the enjoyment of rights protected by the Covenant; the exception was the loss of cultural benefits noted above. Article 27 of the Covenant was deemed to be the article directly applicable to these facts. It was noted that, irrespective of the legislation, 'persons who are born and brought up on a reserve, who have kept ties with their community and wish to maintain those ties must normally be considered as belonging to that minority within the meaning of the Covenant.'[15] In the Committee's opinion, Mrs Lovelace 'belonged' to the minority and could claim rights under Article 27. Further, her right of access to her native culture and language in community with other members of her group was subject to continuing interference 'because there is no place outside the Tobique Reserve where such a community exists'.[16] Not every interference could be regarded as a denial of rights under the article, and national legislation might legitimately define rights of residence to protect resources and preserve the identity of a people. Restrictions on rights of residence had to have 'a reasonable and objective justification'[17] and be consistent with the other provisions of the Covenant read as a whole. Thus, Article 27 had to be construed in relation, especially, to Articles 12, 17, 18[18] and 23.[19] But general determinations of compatibility were not required in view of the special circumstances of the case.

The Committee concluded:

Whatever may be the merits of the Indian Act in other respects, it does not seem . . . that to deny Sandra Lovelace the right to reside on the reserve is reasonable or necessary to preserve the identity of the tribe . . . therefore . . . to prevent her recognition as belonging to the band is an unjustifiable denial of her rights under Article 27 of the Covenant, read in the context of the other provisions referred to.[20]

In view of the direct applicability of Article 27 it was considered unnecessary to examine the question of separate violations of the other Articles of the Covenant. One member of the Committee dissented on this point,[21] arguing that the discriminatory effects of the Indian Act should have been

---

[13] Ibid. [14] Ibid.
[15] UN Doc A/36/40, para. 14.
[16] Para. 15. [17] Para. 16.
[18] Article 12 defines the right to liberty of movement and freedom to choose a residence; Article 17 provides for protection against arbitrary or unlawful interference with privacy, family, home, or correspondence and unlawful attacks on honour and reputation.
[19] *Supra*, n. 4.
[20] UN Doc A/36/40, 174, para. 17.
[21] Ibid., 175, individual opinion of Mr Nejib Bouziri.

examined because they affected Mrs Lovelace in areas not covered by
Article 27.

Comment

It is submitted that this case confirms many of the observations made in the
present chapter. One point clearly affirmed is the prevalence of the international standard over national definitions of minority status. It was pointed
out above[22] that the 'existence' of a minority cannot be exclusively
determined by national legislation, and this control by international law
extends to the question of individual membership of a minority group.
There was no discussion of the application of the term 'minority' to the
cultural group to which Mrs Lovelace belonged; this was simply assumed by
the Committee, though the Canadian legislation, which distinguishes
Indians from other groups, is itself evidence of the existence of minority
groups and the Canadian Government did not dispute this point. The significance of this determination may well lie outside the Canadian context: it
is to be hoped that if cases come before the Committee dealing with tribal
populations in Latin American States under Article 27, the Committee will
make the same assumptions even in the absence of an 'official' international
definition of minority, and despite predictable opposition from such States
as to the 'non-existence' of minorities. Secondly, the stress is laid by the
Committee in the case on the individual's rights under Article 27, although
the community dimension of that right is also given consideration. While
the rights of Sandra Lovelace were deemed to have been violated, the
Committee also recognized that the need 'to preserve the identity of the
tribe'[23] was a legitimate objective of the Canadian legislation, and in other
cases might run contrary to the aspirations of individuals. The Committee
refrained from making generalizations on this point and stressed that the
circumstances were special. It is, however, to be expected in the application
of such a 'hybrid' right that the individual and collective components of the
right will require constant adjustment and balance.[24] Thirdly, Article 27,
besides being interpreted in an internally coherent fashion, needs to be
considered in the overall context of the Covenant. Though not subject to
specific limitations, such limitations may, as argued above, be deduced from
other Articles in the Covenant; this applies equally to general determinations of its scope and to such determinations in the circumstances of a
specific case. Lastly, it may be remarked that the presentation and consideration of a communication on Article 27 goes some way to demonstrat-

---

[22] *Supra*, ch. 16.
[23] UN Doc A/36/40, 175, para. 17.
[24] In the *Kitok Case* (*infra*, text following n. 34), the Human Rights Committee described its
version of the *ratio decidendi* of *Lovelace*.

ing that the rights contained therein are in no way extraordinary or egregious when compared to other human rights.

Kitok *v.* Sweden

On 27 July 1988 the Human Rights Committee adopted its views under the Optional Protocol concerning Communication No. 197/1985[25] the author of which was Ivan Kitok, a member of a Sami family which had been involved in reindeer breeding for, it was stated, 100 years. The substance of Kitok's allegation was that he had inherited rights to reindeer breeding, land, and water in Sörkaitum Sami Village, but was denied the exercise of these rights because of loss of membership in the village under the operation of Swedish law. Membership of a Sami village (*Sameby* or *Lappby*) for purposes of exercising Sami rights to reindeer breeding is lost by a Sami if he engages in any other profession for a period of three years. Swedish law, through the creation of Sami communities as legal entities, effectively divided Sami into two groups: those who engaged in reindeer herding and those who did not: 'The *ratio legis* for this legislation is to improve the living conditions for the Sami who have reindeer husbandry as their primary income, and to make the existence of reindeer husbandry safe for the future . . . Reindeer husbandry was considered necessary to protect and preserve the whole culture of the Sami . . .'[26] Those with Sami rights were estimated by the government to number 2,500 out of a total Sami population of between 15,000 and 20,000; the majority of ethnic Sami, therefore, had 'no special rights under the present law. These other Sami have found it more difficult to maintain their Sami identity and many of them are today assimilated into Swedish society.'[27]

Kitok claimed violations of the Covenant under Articles 1 and 27. The claim under Article 1 was declared inadmissible, the Committee observing that 'the author, as an individual, could not claim to be the victim of a violation of the right of self-determination . . . Whereas the Optional Protocol provides a recourse procedure for individuals claiming that their rights have been violated, Article 1 . . . deals with rights conferred upon peoples as such.'[28] The communication was declared admissible in so far as it raised

---

[25] CCPR/C/33/D/197/1985, 10 August 1988, Human Rights Committee, 33rd Session. Prior decisions: CCPR/C/WG/27/D/197/1985; CCPR/C/29/D/197/1985 (admissibility, 25 March 1987).

[26] Para. 4.2, submission by State party.   [27] Ibid.

[28] Para. 6.3. The Committee did not venture further comment of self-determination, confining itself to this essentially procedural point: cf. the *Micmaq Case*, *infra*, ch. 24. The author of the complaint submitted (para. 5.2) that the Sami people had the right to self-determination, and that the existence of Sami in countries other than Sweden should not be allowed to diminish the right to self-determination of Swedish Sami. The State Party's response (para. 4.1) was unequivocal: 'in the Government's opinion, the Sami do not constitute a "people" within the meaning given to the word in Article 1 of the Covenant'.

issues under Article 27, since 'the author had made a reasonable effort to substantiate his allegations that he was the victim of a violation of his right to enjoy the same rights enjoyed by other members of the Sami community.'[29] On the merits of the claim, the Committee considered whether Kitok had been denied the right to enjoy his own culture, observing that 'The regulation of an economic activity is normally a matter for the State alone. However, where that activity is an essential element in the culture of an ethnic community, its application to an individual may fall under Article 27 . . .'[30] The Committee stated that the right to enjoy culture cannot be determined *in abstracto* but has to be placed in context.[31] The Committee was thus called to consider statutory restrictions on membership of the communities and accepted that the law had as its *raison d'être* the preservation and well-being of the Sami minority. Therefore, it took the view that 'all these objectives and measures are reasonable and consistent with Article 27 of the Covenant'.[32]

The succeeding paragraphs of the opinion none the less cast doubt on certain sections of the legislation in their application to Kitok. The Committee cited sections 11 and 12 of the Reindeer Husbandry Act 1971: section 11 limits membership of a Sami community to those participating in reindeer husbandry within the pasture area of the community, those who have so participated and have not turned to another main economic activity, and specified relations of qualified persons; section 12 provides that others can be accepted as members with a right of appeal in the case of a refusal for special reasons. The Committee declared:

It can . . . be seen that the Act provides certain criteria for participation in the life of an ethnic minority whereby a person who is ethnically a Sami can be held not to be a Sami for the purposes of the Act. The Committee has been concerned that the ignoring of objective ethnic criteria in determining membership of a minority, and the application to Mr Kitok of the designated rules, may have been disproportionate to the legitimate ends sought by the legislation. It was further noted that Mr Kitok has always retained some links with the Sami community . . .[33]

Despite this critique of the impact of the law on the applicant, the Committee, in a very brief resolution of the issue, stated:

In . . . this problem, in which there is an apparent conflict between the legislation, which seems to protect the rights of the minority as a whole, and its application to a single member of that minority, the Committee has been guided by the *ratio decidendi* in the *Lovelace* case . . . namely, that a restriction upon the right of an individual member of a minority must be shown to have a reasonable and objective justification and to be necessary for the continued viability and welfare of the minority as a whole . . . the Committee is of the view that there is no violation of

---

[29] Paras. 5.1, 5.2, 5.3, 5.4 outline Kitok's position.
[30] Para. 9.2.   [31] Para. 9.3.   [32] Para. 9.5.
[33] Para. 9.7. Other legislation is referred to at various points by the author.

Article 27 . . . In this context, the Committee notes that Mr Kitok is permitted, albeit not as of right, to graze and farm his reindeer, to hunt and to fish.[34]

This, the second case with Article 27 as a focus, is again linked to an indigenous people, demonstrating that the article applies *de minimis*, whatever further norms may be relevant. The result is, however, not entirely laudable. The key issue is how far the preservation of communities may emarginate rights of individuals. The terms 'reasonable', 'objective' and 'proportionality' are deployed to decide the issue, but the tensions are clear. The Committee had 'grave doubts' about aspects of the legislation, and the point about unduly restrictive 'national' definitions of group membership might have been pressed. Both cases are contextual and avoid setting broad precedents. However, the Swedish argument on the rôle of the law (and the Committee's acceptance of this) in preservation of Sami identity is difficult to square with the admission that assimilation is the fate of the Sami majority; Article 27 projects its rights at ethnic groups, not ethnic fragments. The effect of the legislation appears unduly divisive to the present author, and the interpretation too favourable to the respondent State.

[34] Para. 9.8.

24. Self-Determination in the Covenants: A Note

Article 1 of both UN Human Rights Covenants commences with 'All peoples have the right of self-determination'. The other paragraphs refer to economic self-determination (paragraph 2); and to the duty of States Parties to the Covenants to promote self-determination (paragraph 3): 'The States Parties to the present Covenant, including those having responsibility for the administration of Non-Self-Governing and Trust Territories, shall promote the realization of the right of self-determination, and shall respect that right, in conformity with the provisions of the Charter of the United Nations.'

The right of self-determination in the Covenants is universal. The text and *travaux* support the view that the Covenants reach beyond the colonial situation,[1] though there are indications of narrower views.[2] Some interest in this respect attaches to the declaration made by India on Article 1: 'the Government of the Republic of India declares that the words "the right of self-determination" . . . apply only to the peoples under foreign domination and that these words do not apply to sovereign independent States or to a section of the people or nation—which is the essence of national integrity.' Other States have objected to the declaration, which clearly curtails the scope of the article.[3] The Netherlands objection reads, in part: 'Any attempt to limit the scope of [the] . . . right or to attach conditions . . . would undermine the concept of self-determination itself and would . . . seriously weaken its universally acceptable character.'[4] The position of India has, however, been marked by inconsistency.[5] Its delegate had earlier stated in the General Assembly's Third Committee that: 'although there were good

---

[1] Cf. Article 1(3): 'The States parties to the present Covenant, including those having responsibility for . . . the Non-Self-Governing and Trust territories, shall promote the realization of the right of self-determination . . .' The post-colonial future of self-determination was a matter of relative unconcern to many States, though Western States insisted on a continuing function. Among other States, we may note the forthright statement of Afghanistan that self-determination 'will have to be proclaimed even in a world from which colonial territories have vanished', UN Doc A/C.3/SR.644, para. 10.

[2] Europe 'had reached the ultimate goal where self-determination was concerned; now that European Powers were denying the right of self-determination to Asian and African peoples, there could be no doubt that the question of the inclusion of Article 1 of the Covenants was a purely colonial issue', UN Doc A/C.3/SR.648, para. 8 (Syria). Many States expressed the view that the Colonies would be the first beneficiaries of self-determination. This does not rule out later beneficiaries.

[3] UN Doc ST/HR/R/Rev.4, 44 ff.   [4] Ibid. 64.

[5] Franck and Rodley, 'After Bangladesh: The Law of Humanitarian Intervention by Military Force', *AJIL*, 67 (1973), 275.

reasons to make special reference to the peoples of non-self-governing territories, it must be recognized that the field of application of the principle of self-determination was wider than that'.[6] There is little reason to doubt the view that the Covenants mean what they say: that Article 1 applies to all peoples, and is not confined to colonial territories.

The 'broad' view of the applicability of Article 1 is a fundamental assumption underlying the 'General Comment' issued by the Human Rights Committee: 'it imposes specific obligations on States Parties, not only in relation to their own peoples but vis-à-vis all peoples which have not been able to exercise or have been deprived of the possibility of their right to self-determination.'[7] This makes it clear that the right is universal, as can be expected in a document of Human Rights. The promotion of self-determination must be consistent with other provisions of International Law: 'in particular, States must refrain from interfering in the internal affairs of other States and thereby adversely affecting the exercise of the right . . .'. Self-determination in the Covenants includes internal self-determination. The Comment alludes to this: 'With regard to paragraph 1 of Article 1, States Parties should describe the constitutional and political processes which in practice allow the exercise of [self-determination].' The Committee complains that many States in their reports 'completely ignore Article 1, provide inadequate information in relation to it or confine themselves to a reference to election laws'. The comment makes no contribution to the elucidation of any people and minority distinction. The assumption appears to be that minorities are covered by Article 27.

The tension between 'people' and 'minority' is apparent at various stages in the drafting. Afghanistan and Saudi Arabia, authors of a Draft Resolution on self-determination, at one time deleted the term 'peoples' from their draft. This was at the suggestion of delegations who feared that the term 'might encourage minorities within a State to ask for the right to self-determination'.[8] On the other hand, India argued that the problem of minorities should not be raised in the context of self-determination.[9] China declared that the issue 'was that of national majorities and not of minorities'.[10] The reference to 'majorities' reflected the views of many in the debates; it may be taken as an infelicitous expression of the conviction that the right of self-determination is one for whole peoples, and not for sections of them. This view of self-determination dominates the *travaux*, despite occasional hesitations.[11]

Article 27 describes limited rights in a limited cultural sphere. Self-

[6] UN Doc A/C.3/SR.399, para. 4.

[7] There is a useful collection of these comments by the Human Rights Committee in *EHRR*, 9, 169. The comment on self-determination was adopted by the Committee on 12 April 1984.

[8] A/C.3/SR.310, para. 3.

[9] A/C.3/SR.399, paras. 5–6.   [10] A/C.3/SR.369, para. 13.

[11] E.g., Yugoslavia professed unconcern at whether self-determination applied to minorities, dismissing this as a 'legalistic' argument. A/C.3/SR.647, para. 40.

determination is related to broader control by a people of its political, social, and cultural arrangements; full, not partial rights. In the light of the limitations of Article 27, it appears ambitious to argue for a connection between minorities and self-determination. There are, however, at least two possibilities of 'positive' interpretation implying a connection: (a) minorities are peoples within the meaning of Article 1 — a view which is not supported by the *travaux*; or (b) attribution of rights to whole peoples benefits minorities *indirectly*. There is also a negative possibility: (c) self-determination is best understood as external, and internal self-determination is supererogatory.

In relation to (a), the practice of the Human Rights Committee is equivocal, but may be taken to buttress the view that minorities are not peoples. Questions on individual groups in a State which might imply that they are covered by Article 1 are often 'fielded' by that State under Article 27.[12] In the 'communication' to the Committee by the Grand Captain of the Mikmaq Tribal Society, the applicant focused on Article 1 rather than Article 27. The communication was rejected at the admissibility stage because the author had 'not proven that he is authorised to act as a representative ... of the Mikmaq tribal society. In addition, the author has failed to advance any pertinent facts supporting his claim that he is personally a victim of any rights contained in the Covenant.'[13] The impediments to his claim may have been procedural or substantive: the Committee's statement is not clear. This statement is hardly a basis for broad claims on the applicability of Article 1. On the other hand, another communication involving Canadian Indians, that of Sandra Lovelace, has produced an unequivocal response from the Committee on the applicability of Article 27.[14] The case contrasts vividly with the uncertainty engendered by the Mikmaq case. Whatever the 'self-descriptive' terms employed by the indigenous groups, the Covenant as construed at present accommodates them better under Article 27 than Article 1.

But if minorities are not the 'peoples' of the Covenants, self-determination may still be relevant. As noted in the introduction to this work, the internal aspect of self-determination may have some incidence upon the fortunes of the groups, even though the formal subject of the right is the whole

---

[12] The reference here is to the reporting procedure under the Covenant. For a recent example, see the report of the Human Rights Committee for 1987, where a question on Article 1 of the Covenant raised the issue of the status of the Kurds: the reply of Iraq stated that the Constitution 'recognised the ethnic rights of the Kurdish people as well as the legitimate rights of all minorities ... the Kurds were part and parcel of the Iraqi people'. Iraq dealt with the Kurdish question in later paragraphs under Article 27. UN Doc A/42/40, paras. 352, 353, 385, 386.

[13] UN Doc A/39/40 (1984) 200, 203; Communication No.78/1980. Cf. the *Kitok Case* (*supra*, ch. 23, text accompanying nn. 25–34).

[14] UN Doc A/36/40 (1981), 166; Communication No.R6/24; Selected Decisions under the Optional Protocol, 2nd to 16th Sessions (New York: United Nations, 1985), 10, 37 and 83, UN Doc CCPR/C/OP/1 *supra*. 207–11.

people; the greater includes the lesser. Internal self-determination is favoured by Western States, reflecting their notions of democracy; President Wilson's early use of the term depended very much on American constitutional tradition.[15] From a Socialist point of view, Lenin wrote that 'in reality, the recognition of the right of all nations to self-determination implies the maximum of democracy and the minimum of nationalism.'[16] For the States of the Third World, concerned with ridding themselves of Western domination, self-determination is externally orientated, and, in so far as it has an internal aspect, this is to do with majority rule (rule of the 'whole people') and the avoidance of rule by minorities, especially white minorities.[17] The question is to what extent may any of these conceptions be taken to govern the Covenants? The comment of the Human Rights Committee is neither optimistic nor very illuminating. States do not find much use for Article 1 'internally'. But the Committee's comment also incorporates a view about self-determination 'underlying' Human Rights: 'The right of self-determination is of particular importance because its realisation is an essential condition for the effective guarantee and observance of individual human rights.' This could be read together with the reference to 'political and constitutional processes' to signify that States must organize these processes to support the programme of Human Rights contained in the Covenants. This stresses the collective aspect of the principle, moving from individuals to the society at large. The application of internal self-determination is gauged with reference to Human Rights, not to ideologies beyond it; violations of self-determination are violations of Human Rights. The 'democracy' of the Covenants can be none other than commitment to the global implementation of their provisions.

Such an interpretation appears to do little more than reiterate existing rights. It does, however, direct attention to the organization of the State as a whole and how that organization favours or disfavours human values to the benefit of all within the State, minorities included. It is probably in advance of the opinions of most States Parties, which leads to possibility (c): perhaps the truth is that self-determination has little to do with human rights. The implementation of the Covenant has not succeeded in showing how self-determination can be effective 'internally'. Frequently, the questions of the Human Rights Committee are directed to divining the attitude of States to apartheid, Namibia, and Palestine, rather than to their own peoples, who should be the primary focus of concern.

---

[15] Miller, *The Drafting of the Covenant.*

[16] *The Right of Nations to Self-Determination* English edn. (Moscow: Progress Publishers, 1947) 45. The Constitution of the USSR 1977, Article 72 provides: 'Each Union Republic shall retain the right freely to secede from the USSR.' Lenin and Stalin (the Bolshevik 'expert' on the nationalities question) both warned that the exercise of self-determination by Soviet nationalities must not prejudice the greater interests of socialism: Stalin, *Marxism and the National Question* (Moscow: Foreign Languages Publishing House, 1950).

[17] The examples of South Africa and the former Southern Rhodesia may be noted.

The limited interpretation of Article 1 offered in this chapter is intended to reflect *lex lata*. In the continuing process of interpretation and implementation of the Covenant right of self-determination, a gradual enhancement of State appreciation of expansive constructions more available to minorities may succeed the present uncertainty. In some interpretations, internal self-determination creates possibilities of autonomy for minorities[18] in partial recognition of the claims of a collectivity. The resistance by some States to any enhanced 'collective' element in the elaboration of a regime for minorities to supplement Article 27 makes this a rather optimistic assessment; 'possibilistic' rather than 'probabilistic'. The answer to claims of autonomy may be to start with what there is and work from the existing base of human rights, including Article 27 in a flexible and supple interpretation of that article, with all its difficulties, rather than confront States with maximalist demands based on self-determination.[19]

---

[18] 'The recognition of group rights, more especially when this is related to territoral rights and regional autonomy, represents the practical and internal working out of the concept of self-determination. Such recognition is therefore the internal application of the concept of self-determination': Brownlie, *The Rights of Peoples*, 6.

[19] See *infra*, ch. 41, on self-determination and indigenous populations.

25. Article 27 as General International Law: Views of Jurists

Capotorti, in a passage not entirely free from ambiguity, states, apropos of Article 27, that

while this article is not a source of legal obligations for States which have not yet ratified the Covenant, the approval of the Covenant by the General Assembly of the United Nations has conferred upon the articles the value of general principles no less significant than those set forth in solemn United Nations Declarations. From this point of view, the right granted by Article 27 to persons belonging to . . . minorities can be considered as forming an integral part of the system of protection of human rights and fundamental freedoms instituted after the Second World War . . .[1]

On the one hand, the Special Rapporteur says that Article 27 does not *oblige* States not parties to the Covenant, but, none the less, the text of the article, and all other articles in the Covenant, have the value of general principles through adoption by the General Assembly. Since 'general principles', in the sense of Article 38(1)(c) of the Statute of the International Court of Justice, are a source of legal obligation, the reference to Article 27, in order not to be illogical, should refer to the rule or maxim *pacta tertiis nec nocent nec prosunt*, now expressed in Article 34 of the Vienna Convention on the Law of Treaties: 'A treaty does not create either obligations or rights for a third State without its consent.'[2] On the other hand, it is not clear that to attribute 'significance' to the principle in solemn United Nations Declarations is quite the same as attributing legal effect—so that the Special Rapporteur may perhaps be describing general effects in the area of 'soft' rather than 'hard' law. Some kind of obligation or effect is hinted at in the reference to 'integral part of the system of protection of human rights'. The place accorded to Article 27 is logically the place accorded to the whole human rights system so that the Article has as much general 'significance' as any other part.

Capotorti's tentative formula may be contrasted with the vigorous assertion of Dinstein that Article 27 is 'declaratory in nature and reflects a minimum of rights recognised by customary law'.[3] Dinstein also asserts that 'International law accords rights—on a collective basis—to ethnic, religious

---

[1] UN Doc E/CN.4/Sub.2/384/Add.4, Para. 1.
[2] *ILM*, 8 (1969), 679.
[3] Dinstein, 'Collective Human Rights of Peoples and Minorities', at 118.

and linguistic minorities.'[4] In relation to the first statement, he considers that Article 27 is a framework provision only, but that concretization was achieved to some extent in the UNESCO Convention against Discrimination in Education, 1960.[5] The lack of concretization is none the less particularly 'glaring' in the cases of linguistic minorities, and it is also evident in the case of religious minorities. The author's statements are perhaps too confident and lack demonstration. The reference to customary international law is illustrated with regard to the case of the *Minority Schools in Albania*[6] and against the background of the League of Nations Minority System, which, the author agrees, is defunct. Customary or general international law is hardly adverted to in the context of the article as a whole except by way of assertion. The author's strong emphasis on the collective right is also more or less unqualified. In view of past and present antipathy to minority rights on the part of States, and particularly to the notion of collective rights, greater caution would have been justified.

Brownlie, in the context of a dispute centred on Canada, also agrees that the principles of Article 27 represent general international law.[7] When his statement was made, Canada was not a party to the Covenant, but 'whilst Canada is not bound by the Covenant in terms of treaty obligations, the International Covenant—in its standard-setting aspects—binds Canada, since the principles set forth in the Covenant constitute general international law'.[8] The steps in the argument are that principles concerning basic human rights generate obligations *erga omnes*, and the rights of minorities are fundamental in at least one sense: 'When cultural and linguistic identity or character is lost or degraded, the change tends to be irreversible.'[9] This distinguishes the right in Article 27 from other rights for the violation of which specific relief may be possible. Secondly, the Sub-Commission on Prevention of Discrimination and Protection of Minorities 'did not regard the principle of Article 27 to be mere *lex ferenda* and novel'. He also cites the ILO Convention on Indigenous Populations[10] and other international instruments[11] as recognizing the 'special position' of ethnic and linguistic groups. While the whole evidence marshalled by Brownlie for his propositions is not of overwhelming cogency, the argument that cultural degradation may be irreversible is important and noteworthy. The effect is to promote the recognition that the right to an identity is a fundamental notion, from at least this point of view. He compares it with the right not to

---

[4] Ibid. 111.
[5] Discuss, *infra*, ch. 32.
[6] *Supra*, ch. 3.
[7] *Re the Mackenzie Valley Pipeline Enquiry: Considerations of Public International Law Concerning the Rights of the Dene and Inuit as the Indigenous Peoples of the North West Territories of Canada*, Opinion (March, 1976).
[8] Ibid. 9.
[9] Ibid.
[10] *Infra*, ch. 39.
[11] UN, Protection of Minorities, *supra*, ch. 9, n. 8.

be detained without trial for which redress may be available (though the detainee's loss of liberty is, *stricto sensu*, irrecoverable). On the other hand, Brownlie's demonstration of the customary law status of the principle of non-discrimination (as opposed to the principle of identity) is more specific. The evidence is that that principle has '*received recognition by States generally*'[12] and non-discrimination 'is *widely regarded* as a part of customary or general international law'. Further evidence includes the principles expressed by the Permanent Court of International Justice in the case of *Minority Schools in Albania*, the *South West Africa Cases*, the 'constant appearance [of the principle of non-discrimination] in multilateral instruments relating to human rights',[13] the *Barcelona Traction Case*, etc. Thus, Article 2 of the UN Covenant on Civil and Political Rights is described as 'declaratory of an existing principle of international law'.[14] It may be guessed that this recital of evidence is more complete than for Article 27 because the weight of evidence is greater.

Vukas is another writer with a clear view of the law: 'We consider that today there exist some general principles guaranteeing minorities the rights necessary for their existence.'[15] He reaches this conclusion on the basis of some 'developments in international and municipal law'.[16] Thus, he asserts that despite their failure as positive law the Minorities Treaties under the League of Nations 'left a lasting imprint on legal consciousness'.[17] He has in mind the fundamental provisions incorporated in all the treaties. Vukas also mentions the 'solutions repeatedly contained in numerous postwar bilateral treaties'[18] on particular minorities, and multilateral treaties 'which explicitly mention the rights of minorities'[19] (the Genocide Convention, the Covenant on Civil and Political Rights, etc.). Another factor is the emergence of human rights stemming from the UN Charter and the Universal Declaration of Human Rights, and in particular the principle of non-discrimination. Finally, the constitutional rules of many countries having minorities are cited: in addition to general rules of non-discrimination, many States demonstrate particular concern in law for their minorities—the States of the Eastern bloc are mentioned here, as well as Italy, Austria, Denmark, Finland, Belgium, and Switzerland. He admits that all constitutions do not grant identical rights to minorities but that some rights are 'almost regularly'[20] mentioned: the right to opt for a minority, the right to equal treatment before the law, the right to use a minority language in communication with State agencies, the right to instruction in the language of the minority, and the right to the development of culture in the mother tongue.

He therefore finds some general principles of law in the sense of Article 38(1)(c) of the Statute of the International Court of Justice: 'the principles

---

[12] *Supra*, n. 7, 11.   [13] Ibid. 18.   [14] Ibid. 19.
[15] 'General International Law and the Protection of Minorities', *RDH* VIII–I (1975), 41.
[16] Ibid.   [17] Ibid.   [18] Ibid. 43.
[19] Ibid.   [20] Ibid. 46.

... have come into being through the mutual and parallel interaction of internal and international law'.[21] The list of general principles is, to the present author, surprisingly extensive and detailed. Besides the above-mentioned rights, and such rights as to physical existence, the author finds 'The right to schools of all levels with instruction in the languages of minorities. Instruction must be so organised that persons belonging to minorities can master the language of the majority and learn the achievements of its culture.'[22] There is also the right to 'voluntary self-financing, and . . . the right to an equitable portion of State budgetary resources for all activities aimed at the preservation of minorities (schooling, culture, administration) etc.'.[23] General principles of law also give rise to duties for minorities: 'The duty to refrain from acts directed against the preservation of the territorial integrity or political independence of the State in which they live.'[24] States have a duty: 'to prevent the propaganda and practice of discrimination against minorities and to forbid organizations based on the ideas of racial, national, ethnic and religious inequality'.[25] From his point of view, the adoption of new instruments on the protection of minorities could not only constitute progressive development but also, clearly, codification of existing law.

Two more writers may briefly be mentioned. Kelly describes Article 27 as 'by far the most persuasive contemporary *codification* of [the] . . . international right to exist as a minority'.[26] This implies that there is law to codify, so that Article 27 may be described as declaratory. He cites the views of the UN Sub-Commission on Prevention of Discrimination and Protection of Minorities that Article 27 is not only a sound conventional rule for the protection of minorities, but also a source of principles that could be applied regardless of the entry into force of the Covenant.[27] He also mentions various multilateral and bilateral treaties in support of his argument.[28] The fact that some States are publicly assimilationist does not deflect his argument. He notes that 'Even in the assimilationist minded United States, national minorities have achieved a special status.[29] In terms of contemporary legislation, he cites Title VII of the 1964 Civil Rights Act exempting Indian tribes from non-discriminatory employment rules.[30] Further evidence includes the fact that in parts of the world (Eastern and Central Europe are mentioned) the right not to be assimilated is considered a basic human right. He summarizes his view in terms of the distinction between tolerance and encouragement: 'At the most, international law currently gives minority

---

[21] Ibid. 47.   [22] Ibid. 48.
[23] Ibid.   [24] Ibid.   [25] Ibid.
[26] 'National Minorities in International Law', *Journal of International Law and Policy*, 3 (1973), 253 at 266.
[27] UN Doc E/CN.4/Sub.2/SR.647, 150.
[28] The UNESCO Convention against Discrimination, the European Convention on Human Rights.
[29] Kelly, 267–8.   [30] 42 USC 8200B (1970).

groups the right to be tolerated.'[31] Thus, the general law reflects Article 27 only as far as the negative interpretation of that Article[32] and does not require positive encouragement of minorities.

De Nova, on the other hand, conducting a survey which resembles Kelly's, reaches a different conclusion.[33] For De Nova, protection of minorities is only a 'technique'[34] for lessening internal and international tensions; this technique is to be used sparingly and cautiously, that is, 'when local situations seem to require and allow it'.[35] On this understanding, there is a clear view that there are no general normative rules relating to minorities — instead the 'technique' is to be applied on a case by case basis. His lists of treaties and declarations relating to minorities[36] do not transmute themselves into universal categories. Only individual human rights along the lines of the Universal Declaration of Human Rights are 'universalizable' — though even in this case such rules have 'exhortatory rather than imperative character'.[37] This reference may be explained by the fact that De Nova's article was published in 1965, before the adoption of the UN Covenants on Human Rights, these have added clear normative character to human rights law as well as lending weight to a trend to regard the principles of the Universal Declaration as customary law.

---

[31] Kelly, 270.

[32] *Supra*, ch. 18.

[33] 'The International Protection of Minorities and Human Rights', *Howard Law Journal*, 11 (1965), 275.

[34] Ibid. 289.

[35] Ibid.

[36] Similar to Kelly, including the Minorities Treaties of the League of Nations.

[37] De Nova, 289.

26. Assessment and Analysis: Human Rights as General International Law

The fact that propositions favouring the idea of Article 27 as generally applicable law derive from reputable jurists makes it expedient to recall that juristic opinion is itself a subsidiary source of international law under Article 38(1)(d), of the Statute of the International Court of Justice.[1] The evidence of law provided through the opinions of writers must be assessed critically as must other 'sources'. Remarks have been made in the present text on the relative lack of demonstration in the legal propositions. None the less, the argument that Article 27 represents general international law is assisted by the opinions outlined, bearing in mind, however, that this sample of writers is limited. Other writers, while they do not deal specifically with the question of the generality of Article 27, might be expected to arrive at different conclusions.[2] It appears largely presupposed by the writers that the international law of human rights has gained acceptance by the international community, clothing it with the character of generally binding international law.

The United Nations Charter is the fountain of law in the case of the modern doctrine. The Charter refers to human rights in its Preamble and in six articles. In the Preamble, the peoples of the United Nations express their determination 'to reaffirm faith in fundamental human rights, in the dignity and worth of the human person . . .'. Article 1(3) describes as a 'Purpose of the United Nations' the promotion and encouragement of 'respect for human rights and . . . fundamental freedoms for all the [non-discrimination formula follows] . . .'. Article 55 provides that the United Nations shall promote: 'Universal respect for, and observance of human rights and fundamental freedoms for all without distinction as to race, sex, language or religion.' Article 56 complements this by providing that 'All Members [of the United Nations] pledge themselves to take joint and separate action in co-operation with the Organization for the achievement of the purposes set forth in Article 55.' Further, Article 13 of the Charter authorizes the General Assembly to initiate studies and make recommendations for the purpose of 'assisting in the realisation of human rights and fundamental

---

[1] Consult Akehurst, *A Modern Introduction to International Law* (6th edn., 1987), ch. 3, and 'The Hierarchy of the Sources of International Law'; Van Hoof, *Rethinking the Sources of International Law*, 176 ff.

[2] See the views of Vierdag in *The Concept of Discrimination*, set out, *infra*, Part V.

freedoms for all [this is followed by the non-discrimination formula]'.[3] Similarly, the Economic and Social Council is empowered, under Article 62, to 'make recommendations for the purpose of promoting respect for, and observance of, human rights and fundamental freedoms for all'. Article 68 empowers the Economic and Social Council to set up Commissions for the promotion of human rights—the Commission on Human Rights and the Sub-Commission on Prevention of Discrimination and Protection of Minorities are referred to extensively in the present work.[4] Finally, Article 76 declares that one of the basic objectives of the Trusteeship System shall be to encourage respect for human rights and fundamental freedoms.

These generalized references to human rights are clearly of great importance. Although not a 'principle' of the Charter, the promotion of human rights is a 'purpose'. The Rapporteur of Committee I of Commission I at San Francisco stated that the 'purposes' 'constitute the *raison d'être* of the Organization'. They are 'the aggregation of the common ends on which our minds met; hence, the cause and object of the Charter to which Member States collectively and severally subscribed.'[5] He regarded the Preamble as setting out 'declared common intentions'. Thus the various provisions of the Charter 'are equally valid and operative. The rights, duties, privileges and obligations of the Organization and its Members match with one another and complement one another to make a whole'.[6]

The importance of inserting a reference to human rights in the 'purposes' of the Charter is evident from the above remarks. The promotion of human rights is a *raison d'être* of the United Nations.[7] However, to what extent any of this constitutes a binding legal obligation on the Members of the United Nations has been, and remains, a matter of dispute. Recalling the hortatory language of the Charter, 'promote', 'encourage', etc., Hudson denied that the Charter imposed legal obligations—human rights were simply an aim to be achieved.[8] Kelsen stated that

The Charter does not impose upon the Members a strict obligation to grant to their subjects the rights and freedoms mentioned in the Preamble or in the text of the Charter. The language used . . . does not allow the interpretation that the Members are under legal obligations regarding the rights and freedoms of their subjects . . . Besides, the Charter does in no way specify the rights and freedoms to which it refers.[9]

---

[3] See the discussion of the Charter articles on non-discrimination, *supra*, ch. 12.

[4] See Salzberg, *UN Sub-Commission*.

[5] *UNCIO Docs.*, vol. vi, 387–89.   [6] Ibid.

[7] A number of writers have distinguished, perhaps rather too sharply, between the Purposes and the Principles of the UN Charter, in order to question to what extent legal obligations may be deduced from the Purposes. See Pomerance, *Self-Determination in Law and Practice: The New Doctrine at the United Nations*, 9. Also, Bentwich and Martin, *A Commentary on the Charter of the United Nations* (London: Routledge and Kegan Paul, 1950).

[8] Hudson, 'Integrity of International Instruments', *AJIL*, 42 (1948), 105.

[9] *The Law of the United Nations* (London: Stevens and Sons, 1951), 29–32. See also Kelsen, *Principles of International Law*, 226 and 237 (New York: Tucker, 1966).

On the other hand, Lauterpacht declared that views claiming a lack of obligation were rather facile, and noted, apropos of Articles 55 and 56, that these 'appear to place Member States under an obligation to co-operate with the United Nations in the carrying out of its function, which is stated as being the promotion of universal respect for, and observance of, human rights and fundamental freedoms'.[10] He said also that 'any construction of the Charter according to which Members of the United Nations are, in law, entitled to disregard—and to violate—human rights and fundamental freedoms is destructive of both the legal and moral authority of the Charter ... [and] ... runs counter to a cardinal principle of construction according to which treaties must be interpreted in good faith'.[11] Lauterpacht's response to the point about the lack of definition of the rights and freedoms referred to in the Charter was that 'There is a difference between urging that the legal character of a rule is destroyed and admitting that its effectiveness is diminished as the result of the absence of a full measure of definition.'[12] Higgins has remarked appropriately that 'the Charter is not in the habit of defining its terms, and if a definition were a pre-requisite to obligation, virtually all the articles of the Charter would be rendered meaningless'.[13] A key word appears to be 'pledge' in Article 56 which suggests some degree of legal obligation.[14] Sloan argued that the 'pledge' in Article 56 cannot be reduced to a platitude, and it is a principle of the Charter that all Members shall fulfil in good faith their obligations[15] (Article 2(2)). Wright deduced the following meanings from Articles 55 and 56:[16]

Article 55 imposes an obligation upon the United Nations as a collective entity to promote universal respect for, and observance of, human rights, while Article 56 imposes an obligation upon its Members to take joint or separate action, in co-operation with the Organization, for the achievement of universal respect for, and observance of, human rights. Certainly, the latter obligation requires Members to see that their organs of government respect and observe human rights in carrying out their normal functions.[17]

---

[10] *International Law and Human Rights* (London: Stevens and Sons, 1950), 149.

[11] Ibid. See now Article 31(1) of the Vienna Convention on the Law of Treaties 1969.

[12] *Supra*, n. 10, 148–9.

[13] Higgins, *The Development of International Law Through the Political Organs of the United Nations* (London: OUP, 1963), 119.

[14] Wright, 'Recognition and Self-Determination', *Procs. ASIL (1954)*, 23; Higgins, 118 ff.

[15] 'Human Rights, the United Nations and International Law', 20 *Nordisk Tidsskrift for International Ret, Acta Scandinavica Juris Gentium* (1950), 30–31. Further 'positive' views of legal obligations on Human Rights flowing from the Charter are essayed in Schwelb, 'International Court of Justice and the Human Rights Clauses of the United Nations Charter', *AJIL*, 66 (1972), 337.

[16] See also Lauterpacht (*supra*, n. 10), 152: 'the legal duty to promote Human Rights includes the legal duty to respect them'.

[17] 'National Courts and Human Rights—The Fujii Case', *AJIL*, 45 (1951), 62 at 73. The *travaux* show a degree of narrowing of the 'pledge' from an original proposal by a Drafting Sub-Committee that the Members of the UN should pledge themselves 'to take separate and joint action and to co-operate with the Organisation and with each other to achieve [the

There is, as noted, no catalogue of human rights in the United Nations Charter. Some delegates at the San Francisco Conference proposed that the Charter define human rights, and Panama urged the incorporation of a Bill of Rights, but none of this was accepted. It may be said that there was a general unwillingness on the part of States to include anything more than general references. The Charter articles on human rights were shaped by concern about national sovereignty, apprehension about the potential coercive power of the United Nations, fears about raising popular expectations too high in the field of human rights, as well as by enthusiasm for human rights. Further, in practical terms, States felt that the detailed drafting of a Bill of Rights should be deferred.[18] Lauterpacht remarked, in a trenchant paragraph, that 'It would have been obtuse to the point of pedantry for the draftsmen of the Charter to incorporate an explicit provision of this nature in a document in which the principle of respect for, and observance of, human rights and fundamental freedoms is one of the main pillars of the structure of the Organization created by the Charter.'[19]

Subject to remarks below on the definition of the rights and freedoms set out in the Charter, it may be said that while the obligation imposed by the Charter is rather general, given the legal quality of the pledge in respect of human rights and fundamental freedoms, the obligation to 'promote' human rights is inconsistent with massive violations of human rights committed by the authorities of the State. It is probably unnecessary to invoke aspects of the Charter dealing with international peace and security to find that at least large scale violations infringe the Charter.[20] Whereas it may be argued that a poor performance by States in respect of some rights may none the less be in general compatible with progress towards human rights in a State, this is presumptively not the case with systematic, regressive policies. Lauterpacht noted that with the advent of the United Nations Charter, it could not be demanded that all human rights be put into effect 'at a stroke'. But, for example, a State 'would act contrary to its clear legal obligations under the Charter if it were to impose fresh discrimination on a religious, ethnical or racial group. And there would be no doubt a flagrant breach of its legal obligations if it were to embark upon active persecution

objectives of Article 55]'. This was interpreted by the UK as implying a threefold pledge: for joint action, for separate action, and action in co-operation with the United Nations; a pledge to take separate action might mean that the internal affairs of a State would be subject to international scrutiny. However, a plain reading of the text would seem to leave little doubt that States should individually co-ordinate their policies in line with those of the UN in order to fulfil the Purposes of the Organization. Consult Sohn, in Sohn and Buergenthal, *International Protection of Human Rights*, 505.

[18] Sohn and Buergenthal, ibid. Also Humphrey, 'The Universal Declaration of Human Rights: its History, Impact and Juridical Character', in Ramcharan (ed.), *Human Rights Thirty Years after the Universal Declaration*, 21 (The Hague: M. Nijhoff, 1979).

[19] *Supra*, n. 10, 151.

[20] See *The Effects of Gross Violations of Human Rights on International Peace and Security*, Report of the Secretary-General, UN Doc E/CN.4/Sub.2/1984/1.

of persons under its jurisdiction on account of their race, language or religion.'[21] Lauterpacht's statement on this point is open to the interpretation that if a State, instead of 'embarking upon' 'fresh discrimination', were merely to continue as existing institutionalized systematic discrimination, it might not be in violation of the Charter. Waldock, it is submitted, states the point rather better:

> It is one thing to say that a State does not, by the working of Articles 55 and 56, engage itself to answer every complaint of an alleged infringement of a human right ... It is quite another thing to hold that it may flagrantly or persistently violate human rights without involving itself in a contravention of those articles. Such conduct would appear to be wholly incompatible with an obligation to *promote* observance of human rights.[22]

In another paragraph, the latter author refers to 'conduct manifestly incompatible with [the] obligation to promote observance of human rights'.[23] Brownlie expresses a similar view: under the Charter, the State is responsible for substantial infringements of human rights 'especially where a class of persons or pattern of activity is involved'.[24]

At the San Francisco Conference, the Soviet delegate considered that 'pledge' (Article 56) was the appropriate verb for a general obligation; a verb such as 'undertake' would have been more appropriate for specific obligations.[25] Thus, to recall the wording of Economic and Social Council Resolution 1503(XLVIII) 'a consistent pattern of gross . . . violations of human rights' by the State would certainly infringe the Charter, even if the State concerned was not a party to any convention on human rights. The '1503 Procedure' (confidential) and the (non-confidential) procedure under Economic and Social Council Resolution 1235(XLII) have been developed from the United Nations Charter itself.[26] Individual violations of human rights would, in general, be left appropriately to the instruments on human rights. Thus, the Soviet Union has opposed scrutiny under the 'Charter procedures' of the relationship between governments and individual citizens,[27] and proposed the discontinuance of such procedures when the United Nations Covenants came into force in 1976.[28] However, the appropriateness of the Charter procedures, with all their difficulties,[29] for mass violations of human rights has been sustained.

The Charter brings the obligation in respect of human rights and the

---

[21] 153.

[22] General Course in Public International Law, *Rec. des Cours*, 106 (1962 vol. ii), 199–200.

[23] Ibid. 200.

[24] *Principles of Public International Law* (Oxford: OUP, 1979), 570.

[25] Sohn and Buergenthal (*supra*, n. 17), 513.

[26] Humphrey, 'The Implementation of International Human Rights Law'; Tolley, 'The Concealed Crack in the Citadel' *Human Rights Quarterly*, 6 (1984), 420.

[27] Tedin, 'The Development of the Soviet Attitude towards Implementing Human Rights under the United Nations Charter', *RDH*, 5 (1972), 399.

[28] Tolley (*supra*, n. 26), 459.   [29] Ibid.

concept of domestic jurisdiction into a relationship which has been troublesome for the development of human rights, but has not frustrated it. Article 2(7) of the Charter states that 'Nothing contained in the present Charter shall authorise the United Nations to intervene in matters which are essentially within the domestic jurisdiction of any State or shall require the members to submit such matters to settlement under the present Charter, but this principle shall not prejudice the application of enforcement measures under Chapter VII.'[30] During the drafting of the Charter, many States were apprehensive about the implications of the 'new' universal programme of human rights for their treatment of their own citizens, and insisted upon the importance of the concept of domestic jurisdiction.[31] As noted above,[32] the international legal obligations undertaken by States to deal with minorities were in effect being broadened to encompass potentially all States. States thus expressed similar feelings of apprehension to those expressed by the Minorities States undertaking international obligations in the League period, though without the same intensity, since these new obligations were voluntary in character. It may be stated that a treaty has the effect of taking matters out of domestic jurisdiction only to the extent of the obligations created by the treaty.[33] If this is the case, the problem of the limits of domestic jurisdiction resolves itself into one of determining the extent of the obligations undertaken by Member States in the Charter. If Articles 55 and 56 had been subjected to very 'restrictive' views (that they were limited to the general furtherance of human rights through studies, preparation of conventions, and general recommendations, etc.) Article 2(7) would have placed human rights almost completely under domestic jurisdiction, and would have excluded consideration of violations by individual States. In practice this has not been allowed to happen and the General Assembly and other organs of the United Nations have scrutinized and condemned violations by individual States.[34] As Fawcett has noted:

Since its earliest days, objections raised by UN Members to discussions or recommendations in the General Assembly or Security Council on the ground that they interfered with the domestic policy or practices of a country, have been constantly rejected by the majority where the maintenance of human rights was seen to be in question ... The United Nations ... has ... constantly intervened in countries by

[30] Chapter VII is entitled 'Action with Respect to Threats to the Peace, Breaches of the Peace, and Acts of Aggression'. Security Council action with an element of Human Rights motivation has been evident in connection with Namibia, South Africa generally, and Southern Rhodesia: *UN Action in the Field of Human Rights*, UN Sales. No. E.79.XIV.6 (New York, 1980).
[31] Sohn, in Sohn and Buergenthal, (*supra*, n. 17). Also, Huston, 'Human Rights Enforcement Issues at the UN Conference on International Organisations'.
[32] *Supra*, ch. 10.
[33] Waldock, (*supra*, n. 21), 184 ff. Also, D'Amato, 'The Concept of Human Rights in International Law' *Columbia Law Review*, 82 (1982), 1110 at 1125: 'Domestic Jurisdiction is a residual concept; it is simply a way of saying that International Law does not apply'.
[34] Higgins (*supra*, n. 14), 118 ff.

inquiry, discussion and recommendation on their practices involving human rights.[35]

However, he noted also that more direct forms of intervention have required justification in terms of peace keeping operations.[36]

Despite its lack of specification of human rights and fundamental freedoms, the United Nations Charter was of some assistance to domestic tribunals shortly after its promulgation. In the Canadian case, *Re Drummond Wren*,[37] the applicant undertook to have removed some restrictive covenants on land, which were 'not to be sold to Jews or persons of objectionable nationality'. The High Court of Ontario declared the restrictions void on grounds of public policy, praying in aid of its interpretation 'the recent San Francisco Charter' which was 'of profound significance'. In *Oyama* v. *State of California*,[38] the United States Supreme Court found that a Californian statute excluding citizens of Japanese origin from certain categories of land ownership violated the United States Constitution, interpreted in the light of the non-discrimination provisions of the United Nations Charter. On the other hand, in *Sei Fujii* v. *State of California*,[39] the human rights provisions of the Charter were deemed not to be self-executing in terms of United States law and did not overrule a law preventing aliens from owning land in California. The Charter articles, in the opinion of the Supreme Court of California, were not sufficiently specific to be applied directly without implementing legislation. The lower court in California had stated that 'Clearly . . . discrimination against a people of one race is contrary both to the letter and to the spirit of the Charter . . .', but the Californian Supreme Court did not endorse this. The Supreme Court only accepted that the above provisions of the Charter stated 'general purposes and objectives of the United Nations' and appeared to deny any legal obligations flowing from the human rights clauses of the Charter 'on the individual member nations'. However, the main thrust of the judgment is not the denial of legal obligations, but rather that the Charter provisions are not sufficiently definite to 'indicate an intent to create justiciable rights in private persons immediately upon ratification'. The Supreme Court of California did not, as the lower court had done, utilize the provisions of the Universal Declaration of Human Rights to guide its determination of the meaning of the Charter articles. However, later cases have adopted this approach.[40] The case, while it has been subject to much criticism,[41] may be explained or justified in the sense that 'decades of UN practice under the

---

[35] *The International Protection of Minorities*, Minority Rights Group Report No. 41, 9.
[36] Ibid., 12. Also Henkin, 'Human Rights and Domestic Jurisdiction', in Buergenthal and Hall (eds.), *Human Rights, International Law and the Helsinki Accord*, 21.
[37] (1945) *Ontario Rep.* 778; *Dominion Law Reports*, 4 (1943–5), 674.
[38] *332 US*, 663 (1948); Sohn and Buergenthal, (*supra*, n. 17), 944 ff.
[39] Ibid. 934 ff.
[40] *Infra*, text following n. 71.
[41] Wright (*supra*, n. 17); Schwelb (*supra*, n. 15); Sohn and Buergenthal (*supra*, n. 17), 946.

human rights provisions of the Charter may be deemed to have supplied the precision regarding their meaning, scope and mandatory character'[42] and such practice had not developed sufficiently at the time of the *Sei Fujii* judgment. Thus, while the United Nations Charter provided, it is submitted, a legal obligation to promote human rights and to refrain from at least large scale violations of these rights, it did not define them, but provided only that they be accorded without distinction as to 'race, sex, language or religion'.[43]

The Universal Declaration

However, the Members of the United Nations, acting in the General Assembly and other organs,[44] have sought to give the Charter a more specific meaning. The Universal Declaration of Human Rights represents the first major attempt to distil more specific meanings from the Charter. It is also widely claimed to represent customary international law.[45] Firstly, the Declaration, in its Preamble, recalls that, in the Charter, the peoples of the United Nations have reaffirmed their faith in fundamental human rights and have 'pledged themselves to achieve, in co-operation with the United Nations, the promotion of universal respect for and observance of human rights and fundamental freedoms'. The Preamble recites further that 'a common understanding of these rights and freedoms is of the greatest importance for the full realisation of this pledge'. The first quoted phrase uses the wording of Articles 55 and 56 of the Charter and may thus be taken as a reference back to these articles. The reference to the 'common understanding' of the peoples of the United Nations refers forward to the catalogue of rights in the Declaration. It is thus a not unreasonable reading of the legal import of the Declaration to claim that the 'pledge' of the Members of the United Nations to observe human rights in Article 56 of the Charter is to be fulfilled or redeemed by observing the catalogue of rights set out in the Universal Declaration. The catalogue of rights in the Declaration is, as it were, incorporated in the United Nations Charter.

Many delegates to the General Assembly made it clear that they did not regard the Universal Declaration as a legally binding instrument either in itself or 'through' the Charter. According to the Delegate of the United States to the General Assembly's Third Committee, the draft Declaration was 'not a treaty or international agreement and did not impose legal

---

[42] Sohn and Buergenthal (*supra, n. 17*), 947.

[43] A later United States court described the Charter articles as '. . . not . . . wholly self-executing', but proceeded to find evidence to interpret the 'broad mandate' of the Charter: *Filartiga* v. *Pena-Irala, ILM (1980)*, 966 at 971.

[44] Subsequent practice is an important ingredient in the interpretation of treaties, particularly treaties setting up international organizations which are to endure over a long period of time: Akehurst, *A Modern Introduction to International Law*, ch. 13.

[45] Humphrey, (*supra, n. 18*).

obligations'; it was rather 'a statement of basic principles of inalienable human rights setting up a common standard of achievement for all peoples and all nations'. Although it was not legally binding, the Declaration would nevertheless 'have considerable weight'.[46] The Delegate of the Soviet Union argued that, far from having binding authority, the Declaration violated the United Nations Charter—the reference here was to the principle of domestic jurisdiction in Article 2(7) of the Charter.[47] The Representative of Australia stated that the Declaration represented a common ideal, but had no binding character.[48] On the other hand, some delegations discerned 'sparks of juridical validity'[49] in the Declaration. The Representative of Chile declared forthrightly that 'violation by any State of the rights enumerated in the Declaration would mean violation of the principles of the United Nations.'[50] The Chairman of the General Assembly, Mr Malik (Lebanon) stated that

'Members of the United Nations have already solemnly pledged themselves under the Charter to promote human rights and fundamental freedoms, but that is the first time human rights and freedoms have been set forth in detail. Hence, every Government knew at present to what extent exactly it had pledged itself, and every citizen could protest to his Government if the latter did not fulfil its obligations.[51]

South Africa and France took a similar view of the relationship between the Charter and the Declaration.[52] One writer remarks that these 'first official *dicta* were the beginning of a now developed practice of regarding the Declaration as an authoritative and therefore binding interpretation of the Charter'.[53]

A variation of this claim is made by Judge Tanaka in his dissenting opinion in the *South-West Africa Cases (Second Phase)*: the Declaration 'although not binding in itself, constitutes evidence of the interpretation and application of the relevant Charter provisions'.[54] This is a reasonable view, since the claim is made in the context of an argument about interpretation, which is an art rather than a science. If the subsequent practice of States reveals a disposition to regard the Universal Declaration as the agreed catalogue of Charter rights and freedoms, this may be cited as evidence of the true interpretation of the Charter. A particularly apt summary of this aspect of the Declaration was given by the Delegate of Uruguay to the General Assembly. He stated that, under the Charter: 'States assumed the international obligations to promote and develop [human] rights and there-

---

[46] *GAOR*, 3rd Session, Part I, Third Committee, 32.
[47] Ibid. 92nd and 93rd meetings.
[48] For a detailed account of delegates' views, see Lauterpacht, 'The Universal Declaration of Human Rights', *BYIL*, 25 (1948), 354.
[49] Humphrey (*supra*, n. 18), 32.
[50] A/C.3/SR.91, 97.
[51] *GAOR*, 3rd Session, Part I, Plenary Session, 860.
[52] Humphrey (*supra*, n. 18), 32.
[53] Ibid. 33.
[54] ICJ Reports, 1966, text in Brownlie, *Basic Documents on Human Rights*, 441 at 449.

fore to respect them scrupulously'. In relation to the Declaration he stated that it had 'great moral force; it defined, specified and enumerated the rights globally and generically enshrined in the Charter; it had indirect legal authority and, therefore, through the Declaration, the Charter principles were made applicable . . .'[55]

Another, bolder claim is made for the Charter by some authors. Humphrey[56] is among those who claim for the Declaration the status of customary international law. Similarly, Waldock states that the constant and widespread recognition of the principles of the Universal Declaration 'clothes it in my opinion, in the character of customary international law'.[57] Waldock made a more modest claim in an earlier work, arguing only that the Declaration may be referred to 'for indications of the content of the human rights envisaged in the Charter'.[58] Even the more 'vigorous' formulation is followed immediately by the tentative statement: 'Be that as it may, the Declaration has acquired a status inside and outside the United Nations which gives it high authority as the accepted formulation of the common standards of human rights.' Sohn is perhaps the most forthright of all: 'In a relatively short time the Universal Declaration . . . has . . . become a part of the constitutional law of the world community; and together with the Charter of the United Nations, it has achieved the character of a world law superior to all other international instruments and to domestic laws.'[59] The hesitations of some States expressed in debates on the legal force of the General Assembly's 'genocide resolution' (96(1)) will be recalled,[60] and a great deal of caution must be exercised in attributing binding character to any such resolutions.[61] The Charter does not attribute binding force to General Assembly resolutions except in so-called 'housekeeping' resolu-

---

[55] *GAOR*, 21st Session, Plenary meetings, vol. I, meeting 1495. Brownlie, (*supra*, n. 23), 571, expresses a similar view on the indirect legal effect of the Declaration in relation to the Charter. He speaks of it as an 'authoritative guide' to the Charter. This is a less ambitious claim than that made by Humphrey: that the Declaration is an 'authoritative and binding interpretation' of the Charter. The latter suggests a document binding *per se*, whereas the former reflects a more flexible position, in keeping with the context of interpretation and evidence of interpretation. The Brownlie formula also gives a clearer indication that the Human Rights content of the Charter is not necessarily exhausted by this 'guide'.

[56] Humphrey (*supra*, n. 18).

[57] 'Human Rights in Contemporary International Law and the Significance of the European Convention', *ICLQ Sp. Supp. No. 11* (1965), 1 at 15.

[58] *Supra*, n. 22, 199.

[59] 'The Universal Declaration of Human Rights: A Common Standard of Achievement', *Journal of the International Commission of Jurists*, 8 (1967), No. 2, 17 at 26.

[60] *Supra*, chs. 6 and 7.

[61] Akehurst, *Custom as a Source of International Law*; Johnson, 'The Effect of Resolutions of the General Assembly of the United Nations', *BYIL*, 32 (1955–56), 97; Cheng, 'United Nations Resolutions on Outer Space, "Instant" International Customary Law?', *Indian Journal of International Law*, 5 (1965), 23; Sloan, 'The Binding Force of a "Recommendation" of the General Assembly of the United Nations', *BYIL*, 25 (1948), 1; Schwebel, 'The Effect of Resolutions of the UN General Assembly on Customary International Law', *Procs. ASIL* (1979), 300.

tions.[62] Apart from this limited class of cases, the powers granted by the Charter to the General Assembly are essentially recommendatory in character. The assumption of the present work is not that the General Assembly's (non-housekeeping) resolutions are somehow binding qua General Assembly resolutions,[63] but that in certain cases they can represent the best possible evidence of customary international law. The resolutions must deal with a legal matter, they must be overwhelmingly supported and they must at least purport to state the law; they must, in summary, convincingly demonstrate the necessary *opino juris* required for the formation of customary law.[64] On this basis, it may be doubted if, at the time of its promulgation, the Declaration represented customary law. States, as noted, expressed views to the effect that it was not a legally binding instrument, and whilst no votes were cast against the Declaration, six Communist States, Saudi Arabia, and South Africa abstained.[65]

The claim of the above cited writers is not, however, that the Declaration was immediately binding, but that it has become binding through constant invocation. Humphrey states that: 'Nothing could be clearer than that the Declaration was never meant to be binding as part of international law nor could it be simply by virtue of its having been adopted as a resolution of the General Assembly . . . .'[66] The fact that this particular resolution is styled a 'Declaration' does not make any difference to its binding quality or lack of it. According to a memorandum of the Secretary-General of the United Nations, 'A "declaration" or a "recommendation" is adopted by a resolu-

---

[62] See Articles 17(1) and 21 of the Charter as examples; compare with Article 13.

[63] Much of the effort of delegates to deny the binding quality of the resolutions is attributable to the efforts of enthusiasts to elevate the Assembly into a kind of world legislature. Rejection of this does not imply rejection of the view that the resolutions can sometimes function as a vehicle to demonstrate an unequivocal *opinio juris generalis*.

[64] The position was well stated by the representative of Italy to the legal Sub-Committee of the Committee on the Peaceful Uses of Outer Space: 'In international law, rules were binding primarily because States considered themselves bound by such rules, whatever their origin. From that point of view, recommendations of the General Assembly undoubtedly had binding force', UN Doc A/AC.105/C.2/SR.20, 7.

[65] In the case of the Communist States, the lack of support stemmed from Cold War politics and because, in their view, the document did not sufficiently emphasize economic, social, and cultural rights. Among Islamic States, Saudi Arabia claimed that Article 18 of the Declaration, which includes the right of persons to change their religion, was contrary to the Koran. Egypt also expressed reservations. However, the delegate of Pakistan, Sir Mohammed Zafrullah Khan, expressed full support for the principles of the Declaration, and Egypt and Pakistan voted to adopt it: Galindo Pohl, Report on the Human Rights Situation in the Islamic Republic of Iran by the Special Representative of the Human Rights Commission, Mr Reynaldo Galindo Pohl, UN Doc E/CN.4/1986/24, 9–11. Iran has recently stated that 'no Islamic scholar or Muslim jurisprudent had a chance to participate [in the preparation of the UDHR]. Therefore Islamic States . . . have the right to reserve their views on the validity or applicability of those provisions', Galindo Pohl, para. 44. Galindo Pohl agrees that participation by Islamic scholars was extremely limited, citing only one scholar, M. Humayun Kabir, consulted by UNESCO. It may be noted that the Eastern Bloc States later voted to adopt UNGA Res. 1514(XV), which declared, *inter alia*, that all States 'shall observe faithfully and strictly the provisions of . . . the Universal Declaration of Human Rights'.

[66] Humphrey, (*supra.*, n. 18), 32.

tion of a United Nations organ. As such, it cannot be made binding upon Member States, in the sense that a treaty or convention is binding upon the parties to it, purely by the device of terming it a declaration rather than a recommendation.'[67] The memorandum attaches an important rider to this statement, asserting that

However, in view of the greater solemnity and significance of 'declaration', it may be considered to impart, on behalf of the organ adopting it, a strong expectation that members of the international community will abide by it. Consequently, in so far as the expectation is gradually justified by State practice, a declaration may by custom become recognised as laying down rules binding upon States.

Logically speaking, there need be no difference between resolutions termed 'recommendations', and 'declarations', in this respect. It is submitted that both are recommendations in the technical sense, as the Secretariat's memorandum makes clear, and that both can under the right conditions effectively reflect international law. The titles of the documents are, *stricto sensu*, irrelevant—General Assembly Resolution 96(1) was not styled a 'Declaration', though it declared the law. What is required is that the international community declares unequivocally that the principles are principles of *lex lata* rather than *lex ferenda*. The important 'Declarations' of international law may at least be expected to generate such perceptions more consistently and cogently than other resolutions.

It may be noted, therefore, that the Universal Declaration has had a very strong impact on important United Nations decisions in many spheres, and an impact on other United Nations human rights instruments: recitals in the preambles of many treaties and references in the main texts refer to the Universal Declaration as equal to the United Nations Charter as the legal source of human rights.[68] The Declaration has also been cited as a 'source of law' in State constitutions, and in municipal laws.[69] However, the mode of citation varies through the different instruments, and in many cases, the invocation may be pragmatic, advertising that the State is a 'civilised' member of the family of nations, pursuing an enlightened policy of human rights.[70] Much of the language appears to lack the quality of demonstrating a clear acceptance of binding obligations. However, resolutions condemning torture as a violation of human rights have called for 'strict respect' for the Universal Declaration. It may be remarked that the adjective 'strict' would be unusual if it were not intended to convey the message that the Declaration is binding.

[67] E/CN.4/L.610 (1962). Bin Cheng, *supra*, n. 1, writes on 'resolutions' and 'declarations': 'A treaty may call itself a declaration and is not less binding for being so called. A General Assembly resolution which chooses to assume the name "declaration' is not thereby rendered legally more binding than any other recommendation.'

[68] UN Action in the Field of Human Rights (*supra*, n. 30), 14–20.

[69] Ibid.

[70] Including a number of States subject to allegations of genocide: see Kuper, *Genocide. Its Political Use in the Twentieth Century*.

Accordingly in a case centred on allegations of torture, the United States Federal Court of Appeals in *Filartiga* v. *Pena-Irala* stated that the United Nations Charter made it clear that a State's treatment of its own citizens is a matter of international concern, and that, although there is no universal agreement on the precise extent of the rights and freedoms guaranteed by the Charter, there is no dissent from the view that torture is prohibited as a minimum: 'This prohibition has become part of customary international law, *as evidenced and defined by the Universal Declaration of Human Rights*.'[71] The Court said also that: 'The General Assembly has declared that the Charter precepts embodied in this Universal Declaration constitute basic principles of international law' and made reference to General Assembly Resolution 2625(XXV), the Declaration on Principles of International Law concerning Friendly Relations among States in Accordance with the Charter of the United Nations.[72] The Declaration on Principles of International Law states that the 'principles of the Charter which are embodied in this Declaration constitute basic principles of international law', and also that 'every State has the duty to promote through joint and separate action universal respect for the observance of human rights and fundamental freedoms in accordance with the Charter.' It does not, however, make a specific mention of the Universal Declaration of Human Rights. The Court goes on to state that some authors have claimed that the Declaration 'has become, *in toto*, a part of binding customary international law'.[73] The Court did not expressly commit itself to this view, though the tenor of the judgment is not obviously inconsistent with it.[74] The Court found that torture violated the law of nations, on the basis of a series of important contemporary documents, including the United Nations Charter, the Universal Declaration, the Covenant on Civil and Political Rights, and the European and American Conventions on Human Rights.

However, the citations in treaty preambles often merely state that they take into consideration the principles of the Universal Declaration, or recognize its ideals. Thus, the International Covenants on Human Rights state in their preambles that they recognize the ideals of the Declaration, but con-

---

[71] (*Supra*, n. 43), 971.

[72] Adopted by the General Assembly, October 1970, without a vote. See, *inter alios*, Rosenstock, 'The Declaration on Principles of International Law Concerning Friendly Relations: A Survey', *AJIL*, 65, (1971), 713; *Filartiga Case*, ibid. 971.

[73] *Filartiga Case*, ibid. 973.

[74] The judge in the *Filartiga Case*, speaking extra judicially, stated that the case should not be read to support sweeping assertions that all or most international norms of Human Rights are customary law: cited by Lillich, in Hannum (ed.), *Guide to International Human Rights Practice*, 234. US Courts have since vacillated on appropriate evidence for customary international law and its contents in the area of human rights. See, for example, *Jean v. Nelson*, 727 F. 2d 957 (11th cir., 1984); 105 S. Ct.2992 (1985); *Fernandez-Roque v. Smith*, 622 F. Supp. 887 (ND Ga. 1985); *Forti v. Suarez-Mason*, 672 F. Supp. 1531 (1987). Also, for another view of the statute under which Filartiga was decided, *Tel-Oren v. Libyan Arab Republic*, 726 F. 2d. 774 (DC Cir. 1984), 470 US 1003 (1985), and, generally, Burley, 'The Alien Tort Statute and the Judiciary Act of 1789: A Badge of Honour', *AJIL*, 83 (1989), 461.

sider 'the *obligation* of States under the Charter of the United Nations'. The constitutions of States often 'proclaim the adherence' of the people of the State to the principles of the Declaration, or 'affirm', or 'reaffirm', their 'attachment' to the same. Bin Cheng has drawn attention to the inadequacy of such phrases as 'guided by', 'supports', 'subscribes to', 'will respect', etc., as unequivocal indicators, without more, of a State's acceptance of a rule as binding customary international law.[75]

Some statements of view on the Universal Declaration appear to have this 'harder' quality of a manifestation of the acceptance of binding rules. Most unequivocally, the International Conference on Human Rights at Teheran in 1968, at which eighty-four States were represented, stated in the 'Proclamation of Teheran' that the Universal Declaration of Human Rights 'constitutes an obligation for the Members of the international community'.[76] Professor Humphrey cites a resolution of the United Nations Security Council which spoke of apartheid as in violation of South Africa's 'obligations as a member of the United Nations and of the provisions of the Universal Declaration of Human Rights'.[77] Leaving aside the argument that the limited membership of the Security Council make its resolutions less persuasive as evidence of customary international law than a unanimous General Assembly resolution, it is possible to achieve a syntactical cleavage between '*obligations* as a member of the United Nations', and violation of '*the provisions of*' the Universal Declaration, implying that the provisions of the latter are not binding in the same sense as Charter obligations.

A further citation of the Declaration appears in the practice of the United States. According to the Legal Adviser to the Department of State, 'The Charter of the United Nations and the Universal Declaration of Human Rights are the basic texts in their field. I would point, in particular, to Articles 55 and 56 of the United Nations Charter . . . The United States recognises these obligations and is determined to live up to them.'[78] The President of the United States has described the Universal Declaration as 'the authoritative statement of the meaning of the United Nations Charter, through which Members undertake to promote and respect human rights and fundamental freedoms'.[79]

There is therefore, strong evidence that the Universal Declaration has

[75] *Supra*, n. 61.

[76] Text in Joyce (ed.), *Human Rights: International Documents*, vol. i, 27 (Alphen aan den Rijn: Sijthoff and Noordhoff, 1978).

[77] *Supra*, n. 18, 35 (S/5471). Also Sohn, 'Enforcing the Universal Declaration of Human Rights', *ICLQ*, 22 (1973), 161.

[78] *Digest of US Practice in International Law* (1975), 125.

[79] Address to the UN, 1977 Public Papers of the President of the United States, 449–50. US practice has not been very consistent on this point, although it may be taken to have developed towards the above position. Compare the statement of the US Ambassador to the UN as late as 1967 (cited by Van Dyke, *Human Rights. The United States and the World Community*, 124: 'The Declaration of Human Rights . . . is at best . . . a moral obligation as distinguished from a legal obligation'.

become part of customary international law, and that it is the most valid interpretation of the human rights and freedoms which the Members of the United Nations pledge to promote. This would appear to be supported by the judgment of the International Court of Justice in the *Hostages* case (US *v.* Iran)[80] where it stated that: 'Wrongfully to deprive human beings of their freedom and to subject them to physical constraint in conditions of hardship is in itself manifestly incompatible with the principles of the Charter of the United Nations as well as with the fundamental principles enunciated in the Universal Declaration of Human Rights.' This was the only reference to human rights in a judgment expressly based on violations of the law relating to diplomatic and consular immunities. The Court was much more strenuous in its efforts to underline the fundamental character of the institution of diplomatic immunity than the fundamental character of human rights.[81] The reference to human rights is nevertheless express, though fleeting, and continues the tradition of associating the Charter with the Universal Declaration. The case also appears to suggest that individual violations of human rights, and not only massive ones, may violate the United Nations Charter. However, the total conduct of the Iranian authorities in that case may plausibly be argued to constitute, in Brownlie's words, a violation of human rights involving a 'class of persons or pattern of activity', and a 'substantial infringement' of human rights. It may be that what is contrary to the principles of the Charter and the Universal Declaration is, precisely, wrongful deprivation of freedom. The United States Memorial in the *Hostages Case* argued more widely and stated that 'the existence of fundamental rights for all human beings . . . and the existence of a corresponding duty on every State to respect and observe them are now reflected, *inter alia*, in the Charter of the United Nations, the Universal Declaration of Human Rights, and the International Covenant on Civil and Political Rights.'[82] The United States cites, as reflecting customary law, Articles 3, 5, 7, 9, 12, and 13 of the

---

[80] *ICJ Reports 1980*, 3, para. 91. See generally, Rodley, 'Human Rights and Humanitarian Intervention: The Case Law of the World Court', *ICLQ*, 38 (1989), 321. The International Court of Justice in the Nicaragua Case, *ICJ Reports 1986*, 14, adopted a somewhat ambiguous stance on the customary status of Human Rights. On the one hand, referring to an accusation that Nicaragua had violated Human Rights, including a 'commitment' to the OAS on free elections, etc., the Court said (para. 267): 'The particular point requires to be studied independently of the question of . . . a "legal commitment" by Nicaragua towards the Organisation of American States to respect these rights; the absence of such a commitment would not mean that Nicaragua could with impunity violate human rights'. On the other hand, the same paragraph uses language that might appear to confine Human Rights to specific treaties: 'However, where human rights are protected by international conventions, that protection takes the form of such arrangements for monitoring or ensuring respect for human rights as are provided for in the conventions themselves.' This is, however, directed to the question of implementation of rights, rather than international obligations.

[81] The above quoted paragraph continued: 'But what has above all to be emphasised is the extent and seriousness of the conflict between the Iranian State and its obligations under the whole corpus of the international rules of which diplomatic and consular law is comprised, rules the fundamental character of which the Court must here again strongly affirm.'

[82] Lillich (*supra*, n. 74), 243.

Universal Declaration of Human Rights,[83] and Articles 7, 9, 10, and 11 of the International Covenant on Civil and Political Rights.[84] All of these rights relate to the particular circumstances of the case, so that it may be deduced that, if circumstances were different, a different catalogue of rights would be regarded as customary law.

A narrower reading of this catalogue and its significance may be implied from the restatement of the Foreign Relations Law of the United States. According to this source:

A State violates international law if, as a matter of State policy, it practises, encourages or condones: (a) genocide, (b) slavery or the slave trade, (c) the murder or causing the disappearance of individuals, (d) torture or other cruel, inhuman or degrading treatment or punishment, (e) prolonged arbitrary detention, (f) systematic racial discrimination, or (g) consistent patterns of gross violations of internationally recognized human rights.[85]

The logic of this set of rules is that they recognize that violation of the customary international law of human rights occurs when rights of a certain quality are violated, or internationally recognized rights are violated in quantity. Thus, torture, even in the case of an official of a State torturing one individual, may, by reason of its quality as a violation of human dignity and integrity, constitute a breach of international customary law. Genocide has both qualitative and quantitative aspects in this spectrum of violations; slavery and the slave trade have, for some time, been regarded as an affront to civilized nations and an offence against human dignity; a government policy of deliberate murder or causing the 'disappearance'[86] of individuals has qualitative and quantitative aspects; prolonged arbitrary detention violates, even in the case of an individual, an essential human freedom; systematic racial discrimination is an offensive denial of human equality. The final category, the quantitative category *per se*, opens the way for an expansive definition of the customary law of human rights, subject, *inter alia*, to the definition of internationally recognized rights. Because the context of the list is international customary law, 'internationally recognized rights' presumably means rights universally recognized, because there are many human rights set out in a variety of human rights instruments which would be unlikely candidates for customary law status.[87]

---

[83] These articles deal with, respectively: the right to life, liberty, and security; the prohibition of torture; the right to equality and non-discrimination; freedom from arbitrary arrest and detention, non-interference with privacy; and freedom of movement.

[84] Rights and freedoms concerning, respectively, torture, liberty, and security of person, treatment in detention, and freedom from imprisonment for inability to fulfil a contractual obligation.

[85] Cited in *AJIL*, 77 (1983), 592.

[86] The UN Human Rights Commission set up a working group on disappearances in 1980. For a review of its activities, see Rodley, *The Treatment of Prisoners in International Law* (Oxford:, 1987).

[87] See Alston, 'Conjuring up New Human Rights: A Proposal for Quality Control', *AJIL*, 78 (1984), 607. All of these rights have, as it were, a 'track record' in international law in the sense

Whatever the ultimate merits of this list as customary law, its exiguous nature (subject to the above interpretation) indicates that sweeping assertions should not be made concerning customary law status, despite the enthusiasm of some commentators. Here, as elsewhere, the wish may be father to the thought. It is with this caveat in mind that one may examine the issue of customary law as it relates to the right to an identity.

of repeated invocations in international instruments as well as, in some cases, specific instruments elaborating a particular right. See generally, UN Action, *supra*, n. 30; and Sieghart, *The International Law of Human Rights.* Further expansion of the 'catalogue' of universally recognized rights on a 'qualitative' basis might include, for example, the prohibition of the State executing children, regarded as a prohibition in *Jus Cogens* by the Inter-American Commission on Human Rights: *Roach and Pinkerton* v. *United States*, Res. No. 3/87, Case 9647, Annual Report of the Inter-American Commission on Human Rights, 1986–87, OAS/Ser.L/VII.71, Doc. 9, rev. 1, at 147 (1987). The evidence for *Jus Cogens* was, in this case, mainly regional in nature, the Commission concentrating on developments in the Americas—ibid., para. 36. The prohibition of retroactive penal legislation, the principle of non-refoulement in the case of torture, and the *ne bis in idem* rule are other candidates. See Sieghart, *supra*, for the specification of the non-retroactive rule; on the non-refoulement principle, see Hailbronner, 'Non-Refoulement and "Humanitarian" Refugees: Customary International Law or Wishful Thinking?', *Virginia Journal of International Law*, 26 (1986), 857; on *ne bis in idem*, see the case before the German Bundesverfassungsgericht in *1987 Neue juristiche Wochenschrift*, 2155.

27. The Principles of Article 27 of the Covenant on Civil and Political Rights as General International Law?

From the point of view of the right of minorities to an identity, it is clear that there are serious limitations in the Universal Declaration of Human Rights—assuming its status in general international law. As noted, it does not contain a 'minorities' article as such. It does, however, contain an article on non-discrimination (Article 2) and an article on equality (Article 7). There are also articles guaranteeing freedom of thought, conscience, and religion (Article 18); freedom of opinion and expression (Article 19); the right to an education, which 'shall promote understanding, tolerance and friendship among all nations, racial or religious groups . . .'; and 'the right freely to participate in the cultural life of the community . . .'.[1] All of these rights stand in some relationship to Article 27 and may be regarded as supporting the freedom of minorities, though they lack the specific group reference.[2] It is difficult to believe that a very systematic and, certainly, forcible campaign of assimilation embarked upon by the authorities of the State would not violate many of the articles in the Declaration relating to freedom of thought, conscience, religion, and expression; and it would, probably, involve overt practices of discrimination. Further, assuming that such a campaign could be described as involving a 'class of persons or pattern of activity' to quote again Brownlie's phrase, it would directly violate the letter and spirit of the United Nations Charter, in the interpretation offered above.[3] Indeed, the notion of the elimination of the identity of a group pursued as a deliberate policy itself suggests action against 'a class of persons or pattern of activity' as a logical and practical prerequisite. It may be, further, that there would be elements of 'true' genocide amidst a forcible assimilation policy—which may be described as cultural genocide.[4]

None the less, despite these positive aspects, there is nothing in the Declaration to make obligatory the adoption of positive policies to safeguard the identity of minorities against less dramatic but still insidious threats. There is no obligation therein to recognize any other identity

---

[1] Article 27 of the Universal Declaration.
[2] The phrasing is very 'individualist'.
[3] *Supra*, ch. 26.
[4] *Supra*, chs. 6 and 7 (genocide).

besides the identity as a citizen or inhabitant of the State. In short, such an 'egalitarian' document as the Universal Declaration may itself, in so far as it is incorporated into the law and policy of the State, become a vehicle of assimilation and the extinction of group identity. These points are discussed further in the section on non-discrimination.[5]

The minority right to an identity was omitted from the Declaration because of the negative repercussions of the League regime, cold war politics, and a rather euphoric belief that the ascription of rights to individuals *qua* individuals, without setting them in their full cultural or religious group contexts, was necessary and sufficient to meet post-war conditions. The Covenant on Civil and Political Rights marks an advance over that view. Besides the rights of minorities, it includes other rights omitted from the Universal Declaration, most notably the right to self-determination,[6] but also freedom from imprisonment for debt,[7] and the rights of children.[8] The Covenant also prohibits propaganda for war and incitement to national, racial, or religious hatred.[9] Many new human rights are now being asserted in international *fora* which had no place in the Universal Declaration.[10] These differences between the Covenant and the Universal Declaration indicate at least that one is not dealing with a static picture, so that, perhaps, the omission of a right from the Universal Declaration is not an insuperable barrier to further cogent interpretations of the meaning of the United Nations Charter, or elaboration of the customary law.

To take the latter point first, a treaty or its provisions may represent, in whole or in part, customary international law. Of the authors discussing the general effect of Article 27, Dinstein took the clearest view that the article represented customary international law. In principle, the rules for the formation of customary international law from international treaties follow the general requirements for the formation of customary law.[11] The clearest case of a treaty claiming to generate rules of customary law is where the text or the *travaux préparatoires* contain statements that the treaty is declaratory of existing law, statements, that is, of *opinio juris*. Statements subsequent to the treaty may similarly demonstrate *opinio juris*. Article 38 of the Statute of the International Court of Justice emphasizes that acceptance by States is the necessary requirement for the emergence of customary law.[12] The formation of general rules from rules of treaty is not an automatic process: State practice accompanied by *opinio juris* are the necessary requirements for this to happen. As the International Court of Justice stated in the *North Sea Continental Shelf* cases, when judging whether a rule corresponding to Article 6 of the Geneva Convention on the

---

[5] *Infra*, Part V. [6] Article 1. [7] Article 11.
[8] Article 24. [9] Article 20.
[10] Alston, 'Conjuring up New Human Rights'.
[11] *Supra*, ch. 7. [12] Article 38 (1) (b)

Continental Shelf had passed into customary international law, 'State practice . . . should . . . have occurred in such a way as to show a *general
recognition* that a rule of law or legal obligation is involved.'[13]

The Covenants on Human Rights were adopted by the General Assembly
of the United Nations by overwhelming majorities, without abstentions: by
106 votes to none in the case of the Covenant on Economic, Social, and
Cultural Rights, and by 105 votes to none for the Covenant on Civil and
Political Rights.[14] However, it seems quite clear that the delegates at the
Assembly did not regard themselves as thereby creating, by a magical pro-
cess of transmutation, an 'instant' customary law. The Representative of the
Philippines spoke of the Covenants as 'standards of achievement'[15] for
States. The Representative of Czechoslovakia spoke of them as anchoring
an international standard. The Representative of Colombia described the
Covenants as 'a guide and standard for our leaders'.[16] Other representatives
related the Covenants to the United Nations Charter and the Universal
Declaration. They were an effective means to 'implement the purposes and
principles of the Charter',[17] according to the Representative of China. The
Representative of Egypt described them as giving 'legal definition to the
principles proclaimed in the Universal Declaration of Human Rights'.[18] The
Representative of Indonesia described the Covenants as giving 'legal force to
the moral obligations proclaimed in the Charter of the United Nations and
the Universal Declaration . . .'.[19] A number of representatives also made
clear the limitations of the generous vote. Thus, the Representative of Japan
stated that, while Japan would vote for the Covenant as a whole, if the
matter of a vote on specific articles were to arise, Japan would vote against
some and abstain on others.[20] The Representative of the United States
declared that 'our affirmative votes do not of course express our agreement
with or approval of every part of the Covenant'.[21] This indicates that, before
claiming that a particular rule in the Covenant is part of customary law, it
must not be assumed that it is such simply in virtue of its inclusion in the
Covenant.

There is no recitation in the Covenants that, in a general sense, they
'confirm' customary law (cf. the Genocide Convention, 1948). They do,
however, refer in the Preambles to the Principles of the United Nations
Charter, and 'the obligations of States under the Charter of the United
Nations to promote universal respect for, and observance of human rights

---

[13] *ICJ Reports 1969*, 3 at 43; see generally, Akehurst, 'Custom as a Source of International
Law', section V; Bin Cheng, 'Custom: The Future of General State Practice in a Divided
World', in MacDonald and Johnston (eds.), *The Structure and Process of International Law*,
513 (Dordrecht, Boston, Lancaster: M. Nijhoff, 1986); Shihata, 'The Treaty as a Law-Declaring and Custom-Making Instrument' *Revue Egyptienne de Droit International*, 22 (1966), 51.
[14] *GAOR*, 21st Session, Plenary meeting 1496.
[15] Ibid., 1495th meeting.   [16] Ibid.
[17] *GAOR*, 9th Session, UN Doc A/C.3/SR.570.
[18] Ibid., SR.571, para. 9.   [19] Ibid., SR.573, para. 3.
[20] *Supra*, n. 15.   [21] Ibid.

and freedoms'. The Covenants are seen as the continuation of the international human rights movement into a broader regime of specific rules.

There is little in Article 27 to suggest that it merely confirms a pre-existing right. This is not necessarily the case with some articles of the Covenant. Thus, Article 6 of the Covenant on Civil and Political Rights states that '1. Every human being has the inherent right to life. This right shall be protected by law . . .' One author suggests that: 'The term "inherent" may indicate . . . that the framers of the Covenant felt that the human right to life is entrenched in customary international law, so that Article 6 is merely declaratory in nature.'[22] However, the linguistic basis of his assertion is open to other interpretations. Thus, the Preambles to the Covenants refer to the recognition that 'these rights derive from the inherent dignity of the human being'; and recite their recognition 'of the inherent dignity and of the equal and inalienable rights of all members of the human family . . .'. As with the Universal Declaration, it is submitted that these recitals refer to a moral order, perhaps that of natural law, rather than to any claim of pre-existing customary law. In the case of Article 27, the article's language is not sufficiently distinctive to warrant assertions of extra-Convention status on the basis of language alone.[23] The *travaux préparatoires* are quite illuminating on the issue. Positively, they dispel the view that the minority right to an identity is somehow 'unfit' for inclusion in a document devoted to human rights. It is clear, for example, that Article 27 was regarded as on the same level as the other rights; it was a 'fundamental right'.[24] In fact one Representative stated that her delegation (Pakistan) considered this Article to be 'the most important in the whole Covenant'.[25] Brazil insisted, perhaps surprisingly, that the human rights in the Covenant would be incomplete without any mention of collective rights—the Representative was speaking on the draft Article 27.[26] In a plenary session of the General Assembly, the Representative of Israel noted that 'there is room for concern lest the swing from minority rights to individual rights should go too far'; accordingly, his delegation 'welcomed in particular' Article 27.[27] None of these statements may be taken to evidence customary law. They do not make a claim that the Article reflects obligations on States *erga omnes*, and point rather to the fundamental status of the article in the Covenant, as a logical completion of the treaty, given its comprehensive nature in the field of civil and political rights.

Despite this, many delegates, as already noted,[28] did not regard Article 27

---

[22] Dinstein, in Henkin (ed.), *The International Bill of Rights*, 114 at 115.

[23] As already noted, Article 18 is non-derogable: a point of importance to minorities.

[24] See, for example, the statement of Cambodia to the 3rd Committee, UN Doc A/C.3/SR.1103, para. 58.   [25] A/C.3/SR.1104, para. 15.

[26] Ibid., para. 18. This does not mean, of course, that the Representative agrees that the article has any relevance to Brazil.

[27] GAOR 21st Session, Plenary meeting, 1495.

[28] In the analysis of Article 27 in its treaty context.

as universal in scope. The views expressed by Latin American States, that the minorities issue was one which 'arose in some European and Asian countries' (Chile),[29] that the 'minority problem did not arise [in Venezuela]',[30] that 'Latin America had no minority problem' (Peru)[31] will be recalled. This fact that many States do not regard the article as having a universal character goes some way to explain the relative paucity of reservations to the article. A large number of reservations to an article may indicate that States do not regard it as of general application, but the converse argument does not convince in this case. Article 27 has attracted only one reservation: that of France. The reservation states 'In the light of Article 2 of the Constitution of the French Republic, the French Government declares that Article 27 is not applicable so far as the Republic is concerned.'[32] The reasons for this are elaborated in a report submitted by France under Article 40 of the Covenant to the Human Rights Committee:

Article 2 [of the French Constitution] declares that France shall be a Republic, indivisible, secular, democratic and social. It shall ensure the equality of all citizens before the law, without distinction . . . of origin, race or religion. It shall respect all beliefs. Since the basic principles of public law prohibit distinction between citizens on grounds of origin, race or religion, France is a country in which there are no minorities and, as stated in the declaration made by France, Article 27 is not applicable as far as the Republic is concerned.[33]

The declaration made by the Federal Republic of Germany interpreting the French statement is interesting in that it has the effect of enhancing the status of Article 27. Germany 'stresses . . . the great importance attaching to the rights guaranteed by Article 27. It interprets the French declaration as meaning that the Constitution of the French Republic already fully guarantees the individual rights protected by Article 27.'[34] It would appear, however, that the German statement includes a rather forced interpretation of the provisions of the French Constitution. The principles of Article 27 are: implicit recognition of a minority group through the formal attribution on rights to the members of that group; the right to maintain identity through the common activity of members of the group in the cultural, religious, and linguistic spheres; and positive service on the part of the State in support of this identity. It has already been mentioned and it is also submitted in the following section that the principle of non-discrimination is a necessary, though not sufficient, protection for minorities. Thus, the French Constitution, or any other constitution containing only a principle of non-discrimination, is not a sufficient instrument to fulfil the demands of Article 27. One is inclined, therefore, to take the French reservation for what it is, a negative view of Article 27, and further evidence that it is not a universal right.

[29] A/C.3/SR.1103, para. 19.
[30] Ibid., para. 28.
[31] A/C.3/SR.1104, para. 4.
[32] ST/HR 5 (1987), 35.
[33] CCPR/C/22/Add.2.
[34] ST/HR 5 (1987), 88.

Subsequent events do not disturb the above opinion. In the views of governments submitted to the United Nations Human Rights Commission on the Yugoslav Draft Declaration on Minorities, which amplifies Article 27, Finland stated that: 'The draft declaration supplements the Universal Declaration by introducing principles concerning minorities . . . [the draft declaration] would express *universally recognised* principles'.[35] Finland did not, however, accept that group rights would be involved, but only individual rights.[36] Yugoslavia stated that a goal of the Declaration was to 'reaffirm and promote the principles and provisions concerning the rights of minorities that are contained in international instruments on human rights and racial discrimination, which have been adopted within the framework of the United Nations or at the regional or bilateral level, proceeding from Article 27 of the . . . Covenant on Civil and Political Rights'.[37] The reference to reaffirming principles is ultimately qualified by the reference to Article 27, so that the whole statement does not add up to an affirmation of universally binding principles. Yugoslavia also referred to the broad support given to their draft by States. This, however, does not mean that States accepted any general customary law—thus far. Of course, a broadly supported Declaration couched in sufficiently clear language may still emerge to 'affirm' or 'confirm' the customary law status of Article 27, but it has not as yet emerged.

Article 27 of the Covenant on Civil and Political Rights thus appears to be a right granted by treaty without wider repercussions in customary law. In view of what has been said above on the possibly very limited number of customary rules relating to human rights, this conclusion is not entirely unexpected. The arguments of the jurists cited above on the general status of Article 27 are thus somewhat overstated in relation to customary law.[38] Considering Brownlie's proposition[39] as regards human rights generating obligations *erga omnes*, it is true that, in the *Barcelona Traction Case*, the International Court of Justice described as involving obligations *erga omnes*

---

[35] UN Doc E/CN.4/1984/42, 3.   [36] Ibid. 7.   [37] Ibid.

[38] In parallel with similar arguments on the UDHR, proponents of the general law status of Article 27 could cite the dissenting opinion of Judge Tanaka in the *South West Africa Cases* (Second Phase) that the international covenants constitute 'evidence of the interpretation and application of the relevant Charter provisions'. (*ICJ Reports* 1966, 6 at 284–316). Tanaka suggests a number of other international instruments as similar evidence. The Covenants are part of the International Bill of Rights and thus deserve consideration from this point of view. Tanaka's pronouncement was based on the repeated invocation of the norm of non-discrimination in a wide range of international instruments, and whereas examination of the *travaux* of the UN Charter clearly indicates that the norm of non-discrimination was a major concern, the same cannot be said of the principle of identity in relation to minorities. Further, some States have made it clear that, in their view, the Charter does not impose obligations on the identity of minorities: see remarks of the delegates of Argentina, Brazil, Bolivia, Peru, and Lebanon in the Special Political Committee of the General Assembly in 1960: UN Doc A/SPC/SR.177, paras. 8–9; SR.179, para. 9; SR.180, para. 3; SR.182, para. 35; SR.181, paras. 15–17. The delegate of Libya, SR.182, para. 31, stated that 'it was indisputable that international law did not grant any special rights to minorities unless there was a treaty to that effect concluded between two or more sovereign States'.   [39] *Supra*, ch. 25.

'. . . the outlawing of . . . genocide . . . [and] . . . the principles and rules concerning the basic rights of the human person, including protection from slavery and racial discrimination'.[40] The passage suggests that the rights mentioned constitute obligations of customary international law, and the description of these is couched in the widest possible terms: 'the basic rights of the human person'. However, the list of examples of such human rights in the paragraph is limited to the prohibition of genocide, slavery, and racial discrimination, all of which are strongly evidenced examples of denials of human rights. This may be taken to manifest a rather cautious attitude rather than to make a sweeping claim about all human rights as constituting part of customary law.

Vukas adopts 'general principles of international and national law' as the basis for his demonstration of the universal character of the right of minorities. Many States, to regulate practical concerns, make constitutional and other legal arrangements concerning particular minorities, including States who declare in international *fora* that they do not have minorities on their territory. Even Latin American States may make pragmatic arrangements in favour of, or at least in recognition of, particular groups, such as indigenous populations.[41] There is no evidence to suggest that these arrangements are made in pursuance of a general obligation to do so under international law. In any case, many other States may not make such arrangements. Vukas's claims on the basis of general principles of law are essentially generalizations of European activity and experience in the protection of minorities. There are existing examples of bilateral and multilateral treaties among European States to regulate problems of mutual concern.[42] Such arrangements are only occasionally duplicated in other continents.[43] Most existing examples of autonomy accorded to minorities may also be found in Europe.[44] In any case, general principles of law are, as a source of international law, secondary to treaties and custom. While there is much academic discussion of the exact nature and incidence of general principles,[45] it would be an odd claim that a State is somehow bound by a 'general principle of law' if it has consistently rejected that principle as one of customary international law.

---

[40] *ICJ Reports 1970*, 3, para. 34.

[41] See the chapters on indigenous populations, *infra*, chs. 38 ff.

[42] A list of such instruments is provided in UN, *Protection of Minorities*. The treaty of Osimo between Italy and Yugoslavia 1975, settling the question of Trieste, is not included in this publication. See Udina, *Gli Accordi di Osimo* (Trieste: Edizioni Lint, 1979); Caggiano, 'Some Reflections on the Treaty of Osimo' *Italian Year Book of International Law*, 2 (1976), 248.

[43] See, for example, the Agreement between Pakistan and India (1950), *UNTS*, 131, 4 *Infra*, Appendix 2.

[44] There is a comparative study of autonomies by Hannum and Lillich in *AJIL*, 74 (1980), 858.

[45] Akehurst, 'Equity and General Principles of Law', *ICLQ*, 25 (1976), 801; Van Hoof, *Rethinking the Sources of International Law*, 131 ff, and extensive references therein.

28. The Helsinki Final Act and Minorities: A Note

The Final Act of the Conference on Security and Co-operation in Europe, 1975,[1] is one other major document of modern international relations which makes references to 'minorities' in its text. The Final Act was signed by representatives of thirty-four States, including the United States and the USSR, and by the Holy See.[2]

The Final Act is not a treaty; the signatories did not wish to bind themselves by an international treaty. A paragraph in the concluding part of the document is clear on this: 'The Government of the Republic of Finland is requested to transmit to the Secretary-General of the United Nations the text of the Final Act, which *is not eligible for registration* under Article 102 of the Charter of the United Nations . . . .' Article 102 of the Charter provides that every treaty entered into by any member of the United Nations must be registered with the Secretariat and published by it. The non-treaty nature of the Final Act[3] is borne out by language used elsewhere which lacks the 'hard edge' of legal obligation; in the concluding part of the document, the States 'declare their resolve' to undertake actions either unilaterally 'in all cases which lend themselves to such action' or bilaterally 'by negotiations with other participating States'. The Preamble notes that the Representatives are motivated by the political will to improve their relations in the interests of peace.[4]

The fact that the Final Act is not a treaty has not deterred some commentators from attributing legal significance to it. On the Soviet side, an extreme expression of the 'legal significance' view is formulated by Ignatenko and Ostapenko:

The Final Act of the Conference on Security and Cooperation in Europe, signed by the supreme representative of 35 states in Helsinki on August 1, 1975 has a special political and legal significance. The Final Act is the result of the coordination of the

---

[1] Edited text in Brownlie, *Basic Documents on Human Rights*, 320; full text in *ILM*, 14 (1975), 1292.

[2] Albania was the only non-participating European State.

[3] Schachter, 'The Twilight Existence of Non-Binding International Agreements', *AJIL*, 71 (1977), 296; Russell, 'The Helsinki Declaration: Brobdingnag or Lilliput?, *AJIL*, 70 (1976), 242; Buergenthal and Hall (eds.), *Human Rights, International Law and the Helsinki Accord*; Ferraris (ed.), *Report on a Negotiation, Helsinki–Geneva–Helsinki 1972–75* (Alphen aan den Rijn: Sijthoff and Noordhoff, 1979); Van Dijk, 'The Final Act of Helsinki—Basis for a Pan-European System?' *Netherlands Yearbook of International Law*, 11 (1980), 97.

[4] White, *East–West Détente and International Law, Language and Substance* (Thomas Percival Lecture, 1978) essays comment on the language on the Final Act: White notes, *inter alia*, reference to the 'Participating States' (non-treaty), rather than to 'States Parties' (treaty).

wills and the foreign policy positions of European states as well as the United States and Canada. The participants of the Conference arrived at a generally acceptable position on each of the questions discussed therein. The heart of the Final Act was the Declaration of Principles by which the conduct of the participants was to be governed. The Final Act in its totality (and especially its Declaration of Principles) contains independent normative rules and as such grants a multilateral all-European normative character to all previously existing bilateral treaties and other documents . . . Accordingly, the provisions of this Act were officially recognised by all participating states as constituting a component part of the international law in force.[5]

These views are stated in the context of a doctrine which claims that resolutions of certain international conferences can amount to a specific source of law in relation to those States which consent to be bound. This appears to be a minority view among Soviet writers.[6]

Western writers, including Fawcett[7] and Schachter,[8] debate the difference between 'binding' and 'non-binding' agreements with reference to the Final Act, though their contributions reveal little practical difference in the results to be expected from States in their performance of the two kinds of agreement.[9] Russell views the Final Act as 'consistent with international law and, given the level at which it was concluded, many observers think that it may become in fact one of the most widely quoted sources of customary international law'.[10] Van Dijk categorizes the Final Act as a 'not binding international agreement'.[11] White writes that: 'The participating States declined to give their agreed formulation the status of an international treaty, but they seem to be saying rather clearly that these principles are normative in character. They are guides which ought to be followed in the actual conduct of international relations.'[12] The author also states the opinion that 'the gulf between [the above] situation and the situations comprised in the traditional notion of *opinio juris* is not so very great.'[13] Many writers, in fact, opt for the 'soft law' approach: that the Final Act, or most of it, distils some kind of moral and political obligation on States, if not a strictly legal one.

But, besides setting new standards of 'soft law', the Final Act quite clearly also reaffirms some existing standards, in the field of human rights and

---

[5] International Law (1978), cited by Osakwe, 'Contemporary Soviet Doctrine on the Sources of General International Law', *Procs. ASIL*, 1979, 310 at 322; also Mullerson, 'Sources of International Law: New Tendencies in Soviet Thinking', *AJIL*, 83 (1989), 494.

[6] Osakwe, ibid.

[7] 'The Belgrade conference: Recycled Paper', *VII Millennium*, Journal of International Studies, No. 1, 52.

[8] *Supra*, no. 1, 52.

[9] Schachter discerns two kinds of commitment on States to act to fulfil the demands of the Final Act: 'One is internal in the sense that the commitment of the State is "internalised" as an instruction to its officials to act accordingly; the other is "external" in the sense that the fact that . . . the States have entered into mutual engagements confers an entitlement on each party to make representations to the others on the execution of those engagements', ibid., 304.

[10] *Supra*, n. 3, 248. [11] Ibid. 110.

[12] White, 11. [13] Ibid.

elsewhere. The Final Act contains a 'Declaration on Principles Guiding Relations between Participating States' which are stated to be 'in conformity with the Charter of the United Nations' and are also to be applied 'in conformity with the purposes and principles of the Charter of the United Nations'. In many places, the Final Act explicitly mentions the existing obligations of States under international law, and Principle X of the Declaration on Principles (Fulfilment in Good Faith of Obligations under International Law) provides, *inter alia*, that 'The Participating States will fulfil in good faith their obligations under international law, both those obligations arising from the generally recognised principles and rules of international law and those obligations arising from treaties and other agreements . . . to which they are parties.' The Declaration on Principles is not primarily intended as innovative; it is explicative in character, and what it explicates are the existing rules and principles of international law, stemming from the United Nations Charter and other sources. The meaning of the promise to fulfil their obligations may, in the words of one writer, amount to an indication 'that the participating States, or at least some of them, did not observe their duties in the past, and implies a promise that in the future they "will fulfil in good faith their obligations under international law".'[14]

Principle X is followed by a statement that the participating States 'paying due regard to the principles above and in particular to the first sentence of the tenth principle . . . note that the present Declaration does not affect their rights and obligations, nor the corresponding treaties and other agreements and arrangements'. Thus, the Representative of Greece to the Conference regarded the Declaration on Principles as a reaffirmation of the tenets of the United Nations Charter by giving them 'a new dimension in European space'.[15]

The Declaration on Principles, calculated to elucidate norms of international law in a European context, does not constitute the whole of the Final Act, which consists of a Preamble, four main parts, and a concluding part. The references to minorities are contained in the Declaration on Principles and in the part on 'Co-operation in Humanitarian and other fields'. The reference in the Declaration on Principles is contained in Principle VII: 'Respect for Human Rights and . . . Freedoms, including the Freedom of Thought, Conscience, Religion or Belief.' The whole section reads:

The Participating States will respect human rights and fundamental freedoms, including the freedom of thought, conscience, religion or belief, for all without distinction as to race, sex, language or religion.

They will promote and encourage the effective exercise of civil, political, economic,

---

[14] *Human Rights: Soviet Theory and Practice*, Institute for the Study of Conflict, Conflict Studies No. 83 (London, 1977), 5.

[15] Cited by Cassese, 'The Helsinki Declaration and Self-Determination', in Buergenthal and Hall (eds.), 'Human Rights, International Law, and the Helsinki Accord', 105.

social, cultural and other rights and freedoms all of which derive from the inherent dignity of the human person and are essential for his free and full development.

Within this framework the participating States will recognise and respect the freedom of the individual to profess and practise, alone or in community with others, religion or belief acting in accordance with the dictates of his own conscience.

The Participating States on whose territory national minorities exist will respect the right of persons belonging to such minorities to equality before the law, will afford them the full opportunity for the actual enjoyment of human rights and fundamental freedoms and will, in this manner, protect their legitimate interests in this sphere.

The Participating States recognise the universal significance of human rights and fundamental freedoms, respect for which is an essential factor for the peace, justice and well-being necessary to ensure the development of friendly relations and co-operation among themselves as among all States.

They will constantly respect these rights and freedoms in their mutual relations and will endeavour jointly and separately, including in co-operation with the United Nations, to promote universal and effective respect for them.

They confirm the right of the individual to know and act upon his rights and duties in this field.

In the field of human rights and fundamental freedoms, the Participating States will act in conformity with the purposes and principles of the Charter of the United Nations and with the Universal Declaration of Human Rights. They will also fulfil their obligations as set forth in the international declarations and agreements in this field, including *inter alia* the International Covenants on Human Rights, by which they may be bound.

In relation to the 'minorities paragraph', some reflections on its preparation are in order. While there are no published *travaux préparatoires* of the Final Act, a group of independent scholars 'reconstructed' the various discussions through interviews with many of the participants.[16] As elsewhere, the initiative on minorities was prepared by the delegation of Yugoslavia. The Yugoslavian delegation endeavoured to achieve a separate resolution on the minorities question but was eventually content with a clear reference in the Context of Principle VII. Yugoslavia's early proposal for the above paragraph is markedly different from the finished product and was formulated as follows: 'The participating States respect the interests of national, ethnic and linguistic minorities and their right to free development, in such a way that such minorities might contribute to [the] free development of friendship and co-operation between the countries and peoples concerned.'[17]

According to the recollections of the scholars, Yugoslavia wanted a reference to 'national minorities' with their mother country in another State, whereas the USSR preferred 'ethnic group'; a number of delegations, including Italy, preferred a reference to all minorities, which apparently included

---

[16] Ferraris (*supra*, n. 3).   [17] Ibid. 136.

'ideological' groups.[18] There were difficulties over the reference to minorities as groups. To counter the Yugoslav proposal, Greece proposed a different text: 'The Participating States respect the legitimate interests of people belonging to minorities already recognised by bilateral treaties or by internal legislation.' The Greek proposal served a dialectical function in the discussions. Yugoslavia accepted a reference to 'people belonging to minorities' instead of to the groups themselves, and preferred that emphasis be placed on equality of rights. The pledge to minorities was not to go beyond the possibility of an effective enjoyment of human rights.[19] The Yugoslav proposal as it then stood resembled the eventual text, except that before the word 'interests' in the last part, the adjectives 'individual and collective' were included. This was unacceptable, particularly to the French delegation, and was eventually deleted.

The limited *travaux préparatoires* show at least the narrowing down of the reference from 'national, ethnic, and linguistic' minorities to 'national' minorities, supporting a restrictive interpretation.[20] Because the final text makes no reference to the connections of such groups with kin States, it must be assumed that Yugoslav proposals on this are not in accordance with the final text. The final text is inconsistent with the Greek proposal to limit the group covered by the paragraph to those minorities recognized in some legal fashion. Neither Article 27 nor the present text should be restricted in this way.

The other reference to minorities in the text is as follows: '*National Minorities or Regional Cultures.* The Participating States, recognising the contribution that national minorities or regional cultures can make to co-operation among them in various fields of culture, intend, when such minorities or cultures exist within their territory, to facilitate this contribution, taking into account the legitimate interests of their members.' In the corresponding section on education, 'fields of culture' is replaced by 'fields of education'. These paragraphs are not contained in the Declaration on Principles and are clearly, as evidenced by their language, part of the political 'soft law' aspect of the Final Act and amount to a declaration of the will or intention of States rather than a statement of obligation.

In the Declaration on Principles, which, as has been noted, is regarded as being in conformity with the United Nations Charter, the rights of persons belonging to minorities (as well as 'legitimate interests') are underlined. The whole of section VII contains both a non-discrimination clause and a specific minorities paragraph, which might be supposed to reflect the right of minorities to an identity. Article 27 of the Covenant on Civil and Political Rights has been criticized in the present work as being little more than a framework provision,[21] though its logical structure and situation in the United Nations Covenant permits reflection on more detailed obligations

---

[18] Ibid.
[20] *Infra*, text following n. 21.

[19] Ibid. 138.
[21] *Supra*, chs. 14 ff.

stemming from its meagre text. Such considerations apply, *a fortiori*, to the minorities paragraph in the Final Act. In the first place, it is even narrower than Article 27, applying only to 'national minorities', and not 'ethnic, religious, or linguistic minorities'.[22] Secondly, there is no mention in the Final Act of any 'right to an identity'; instead, the reference is to 'equality before the law', and 'to full opportunity for the actual enjoyment of [unspecified] human rights and fundamental freedoms'. These rights of persons are apparently intended to protect their 'legitimate interests'. The syntax of the paragraph does not enable one, in fact, to distinguish between 'legitimate interests of minorities' and 'legitimate interests of members of minorities'—but the latter meaning is set out in the paragraphs elsewhere in the Final Act. In the 'follow-up' Conference on Security and Co-operation in Europe at Madrid, the latter meaning of 'legitimate interests' is clearly asserted.[23]

Both Article 27 and the text of the Final Act invite reflections on the existence or non-existence of minority groups. In the context of Article 27, this has invited disclaimers from States on the existence of relevant groups.[24] However, in both cases 'existence' should be interpreted in a factual sense: minorities are not 'born' or extinguished simply through some act of their host State. The emphasis on actual enjoyment of human rights by members of minorities is to be welcomed and represents a theme which runs through the Declaration on Principles. While they are unspecified human rights, they must be 'civil, political, economic, social and cultural and other rights and freedoms . . .' to cite the text of Principle VII. They include the principles of Article 27 of the Covenant on Civil and Political Rights the 'international Covenants' are specifically mentioned.

However, it is a misreading of an admittedly tortuous and badly assembled text to suggest that some States which were not parties to the Covenants were committing themselves as a matter of legal obligation to observe their provisions. The reference to 'obligations' in the text describes 'obligations as set forth in the international declarations and agreements in this field, including *inter alia* the International Covenants on Human Rights, by which they may be bound'. The States promise to fulfil these 'obligations'. As Lapenna noted, because the States are already legally bound to fulfil 'obligations', the term in any case can only carry the connotation of fulfilment in good faith: the States' promise here is a promise to 'do better'. The official Soviet view of 'obligations' *vis-à-vis* the whole of the Declaration on Principles is that they 'confirm the corresponding provisions already having juridical force which [have] been previously included into the

---

[22] The USSR defines the expression to mean a group with, *inter alia*, a common territory and common economic life. 'Nation' in any case suggests a larger grouping than, say, ethnic group. See Cassese, (*supra*, n. 15); *Leninism and the National Question*, Institute of Marxism (Moscow: Progress Publishers, 1977).

[23] Conference on Security and Co-Operation in Europe: Madrid Session, *ILM*, 22 (1983), 1395 at 1399.   [24] *Supra*, ch. 16.

bilateral inter-State treaties and other documents, concluded [by the Soviet Union and other States'.[25] This echoes the statement by commentators that the Soviet Union was anxious 'not to extend the obligations undertaken at the [Conference] with reference to human rights over and above those already *agreed to* in regard to other international documents'.[26] The provisions in the Final Act may perhaps be used to interpret the human rights provisions of the Covenants,[27] but in the particular case of Article 27 this is not a useful proposal in view of the limitations of text in the Final Act; 'interpretation' would normally only be advanced by a clearer or more detailed subsequent text, which is not the case here. The procedure envisaged cannot be compared with, for example, the 'interpretation' of the human rights provisions, of the United Nations Charter by the Universal Declaration of Human Rights.

In summary, the provisions of the Helsinki Final Act are a welcome recognition of the relevance of minorities to the agenda of international relations. It is not inherently surprising to see such a reference in the context of Europe, since, for example, many European States describe particular groups in their constitutions,[28] and some bilateral or limited multilateral[29] treaties also refer to them. The promises to honour obligations on human rights are encouraging, although in the case of States such as the United States of America, which relies heavily on the Final Act in its diplomacy, the cause of human rights would perhaps be better served by becoming a party to the International Covenants.[30]

---

[25] Official Gazette of the Supreme Soviet, No. 33 1975; Pravda, 2 August 1975.

[26] Ferraris (*supra*, n. 3), 132.

[27] Frowein, 'The Interrelationship between the Helsinki Final Act, The International Covenants on Human Rights, and the European Convention on Human Rights', in Buergenthal and Hall, *Human Rights, International Law and the Helsinki Accord*, 73. Frowein cites Article 31(3)(a) of the Vienna Convention on the Law of Treaties in this context (74).

[28] See the references to various Constitutions in the Capotorti Report, Add. 4. These include, *inter alia*, the Constitutions of the USSR, Yugoslavia, Romania, Finland, Italy, Belgium, and Switzerland. The Constitution of Spain 1978 also makes extensive provisions for minority groups: Spanish Constitution 1978 (Ministero de Asuntos Exteriores, Officina de Informacion Diplomatica, 1979).

[29] UN, *Protection of Minorities*.

[30] The position of minorities is improved in the latest document of the Conference on Security and Co-operation in Europe held at Vienna—*ILM* 28 (1989), 527. The focus of the document is still on national minorities, and where rights are mentioned, they remain the rights of persons belonging to minorities. However, the representation of the right to identity is more explicit: whereas Principle 18 essentially reiterates existing promises to national minorities in the Helsinki and Madrid documents, Principle 19 reflects a more advanced view, providing that the participating States 'will protect and create conditions for the promotion of the ethnic, cultural, linguistic and religious identity of national minorities on their territory. They will respect the free exercise of rights by persons belonging to such minorities and ensure their full equality with others'. Provisions on religious communities are also expanded (Principle 16). Principle 19 is complemented by paragraphs 59 and 68 in the sections on 'Co-operation and Exchanges in the Field of Culture' and 'Co-operation and Exchanges in the Field of Education', respectively. It remains to be seen to what extent the more positive nuances translate into political and legal reality, particularly in the case of States such as Turkey whose approach to minorities has often been draconian: text extracts in Appendix 6 to the present work.

PART V

The Right Not to be Discriminated Against

29. *United Nations Instruments on Racial Discrimination*

The Declaration on the Elimination of All Forms of Racial Discrimination

On 20 November 1963, the United Nations General Assembly in Resolution 1904(XVIII) proclaimed the Declaration on the Elimination of All Forms of Racial Discrimination. It had previously been suggested at the Sub-Commission's session in 1961 that the Assembly should be encouraged to undertake the preparation of an international convention which would impose specific legal obligations on the parties to prohibit manifestations of racial and national hatred.[1] The Economic and Social Council recommended to the General Assembly the adoption of a draft resolution on 'Manifestations of Racial Prejudice and National and Religious Intolerance'.[2] The item was allocated to the Third Committee of the General Assembly which decided to split the issues of racial discrimination and religious intolerance,[3] adopting separate resolutions on the two issues. Resolution 1780(XVIII) requested the Economic and Social Council to ask the Commission on Human Rights to prepare a draft declaration on the elimination of all forms of racial discrimination and a draft international convention on the same topic.

Article 1 of the Declaration states that

Discrimination between human beings on the grounds of race, colour or ethnic origin is an offence to human dignity and shall be condemned as a denial of the principles of the Charter of the United Nations, as a violation of the human rights and fundamental freedom proclaimed in the Universal Declaration of Human Rights, as an obstacle to friendly and peaceful relations among nations and as a fact capable of disturbing peace and security among peoples.

The term 'discrimination' is not defined. The Preamble, however, expresses the consideration that the Charter of the United Nations 'is based on the dignity and equality of all human beings'; the Universal Declaration of Human Rights is cited for its proclamation 'that all human beings are born free and equal in dignity and rights'. It can therefore be deduced from these

---

[1] UN Doc E/CN.4/815, paras. 176 and 185.

[2] Res. 826B(XXXII).

[3] Res. 1780(XVII) and 1781(XVII), respectively. See generally Schwelb, 'The International Convention on the Elimination of All Forms of Racial Discrimination', *ICLQ*, 15 (1966), 996; Lerner, *The UN Convention on the Elimination of All Forms of Racial Discrimination* (Alphen aan den Rijn: Sijthoff and Noordhoff, 1980).

references and others in the operative part of the text[4] that discrimination is treatment which offends against the principle of the equality and dignity of human beings. Article 2(1) forbids discrimination by any 'State, institution, group or individual . . . in matters of human rights and fundamental freedoms'; Article 2(2) provides that no State shall lend its support to such discrimination. The Declaration contains further provisions to ensure that the laws of States function in a non-discriminatory manner, with a particular reference made to policies of racial segregation and apartheid; and that steps be taken to educate State populations to eliminate racial discrimination and prejudice, and promote understanding. Effective national remedies against acts of discrimination are also called for, as well as national suppression of racist organizations.

Article 2(3) is an interesting provision in the context of the present discussion. It provides that:

Special concrete measures shall be taken in appropriate circumstances in order to secure adequate development or protection of individuals belonging to certain racial groups with the object of ensuring the full enjoyment by such individuals of human rights and fundamental freedoms. These measures shall in no circumstances have as a consequence the maintenance of unequal or separate rights for different racial groups.

The Declaration is described by McKean as a preliminary reconnaissance of the content of the principle of non-discrimination,[5] and indeed the themes present in the Declaration reappear in later instruments. Article 2(3) is deserving of some comment, as is the general effect on this and related instruments of the political regime in South Africa. The Article provides for 'affirmative action' to meet the needs of racial groups existing in a state of underdevelopment. The measures are intended to be only of limited duration. Although the, unspecified, measures would appear to amount to a temporary offence to the principle of equality, this is at the same time forbidden by the article, which demands that the measures shall not have as a consequence the maintenance of unequal rights. Perhaps what is objected to here, and assuming that the stress of the sentence falls upon the 'maintenance' of these rights, rather than on that characteristic of being 'unequal', is something like the system prevailing in South Africa which is to be avoided. The article relates to measures which 'shall be taken' by the State; there is no mention of the consent of the groups involved. The article also falls far short of the type of article one would associate with 'the right to identity' in that it does not deal explicitly with distinctions between racial, or ethnic, groups which are voluntarily maintained—though a possible implication of the article is that it would ultimately favour assimilation of diverse 'racial' groups rather than contribute to the maintenance of their

---

[4] For example, Article 7.
[5] McKean, *Equality and Discrimination under International Law.*

identity. It does not expressly mention cultural, as opposed to economic underdevelopment, though the reference to enabling individuals to enjoy 'human rights and fundamental freedoms' is wide enough to encompass both aspects. The outcome is a very tentative endorsement of 'special measures'. Members of minorities are thus promised 'equal treatment' across a broad spectrum of rights, but the sense in which 'equality' is used is perhaps formal and legalistic rather than substantive or factual.

The International Convention on the Elimination of All Forms of Racial Discrimination

General Assembly Resolution 1906(XVIII), passed on the same day as the adoption of the Declaration on Racial Discrimination, requested the Sub-Commission and the Commission to give absolute priority to preparing a draft convention. Drafts were prepared by the Sub-Commission and the Commission on Human Rights; the Commission devoted its 775th to 810th meetings[6] to the work and adopted the substantive articles, and, on its recommendation, the Economic and Social Council submitted to the General Assembly the draft articles and other materials.[7] The item was allocated to the Third Committee of the General Assembly which devoted forty-three meetings to it and submitted its report to the General Assembly on 21 December 1965.[8] The Convention was adopted by 106 votes to none[9] with Mexico abstaining, though Mexico later declared that it would give an affirmative vote.[10] It is clear from the history of the preparation of the Convention that it received a thorough consideration at various levels in the United Nations hierarchy and constitutes as near an authentic expression as possible of the general view at the United Nations in 1965. On 1 September 1988 124 States had become parties to the Convention, and seven States had signed but not ratified: Benin, Bhutan, Grenada, Ireland, Mauritania, Turkey, and the USA.[11] The Convention is supported by States to a greater extent than any comparable Human Rights instrument.

The themes of the Declaration are taken up, modified, and extended in the Convention which includes measures of implementation as well as sub-stantive articles. The Preamble lays considerable stress, as did that of the Declaration, on the equality and dignity of human beings, declared as 'inherent in all human beings', and on the deleterious consequences of racial discrimination for world order and for 'the harmony of persons living side by side even within one and the same State'. The statement in the Preamble

---

[6] Larner (*supra*, n. 3), 4–5.
[7] ECOSOC Res. 1015B(XXXVIII); UN Doc E/CN.4/873.
[8] UN Doc A/6181 (report of the 3rd Committee, December 1966).
[9] UNGA Res. 2106A(XX).
[10] UN Doc A/PV.1408.   [11] ST/HR/5, November 1988.

that 'the existence of racial barriers is repugnant to the ideals of any human society' is a novelty not found in the Preamble to the Declaration. The reference was introduced in the Third Committee of the General Assembly[12] by Brazil, Colombia, and Senegal, their original text referring to 'civilised society' rather than the 'human society' of the final version.[13] The Representative of Senegal in the Third Committee explained the term, saying that racial barriers existed 'wherever communities were separated from each other on the basis of racial criteria, as was the case in South Africa where autonomous indigenous communities were being created. For those who were the victims of that form of discrimination the idea of racial barriers was as specific as that of geographical or customs barriers for others'.[14] The Representative of Brazil[15] elaborated this explanation: 'If racial discrimination was treated on an entirely negative basis and no attempt was made to promote race relations by abolishing the barriers which prevented solidarity between persons within the same community, the [Third] Committee's work would not be complete.' The term drew attention to one of the main causes of racial discrimination.

The Representative of Austria, however, discussed the new phrase in terms pertinent to the present discussion.[16] While sympathizing with the spirit underlying the racial barriers amendment, Austria could not support it; the amendment

might be understood to refer to barriers between national and ethnic groups within one country. Such groups were covered by the definition of 'racial discrimination' in Article 1 [below] and were . . . entitled to freedom from interference in their cultural and linguistic traditions, but the term 'racial barriers' was not defined and had not been used previously in any legal instrument. The wording of the amendment was not in harmony with the fundamental rights of national and ethnic minorities.

The implications of this are clear. The primary target of the amendment in the opinion of the Senegalese co-sponsor was the system prevailing in South Africa where 'autonomous indigenous communities' were created by act of the Government. The creation of such communities proceeded from the basic philosophy of apartheid and was achieved through the political, military, and police power of the dominant white minority. There is however a difference between the creation of such communities through repression of the races forced to live in such communities, and the situation where a racial or ethnic group itself wishes for a measure of self-government or autonomy to preserve its cultural or linguistic heritage. The latter situation is also the one identified by the Representative of Austria. Set apart from the situation in South Africa, the Representative correctly identified the possible repercussions of introducing such a novel term, in particular its potential

---

[12] UN Doc A/C.3/L.1217.
[14] UN Doc A/C.3/SR.1301, para. 62.
[16] Ibid. para. 5.

[13] Lerner, (*supra*, n. 3), 20.
[15] UN Doc A/C.3/SR.1302, para. 1.

force for justifying a policy of assimilation. While the argument of Senegal set its sights on South Africa, that of Brazil once more contains a strong sense of the 'melting pot' argument. The difference in this case between their traditional stance and the argument in this context is that the Convention was intended to have universal rather than regional application. The 'racial barriers' reference was in any case supererogatory since 'positive action' to promote racial harmony is envisaged by another paragraph of the Preamble wherein the States Parties declare themselves 'Resolved to adopt all necessary measures for speedily eliminating racial discrimination in all its forms and manifestations, and to prevent and combat racist doctrines and practice *in order to promote understanding between races . . .* '. The phrase in italics is quite as 'positive' as the reference to racial barriers and less open to misunderstanding.

Unlike the United Nations Declaration on Race, the Convention provides a definition of racial discrimination. Discrimination is not differentiating between individuals, but, as the Secretary-General's memorandum put it, was limited to 'any conduct based on a distinction made on grounds of natural or social categories which have no relation either to individual capacities or merits or to the concrete behaviour of the individual person';[17] discrimination meant 'unwanted, unreasonable, arbitrary or invidious differences'[18] made between one individual and another. Thus, Article 1(1) of the Convention defines 'racial discrimination' as 'any distinction, exclusion, restriction or preference based on race, colour, descent, or national or ethnic origin which has the purpose or effect of nullifying or impairing the recognition, enjoyment or exercise, on an equal footing, of human rights and fundamental freedoms in the political, economic, social, cultural or any other field of public life'. The second and third paragraphs of the article describe cases where the Convention does not apply; distinctions 'between citizens and non-citizens' (paragraph 2), and laws regulating nationality, citizenship, or naturalization, 'provided that such provisions do not discriminate against any particular nationality' (paragraph 3). It may be noted that the term 'preference' is used in Article 1(1); a preference will only fall within the prohibitions in the Convention if it is not one of the 'special measures' envisaged in Articles 1(4) and 2(2) of the Convention.[19]

The definition of 'racial discrimination' in the Convention is a broad one and includes discrimination based on race, colour, descent, national and ethnic origin. The word 'descent' does not appear in related international instruments on discrimination including the UN Declaration on Race, and did not appear in the draft submitted by the Sub-Commission or the Commission on Human Rights. The term was suggested by India in the Third

---

[17] UN Doc E/CN.4/Sub.2/40.
[18] ECOSOC OR. 6th Session, Supp. No.11.
[19] See also the UNESCO Convention against Discrimination, *infra*, ch. 32.

Committee of the General Assembly[20] and was later unanimously approved. The drafting record does not indicate in what way 'descent' could be regarded as different from 'national origin' or 'ethnic origin'. Schwelb[21] comments that 'it is reasonable to assume that "descent" includes the notion of "caste" which is a prohibited ground of discrimination in Indian constitutional law, which, however, also uses the expression "descent" side by side with "caste" . . .' 'Descent' may indeed add something because, as McKean remarks, it 'is not easily subsumed under the concepts of national or ethnic origin'.[22]

The phrase 'national origin' was used in the Preamble to the Race Declaration but not in its operative part. The words provoked discussion during the drafting stages, and much confusion. Weis wrote that '"nationality" . . . is a politico-legal term denoting membership of a State. It must be distinguished from nationality as a historico-biological term denoting membership of a nation.'[23] The distinction was not always made in the debates, and the Representative of Ghana in the Third Committee rightly observed[24] that 'nationality' did not have a universally accepted meaning. The Representative of Hungary[25] argued for a clear phraseology forbidding discrimination against those who were citizens of a State, but had a different 'nationality' from other citizens, by which he meant a different mother tongue, cultural traditions, etc.[26] The Representative of Austria argued in similar vein,[27] urging that the term be retained, otherwise the rights of such groups would only be the subject of uncertainty and perhaps ultimate denial. Like Hungary, Austria mentioned the distinction between 'nationality' as State citizenship and the other meaning of 'nationality' as a phenomenon of language, culture, and tradition. The Representative of the United States made a comprehensive effort to distinguish 'national origin' as a term separable both from 'nationality' and from 'ethnic origin'. 'National origin' differed from 'nationality' in that it related to the past, whereas nationality described a present status. By 'the past' was meant the previous 'legal-political' status of the group rather than its cultural and historical traditions. 'National origin' was a narrower term than 'ethnic origin' which was associated with racial and cultural characteristics, and a reference to it would not necessarily cover persons resident in foreign countries where their national origins were not respected.[28] The Representative of India stressed that no one was suggesting that the rights guaranteed and the duties imposed under national constitutions should be extended to aliens.[29]

[20] UN Doc A/C.3/L.1216, and L.1238; UN Doc A/6181, paras. 33, 37, 41(a).

[21] Schwelb (*supra*, n. 3), n. 43.

[22] McKean, *Equality and Discrimination under International Law*, 156.

[23] Weis, *Nationality and Statelessness in International Law*, 3 (London: Stevens and Sons, 1956; 2nd edition, Alphen aan den Rijn: Sijthoff and Noordhoff, 1979).

[24] UN Doc A/C.3/SR.1306.   [25] Schwelb (*supra*, n. 3), 1006.

[26] UN Doc A/C.3/SR.1304.   [27] Ibid.

[28] Ibid.   [29] Ibid.

Reviewing the *travaux préparatoires* of the Convention, Schwelb summarizes that 'the three terms "descent", "national origin" and "ethnic origin" among them cover distinctions both on the ground of *present* or *previous* "nationality" in the ethnographical sense and on the ground of *previous* nationality in the politico-legal sense of citizenship.'[30]

Article 1(2) of the Convention does permit distinctions based on the fact that a person is or is not a citizen, but has nothing to say about internal legislation to this effect; neither does it control laws relating to nationality, citizenship, or naturalization, provided they do not discriminate against a particular nationality.[31] The meaning of 'nationality' is again unclear in this paragraph, though it would seem unlikely that two different senses of 'nationality' were intended in this same sentence. While the Convention is not generous as regards aliens,[32] paragraphs 2 and 3 imply that differences of treatment are allowed only on grounds of citizenship or lack of it, distinctions in respect of aliens on the basis of race, colour, etc., are prohibited; also, while naturalization may be refused on the basis of race (paragraph 1(3)), it would appear that a person may not be deprived of his nationality on racial grounds, under Article 5 by which States parties guarantee 'the right of everyone, without distinction as to race, colour, or national or ethnic origin, to equality before the law, notably in the enjoyment of the following rights . . . the right to nationality'. If this limited interpretation is not adopted, no effective meaning can be given to Article 5 in the face of Article 1(3). The prohibition on deprivation of nationality on racial grounds which results is important in the context of minorities who derive particular rights under Article 27 of the UN Covenant on Civil and Political Rights on the basis of their being nationals of a State. While it has been discussed in that context, it is instructive to see this principle emerge from a basic anti-discrimination provision, such as the one under review, though it would have been more direct and reassuring to have incorporated a provision in the Convention similar to Article 9 of the Statelessness Convention of 1961[33] by which a contracting State may not deprive any person or group of persons of their nationality on racial, ethnic, religious, or political grounds.[34]

Apart from provisions relating to aliens, the Convention conceives the grounds upon which discrimination is not permissible in a broad fashion suitable to protect racial, ethnic, and linguistic groups. In view of the importance which the United Nations has attached to the evils of racism, it

---

[30] Schwelb, (*supra*. n. 3), 1007. Subject to an exception in relation to naturalized citizens: Article 1(3).

[31] Schwelb, (*supra*, n. 3), 1009, says that this is politico-legal nationality; Lerner, (*supra*, n. 3), 30 says that it is equivalent to the meaning in 'national origin'.

[32] McKean (*supra*, n. 5), 158.

[33] Convention on the reduction of Statelessness, A/CONF.9/15 (1961), text in Brownlie, *Basic Documents on Human Rights*, 83.

[34] Article 9.

would seem that generosity of interpretation of basic terms would contribute to the effectiveness of the Convention: doubts should be resolved in
favour of giving words their broadest significance.

The Convention does not explicitly deal with religious groups, it deals
with 'racial' discrimination and gives the term a wide meaning. It seems
clear that in the Racial Discrimination Convention, racial discrimination
disguised as discrimination on religious grounds is not permissible; 'purely'
religious discrimination falls to be dealt with by other international instruments. The distinction between the forms of discriminatory practice
featured to some extent in discussions relating to anti-Semitism. There is no
specific reference to anti-Semitism in the Convention despite efforts to have
one inserted.[35] The reasons for the omission are political rather than technical, though they also illuminate the question of how far the Convention
extends. Thus, the United States representative to the Commission on
Human Rights proposed an amendment to Article 3 of the Convention
under which 'States parties particularly condemn racial segregation and
Apartheid' by inserting 'and anti-Semitism'[36] after '*apartheid*'. The USA
later suggested an Article specifically condemning anti-Semitism. A sub-
amendment was proposed by the USSR which would have condemned
'Nazism, including all its new manifestations (neo-Nazism), genocide, anti-
Semitism, as also other forms of racial discrimination . . .'.[37] The United
States argued that the Convention would not be complete if it failed to
recognize the programme of annihilation which had destroyed so many
Jews, and that besides a religion the Jews also shared a historic and cultural
past which constituted a common ethnic origin. Poland and Ecuador
remarked that anti-Semitism was a form of racial discrimination, Ecuador
noting that, under the definition in Article 1, discrimination based on ethnic
origin was racial discrimination.[38] The USA and USSR amendments were
transmitted to the General Assembly and the problem was considered in the
Third Committee. Here, the matter became strongly politicized, with the
USSR submitting a controversial amendment to the effect that States Parties
condemned 'anti-Semitism, Zionism, Nazism, neo-Nazism and all other
forms of the policy and ideology of colonialism, national and race hatred
and exclusiveness . . .'.[39] During the debates in the Committee, the
Representative of Hungary

considered that anti-Semitism should not be regarded as a form of racial discrimination. As Judaism was primarily a religion, it would be more appropriate to refer

[35] Generally, Coleman, 'The Problem of Anti-Semitism under the International Convention
on the Elimination of All Forms of Racial Discrimination', *RDH*, 2 (1969), 609; Roth, 'Anti-
Semitism and International Law' *Israel Yearbook on Human Rights*, 13 (1983), 208.
[36] UN Doc E/CN.4/L.701/Rev. 2.
[37] UN Doc E/CN.4/L.710, E/3873, para. 272; E/CN.4/L.710/Rev.1, UN Doc E/3873, para,
274 (revised version).
[38] Schwelb (*supra*, n. 3), 1012.
[39] UN Doc A/C.3/L.1231, A/6181, para. 101(a).

to anti-Semitism in the context of the discussion of religious intolerance. It was Nazism which had made anti-Semitism a political viewpoint and had created the aberrant doctrine according to which the Jews were not the followers of a particular religion but members of a separate racial group.[40]

As anti-Semitism was only one aspect of Nazism, it was the latter rather than the former practice which deserved a specific reference. However, the Hungarian opinion that anti-Semitism was not racial but religious discrimination appears to have been a minority view. The majority viewpoint was clearly that it was racial discrimination though it was undesirable to mention it specifically in a general text, otherwise it would be necessary to list all possible forms and manifestations which was impossible; any enumeration would be incomplete. Arab States were anxious to guard against charges of anti-Semitism as well as to condemn Zionism; the representative of Sudan emphasized that the Arab-Israeli conflict was 'not an expression of anti-Semitism in a religious or racial sense, but a dispute between Arabs on the one hand and Zionism as a political movement and Israel as a State on the other'.[41]

Article 1(4) is an important provision on disadvantaged groups which is relevant to many minorities; in the context of the distinction between 'protection of minorities' and 'prevention of discrimination', it marks out the boundaries of a distinction between the two concepts for the purpose of the Convention. It is clearly in direct line of descent from Article 2(3) of the United Nations Declaration on Race and reads as follows:

Special measures taken for the sole purpose of securing adequate advancement of certain racial or ethnic groups or individuals requiring such protection as may be necessary in order to ensure to such groups or individuals equal enjoyment or exercise of human rights and fundamental freedoms shall not be deemed racial discrimination, provided, however, that such measures do not, as a consequence, lead to the maintenance of separate rights for different racial groups and that they shall not be continued after the objectives for which they were taken have been achieved.

Article 1(4) is contextually a development of the definition of discrimination by the Convention; it is complemented by Article 2(2) which represents a detail of the obligations undertaken by States parties who:

shall, when the circumstances so warrant, take, in the social, economic, cultural and other fields, special and concrete measures to ensure the adequate development and protection of certain racial groups or individuals belonging to them, for the purpose of guaranteeing them the full and equal enjoyment of human rights and fundamental freedoms. These measures shall in no case entail as a consequence the maintenance of unequal or separate rights for different racial groups after the objectives for which they were taken have been achieved.

---

[40] UN Doc A/C.3/SR.1301, para. 22.   [41] UN Doc A/C.3/SR.1302, para. 16.

McKean's judgment of Articles 1(4) and 2(2) is that a definition of discrimination 'which incorporates the notion of special temporary measures, not as an exception to the principle but as a corollary to it, demonstrates the fruition of the work of the Sub-Commission and the method *by which the twin concepts of discrimination and minority protection can be fused into the principle of equality*'.[42] This is a sweeping claim and must be treated with caution; it is tantamount to saying, as with Vierdag,[43] that ' protection of minorities' does not and need not reach beyond the formulae set out in the two paragraphs. For reasons set out above, this must be doubted, and a reading of the text together with the preparatory materials leads to the conclusion that this limited concession in the definition of discrimination in favour of disadvantaged groups should not be idealized into a substitute for the protection of minorities, which is a wider notion.

On the incorporation of 'special measures' in the definition, some delegations were unconvinced even by the notion that these limited measures did not constitute discrimination in themselves. The Representative of Ivory Coast in the Third Committee remarked that the phrase in the draft under discussion 'adequate development or protection of certain under-developed racial groups or individuals belonging to them' had often in the past been invoked to justify colonialism; 'moreover, the principle still represented discrimination, even though the aims might be good and even though limits were set for the length of time such special measures would be in effect'.[44] She described the paragraph (1(4)) as opening the door to all sorts of 'legal manœuvring to justify various kinds of racial discrimination',[45] and as favouring the racists more than their victims. The Representative of Nigeria argued that, in any case, 'underdeveloped' was not a suitable description of human individuals or groups.[46] Neither was 'underprivileged' a suitable term because it would imply, according to the Representative of India,[47]

---

[42] McKean (*supra*, n. 22), 159.   [43] Vierdag, *Concept of Discrimination*.

[44] UN Doc A/C.3/SR.1306, para. 23.

[45] Ibid. cf. *Gerhardy* v. *Brown, 57 ALR 472*, a decision of the High Court of Australia. The Racial Discrimination Act 1975 implements the UN Racial Discrimination Convention; section 8(1) of the Act reflects Article 1(4) of the Convention. The issue in the case was whether provisions under the South Australian Pitjantjatjara Land Rights Act 1978 were discriminatory under the Racial Discrimination Act. The Land Rights Act prevented anyone other than a member of the Pitjantjatjara entering their land without permission of the corporate body of the Pitjantjatjara; it was held that it was not in conflict with the Commonwealth Act because it was a special measure under Article 1(4) and section 8(1). However, five of seven judges held that it would have been discriminatory in the absence of a special measures provision since it distinguished between a Pitjantjatjara and a non-Pitjantjatjara and included the proposition that to be a Pitjantjatjara was to be a member of a race. The Racial Discrimination Act was treated as forbidding any discrimination employing race as a criterion. The case demonstrates the utility of a special measures provision in cases of otherwise absolute refusal to employ race as a criterion in legislation irrespective of reasonableness and appropriateness in a particular case. For further comment, see Brownlie in Crawford (ed.), *The Rights of Peoples*, 8–10.

[46] UN Doc A/C.3/SR.1306, para. 30.

[47] Ibid., para. 26.

that the special measures were privileges. The Representative of India expressed strong support for the inclusion of 'special measures' in the Convention and gave a detailed explanation of India's understanding of the need for such a paragraph. Paragraph 1(4) had been included:

in order to provide for special and temporary measures to help certain groups of people . . . who, though of the same racial stock and ethnic origin as their fellow citizens, had for centuries been relegated by the caste system to a miserable and downtrodden condition . . . they had for centuries been denied those advantages that were essential for the full development of the human personality.[48]

He pointed to efforts made by India since independence to deal with the caste problem through equality before the law and the removal of barriers to advancement.[49] This had not been sufficient; the allocation of special rights to raise educational, social, and economic status had also been necessary. It may be noted that the Constitution of India expressly authorizes special measures to protect backward groups. The full extent of these measures was set out by the Government of India in a document submitted to the Commission on Human Rights.[50] The document distinguishes between rights of minorities, and the 'Scheduled Castes and Scheduled Tribes'. While the constitutional and legal rights of minorities have an element of permanence and include such things as the establishment and maintenance of schools, conservation of language and culture, management of religious affairs, etc., the rights relating to the Scheduled Castes and Scheduled Tribes are envisaged as temporary and exceptional measures to reduce the inequalities between communities. In relation to the Scheduled Tribes, the problem was 'to evolve ways and means of their gradual *assimilation* in to [the] general life of the country without undue and hasty disruption of their way of life'.[51] For the Scheduled Castes, the problem was 'to eradicate the scourge of untouchability and to improve the economic and social position of the Untouchables'.[52] Elsewhere it was said that 'the real protection of these weaker sections lies in their improved economic standards'.[53] Accordingly, it would also appear that, unlike the minorities question which is often seen as a cultural issue, that of the Scheduled Castes and Scheduled Tribes is seen primarily as a social and economic issue. Thus, the references by the Indian representative in the Third Committee are to the kind of measures associated with amelioration of the social position of castes and tribes rather than general 'minorities' questions; the two issues are distinguishable and one set of norms will not do the work of the other.

The key to the Indian interpretation of Articles 1(4) and 2(2) is the desirability of integrating certain groups into the nation, though from the quotation above in relation to the Tribes, integration may be a euphemism

[48] Ibid., para. 25.
[49] McKean, *supra*, n. 22, ch. xiii.
[50] UN Doc E/CN.4/1298/Add.2, 4–9.
[51] Ibid. 7, para. 16. See *infra*, chs. 38 ff.
[52] Ibid., para. 15.
[53] Para. 22.

for assimilation. There is a general emphasis in the Convention on integration: Article 2(1)(e), for example, provides that the States parties 'undertake to encourage, where appropriate, integrationist multiracial organizations and movements and other means of eliminating barriers between races, and to discourage anything which tends to strengthen racial division'. The objectives of the Convention are laudable provided integration is given a limited meaning on behalf of groups willing to participate in the wider society, but without the loss of distinctive identity. In general, it may also be said that special measures of protection represent a progressive impulse in the development of anti-discrimination norms. If integration and *de facto* equality between groups are truly desired by all, relative levels of advancement must be taken into account. Special measures are a necessity, and they are not incompatible with integration. The 'countries of immigration', however, may see things differently. Integration may here have a 'harder' meaning, tantamount to assimilation.

In discussions on the draft Convention, special measures were objected to in the South American context by Mr Santa Cruz (Chile) because they served only to maintain and perpetuate the separation of the protected groups from the wider community.[54] For similar reasons, it may be recalled, South American States opposed even the notion that minorities existed on their territories. Capotorti's perception of the indispensability of a rule of non-discrimination, a necessary but not a sufficient rule for the protection of minorities, assumes validity as the perception of a rule necessary to combat this type of attitude. But if States reject or accept with reluctance even the limited concept of special temporary measures to aid disadvantaged groups, there is little hope for permanent measures necessary to preserve group identities.

Finally, on special measures, although the Convention Articles are based on the United Nations Declaration on Race, one interesting difference reveals itself on a comparison of texts: the United Nations Declaration is more markedly individualistic in its description of the objects of the measures, they are 'individuals belonging to certain racial groups', rather than the groups as such. In the limited context of 'special measures', the Convention speaks directly of 'certain racial or ethnic *groups*' or individuals belonging to them. It thus confronts the question of an intermediate level of social reality between State and individual in a more direct way than the most important contemporary legal text relevant to the protection of the identity of minority groups—Article 27. The explanation in this case may lie in the limited, temporary nature of State obligations in the Convention on Racial Discrimination.

The remaining articles of the Convention require only brief description. Article 2 sets out State obligations in detail; the general aim of the measures

---

[54] E/CN.4/Sub.2/SR.416, para. 13.

is 'to pursue by all appropriate means and without delay, a policy of eliminating racial discrimination in all its forms and promoting understanding among all races . . .'.[55] To this end the State itself and its subordinate public bodies are forbidden to discriminate,[56] and the State is not 'to sponsor, defend or support racial discrimination by any persons or organizations'.[57] The State is also expected to bring its laws into conformity with the Convention's requirements.[58] Article 2(1)(d) is particularly strong: 'Each State Party shall prohibit and bring to an end, by all appropriate means, including legislation as required by circumstances, racial discrimination by any persons, group or organization.' Racial segregation and apartheid are singled out for special condemnation by Article 3. Article 4 sets up something of a conflict between the elimination of racial discrimination and freedom of expression by requiring that States parties 'condemn all propaganda and all organizations which are based on ideas or theories of superiority of one race or group of persons of one colour or ethnic origin' or which attempt to justify or promote racial hatred and discrimination in any form; the States undertake to adopt immediate and positive measures designed to eliminate such discrimination. However, the States' obligations here are to be exercised with due regard to 'the principles embodied in the Universal Declaration of Human Rights and the rights expressly set forth in Article 5 of this Convention.'[59]

The broad obligations set out in Article 2 are set out in detail by Article 5, whereby 'States parties undertake to prohibit and to eliminate racial discrimination in all its forms and to guarantee the right of everyone, without distinction as to race, colour, or national or ethnic origin, to equality before the law, notably in the enjoyment of the following rights' and a list of rights follows which is taken primarily from the Universal Declaration of Human Rights and includes both civil rights, and economic, social, and cultural rights.[60] Article 6 requires the States to provide effective national remedies for acts of discrimination. Article 7 imposes on States parties an obligation to educate their populations to combat prejudices leading to discrimination and to promote inter-racial understanding.

Measures of implementation are provided for by Part II. The vehicle for implementation is the Committee on the Elimination of Racial Discrimination which consists of 'eighteen experts of high moral standing and acknowledged impartiality elected by States parties who shall serve in their

---

[55] Article 2(1).   [56] Article 2(1)(a).
[57] Article 2(1)(b).   [58] Article 2(1)(c).
[59] Australia, Bahamas, Belgium, Fiji, France, Italy, Malta, Nepal, Papua New Guinea, Tonga, and the UK have all made reservations or given 'interpretations' of Article 4: ST/HR/5, 99 ff.
[60] They include equality before the law, security of the person (political rights), freedom of movement, freedoms of thought, conscience, opinion, expression, and peaceful assembly (civil rights), and rights to work, to housing, health, education and equal participation in cultural activities (economic, social, and cultural rights).

personal capacity, consideration being given to equitable geographical distribution and to the representation of the different forms of civilization as well as of the principal legal systems'.[61] By Article 9(1), States parties are obliged to submit reports on the progress they have made in implementing the Convention '(*a*) within one year after the entry into force of the Convention for the State concerned; and (*b*) thereafter every two years and whenever the Committee so requests'. Article 9(2) provides for annual reports by the Committee through the Secretary-General to the General Assembly, and the Committee 'may make suggestions and general recommendations based on the examination of the reports and information received from the States parties'. Apart from the reporting procedure, there is an interstate complaints procedure under Articles 11 to 13 which is supervised by the Committee; with provisions for a subordinate *ad hoc* Conciliation Commission in the case of more intractable disputes. Article 14 provides yet another procedural limb, whereby a State party 'may at any time declare that it recognizes the competence of the Committee to receive and consider communications from individuals or groups of individuals within its jurisdiction claiming to be victims of a violation by that State party of any of the rights set forth in this Convention'. Article 14(2) provides that a State party agreeing to this procedure 'may establish or indicate a body within its national legal order which shall be competent to receive and consider petitions from individuals or groups of individuals within its jurisdiction who claim to be victims . . .'. There is therefore the possibility of a double safeguard against the embarrassment which may be caused to a State party by individual petitions. Concern for the dignity and prerogatives of sovereign States is a prominent feature of all international petitioning procedures, and the precautions evident in this procedure represent an interesting manifestation of the lengths to which such concern can be taken while still admitting the validity of the procedure;[62] the procedure is also, as the Convention makes clear, only optional, whereas other procedures are basic to the Convention. The Representative of Ghana in the Third Committee pointed out that it was important to reconcile 'the sincere wish of many delegations to use the right of petition and communication as an effective weapon against discrimination'[63] with the fact that States were 'jealous of their sovereignty and . . . reluctant to acknowledge that right'.

---

[61] Article 8. See Lerner, 'Curbing Racial Discrimination—Fifteen Years CERD' *Israel Yearbook on Human Rights*, 13 (1983), 170.

[62] The representative of Canada remarked to the General Assembly's 3rd Committee that the procedure 'could not be more optional than it was': UN Doc A/C.3/SR.1335, para. 10. Costa Rica, Denmark, Ecuador, France, Iceland, Italy, Netherlands, Norway, Peru, Senegal, Sweden, and Uruguay have made declarations recognizing the competence of CERD under Article 14: ST/HR/5. The 10th declaration necessary to bring this procedure into force was made in 1982. See also Article 15 of the Convention, discussed in Lerner, (*supra*, n. 61), 176–7.

[63] UN Doc A/C.3/SR.1335.

The achievement of such procedures[64] is, however, a progressive moment in international human rights law, even if the procedure is cautious. The inclusion of petitions from groups is an important advance; the United Nations Covenant on Civil and Political Rights grants the right only to individuals, but the Convention on Racial Discrimination pursues the logic of allocating recognition to the needs of 'racial or ethnic groups' (Article 1(4)) in the text by extending the right of petition to groups. The words 'groups of individuals' appear to be 'general and comprehensive'[65] and so could include the racial, ethnic, and linguistic groups within the purview of this work.[66]

Finally, Article 22 provides that

Any dispute between two or more States parties over the interpretation or application of this Convention, which is not settled by negotiation or by the procedures expressly provided for in this Convention, shall, at the request of any of the parties to the dispute, be referred to the International Court of Justice for decision, unless the disputants agree to another mode of settlement.

The Communist States parties to the Convention among others, have made reservations to this article, on the basis that no such reference can be made without the consent of all States parties to the dispute.[67]

---

[64] See also Article 25 of the European Convention on Human Rights, and Article 44 of the American Convention on Human Rights.

[65] Lerner, *The UN Convention on the Elimination of Discrimination*, 84.

[66] Lerner (*supra*, n. 61), 179–83.

[67] ST/HR/5, 99 ff.

30. Interpretation of Treaty Articles in the Proceedings of the Committee on the Elimination of Racial Discrimination

The Convention on the Elimination of All Forms of Racial Discrimination is concerned with racial groups in general and not specifically with minorities. None the less, minorities are the natural victims of racial discrimination in most States, and have been frequently discussed in the reporting procedure under the Convention. The reporting procedure by which the State describes the progress made in its legislation and administration is perhaps better adapted to securing an overview of group problems than the more sharply focused individual complaints procedures, and thus to emphasize the collective aspects of discrimination as they affect minorities. The Committee has filled out some of the implications of the Convention as matters of general interpretation and contributed to a better understanding of its virtues and limitations as a legal text to support the interests of minority groups. Its practice is comparable to the practice of the less experienced Human Rights Committee under the Covenant on Civil and Political Rights, and a number of problems common to the two instruments appear and reappear in the proceedings. For example, while many States deny the existence of minorities on their territory in reports with reference to Article 27 of the Covenant on Civil and Political Rights, they also do this in reports to the Committee on the Elimination of Racial Discrimination, or, while admitting the presence of diverse ethnic groups in their territory, deny that there is any question of racial discrimination.[1] The Committee has, accordingly, developed a practice of requesting information from States on the ethnic composition of their populations. The initial report of Brazil stated that: 'in spite of the multiplicity of races living within its boundaries, racial problems are simply non-existent';[2] Brazil expressed irritation at the Committee's repeated requests for more information on measures to comply with the Convention. The Committee's response was to emphasize the demands of the Convention, and, perhaps with a degree of irony, to emphasize that 'in the light of the situation of racial harmony which

---

[1] This parallels assertions before the Human Rights Committee that, while there may be minorities in the State, there is no minority 'problem'.

[2] Para. 18, cited UN Doc A/9018, para. 124.

prevailed in Brazil, the requests for additional information on the measures taken to attain, preserve and promote such harmony should be regarded not as a nuisance but as an opportunity to help other countries which might be faced with similar tasks . . .'.[3] The report of Pakistan, discussed by the Committee in 1973, asserted that in relation to 'the recent tragic events in East Pakistan', 'at no time was the imputation of racial discrimination or differentiation a component of [the] grievances or a cause of friction between the regions of Pakistan . . .'.[4] This was a surprising statement in the face of much evidence and was disbelieved by some members of the Committee. A strong claim to a discrimination-free society was made by Venezuela, whose Representative explained to the Committee that his government 'found it difficult to provide information on racial discrimination which did not and could not exist in Venezuela', because the majority of Venezuelans 'did not belong to a particular race, but were part white, black or Indian; and there were no official statistics on the ethnic composition of the population'.[5] Rather inconsistently with this position, which again was not accepted by members of the Committee, the Representative of Venezuela explained that even 'a specific mention of racial discrimination [in legislation] would create a problem that had not existed before . . .'[6]—presumably by 'creating' a racial or ethnic group which had no existence previous to the legislation. Burundi was another State claiming a homogeneous population, a view offered in the absence of demographic information supplied by its government, and implicitly challenged by the Committee.[7] According to the sixth periodic report of Bulgaria,[8] that country had historically been the home of other nationalities which apparently no longer existed. Members of the Committee therefore asked how the Government of Bulgaria could provide for ethnic groups if it did not acknowledge their existence.[9]

The 'no racial discrimination' States usually claim either a homogeneous society, or a heterogeneous society but without racial discrimination. Another approach to deflect the thrust of the Convention is to emphasize the limited scope of the Convention in terms of protected groups. Thus, the Representative of Spain, replying to the Committee's questions, stated that issues concerning the Basques and Catalans were dealt with in various legal texts;[10] however, the Basques and the Catalans 'were not treated as separate

---

[3] Ibid.

[4] A/9018, para. 164. The reference was, of course, to the events leading to the establishment of the State of Bangladesh.

[5] UN Doc A/31/18, para. 126.

[6] Ibid.

[7] UN Doc A/36/18, para. 236: the 2nd report of Burundi is CERD/C/62/Add.1.

[8] CERD/C/66/Add.28.

[9] UN Doc A/36/18, para. 251. For claims to 'discrimination-free' societies in the more limited sense that no cases of discrimination have ever been brought to the courts, see for example, CERD/C/SR.779 (Soviet Union), CERD/C/SR.782 (Trinidad and Tobago).

[10] A/37/18, para. 286: the Spanish report is CERD/C/91/Add.6.

races and, therefore, did not fall within the scope of the Convention'. Article 14 of the Spanish Constitution dealt with racial discrimination and did not define 'racial' in the wide terms adopted by the Convention. The terms of the Convention would, however, appear to cover the cases of the Basques and Catalans adequately and this was indicated by a member of the Committee. In similar vein, Pakistan reported to the Committee that there were no ethnic minorities, but only religious minorities in Pakistan. Some members expressed doubts that the entire population of Pakistan was racially and ethnically homogeneous; others wondered whether differences,[11] which may have been in their origin purely religious, 'had not given rise over the centuries to ethnic diversity as well'.[12] The attitude of Pakistan does not appear to be marked by absolute consistency. In response to questions of the Commission on Human Rights on the 'Rights of Persons Belonging to National, Ethnic, Religious and Linguistic Minorities', Pakistan listed the measures by which the 'rights and privileges of minorities' are safeguarded, in such a manner as to imply that culture as well as religion was a component part of minority identity. Thus, the 'Declaration on Minorities' issued by the Government of Pakistan in 1976 provided that '. . . the Minorities shall be integrated and accepted in the general stream of national life, without affecting their religious and cultural identities';[13] '. . . that special measures shall be adopted to help and support the underprivileged sections of the society, irrespective of their *creed, caste or colour*'. Further, one of the 'major steps' taken for the welfare of minorities was the 'Constitution of a *cultural* council for the advancement of the *cultural* activities of minorities'.[14] It appears that a cultural minority identity is in fact recognized in Pakistan in practice, and this is caught by the term 'ethnic' in Article 1 of the Convention. These observations are echoed in the questions of members of the Committee.[15] One quoted the report of Pakistan which stated that 'the minorities in Pakistan are essentially religious minorities'; this seemed to him to imply that there were other minorities besides religious ones. He also quoted the second periodic report of Pakistan which contained information about populations observing tribal laws or customs; to the extent that such customs 'only arose among populations of a different ethnic origin, the impression was given that different ethnic groups did exist and needed to be protected by special laws'.[16] Another noted that Pakistan had created autonomous regions in order to develop the economy 'and that measure perhaps amounted to an implicit acknowledgement of the fact that several ethnic groups did exist'.[17] One Committee member gave a clear description of the minorities existing in Pakistan and noted that they were ethnic minorities and that ethnic groups such as the Pathans of the North-

---

[11] UN Doc A/32/18, para. 99.
[12] Ibid.
[13] UN Doc E/CN.4/1298/Add.3, para. 3.
[14] Ibid., para. 4.
[15] Discussion of 4th report of Pakistan, CERD/C/R.90/Add.22, in CERD/C/SR.322.
[16] Para. 7 (Mr Nettel).
[17] Para. 10 (Mr Blischenko).

West Frontier were omitted from consideration in Pakistan's report.[18] The response of the Representative of Pakistan was to defend the classifications,[19] for example, to meet the questions of one member on 'essentially religious' minorities, his proposition was simply to delete the word 'essentially'. Racial discrimination simply had no part in the traditions or history of the country.[20]

The meaning of 'ethnic' has been extensively discussed in this work and has a core of reasonably clear applications. The attitude of Pakistan before the Committee illustrates the difficulty of separating ethnicity from religion the Convention does not condemn religious discrimination. Members of the Committee have attempted to distinguish the 'religious' from the 'ethnic' or 'racial' question, particularly in the case of the Jews.[21] Neither does the Convention condemn discrimination on grounds of language, and this too has been asserted to make it inapplicable, despite the obviously close and overlapping relationship between cultural and linguistic minorities in most conceivable instances. The Representative of Austria, presenting the initial report of that State to the Committee, explained that there were no distinct national or ethnic groups in Austria, although there were religious and linguistic minorities.[22] This was reiterated in his response to questioning by the Committee.[23] Similarly, India's view of its minorities, as presented to the Committee, was that these groups, apart from a small ethnic minority, the Anglo-Indians, were religious and linguistic.[24] The Government of India set up a Minorities Commission in 1978 to safeguard the interests of minorities. The linguistic minorities have various rights under the Indian Constitution,[25] which shows the thinness of the distinction between linguistic and ethnic groups; by Article 29(i), the minorities have the right to conserve their language, script, and culture, and, by Article 30(i), to establish and administer educational institutions of their choice-which would presumably impart culture as well as language. Following the division of India into linguistic States, constitutional safeguards were provided in Article 350A to linguistic minorities in all States for the provision of adequate facilities for instruction in the mother tongue at the primary level of education. There is

---

[18] Paras. 21–7 (Mr Dechezelles).

[19] Para. 37 (Mr Sayegh).

[20] Paras. 42 and 43. Para. 13 of the 9th Periodic Report of Pakistan (CERD/C/149/Add. 12 and Corr. 1) stated that Pakistan had no linguistic minorities. However, para. 4 of the 8th Periodic Report (CERD/C/118/Add.15) gave percentages of people speaking 8 different languages. See discussion of this discrepancy in CERD/C/SR.797. Pakistan defended the statement by defining 'minority': 'The statement . . . that there were no linguistic minorities in Pakistan was true, since there was no single linguistic majority, the most common language being spoken by less than half the population': CERD/C/SR.797, para. 39.

[21] See discussion of the 3rd Periodic Report of Iraq, UN Doc A/31/18, para. 70; and that of Jamaica, ibid., para. 61.

[22] GAOR, 29th Session, Supp. No.18, para. 135, UN Doc A/9618.

[23] Ibid.

[24] UN Doc E/CN.4/1298/Add.2, paras. 1–14.

[25] Ibid.

also a Commissioner for Linguistic Minorities as well as the Minorities Commission. The prime reference is thus to linguistic groups; the Indian Government did not recognize the right of the Committee to discuss issues relating to the Minorities Commission, though it provided information on this in accordance with its policy on co-operation with the Committee.[26]

The negative responses of some States to such basic questions as the existence of racial and ethnic groups on their territory and the existence of racial discrimination does not augur well for broad interpretations of obligations under Article 2(2) of the Convention, although the opinions of States show considerable variation. The Committee members interpret Article 2(2) in a strict fashion in some aspects. Thus, when the fourth periodic report of Fiji[27] was under discussion, members pointed out that the 'special treatment accorded to certain racial groups did not appear to have specified limited duration . . . in order to satisfy the Convention, a more categorical undertaking should have been given that the unequal rights for different racial groups would not be maintained after the objectives for which they were intended had been achieved'.[28] It is clear from this reminder to Fiji that there is a difference between the regime of the Convention and a 'minorities' article which, as suggested above, could require permanent measures. In the context of the Convention, the Committee is correct to insist on a narrow interpretation of Article 2(2); the philosophy of the Convention is 'integrationist' and any manifestation of a different philosophy is an object of suspicion.[29]

States and members of the Committee display an occasional appreciation of the distinction between integration and assimilation, though the distinction is frequently blurred. Some dilemmas of an enlightened policy on ethnic groups are properly expressed in the discussion of the fifth periodic report of Canada.[30] The report noted that the Federal Government's relationship with Indians 'was based on the concept of *Indian identity within Canadian society* rather than on *separation* from that society or *assimilation* into it . . .'.[31] It was pertinently asked 'whether the efforts of the Canadian authorities to enable the Inuit to benefit from North American civilisation were not undermining that people's own civilisation and causing it to lose its true identity?' The Representative of Canada replied that measures had been taken to help maintain the cultural identity of the Inuit through, *inter alia*,

[26] A/9618, paras. 394–6. Cf. discussion of the 9th Periodic Report of the UK on the situation in Northern Ireland: could it be regarded as having 'racial nuances' or was it only a political/religious issue? CERD/C/SR.793. The UK Report is CERD/C/149/Add/ 7.

[27] CERD/C/64/Add.4.

[28] UN Doc A/37/18, para. 101.

[29] See for example A/37/18 (Finland); A/32/18 (Australia).

[30] A/36/18, para. 2; the report is CERD/C/50/Adds. 6 and 7.

[31] Para. 313. See also CERD/C/SR.781, discussing the 7th and 8th Periodic Reports of Canada. The Canadian representative stated in para. 25 that: 'Canada had no melting-pot philosophy; it was endeavouring to build a multiracial society, a mosaic'. The Canadian Reports are CERD/D/107/Add.8 and CERD/C.132/Add.3.

committing their languages to writing.[32] It is instructive that the maintenance of identity in the context of integration was mentioned by the
Committee and by Canada, because the identity of groups is not an explicit
concern of the Convention. A similar appreciation of policy difficulties was
expressed in Committee discussions of the third periodic report of Ethiopia.[33] Questions to the Representative of Ethiopia demanded information
on whether 'the various ethnic groups [were to be brought] into the national
mainstream while enabling them to retain their distinctive cultures . . .'.[34] A
question was also directed to the issue of regional autonomy, as well as on
language teaching in schools and official recognition of languages. The
Representative merely stated that 'regional autonomy must not be allowed
to be divisive and Ethiopia's problems had to be solved within a national
framework and . . . the trend was towards integration rather than separation'.[35] One may deduce from this that the Representative did not fully note
the Committee's concern about maintaining group identities and replied
simply in terms of preferring integration to separation.

In the light of this, it would appear that there is no consensus on the
policy of the Convention on minority groups; or it may be the case that
States and members of the Committee express 'liberal' views on minority
policy in terms which the Convention does not fully warrant. In discussions
of the third periodic report of Iraq which dealt with the Kurds, whereas
some members of the Committee were concerned to know 'whether the
Government of Iraq contemplated further steps to integrate the Kurds into
Iraq's society (as envisaged in the final sentence of Article 2, para 2, of the
Convention). . .'[36] others took the view that 'the recognition of a distinct
Kurdish nationality and the establishment of autonomy in areas where the
majority of the population were Kurds [was] fully in accord with the will of
the Kurds themselves *as well as the principles of the Convention.*' Whilst the
Representative of Iraq made no comment on 'the principles of the Convention', it is clear that the Committee members did not speak with one voice
on this question.

The various Bulgarian reports produced heated debate in the Committee
on the exact nature of the 'principles of the Convention' in relation to
minorities. The fourth periodic report provoked the Committee[37] to ask
how they should interpret the statement in the report that 'all citizens . . .
enjoy the right to develop their own culture, based on their own traditions
and customs':

if the main objective of the policy of the State and the Party—as reflected in the . . .
decree on Civil Status, adopted on 30 August, 1975—was the creation of the unity of
the Bulgarian nation on the basis of citizenship, which implied the gradual disap-

---

[32] Para. 320.

[33] A/37/18, paras. 195 ff; the report is CERD/C/73/Add.2.

[34] Para. 197.

[35] Para. 201.

[36] A/31/18, para. 70.

[37] A/31/18, paras. 172 ff.

pearance of the Turkish, Macedonian, Romanian, Jewish and Gypsy national minorities and their assimilation into the Bulgarian nation.[38]

On the other hand, it was claimed in relation to the Macedonian people that 'nowadays, all of those people declared themselves to be Bulgarians',[39] and that 'persistent attempts to question that reality' were harmful to friendly relations between nations, Bulgaria and Yugoslavia, and did not contribute[40] to the fruitful work of the Committee. The summary of the discussion records simply that 'there was wide divergence of views among .. . members of the Committee regarding their interpretation of the aims and objectives of the Convention with respect of minorities.'[41]

The reference to 'divergence of views' is a bland description of a heated discussion[42] of policy issues inspired by a basic disagreement between Bulgaria and a Yugoslav member of the Committee (Mr Devetak) on the Macedonian population in Bulgaria. The Committee member recalled[43] earlier explanations of Bulgaria in discussions of its second periodic report to the Committee to the effect that Bulgaria was not a multiracial country and there was no Macedonian national minority in Bulgaria. The member cited Bulgarian historical documents to prove otherwise, remarking that 'the Committee could not accept that a State member of the United Nations or a party to the Convention should deny the existence of part of a nation living within its boundaries'. He went on to discuss 'one of the basic principles of the Convention',[44] the elimination of discrimination based on national or ethnic origin, which was manifested, *inter alia*, in 'obstacles to the cultural, social and economic development of certain national, ethnic and linguistic groups, namely, minorities, in the non-recognition of the basic human rights of the members of those groups, in the discrimination with regard to their national or ethnic features and in the denial of the existence of certain of those groups'. Summing up his criticism of Bulgarian policy, the member declared that 'slogans on the creation of a unitary Socialist nation and a unitary socialist culture would serve to disguise hegemonistic, assimilationist and integrationist tendencies on the part of one or several nations vis-à-vis others'.[45] Abstracted from the context of the particular

---

[38] Ibid., para. 175.
[39] See also UN Doc A/36/18, para. 255: 'The concept of Macedonia is a geographical one— the people in that area 'had no other cultural or national sentiments'. Bulgaria lists 3 main ethnic minorities: Jews, Armenians, and Gypsies, and Bulgarian Moslems as a religious minority (*infra*, n. 49). In a later report to CERD, the Macedonians were referred to as 'a non-existent minority': A/42/18, para. 221, discussing Bulgaria's 8th Periodic Report, CERD/C/118/Add.17/Rev.1.

[40] UN Doc A/31/18, para. 175.   [41] Ibid., para. 176.
[42] CERD/C/SR.296/97.   [43] SR.296, para. 24.
[44] Ibid., para. 25.

[45] Para. 26. Cf. the statement of Romania, heavily criticized for the treatment of its Hungarian minority, including plans to raze villages and concentrate populations: 'The Government recognised the right of minorities to be different and there was no policy of assimilating ethnic Hungarians to Romanians or of destroying their cultural identity. The

dispute, this represents a progressive assessment of the policy of the Convention towards minorities. Perhaps not surprisingly, the Yugoslav point of view attracted criticism in turn. Another member pointed out that the fundamental objective of the Convention was to eliminate racial discrimination and not strengthen racial division;[46] different treatment for racial or ethnic groups was an exceptional measure and, although it should be recognized that the authors of the Convention knew that exceptions were necessary, 'it was no less certain that the objective of the Convention was not to maintain the divisions but to integrate the various groups into the society to which they belonged'.[47] The member defended Bulgaria, which had been accused of not taking the Convention into account by eliminating from its civil laws certain provisions applicable to minorities. But, in his own view, 'that was precisely what should be done to give effect to the Convention'.[48] Another member of the Committee struck a middle position between the two main disputants. In the Bulgarian case, what was objectionable was not that 'the integration of those minorities into the society in which they belonged was being promoted, but that the minorities were being assimilated against their wishes'.[49] In his view the Convention did not stipulate that the differences between the ethnic minorities should be eliminated; special measures for minorities were consistent with Convention policy.[50] The Soviet member of the Committee defended Bulgaria though he did agree that it was understandable that differing opinions were possible on the interpretation of the Convention.

In discussions on the fourth periodic Yugoslav report,[51] the view was expressed that the Committee was not required to concern itself with groups, their specific rights, and measures to preserve their identity, but with discrimination against the individual. The measures to help groups

object was to place them on an equal footing with the rest of the population': A/43/18, para. 135.

[46] SR. 296, 36−7.

[47] Para. 37.

[48] Para. 38. For a review of some of these difficulties on the aim of the Convention, see Meron, 'The Meaning and Reach of the International Convention on the Elimination of All Forms of Racial Discrimination', *AJIL*, 79 (1985), 283, and *Human Rights Law-Making in the UN: A Critique of Instruments and Process* (Oxford: OUP, 1986) ch. 1.

[49] SR.296, para. 43. The position of the Turkish or Muslim minority in Bulgaria following reports of attempts to assimilate them, has also provoked heated debate: UN Doc A/42/18, paras. 199−226. Bulgaria was prepared to recognize the Muslims as a religious minority but did not recognize a Turkish ethnic minority. Bulgaria and Turkey have since concluded a Protocol providing for bilateral negotiations to settle this question: this was signed in Belgrade on 23 February 1988. At the 44th Session of the Human Rights Commission, the Representative of Turkey expressed the hope that 'the process of bilateral negotiations set up under the Protocol would contribute to restoring the legitimate cultural and minority rights of Turks in Bulgaria . . .': UN Doc E/CN.4/1988/SR.47, para. 69. This perhaps foreshadows some modification of the Bulgarian position.

[50] SR.296, para. 44.

[51] CERD/C/90/Add.7.

were exceptional—the Committee should be clear about the [restricted] scope of its mandate and competence on this question.[52]

Policy confusions are apparent in the discussions on the seventh report of Czechoslovakia,[53] particularly in relation to the gypsies. In the context of general satisfaction expressed by the Committee members with the information in the report, some members expressed surprise at the statement in the report that there were no gypsies resisting integration 'given the traditional desire of the gypsy population to be different and to enjoy unrestricted freedom'.[54] The report used the term 're-education' in relation to the gypsies, which suggested that a way of life was being imposed upon a group of people. The Representative of Czechoslovakia replied that 're-education' referred specifically to their voluntary integration and no compulsion whatsoever was involved. The Representative then said, rightly, that the process of integration was a complex one which had to take into account the traditions and ways of the gypsy population, a view which also states a correct assumption for groups other than gypsies. None the less, the Representative regarded as a 'favourable development':[55] 'the very fact that many gypsies had abandoned their nomadic way of life'. The reply confirmed the doubts entertained by the member of the Committee about the attitude of the Czechoslovakian authorities; integration does not distinguish itself readily from assimilation through abandonment of basic cultural practices. The point at present is not to applaud or condemn such attitudes, but merely to indicate that there is little in the Convention to assist in formulating a point of view except its overall attitude favouring 'integration'.

---

[52] CERD/C/SR.283, 178.

[53] CERD/C/91/Add.14.

[54] A/37/18, para. 384.

[55] Ibid., para. 393. There is further illuminating discussion of gypsies in relation to the 9th Periodic Report of Czechoslovakia in CERD/C/SR.785: the report is CERD/C/149/Add.2. A few members of CERD expressed their satisfaction with the sedentarization process. However, one member, Mr Oberg, questioned whether the Czech measures amounted to a 'modified assimilation'. In the general reply (para. 72), the Czech representative stated: 'The Government's first task had been to remove the differences in development between the various ethnic groups and to integrate them into the general population, while allowing them to maintain their own traditions.' On gypsies, it was stated (para. 73) that an Act of 1958 (providing, *inter alia*, for 5 years imprisonment for refusal to accept a flat assigned by the authorities) 'merely prohibited a nomadic way of life and applied to gypsies and non-gypsies alike'. Compare the response of Romania, heavily criticized for its actions with regard to its Hungarian minority (*supra*, n. 45): 'nomadic gypsies were allowed to continue their nomadic existence and to preserve their traditions': A/43/18, para. 135.

31. The United Nations Covenants on Human Rights

The concepts of non-discrimination and equality are asserted throughout the two UN Covenants on Human Rights. In almost identically worded Preambles, the 'equal and inalienable rights of all members of the human family' are recognized as the foundation of freedom, justice and peace in the world. In Article 2(1) of the Covenant on Civil and Political Rights, the States parties undertake 'to respect and to ensure' to all individuals within their territory and subject to their jurisdiction the rights recognized in the Covenant 'without distinction of any kind, such as race, colour, sex, language, religion, political or other opinion, national or social origin, property, birth or other status . . .'. It is clear that other kinds of 'distinctions' may infringe the article besides those specified. The unmentioned distinctions must logically be *in pari materia* with those listed, that is, distinctions unrelated to an individual's merit, abilities, or efforts.[1]

In the Covenant on Economic, Social, and Cultural Rights, the obligation on States parties is to 'guarantee' the rights without discrimination—the list of grounds on which discrimination is objectionable is the same in both Covenants, though the Covenant on Civil and Political Rights uses the term 'distinction' whereas the other Covenant uses 'discrimination'. The representative of Italy made the suggestion to replace[2] 'distinction' with 'discrimination' on a number of occasions during the drafting of the Covenant on Civil and Political Rights, but these were opposed. He argued for 'discrimination' as the most suitable term because there were instances in which the law 'was justified in making distinctions between individuals or groups, but the purpose of the Articles was to prohibit discrimination, in the sense of unfavourable and odious distinctions which lacked any reasonable or objective basis'.[3] Elsewhere he explained that a measure taken on behalf of a backward group might be called a 'distinction' but could in no sense be called 'discrimination', and he wished to guard against any interpretation which would make such measures questionable under the terms of the Covenant.[4] Such arguments were accepted in relation to the Covenant on Economic, Social and Cultural Rights at another session of the Third Committee.[5] The argument against 'discrimination' was put by the USSR: if it was used, 'a State might apply unequal treatment to different groups of

---

[1] *Supra*, ch. 29, text following n. 17.
[2] UN Doc A/C.3/SR.1099, para. 10; A/C.3/SR.1258, para. 27.
[3] UN Doc A/C.3/SR.1099, para. 10.
[4] A/C.3/SR.1258, para. 27.   [5] A/C.3/SR.1206.

people and claim that this did not constitute discrimination but distinct treatment of distinct groups.'[6] The danger was all the greater because there was no 'generally adopted' test of discrimination.[7]

It is instructive that this debate took its character from the related themes of separate, disadvantaged groups, and how to cater for them, and the danger of condoning a system like apartheid or separate development for different racial groups. While the Convention on Racial Discrimination provides a definition of discrimination and allows 'special measures' for disadvantaged groups, the Covenants do neither of these things, so that interpretation is more than normally difficult. If the difficulty in using 'discrimination' is that it would permit the apartheid system to be justified as implying only distinctions and not discrimination, the difficulty with 'distinction' was discussed in another context by the European Court of Human Rights in the *Belgian Linguistics Case*.[8] Whereas the French text of Article 14 of the European Convention on Human Rights uses the term '*sans distinction aucune*' in relation to any enjoyment of rights, the English text refers simply to 'without discrimination'. Preferring the English to the French text, the Court remarked that, using 'distinction' as the legal criterion, one would be led to judge as contrary to the Convention

every one of the many legal and administrative provisions which do not secure to everyone complete equality of treatment in the enjoyment of the rights and freedoms recognized . . . national authorities are frequently confronted with situations and problems which, on account of differences inherent therein, call for different legal solutions; moreover certain legal inequalities tend only to correct factual inequalities.

While it is clear that both words refer to arbitrary or unjust distinctions or discrimination, it is also clear that the coalitions of States supporting the different terms were influenced by the notion of providing different rights for different groups; arguments in favour of the term 'discrimination' support the desirability of special measures or 'affirmative action'. Such measures were defended by the Representative of India in the Third Committee who argued that in relation to certain socially or educationally backward sectors of the population, 'something like "positive discrimination" might be necessary in order to ensure eventual fuller participation by such groups in civil and political life'.[9] He suggested, therefore, that in relation to the draft article in the Covenant on Civil and Political Rights, an explanatory paragraph should be added reading: 'Special measures for the advancement of any socially and educationally backward sections of society shall not be construed as distinctions under this article.'[10] He further explained the point, in a manner which draws a line between such measures

---

[6] Ibid., para. 16.   [7] Ibid.
[8] European Court of Human Rights, Judgment, July 1968.
[9] A/C.3/SR.1257, para. 18.   [10] Ibid.

and Article 27 of the Covenant: the measures were necessary because, owing to past treatment or historical circumstances, 'a certain section of the people had to be given greater privileges and protection only for a certain period of time, in order to promote the rights of those people to re-establish their equality and conditions under which there would remain no need for such provisions . . .'.[11] The interpretation advanced by India was supported by many States,[12] some of which pointed to the Draft Declaration on Racial Discrimination. The Representative of the United Arab Republic reported the widely held view in the Third Committee that 'special measures for the benefit of retarded population groups would in no case be regarded as establishing distinctions within the meaning of Article 2 of the Draft Covenant on Civil and Political Rights.' On the other hand, some delegations were not convinced: the Representative of the United Kingdom in the Third Committee went so far as to suggest that the best way to meet the difficulty pointed out by the Indian Representative would be to make provision for a reservations clause. The United Kingdom has not subsequently made a reservation on this point although among the 'Declarations and Reservations' made by Australia upon ratification of the Covenant on Civil and Political Rights there appears the following:

Discrimination and Distinction. The provisions of Articles 2(1) [and 24(1), 25 and 26] relating to discrimination and distinction between persons shall be without prejudice to laws designed to achieve for the members of some class or classes of persons equal enjoyment of the rights defined in the Covenant. Australia accepts Article 26 on the basis that the object of the provisions is to confirm the right of each person to equal treatment in the application of the law.[13]

It is a matter of some surprise and regret that Australia found it necessary to enter such a statement. Part of the reason is no doubt the selection of the term 'distinction' in the Covenant instead of 'discrimination', but the other articles cited in the statement refer to discrimination which would generally be taken to have a clearer legal meaning of unjust, unfavourable, distinctions which do not have objective justification.[14]

Despite these doubts, majority opinion favours the view that measures to favour disadvantaged groups do not constitute 'distinctions' in the sense of Article 2. Statements to this effect were included in the report of the Third Committee. The matter might have been pressed harder by the Italian Representative[15] had he (and others) not understood that a committee would be established to harmonize the Covenants after adoption. Such a committee never functioned; accordingly these differences remain.

The practice of the Human Rights Committee lends support to the view

---

[11] Ibid.
[12] E.g., Australia, A/C.3/SR.1258, para. 44; UAR, ibid., para. 47.
[13] ST/HR/4/Rev.4, 45. This reservation has since been withdrawn: *ST/HR/5*, 86–88.
[14] *Belgian Linguistics Case, supra.*
[15] A/C.3/SR.1258, para. 27; also A/C.3/SR.1258, para. 48.

that affirmative action is consistent with the Covenant on Civil and Political Rights. The essential nature of such actions was pointed out by members of the Committee[16] addressing the Representative of Sweden who accepted them as correct. Commentaries[17] on the Covenant also stress the incorrectness of regarding affirmative action as contrary to their terms.

It is submitted that practice and principle favour the concept of affirmative action; that 'privileging the underprivileged' is not contrary to the law of the Covenants. There would otherwise be a quite extraordinary lack of congruence between the Covenants and the other major document on racial discrimination, the UN Convention on the Elimination of All Forms of Racial Discrimination, as well as with other instruments.[18] The acceptance of that does not, however, permit the ignoring of the limits of affirmative action sanctioned by the Conventions. Affirmative action has been shown above to deal with a set of measures which are limited in various ways, but especially in time, and which must not result in what is termed 'separation'. The time limitation was expressly referred to by the Representative of India in the Third Committee, and the question of separation is one of the key issues underlying the whole debate. While there is a remarkable absence of explicit reference to minorities in the *travaux préparatoires* of the articles on discrimination and equality, they reveal the differences between protection of minorities and prevention of discrimination: the limited protection afforded by Article 27 seems all the more necessary when considering the limited nature of the rule of non-discrimination in the Covenant on Human Rights.

Article 26 of the Covenant on Civil and Political Rights has been referred to. In as much as its terms are not self-defining, there is again an absence of further definition. The original draft prepared by the Human Rights Commission read: 'All persons are equal before the law. The law shall prohibit any discrimination and shall guarantee to all persons equal and effective protection against discrimination on any ground such as race, colour, sex, language, religion, political or other opinion, national or social origin, property, birth or other status.' There was debate on the phrase 'equal before the law' which had been used in Article 7 of the Universal Declaration of Human Rights; the substance of the discussion was to what extent this meant that the law should be the same for all, so as to preclude the imposition of certain disabilities on categories such as minors. It was explained that the phrase meant equality, not identity of treatment, which did not preclude reasonable differentiation between individuals and groups.[19] The Third Committee inserted 'equal protection of the law' to

---

[16] In connection with Articles 3 and 26; CCPR/C/SR.1809, para. 10.

[17] McKean, (*supra*, ch. 29, n. 5), 136; Ramcharan, 'Equality and Non-Discrimination', in Henkin (ed.), *The International Bill of Rights*.

[18] UNESCO Convention against Discrimination in Education.

[19] UN Doc A/2929, para. 179, *GAOR*, 10th Session, Annexes.

supplement 'equal before the law', so that the first sentence of Article 26 reproduces the first sentence of Article 7 of the Universal Declaration. The phrase 'equal before the law' is narrower than 'equal protection of the law'; the former reflects the notion of equality before the courts, whereas the latter incorporates a general prohibition of discrimination on forbidden grounds, not only in court, but wherever it manifests itself in law; as McKean writes: 'The essence of the [equal protection of the law] . . . principle is that the law should treat people in the same way except where there is reasonable justification for not doing so.'[20] The practice of the Human Rights Committee appears to support the wider view of the meaning of equality. In connection with the report of Sweden, the Swedish Representative agreed with the Committee that Article 26 did not only refer to the passive aspect of prevention of discrimination through guarantees of equality before the law, but called for positive action for the elimination of discrimination.[21]

The article is badly drafted in many respects. The second sentence adds little or nothing to the first, and the article has been described by one writer as an 'accumulation of tautologies'.[22] Its relationship to Article 2(1) appears to be that, in order to avoid abusing the general mandate of equality in Article 26 (in so far as equality means equal treatment of equals and unequal treatment of unequals so that differential treatment is permissible on the interpretation of 'equality' and 'equals'), Article 2(1) makes it clear that unequal treatment on the listed grounds is impermissible. Article 27 of the Covenant on Civil and Political Rights also deals with aspects of equality, which is in fact its true purpose; within its limits, extensively discussed already, it endeavours to achieve *de facto* equality between members of the majority and the minority in the limited area of culture, religion, and language. In relation to the other rights listed in the UN Covenant, members of minorities have the right not to be discriminated against and the general right under Article 26 to equal protection of the law, though they do not have these rights as members of minorities but as 'persons' or individuals, the rights appertaining to 'all persons' or 'all individuals' under Article 26 and Article 2(1) respectively. The hesitantly expressed group dimension in Article 27 where individual rights are deemed to be exercised 'in community with other members of the group' finds no reflection in Article 2(1) or 26: the essence of the non-discrimination principle as expressed therein is that membership of a group is not a permissible basis for the denial of rights to individuals.

Despite its imperfections, the Covenant on Civil and Political Rights is an important text. It is unique among modern treaties in its explicit reference to

---

[20] 139.
[21] Report of the Human Rights Committee, *GAOR*, 34th Session, Supp. No. 40, para. 325.
[22] Schwelb, 'The International Convention on the Elimination of All Forms of Racial Discrimination', 1019.

independent rights of minorities. While there are difficulties in the interpretation of the non-discrimination and minorities articles in the Covenant in terms of a tension between 'equality' and 'differentiation', the potential contribution of such a weakly drafted article as Article 27 becomes even more apparent on comparison of the Covenant with others such as the UN Convention on Race. In the latter Convention, while the protection of minorities may be given a liberal interpretation by the Committee on the Elimination of Racial Discrimination, its policy on minorities is either simply unclear or clear in a manner which is detrimental to minorities. Its overall 'integrationist' philosophy may be perhaps interpreted in a manner which distinguishes such a philosophy from an assimilationist one; on the other hand minorities can offer little in the way of a 'textual barrier' based on the Convention against States determined to assimilate them. At least the Covenant on Civil and Political Rights cannot be construed to favour such a policy; Article 27 does furnish such a 'textual barrier' to defend minority identity. It provides a clear limitation on the 'levelling' or 'equalizing' force of rights granted to 'all persons' or 'all individuals' without distinction. Because such a barrier exists, the non-discrimination provisions can be construed as a genuine advantage to minorities and not as an advantage which is premised on a non-recognition of the right to an identity.

32. The UNESCO Convention Against Discrimination in Education

The UNESCO Convention against Discrimination was adopted by the UNESCO General Conference in 1960 and entered into force in 1962.[1] The Convention is of importance to minorities in that it deals with the most important general means of preserving the identity of the group. UNESCO is a specialized agency of the United Nations; its competence relates to education, science, culture, and communication, and it is by reference to these four aspects that the organization's interest in human rights is circumscribed. The purpose of UNESCO as laid down in its constitution[2] is:

to contribute to peace and security by promoting collaboration among the nations through education, science and culture in order to further universal respect for justice, for the rule of law and for the human rights and fundamental freedoms which are affirmed for the peoples of the world, without distinction of race, sex, language or religion, by the Charter of the United Nations.

In partial fulfilment of its mandate, UNESCO has prepared a number of conventions and recommendations relating to human rights.[3] UNESCO has also exhibited a considerable interest in race and racial discrimination, and has adopted 'statements' on the race question. These statements are the 1950 Statement on Race; the 1951 Statement on the Nature of Race and Race Differences; the 1964 Propositions on the Biological Aspects of Race, and the 1967 Statement on Race and Racial Prejudice.[4] The first two statements are chiefly anthropological; the 1964 Propositions reject the notion of innate differences generating differences in cultural achievement; the 1967 Statement analyses racialist theories and prejudices. UNESCO also adopted, at its General Conference in 1978, the important Declaration on Race and Racial Prejudice.[5] The Convention against Discrimination in Education includes racial discrimination, directing itself against any 'distinction, exclusion, limitation or preference which, being based on race, colour, sex, language, religion, political or other opinion, national or social origin,

---

[1] 11th General Conference 1960, *UNTS*, 429, 93, in force May 1962. See generally, Marks, 'UNESCO and Human Rights', *Texas International Law Journal*, 13 (1977), 35.

[2] *UNTS*, 4, 275.

[3] Marks, (*supra*, n. 1).

[4] UNESCO, *Four Statements on the Race Question* (Paris, 1969).

[5] Lerner, 'New Concepts in the UNESCO Declaration on Race and Racial Prejudice', *Human Rights, Quarterly*, 3 (1981), 48.

economic condition or birth, has the purpose or effect of nullifying or impairing equality of treatment in education . . .'.[6]

The origins of the Convention demonstrate the influence of the UN Sub-Commission on Prevention of Discrimination and Protection of Minorities, and the Commission on Human Rights.[7] The Convention was preceded by a Sub-Commission study of discrimination in education.[8] The Special Rapporteur recommended that an international convention for the prevention of discrimination should be prepared, which would include machinery to deal with complaints relating to its implementation. UNESCO was willing to undertake the task, and emphasized the need for a detailed definition of obligations, though some division of opinion manifested itself in the Sub-Commission as to the merits of a Convention in view of the fact that the draft UN Covenants on Human Rights were in preparation; the Convention might be an unnecessary distraction.[9] The Commission on Human Rights, however, decided that UNESCO should be invited to prepare an appropriate international instrument. UNESCO produced the Convention, declaring that the Sub-Commission's study of discrimination in education was 'a basic and permanent source of inspiration, along with the draft covenants, the Universal Declaration of Human Rights and, *inter alia*, the work of the Commission on Human Rights and the Sub-Commission'.[10]

The Convention confronts the question of minorities by describing them as minorities, in this case 'national minorities', whereas the Race Convention spoke only of racial or ethnic groups requiring protection. There is therefore a possibility that the limits of the anti-discrimination rules in relation to minorities can be more clearly perceived. Analysis of the Education Convention reveals an instrument which provides more liberally than the Convention on Race for some needs of minorities, but is more restrictive in the prerogatives it retains for States claiming to override certain freedoms in the name of public policy. Part of the basic definition of discrimination has been quoted; following that basic premise, Article 1(1) of the Convention 'in particular' declares against:

(*a*) . . . depriving any person or group of persons of access to education of any type or at any level; (*b*) . . . limiting any person or group of persons to education of an inferior standard; (*c*) Subject to the provisions of Article 2 of this Convention, . . . establishing or maintaining separate educational systems or institutions for persons or groups of persons; or (*d*) . . . inflicting on any person or group of persons conditions which are incompatible with the dignity of man.

All four sub-paragraphs of the article refer to discrimination against groups

---

[6] Article 1.

[7] *Supra*, ch. 13.

[8] *Study of Discrimination in Education*, Special Rapporteur Ammoun, UN Doc E/CN.4/Sub.2/181/Rev.1.

[9] UN Doc E/CN.4/740.

[10] UNESCO Doc 11C/15, paras. 18–20.

rather than simply individuals. The group dimension of discrimination is also present in the Convention on Race but it is a more insistent theme in the Convention of 1960; the latter Convention is not as 'individualist' in character as the Convention on Race and recognizes the group character of educational rights. Article 1(c) is subject to Article 2 of the Convention which declares that the following situations, *inter alia*, shall not amount to discrimination:

(b) The establishment or maintenance, for religious or linguistic reasons, of separate educational systems or institutions offering an education which is in keeping with the wishes of the pupils' parents or legal guardians, if participation in such systems or attendance at such institutions is optional and if the education provided conforms to such standards as may be laid down or approved by the competent authorities, in particular for education of the same level.

The provision is not specifically aimed at minorities, but includes them. It is supplemented by Article 5(1)(c) whereby States parties agree that it:

is essential to recognize the right of members of national minorities to carry on their own educational activities, including the maintenance of schools and, depending on the educational policy of each State, the use or the teaching of their own language, provided however:

1. That this right is not exercised in a manner which prevents the members of these minorities from understanding the language of the community as a whole and from participating in its activities, or which prejudices national sovereignty;
2. That the standard of education is not lower than the general standard laid down or approved by the competent authorities; and
3. That attendance at such school is optional.

This provision specifically relates to minorities, unlike Article 2(b); in both cases the restriction on the manner in which rights may be exercised is apparent. Despite the provisions in Article 1 giving overriding force to Article 2, the inclusion of establishing or maintaining separate educational systems in the overall definition of discrimination is influential in determining the character of subsequent articles. Separate education is only grudgingly admitted in the Convention. Thus, both Article 2(b) and 5(1)(c) provide that such education is optional, not compulsory; this contrasts with the general undertaking by States in Article 4(a) 'To make primary education free and compulsory'. Further, both articles provide specific limitations reflecting a general integrationist philosophy which give latitude to the State in implementing requirements. The separate systems of education must conform 'to such standards as may be laid down or approved by the competent authorities' (Article 2(b)). No indication is given as to the content of such 'standards', except that they are related to the provision of 'education of the same level' as the separate systems or institutions. The rights of national minorities in the linguistic field are made to depend 'on the educational policy of each State' by Article 5; they are obliged to provide an education which does not dissociate them from the culture and language of 'the community as a whole' or prevent them from participating in its activities — although, rather alarmingly, even this restricted exercise of rights is under suspicion, so it must not prejudice 'national sovereignty'. The notion of a minority language as in effect a subversive activity has affected the drafting of the Article; it would be difficult to call States to account if a language were to be suppressed provided the State took care to invoke the danger to 'sovereignty' as its justification. The right of national minorities in Article 5 is 'to carry on their own' educational activities — there is no suggestion that the State is *obliged* to provide financial or other assistance to the group, so that it is very much a case of a negative rather than a positive freedom.[11] This is reinforced by Article 3(d) of the Convention by which States undertake 'Not to allow, in any form of assistance granted by the public authorities to educational institutions, any restrictions *or preference* based solely on the ground that pupils belong to a particular group'. The equality and non-discrimination promised by the Convention to minority groups is the equality and non-discrimination provided for the community as a whole with little respect for cultural differences. In any dispute about the abuse of rights based upon the interpretation of the Convention, the balance is clearly in favour of the State, which can find ample scope to deny their practical exercise.

The Convention, despite its defects, may at least be considered valuable in so far as it provides a basis upon which to build a more advanced conception of the rights of groups not forming part of the cultural majority in a State. The Convention only recognizes those rights in a cautious and fearful way; there is a strong suggestion that minority rights are a Pandora's box of dangers to the sovereign State.

[11] See UNESCO General Conference 11C/15, ibid., UN Doc E/CN.4/Sub.2/210, 22, according to whose analysis Article 5 does not support the notion that the States are obliged to provide public or publicly supported schools.

33. The UNESCO Declaration on Race and Racial Prejudice

The Declaration on Race and Racial Prejudice was adopted by the UNESCO General Conference in 1978[1] at its twentieth session. It represents part of UNESCO's effort to play, in the words of the Preamble, 'a vigorous and constructive part in the implementation of the programme of the Decade for Action to Combat Racism and Racial Discrimination' as defined by the General Assembly of the UN at its twenty-eighth session.[2] It is not simply about discrimination, but is a more comprehensive instrument covering various aspects of race and racism which summarizes UNESCO's approach.[3] It includes a number of references to racial discrimination, genocide, and apartheid, and the preamble recalls, *inter alia*, the UN Declaration and Convention on the Elimination of All Forms of Racial Discrimination, as well as the Convention against Discrimination in Education. In so far as the limits of the anti-discrimination approach to benefit minorities have been pointed out in the preceding discussion, the concepts outlined in this later UNESCO instrument promise to transcend these limits, and provide the basis of a positive appreciation of the potential contribution of minorities to multinational States.

The text cannot readily be classified into 'prevention of discrimination' or 'protection of minorities', but is something of a *tertium quid*. It is none the less appropriate to discuss it in the present section because it is buried in the interstices of UN action to combat racism and proclaims its affinity with the leading texts on racial discrimination. The Declaration is not a binding treaty, but was widely supported, being adopted unanimously and by acclamation.[4] It is accompanied by a resolution of the General Conference for its implementation, in which Member States are urged to consider ratifying the leading international instruments on racial discrimination if they have not already done so, and to take appropriate measures, guided by Articles 4 and 6 of the UN Convention on Race, 'with a view to preventing and punishing acts of racial discrimination and ensuring that fair and adequate reparation is made to the victims of racial discrimination'.[5] It is

---

[1] Text in Lerner, *The UN Convention on the Elimination of All Forms of Racial Discrimination*, Appendix 3.

[2] The United Nations and Human Rights (New York: UN, 1978), UN Sales No. E.78.1.18.

[3] According to Vasak, former Director of the Human Rights Division of UNESCO, cited in Lerner, (*Supra*, ch. 32, n. 5). 'New Concepts in the UNESCO Declaration', *Human Rights Quarterly* 3, no. 1 (1981) 48, n. 9.

[4] Lerner, *supra*, n. 1.

[5] Text in Appendix 4 to the present work.

also a 'declaration' which is regarded in UN practice as of greater weight and significance than a mere recommendation.[6]

At its eighteenth session, the General Conference of UNESCO decided to prepare a draft Declaration on Race and Racial Prejudice for submission to the next General Conference; the text to be prepared by a meeting of experts. The meeting of experts was not held until March 1978 and was attended by representatives from over one hundred States. The meeting had the benefit of a working paper prepared by a committee of specialists in human rights under the Director-General of UNESCO. The draft was adopted by consensus and a report submitted to the General Conference which also had before it an explanatory memorandum prepared by the Director-General.[7] The Preamble to the Declaration recalls the Constitution of UNESCO and its commitment to human rights 'without distinction of race, sex, language or religion'. The Preamble also recites that 'all peoples and all human groups, whatever their composition or ethnic origin, contribute according to their own genius to the progress of civilizations and cultures which, in their plurality and as a result of their interpenetration, constitute the common heritage of mankind'. This represents a vigorous affirmation of the value of diversity in the progress of humanity and the importance of conserving as much as possible of this diversity as the inheritance of human beings. The reference to the dynamics of 'interpenetration' also reflects the assumption that the process of conservation is not a process of attempted cultural ossification, nor a futile exercise in archaism. Development, cultural change, or progress can be forced upon recalcitrant groups, so that the modernism of this approach needs to be tempered by reference to group choice and a restriction upon mechanisms of repression that may be used to engineer change.

Thus, the Preamble reaffirms attachment to the UN Charter and the Universal Declaration of Human Rights, the Conventions on Genocide and Apartheid and other human rights texts, and also, in strong phraseology, notes that racism and related evils continue to manifest themselves in constantly changing forms through unjust practices and structures 'characterized by injustice and contempt for human beings and leading to the exclusion, humiliation, and exploitation, *or to the forced assimilation*, of the members of disadvantaged groups . . .'. The emphasized reference is a fresh development. This is a necessary reinforcement of the general approval of cultural diversity, implying choices for the groups concerned. Forced assimilation is listed in the catalogue of basic violations of human rights, as an expression of 'injustice and contempt for human beings', placed in the same paragraph as colonialism and apartheid, all characterized in the succeeding preambular paragraph as 'offences against human dignity' which

---

[6] *Supra*, ch. 26.
[7] UNESCO, Explanatory Report, Doc 20/C/18, annex.

reduce the possibility of mutual understanding between peoples and threaten international peace and security.

The outstanding feature of Article 1 of the Declaration, which commences with the statement that all human beings are descended from a common stock and are born 'equal in dignity and rights' (Article 1(1)), is the proclamation in the second paragraph that 'All individuals and groups have the right to be different, to consider themselves as different and to be regarded as such'. The right to be different should not, however, 'serve as a pretext for racial prejudice' nor justify discriminatory practices, nor provide a ground for the policy of apartheid. The succeeding paragraph (Article 1(3)) states that 'Identity of origin in no way affects the fact that human beings can and may live differently, nor does it preclude the existence of differences based on cultural, environmental, and historical diversity nor the right to maintain cultural identity.' The article represents a courageous attempt to revalue differences between individuals and groups, developing the concept outlined in the Preamble to a culminatory 'right to be different', while endeavouring to ensure that differences are not used as the basis for discriminatory practices and apartheid. The right to be different has as its corollary 'the right to maintain cultural identity' (Article 1(3)). This aspect is reminiscent of the 'right to identity' described in Article 27 of the UN Covenant on Civil and Political Rights, though the Declaration applies to all groups and not only minorities.[8] Article 27 was read to impose duties on States to help in the maintenance of the identity of minority groups, but there is nothing in the internal logic of the Declaration to assist such an interpretation. Thus the recognition of the right may be a maximum, though it is progressive to see it so clearly stated. There is a close connection between the right and the condemnation of practices of forced assimilation expressed in the Preamble. A significant aspect of the article and the Declaration is the emphasis on group identities. The Preamble recites that 'all peoples and all *human groups*' contribute to civilization and condemns forced assimilation 'of the members of disadvantaged *groups*'. The right to be different is a right of 'all individuals and *groups*'. The theme of the group is carried on in other Articles; 'human beings', and 'groups' and 'peoples' are deemed to have other rights in the Declaration such as the right to full development in Article 3; according to Article 6, human rights are to be assured by the State 'on an entirely equal footing in dignity and rights for all individuals and all *groups*'. The group dimension is only allowed to surface occasionally in the main texts on non-discrimination and then only with reservations. Even Article 27 of the Covenant on Civil and Political Rights is more individualist in character, recognizing that where minorities (groups) exist, persons belonging to the minorities (individuals) have certain rights. The reality of the group is implied in the rights set out in Article 27, but the

---

[8] In practice, of course, dominant majority groups holding political power will avail themselves of the right without support of international human rights law.

Declaration is more frank in attributing the rights directly to the collectivity as well as to the individuals composing it. The attribution gives the Declaration a special character.

The meaning of the right to be different is not elaborated. The Director-General's explanatory report pointed out that the right should be interpreted as involving the possibility for individuals and groups to lead their lives 'without needing to abandon their essential identity'.[9] Lerner interprets the puzzle of attributing such a right to individuals to mean the individual as member of a group, 'otherwise it would imply the recognition of a right to extravagant behaviour, which it certainly was not the intention of the drafters to proclaim'.[10] None the less, the right is for both individuals and groups, 'all individuals *and* groups', without restriction. The 'essential identity' of individuals may be expressed within a group but also outside the group. While the Declaration cannot, as Lerner suggests, be interpreted as a recipe for unlimited individual eccentricity, its focus would appear to be rather on the limitation of 'group rights' which appears also in Article 27 of the UN Covenant on Civil and Political Rights, namely on excluding 'group determinism' by accenting the right of individual choice. What the Declaration reveals is an equality of rights for individuals and groups; conflicts between the two would be resolved by whatever means were possible. They are not, *prima facie*, resolved in the Declaration by subordinating the group to the individual; neither are they resolved, as Lerner suggests, by suggesting that the individual only possesses the right to be different as a member of a group. It was suggested in relation to Article 27 that individuals could not by a pure act of personal choice simply regard themselves as members of a minority with which they had no cultural, linguistic, or religious affinity; but that, asymmetrically, they could *renounce* minority rights as their personal preference. A similar interpretation may be offered here in relation to the naming of 'all individuals' and 'all groups' as holders of the right to be different.

Article 2 also rebuts the legitimation of certain types of domination: 'Any theory which involves the claim that racial or ethnic groups are inherently superior or inferior, thus implying that some would be entitled to dominate or eliminate others, presumed to be inferior, or which bases value judgements on racial differentiation, has no scientific foundation and is contrary to the moral and ethical principles of humanity.'[11] This is followed by a listing of racist practices and a warning of their deleterious consequences for international order. Article 3 introduces 'the right to full development' which implies 'equal access to the means of personal and collective advancement and fulfilment in a climate of respect for the values of civilizations and cultures, both national and world-wide'; as noted above, the right to full development is a right of individuals and groups. The article continues the

---

[9] *Supra*, n. 7.   [10] *Supra*, n. 3, 53, n. 21.   [11] Article 2(1).

theme of respect for diversity; the reference to respect for 'national culture' which might be a restrictive concept is qualified by the reference earlier in the Article to the right of 'every human being and group' to full development. In the context of a multinational State the notion of national culture should be interpreted to mean the various cultures of that State along with whatever overall national culture is supported by its people. Article 3 also condemns distinctions, exclusions, or preferences based on race, colour, ethnic, or national origin, '*or religious intolerance*' motivated by racist considerations. The UNESCO Convention against Discrimination in Education contains a reference to religion as a prohibited ground of discrimination, but the UN Convention on Race does not; it may seem rather strange to find a reference to religion in a document dealing with questions of race, though the Declaration is concerned not with religious intolerance *per se* but with religious intolerance motivated by racist considerations. There is no real definition of racism in the Declaration, only a list of racist practices, but the whole context of the document and the repeated references to race or ethnic groups indicates that racism has a wide meaning, so that it .includes a condemnation of religious intolerance where the adherents of the religion also constitute a distinct ethnic group or minority.

Article 4 is centred on attacking apartheid, equated with genocide as a crime against humanity.[12] Apart from other demerits of apartheid, it is here condemned as a serious violation of the principle favouring 'self-fulfilment of human beings and free communication between them'. This integrates with the general theme of the Declaration of equality, openness of communication between cultures, non-domination of one group by another, and the value of diversity. Cultures held in equal regard can communicate with each other in a spirit of mutual enrichment. Apartheid, like genocide, is not a philosophy of communication between diverse cultures, but, in the realities of its practice, a philosophy which takes cultural diversity as inequality between cultures and excuses domination of one group by another. Communication between cultural groups is only possible where there is parity of esteem.

Article 5 states the broad concern of UNESCO with culture, education, and racial discrimination in three lengthy paragraphs. The first paragraph restates, in unequivocal terms, the need to respect 'the right of all groups to their own cultural identity and the development of that distinctive cultural life within the national and international context, it being understood that it rests with each group to decide in complete freedom on the maintenance and, if appropriate, the adaptation or enrichment of the values which it regards as essential to its identity'. This represents the highest development in the Declaration, and among contemporary legal instruments, of the notion of group rights. It expresses what is implied in Article 27 of the

---

[12] *Supra*, chs. 6 and 7.

Covenant on Civil and Political Rights. The individualist bias in contemporary international law is here completely dissipated. Again, the emphasis is dynamic: groups have the right to maintain the values which they regard as essential to their identity, but they can also choose 'the adaptation or enrichment' of these values. This emphasis on progress is complemented by an emphasis on choice—change can be accepted or rejected by the group, as the group wishes.[13]

The language of the paragraph is 'universalist'; '*all* groups' have the right to a cultural identity. The universalist language, which pervades the Declaration, in many ways is beneficial to minorities but may none the less have some drawbacks. The discussion of Article 3 made the point that the multinational State should value all its cultures including the overall national culture in the delineation of the right to full development of '*every* human being and group'. Article 5 is similarly concerned with '*all* groups' whereas Article 27 of the Covenant on Civil and Political Rights deals with minorities only. The attribution of rights specifically to a non-dominant minority group identifies the group as a holder of rights and asserts its claim against a dominant majority whose culture may be identified with that of the State. On the other hand, the attribution of rights to 'all groups' whether dominant or not may simply ensure the continuation of a *de facto* dominance—to the extent that it strengthens the hand of a minority group, so also may it strengthen that of the majority.[14] This situation becomes acute for a minority when its culture, existence, and sense of identity is in competition with those of the majority. Some States tend to see only one culture in their domain (the States of Latin America);[15] clearly, they would claim the right to identity, diversity, development, etc. as one group, effectively cancelling the existence as well as the rights of groups asserting a separate, minority identity. The present right needs acutely to be supplemented by some legal effort, perhaps in the form of a definition, to identify which groups are envisaged. The definition, one supposes, can be transposed from other contexts such as the international legislation *in pari materia* on racial discrimination. Subsequent interpretation, and *travaux préparatoires* of, for example, the UN Convention on Race, reveal the outlines of definitions, though the number of contested cases is great. Good faith and some self-denial by States would eliminate some conflicts of identity asserted more for political than logical reasons. But legal instruments can assist rational processes of conflict solving by providing clearer and more specific definitions and descriptions of those who hold rights. The problem is acute enough in relation to Article 27, where the existence of minority groups can be, and is, denied; but it is likely to be even more so in universal instruments which speak in grandiose but unspecific terms of all human beings and all groups as holding rights.

[13] References, *supra*, ch. 1, to 'ethnodevelopment'.
[14] *Supra*, n. 8.   [15] *Supra*, ch. 16.

None of this is intended to detract from the desirability of the principles in the Declaration, but only to indicate the limits of their efficacy in relation to minorities, and to indicate where further legal work may profitably be done. Such considerations, in relation to the right of 'all groups' or, as in general human rights terminology, of 'all individuals' or 'all human beings', point to the desirability of continuing to identify 'minority groups' or 'individuals belonging to minority groups' as holders of rights. The philosophy of catering for all sections of society does not necessarily remedy the specific grievances of disadvantaged groups. The Director-General's Explanatory Report on the Declaration interpreted Article 5(1) to mean that every minority group has the right to decide the extent to which it desires to preserve and develop its own culture, or, if it prefers to, to join the dominant culture.[16] Such a beneficial interpretation, which is just and logical, would generate greater confidence in its authenticity if the term 'minority' were mentioned on the face of the Declaration.

Article 5(1) is a peculiar article in one respect—only groups, and not individuals, are holders of rights here. If there is not to be a suggestion of 'group determinism', one can only surmise that the article should be interpreted as allowing for individual choices of those who wish to dissociate themselves from the group even at the expense of the group identity.[17] To interpret the Article otherwise would be out of line with all the contemporary human rights legislation.

Paragraph 2 points out the duties of States in education against racism and contains a clause on general 'affirmative action': States should take 'appropriate steps to remedy the handicaps from which certain racial or ethnic groups suffer with regard to their level of education and standard of living and in particular to prevent such handicaps from being passed on to children'. Paragraph 3 deals with the contribution of the mass media in the elimination of racism. The responsibilities of States are again the theme of Article 6: the State has primary responsibility for ensuring human rights 'for all individuals and all groups'; in so far as legislation is insufficient, it must be supplemented by administration, education, and research to combat racism, and by 'programmes of positive political, social, educational and cultural measures calculated to promote genuine mutual respect among groups'. Article 7 expands upon the role of law in combating prejudice. Article 8 deals with the duties of individuals in the elimination of racism; the duties listed are not ones which reduce the benefits of rights by restricting their exercise, but positive duties to promote harmony among peoples and combat racism. Article 9(1) asserts that racial discrimination by the State 'constitutes a violation of international law giving rise to . . . international responsibility' and that 'the equality in dignity and rights of all human beings and all peoples, irrespective of race, colour and origin, is a generally

[16] Explanatory Report (*supra*, n. 7), 4–5.   [17] *Supra*, ch. 17.

accepted and recognized principle of international law'. Article 9(2) restates the theme of 'special measures'; in this case the formula is that special measures for individuals and groups are to be taken wherever necessary, provided 'that they are not such as to appear racially discriminatory'. The measures envisaged are social and economic, but they also involve an obligation 'to respect the authenticity of their [the disadvantaged groups and individuals] culture and values'. The operative part of the Declaration concludes with a resounding call to international organizations to assist in implementing the Declaration.

There is no special machinery envisaged to implement the Declaration. The accompanying Resolution for Implementation of the Declaration, urges ratification of relevant anti-discrimination instruments and the taking of measures in the municipal legal systems of Member States. States are also urged 'to communicate to the Director-General all necessary information concerning the steps they have taken to give effect to the principles set forth in the Declaration'. This raises the possibility of overlap between UNESCO and the work of the Committee on the Elimination of Racial Discrimination. Accordingly, the Committee suggested to the Director-General of UNESCO that he takes into account the reporting obligations of States Parties to the UN Convention on Race when requesting information from States, 'with a view to avoiding duplication'.[18]

[18] Lerner (*supra*, n. 3), 60.

34. The Anti-Discrimination Provision of the European Convention on Human Rights

The European Convention on Human Rights and Fundamental Freedoms[1] contains a basic anti-discrimination clause in Article 14:

The enjoyment of the rights and freedoms set forth in this Convention shall be secured without discrimination on any ground such as sex, race, colour, language, religion, political or other opinion, national or social origin, association with a national minority, property, birth or other status.

There is no reference to the principle of non-discrimination in the Preamble to the Convention, neither is there any specific article on equality; Article 14, therefore, stands alone in the Convention, supplemented by a cross-reference in Article 16 which states that: 'Nothing in Articles 10,[2] 11,[3] and 14 shall be regarded as preventing the High Contracting Parties from imposing restrictions on the political activity of aliens.'

The machinery established for the protection of the rights and freedoms consists mainly of three bodies: the European Commission of Human Rights, the European Court of Human Rights, and the Committee of Ministers of the Council of Europe. The task of the Commission is to examine alleged violations of the Convention by the contracting States; it has an obligatory competence to receive applications lodged by other contracting parties and an optional competence to receive applications from individuals, non-governmental organizations, or groups of individuals.[4] The Commis-

---

[1] *UNTS*, 213, 221, signed in Rome, 4 November 1950, entered into force 3 September 1953; reprinted in Brownlie, *Basic Documents on Human Rights*, 242. For general reviews of the Convention, see Fawcett, *The Application of the European Convention on Human Rights* (Oxford: OUP, 1987); Jacobs, *The European Convention on Human Rights* (Oxford: OUP, 1975); Van Dijk and Van Hoof, *Theory and Practice of the European Convention on Human Rights* (Deventer: Kluwer, 1984). See also *Stock-Taking on the European Convention on Human Rights,* a periodic note by the Secretary to the European Commission on the concrete results achieved under the Convention covering the first 30 years from 1954 to 1984 (Strasbourg: Council of Europe, 1985) with supplements to November 1987 (Strasbourg: Council of Europe, 1988). The Convention has been ratified by all 22 Member States of the Council of Europe. There are eight Protocols supplementing the norms and procedures of the Convention, summarized in *Stocktaking*, Supplement 1987, vi–vii. On the specific issue of minorities, see Ermacora, 'Minority Rights', *Forum*, Council of Europe 1/80, xx–xxi.

[2] On freedom of expression.

[3] Freedom of assembly.

[4] Article 24 (inter-State procedure); Article 25 (individual petition procedure). See also Article 57 of the Convention which provides for a reporting procedure: 'On receipt of a request from the Secretary-General of the Council of Europe any High Contracting Party shall furnish an explanation of the manner in which its internal law ensures the effective implementation of

sion decides the admissibility of applications based upon certain tests;[5] if the application is declared admissible, the Commission will ascertain the facts and try to reach a friendly settlement between the parties, which must, according to Article 28 of the Convention, be based on respect for human rights as they are defined in the Convention. Unless a settlement is achieved, the Commission draws up a report in which it declares its opinion as to whether a breach of the Convention has been found.[6] The Commission, or any government converned, may refer the case to the European Court of Human Rights[7] or to the Committee of Ministers of the Council of Europe to obtain a decision. The latter body may decide by a two-thirds majority if there has been a violation and if so it may prescribe a period in which the State concerned must take remedial measures.[8] The Court of Human Rights has the power to pronounce judgment on any violation of human rights, and the power to afford 'just satisfaction' to any injured party under Article 50. The execution of judgments is supervised by the Committee of Ministers of the Council of Europe.

The Commission of Human Rights holds that Article 14 only sanctions the principle of non-discrimination as regards enjoyment of the rights and freedoms set out in the Convention,[9] and initially held that violations of Article 14 presupposed violations of another article of the Convention.[10] But in the *Grandrath Case*,[11] the Commission took the view that Article 14 does not depend for its application upon a finding that a violation of another Article has occurred. Also it is clear that Article 14 may be violated in an area dealt with by another article in the Convention even though there has been no violation of that article otherwise.[12] The article has now been considered by the Commission and the Court in connection with most of the rights and freedoms defined in the Convention.[13] The leading case on dis-

---

any of the provisions of this Convention': this appears to have little effect, in contrast to other reporting procedures set out in the present work.

[5] Articles 26 (non-exhaustion of domestic remedies) and 27 (refusal of petitions which are anonymous, repetitive, incompatible with the ECHR, manifestly ill-founded, or an abuse of the right of petition).

[6] Articles 28 and 30.

[7] If the defendant State has accepted the jurisdiction of the Court: Article 46. At the time of writing, 20 States are known to have accepted the Court's jurisdiction.

[8] Article 32.

[9] Applications 86/55, *YBECHR*, 198; 107/56, ibid., 235; 436/58, 1, *YBECHR*, 2, 385; 2373/64, *CD* 16, 58; 2145/64, *CD* 18, 1; 3325/67, *YBECHR*, 10, 528; 6745/74, 6746/74, *DR*, 2, 110 and 116.

[10] Appln. 808/60.

[11] *YBECHR*, 8, 324 (admissibility); Commission Report and Decision of Committee of Ministers, *YBECHR*, 10, 626 and 694.

[12] Eissen, 'L'Autonomie de l'Article 14', in *Mélanges Offerts à Polys Modinos* (Paris: Editions A. Pedone, 1968), 122. It is correct to say that the Convention does not prevent discrimination as such, but only discrimination in the securing of rights under the Convention.

[13] For a list, consult Sieghart, *The International Law of Human Rights*, 78–9 (Oxford: OUP, 1983). For an encapsulation of cases dealing with discrimination on grounds of race, sex,

crimination remains the *Belgian Linguistics Case*.[14] The applicants were the parents of families in Belgium who applied both on their own behalf, and on behalf of children under age. The gravamen of their complaint was that, as French speakers, they wanted their children to be educated in that language despite living in a region considered by Belgian law to be Dutch speaking and thus requiring that public education be conducted in the official language of the region. The case raised issues relating to the First Protocol to the Convention, Article 2 of which provides that 'No person shall be denied the right to education. In the exercise of any functions which it assumes in relation to education and to teaching, the State shall respect the right of parents to ensure such education and teaching in conformity with their own religious and philosophical convictions'; as well as Article 8 of the Convention (respect for private and family life) and Article 14.

The Court pointed out that despite the very general wording of the French version of Article 14 ('sans distinction aucune'), the Article does not forbid every difference in treatment in the exercise of the rights and freedoms recognized, and to hold that it does so would produce absurd results in that every legal and administrative provision which did not secure to everyone complete equality of treatment in the enjoyment of the rights and freedoms recognized would be contrary to the Convention. The Court went on to say that the competent national authorities are frequently confronted with situations and problems which, on account of differences inherent therein, call for different legal solutions. The question thus became one of determining the criteria by which differences of treatment would infringe Article 14 or not infringe it. The Court drew on 'principles which may be extracted from the legal practice of a large number of democratic States', and held that 'the principle of equality of treatment is violated if the distinction has no objective and reasonable justification.' Further, the existence of such a justification must be assessed in relation to the aim and effect of the measure, regard being had to the principles which normally prevail in democratic societies. A difference of treatment in the exercise of a right laid down in the Convention must not only pursue a legitimate aim: Article 14 is likewise violated when it is clearly established that 'there is no reasonable relationship of proportionality between the means employed and the aims sought to be realised'. The Court then made some remarks about the respective roles of the States parties and the enforcement machinery of the Convention— pointing out the subsidiary nature of the latter in reviewing the measures chosen by the States to implement the Convention. Article 14 of the

and religion, see Greenberg, in Meron (ed.), *Human Rights in International Law: Legal and Policy Issues*, 333, n. 177.

[14] *Case Relating to Certain Aspects of the Laws on the Use of Languages in Belgium,* Judgment, 23 July 1968, *European Court of Human Rights Ser. A No. 6.* There is a succinct account of the case and a critique in Van Dyke, *Human Rights, Ethnicity and Discrimination,* 24 ff.

Convention and Article 2 of the Protocol *did not produce the effect of guaranteeing to a child or to his parents the right to obtain instruction in a language of his choice*.[15] The object of the articles was more limited: to ensure that the right to education shall be secured by each contracting party to everyone within its jurisdiction without discrimination. Furthermore, 'to interpret the two provisions as conferring on everyone within the jurisdiction of a State a right to obtain education in the language of his own choice would lead to absurd results, for it would be open to anyone to claim any language of instruction in any of the territories of the contracting parties'. The Court mentioned cases where the Convention had conferred specific language rights, including Article 5(2),[16] stating that 'if they had intended to create for everyone within their jurisdiction a specific right with respect to the language of instruction, they would have done so in express terms in Article 2 of the Protocol.'

The Court found nothing to contravene the Convention in the establishment and State funding of schools in the major Dutch and French linguistic regions of Belgium which employed the language of each region as the language of instruction. The purpose of the law was 'to achieve linguistic unity within the two large regions of Belgium in which a large majority of the population speaks only one of the two national languages'. The Convention was also not broken by legislation withdrawing subsidies from public schools in the Dutch unilingual region which provided education in French; despite the harshness of this measure, it was not an arbitrary distinction. Private organization of French-speaking education was not affected. However, the Court did find discrimination in the access to education in six communes on the periphery of Brussels: Dutch-speaking children resident in the French unilingual region had access to schools in the six communes; whereas French-speaking children living in the Dutch unilingual region were refused access to French-language schools in those communes. The discrimination between the two groups was founded on language, which is referred to in Article 14, and was not simply a question of residence. The problems of the French-speaking children were compounded by the fact that there were no French-speaking schools in the areas where they lived. This was the only breach of the Convention found by the Court.[17]

One feature of the Convention jurisprudence is worthy of mention before discussing the relationship between the anti-discrimination Article 14 and the efforts to write a minorities protection article into the Convention. The assumption of anti-discrimination law in general is that the grounds upon

[15] Author's emphasis.
[16] 'Everyone who is arrested shall be informed promptly, in a language which he understands, of the reasons for his arrest and of any charge against him.'
[17] The political and linguistic arrangements in Belgium are concisely set out by the European Court in the case of *Mathieu-Mohin and Clerfayt (99/1985/95/143)*, Judgment, 2 March 1987, 3—12.

which no discrimination shall be permitted are of equal value: to discriminate on the grounds of race is as reprehensible as discriminating on grounds of sex, language or religion. However, the Commission of Human Rights has introduced a hierarchy into the prohibited grounds. In its report on 31 Applications Lodged by East African Asians against the United Kingdom,[18] the Commission stated that

as generally recognised, a special importance should be attached to discrimination based on race; that publicly to single out a group of persons for differential treatment on the basis of race might, in certain circumstances, constitute a special form of affront to human dignity; and that differential treatment of a group of persons on the basis of race might therefore be capable of constituting degrading treatment when differential treatment on some other ground would raise no such question.[19]

The Commission qualified its reference by mentioning special circumstances, which, in the cases of the Asians expelled from East Africa in consequence of 'Africanization' policies, included the fact that, as citizens of the United Kingdom, they had no other country to which they could make out a claim for admission, and that they had been deprived of their livelihood and rendered destitute.[20] While this affirmation of discrimination as degrading treatment (prohibited under Article 3 of the Convention) rightly underlines the importance of non-discrimination to universal human rights, the implied distinction between race and other grounds is not as welcome. The other grounds are not listed in the Report, but by implication would include all those grounds listed in Article 14. The Commission's decision[21] on admissibility mentioned 'language' as a possible case where differential treatment might not be so reprehensible. While it is true that in the present age 'race' is the aspect of discrimination singled out most frequently in international and municipal law, this should not be taken to imply that discrimination on some other ground is less reprehensible. Religion, nationality, and ethnic or linguistic group membership (association with a national minority) have been quite as productive of repression, injustice, and conflict as 'race'. It is not entirely clear what is meant by 'race' in the remarks of the Commission; on the facts, the 'race' of the applicants is clear enough, but the Commission also referred to the condemnation of racial discrimination 'as generally recognised' which would include its recognition in such instruments as the International Convention on the Elimination of All Forms of Racial Discrimination where racial discrimination is deemed to include discrimination on grounds of 'colour, descent, or national or ethnic origin'.[22] The grounds of discrimination forbidden in international law are

---

[18] *3 EHRR. 76.* The Commission's report was not published (its date is 1973) until 1979 when it was 'leaked'. See Joint Council for the Welfare of Immigrants, *The Unpublished Report, the European Commission of Human Rights and British Immigration Policy* (London, 1979).

[19] Ibid., para. 207.

[20] Generally, paras. 203–6.

[21] CD 36, 92 at 117.

[22] Article 1, *supra*, ch. 29.

grounds where distinctions are unjust and threaten the good order of society. It would be regressive to introduce hierarchical distinctions between them.

The *Belgian Linguistics Case* brought to an end an attempted development of a minorities article in the European Convention on Human Rights. When the Consultative Assembly of the Council of Europe made proposals in 1949 for the European Convention on Human Rights, it proposed to include a non-discrimination clause based on Article 2 of the Universal Declaration which does not mention 'association with a national minority' as a prohibited ground of discrimination. On the proposal of M. Lannung[23] the phrase 'affiliation to a national minority' was added; the basic idea was retained with the change from 'affiliation to' to 'association with' in the final text.[24] M. Lannung was the Danish delegate in the Consultative Assembly and the action was taken with the position of the Danish minority in South Schleswig in mind,[25] and following what he described as the 'disappointing experience'[26] concerning United Nations efforts to secure a regime of protection of the rights of minorities. The insertion of the reference to minorities in Article 14 was designed, according to M. Lannung, to secure the first requirement of minorities, that is equality with other nationals of the State. The harder task remained, to ensure for them 'suitable means for the preservation of their racial peculiarities, their traditions, and their national characteristics'.[27] The 'Teitgen Report', submitted to the Consultative Assembly by the Committee on Legal and Administrative Questions dealing with the Establishment of a Collective Guarantee of Essential Freedoms and Fundamental Rights,[28] had stated that 'the resolution by the Committee specifies that the regime of guaranteed freedoms should prevent any discrimination based on membership of a national minority. After having heard a report by M. Lannung on the problem of the *wider protection of the rights of national minorities*, the Committee unanimously recognised the importance of this problem.'[29] However, it was not until 1956 that any action was taken on minorities, following a reminder in 1954 from the Consultative Assembly that 'a more precise definition of the rights of national minorities was still outstanding'.[30] The creation of a special Sub-Committee of the Legal Committee to study the

---

[23] Lannung, 'The Rights of Minorities', in *Mélanges* (*supra*, n. 12), 181.

[24] Recommendation No. 38, in *Texts Adopted by the Consultative Assembly* 1949.

[25] *Collected Edition of the Travaux Préparatoires of the European Convention*, vol. i, Preparatory Commission of the Council of Europe, Committee of Ministers, Consultative Assembly 11 May–8 September 1949, 54, 68.

[26] Lannung (*supra*, n. 12), 184.

[27] Ibid. 185.

[28] Collected Edition of Travaux (*supra*, n. 24), 216.

[29] Ibid., 220 (para. 11).

[30] Opinion No. 12, para. 42, in *Texts Adopted by the Consultative Assembly*, September 1954.

legislation on minorities in Member States was proposed in April 1956,[31] and the Sub-Committee on Minorities was duly constituted and reported in October 1957.[32] The report proposed a full comparative study of minorities laws and regulations in member States. A report, the Struye Report, was presented to the Assembly in April 1959, and on the basis of a fairly limited range of research (to laws in force in Austria, Denmark, Federal Republic of Germany, and Italy) concluded that the status of national minorities was broadly satisfactory.[33] None the less, an additional Protocol to the Convention was proposed,[34] and was the subject of further work by the Sub-Committee on Minorities. All the issues that arise when minority protection is discussed were considered by the Committee: the fear of encouraging separatism and dissension between Member States; the question of the 'loyalty' of minority members to their host State; the nature and limitations on the rights minorities should have, as well as such drafting questions as to how detailed a specification should be made of the rights. The Sub-Committee drew inspiration from the work done at the United Nations though it rejected the text of the draft Article 27 of the Covenant on Civil and Political Rights as being not sufficiently representative of European conditions, noting in particular that the existence of some minorities was due not so much to markedly different ethnic or linguistic characteristics from the majority as to the vaguer question of 'national sympathies',[35] which is in any case reflected in Article 14 of the Convention in the phrase 'national minority'. The Sub-Committee proposed the following text:

Persons belonging to a national minority shall not be denied the right, in community with the other members of their group, and as far as compatible with public order, to enjoy their own culture, to use their own language, to establish their own schools and receive teaching in the language of their choice, or to profess and practise their own religion.

The proposed article may be instructively compared with Article 27 of the UN Covenant on Civil and Political Rights. In the first place, it is devoid of the phrase in Article 27 'In those States in which ethnic, religious or linguistic minorities exist'; the reference in the Sub-Committee's draft to 'belonging to a national minority' of course implies the existence of a minority group or groups in a State but it does not draw attention to itself in quite as obvious a fashion as the introductory phrase of Article 27 which almost invites State claims that no minorities exist on their territory.[36] The

---

[31] *Docs. of the Assembly*, Doc. 508. [32] M. Rolin, Rapporteur.
[33] *Docs. of the Assembly*, 1002, April 1959. [34] Ibid., 999, April 1959.
[35] Lannung (*supra*, n. 12), 188.
[36] A different type of restriction may result from the choice of 'national minority' (as in Article 14) instead of ethnic groups. 'National' was understood by the Sub-Committee to cover only groups well-defined and long established on the territory of a State, and did not apply to groups which would seek to form separate entities within the State, Lannung (*supra*, n. 12), 187. The Sub-Committee was influenced by rather restrictive interpretations of the UN Covenant, despite its attempt to ground the Protocol in European conditions.

Article follows Article 27 in describing the right as a right of 'persons belonging to' minorities rather than the groups themselves, though, as with Article 27, it is a right to be exercised 'in community with' other members. The text is more restrictive than Article 27 in that it would only allow the exercise of rights 'as far as compatible with public order', which would give considerable latitude to States to deny their exercise.[37] M. Lannung explained that 'we could not expect our governments to give additional rights to members of a minority group if the beneficiaries were not loyal citizens'.[38] The problem of loyalty is discussed elsewhere[39] but it may be remarked here that the formula proposed by the Sub-Committee is rather timid; the impression is created of a rather grudging concession to minority groups rather than any positive valorization of their rights, their place in multinational States, or their potential contribution to improving relations between States. The rights to be exercised are more explicit on the question of education.

The Sub-Committee proposals were transmitted through the Legal Committee to the Parliamentary Assembly in 1961 which recommended[40] that a minorities article should be included in a Protocol. The Committee of Experts drafting the Protocol were, however, distracted from their task by the series of applications in the *Belgian Linguistics Case*, bearing in mind that the Sub-Committee had proposed a right of members of minorities to establish schools and receive teaching in their own language and the case raised a question precisely of that kind. Accordingly, the Committee of Experts agreed to defer the issue and their decision was ratified by the Committee of Ministers.[41] Although the Rapporteur at the Parliamentary Conference on Human Rights in Vienna in 1971[42] wondered whether the governments had not hitherto been too pessimistic about protection of minorities, the Committee of Experts took a negative view in 1973: in view of provisions already present in the Convention, the difficulty of achieving a definition of 'national minority', and the political difficulties from claims to autonomy and separatism, it was not realistic to expect governments to agree on new guarantees of rights.[43]

Petitions to the Council of Europe which concern minorities as groups have therefore been presented to the Convention organs in terms of individual discrimination under Article 14. The minority grievance has to be decided in accordance with the law of the Convention with its limited

---

[37] Limitations on Article 27 discussed, *supra*, ch. 22.

[38] Lannung, 192.

[39] Referring to UN debates, Lannung, 12, 191−2 stated: 'We decided to follow the same line, it being understood that to work by democratic means to achieve self-determination could not be considered as disloyalty'.

[40] Recommendation 285, *Texts Adopted by the Assembly*, April 1961.

[41] *15th Report of the Committee of Ministers to the Assembly*, 1963, para. 279.

[42] Vienna, October 1971, Proceedings published by the Council of Europe 1972.

[43] Robertson, 'The Promotion of Human Rights by the Council of Europe', *RDH*, 8, (1975), 545.

catalogue of rights to be guaranteed on a non-discriminatory basis, rather than under a wider formula which might represent the core of the issue rather better. Thus, in *Rassemblement Jurassien and Unité Jurassienne* v. *Switzerland*, the applicant organizations had planned a demonstration in 1977 to protest against the removal of the reference to the 'People of Jura' from the constitution of the Canton of Bern. The Executive Council of the Canton of Bern had banned political meetings in Moutier where the demonstration was to take place, fearing clashes between separatist (pro-Jura) and anti-separatist (pro-Bern) groups. The applicants contended the well-foundedness of the prohibition in terms of Article 11 of the Convention (freedom of assembly) and Article 14; they alleged that the Bern authorities, in response to pressure from anti-separatist organizations, had taken discriminatory measures. Thus the Articles invoked deal with peripheral aspects of the central dispute, in substance an argument about the extent of the linguistic group's autonomy, rather than its central case. The Commission declared the case to be inadmissible.

Many other cases have also dealt with minority issues: the *Isop Case* and the *Rebernig Case*[44] relate to the Slovenian minority in Carinthia, and a number of inter-State applications have touched upon peripheral aspects of what are essentially minority issues (in a substantially higher proportion than in individual applications), the case of *Ireland* v. *the United Kingdom*[45] and the applications lodged by *Cyprus* v. *Turkey* are examples.[46] Rights to autonomy and self-determination have been canvassed without success before the Commission in cases such as *X* v. *the Federal Republic of Germany*[47] and *X* v. *The Netherlands*.[48] These cases failed on the basis of inadmissibility *ratione materiae*, because the Convention quite clearly does not guarantee any right of self-determination. The former case concerned an applicant who claimed to represent three and a half million Sudeten Germans and claimed that 'normalizing' relations between the Federal Republic of Germany and Czechoslovakia violated their rights in view of their expulsion from Czechoslovakia in 1945. The latter case was brought by a Dutch citizen who became, subsequent to the application, a citizen of Surinam, resident in Paramaribo. He unsuccessfully attempted to invoke the Convention to determine that the independence of Surinam should have been granted only to descendants of the original Indians in the territory, and not to descendants of the former colony's black population. The case law of the Commission has also established that there is no general right of citizens to use their mother tongue in relations with public authorities.[49] The *Isop Case*[50] concerned the right to employ the Slovene language before an Austrian court. The applicant maintained that the court had acted

---

[44] Appln. 8191/78.
[46] Judgment, January 1978.
[48] Appln. 6742/74, *DR*, 3, 98.
[50] Appln. 2333/64, *YBECHR for 1965*, 338.

[45] Appln. 8142/78.
[47] Applns. 6780/74; 6950/75; 8007/77.
[49] 7230/75, *DR*, 7, 109.

improperly in referring back a statement made in the Slovene language. The case was based on Article 6 of the Convention which, combined with the rule against discrimination, entitled the applicant to a fair hearing on the basis of language or association with a national minority. The claim was rejected, since the language had no official status in Austria and the refusal to receive the statement did not violate the Convention which did not state a right of individuals to address themselves to a court in other than the official language. There was a violation neither of Article 6 nor of Article 14. The *Isop Case* is an example of the lacuna in the Convention caused by the absence of a minorities article. Isop was in essence entitled to the rights of only the other Austrian citizens on a non-discriminatory basis under Convention law; he was not entitled to the specifically directed measures which one would expect in a convention which also protected the right of identity of minority groups.[51] Of course, the principle of non-discrimination operates in relation to the rights laid down in the Convention; if the rights were widened, it may be argued, the problem revealed in such cases as the *Isop Case* would disappear. However, it remains true that some rights are appropriate and necessary to minorities as such to protect them from cultural extinction; the generality of the population does not require the same level of protection. One may therefore agree with the statement of the European Court of Human Rights in the *Belgian Linguistics Case* that it would be absurd to interpret the Convention as conferring on everyone within the jurisdiction of the States parties the right to education 'in the language of his own choice'; it is less absurd to attribute this to the members of minorities within a particular jurisdiction, in terms of *their own language* on the basis of equality with the dominant languages in the State.

There is a certain irony in this lack of provision for minority rights in the continental home of the nation State doctrine and 'the minorities question'. The minimal provision in the European Convention is ill-matched with European constitutional arrangements to benefit particular groups. Specific minority rights, forms of autonomy, home rule, separate representation, and federalism are institutionalized in and between many States of the Council of Europe. Besides Belgium, forms of constitutional autonomy are found in, for example, Austria, Denmark, Finland, Italy, Spain, and Switzerland.[52] Inter-State arrangements, overlapping with domestic protection, exist between Denmark and the Federal Republic of Germany, Greece and Turkey, the Republic of Ireland and the UK, Italy and Austria, and Sweden and Finland.[53] The existing scheme manifests the continuing importance of

---

[51] 808/60, *YBECHR for 1962*, 108.

[52] For further comment, see Brownlie, 'The Rights of Peoples in Modern International Law', in Crawford (ed.), *The Rights of Peoples* 1 at 3—4.

[53] Some European arrangements are outlined, specifically and generally, in Blaustein and Flanz, *Constitutions of the Countries of the World* (New York, Dobbs Ferry: Oceana Publications, 1973); Capotorti Report, (*supra*, ch 1, n. 4); *Co-Existence in Some Plural European Societies*, Minority Rights Group Report No. 72; *Constitutional and Legislative Provisions*

ad hoc agreements between States, though this complexity and richness of experience has not been translated into generally applicable international norms. In 'positive' minority rights, it may be argued that general international law contains more than the Convention, despite the greater scale and depth of the problems dealt with.

Concerning the Organisation of Regional Government, Länder, Cantons and Regions in Europe, Council of Europe, Strasbourg; Modeen, *The International Protection of National Minorities in Europe*; Thornberry, *Minorities and Human Rights Law*, Minority Rights Group Report No. 73; Van Dyke (*supra*, n. 14).

[54] The international arrangements to 1967 are canvassed in UN, *Protection of Minorities*, UN Sales No.67.XIV.3; some later treaties are referred to in the Capotorti Report, and Thornberry (*supra*, n. 52). The Anglo-Irish Agreement of 15 November 1985 can also be included: see Bailey (ed.), *Human Rights and Responsibilities in Britain and Ireland* (London: Macmillan, 1988) for a critique. Most of the treaties have been studied in depth: see, for example, Alcock, *The History of the South Tyrol Question*: he considers, *inter alia*, the contribution of the Council of Europe to efforts to resolve disagreement between Italy and Austria on this question, 308—12 (Geneva: Michael Joseph Ltd., 1970); Barros, *The Aaland Islands Question: its Settlement by the League of Nations* (New Haven: Yale UP, 1968). For case law relating to the Cyprus issue, consult Fawcett, (*supra*, n. 1). Other European initiatives on rights of minorities include: (1) the Draft Charter for Regional or Minority Languages in Europe submitted to the Committee of Minorities of the Council of Europe in March 1988: Doc. CPL(23) 8, 14 March 1988; (2) the Community Charter of Rights of Ethnic Minorities adopted by the European Parliament in the framework of the EEC in 1981: *Off. Jnl. of European Communities*, C 287, 9 Nov. 1981.

35. Non-Discrimination in General International Law (I)

Introduction

The brief account[1] of the emergence of the non-discrimination formula in the drafting of the United Nations Charter at San Francisco indicates that, unlike the principle of identity (as applied to minorities), non-discrimination as a concept is capable of appealing to a very broad spectrum of States, including the 'countries of immigration'. The explicit nature of the non-discrimination formula, in contrast to the generalized references to 'human rights and fundamental freedoms' elsewhere in the Charter, and the insistent character of its repeated invocation,[2] promised from the outset that the United Nations would make it a principle of great potency in international law and relations. The gradual coalescence of opinion at San Francisco in favour of the principle was not without elements of political compromise. The Atlantic Charter[3] agreed by the United Kingdom and the United States of America, and the subsequent Declaration of the United Nations[4] made only general statements and were not explicit on the racial discrimination issue. Following the promulgation of these documents, Britain made it clear that it had made no commitments in relation to racial policies in the colonies.[5] There is evidence that the 'racial question' caused nervous responses in other States, including the United States of America[6]—though wartime drafts of the Charter of a new international organization prepared in the United States emphasized the importance of the principle. One early draft in the United States Department of State stated a prohibition of discrimination on the basis of race, nationality, language, political opinion, or religious belief, asserting that the ban on discrimination is fundamental because without it no person's rights are assured and the rights of all may be undermined. The draft also reflected the need to avoid a repetition of the Nazi experience, a regime for which racial discrimination was a major element of law and philosophy: 'The prohibition of discrimination on the grounds of race is intended to prevent the enactment of laws like the notorious Nuremberg laws . . . discriminating against "non-Aryans".'[7]

---

[1] *Supra*, ch. 11.
[2] *Supra*, ch. 26.
[3] Whiteman, *Digest of International Law*, vol. v, 44.
[4] Ibid. 44–5.
[5] Churchill, 'Great Design in Africa', The Times, 11 November 1942.
[6] Lauren, 'First Principles of Racial Equality', *Human Rights Quarterly*, 5 (1983), 1.
[7] Cited by Lauren, ibid. 9.

Such drafts were not, however, introduced into the negotiations at Dumbarton Oaks; nor was a Chinese text proposing as a fundamental principle that 'The . . . equality of all States and all races shall be upheld'.[8] The reservations of States at this stage were not perhaps so much about non-discrimination and racial equality *per se*, as about the dangers of interfering in the internal affairs of States.[9] At the San Francisco Conference, the reaction of many States to the racialism of the Nazis merged with those of the States which had experience of racial discrimination at the hands of colonial powers. India proposed that fundamental liberties should be guaranteed 'for all men and women, irrespective of race, colour, or creed, in all nations and in all international relations and associations of nations one with another'.[10] The Philippines declared the need to establish 'racial equality among nations'.[11] China also referred to the principle of the equality of all races.[12] Among European States, France[13] was the most active in pressing the issue of discrimination and, in a reversal of previous attitudes, the Soviet Union supported the new proposals.[14] The Four-Power amendment to the Dumbarton Oaks proposals accepted the principle of non-discrimination, completing, despite hesitations, the response to the mood of the Conference. President Truman of the United States declared, grandly, in his speech at the closing plenary session, that 'The Charter is dedicated to the achievement and observance of human rights and fundamental freedoms. Unless we can attain those objectives for all men and women everywhere, without regard to race, language or religion—we cannot have permanent peace and security in the world.'[15]

Since the non-discrimination reference was the only specifically mentioned aspect of the human rights programme of the United Nations,[16] it is not surprising that its subsequent elaboration has been a favourite theme in the action of the Organisation. The concept of non-discrimination, especially on grounds of race or ethnic group, has become, almost beyond argument, part of the 'law of the United Nations'. As early as 1946, the General Assembly, in Resolution 103(I), declared that 'it is in the higher interests of humanity to put an immediate end to religious and so-called racial persecution and discrimination, . . . [calling] . . . on the Governments and responsible authorities to conform both to the letter and to the spirit of the Charter of the United Nations. . . .'[17] This concern was developed in relation to particular contexts such as Southern Africa and broader contexts

---

[8] Ibid. 10. [9] *Supra*, ch. 26.
[10] *3 UNCIO Docs.* 527. [11] Ibid. 535.
[12] *10 UNCIO Docs.* 453. [13] *3 UNCIO Docs.* 93–9.
[14] Lauren (*supra*, n. 6), 16. At Dumbarton Oaks, the Soviet representative had opposed any reference to Human Rights and Fundamental Freedoms, arguing that these matters were not germane to the main tasks of an international security organization: *Foreign Relations of the United States 1944*, 1, 789.
[15] *1 UNCIO Docs.* 715–16. [16] *Supra*, ch. 27.
[17] United Nations Action in the Field of Human Rights, (New York: United Nations, 1980).

such as the Non-Self-Governing Territories referred to in Chapter XI of the United Nations Charter. General Assembly Resolution 644(VII) of December 1952 is another early example of growing concern with the 'race issue', wherein the General Assembly, having regard to 'the principles of the Charter and of the Universal Declaration of Human Rights, emphasising the necessity of promoting and encouraging respect for human rights and for fundamental freedoms for all without distinction as to race, sex, language or religion' recommended to those Member States responsible for administering Non-Self-Governing Territories 'the abolition in those Territories of discriminatory laws and practices contrary to the principles of the Charter and of the Universal Declaration of Human Rights'.[18] Racial discrimination has been a potent element in the efforts by the United Nations to achieve self-determination for the peoples of the Non-Self-Governing Territories and other peoples. Calls to implement a right of self-determination have been much assisted by the recognition of a situation involving racial discrimination in a territory of interest to the United Nations. The 'Colonial Declaration' of 1960 requires, *inter alia*, that 'immediate steps shall be taken, in Trust and Non-Self-Governing Territories or all other territories which have not yet attained independence, to transfer all powers to the peoples of those territories . . . in accordance with their freely expressed will and desire, without any distinction as to *race, creed or colour*. . . .'[19]

However, United Nations interest in the question of discrimination has been more broadly focused on discrimination generally. Following manifestations of anti-Semitism and other forms of racial and national hatred in 1959, the United Nations Commission on Human Rights condemned these manifestations as 'violations of the principles embodied in the Charter of the United Nations and in the Universal Declaration of Human Rights, and in particular as a violation of the human rights of the groups against which they are directed . . .'[20] Subsequently, the Assembly condemned 'all manifestations and practices of racial, religious and national hatred . . . as violations of the Charter of the United Nations and the Universal Declaration of Human Rights'.[21] A series of resolutions to follow up this issue resulted in the adoption by the General Assembly of the Declaration on the Elimination of All Forms of Racial Discrimination.[22] Subsequently, the International Convention on the Elimination of All Forms of Racial Discrimination stated the considerations borne in mind by the General Assembly in drafting the instrument, including the consideration that:

the Charter of the United Nations is based on the principles of the dignity and equality inherent in all human beings, and that all Member States have pledged

---

[18] Ibid.   [19] UNGA Res. 1514(XV). See remarks, *supra*, ch. 1.
[20] Res. 6(XVI), UN Action, 47.
[21] Res. 1510(XV), UN Action, ibid.
[22] *Supra*, ch. 30.

themselves to take joint and separate action . . . for the achievement of one of the Purposes of the United Nations which is to promote and encourage universal respect for and observance of human rights and fundamental freedoms for all, without distinction as to race, sex, language or religion.

This wording echoes that of Articles 55 and 56 of the United Nations Charter.

In language which recalls that of the delegates speaking to the legal force (or lack of it) of the Universal Declaration of Human Rights, the 'force' of the Declaration on Race was stated variously by different representatives. According to the Representative of Chile to the General Assembly, the Declaration on Race 'will have a moral impact on the world and is a document no less important than the United Nations Charter, the Universal Declaration of Human Rights and [General Assembly] Resolution 1514(XV) on decolonisation'.[23] The Representative of South Africa, on the other hand, reminded the General Assembly that 'this document is a Declaration and therefore does not have the legal status of a covenant or an international agreement'.[24] The Representative of Finland also stated that the Declaration was 'a statement of principles, not a set of binding rules'.[25] This was echoed by the Representative of the United Kingdom who stated that 'we do not believe that it imposes legal obligations',[26] and by the Representative of Australia: 'it has no legal binding force'.[27] On the other hand, the Representative of Byelorussia regarded the Declaration as 'a logical development of and a complement to the Universal Declaration of Human Rights . . .'.[28] African and Asian States tended to state that the Declaration was equivalent to the Universal Declaration of Human Rights, without explicitly claiming that it had legal force.

---

[23] *GAOR* 18th Session, UN Doc A/PV.1262, para. 17.   [24] Ibid., para. 35.
[25] Ibid., para. 49.   [26] Para. 73.   [27] Para. 151.
[28] Para. 189.

36. Judge Tanaka's Dissenting Opinion in The South-West Africa Cases (Second Phase) (II)

The dissenting opinion of Judge Tanaka[1] is described as 'profound and eloquent'[2] by Professors McDougal, Lasswell, and Chen, and as 'probably the best exposition of the concept of equality in existing literature'[3] by Professor Brownlie. In this case, the International Court of Justice failed to deal with the merits of the submission by applicant States Ethiopia and Liberia that South Africa had violated her international obligations in relation to the territory of South-West Africa. Paragraphs 3 and 4 of the applicants' final submissions to the Court had alleged that the respondent (South Africa) had practised apartheid, that is, had 'distinguished as to race, colour, national or tribal origin in establishing the rights and duties of the inhabitants of the Territory' in violation of Article 2 of the Mandate and Article 22 of the Covenant of the League of Nations. South Africa had 'in the light of applicable international standards or international legal norms, or both, failed to promote to the utmost the material and moral well-being and social progress of the inhabitants of the Territory'[4] in violation of its legal obligations vis-à-vis the Territory. The applicants thus asserted the existence of a norm or standards prohibiting apartheid—the norm or standards, as Judge Tanaka repeatedly referred to, of 'non-discrimination or non-separation'. Apartheid, according to the applicants, meant a system under which 'the status, rights, duties, opportunities and burdens of the population are determined and allotted arbitrarily on the basis of race, colour and tribe', in a pattern which 'ignores the needs and capacities of the groups and individuals affected, and subordinates the interests and rights of the great majority of the people to the preferences of a minority . . .'.[5] Judge Tanaka's opinion is a detailed examination of the basic issue as to whether there exists a general norm of non-discrimination, and draws upon the sources of international law in a systematic fashion. Thus, the various treaties which contain references to the non-discrimination principle are listed and commented upon, including, most importantly, the United Nations Charter.[6] Judge Tanaka concluded that

[1] *ICJ Reports 1966*, 4 at 284–316.
[2] McDougal, Lasswell and Chen, *Human Rights and World Public Order*, 599.
[3] Brownlie, *Basic Documents on Human Rights*, 439.
[4] Applicants' Final Submissions, May 1965, CR/65/35, 69–70.
[5] South West Africa, Pleadings, Memorials, 108.
[6] *Supra*, ch. 11.

the equality principle, as an integral part of the Charter of the United Nations or as an independent source of general international law, can be directly applied to the matter of the Mandate either as constituting a kind of law of the Mandate *in sensu lato* or, at least in respect of standards, as a principle of interpretation of the mandate agreement.

In relation to customary international law under Article 38 1(b) of the Statute of the International Court of Justice, the applicants cited numerous resolutions of the General Assembly of the United Nations and the Security Council, the agreements governing Trust Territories, the Universal Declaration of Human Rights, the [then] draft United Nations Covenants on Human Rights, the International Law Commission's Draft Declaration on Rights and Duties of States 1949, and regional treaties and declarations — including the European Convention on Human Rights and Fundamental Freedoms. Judge Tanaka concluded that 'the norm of non-discrimination or non-separation on the basis of race has become a rule of customary international law . . .'.

In relation to the respondent's argument on the non-retroactive nature of customary law and thus its inapplicability to the Mandate over South-West Africa, the judge's view was that the customary law of non-discrimination simply clarified the situation existing at the time of the Mandate and thus 'what ought to have been clear 40 years ago has been revealed by the creation of a new customary law which plays the role of authentic interpretation the effect of which is retroactive.'

An interesting aspect of the case as a whole is the respondent's attempt to justify the system of apartheid, denying the existence of 'any norm of non-discrimination of an absolute character' and arguing the necessity of group differentiation in the administration of a multiracial, multinational, or multi-lingual community. The point raised by South Africa is of the highest relevance to any argument relating to minorities and their legal treatment. South Africa contended that geographical, historical, ethnological, economic, and cultural differences and variations between population groups necessitated the adoption of a policy of separate development which was the best method of achieving well-being and social progress.[7] The mixed integral society in the sense of Western democracy was to be rejected in their case because it would necessarily lead to competition, friction, struggle, chaos, etc., as had happened in many African countries.[8] In the governance of South-West Africa, therefore, indirect rule, utilizing the merits of tribalism,

---

[7] Richardson, 'Self-Determination, International Law and the South African Bantustan Policy', *Columbia Journal of Transnational Law*, 17 (1978), 185. According to a South African Representative to the UN General Assembly, UN Doc A/6688: 'South Africa's policy of autonomous development is designed to benefit all the nations of South Africa. The purpose is to maintain the self-determination of all her peoples. The policy is not based on any concept of superiority or inferiority, but on the fact that people differ particularly in their group associations, loyalties, cultures, outlook, modes of life and standards of development.'

[8] Tanaka, in Brownlie, *Basic Documents*, 459.

was most appropriate. Contrary to the view of the applicants who contended that the policy was illegal, South Africa regarded it as neutral, merely a tool to attain a particular end.

To meet these arguments, Judge Tanaka sought to distinguish permissible from impermissible discrimination. In relation to treaties protecting minorities, he regarded them as prohibiting a State from excluding members of minority groups from participating in 'rights, interests and opportunities which a majority population group can enjoy' and as guaranteeing to the group the exercise of their own religious and educational activities. The guarantee, he stated, was conferred on group members to protect their interests and not from the motive of discrimination itself. It was an essential part of such a guarantee that such protection 'cannot be *imposed* upon members of minority groups, and consequently they have the choice to accept it or not'. Thus, members of a minority group, enjoying citizenship on equal terms with members of majority groups 'have conferred on them the possibility of cultivating their own religious, educational or linguistic values as a recognition of their fundamental human rights and freedoms'. Thus, 'the spirit of the minorities treaties . . . is not negative and prohibitive, but positive and permissive'.

The South African arguments and their attempted refutation pin-point the area of difficulty; minority rights operate between 'the unqualified application of the norm of non-discrimination or non-separation' and the kind of separation favoured as apartheid.[9] Judge Tanaka stresses individual, not group rights, and his approach follows Article 27 of the Covenant on Civil and Political Rights; thus, the individual must be free to reject the opportunity given to cultivate differences.[10] He correctly identifies the positive nature of minorities treaties. There is, however, a certain tension in his argument which demonstrates that the South African contention may have been difficult to overcome. The basic normative starting point 'non-discrimination or non-separation' is a strong formulation which renders difficult the justification of exceptions. He is constrained to deny group status to minorities: 'what is protected is not the religious or linguistic group as a whole, but the individuals belonging to this group, *the former being nothing but a name and not a group.*' He admits that in some cases, however, a necessity may arise to treat one race differently from another, but this could not be justified by reference to race or colour but by 'differences of religion, language, education, custom, etc.', and since South Africa had tried to incorporate this distinction in its own submissions by reference to 'cultural population groups', he referred to their claims as 'dissimulating the underlying racial intention'. Thus, different treatment is justifiable in some cases, and he admits that even within the system of apartheid, the motive of which is evil overall, not all distinctions of treatment can be condemned: whereas

---

[9] *Supra*, ch. 1.   [10] *Supra*, ch. 17.

separate education and schooling could be reasonable, the same could not be said of separation in the public use of such facilities as hotels and buses; none the less it was not possible to 'condemn all measures derived from the respondent's policy of *Apartheid* or separate development . . .'. Some measures within the system could be equated with those in minorities treaties; positive measures to protect natives could be regarded as reasonable in some cases but the system was typified rather by the restrictions in many areas of life which violated the principle of equality. Justifications for differences in treatment should not be given arbitrarily; they must be reasonable, or 'in conformity with justice— as in the treatment of minorities . . .'. In the case of apartheid, 'the necessary logical and material link between . . . difference . . . and different treatment, which can justify such treatment in the case of . . . minorities . . . does not exist.' Apartheid was fundamentally unreasonable and unjust.

The judgment is an interesting and intelligent attempt to disentangle apartheid from related concepts of forms of separation which are none the less fundamentally different from it, such as the protection of minorities. The latter combines the concept of equality with that of liberty to choose whether or not to be different;[11] apartheid denies both equality and liberty —it is an imposed system, the intention of which is the maintenance of the monopoly of wealth and power by the white minority in South Africa to the detriment of other groups. While stating the fundamental norm in terms of non-discrimination and non-separation there is an implicit recognition that the justice of the minorities'[12] case may require permanent measures of protection. This justification of the minorities' case is not achieved without difficulty, and the Opinion demonstrates the tension between a concept of equality, which is not coherent enough to recognize the justice of certain exceptions, and one which does recognize and embrace their case. The judge goes too far in his denial of the realities of group identity which is subject to increasing recognition in later international instruments.[13]

Whilst Judge Tanaka's disentanglement of minority rights from apartheid is crucial in the understanding of these concepts, the demonstration of the customary law status of the norm of non-discrimination functions, it must be recalled, in the context of a dissenting Opinion. The contentions of the applicants, supported by references to many General Assembly resolutions condemning racial discrimination and apartheid, that there existed a norm of non-discrimination in general international law, were rejected by Judge Jessup on the grounds that such bodies as the General Assembly lack a true legislative character.[14] Judge Jessup refused to hold that apartheid was

---

[11] *Supra*, ch. 17.

[12] The norm was referred to by South Africa in the Pleadings as the norm of 'non-differentiation' which clearly would have made nonsense of the Applicants' case.

[13] See particularly the UNESCO Declaration on Race and Racial Prejudice *supra*, ch. 33.

[14] Judge Tanaka also utilized the formula of 'General Principles of Law recognized by

contrary to a norm of international law, though he admitted that United Nations resolutions might be used to interpret the Mandate. McKean states that, therefore, Judge Jessup 'must also admit them to assist in the interpretation of the Charter . . . to which South Africa is a party'.[15] This is not, however, set out explicitly in the case. Confirmation of the points made by Judge Tanaka was not forthcoming until the International Court's Advisory Opinion in the Namibia Case and, even here, not to the fullest extent.

Civilised Nations' (Article 38(1)(c) of the Statute of the International Court of Justice) to demonstrate the general status of the norm of non-discrimination. He noted that the principle of equality before the law is recognized by the municipal law of virtually every State. However, Judge Van Wyk stated that Article 38 does not mean that a majority of civilized nations, by legislating on a particular matter, could compel a minority to introduce similar legislation: *ICJ Reports* 1966, 170.

[15] McKean, *Equality and Discrimination*, 269.

37. The Advisory Opinion on Namibia 1971 (III)

Authors who declare that the principle of non-discrimination is part of general international law often place the Advisory Opinion of the International Court of Justice on Namibia at the centre of their arguments.[1] Resolution 2145(XXI) of the General Assembly of the United Nations[2] terminated South Africa's Mandate in South-West Africa. In this Resolution, the Assembly recited its conviction that 'the administration of the Mandated Territory of South Africa [had] been conducted in a manner contrary to the Mandate, the Charter of the United Nations[3] and the Universal Declaration.' In explanation, the General Assembly reaffirmed its condemnation of apartheid and racial discrimination as practised by the Government of South Africa—policies which constituted a crime against humanity. South Africa had failed to fulfil its obligations 'to ensure the moral and material well-being and security of the indigenous inhabitants of South-West Africa and [had] in fact, disavowed the Mandate'. The Resolution declared that, accordingly, the administration of the Territory came under the direct responsibility of the United Nations. The Resolution was adopted by 114 votes to 2, with 3 abstentions (France, Malawi, and the United Kingdom).[4]

Despite further action by the United Nations (including Security Council Resolution 276[5] which declared the continued presence of South Africa in South-West Africa, Namibia, illegal), South Africa was not reconciled to the views of the United Nations. Accordingly, the Security Council requested an Advisory Opinion from the International Court of Justice: 'What are the legal consequences for States of the continued presence of South Africa in Namibia, notwithstanding Security Council Resolution 276 (1970).'[6]

Paragraph 131 of the Opinion has been widely cited:

Under the Charter of the United Nations, the former Mandatory had pledged itself to observe and respect, in a territory having an international status, human rights and fundamental freedoms for all without distinction as to race. To establish instead, and to enforce, distinctions, exclusions, restrictions and limitations

[1] McKean, *supra* ch. 10, n. 37, ch. XV; Schwelb, 'International Court of Justice and the Human Rights Clauses of the United Nations Charter'.
[2] GAOR, 21st Session, Supp. No. 16, 2–3.
[3] GAOR, 22nd Session, Annexes (1967).
[4] ICJ Reports 1971, 16. The proceedings leading up to the adoption of UNGA Res. 2145(XXI) are reviewed by the UN Secretary-General in the case *Pleadings*, 123.
[5] Text in Sohn and Buergenthal, 'International Protection of Human Rights', 453.
[6] Security Council Res. 284, SCOR, 25 (1970), 4.

exclusively based on grounds of race, colour, descent or national or ethnic origin which constitute a denial of fundamental human rights is a flagrant violation of the Purposes and Principles of the Charter.

Further, in response to a request by South Africa that her acts had no other motives than to promote the interests of the inhabitants of Namibia, the Court replied that

no factual evidence is needed for the purpose of determining whether the policy of *Apartheid* as applied by South Africa in Namibia is in conformity with the international obligations assumed by South Africa under the Charter of the United Nations. In order to determine whether the laws and decrees applied by South Africa in Namibia, which are a matter of public record, constitute a violation of the Purposes and Principles of the Charter of the United Nations, the question of intent . . . is not relevant.[7]

South Africa had stated that it was accused of 'discriminating, in the pejorative sense of suppressing one [ethnic or racial] group for the benefit of another', and that 'that is what is meant by racial discrimination'. South Africa disputed this in fact, adding that if South Africa were indeed doing what the accusers claimed, it would violate the Mandate and the United Nations Charter. South Africa has made similar statements elsewhere in the context of disputes about racial discrimination.[8] South Africa argued that the human rights provisions in the United Nations Charter do not, in any case, 'mechanically prohibit distinctions', but indicated that States must not make distinctions in 'the concern which will be shown to . . . people belonging to various groups'. South Africa stated that it was not a party to any treaty accepting such an absolute norm as binding.[9]

The Advisory Opinion is not absolutely clear on the general law status of the norm of non-discrimination. The strongest paragraph, 131, apparently qualifies the reference to human rights and non-discrimination with 'in a territory having an international status', suggesting some legal and geographical restriction on its scope. Schwelb argues that, on the contrary, if Namibia had not had an international status, the matter would not have been submitted to the Court, and that the location of the South African acts in such a territory may be seen rather as an aggravating factor—in view of the Mandate's concept of the 'sacred trust of civilization'. Be that as it may, it can hardly be contended that if such acts had been perpetrated elsewhere, they would be permissible by international law. The Charter speaks of promoting respect for human rights and fundamental freedoms 'for all', that is, universal respect. Schwelb makes the correct point when he states that 'what is a flagrant violation of the Purposes and Principles of the Charter

---

[7] Para. 129.

[8] See for example, *GAOR*, 18th Session, Plenary Session, UN Doc A/PV.1261, paras. 31–5 (debate on the UN Declaration on the Elimination of Racial Discrimination).

[9] Tanaka opinion.

when committed in Namibia, is also such a violation when committed in South Africa proper, or for that matter, in any other sovereign Member State, or a Non-Self-Governing or Trust Territory'.[10]

The case does, however, make a clear statement on the law of the Charter: South Africa's actions violate the 'Purposes and Principles' of the Charter, not just the Purposes; the Court also refers to the 'pledge' of the former Mandatory, a reference presumably to Article 56 of the Charter. The Court appears, in effect, to be referring to the Charter as a whole and states that such conduct as South Africa's is in 'flagrant violation' of the Charter. Both dissenting opinions in the case (Gros and Fitzmaurice) dealt with matters unconnected with paragraph 131, and may not, therefore, be used to cast doubt on the points under discussion. Judge Ammoun was more explicit in his separate opinion that South Africa had violated its obligations under the Charter 'and the Universal Declaration of Human Rights'.[11] He spoke also of the 'imperative character'[12] of the human rights violated by South Africa—perhaps suggesting *jus cogens*. In response to the written statement of the French Government, which had argued that violation of the Universal Declaration was not violation of a treaty and did not sanction the revocation of the Mandate, Judge Ammoun referred to the possibility of the norms of the Universal Declaration becoming customary law, and concluded that: 'one right which must certainly be considered a pre-existing binding customary norm which the Universal Declaration of Human Rights codified is the right to equality . . .'.[13] Other judges taking a strong line on South Africa were not so explicit about customary law. Judge Nervo referred to the rules binding South Africa's administration of Namibia as including 'declarations and resolutions formally adopted by the principal organs of the United Nations Charter which represent generally accepted interpretations and applications of the United Nations Charter, and which either are of general application, or are stated to have specific reference to the situation of Namibia'.[14] Judge De Castro's remarks also deal primarily with the interpretation of the Charter.[15] Schwelb's summary of the opinion is thus substantially correct, if rather limited in its effects; the Court's Opinion vindicates the arguments of Lauterpacht and others that the Charter imposes legal obligations in the human rights field.[16] McDougal, Lasswell, and Chen speak of the 'unequivocal condemnation'[17] of racial discrimination and the definition by the Court of apartheid as a violation of the Charter of the United Nations and of the Universal Declaration of Human Rights.

---

[10] Schwelb (*supra*, n. 1), 349.
[12] Ibid. 62.
[14] Ibid. 109.
[16] *Supra*, ch. 26.

[11] *ILR* 49, 61.
[13] Ibid. 66.
[15] Ibid. 174–5.
[17] *Human Rights and World Public Order*, 599.

From the Namibia Opinion to Customary Law?

The First World Conference on Race and Racial Discrimination held at Geneva in 1978,[18] at which 125 States were represented, stated, in paragraphs of its 'Declaration' which were adopted without a vote, that 'racialism and racial discrimination are serious violations of fundamental human rights'. Further, racism, racial discrimination, and apartheid were 'gross violations of human rights', and the elimination of racial discrimination was 'an imperative norm of the world community'—a phrase which suggests that racial discrimination is a violation of *jus cogens*. In an address to the Conference, the delegate of Switzerland referred to the 'two fundamental and complementary principles of international law'—the right to equality and the principle of non-discrimination. Citing the Namibia Advisory Opinion, the delegate stated that the prohibition of discrimination has become a norm of positive law. In this context, it may also be recalled that the recent Restatement of Foreign Relations Law of the United States included 'systematic racial discrimination'[19] as an example of a violation of customary law. *The Barcelona Traction Case*, in its description of the basic rights of the human person in 'contemporary international law' referred to 'protection from . . . racial discrimination'.[20] The Proclamation of Teheran,[21] which affirms the obligation of States to respect the principles of the Universal Declaration of Human Rights, does not expressly include the principle of non-discrimination in this statement of 'obligation'. It was submitted previously[22] that, despite the general statement about the Universal Declaration, it must not be assumed without more that any and every human right referred to therein is part of customary international law. However, the prohibition of discrimination occupies a special place in the sense that it determines the field of application of the rights in the Declaration: it is a structural, formal, or architectural aspect of the Universal Declaration, and of the other general international instruments of human rights, rather than merely another right.[23] It is plausible to assert that the non-discrimination principle partakes of whatever is the maximum status of the Universal Declaration in customary law.

However, this logical reading of the status of non-discrimination is not fully reflected in practice. It is undoubtedly the case that the clearest evidence of rules of general international law relates to *racial* discrim-

---

[18] A/CONF.92/40. See conclusions to the present work.
[19] *Supra*, ch. 26. See also *Koowarta v. Bjelke-Petersen*, ALR 39, (1982), 417 at 455–6, per Stephen J.
[20] *Supra*, ch. 26.
[21] *Supra*, ch. 26.
[22] *Supra*, ch. 26.
[23] Partsch, in Vasak and Alston (eds.), *The International Dimensions of Human Rights* (Paris: UNESCO, 1982), vol. i, 61.

ination; there is a strong case for claiming that customary law forbids racial discrimination. Members of racial or ethnic minorities would thus be entitled to protection from discrimination on the ground of membership of a race or ethnic group irrespective of any particular treaty to which their State is a party. The members of religious and linguistic groups have not been the focus of comparable international interest, though in view of the close connection between language and ethnicity, the lacuna, if any, in the case of the latter group is not profound. The enhanced status of the prohibition of racial discrimination is not, however, reflected in the United Nations Charter. The pledge to promote and encourage respect for human rights in the Charter is a pledge to act in this regard without distinction as to 'race, sex, language or religion'. 'Race' may be placed first in this list of grounds, but the other grounds are there also. If there is a 'law' of human rights in the Charter, and if words mean anything, discrimination on the grounds of language and religion is contrary to the law of the Charter. Thus, in line with the interpretation of the Charter offered above, serious and systematic discrimination on such grounds is prohibited to Members of the United Nations.

It was noted above that 'racial' issues surfaced at San Francisco and became important because of revulsion from Nazi racialist doctrines and because of the sensitivities of those States which were formerly colonies of the Powers to notions of national inferiority.[24] These motives, especially in more recent times, the colonial or racial motive, have ensured that racial discrimination has been the primary focus of United Nations action.[25] Discrimination on grounds of religion has raised different issues for States, although the difficulties in elaborating a norm of religious non-discrimination have had more to do with the limits of the general human right of religious freedom rather than with religious discrimination *per se*.[26] It is relatively easy for a State to concede that it should not discriminate against a person on grounds of religious belief: it is not so easy when one considers manifestations of religion, or, *a fortiori*, proselytizing on behalf of a religion, the latter aspects raise the spectre of organized communities of believers whose loyalties may transcend their loyalty to the State. Thus, as in the case of minorities generally, it is the community aspects of rights that are feared by the States.

Some of the problems implicit in the question of religious minorities have

---

[24] Lauren, 'First Principles of Racial Equality'.

[25] UN Action, *Supra*, ch. 35, n. 17.

[26] Neff, 'An Evolving International Legal Norm of Religious Freedom: Problems and Prospects', *California Western International Law Journal*, 7 (1979), 543; Clark, 'The United Nations and Religious Freedom', *New York University Journal of International Law and Politics*, 11 (1978), 197; McDougal, Lasswell and Chen, 'The Right to Religious Freedom and World Public Order', *Michigan Law Review*, 74 (1976), 765; McKean, *Equality and Discrimination*, 121.

already been touched on.[27] They have also appeared in the various stages of the elaboration of the Declaration on the Elimination of All Forms of Intolerance and of Discrimination Based on Religion or Belief[28] and in the attempts to produce a Convention on this question.[29] The presentation of a draft Convention to the United Nations General Assembly in 1967 raised the usual arguments about proselytizing, and the work of missionaries.[30] States were also concerned about pilgrimages on or through their territory. The possibility of withdrawing from State school systems to gain an alternative religious education was also a preoccupation, with Soviet bloc States making some effort to undercut the legitimacy of Church schools. In the Declaration on Religious Intolerance, a paragraph in the Preamble, suggested by Byelorussia,[31] proclaims that freedom of religion and belief should also contribute to world peace, social justice, and friendship. Rival drafts presented by the Holy See and by Western States had provided only that religion could make such a contribution. The paragraph actually adopted may be interpreted to reduce the value of freedom of religion as an autonomous freedom, subordinating it to the achievement of other goals. Substantive articles in the text also betray a certain nervousness about the full implications of an elaborated norm of religious non-discrimination and of religious freedom.[32] The question of religion takes international law to the limits of human rights, at least in so far as the law functions in a community of States. It is quite meaningless, for example, to the adherents of a religion to have their beliefs or practices declared to be contrary to 'public morality'. To the believer, religion is morality itself and its transcendental foundation grounds it more firmly in terms of obligation than any secular rival, or the tenets of other religions. All religions are to a greater or lesser extent 'fundamentalist' in character in that they recognize that theirs is the just rule, the correct avenue to truth. When the State and the dominant religion are in harmony with each other, friction is minimized, but in States determined to carry the secular, anti-religious approach to a position of dominance, or, in the case of minority religions struggling to survive in a State dominated by adherents of a majority group, conflict is always possible and frequently occurs. No such considerations militate against the international proscription of racial discrimination.

[27] See the analysis of Article 27 of the Covenant on Civil and Political Rights in the present work.

[28] *Supra*, ch. 20.

[29] See Draft Convention on the Elimination of All Forms of Religious Intolerance, in Brownlie, *Basic Documents on Human Rights*, 111.

[30] *Debates in GAOR*, 22nd Session, 3rd Committee, meetings 1486–1514.

[31] Neff (*supra*, n. 26), 577.

[32] Thus, for example, Article 1(3) of the Declaration on Religious Intolerance states that freedom to manifest religion or beliefs may be subject 'only to such limitations as are prescribed by law and are necessary to protect public safety, order, health or morals . . .'. This strikes the present author as a catch-all sentence, and is subject to what is said in the text, *infra*, about judging religion in terms of 'morals'.

In making the assertion that a policy of racial discrimination violates customary law, it may be that a more detailed assessment of the meaning of discrimination in customary law cannot be made with any degree of cogency. Writers who have commented on racial discrimination as customary law vary in their assessment of its content. Brownlie writes that 'there is well nigh universal acceptance of the principle of non-discrimination . . . in racial matters. The principle is, of course, to be applied in accordance with the concept of effective equality . . .'[33] (he cites the case of the Minority Schools in Albania).[34] McKean also considers that discrimination in international law requires 'a substantial and genuine equality in fact' and affirmative action.[35] Meron refers merely to the 'fundamental norm of the United Nations Charter—by now accepted into the corpus of customary international law—requiring respect for and observance of human rights and fundamental freedoms for all, without distinction as to race'.[36] In his review of the Namibia Advisory Opinion and its significance, Schwelb remarks that the Convention on Race is to 'a large extent'[37] declaratory of the Law of the Charter, but does not elaborate on this. It may be stated, in the light of the discussion of the customary law status of the norm of the Genocide Convention[38] that many norms in a particular treaty constitute only a binding promise of future conduct and do not have significance as declaring customary law. Apart from 'organizational' norms in a treaty, doubts may be expressed concerning the customary status of other rules of non-discrimination such as the obligation to outlaw organizations that incite racism. For example, a number of States have made specific reservations to, and interpretations of, Article 4 of the International Convention on the Elimination of All Forms of Racial Discrimination.[39] A typical example is provided by Italy:

(a) The positive measures, provided for in Article 4 of the Convention and specifically described in subparagraphs (a) and (b) of that Article, designed to eradicate all incitement to, or acts of, discrimination, are to be interpreted, as that Article provides, 'with due regard to the principles embodied in the Universal Declaration of Human Rights and the rights expressly set forth in Article 5 of the Convention. Consequently, the obligations deriving from the afore-mentioned Article 4 are not to jeopardize the right to freedom of opinion and expression and the right to peaceful assembly and association, which are laid down in Articles 19 and 20 of the Universal Declaration of Human Rights . . . .'[40]

The reservation of the United States of America (made upon signature, the

---

[33] Opinion on the Dene Indians, *In Re the Mackenzie Valley Pipeline Inquiry*, March 1976.
[34] PCIJ Ser. A/B No. 64.
[35] McKean, *Equality and Discrimination*, 288.
[36] Meron, *International Convention on the Elimination of Racial Discrimination*, 283.
[37] Schwelb, 'ICJ and Human Rights', 351.
[38] *Supra*, ch. 7.
[39] *Supra*, ch. 29, n. 59.
[40] Ibid. 75–6.

United States has not ratified the Convention) does not refer expressly to Article 4 of the Convention but clearly implies such a reference: 'The Constitution of the United States contains provisions for the protection of individual rights, such as the right of free speech, and nothing in the Convention shall be deemed to require or to authorize legislation or other action by the United States of America incompatible with the provisions of the Constitution of the United States. . .'[41] The rule in Article 4 is in all probability a rule of treaty rather than of customary law.

Bearing in mind the references to 'systematic' racial discrimination and the close connection in the case law between racial discrimination and apartheid, it may be that the basic proscription of racial discrimination in the customary law is of a rather general kind, directed to systems and practices of discrimination. The detailed forms of the elaboration of the anti-discrimination rule in treaties cannot, without more, be transposed into customary law. For example, affirmative action may, in the present author's view, certainly be permitted by customary law, but it is only doubtfully required by that law. Where a treaty deals with non-discrimination and equality, but without elaborating the meaning of these concepts, as do the United Nations Covenants on Human Rights, States have been reluctant to read in directions to engage in 'affirmation action'.[42] Analogically, it may be that customary law is also rather limited in this respect. Many States, it may be pointed out, offer more in their municipal law in terms of rules against discrimination than the basic normative requirements of customary law, but without necessarily being obliged to do so.[43]

From Customary Law to *Jus Cogens*?

Some authorities go much further than the tentative assertions in the present work, in favour of the claim that non-discrimination in international law is a rule of *jus cogens* rather than *jus dispositivum*. McKean argues that there are good reasons 'for accepting that the principles of equality and non-discrimination, in view of their nature as fundamental constituents of the international law of human rights, are part of the *jus cogens*'.[44] McKean reads the *Barcelona Traction Case* on obligations *erga omnes* to mean that 'basic human rights and racial discrimination in particular are placed in the

---

[41] ST/HR/5, 108. For similar criticisms of the Declaration on Race, see remarks in *GAOR*, 18th Session, Plenary Session, UN Doc A/PV.1281, by the delegates of Greece (para. 107), Belgium (para. 117), USA (para. 132), and Ireland (para. 202).

[42] *Supra*, ch. 29.

[43] The Capotorti Report stated, Add. 3, para. 78, that 'The constitutions or the laws of all the countries surveyed contain provisions which proclaim the principles of equality and non-discrimination'. See also McKean, Ch. XII.

[44] Ibid. 283.

same category as matters generally acknowledged to form part of *jus cogens*, that is, the outlawing of aggression and genocide . . .'.[45] This statement contrasts with the author's earlier, more tentative assertion that the principle of non-discrimination 'would be a strong candidate for inclusion under the heading [rules of *jus cogens*], if it is correct that the widely repeated condemnations of discrimination have ripened into a rule of customary international law'.[46] The author thus appears to take a qualitative leap from a tentative claim that non-discrimination is part of customary international law, to a confident claim that the rule is part of the *jus cogens*. McKean does not unequivocally claim that respect for human rights as such is part of *jus cogens*, though some are prepared to do so.[47] However, the fact that derogations are often permitted from rules of human rights is fatal to this argument, though it may not be fatal to the more limited claim that the rule of non-discrimination is part of *jus cogens*, since it is not uncommon in human rights treaties to include a restriction on measures taken by the State in derogation of treaty obligations, that is, the measures must not involve 'discrimination solely on the ground of race, colour, sex, language, religion or social origin' (Article 4 (1) of the UN Covenant on Civil and Political Rights, and, with the omission of 'solely', Article 27 (1) of the American Convention on Human Rights). The claim by McKean in favour of the rule of non-discrimination is supported by Professor Brownlie who argues that the 'least controversial' examples of *jus cogens* are provided by the prohibition of genocide, and discrimination on the basis of race, religion and sex.[48] Schwelb makes a similar claim for racial discrimination.[49]

At the Vienna Conference on the Law of Treaties a number of delegates favoured the idea of human rights as *jus cogens*. In his dissenting opinion in the *South-West Africa Cases (Second Phase)*, Judge Tanaka also gave expression to this view. Other delegates, as noted above, specifically referred to the prohibition of racial discrimination as part of *jus cogens*.[50] Not all the delegates at the Vienna Conference indicated views on a specific rule or rules as part of *jus cogens*, and while some delegates who were prepared to provide a list included in it the prohibition of racial discrimination, others omitted mention of this rule.

In a previous section of this work, dealing with genocide, some criteria for recognition of a rule of international law as *jus cogens* were referred to:[51] above all, there must be acceptance and recognition by the international community of States as a whole of the norm in question as one from which

---

[45] Ibid.

[46] Ibid. 279.

[47] Ibid. 280, n. 89.

[48] *Principles of Public International Law*, 513.

[49] 'Some Aspects of International Jus Cogens as Formulated by the International Law Commission', *AJIL*, 61 (1967), 946 at 956.

[50] *Supra*, ch. 7.

[51] *Supra*, ch. 7.

no derogation is permitted (Article 53 of the Vienna Convention on the Law of Treaties). Perhaps no absolutely mechanical test can be devised for proving such acceptance and recognition; though recognition would appear to be a logical and practical prerequisite. In this, there is a danger in attempting to transpose the urgent concerns of one group of States into a universal formula for a peremptory norm. No doubt, many ex-colonial States would assert the fundamental quality of the prohibition of at least racial discrimination. There is also a logical connection between the prohibition of genocide, a crime which is the most fundamental denial of human dignity and equality, and the prohibition of racial and religious discrimination, which lends weight to the latter prohibition. The 'architectural' or 'structural' quality of the prohibition of discrimination in the area of human rights has also been referred to. Further, the International Convention on the Elimination of All Forms of Racial Discrimination has been suggested as suitable for inclusion in an international criminal code.[52] Despite these claims, it is not the case that every rule of established *jus dispositivum* elevates itself automatically into the category of *jus cogens*. There is some, but not conclusive evidence that the rule of non-discrimination has achieved such status: it is, as it were, a case 'not proven'. While such a claim is made in the present work for genocide, discrimination, while related to genocide, is not the same as genocide: it is not, on any probable humanitarian scale, as qualitatively repugnant to the sense of justice as the extermination of racial groups. Even in the pernicious form of apartheid, States continue to express reservations as to whether this practice constitutes, for example, a crime against humanity in the same sense as the Nuremberg Principles. It may be, in fact, that there are very few rules of *jus cogens* in international law. Of the humanitarian rules canvassed in the present work, the prohibition of discrimination is probably the best candidate, but it would probably relate, in the *lex lata*, to cases where the denial of rights on a racial basis was so extreme as to contain within it aspects of the genocidal process.

[52] McKean, 279.

PART VI

Rights of Indigenous Peoples

38. Indigenous Peoples: An Introduction

Indigenous peoples are referred to at many points in the present work. Sections and chapters on the definition of minority,[1] State policies towards groups,[2] self-determination,[3] genocide,[4] the application of Article 27, including the cases under the Optional Protocol,[5] and the non-discrimination principle[6] have all considered questions relating to indigenous groups. There is clearly an overlap between the general case of minorities and the specific issue of indigenous groups. But indigenous peoples claim to be more than, or different to, minorities. Deschênes dismisses the case of indigenous peoples from his quest for a definition of 'minority' as a 'non-problem', citing a representative of the International Indian Treaty Council before the UN Working Group on Indigenous Populations: 'The ultimate goal of their colonizers would be achieved by referring to indigenous peoples as minorities'.[7] The Independent Commission on International Humanitarian Issues stated the matter thus:

Although there is overlap in the distinction between indigenous peoples and minorities, in general, indigenous refers to peoples affected by the past 500 years of colonialism. Therefore, minorities within the European continent itself—Basques, Catalans, Romany (Gypsies), migrant workers, and others such as the Kurds, are not included in the United Nations' working definition of indigenous populations[8] but rather are considered national minorities, even though the problems they face may be similar to those of the indigenous. On the other hand, the hunting and fishing peoples of the Arctic Circle . . . consider themselves and are accepted as indigenous.[9]

However, although many minorities may not satisfy the definition, if any, of indigenous, the converse is not the case. Most indigenous groups easily satisfy definitions of 'minority'; hence, *inter alia*, their regular appearance in proceedings relating to Article 27 of the Covenant on Civil and Political Rights. Whatever the exigencies of definition, the rules of international law

---

[1] *Supra*, chs. 1 and 16.   [2] *Supra*, ch. 1.
[3] *Supra*, chs. 1 and 24.   [4] *Supra*, chs. 5 ff.
[5] Recalling that the *Lovelace* and *Kitok Cases, supra*, ch. 23, both involve indigenous persons.
[6] *Supra*, Part V.
[7] Deschênes, 'Proposal Concerning a Definition of the Term "Minority" ', UN Doc E/CN. 4/Sub. 2/1985/31, paras. 24–38. The quotation is from UN Doc E/CN.4/L.1540. See also *infra*, ch. 40–1.
[8] *Infra*, ch. 41.
[9] *Indigenous Peoples: A Global Quest for Justice* (London and New Jersey: Zed Books, 1987), 8.

relating to human rights in general, minority rights, the protection of existence through the Genocide Convention, and the rule of non-discrimination apply to indigenous groups as a matter of logical and literal interpretation of texts. This is without prejudice to whatever further or special rights or institutions exist or may be developed to accommodate the interests of the groups.

In a broad sense, the history of indigenous peoples is a history of colonialism. The general issue of colonialism has been largely transformed through the emergence of a legal doctrine of self-determination, questioning its legitimacy and reducing its scope, though its long-term effects are likely to be profound.[10] The indigenous groups have been subjected to all the excesses associated with the colonial enterprise. The legal discourse on the indigenous has moved through consideration of the rights of infidels,[11] native sovereignty,[12] the doctrine of *terra nullius*,[13] 'Christian right',[14] the 'empty lands' doctrine,[15] the paternalistic doctrine of guardianship,[16] and all the incidents of the civilizing mission of the Powers. Indigenous groups entered the twentieth century with hardly a remnant of any former 'subject' status in international law.[17] Their treatment reflects, in a striking manner,

[10] Particularly in the sense that it has created States which are ethnic, religious, and linguistic conglomerates: *supra*, ch. 1.

[11] The history of the relations between European Powers and indigenous peoples is chronicled by Lindley, *The Acquisition and Government of Backward Territory in International Law* (New York: Negro Universities Press, 1969); Snow, *The Question of Aborigines in the Law and Practice of Nations* (Northbrook, Illinois: Metro Books, 1972). See also Merrills, 'Francisco de Vitoria and the Spanish Conquest of the New World', *Irish Jurist*, 3 (1968), 187. Chief protagonists in the sixteenth century legal argument on the status of the Indians of the New World were: Vitoria, *De Indis et de Jure Belli Relectiones*, English transl. (Washington: Nys, 1917), Spanish transl. *Relecciones de Indios y del derecho de la Guerra* (Madrid: Espasa Calpe, 1928); Sepulveda, *Democrates Secundus*, Spanish transl. *Democrates segundo o de las Justas Causas de la Guerra Contro los Indios* (Madrid: CSIC, 1951); Las Casas, *Brevisima Relación de la Destrucción de los Indios* (Madrid: Real Academia Española, 1943–58). See also Midgley, *The Natural Law Tradition and the Theory of International Relations* (London: Paul Elek, 1975), Alexandrowicz, 'Paulus Vladimiri and the Development of the Doctrine of Co-Existence of Christian and Non-Christian Countries', *BYIL*, 34 (1963), 441.

[12] Lindley, ibid.; Bennett, *Aboriginal Rights in International Law*, (Royal Anthropological Institute, London, 1978).

[13] Lindley remains the outstanding work on the operation of the *terra nullius* doctrine in State practice. Also Alexandrowicz, *An Introduction to the History of the Law of Nations in the East Indies* (Oxford: OUP, 1967); Berman, 'The Concept of Aboriginal Rights in the Early Legal History of the United States', *Buffalo Law Review*, 27 (1978), 637; Evatt, 'The Acquisition of Territory in Australia and New Zealand', in Alexandrowicz (ed.), *Grotian Society Papers* (The Hague: M. Nijhoff, 1970). For a modern statement, consult the Advisory Opinion of the International Court of Justice in the *Western Sahara Case*, *ICJ Reports 1975*, 12; Shaw, 'The Western Sahara Case', *BYIL*, 49 (1978), 119.

[14] Lindley (*supra*, n. 11), ch. 3.

[15] See for example Fiore, *Nouveau Droit International Public*, Vol. i, 379–80 (Paris: Durand et Lauriel, 1868); also the references to Vattel, Phillimore, and Ortolan in Lindley (*supra*, n. 11), 17.

[16] Snow (*supra*, n. 11); Bennett (*supra*, n. 12). Note Article 23(b) of the Covenant of the League providing, *inter alia*, that Member States should secure the just treatment of the native inhabitants of territories under their control.

[17] The *Cayuga Indians Case*, *RIAA*, 6 (1926), 173; the *Island of Palmas Case*, *RIAA*, 2

the racist and hierarchical assumptions about the lack of value in particular 'undeveloped' or 'primitive' cultures and the attempt to extinguish or 'modernize' them.[18] The present section analyses the major text of international law dealing specifically with indigenous groups: the International Labour Organization's Convention No. 107 of 1957 concerning the Protection and Integration of Indigenous and other Tribal and Semi-Tribal Populations in Independent Countries. The Convention, which expresses what may be regarded as anachronistic assumptions about the integration and modernization of indigenous peoples, has been subjected to vigorous criticism by indigenous organizations, and is to be revised: however, the speed of ratifications of any revised document is difficult to assess, and some Governments have expressed satisfaction with the instrument as it stands.[19] The Convention is then measured against indigenous claims, and the resoponse of international law is assessed. Emphasis is placed on the issues informing the present work: basic group protection, individual and collective rights, culture and identity, with special reference in this case to land issues and self-determination. The proposals to rectify the law on indigenous peoples reflect developments in thinking about minorities and collective rights generally. The two issues cannot be finally separated, despite the tendency of the international community to develop separate bodies of law.

(1928), 831; the *Eastern Greenland Case, PCIJ Rep. Ser. A/B No. 53* (1933). Treaties between indigenous groups and colonizing States led to extinction of international personality as much as any doctrine of *terra nullius*, which may, in some respects, have been an academic conceit rather than a doctrine operating in the diplomatic sphere. The UN Sub-Commission on the Prevention of Discrimination and Protection of Minorities proposed that a study be undertaken on 'Treaties, Agreements and Other Constructive Arrangements between States and Indigenous Populations'. The proposal was modified by the Commission on Human Rights to an 'outline' of a study, with a warning not to touch the inviolability of State sovereignty and territorial integrity. The 1988 session of the Sub-Commission endorsed the 'outline': *The Review of the International Commission of Jurists*, No. 40 (June 1988) and 41 (December 1988).

[18] Falk, 'The Rights of Peoples (In Particular Indigenous Peoples)', in Crawford (ed.), *The Rights of Peoples*, 17. A brief account of racism as (recent) doctrine is given by Vincent in Bull and Watson (eds.), *The Expansion of International Society* (Oxford: OUP, 1984), 239.

[19] Chile, General Observations, in International Labour Conference 75th Session 1988, Report VI(2), *Partial Revision of the Indigenous and Tribal Populations Convention, 1957 (No. 107)*, 4.

39. The ILO and Indigenous Populations: The Convention and Recommendation of 1957

The International Labour Organization has exhibited an interest in the condition of indigenous populations since its inception. In a description of its work submitted to the Special Rapporteur of the UN Sub-Commission on Prevention of Discrimination and Protection of Minorities on the question of discrimination against indigenous populations,[1] it stated that as early as 1921, the International Labour Office had carried out studies on indigenous workers in independent countries. Following the establishment of a Committee of Experts on Native Labour in 1926, a series of conventions and recommendations were adopted by the ILO Conference at its fourteenth, twentieth, and twenty-fifth sessions. These are: the Forced Labour Convention, 1930;[2] the Forced Labour (Indirect Compulsion) Recommendation, 1930;[3] the Forced Labour (Regulation) Recommendation, 1930;[4] the Recruiting of Indigenous Workers Convention, 1936;[5] the Elimination of Recruiting Recommendation, 1936;[6] the Contracts of Employment (Indigenous Workers) Convention, 1939;[7] the Penal Sanctions (Indigenous Workers) Convention, 1939;[8] the Contracts of Employment (Indigenous Workers) Recommendation, 1939;[9] and the Labour Inspectorates (Indigenous Workers) Recommendation, 1939.[10] The recurring phrase 'Indigenous Workers' is defined in Article 2(b) of the Recruiting of Indigenous Workers Convention, 1936 as 'workers belonging to or assimilated to the dependent indigenous population of the home territories of Members of the Organization'. This definition is also used in the Contracts of Employment (Indigenous Workers) Convention, 1939 (Article 1(a)), and the Penal Sanctions (Indigenous Workers) Convention, 1939 (Article 1.1). The conventions there apply not only to indigenous workers in Non-Self-Governing Territories, but also to independent countries.

Following prompting from Regional Conferences of American States Members of the ILO, the Governing Body of the ILO decided in 1945 to set up a Committee of Experts on social policy in non-metropolitan ter-

---

[1] UN Doc E/CN.4/Sub.2/1982/Add.1 (May 1982), para. 34 (Martinez-Cobo Report).
[2] No. 29, *Conventions and Recommendations Adopted by the International Labour Conference 1919–66* (Geneva: ILO, 1966), 155.
[3] No. 35, ibid. 164. [4] No. 36, ibid. 166.
[5] No. 50, ibid. 301. [6] No. 46, ibid. 309.
[7] No. 64, ibid. 421. [8] No. 65, ibid. 430.
[9] No. 15, ibid. 433. [10] No. 59, ibid. 434.

ritories.[11] Subsequently, the ILO established a Committee of Experts on Indigenous Labour on the social problems of the indigenous populations of the world, which gave special prominence to Latin American countries. The Fourth Conference of American States Members of the ILO supplied the Committee of Experts on Indigenous Labour with many of the principal themes in the field of aboriginal protection, including the principles of equality of rights and opportunities without distinction of race or nationality.[12] The Committee adopted resolutions inspired by the idea of extending the legislation of States to all sections of its population, including the aboriginals, who had hitherto been excluded from its scope.[13] Resolutions of the Committee stressed certain desiderata for aboriginal peoples in terms of general education, vocational training, social security, protection of handcrafts, etc. The work of the ILO was animated by the conviction, expressed at the Fourth Conference of American States Members, that the problems affecting aboriginal populations, and the measures required to solve them, were essentially social and economic in character.[14]

In one of its resolutions, the Experts suggested that the International Labour Office should prepare a major survey of the conditions of aboriginal populations throughout the world. The work was published in 1953 under the title of Indigenous Peoples: Living and Working Conditions of Aboriginal Populations in Independent Countries.[15] A proposed complementary book on nomadic and semi-nomadic populations was not published.[16] The study dealt with the definition of 'indigenous' in the legal and administrative practice of Latin American States, the United States, Canada, Asia, and Australasia, as well as the theoretical aspects of the problem. The study's authors decided, following their definitional survey, to 'lay aside the complex problem of *a priori* definitions'[17] of 'indigenous' and give an empirical 'guide to the identification of indigenous groups in independent countries'[18] as follows:

Indigenous persons are descendants of the aboriginal population living in a given country at the time of settlement or conquest (or of successive waves of conquest) by some of the ancestors of the non-indigenous groups in whose hand political and economic power at present lies. In general these descendants tend to live more in conformity with the social, economic and cultural institutions which existed before colonisation or conquest . . . than with the culture of the nation to which they

[11] ILO, *Minutes of 95th Session of Governing Body*, 113, 114, 208, 209; *94th Session*, 109, 110.

[12] Martinez-Cobo (*supra*, n. 1), paras. 45 ff.

[13] ILO, *Minutes of 114th Session of Governing Body*, Appendix V, 85; 'First Session of the ILO Committee of Experts on Indigenous Labour', LXIV *International Labour Review*, No. 1 (1951).

[14] Martinez-Cobo (*supra*, n. 1), para. 45.

[15] *Studies and Reports*, New Series No. 35 (Geneva: International Labour Office, 1953).

[16] Martinez-Cobo (*supra*, n. 1), para. 63.

[17] ILO Study (*supra*, n. 15), 25.

[18] Ibid. 25–6.

belong; they do not fully share in the national economy and culture owing to barriers of language, customs, creed, prejudice, and often to an out-of-date and unjust system of worker–employer relationship and other social and political factors. When their full participation in national life is not hindered by one of the obstacles mentioned above, it is restricted by historical influences producing in them an attitude of overriding loyalty to their position as members of a given tribe; in the case of marginal indigenous persons or groups, the problem arises from the fact that they are not accepted into, or cannot or will not participate in, the organised life of either the nation or the indigenous society.[19]

The influence of this empirical identification of indigenous groups on subsequent international standards is clear. The International Labour Organization at its fortieth session in 1957 adopted two texts on indigenous and other tribal and semi-tribal populations in independent countries which became ILO Convention No. 107, concerning the Protection and Integration of Indigenous and other Tribal and Semi-Tribal Populations in Independent Countries,[20] and Recommendation No. 104[21] which bears the same title as the Convention. The Convention entered into force in June 1959 and at the time of writing has been ratified by twenty-seven States.[22]

The Convention[23] is structured as follows: the Preamble is followed by

[19] ILO Study, 25–6.

[20] Conventions and Recommendations 1919–66 (*supra*, n. 2), 901; *UNTS*, 328, 247 (1957).

[21] Ibid. 909. Certain other Conventions have been adopted, which have a particular effect on indigenous and tribal peoples, including the Plantations Convention 1958 (No. 110), the Discrimination (Employment and Occupation) Convention 1958 (No. 111), the Employment Policy Convention 1964 (No. 122) and the Rural Workers' Organisations Convention 1975 (No. 141). Convention No. 107 and Recommendation No. 104 today remain the only international instruments in force for the protection of indigenous and tribal populations. The revision process in relation to Convention 107 is considered, *infra*, ch. 41.

[22] List of States Parties in Appendix 8 to the present work. The Convention has been ratified by 27 States, 14 of them in Latin America and the Caribbean. The majority of these ratifications were registered in the 1950s and 1960s. The only ratifications since 1970 are Panama (1971), Bangladesh (1972), Angola (1976), Guinea-Bissau (1977) (the last three confirming obligations undertaken on their behalf before independence), and Iraq in 1986. According to the ILO Report, 75th Session 1988, Report VI(1), *Partial Revision of the Indigenous and Tribal Population Convention, 1957 (No. 107)* 5: 'The virtual absence of ratifications in recent years can be traced to the reservations of governments and others with regard to the instrument's basic orientation'. The Report comments further (ibid. 18): 'In 1956 and 1957 . . . it was felt that integration into the dominant national society offered the best chance for these groups to become a part of the development process . . . it [integration] has become a destructive concept, owing in part to the way it has been interpreted by Governments . . . The implications of this principle have also discouraged indigenous and tribal organisations from taking full advantage of the strong protection offered by other aspects of the instrument, as they have fostered a certain distrust of the instrument.' Non-party States with significant indigenous populations include Australia, Canada, China, New Zealand, Norway, and the United States of America. Other aspects of ILO activity relevant to indigenous peoples, including programmes of technical assistance, rural development, and studies of the effects of development programmes on indigenous groups are outlined in this Report, 5–7.

[23] The main source of information on the implementation of ILO Conventions is the system of reports instituted in accordance with Article 22 of the ILO Constitution: 'Each of the Members agrees to make an annual report to the International Labour Office on the measures which it has taken to give effect to the provisions of Conventions to which it is a party. These

Part I which describes its general policy; Part II deals with various rights relating to land; Part III with 'Recruitment and Conditions of Employment'; Part IV with 'Vocational Training, Handicrafts and Rural Industries'; Part V with 'Social Security and Health'; Part VI with 'Education and Means of Communication'; Part VII with 'Administration'; Part VIII with residual 'General Provisions'. The main focus of this chapter will be on the general provisions in the Convention, and the sections on 'Education and Means of Communication'; this will keep the discussion broadly in step with discussions elsewhere in this work. However, in view of the importance accorded to land rights in contemporary discussions of the rights of indigenous groups, the Convention provisions on land must also be discussed. Recommendation 104 displays a similar structure, though, *inter alia*, 'Education' is featured separately from 'Languages and Other Means of Communication', and there is a separate section on 'Tribal Groups in Frontier Zones'.

The reasons for the Convention are set out in the Preamble; it is premised on the consideration that 'all human beings have the right to pursue both their material well-being and their spiritual development in conditions of freedom and dignity, of economic security and equal opportunity . . .'.[24] The concern of the Convention is not only humanitarian with respect to the populations it deals with, it is also 'in the interests of the countries concerned'[25] to improve the living and working conditions of the population. The Preamble refers to one of the great themes of the Convention, the 'integration' of the populations into the national community: it relates to indigenous and other tribal and semi-tribal populations which are 'not yet integrated'[26] into the community and consequently do not benefit from 'the rights and advantages enjoyed by other elements of the population'.[27] The major themes are thus 'the protection of the populations concerned, their progressive integration into their respective national communities and the improvement of their living and working conditions'.[28] The Preamble to

reports shall be made in such form and shall contain such particulars as the Governing Body may request.' See generally, *Report Form on the Indigenous and Tribal Populations Convention 1957* (No. 107) (Geneva: International Labour Office, 1973). The Form appends the text of Recommendation 104, but provides that the report on the Convention does not have to include information on the implementation of the recommendation as such; such information may, however, be offered if the State concerned deems it useful and the information illuminates issues on the Convention. Reports are scrutinized by the Committee of Experts on the Application of Conventions and Recommendations. For a detailed account of the procedures adopted by the ILO Committee of Experts, the Conference Committee, and for 'contentious' representations and complaints, see International Labour Office, *Manual of Procedures Relating to International Labour Conventions and Recommendations*, Doc. D.31.1965 (rev. 1980) (Geneva:, 1980). See also Wolf, 'Human Rights and The International Labour Organization', in Meron (ed.), *Human Rights in International Law: Legal and Policy Issues*, 273; also Samson, 'The Changing Pattern of ILO Supervision', *International Labour Review*, 118, 569; Bennett, *Aboriginal Rights*, 43 ff.

[24] Para. 5.   [25] Para. 7.   [26] Para. 6.
[27] Ibid.   [28] Para. 8.

Recommendation 104 also refers to 'protection and integration' of the populations.[29]

Article I(1) of the Convention provides in its first paragraph the basic definition of the groups of which it applies:

(a) members of tribal or semi-tribal populations in independent countries whose social and economic conditions are at a less advanced stage than the stage reached by the other sections of the national community, and whose status is regulated wholly or partially by their own customs or traditions or by special laws or regulations;

(b) members of tribal or semi-tribal populations in independent countries which are regarded as indigenous on account of their descent from the populations which inhabited the country, or a geographical region to which the country belongs, at the time of conquest or colonisation and which, irrespective of their legal status, live more in conformity with the social, economic and cultural institutions of that time than with the institutions of the nation to which they belong.

Paragraph 2 of the article defines the term 'semi-tribal' as including 'groups and persons who, although they are in the process of losing their tribal characteristics, are not yet integrated into the national community'. This rather long and complex definition is an attempt to bring some degree of order into what had been a matter of confusion, certainly as regards national laws defining indigenous populations. The ILO Study of 1953 recorded the complaint of the Director of the Inter-American Indian Institute about 'the confused and illogical classification, quantitative as well as qualitative, encountered in almost all the American countries regarding the aboriginal populations which prevents proper definition of the persons to whom indigenous policy should apply'.[30] The Study then recorded a number of these varying definitions in Latin America and elsewhere, based, *inter alia*, on descent, race, culture, language, tribal or clan organizations, original habitation in the country concerned, residence in jungle, forest or other remote areas, inheritance of certain types of land grants dating from early colonial times, primitive way of life, nomadism, or an existence based primarily on hunting and gathering, and animistic religion. The study records a bewildering list of such criteria,[31] used singly or in combinations. It records, for example, six different definitions used by Mexico between 1895 and 1940 for population classification, and some extraordinary suggestions, *de lege ferenda*, made by various Indian States to improve the basic definition of the Scheduled Tribes in Article 342 of the Indian Constitution, including, from the Government of Vindhya Pradesh, 'dark skin and flat noses, preference for fruits, roots and animal flesh rather than food grains, the use of bark and leaves of trees as clothes on ceremonial occasions, nomadism, witch-doctoring, and the worship of ghosts and spirits'[32]

---

[29] Para. 3.
[31] Ibid. 13–14.
[30] *Supra*, n. 15, 8.
[32] Ibid. 13. On Mexico, see *infra*, n. 50.

Article I(1)(a) of the Convention relates primarily to Asia and Africa where, generally speaking, the struggles of the more 'advanced' elements in the population produced independence. On the other hand, Article I(1)(b) describes better the situation in Latin America where independence was achieved through the efforts of European colonists and their descendants, rather than by the indigenous population itself. One author summarizes the Convention's definition as being in terms of the populations' 'living conditions rather than by reference to their racial or cultural characteristics . . . indigenous peoples, it is said, require assistance not because they are indigenous but because their standards of living are inferior to those of other social groups'.[33] However, it is not the case that the definition neglects the specific differentiae of the populations—the references to 'tribal' and 'semi-tribal' are plain and set the groups apart from the population at large, as well as their 'customs and traditions' or 'social, economic and cultural institutions'. 'Inferiority is not mentioned as such in the definition, though the phrase 'less advanced' in section I(1)(a) gives an unfortunate impression that the cultures described therein require advancement and are not valued in their own terms. The definition has other noteworthy features: Articles I(1)(a) and I(1)(b) refer to 'members' of tribal or semi-tribal populations rather than the populations themselves, reflecting the familiar tension between collective and individual rights.[34] The Indigenous and Tribal Populations Convention is not particularly consistent on this point; thus, while the term 'tribal' is not defined, the term 'semi-tribal' is defined in Article I(2) as including 'groups and persons who, although they are in the process of losing their tribal characteristics, are not yet integrated into the national community'. The substantive articles of the Convention also display variation of terminology, addressing 'groups' and 'individuals' with equal facility.[35] A further point is that, despite the title of the Convention, 'Indigenous and Tribal', the term 'indigenous' occurs only in Article I(1)(b) in the definition and not in Article I(1)(a). Thus, provided a group can be described as 'tribal' or 'semi-tribal', it is not *ex facie* ruled out from contemplation by the Convention in virtue of the fact that it is an immigrant community or a nomadic one with a non-historic presence in a particular State. This interpretation does not necessarily provoke the antipathy of the 'countries of immigration' to special rights for immigrant groups—what they fear is the disruptive effect of the arrival of new 'advanced' elements into the populations claiming to set themselves apart from the mainstream of the host culture, rather than any demands that might be made in terms of the ILO Convention by such as the Bush Negroes of African descent who established tribal groups in Colombia and Surinam after the abolition of

---

[33] Bennett (*supra*, n. 23), 17.
[34] See discussion in the present work relating to Article 27 of the Covenant on Civil and Political Rights.
[35] *Infra*, text following n. 114.

slavery.[36] None the less, a suggested redraft of Article 1 by the United Kingdom, to the effect that 'the term "indigenous peoples" includes immigrants whose social and economic conditions are comparable to . . .' indigenous groups which have retained their separate identities and in consequence lag behind the rest of the population, was not incorporated into the final version.[37]

The looseness of the Convention formula has encouraged States to adopt their own approaches to its meaning. Brazil[38] considered that it applied 'only to the forest-dwelling' populations. It formulated replies to suggested drafts of the Convention 'on the explicit understanding that' its replies related only to these groups.[39] Bolivia has taken a similar view. The Committee has addressed questions to the Bolivian Government based on the view that the indigenous populations of Bolivia are divided into two groups, those living in the Sierra regions which form the more settled rural portion of those populations, and the forest dwelling populations.[40] The Committee took the view that the Convention did not apply to the settled rural populations 'to the same extent or in all the same ways as it does to the forest-dwelling indigenous populations . . . [but] . . . those [rural] populations are . . . still covered by the Convention'.[41]

El Salvador took the denial one step further by claiming that it had no relevant populations in its territory to whom the Convention might apply.[42] The genuineness of this claim may be tested by reference to recently compiled statistics designed to assist the Special Rapporteur for the UN Sub-Commission on Prevention of Discrimination and Protection of Minorities, M. Martinez-Cobo, in the preparation of his study on 'The Problem of Discrimination against Indigenous Populations'.[43] The Special Rapporteur, in explaining the statistics, noted that 'an attempt has been made to present proven statistics derived either from censuses officially conducted and recorded in the countries under consideration, or from official estimates and calculations, or from unofficial estimates and calculations which can be regarded as reliable'.[44] For El Salvador, with an estimated total population

---

[36] Bennett, *Aboriginal Rights*, 18. It may also be noted that in South and South-East Asia, the term 'indigenous' is not generally used; rather, States employ the term 'tribal'.

[37] ILO, *International Labour Conference, 40th Session (1957), Report VI (2)*, Protection and Integration of Indigenous and other Tribal and Semi-Tribal Populations in Independent Countries, 10.

[38] Martinez-Cobo, UN Doc E/CN.4/Sub.2/1982/2/Add.6, para. 272.

[39] *International Labour Conference, 39th Session (1956), Report VIII (2)*, Living and Working Conditions of Indigenous Populations in Independent Countries, 9–10.

[40] ILO Committee of Experts on the Implementation of Conventions and Recommendations, *Report to the International Labour Conference 1981*, 84 ff.

[41] Committee of Experts, *Report*, 1983, 198. See also Partial Revision, (*supra*, n. 22), ch. III.

[42] ILO Summary of Reports of Ratified Conventions, Report III (1), International Labour Conference, 45th Session (1961), 131; ibid., 53rd Session (1969), 196; Swepston, 'The Indian in Latin America:Approaches to Administration, Integration and Protection', *Buffalo Law Review*, 27 (1978), 715.

[43] UN Doc E/CN.4/Sub.2/476, Add. 1.　　　　[44] Ibid., para. 3.

of over four million people in 1975, some 400,000 were unofficially estimated to come within the indigenous category, though the latter figure is reduced according to a study in 1978.[45] Over half the population of Bolivia is classified as indigenous according to the 1978 Study (59.2% of the population).[46] Malawi[47] has taken a similar view to that of El Salvador: both countries are parties to the Convention.[48] Other countries, however, have taken a more generous view of the applicability of the Convention to their indigenous groups.[49] Peru has regarded the Convention as applicable to almost half of its population,[50] and Mexico also adopts a broad view.[51]

The definition in ILO 107 overlaps considerably with definitions of 'minority' advanced with particular reference to Article 27 of the Covenant on Civil and Political Rights.[52] There is not, of course, a complete identity between the definition of minority advanced by Special Rapporteur Capotorti and the ILO Convention definition. Martinez-Cobo advanced a 'working definition' which was closer to the Capotorti formula:

Indigenous populations are composed of the existing descendants of the peoples who inhabited the present territory of a country wholly or partially at the time when persons of a different culture or ethnic origin arrived there from other parts of the world, overcame them and, by conquest, settlement or other means reduced them to a non-dominant or colonial condition; who today live more in conformity with their particular social, economic and cultural customs and traditions than with the institutions of the country of which they now form part, under a State structure which incorporates mainly the national, social and cultural characteristics of other sections of the populations which are predominant.[53]

[45] Ibid. 5–6. The first estimate is an unofficial estimate of 1975; the revised figure is provided in *XXXIX America Indigena*, No. 2 (1979), 217.

[46] *XXXIX America Indigena*, ibid.

[47] Summary of reports, (*supra*, n. 42), International Labour Conference, 42nd Session (1958), 201. Guinea-Bissau, another Party to ILO 107, is listed among States declaring that the revision of this Convention is of no concern, and/or that it had no indigenous and tribal populations within the meaning of the text: International Labour Conference, 75th Session 1988, Report VI(2), *Partial Revision of the Indigenous and Tribal Populations Convention, 1957 (No. 107)*, 3.

[48] Also Haiti, *Report to the ILO* (1969).

[49] India, for example, regards the Convention as applicable to all its tribal peoples, numbering some 38 millions according to a census of 1971: cited by Martinez-Cobo, UN Doc E/CN.4/Sub.2/476/Add.1, 5–6; Bennett, (*supra*, n. 23), 17.

[50] Bennett, ibid.; Martinez-Cobo, ibid., 5–6. However, one commentator notes that 'even though Mexico has a government policy designed to improve the situation of Indian communities (called *indigenismo* in the Latin American countries), there exists no legal definition of Indians, and there is no statistical definition either. This has led some observers to speak of "statistical ethnocide" of Indians, that is, the systematic under-enumeration of Indians in the national censuses': Stavenhagen, 'Indigenous Peoples, The State and The UN System: Claims, Issues and Proposals', *The Thatched Patio*, vol. 2, no. 3 (May 1989), 1.

[51] Martinez-Cobo, ibid.

[52] *Supra*, chs. 1 and 16.

[53] Martinez-Cobo, UN Doc E/CN.4/Sub.2/L.556. Isolated and marginal groups were also to be included in the definition of 'indigenous': 'Although they have not suffered conquest or colonisation, isolated or marginal groups exisating in a country should also be regarded as covered by the notion of "indigenous populations" for the following reasons: (a) they are

In particular, the reference to 'non-dominant' elements in the population recalls Capotorti. The reference to a 'colonial condition' is an echo of the vocabulary of self-determination; it suggests the relevance of the modern norms of self-determination to indigenous peoples as was once advanced in the 'Belgian Thesis',[54] though the relevance of self-determination to indigenous peoples is controversial.[55] There is no reference to any numerical requirement like that in the Capotorti definition, stating a minority is numerically inferior to the rest of the State's population. In theory, therefore, an indigenous group could constitute a majority in the State although this is not normally the case.[56] In most cases, an indigenous group would be entitled to two 'sets' of rights, one as indigenous group, the other as minority.

The Martinez-Cobo definition also dispensed with any reference to the populations being at a 'less advanced stage' of development than the newcomers; the effect is to invest the 'old' and the 'new' cultures with parity of esteem. A corollary of any ultimate international instrument which took this definition as its focus, would be to ease the pressure towards integration or assimilation; if the cultures of humankind form a horizontal pattern of equality rather than a vertical pattern of 'superiority' and 'inferiority', why should it be considered valuable to ensure the merging of one in another except in terms of the choice of the people concerned opting for cultural change? M. Martinez-Cobo later produced a 'definition of indigenous populations from the international point of view'.[57] The suggested principles 'are for use as a point of departure and for criticism and modification in the approach to a more precise draft definition of the concept of indigenous populations'. Thus:

Indigenous communities, peoples and nations are those which, having a historical continuity with pre-invasion and pre-colonial societies that developed on their territories, consider themselves distinct from other sectors of the societies now prevailing in those territories, or parts of them. They form at present non-dominant sectors of society and are determined to preserve, develop and transmit to future generations their ancestral territories, and their ethnic identity, as the basis of their continued existence as peoples, in accordance with their own cultural patterns, social institutions and legal systems.

descendants of groups which were in the territory of the country at the time when other groups of different cultures or ethnic origins arrived there; (*b*) precisely because of their isolation from other segments of the country's population they have almost preserved intact the customs and traditions of their ancestors which are similar to those characterised as indigenous; (*c*) they are, if only formally, placed under a State structure which incorporates national, social and cultural characteristics alien to their own': UN Doc E/CN.4/Sub.2/1983/21, Add. 8, para. 379.

[54] *Supra*, ch. 1.

[55] The term 'peoples' in its application to indigenous groups in the revision process of ILO 107 and elsewhere is discussed *infra*, ch. 41.

[56] Martinez-Cobo, UN Doc E/CN.4/Sub.2/476, Add. 1, 5–6: of 37 States listed in the table of indigenous populations, only Bolivia and Guatemala were estimated to have indigenous groups representing a majority in the State, 59.20%, and 59.70%, respectively.

[57] UN Doc E/CN.4/Sub.2/1982/2/Add.6, para. 1.

The historical continuity referred to in the definition may consist of any of the following factors: occupation of ancestral lands, common ancestry with the original occupants of the lands, distinctive cultural forms, language, and residence in certain regions. The above refers essentially to the group and is complemented by a reference to individuals: 'On an individual basis, an indigenous person is one who belongs to those indigenous populations through self-identification as indigenous . . . and is recognised and accepted by those populations as one of its members'.[58]

Article 2: Protection and Integration

The themes identified in the Preamble, protection and integration, are elaborated in Article 2. Article 2(1) declares that governments have the primary responsibility for developing co-ordinated and systematic action for the protection of the populations concerned and their progressive integration into the life of their respective countries. Such action, according to Article 2(2), shall include measures for enabling the populations 'to benefit on an equal footing from the rights and opportunities which national laws or regulations grant to the other elements of the population', and for promoting their social, economic, and cultural development, and raising their standard of living. Article 2(2) also attempts to distinguish between objectives of governments: State measures are to aim at 'creating possibilities of national integration to the exclusion of measures tending towards the *artificial assimilation* of those populations'. There is, therefore, a distinction between 'integration' and 'assimilation'; however, assimilation is not an undesirable objective, only 'artificial' assimilation is regarded as improper. The objective of State action in general is 'the fostering of individual dignity' and 'the advancement of individual usefulness and initiative' (Article 2(3)). Article 2(4) provides another element of protection: 'Recourse to force or coercion as a means of promoting the integration of these populations into the national community shall be excluded'.

A 'special measures' clause similar in intention to such clauses in treaties against discrimination[59] is provided by Article 3. Like the anti-discrimination articles in general, the measures envisaged are temporary. In the first place they are premised on the condition that 'the social, economic and

---

[58] UN Doc E/CN.4/Sub.2/1983/21/Add.8, para. 366. The definition is at paras. 379–81. For the revised ILO definition, see *infra*, ch. 41 (*inter alios*, self-definition as indigenous is included in the text). The UN Working Group on Indigenous Populations has discussed the question of definition. For all practical purposes, it has deferred the question and uses the definition and criteria set out by Martinez-Cobo. The Draft Universal Declaration on Indigenous Rights (*infra*, ch. 41) has not, thus far, essayed a definition.

[59] *Supra*, 29 ff. Bolivia (ILO Report, (*supra*, n. 47), 24) has objected to the revision of Article 3, which 'would result in a paternalistic approach, since "special measures" would have a permanent character'.

cultural conditions of the populations concerned prevent them from enjoying the benefit of the general laws of the country to which they belong' (Article 3(1)). The special measures shall be adopted to protect the 'institutions, persons, property and labour' of the indigenous groups. However, the special measures shall not be used 'as a means of creating or prolonging a state of segregation' (Article 3(2)), and will be continued only as long as there is a need for them.

Article 4 sets further limits to the integration process by providing that, in applying the convention, 'due account' is to be taken by the States Parties of the 'cultural and religious values and . . . forms of social control' existing among the populations, and of the nature of the problems facing groups and individuals who undergo social and economic change. Due account is also to be taken of the danger of disrupting 'the values and institutions' of indigenous groups 'unless they can be replaced by appropriate substitutes which the groups concerned are willing to accept'. Article 5 obliges governments, in relation both to the integration and to the protection aspects of the Convention, to seek the collaboration of the populations and their representatives and to 'stimulate by all possible means the development among these populations of civil liberties and of participation in elective institutions'.

Some further, if qualified, recognition of indigenous institutions and values is provided by subsequent articles. Article 7(1) requires that in defining the rights and duties of indigenous groups, 'regard shall be had to their customary laws'. Article 7(2), however, constitutes a severe obstacle to the retention of indigenous institutions and is phrased in such a manner as to indicate that indigenous institutions are not valued in their own terms: indigenous populations 'shall be allowed to retain their own customs and institutions where these are not incompatible with the national legal system or the objectives of integration programmes'. Article 8 requires that the methods of social control practised by indigenous groups 'shall be used as far as possible' to deal with offences committed by members of those populations, but that where this is not feasible, the customs of the populations in penal matters are to be borne in mind by public authorities and the courts. But these concessions are qualified by Article 8 in that both are limited by the criterion of consistency with 'the interests of the national community and with the national legal system'.

Comment: Protection and Integration

Bennett, in commenting on the Convention finds a 'duty to integrate'[60] and a 'duty to protect'. He regards 'protection' and 'integration' as complementary:

---

[60] Bennett, *Aboriginal Rights*, 18 ff.

On the one hand, the effective integration of indigenous peoples is impossible unless their social institutions, persons, property and labour are sheltered from the destructive consequences of unregulated contact with the non-indigenous society . . . On the other hand, runs the argument, in the long term tribes can only secure themselves against exploitation and oppression by integrating themselves into the national society; too strong a dependence on government protection will frustrate integration.[61]

In his view of the Convention, 'Integration . . . is the primary goal to which protective policies are to be subordinated.'[62] Capotorti[63] takes a similar view: the main purpose of the Convention is to promote the integration of indigenous groups into the national community to enable them to benefit fully from the rights enjoyed by other elements of the population;[64] the safeguarding of the ethnic, social, and cultural identity of protected groups is 'a second priority'. His summary is that 'the classic features of the protection of minorities (respect for the religion, language, institutions and values of the protected groups) are all touched upon in Convention 107 but they are *qualified by the main objectives of integration and development.'*[65]

The term 'integration', though used extensively in Convention 107, is not defined. Portugal suggested a definition of integration in the preparatory stages of the Convention: '. . . integration means the progressive incorporation of indigenous populations into the national community through measures aimed at guaranteeing for them the same rights and obligations as are established by law for the whole of the community.'[66] The International Labour Office decided against any definition because it would 'necessarily be restrictive and therefore might not cover all the many aspects of the problem'.[67] It was considered that the meaning was sufficiently clear from the text as a whole. The term is used six times in the section on general policy in the Convention, Articles 1–10 inclusive. In their comments on various stages of the text, many governments set out interpretations. Mexico distinguished between integration and segregation,[68]—which it related to the application in a permanent sense of special measures. All States replying to the International Labour Office stressed the transitional nature of special measures; Pakistan proposed a time limit of twenty years for special measures as a reference point which could be shortened or lengthened—this was to 'avoid perpetuation of a state of segregation'.[69]

---

[61] Ibid. 18.
[62] Ibid.
[63] Capotorti, 'The Protection of Minorities under Multilateral Agreements on Human Rights', 3.
[64] Ibid. 7.
[65] Ibid. 8 (present author's emphasis).
[66] Report VI(2) (*supra*, n. 37). See also the definition of 'integration' outlined in the opening chapter of the present work.
[67] Ibid. 15.
[68] Report VIII(2) (*supra*, n. 39), 14.
[69] Ibid. 17.

The relationship between 'integration' and the cultural integrity of the indigenous population was expressed in different terms by the States. Mexico described the aim of indigenous policy in general as modification of the way of life of indigenous communities[70] in order that they may improve their present conditions, 'strengthened in this by their cultural values', and enjoy protection against dispossession by economically or politically powerful individuals or groups. New Zealand took the view that protection of indigenous populations should not be a bar to the 'development and modification of indigenous institutions', by implication,[71] development by agencies other than the indigenous communities themselves. Ecuador referred to the existing values of indigenous communities requiring accurate assessment 'if they are to be successfully changed in a gradual and methodical way';[72] this approach might be termed, to adapt a metaphor, 'cultural engineering', or 'value engineering'.[73] Colombia described the need to support groups 'governed by Western standards of culture' because of the part they can play 'in speeding up the process of acculturation of the indigenous people'.[74] 'Acculturation' may be defined as culture change that emerges from the interaction of two or more societies or groups with different cultural traditions.[75] On a mild interpretation, the Colombian reference would simply mean speeding up the process of cultural contact between indigenous and other groups, but the context of the Colombian statement seems to indicate assimilation, replacing native values with 'Western standards of culture'.[76]

One may legitimately question the extent to which such approaches to integration can be reconciled with the wording of Article 2(2)(c) of the Convention which excludes measures tending towards artificial assimilation. Article 2(4) seems to have, at first sight, a legal 'cutting edge' in its prohibition of recourse to force or coercion to promote integration. Some States have not regarded this as a bar to certain policies. Whereas Honduras replied to the International Labour Office that: 'Not only has force never served the purpose of integration, but it has . . . had the contrary effect',[77] Ecuador stated the matter differently: 'Moral, ethical or spiritual action cannot be based on force or physical compulsion. On the other hand, legal action necessarily implies the use of force in support of the law. In the case of indigenous peoples, educational and cultural methods appear prefer-

---

[70] Ibid. 15.   [71] Ibid. 16.   [72] Ibid. 19.

[73] From 'social engineering': the planning of social changes in a methodical fashion as opposed to allowing spontaneous development. See Popper, *The Poverty of Historicism* (London: Routledge and Kegan Paul, 1957).

[74] Report VIII(2) (*supra*, n. 39), 24.

[75] Bullock and Stallybrass (eds.), *The Fontana Dictionary of Modern Thought* (London: Fontana/Collins, 1977), 5.

[76] Batalla, 'The Indian and the Colonial Situation: the Context of Indigenous Policy in Latin America', in *The Situation of the Indian in South America* (Geneva: World Council of Churches, 1972), 21.

[77] Report VIII(2) (*supra*, n. 39).

able'[78] to forcible ones, but do not exhaust the possible range of measures. India gave another ambiguous response to the International Labour Office: 'Recourse to force should be excluded; but a cultural trait injurious to the tribal community *should not be retained indefinitely* . . . .'[79] The Indian preference was for propaganda rather than physical coercion; propaganda for change 'should not be considered as moral coercion'. The line between persuasion (propaganda) and 'moral coercion' may be a very fine one. In the reply of Colombia to the International Labour Office on the need to pay attention to indigenous leadership in obtaining co-operation with the communities for the purpose of integration, the proposal was made that account should be taken of indigenous leaders 'in so far as they represent the traditions of a group or community but any isolationist attitude or hostility to acculturation displayed by them should be *fought*'.[80] Does this imply 'physical coercion', 'moral coercion' or 'propaganda'?

Martinez-Cobo provides further evidence on States' views on coercion. He considers that 'Violence or intimidation, suggestion by coercion, material incentives, explicit and violent condemnation of the indigenous culture as a whole should be regarded as illegitimate means of exerting influence and of bringing about cultural or religious changes. The use of these methods is tantamount to ethnocide.'[81] The reports of States to the Special Rapporteur present a bland picture. Malaysia reported its policy on the Orang Asli in terms which merely reproduce the content of ILO Convention 107: 'The social, economic and cultural development of the aborigines should be promoted with the ultimate object of natural integration as opposed to artificial assimilation. The primary objective should be the fostering of individual dignity and the advancement of individual usefulness and initiative. Recourse to force or coercion as a means of promoting integration shall be excluded.'[82] Other States reported the absence of any measures to prevent force or coercion against indigenious populations because this is unknown in their countries.[83] The Special Rapporteur, however, noted laws limiting the freedom of indigenous groups to carry out traditional practices;[84] this raises, but does not dispose of, a general point about the relationship between humanitarian considerations and cultural respect:[85] 'Systematic and deliberate opposition to certain social or religious customs of the indigenous population would be acceptable only as a way of discouraging, by appropriate means, certain practices which violate the

---

[78] Ibid. 18.   [79] Ibid. 19.
[80] Ibid. 21 (present author's emphasis).
[81] UN Doc E/CN.4/Sub.2/1983/21/Add.3, para. 77.
[82] Ibid., para. 81.
[83] Australia, New Zealand, Norway, ibid., para. 85.
[84] Ibid., para. 87.
[85] Ibid., para. 79: he adds in a footnote (35) that systematic and deliberate opposition to social or religious customs 'would not perhaps be advisable as a means of inducing the group in question to abandon such customs altogether'.

sanctity of human life even though they may be associated with a particular religion, as may happen in very exceptional cases.'[86]

In most of the articles of the Convention which deal with the process of integration, one seeks in vain for any hard obligation to ensure the participation of indigenous groups in decision making about integration. Article 2 places on governments 'the primary responsibility' for integration and protection of indigenous groups. The phrase may indicate a 'secondary' responsibility, but there is no indication as to where this might lie. One authority (Bennett) interprets the phrase as prohibiting delegation of responsibility to missionary or charitable organizations. The ILO Committee of Experts has addressed questions to the Government of Bolivia on a number of occasions relating to its delegation of responsibilities for the forest-dwelling Indian populations to the Summer Institute of Linguistics, a religious missionary organization.[87] From the 'indigenous' point of view, the Report of the International NGO Conference on Discrimination against Indigenous Populations in the Americas[88] stated that in general, the

survival of indigenous cultures, and through it the physical integrity of indigenous communities, is threatened most especially by the direct importation and promotion of foreign values, beliefs and ideals among the Indian peoples. Ample testimony has been received as to the forcible character of this cultural transposition, particularly in the vast backing given by private and public sources for the missionary activity of the various Christian denominations.

The delegation of State functions to missionary organizations merely compounds the danger thus described though many States have themselves been devoted to 'cultural transposition'.[89] Bolivia is not the only State which entrusts responsibilities to religious organizations. By a Statute of 1892, Colombia delegated authority over areas containing non-integrated forest-dwelling Indians to the Catholic Church.[90] Further, by a succession of so-called 'Mission Agreements' concluded between the Government of Colombia and the Holy See since 1888, mission territories were placed under the exclusive educational, religious, and political control of the missions. The ILO has asked Colombia to clarify the legal position of indigenous populations in the mission territories.[91]

---

[86] Conclusions to the present work.

[87] See the Committee of Experts Report to the International Labour Conference 1983.

[88] Palais des Nations, Geneva 1977, 22.

[89] Martinez-Cobo, UN Doc E/CN.4/Sub.2/1983/21/Add.1, para. 41, comments 'on the one hand . . . missionary organisations have transcribed and preserved indigenous languages, and have provided the resources for intercultural contact and the dissemination of traditional values and customs, which might otherwise have been beyond the powers of many States, on the other hand, they have also been found to have applied in the past clear policies of forced assimilation with intimidatory and outright punitive measures . . . and [of] having opened these communities to all kinds of destabilisation and acculturation pressures'.

[90] Colombia Act No. 72, 1892, published in Ministerio de Gobierno, *Direccíon General de Integracíon y Desarrollo de la Comunidad*, Legislacíon Nacional sobre Indígenas (Bogotá: Imprenta Nacional, 1970), cited Swepston, (*supra*, n. 42), 723.

[91] Swepston (*supra*, n. 42), 723–4. See further Bunyard, *The Colombian Amazon* (Bodmin: The Ecological Press, 1990).

During the drafting of the Convention, the Government of the Philippines proposed the insertion of a paragraph in the article on General Policy: 'The progressive integration of indigenous and other tribal populations into the life of their respective countries should be *mainly at their own initiative*.'[92] The USSR proposed that the proper conditions 'should be created for the development of indigenous populations according to their desires'.[93] The International Labour Office indicated its view that Article 4 of the Convention satisfied the Philippine and Soviet requirements; it requires that 'due account' is taken of the cultural and religious values of the indigenous groups and of the danger of disrupting their values and institutions.[94] But an obligation to 'take due account' of indigenous values and a warning against the danger of cultural disturbance requires neither the co-operation nor the participation of indigenous groups in decision-making processes. A State can take due account of values and then proceed to 'engineer' them out of existence. The exception to 'soft' obligations is section 5 whereby governments 'shall . . . seek the collaboration of those populations and of their representatives'. Whereas for Ecuador consultation with indigenous leaders was 'wise and profitable',[95] and their consent to integration should be obtained, Egypt would only concern itself with 'progressive and democratic leadership'.[96] The Egyptian suggestion to the International Labour Office included the advice that 'due care should be taken to avoid any attempt by traditional leaders . . . to maintain any exceptional privileges which would hinder . . . integration.'[97] Lebanon envisaged a different restriction, consultation with traditional leadership was desirable in principle 'provided that the authority exercised by tribal leaders [was] supervised . . . to ensure that it facilitates the process of integration'.[98] New Zealand envisaged a purely 'nominal' role for traditional leadership.[99] Yugoslavia advocated consultation with leaders only 'where it meets their need for cultural and political progress'.[100] The Philippines gave its unqualified approval of consultation with traditional leadership, regarding the co-operation 'freely offered by chiefs and other leaders of the indigenous groups' as 'indispensable to the process of integration'.[101]

The 'hardness' of the legal obligation in Article 5 is considerably 'softened' by the insertion of 'populations' to be consulted as well as 'their representatives'. On the surface, this may appear to be more 'democratic' when considering an 'unrepresentative' leadership. But this bypassing of traditional leadership can effectively set aside the consultation process—how does a State agency 'consult' with an indigenous group directly without

---

[92] Report VI(2) (*supra*, n. 37), 12 (present author's emphasis).
[93] Ibid.
[94] Ibid. 12–13.
[95] Report VIII(2), 21. Ecuador considers that Article 5 should remain untouched by any revision: Report, *supra*, n. 47, 29.
[96] Report VIII (2), Ibid.
[97] Ibid.   [98] Ibid.   [99] Ibid.
[100] Ibid. 22.   [101] Ibid.

reference to the structure of the group? A likely possibility is to choose 'leaders' who are more responsive to the notion of integration. New Zealand communicated to the International Labour Office: 'Traditional leaders will often be found to be unsuitable in new forms of activity and . . . a new type of leader may have to be found.'[102] Further, the extent of the obligation is to 'seek' the collaboration of the populations—what if a government claims that although it has sought collaboration, it has not found it?

Capotorti[103] considered ILO Convention 107 as a 'minorities-type' of instrument, qualified in its approach by emphasis on integration. Bennett questions whether the drafters of the treaty have achieved a proper[104] balance between protection and integration.[105] The Convention makes a number of references to respect for traditional culture. But the protection of institutions is essentially a special measure. Such 'special measures' are temporary remedies—the special measures of protection are justified only as long as the social, economic, and cultural conditions of the populations 'prevent them from enjoying the benefits of the general laws of the country to which they belong' (Article 3(1)). The 'benefits of the general laws' is therefore regarded as the ultimate goal of indigenous policy. The respect for indigenous culture is then a respect for a transitional phenomenon, a respect for a cultural stage of mankind which is to disappear, to be replaced by a 'higher' culture. This attitude appears less like 'respect' for indigenous culture than simple recognition that it exists and is inherently undesirable.

Perhaps this is too bleak a view of ILO Convention 107, but there is little doubt that the 'protection' elements therein are limited. The various articles usually attempt to secure a balance between protection and integration or between integration and what may be termed cultural respect. For example, Article 7(1) requires that in defining the rights and duties of the populations 'regard shall be had' to their customary laws. This is a 'respect' provision, though, again, a weak one. Article 7(1) which hardly contains any threat to national integration programmes is 'balanced' by Article 7(2) which allows indigenous groups to retain their own customs and institutions where these are not incompatible with the national legal systems or 'the objectives of integration programmes',[106] that is not incompatible with law or policy.

A proposed amendment would have made Article 7(1) more restrictive. The USSR proposed that Article 7(1) should be amended to include, after

---

[102] Ibid.

[103] *Supra*, n. 63.

[104] *Supra*, n. 23, 19.

[105] Thornberry, *Minorities and Human Rights Law* (Minority Rights Group, London, 1987), 4–5.

[106] Bennett, *Aboriginal Rights*, 20–21, interprets 'national legal systems' to be a more limited conception than 'laws' so that a custom may not be disallowed merely because it differs from the terms of a particular law. It may be noted that, while the majority of Governments replying to ILO questions wished there to be no change in Article 7(i), a majority favoured changing Article 7(2) to delete the reference to integration programmes; however, Ecuador and the USA preferred to retain Article 7(2) as it stands: Report, (*supra*, n. 47), 37.

the reference therein to customary laws by: 'with the exception of customs which are incompatible with humanitarian principles'.[107] The International Labour Office's comment on this proposal points out the extreme cases of indigenous 'customs' repugnant to modern moral sensibilities, such as cannibalism and head-hunting, which would be prohibited in the USSR's amendment; but, as these were already prohibited by Article 7(2), there was no need for the amendment. However, the problem with Article 7(2) as it has emerged is that it is not limited in any way to 'repugnant' or merely 'offensive' practices of indigenous groups, but catches all aspects of their customary laws which do not cohere with the objective of national integration without being in any way 'morally' offensive. The verb 'allows' in Article 7(2) reflects the stance of the Convention very accurately: indigenous groups are permitted to retain their customary laws by the State; there is no inherent right to retain them, the State does not recognize their pre-existence, that is pre-existing any purported permission of the State, as it does in the case of most instruments on human rights. Article 8 follows a similar pattern to Article 7 in allowing indigenous methods of social control 'as far as possible', but only 'to the extent consistent with the interests of the national community and with the national legal system'. This is a broad framework provision which allows the State almost complete freedom of manœuvre in allowing or disallowing indigenous methods of social control.

Article 8(6) requires that the penal customs of aboriginal groups 'shall be borne in mind' if their methods of social control cannot be adopted—but this too is caught by the broad saving clause for the interests of the national community and the national legal system at the beginning of the article. States have indicated in their annual reports submitted to the ILO what factors they consider relevant in determining whether indigenous methods of social control are to be relied upon; minor offences may be left to be dealt with by the tribal courts, crimes against non-indigenous victims are usually dealt with by the national courts, whereas inter-tribal disputes are settled by the tribes themselves.[108] But there is no obligation in terms of the Convention to adopt any of these criteria.

Compared to other international instruments touching on the issue of minorities, the situation of the population comprehended by ILO Convention 107 is very weak. The general policy section of the Convention would appear to have an integration objective which is similar to anti-discrimination treaties: the goal is some version or other of equality between the citizens in a State, otherwise the indigenous groups will be prevented from 'enjoying the benefits of the general laws'. It may be noted that even this modest aim is not fully achieved in many States. Thus the Constitutions of

---

[107] Report VI(2), 16.
[108] ILO Summary of Reports of Ratified Conventions, Report III(1), *International Labour Conference 48th Session* (1964), 265; *49th Session* (1965), 278; *51st Session* (1967), 184; Report VIII(2) (*supra*, n. 39), 114 ff.

the States Parties to the Convention generally contain anti-discrimination provisions.[109] In the case of Peru, the ILO has found that the promise of equality in the Constitution is not delivered in the criminal law: a distinction is made in the Penal Code between crimes commited by ordinary Peruvians and crimes commited by persons of a lower order of civilization, *salvajes*, a crime commited by one of the latter can lead to a sentence in an agricultural penal colony instead of rigorous imprisonment; the drawback to the apparently more lenient measure is that the penal colony sentence can endure for a longer period than the normal maximum sentence for the crime. Further, the sentence in the colony may be terminated before twenty years if the prisoner becomes assimilated into civilized life.[110] In the case of Brazil, Indians who are not yet integrated into national life are under tutelage, that is, they are legally minors and are under the guardianship of the State. An Indian may be emancipated by application to a magistrate if he fulfils certain conditions, including some knowledge of Portuguese and reasonable comprehension of the usages and customs of the national community.[111] Colombian legislation has a similar disabling rule, providing that 'the general legislation of the Republic shall not apply to savages who are being brought to civilised life by the Missions'.[112]

But the unstated premise of the anti-discrimination treaties is that they are dealing with populations of roughly comparable social and cultural development. Another unstated premise is that groups wish to be integrated. Such equality as is generally favoured in the anti-discrimination treaties[113] will certainly favour the removal of disabilities such as those suffered by Indians in Brazil and Colombia. ILO Convention 107 partakes of this anti-discrimination and equality approach. This is valuable in removing obstacles to equality, but does not go far enough in the attention to be paid to the cultural characteristics of the subject populations. They may or may not wish to integrate while appreciating the removal of disabilities. However, theirs is not the duty or right to integrate; that duty is cast upon the State, and a State assumes a duty to integrate not through consultation with its indigenous population, but by becoming a party to ILO Convention 107. Further, in contrast to general human rights instruments, there is little emphasis on rights, at least in the 'General Policy' articles. Article 7(1) does mention rights, but only as they are to be *defined* by the State Party.[114] Article 5(c) refers to liberties: Governments are to stimulate the development of civil liberties among the populations, and elective institutions. Bennett comments:

[109] Stavenhagen, *Derecho Indígena y Derechos Humanos en América Latina* (El Colegio de Mexico and Instituto Interamericano de Derechos Humanos, Mexico City, 1988).

[110] International Labour Conference, Report of the Committee of Experts on the Application of Conventions and Recommendations, 64th Session 1978.

[111] Indian Statute, Brazil Act No. 6001 (1973), cited Swepston, 721.

[112] Colombia Act No. 89, S.1 (November 1890), Swepston, 723.

[113] *Supra*, ch. 29. [114] (Present author's emphasis) Also Article 7(3).

Isolated hunting and gathering bands generally practise an economy which is in fact more co-operative and egalitarian than anything found in modern societies; individual authority and responsibility are unwanted and avoided in secular affairs, and the so-called chief or leader, if indeed any exists, is often without any personal power. Do such communities really stand in urgent need of Western-style 'civil liberties' or elective institutions?[115]

Article 5(c) does not say whether the elective institutions are to be understood as within the tribe itself or in the wider national society: a State could hardly be said to be acting in violation of the Convention if it preferred the former view. Article 10 does refer to 'fundamental rights of persons belonging to the populations concerned'. The only rights mentioned in the General Policy section are, in essence, 'the rights granted to all citizens (Article 7(3)). There is no description of them in this section as 'fundamental', so perhaps one needs to look elsewhere in the Convention. One may recall the Preamble: 'all human beings have the right to pursue both their material well-being and their spiritual development'. It may be that the Convention provisions should be interpreted in this light to give more substance to such rights as are intimated therein. But what is the right to 'spiritual development' of an individual without reference to the right to spiritual development of a group to which he belongs? Where is this right when customs and institutions, including their religious elements, are merely allowed as an act of generosity by the States parties? To adapt the language of a previous discussion, what is lacking is any firm version of the right to be different.[116]

Further Comment on State Policies

A number of States submitted information to Special Rapporteur Martinez-Cobo on the fundamental policy of the State in relation to indigenous populations. That adherence to ILO Convention 107 can at least exercise a moderating influence on State ambitions to integrate is evidenced, if negatively, by considering the statement of Chile[117] which is not a party to the Convention. Chile sets itself against special legislation which in the past has resulted in retarding the economic and social development of indigenous groups. Its view of indigenous peoples is that:

indigenous peoples are Chilean and must be integrated with the rest of the nation as soon as possible; in turn, society in general must assimilate them as promptly and

---

[115] 21.

[116] *Supra*, ch. 33.

[117] UN Doc E/CN.4/Sub.2/1983/21/Add. 1, para. 111. The Chilean view of the revision of ILO 107 has been bluntly expressed: 'Revision is not considered necessary. In Chile there is no difference between indigenous and non-indigenous peoples, and the Government does not agree with discrimination between Chileans and indigenous persons, or with the new concept of self-determination and individual development of the indigenous populations, in an isolated form separate from the rest of Chilean society': Report (*supra*, n. 47), 4.

completely as possible. It might be regrettable if this process of assimilation involved the loss of indigenous languages and forms of culture . . . but this would in no way be an impediment to the final consolidation of Chilean society, which cannot be other than a single whole.

The statement displays in the clearest manner the metamorphosis of integration into assimilation and implies no respect whatever for indigenous culture and values: there is only one right for the indigenous population *vis-à-vis* such a policy, the right to cease existence as a recognizable group. The preferred policy of most States replying to the Special Rapporteur is the voluntary integration over a period of the populations,[118] with due regard for their cultural values and traditions. This attitude is exemplified by Brazil, the Government of which states that it has 'always taken care to elaborate special laws for their [the indigenous population's] protection while they are living under primitive conditions. These laws are aimed at maintaining their lives and property, as well as progressively integrating them into the national community by appropriate means, which is to say, without violence or any form of coercion.'[119] The Government described its basic legal text as 'Decree No. 5484 of 27 June 1928[120] which established a special code for the Indians, placing them under the guardianship of the State, and providing for a steady pace of progressive emancipation until such time as they are completely integrated into the life of the nation'.[121] Mexico,[122] another State Party to ILO Convention 107, adopts a more positive approach to its indigenous population claiming that its indigenous policy, 'which is regarded as a necessity, is based on the tenet that the strengthening of the national consciousness will be achieved in respecting ethnic pluralism'.[123]

Some governments report a change of view. Guatemala reported that 'a positive change in the attitude of the State is apparent at present . . . cultural pluralism is now recognised as essential to the formation of genuine Guatemalan nationhood.'[124] Other governments claim that they favour greater respect for indigenous culture and values. The Government of Fin-

---

[118] Ibid., para. 105 (Martinez-Cobo Report).

[119] Ibid., para. 106.

[120] The text is complemented by Act 6001, Article 1 of which provides: 'This law regulates the juridical situation of the Indians or forest-dwellers and native communities for the purpose of preserving their culture and integrating them, progressively and harmoniously, in the National community'. The Brazilian Constitution of 1988 includes a chapter on Indian rights for the first time in Brazilian constitutional history, the effects of which will gradually work through to domestic law. The basic provision is Article 266: 'The social organization, customs, and languages, beliefs and traditions of the Indians are recognized, as well as their aboriginal rights to the lands they traditionally occupy, it being within the competence of the Union to demarcate them, protect and guarantee respect for all of their estate' (translation provided to the author by Survival International). See also Stavenhagen, (*supra*, n. 109).

[121] Martinez-Cobo (*supra*, n. 117), para. 112.

[122] Ibid.

[123] Ibid., para. 114.

[124] Ibid., para. 102.

land reported, in relation to the Lapps, that previously the Lapps simply benefited from measures to improve the lot of all population groups in the north of the country. The change is to recognize the Lapps as a distinct group and take steps[125] to preserve their language and culture. Sweden[126] and Norway also report a shift from treating the situation of the Lapps as an economic issue towards taking measures to favour their language and culture.[127] A move from a policy which 'perhaps unconsciously tended towards assimilation' is reported by New Zealand; government policy has now 'recognised the fact that New Zealand society embraces more than one culture in one citizenship'.[128] The Maori is recognized as a full citizen of the State, but one who is 'entitled' to retain his social and cultural institutions, which other citizens should know and respect. Australia also favours full citizenship allied with recognition of distinctive Aboriginal qualities, which are 'living elements in the diverse culture of Australian society'.[129] Australia significantly refers to taking into account 'the expressed wishes of Aboriginal Australians themselves'.[130] Canada refers to the free choice of the Indian peoples in relation to any development programmes for their benefit, and describes them as 'citizens plus'.[131] There is some evidence, therefore, at the level of government formulation of fundamental policy for indigenous groups, that their distinctive character is being more fully recognized.[132]

Land Rights

The issue of land rights has not been dealt with elsewhere in this work[133] because it does not impinge significantly on minorities issues. ILO Convention 107 devotes four articles to this issue and the question assumes a high degree of importance to many indigenous groups.[134] Article 11 provides a right in this Convention which is delineated in a 'strong' manner: 'The right

---

[125] Ibid., para. 101.   [126] Ibid., para. 103.

[127] Ibid., para. 116 and, *supra*, ch. 24 (the Kitok case).

[128] Ibid., para. 115.   [129] Ibid., para. 108.

[130] Ibid.

[131] Ibid., para. 109. For further evidence of changing views, see *infra*, ch. 41. Much of the effort to develop more modern approaches to indigenous issues comes from States which are not parties to the Convention. The International Labour Office has stated: 'Although most North American, Australasian and European States have not ratified Convention No. 107, some of the recent initiatives taken in these States illustrate new approaches to indigenous participation in development and have major implications for the revision of Convention No. 107': Partial Revision, Report VI(1), 21.

[132] *Infra*, ch. 41.

[133] See further the conclusions of the present work.

[134] For a spectrum of views, see *International NGO Conference on Indigenous Peoples and the Land*, Geneva, September 1981, organized by the Sub-Committee on Racism, Racial Discrimination, Apartheid and Decolonisation of the Special NGO Committee on Human Rights (Geneva). The Australian Aboriginal Paper on Land Rights stated: 'land to . . . Aboriginals is the life and the continuation of that life forever. Land . . . is religiously observed by our people in our myths, legends and laws . . . it provided all that was necessary to sustain life'.

of ownership, collective or individual, of the members of the populations concerned over the lands which these populations traditionally occupy shall be recognised.' Article 12 is not quite as categorical, but it none the less contains important constraints on the States Parties' freedom of action: indigenous populations 'shall not be removed without their free consent from their habitual territories except in accordance with national laws and regulations for reasons relating to national security, or in the interest of national economic development or of the health of the said populations' (Article 12(1)). However, if a State should choose to remove populations from their 'habitual territories' as an 'exceptional measure' (Article 12(2)), the populations 'shall be provided with lands of quality at least equal to that of the lands previously occupied by them, suitable to provide for their present needs and future development'. Persons removed are to be 'fully compensated for any resulting loss or injury' (Article 12(3)). Article 13 relates back to the general question of indigenous laws and customs in the context of land rights and provides that procedures for the transmission of rights of ownership and use of land which are 'established by the customs of the populations concerned shall be respected within the framework of national laws and regulations, in so far as they satisfy the needs of these populations and do not hinder their economic and social development' (Article 13(1)). Article 14 is another 'equality' provision—indigenous populations are to have equal treatment under national agrarian programmes in so far as they allocate more land for populations who do not possess 'the essentials of a normal existence' or for any possible increase in their numbers (Article 14(a)), and the programmes provide means to promote the development of land already possessed by the populations.

Comment

The contentious nature of the land question for indigenous groups is immediately apparent from a perusal of the comments made by States to the ILO on the draft articles.[135] Portugal advanced the view that the question was not appropriate for treatment in an international instrument of the ILO, the questions dealt with, for example, by Article 11, were 'a matter for domestic legislation'. The mere adoption of rules in this sphere would 'defeat the very purpose of integration'.[136] The USSR injected a 'socialist' element into this discussion by arguing that the Convention should provide for a redistribution of land to indigenous groups deprived of land through 'seizure or colonisation'.[137] The United Kingdom sought to balance the general principle of securing to the indigenous peoples the use or occupation of land against the rights of those who had obtained or would obtain at

---

[135] Report VI(2), (*supra*, n. 37), 19 ff.
[136] Ibid. 19.   [137] Ibid.

some time in the future 'legitimate interests in land through the due processes of the national law'. The UK interpreted Articles 11 and 14(a) as envisaging land reservations for communities, disapproving of this policy in favour of the individualization of land tenure.[138] The ILO disputed the interpretation by the United Kingdom, pointing out that this part of the Convention 'does not in any way relate to the establishment of land reservations by the populations concerned'.[139] The ILO referred to the fact that Article 11 refers to both collective and individual ownership of land 'without expressing a preference for either system'.[140] Thus, governments were free to recognize ownership in the form most likely to serve the interests of the persons whom it sought to protect.[141] A number of other States expressed views on Article 11. An earlier version of Article 11 referred to the granting by the State of property rights over land traditionally occupied; 'granted' was changed to 'recognized' following a suggestion by Brazil[142] because the former term implied a recognition that the State had a prior and overriding property right which would enable it to concede or grant indigenous land.[143] On the other hand, States such as Egypt[144] and Honduras[145] were apparently satisfied with the term 'grant'.[146]

Article 11 may be neutral on the question of type of ownership, but it deals with ownership rather than possession, which is important for indigenous groups. The original draft of Article 11 referred to 'property' rights rather than ownership; on the suggestion of the United Kingdom, the latter term was inserted.[147] In any case, the use of 'ownership' is consistent with its use in Article 13. States parties are, therefore, obliged to 'recognize' aboriginal title to tribal lands, based on immemorial occupation rather than any grant of the State. Unfettered free disposition by the State of tribal lands is, therefore, ruled out by the Convention, though the rigour of the prohibition is weakened by Article 12.

Consistent with its initial responses, the ILO, through the Committee of Experts, has been flexible in its approach to deciding whether legal arrangements comply with the article. Indigenous societies may have little conception of ownership, individual or collective, and may be ripe for exploitation; collective ownership may, however, be a more comprehensible concept for

[138] Ibid. 19–20.
[139] Ibid. 20. See, however, Report VIII(2) (*supra*, n. 39), 38 ff.
[140] VI(2), 20.
[141] For the position on rights acquired by third parties, see Report VI(2), 21.
[142] VIII(2), 33.
[143] Brazil maintains an extensive system of reserves. These are not to be confused with areas possessed from time immemorial by tribes: Act No. 6001, s.2 (1973).
[144] VIII(2), 34.
[145] Ibid.
[146] On land-holding systems in Mexico, see Fernandez, 'La Tenencia de la Tierra entre los Grupos indígenas de México', *América Indígena*, 33 (1974), 107; for a Mexican appreciation of the relationship between land-holding systems and the indigenous sense of community, see *Report VIII(2)*, 35–6.
[147] VI(2), 21.

many indigenous groups. Swepston[148] considers that restrictions on alienation of land by members of indigenous groups may be more beneficial than
conferment of full title (subject to the principle of Article 3(2)(b) of the
Convention). He considers that some of the reservation systems adopted by
States are only doubtfully compatible with the Convention. For example, in
the Brazilian system mentioned above,[149] while the Indians have permanent
usufruct of these lands, which may not be alienated, Indians are none the
less legally minors, and thus legally incompetent to own the lands, which are
'the inalienable property of the Union'.[150] Full ownership may be obtained
upon emancipation. The Indians are deemed incapable of managing their
lands, that function is carried out by the National Indian Foundation
attached to the Ministry of the Interior (*FUNAI*),[151] frequently using
Indians as labourers.[152] The religious missions figure prominently in land-
holding, as they do in other areas of indigenous concern; in Colombia, for
example, there are mission territories of unknown extent ceded for
acculturating the Indians occupying them, securing their conversion to
Christianity. The missions both own lands where Indians reside and hold
other lands where they are generally responsible for Indians thereon.[153] The
various systems by which lands are dealt with should distinguish between
administration and ownership, and provide at least for the transfer of title
to Indian populations, in order to comply with the Convention.

The question of land ownership is replete with tension between protection and integration. The 'protection' aspects of reservations for Indian
populations may be disabling and paternalistic. On the other hand, greater
self-management in cases of weakly organized, perhaps isolationist Indian
groups may give little protection from outside pressures. The problem with
any choice of ultimate policy is that so far the choices have been made by
States; choices have not always involved an indigenous contribution to the
formulation of the values to be served by any system.[154]

---

[148] Swepston, 'The Land Rights of Indigenous Populations under the ILO's Indigenous and
Tribal Populations Convention . . . and Recommendations in NGO Land Conference', (*supra*,
n. 134), Doc.IPC. Com. 1–7, 2. See also ILO Comment to Martinez-Cobo, UN Doc E/CN.
4/Sub.2/1982/2/Add 1, para. 91.

[149] *Supra*, n. 143, 596.

[150] Act 6001 (*supra*, n. 143), S.22.

[151] Government of Brazil, report to the ILO 1976.

[152] For Paraguay, see Government of Paraguay, Report to the ILO 1976; Bejarano, *Solucio-
nemos Nuestro Problema Indígena con el INDI* (Asuncion, 1976), communicated by the
Government of Paraguay to the ILO. Some recent developments are outlined in Partial
Revision, Report VI(I), 52–3.

[153] Bonilla, 'The Destruction of the Colombian Indian Groups', in World Council of
Churches (*supra*, n. 76), 56–7.

[154] International NGO Conference (*supra*, n. 133). The various position papers of indigenous groups are collected under the serial IPC-Com.I. It is instructive that many groups of
indigenous peoples regard 'outside' imposition of land-holding patterns as potentially or actually ethnocidal in character. Thus, relating to Decree-Law 2568 (1979) of Chile, the Mapuche
Cultural Centre of Chile noted that the law and government declarations contain a 'basic idea:
the Mapuche community does not exist, therefore, there is neither exploitation nor communal

Article 11 does not make a distinction in relation to ownership of land between tribes with a settled territorial base and, for example, semi-nomadic forest tribes. In reply to the International Labour Office, on whether there was a need to secure land ownership to such tribes as 'periodically move for seasonal, climatic or economic reasons' but 'habitually return to the same starting point and generally remain there', States indicated in the main that land rights should be secured. Ecuador regarded it as 'absolutely essential'.[155] Egypt put forward the view that they should be granted such rights in places which are likely to be the centre of their movements. A number of States[156] also supported the concept of 'zones of nomadism' where tribes should have an undisturbed right to graze their herds and flocks, though others, such as Colombia[157] and Pakistan,[158] disagreed. The question of nomadism does not appear on the face of the Convention, but Article 3(1) of Recommendation 104 provides that indigenous populations should be assured of a land reserve 'adequate for the needs of shifting cultivation so long as no better system of cultivation can be introduced'. Article 3(2) provides that: 'Pending the attainment of the objectives of a settlement policy for semi-nomadic groups, zones should be established within which the livestock of such groups can graze without hindrance'. The tone of the recommendation on this point is unfortunate. Shifting cultivation is described in effect as an 'inferior' system of cultivation by Article 3(1). The second paragraph views nomadism as a transitory phenomenon, a policy of 'settlement' is the desired mode of integrating such groups into the fabric of the State. Article 11 of the Convention arguably provides a better line of defence for groups threatened by settlement policies in relation to the lands which they 'traditionally occupy'. Bennett,[159] however, argues that Article 3 of the ILO Recommendation 104 is clearly drafted on the assumption that Article 11 does not cover such groups, Article 3 specifies 'zones' of nomadism instead of lands of traditional occupation and is thus inconsistent with Article 11. However, on a literal reading of Article 11, it is apt to cover the case of nomads: the Convention requires only an indigenous population and describes the rights to lands traditionally occupied. Clearly, there is a difficulty in the case of nomadic populations in settling the spatial extent of lands to which title may be recognized, and in the different types of relationship which nomadic tribes may have to the lands over which they move for the purpose of interpreting

---

property of land. Each family exploits individually a property . . . with regard to which they behave as individual owners . . . '. The fallacy in the Decree-Law is deemed to be the ethnocentric perspective of government, the application of Western 'individualism' in an indigenous context which is ultimately an attempt to destroy the indigenous communities: Indian Philosophy and the Land, Doc. IPC-Com. II-4. See also Docs. IPC-Com.I-I; IPC-Com.II-3; IPC-Com.II-5.

[155] Report VIII (2), 35.
[156] Ibid. 36.   [157] Ibid.   [158] Ibid. 37.
[159] Bennett, *Aboriginal Rights in International Law*, 35.

their 'occupation' of it.[160] But these are difficulties of perception on the part of States, which are, after all, territorially based communities,[161] rather than absolute impediments to the applications of a rule.

Article 12 of ILO Convention 107 states a very important principle for indigenous groups—that their 'free consent' is necessary for their removal from their 'habitual territories'. This last phrase is free from the difficulties of 'traditionally occupy' in Article 11. The principle is important in a general human rights context and represents what may be termed the 'right to remain'. This right may be found in general international law in, for example, Article 3(1) of the Fourth Protocol to the European Convention on Human Rights and Fundamental Freedoms: 'No one shall be expelled, by means either of an individual or of a collective measure, from the territory of the State of which he is a national.'[162] The right to remain in Article 12 of ILO Convention 107 is more restrictive of the rights of the State than the Fourth Protocol to the European Convention,[163] though it limits the State *vis-à-vis* 'populations' rather than individuals. The principle expressed in Article 12 was relatively uncontentious from the viewpoint of most of the States.[164] This, however, may have been due not to sympathy for the principle but satisfaction with the sweeping exceptions to it which are also contemplated. 'National security' and 'national economic development' were supplemented by the reference to 'health' at the insistence of the United Kingdom.[165] These are broad incursions into the right to remain, though at least the removal must be in accordance with 'national laws and

---

[160] See the lengthy discussion of nomadic rights in the Western Sahara Advisory Opinion, *ICJ Reports 1975*. Most States responding to the ILO have stated that, whatever the difficulties, Article 11 should remain unchanged: *Partial Revision*, Report VI(2), 46–7.

[161] See Article 1 of the Montevideo Convention on the Rights and Duties of States 1933, *LNTS*, 165, 19. A number of States, including Egypt and Tunisia, have reported 'successes' in sedentarization of nomadic groups to the ILO; also: 'The Syrian Arab Republic, which has ratified the Convention, reported that most of its Bedouin populations have been fully sedentarised . . . Some of these populations remain nomadic, however, and the Government envisages further measures to encourage them to settle': *Partial Revision*, Report VI(I), 25.

[162] Goodwin-Gill, *International Law and the Movement of Persons Between States*, 202, 213–14, 287 (Oxford: OUP, 1978).

[163] Which deals with expulsions from a State, not deportations within a State. See also the 7th Protocol to the ECHR.

[164] Swepston, Doc IPC-CON 1–7, *supra*, n. 48, 4, states 'It might be argued that there should be no removals of indigenous populations from their "habitual territories", but this is obviously unrealistic. All Governments retain the right in particular circumstances to remove their nationals from the land they inhabit, under any form of title.' The power of removal, must, however, be understood in the light of contemporary standards of Human Rights. See De Zayas, *Nemesis at Potsdam* and 'The Anglo-Americans and the Expulsion of the Germans', and Iyer, 'Mass Expulsion as Violation of Human Rights', *Indian Journal of International Law* 13 (1973), 169.

[165] Report VI(2), 22. States' views were divided on proposals to delete all the words after 'habitual territories' in Article 12(1): *Partial Revision*, Report VI(2), 54. Stringent views were offered by Colombia: 'Yes, it should be revised, but it is necessary to retain the possibility of removing these peoples for reasons of national security'; and Ecuador: 'The implication of this revision would conflict with national interest to the extent of making ratification of the Convention exceedingly inconvenient.'

regulations' which would doubtless exclude actions by State agencies not so clearly grounded.[166] If there is removal from lands habitually occupied by the populations they must be given lands of equal quality (but of undefined spatial extent, there is no reference to 'quantity') and full compensation for any resulting loss or injury. Again, the will of the indigenous populations can be subordinated to a national economic plan which they may have played little or no part in shaping.[167] The problem with 'full compensation' is that there may be no compensation for the loss of traditional lands: for many indigenous communities, their lands have a mythical or religious significance[168] so that to be dispossessed is a contribution to the destruction of the culture and values. 'Western' notions of monetary compensation may be highly inappropriate in this context. However, during the drafting of the Convention, Belgium expressed its disapproval of even the basic principle of compensation, though it did not rule out 'generous assistance and acts of liberality', clearly on an *ex gratia* basis.[169]

The application of Article 12 has from time to time caused concern to the ILO Committee of Experts on the Application of Conventions and Recommendations. In the case of Brazil, for example, the Committee expressed its concern at the gradual encroachment on Indian lands by members of the non-indigenous community—it seems clear from the Committee's remarks on this that they consider that this is contrary to the Convention, though the question of private encroachment is not dealt with as such. The Committee also disapproved of leases to non-Indians of Indian lands, with consequent removals of Indian communities from lands previously occupied, which clearly was in violation of Article 12.[170]

The Recommendation also deals with a matter which may be covered by implication in the Convention,[171] namely mineral resources: Article 4

---

[166] The syntax of Article 12 is peculiar: an unguarded reading might give rise to the supposition that the reference to the limitation of 'national laws and regulations' applies only to matters of national security, and that other grounds of removal are quite unfettered. However, this reading would give rise to an absurd result and is not in keeping with the object and purpose of the Article or the Convention as a whole.

[167] *Supra*, text following n. 92.

[168] See various contributions to the International NGO Conference, (supra, n. 134).

[169] Report VIII(2), 37.

[170] Committee of Experts, *Report to the International Labour Conference, 69th Session* (1983), 186.

[171] Many States, including States Parties to ILO 107, take the view that the Convention does not refer to mineral resources. Current Latin American legislation generally provides that the State retains full rights over sub-surface resources, and examples of indigenous control or participation are rare. For example, Article 27 of the Constitution of Mexico provides that ownership of the lands and waters within the bounds of the national territory is vested originally in the nation, as the direct ownership of all natural resources of the continental shelf, of all mines, solid mineral fuels, and the space above the national territory to the limit fixed by International Law. Exploitation, appropriation, and use may be undertaken by concessions granted by the Federal Government. The ILO has addressed questions to States in terms which suggest that the matter is for a revised convention rather than the present text. Some States have expressed hostility to the inclusion of an explicit provision on mineral resources. Brazil states that the question is outside the mandate of the ILO. Colombia states that a

provides that members of indigenous populations should receive the same treatment as other members of national populations 'in relation to the ownership of underground wealth or to preference rights in the development of such wealth'. Part II of the Recommendation is, like Part II of the Convention, headed simply as 'Land' so that the reference to 'underground wealth' might be regarded as an explanation of its meaning. However, the description of the right holder in Article 4 of the Recommendation is only to: 'Members of the [indigenous] populations concerned' and not to the populations as such. It is difficult to see how the concept of individual rights at this point can be married with the reference to collective ownership in Article 11 of the Convention.

The right to own land is one of the most important rights for indigenous groups. Land is an economic and frequently a cultural necessity. As one writer puts it, when indigenous groups lose their land 'their cultures disintegrate and they are dispersed among the general rural population or they simply die.'[172] 'Western' notions of title may be inappropriate to indigenous groups; the mere appearance of the concept of individual title to land may contribute to the weakening or destruction of tribal institutions.[173]

Education and Languages

In Part VI of the Convention relating to 'Education and Means of Communication' there are a number of principles expressed on the use of indigenous languages, and language is singled out for separate treatment in Recommendation 104. Article 23(3) of the Convention provides that appropriate measures 'shall, as far as possible, be taken to preserve the mother tongue or the vernacular language'. This limited obligation is heavily qualified by the preceding paragraph: 'Provision shall be made for a progressive transition from the mother tongue or the vernacular language to the national language or to one of the official languages of the country.' The degree of logical coherence between a commitment to preserve a language, and one to secure its gradual elimination from use is not great. The commitment to preserve is, to be sure, only to preserve 'as far as possible' so that the balance is tipped in favour of elimination. Part IX of Recommendation 104 does not deal with elimination or retention of a language; it addresses itself rather to the 'improvement' of native languages in the context of integration—which is to be facilitated by, *inter alia*, 'enriching the technical and juridical vocabulary of their [the indigenous populations'] vernacular languages and dialects' and reducing the languages and dialects to writing.

---

resources provision would conflict with the principle of absolute State dominion and would be very dangerous: *Partial Revision*, VI(1), 57 ff; VI(2), 50–1.

[172] Swepston, (*supra*, n. 42), 729.
[173] *Supra*, n. 134.

The *travaux préparatoires* of the Convention indicate a degree of enthusiastic support by States for the linguistic principles outlined above, particularly for the principle of transition. Some States, reflecting their own experience with diverse linguistic groups, opted for bilingualism (or multilingualism as the case may be) as the preferred pattern. Belgium[174] and Yugoslavia[175] are two States in point. However, other States exhibited a zeal to reform linguistic practices. Thus, according to the response of the Government of Haiti to the ILO, the use of the vernacular language was only 'a preliminary stage before *compulsory* transition to the national language'.[176] In the view of Pakistan, the main effort was to teach the national language, the preservation of the original language was to be considered 'only as subsidiary'.[177]

Subsequent practice indicates some change towards recognition of the value of indigenous languages, but negative attitudes continue. In its 1966 Report to the ILO, Costa Rica stated that after an initial period of experiment, teaching in the native languages had been abandoned because it was too slow and because there were too many small ethnic groups. However, by Article 4 of Act No. 5251 of July 1973, the National Commission on Indigenous Affairs established by the Act has, as one of its objectives: '(d) to foster knowledge of indigenous affairs in order to increase awareness of them and thus to be able to stimulate interest in the study of indigenous cultures and, in particular, of indigenous languages, whose use and study shall be actively promoted.' Martinez-Cobo recorded that no relevant information on the application of the Act was provided by the Government of Costa Rica.[178] However, elsewhere he relates that Costa Rica is one State wherein indigenous languages are not used at all in public schools as languages of instruction at any level; education for the indigenous peoples is in Spanish,[179] the official language. Article 50 of the Constitution of Paraguay provides that 'the national languages of the Republic shall be Spanish and Guarani'; Article 92 provides that 'the State shall protect the Guarani language and promote its teaching, development and improvement'.[180] However, it is apparent that Guarani is treated with disdain in Paraguay[181] and many indigenous persons in Paraguay are forced to change their names

---

[174] Report VIII(2), 84.

[175] Ibid. 86.

[176] Ibid. 85 (present author's emphasis).

[177] Ibid.

[178] UN Doc E/CN.4/Sub.2/476/Add.6, paras. 65–6. In its 1977 report to the ILO, Argentina set itself against the introduction of any system of bilingual education, preferring full integration of indigenous groups into the national society. However, Act No. 23302 of 1985 provides for new policies with respect to the indigenous: *inter alios*, education must include teaching in native languages. A National Institute for Indigenous Affairs will implement the Act in co-operation with representatives of communities concerned: *Partial Revision*, VI(1), 22.

[179] Ibid., para. 225.

[180] Martinez-Cobo (*supra*, n. 178), para. 186.

[181] Ibid., para. 187. For an official State view, see *Government of Paraguay, Report to the ILO* (1976).

from the indigenous language into Spanish, despite the fact that 'the name is an inseparable part of the personality and soul'.[182] Paraguayan 'respect' for indigenous languages in practice is evidenced by the complete prohibition of Aché names. Special Rapporteur Martinez-Cobo remarks that 'in the Aché system of religious beliefs, this means that they lose their souls'.[183]

Panama is a party to the Convention, and Article 83 of its Constitution of 1972 lays down the basic requirement of bilingual education for indigenous populations. However, indigenous students in Panamanian schools are reportedly forbidden to use their own languages to communicate with each other, a modern case of linguistic 'aggression' or persecution.[184] Colombia presents an uncertain picture in many respects in its linguistic policy. According to Article 9 of Decree No. 1142 of July 1978, which regulates an earlier law on education for indigenous communities, 'instruction in reading and writing will be given to the communities in their mother-tongue, with provision for the gradual learning of the national language without detriment to the mother-tongue'.[185] The provision reflects a positive reading of Convention 107 (Article 23). However, the implementation of this provision is unclear, a 1960 'Law on the Defence of the National Language' provides that all instruction is to be given in Spanish. Formerly, the situation was perhaps even more confused with a general delegation to missions of responsibility for indigenous education; the delegation was declared unconstitutional in 1967,[186] and, by a new Concordat approved in 1974,[187] responsibility for education passed to the national government. Another aspect of Colombian policy which is noteworthy in the present context is the attempt to devise written vocabularies for indigenous languages. The Colombian Government reports to the United Nations that this is to facilitate communications and education of the Indians 'thereby easing their assimilation into the larger society'.[188]

There is a good deal of evidence of discrimination against indigenous languages in various States, including those party to ILO Convention 107. Besides the examples above, many States do not recognize indigenous languages as official languages, despite the presence of large indigenous groups in their territories. An 'official' language is defined by UNESCO as one used in the business of government: legislative, executive, administrative, and judicial and in the performance of the various other functions of the State.[189] One exception appears to be Peru, which in March 1975 enacted

---

[182] Resolutions of the Cuzco Conference, the first Congress of South American Indian Movements, Cuzco, 1980; UN Doc E/CN.4/Sub.2/476/Add.6, paras. 183 ff.
[183] Ibid., para. 230.
[184] Ibid., para. 232.
[185] *Government of Colombia, Report to the ILO* (1971).
[186] Swepston, (*supra*, n. 42), 724.
[187] Martinez-Cobo (*supra*, n. 178), para. 346.
[188] *Supra*, n. 185.
[189] *The Use of Vernacular Languages in Education* (Paris: UNESCO, 1953).

Decree-Law No. 21,156 recognizing Quechua as an official language of the Republic.[190] The Preamble recites, *inter alia*, that because of the language barrier, large sections of the indigenous population 'have no direct access to knowledge of the laws' and are thus 'unaware of their obligations and limited in the exercise of their rights'. The law proposes that where the parties only speak Quechua legal proceedings shall be conducted in that language, and that the Ministry of Education will provide 'all necessary support for institutions engaged in . . . the teaching and promotion of the language in question'.[191] The teaching of Quechua is declared to be compulsory at 'all levels of education in the Republic'.[192] The aim of the Peruvian measures[193] is to secure 'equality before the law' which is praiseworthy in the context of a State enforcing its laws against indigenous groups who may not understand the language in which the law is recorded.[194]

The stress on integration in ILO Convention 107 is probably consistent, as a general rule, with indigenous language policy, particularly in Latin American States. The Special Rapporteur on Discrimination against Indigenous Populations takes a long-term view and finds 'a growing tendency to recognise the existence and importance of indigenous languages'.[195] 'It is . . . being recognised that these languages are an integral part of the various cultures in the country'.[196] Peru is commonly cited as a progressive example, as are current developments in, for example, Denmark[197] and New Zealand:[198] these last two States are not parties to ILO Convention 107. The Special Rapporteur writes that 'the time has perhaps come, as some States have acknowledged, for countries with large groups of indigenous-language speakers to rethink their linguistic and cultural policies and to place them squarely on a course designed to ensure respect for . . . and use of these languages.'[199]

The references to linguistic strategies in Part VI of the Convention are framed by a general reference to education in Article 21 obliging States to take measures to ensure that members of indigenous populations have the opportunity to acquire education at all levels 'on an equal footing with the rest of the national community'. Educational programmes in general are to be adapted to the stage reached by the populations 'in the process of social, economic and cultural integration' into the national community (Article

---

[190] The text of this statute is reproduced in Martinez-Cobo (*supra*, n. 178), para. 57.
[191] Ibid., para. 58.
[192] *Government of Peru, Report to the ILO* (1977).
[193] See also the annex to the 1970 Report to the ILO in relation to the forest-dwelling Indians.
[194] For an American Indian view, see *American Indian Law Newsletter, Special Issue No. 11*, 1974, 41.
[195] Para. 10.
[196] Ibid.
[197] *IWGIA Newsletter No. 22*, Copenhagen, June 1979, 10.
[198] Martinez-Cobo, (*supra*, n. 178), paras. 81 ff., para. 268.
[199] Ibid., para. 33.

22). The delegation of educational functions to missionary groups makes it extremely difficult to monitor compliance with these provisions,[200] but most States at least concede equality of access to education in formal terms.[201] Generally, however, for both indigenous and non-indigenous minorities, 'education' has not been an unmitigated benefit; on the contrary, it is not the provision of a general right to education that is important but what kind of education, bearing in mind that 'education' can destroy a culture as well as protect it. The report of the Anti-Slavery Society to Martinez-Cobo illustrates the problem in connection with indigenous groups in Paraguay. The Society reports that 'no racist limitations' are imposed on indigenous access to education. None the less, it is noted that groups under missionary control are often forced to send all their children to school.[202]

General Provisions: Part VIII of the Convention

The final part of the Convention contains two articles which affect the substantive rights of the indigenous populations. Thus, Article 28, the 'implementation' provision, is capable of inducing wide variations in the protection of the populations: 'The nature and scope of the measures to be taken to give effect to this Convention shall be determined in a flexible manner, having regard to the conditions characteristic of each country.' The States Parties, therefore, possess a considerable margin of appreciation in the fulfilment of their obligations. The wording of the Convention is, at least when compared with other human rights conventions, reasonably precise and detailed so that this 'flexibility' provision avoids the imposition of a very heavy burden of obligation. However, the obligations of the Convention as a whole are not unduly burdensome, the analysis of the text displays a considerable range of 'exemption clauses' for States in the fulfilment of their duties. Certain further aspects of the text point to the possibility of States graduating their responses to the Convention. The Preamble refers to the interest of the States 'to promote continued action, to improve the living and working conditions' of the population. The references to 'integration' are usually prefixed by the adjective 'progressive', indicating that some, unspecified, time-scale is involved. Article 2 mentions States 'developing co-ordinated and systematic action'. Some of the provisions have a more peremptory character. Compulsory personal services 'shall be prohibited by law' (Article 9); the right of ownership of land 'shall be recognised' (Article 11); populations 'shall not be removed without their free consent' from

---

[200] The ILO Committee of Experts frequently asks questions on this: see, for example, its reports to the 1982 and 1983 International Labour Conferences, 186, and 198, respectively, for the case of Bolivia.
[201] UN Doc E/CN.4/Sub.2/1983/21/Add.2, paras 9–11.
[202] Ibid., para. 29.

habitual territories, etc. The Convention is like most human rights conventions in that it has a 'mixed' character[203] *vis-à-vis* the immediate application and progressive implementation distinction. The particular form of Article 28 reflects a general feature of ILO Convention and Recommendations— flexibility of standards is a desideratum expressed in the ILO Constitution[204] and a separate section is devoted to describing methods of achieving this in the standard ILO 'Manual on Procedure'. Granted, the 'progressive implementation' character of the Convention, and Article 28, the supervisory machinery for the implementation of ILO instruments assumes considerable importance in case the laxity of the Convention translates itself into a lack of any real benefit to indigenous groups.

The ILO seems, in many respects, an organization whose basic concerns and institutional structure are ill-suited to advance the cause of indigenous groups.[205] The organization and its instruments are very 'labour oriented'. While the problems encountered by indigenous groups in the modern world relate to their economic condition, they also relate to their cultural survival. Convention 107 endeavours to deal with these problems largely from an economic and social standpoint. While the Convention remains the only instrument to attempt to deal with a range of indigenous problems, the 'cultural' question is not dealt with adequately. Much of the content and the tone of the Convention appear rather dated; its 'economism' coupled with its paternalistic approach, does not meet the requirements of a modern policy.[206] The stress on integration is too heavy. It reflects the assumptions of the age when it was drafted and does not give adequate autonomy to indigenous peoples. Its 'peculiarity' compared to the normal ILO concerns has caused its neglect by that organization: there was initially much debate as to whether it was even constitutional for the ILO to concern itself with broad indigenous issues.[207] Paradoxically, this relative lack of concern may not have been a wholly bad development: while some basic protections have

---

[203] Thornberry, 'Poverty, Litigation and Fundamental Rights—A European Perspective', *ICLQ*, 29 (1980), 250; *supra*, discussion on Article 27 of the Covenant on Civil and Political Rights.

[204] See Article 19(3) of the ILO Constitution, cited in *ILO Manual of Procedures*, 3.

[205] The worker/employer distinction reflects an industrial economy which may be at some remove from the type of economy practised by indigenous groups. While associations of workers or employers may be expected to concern themselves with indigenous labour as an adjunct to the industrial or agricultural workforce, this may not follow in the case of groups displaying indifference or antipathy towards 'modernization'. The connection between the ILO and the indigenous issue is, however, understandable in historical terms, since many of the most exploited groups of workers have been 'indigenous'. For a discussion of the ILO's role, see Berman, 'The ILO and Indigenous Peoples: Revision of ILO Convention 107', *Review of ICJ*, 41 (1988), 48; replies by Samson and Swepston, *Review of ICJ*, 42 (1989), 43, 44.

[206] *Infra*, ch. 41.

[207] Bennett, 'The ILO Convention on Indigenous and Tribal Populations: The Resolution of a Problem of Vires', *BYIL*, 46 (1972–3), 382. The revision of ILO 107 has brought forth many expressions of opinion by States that particular questions are outside the ILO's competence: see especially International Labour Conference, 75th Session, 1988, *Partial Revision*, Report VI(2), and 76th Session, 1989, Report IV(2A).

suffered to the considerable detriment of the populations, the headlong rush to the 'integration' policy favoured by the Convention would probably have resulted in further and, perhaps irrevocable, damage to its intended beneficiaries.

40. *Beyond ILO Convention 107*

Articulation of Indigenous Peoples' Demands

Many references have been made in the foregoing chapter to the anachronistic nature of ILO Convention 107 and to the need for change. The criticism was essayed from the point of view of humanitarian standards and the equal valuation of cultural contributions to humanity. A vaguely identified indigenous point of view was also mentioned. 'Indigenous groups' are not, of course, a unified body of 'peoples' and many points of view are possible on the scope of a more helpful regime of national and international legislation. However, in recent years a number of indigenous group organizations have emerged to promote their claims on the national and international plane. This is already a significant new area of awareness in international human rights law which shows every sign of further development.[1] Valid criticism and reform of the present international system must incorporate in some form the indigenous peoples' perception of their relationship to international law.

Documents of conferences on indigenous peoples evince a widespread dissatisfaction with both the content of international law and its implementation. ILO Convention 107 has been a particular and obvious target. At the First Congress of Indian Movements in South America,[2] the

[1] Alfredsson, 'International Law, International Organisations and Indigenous Peoples' *Journal of International Affairs*, 36 (1982), 113; Barsh, 'Indigenous Peoples: An Emerging Object of International Law' *AJIL*, 80 (1986), 36, and 'Revision of ILO Convention No. 107', *AJIL*, 81 (1987), 756; Crawford (ed.), *The Rights of Peoples*, articles by Falk and Nettheim, 17 and 107; Cumming, 'The Rights of Indigenous Peoples: A Comparative Analysis', *Procs. ASIL*, 68 (1974), 265; Eggleston, 'Prospects for United Nations Protection of the Human Rights of Indigenous Minorities', *Australian Yearbook of International Law*, 5 (1970–3), 68; Galey, 'Indigenous Peoples, International Consciousness-Raising and the Development of International Law on Human Rights', *RDH*, 8 (1975), 21; Hannum, 'New Developments in Indigenous Rights' *Virginia Journal of International Law*, p. 28 (1988), 649. See also Roy and Alfredon, 'Indigenous Rights: The Literature Explosion', *Transnational Perspective*, 13 (1987), 19; *Analytical Compilation of Existing Legal Instruments and Proposed Draft Standards Relating to Indigenous Rights, prepared by the Secretariat in Accordance with Sub-Commission Resolution 1985/22*, UN Doc M/HR/86/36.

[2] Held at Ollantaytambo (Cuzco, Peru, Feb.–March 1980), cited Martinez-Cobo, UN Doc E/CN.4/Sub.2/476/Add.5, 54, and ibid., Annex V. There are at present 10 indigenous organizations in consultative status with the UN Economic and Social Council (ECOSOC): World Council of Indigenous Peoples, International Indian Treaty Council, Inuit Circumpolar Conference, World Indigenous Association, Indian Law Resource Center, Indian Council of South America, National Indian Youth Council, National Aboriginal and Islander Legal Service Secretariat, Four Directions Council and the Grand Council of the Crees (Quebec). See also *Partial Revision*, Report VI(1), ch. II.

Indian Council of South America declared its belief that the ILO Convention, 'elaborated by oppressive governments, was meant to legalise the colonial oppression of the Indian peoples . . .'.[3] The Council made the following particular criticisms:[4] (1) the Convention was 'made by Governments without the participation of representatives of the Indian peoples'; (2) it did not consider the right of self-determination; (3) its aim was 'integration and assimilation, with total lack of respect for the dignity of every people and its right to freedom; (4) this would result in the total destruction of Indian culture, traditions and languages; (5) the Convention is 'contradictory in its different articles, allowing for wide interpretations and vague definitions'. The last mentioned criticism is not, unfortunately, relevant only to ILO Convention 107, but it may reflect the difficulties in the Convention of reconciling 'protection' with 'integration'. The other criticisms are quite comprehensive in that they strike at the basic purposes of the Convention, finding them destructive rather than constructive.

The critical summation of the Convention is developed in relation to some of its particular articles. Article 2(3), which states that the 'primary objective of an action shall be the fostering of individual dignity, and the advancement of individual usefulness and initiative', is criticized because it 'pretends to encourage dignity, as if the Indian people were lacking in dignity', it 'pretends to promote social usefulness, as if our people had no social organisation to dignify them', and, finally, it 'seeks to promote the individual, which is contrary to the communal spirit of our peoples'.[5] Article 4(b), which mentions the dangers of disrupting indigenous values and institutions unless 'appropriate substitutes' acceptable to the groups are found, is declared to be extremely contradictory, in the sense that it 'speaks about the danger of interfering with the values of our peoples, but . . . it allows their replacement by other values which correspond to the culture of the oppressor'.[6] Article 7(2), populations shall be 'allowed to retain' their own customs provided they are not incompatible with the national legal systems or integration programmes, receives a particularly sharp rebuke: 'We feel that this article clarifies perfectly the spirit of Convention 107, because the legislation imposed by the colonisers does not contemplate the right to maintain one's customs and institutions and the objectives of the integration programmes are the destruction and the death of the Indian peoples.'[7] Further criticism is essayed of Article 23(2), the principle of linguistic transition from the vernacular to the national language, this fosters 'forced acculturation by imposing the language of the coloniser . . .'.[8] Article 24(1), the principle of 'education for integration', 'shows the evident intention of bringing about, at all costs, the disappearance of our peoples,

---

[3] Martinez-Cobo (*supra*, n. 2), Annex V, para. 2.
[4] Ibid.   [5] Ibid., para. 3(*a*).
[6] Ibid., para. 3(*b*).   [7] Ibid. 14, para. 3(*c*).
[8] Ibid., para. 3(*d*).

by destroying the minds of our children, by disuniting our families and . . . the total community.'[9]

This particular conference was only one of a spate of such conferences in recent years.[10] The contemporary demands of indigenous groups on international law were articulated in four major conferences in 1977: the Inuit Circumpolar Conference (Barrow, Alaska);[11] the Barbados II Conference (Bridgetown, Barbados);[12] the Second General Assembly of the World Council of Indigenous Peoples (Kiruna, Sweden);[13] and the International NGO Conference on Discrimination against Indigenous Populations in the Americas (Palais des Nations, Geneva).[14] Other noteworthy conferences demonstrating the modern indigenous viewpoint include the First Congress of South American Indian Movements,[15] the International NGO Conference on Indigenous Peoples and Land,[16] and the Fourth Russell Tribunal on the Rights of the Indians in the Americas.[17] Many of the conferences are of course part of a series, the Inuit Circumpolar Conferences, the General Assemblies of the World Council of Indigenous Peoples (WCIP), etc.

Extensive canvassing of indigenous opinions has also been undertaken by Special Rapporteur Martinez-Cobo for his massive study of Discrimination against Indigenous Populations.[18] A review of the resolutions and conclusions of the conferences reveals a consistent emphasis on a number of themes.[19] Self-determination is one such theme. At the second general

---

[9] Ibid., para. 3.

[10] These are listed in Martinez-Cobo (*supra*, n. 2), with resolutions in Annex V.

[11] See Inuit Circumpolar Conference, June 1977–the Report of the First Inuit Circumpolar Conference, Martinez-Cobo, (*supra*, n. 2), 3–12; Conference resolution in Martinez-Cobo, ibid., Annex 1. The conference was attended by Inuit, and private and government experts from many States.

[12] Martinez-Cobo, (*supra*, n. 2), 13–17, and Annex II. Barbados I was a symposium held in Barbados in 1971 by anthropologists. Unlike Barbados I, Barbados II had significant participation by Indian groups. For recommendations of the first conference, see *Declaration of Barbados I*, IWGIA Document (Copenhagen: International Work Group for Indigenous Affairs, 1971).

[13] Martinez-Cobo (*supra*, n. 2), 18–33.

[14] Ibid. 35–53, and Annex IV; Report of the International NGO Conference on Discrimination against Indigenous Populations (Geneva, 1977); also in *Journal for the Development of Indian Law*, Special Issue, October 1977.

[15] *Supra*, n. 2.

[16] International NGO Conference on Indigenous Peoples and the Land, Palais des Nations, Geneva, September 1981, organized by the Sub-Committee on Racism, Racial Discrimination, Apartheid and Decolonisation of the Special NGO Committee on Human Rights.

[17] *Report of the 4th Russell Tribunal* (Rotterdam, 1980), vol. i (conclusions).

[18] *Study of the Problem of Discrimination against Indigenous Populations*, UN Doc E/CN. 4/Sub/2/476/Add.1–6; 1980/2, Add.1–7, 1983/21, Add.1–8.

[19] The Analytical Compilation (*supra*, n. 1), is divided into 12 chapters, reflecting a more complex classification than is adopted here: Full and Effective Enjoyment of Fundamental Freedoms, Life, Physical Integrity and Security, Freedom of Religion and Traditional Religious Practices, Education, Language, Culture, Traditions and Way of Life, Intercultural Information and Education, Land and Natural Resources, Autonomy, Self-Government and Self-Determination, including Political Representation and Institutions, Treaties and Agreements Concluded between States and Indigenous Populations, Right and Responsibility of Indigenous

assembly of the WCIP, the Declaration on Human Rights describes self-determination as one of the 'irrevocable and inborn rights which are due to us in our capacity as Aboriginals'. A full statement[20] of the content of self-determination is made in the submission of the International Indian Treaty Council to the UN Working Group on Indigenous Populations.[21] In this submission, indigenous populations are described as being subject to 'an economic and/or political and/or social domination which is alien and colonial or neo-colonial in nature'[22] and as being 'composed of nations and peoples, which are collective entities entitled to and requiring self-determination'.[23] Self-determination involves both its external manifestation: 'Indigenous nations and people who so desire should be granted the full rights and obligations of external self-determination'[24] and internal self-determination, which includes control over economic, social, and cultural development in accordance with their traditions, the right to engage in foreign trade, to 'restore, practise and educate their children to their cultures, languages, traditions and way of life', and the right to the ownership of land 'as the territorial base for the existence of indigenous populations as such'.[25] It may be seen from these statements that 'self-determination', as claimed by indigenous groups, is a broad, portmanteau concept embracing education and land rights as well as rights pertinent to external self-determination which is in effect the right to a separate sovereignty. The Treaty Council adopts and elaborates the modern vocabulary of anti-colonialism, applying it to indigenous groups.

Not surprisingly, protection from genocide, 'ethnocide' or 'ethno-genocide' is prominent in indigenous demands. The Second General Assembly of the WCIP noted the 'outright massacres—in the style of those enacted by the conquerers and usurpers of the 15th and 16th centuries', and that: 'almost all the articles in the [Genocide] Convention of 1948 have been violated.'[26] The Congress of Indian Movements of South America described 'ethno-

Populations, As of All Others, to Respect Universally Recognised Human Rights and Fundamental Freedoms.

[20] UN Doc E/CN.4/Sub.2/476/Add.5, Annex III, 2.
[21] UN Doc E/CN.4/Sub.2/A.C.4/1983/5/Add. 2, 3–4. On the Working Group, see *infra*, ch. 41.
[22] Ibid. 3.
[23] Ibid.
[24] Ibid., paras 3–4.
[25] Ibid. 4. Even more sweeping demands are made by some groups. The International NGO Conference on Discrimination against Indigenous Populations in the Americas declared: '1. RECOGNITION OF INDIGENOUS NATIONS. Indigenous peoples shall be accorded recognition as nations, and proper subjects of international law, provided the people concerned desire to be recognised as a nation and meet the fundamental requirements of nationhood, namely: (*a*) Having a permanent population (*b*) Having a defined territory (*c*) Having a government (*d*) Having the ability to enter into relations with other States . . . 4. ACCORDANCE OF INDEPENDENCE. Indigenous nations or groups shall be accorded such degree of independence as they may desire in accordance with international law . . .' (this document is now available in UN Doc E/CN.4/Sub.2/1986/7).
[26] E/CN.4/Sub.2/476/Add. 5, Annex III, 1. Also the Russell Tribunal (*supra*, n. 17).

genocide' against the Indian as involving physical and cultural elements—
the latter described as aggression against 'the cultural values of our
ancestors, such as the prohibition to use our languages, the alienation and
sense of shame about our Indian person and place names, the prohibition of
the practice of our religion.'[27] The physical aspect of the destruction of the
Indians is described as 'systematic extermination',[28] implying a full-scale
and deliberate policy of genocide as this is recognized in the Convention of
1948 and in customary law. Besides violations of their right to existence, the
groups allege widespread denial of human rights at virtually every point in
the spectrum of modern human rights law.

Besides demanding remedies for gross policies of cultural genocide, the
indigenous groups affirm their rights in this field, such as the right to
maintain culture, language, and traditions;[29] the right to respect for indigenous culture 'in all its modes of expression',[30] and the right to 'an
appropriate education in accordance with our culture and our traditions,
without any foreign elements and within the framework of an educational
system which recognises the value of our culture and acknowledges an
official status to our language at all educational levels'.[31]

The land and resources question also figures prominently at the conferences. Article 11 of the Declaration of Principles for the Defence of the
Indigenous Nations and Peoples of the Western Hemisphere summarizes
this concern very well:

It shall be unlawful for any State to make or permit any action or course of conduct
with respect to the territories of an indigenous nation or group which will directly or
indirectly result in the destruction or deterioration of an indigenous nation or group
through the effects of pollution of earth, air, water, or which in any way depletes,
displaces or destroys any natural resource or other resources under the dominion of,
or vital to the livelihood of an indigenous nation or group.[32]

A much amplified version of this was submitted to the UN Working Group
on Indigenous Populations by the International Indian Treaty Council.[33]
The WCIP resolution describes the inherent rights of aboriginal peoples as
including the right 'to recover the land which rightfully and according to
millenary tradition belongs to us, but which has been robbed from us by the
foreign intruders'; and the right 'to occupy land collectively with sole rights
as something irrevocable and non-transferable'.[34] Land rights are also
deemed to include the right to organize the administration of land and

---

[27] UN Doc E/CN.4/Sub.2/476/Add. 5, Annex V, 10.
[28] Ibid.
[29] Ibid., Annex III, 2 (WCIP).
[30] Ibid. 3.
[31] Ibid.
[32] Ibid., Annex IV, 3.
[33] UN Doc E/CN.4/Sub.2/AC.4/1985/5/Add.2, 6.
[34] UN Doc (*supra*, n. 26), 2.

natural resources, the right to demand 'sufficient' land from governments, the right to use natural resources, and the right to demand that laws will be passed to recognize indigenous land ownership.[35]

There is a difference between persuading governments to observe more stringently existing international legal principles and humanitarian standards, and demanding the wholesale 'rectification' of international law by claiming statehood, self-determination, and reinstatement of whatever personality was formerly held by indigenous communities.[36] The changes sought by indigenous groups must be realized against the background of late twentieth century international law, the humanitarian principles of which are in a rapid state of evolution, not least with respect to these groups; they must also be realized in the context of a largely State based system of international law. States will not respond to demands which, if realized, would cancel their existence as integral units. There is however, a particular indigenous problem with respect to human rights, and a developing indigenous point of view. There is clearly a need for a more advanced international instrument than ILO Convention 107, as there is a need for a better focused application of human rights law to indigenous groups. Indigenous peoples are among the most deprived groups in terms of basic rights in the modern world. The tentative international efforts to ameliorate their position are discussed in the following chapter.

[35] UN Doc 2.

[36] *Supra*, introduction to the section on Indigenous Peoples, for historical studies of the question.

41. Indigenous Groups and Contemporary International Standards

There has been a considerable amplification of United Nations activity on indigenous populations following the United Nations Declaration on the Elimination of All Forms of Racial Discrimination[1] and the subsequent Programme for the Decade of Action to Combat Racism and Racial Discrimination[2] (the Decade began on 10 December 1973). One of the objectives of this Programme is declared to be 'to identify, isolate and dispel the fallacious and mythical beliefs, policies and practices that contribute to racism and racial discrimination'. The Programme also looks forward to the ending of racist regimes, and is thus both activity directed and educational. The proposed 'revaluation of values' has a particular potency in the context of indigenous populations, victims of the psychology and vocabulary of prejudice, dehumanization and patronization to as great an extent as any human group. The anti-discrimination movement owes its ideology and modern impetus to the resentment of the new political elites of African and Asian States at old attitudes and practices perceived by them as still existing within many States. These groups were themselves the indigenous peoples of the colonial age; now that the focus shifts to such groups in independent States in the post-colonial age, it is logical that there should be a connection between the anti-discrimination movement in international law and the movement to secure justice to indigenous groups.

Before this development, there was a brief flurry of interest in indigenous groups at the United Nations. General Assembly Resolution 275(III) is entitled 'Study of the Social Problems of the Aboriginal Populations and other Underdeveloped Social Groups of the American Continent'.[3] The Preamble to the Resolution recalls the objectives of the United Nations, in particular, that of promoting 'social progress and higher standards of living throughout the world', and it notes the existence on the American continent of 'a large aboriginal population and other underdeveloped social groups which face peculiar social problems . . .'. The Preamble also recites that 'the material and cultural development of those populations would result in a more profitable utilisation of the natural resources of America to the

---

[1] UNGA Res. 1904(XVIII), November 1963.
[2] For a succinct account of the aims of the 'Decade', consult *The United Nations and Human Rights* (New York, 1978), UN Sales No. E.78.I.18.
[3] GAOR, 3rd Session, pt. II, 208th plenary meeting, 349.

advantage of the world.' The operative part of the resolution hardly addresses those undefined problems, recommending only that the Economic and Social Council, 'with the assistance of the specialised agencies concerned, and in collaboration with the *Instituto Indigenista Interamericano*, study the situation of the aboriginal populations . . . of the States of the American continent requesting such help'. The Secretary-General of the United Nations is invited to co-operate in such studies. Bolivia, it may be noted, had earlier submitted a resolution to the General Assembly proposing that the Economic and Social Council create a special sub-commission to study 'the social problems of the aboriginal populations of the American continent'.[4] This was referred to the Third Committee of the General Assembly[5] and then to the Ad Hoc Political Committee.[6] Resolution 275(III), however, did not refer to the desirability of any sub-commission in its Preamble or substantive part.

In the event, no governmental requests for assistance were received.[7] The USSR and its allies used the proposals on indigenous groups to attack the human rights record of the United States.[8] The Economic and Social Council briefly considered the matter in 1950, adopting Resolution 313(XI)[9] which requested the Secretary-General to render assistance on improving the living standards of indigenous groups to any national or international governmental body requesting such assistance. The general[10] question of indigenous populations did not thereafter claim the attention of the principal organs of the United Nations until the developments in connection with racial discrimination.

Thus, in 1969, the Sub-Commission on Prevention of Discrimination and Protection of Minorities received the report of the Special Rapporteur entitled 'Special Study on Racial Discrimination in the Political, Economic, Social and Cultural Spheres' which included a chapter on measures to protect indigenous populations.[11] Subsequently, the Economic and Social Council passed Resolution 1589(L) of May 1971, where it authorized the preparation of a Study on the Problem of Discrimination Against Indigenous Populations (Special Rapporteur M. Martinez-Cobo).[12] The study in

---

[4] UN Doc A/610.

[5] *GAOR*, 3rd Session, pt. I, 3rd Committee, 180th meeting.

[6] Ibid., pt. II, Ad Hoc Political Committee, 53rd and 54th meetings; UN Doc A/AC.24/71/Rev.1 (Revised Bolivian resolution), and UN Doc A/AC.24/77/Rev.1 (Haitian amendment).

[7] *YBUN 1950*, 610; Report of the UN Secretary-General to the Economic and Social Council, UN Doc E/1691.

[8] Meetings of the Ad Hoc Political Committee (*supra*, n. 6).

[9] 379th plenary meeting, July 1950.

[10] For activities of the United Nations on specific issues such as slavery and forced labour, see Martinez-Cobo, UN Doc E/CN.4/Sub.2/476/Add.4.

[11] UN Sales No. 71.XIV.2 (updated edition is UN Sales No. 76.XIV.2). See also the preliminary report UN Doc E/CN.4/Sub.2/301.

[12] See the preliminary report, UN Doc E/CN.4/Sub.2/L.566, paras. 1–11.

turn inspired the creation of the Working Group on Indigenous Populations of the UN Sub-Commission on Prevention of Discrimination and Protection of Minorities. The Group was set up in May 1982[13] to review developments relating to indigenous populations and to submit conclusions, including views as to what measures will be needed to promote respect for the human rights and fundamental freedoms of such populations. The Group was asked to pay special attention to the evolution of standards, and in particular to consider avenues of recourse at the national, regional, and international levels to guarantee the basic rights of the groups. In carrying out this task, it was requested to take into account both the similarities and differences in the situations and aspirations of indigenous populations throughout the world. The *locus* of the Group within the Sub-Commission and the Commission on Human Rights will ensure that whatever standards may evolve will harmonize with the principal human rights instruments of the United Nations.[14] The United Nations is, therefore, moving from the age of 'consciousness raising'[15] to that of 'standard setting'.

The Working Group has produced a Draft Universal Declaration on Indigenous Rights to be adopted by the General Assembly in 1992.[16] Following the United Nations initiatives towards a declaration of indigenous rights, the governing body of the ILO decided in 1985 to convene a meeting of experts on the Revision of the Indigenous and Tribal Populations Convention. The experts recommended unanimously that the Convention be revised as a matter or urgency, and drew particular attention to the need to review the Convention's basic integrationist approach and its provisions on land rights. They emphasized that the revision of the Convention should be a partial one: 'based on the text of the existing instrument in order to preserve its inherent strengths in so far as possible'.[17] The first discussion on

---

[13] The creation of the Working Group on Indigenous Populations was proposed by the Sub-Commission on the Prevention of Discrimination and Protection of Minorities in its Res. 2(XXXIV) of 8 September 1981, endorsed by the Commission on Human Rights in Res. 1982/19, and authorized by the Economic and Social Council in Res. 1982/34 of 7 May 1982.

[14] See, for example, the information submitted by the Government of Australia to the Working Group, UN Doc E/CN.4/Sub.2/AC.4/1983/2/Add.2. The Government expressed the opinion that the Working Group should not be seen as replacing existing UN Human Rights communications mechanisms. See also UNGA Res. 41/120, 4 December 1986: 'Setting of International Standards in the Field of Human Rights': international instruments in process of development should, *inter alia*, 'be consistent with the existing body of international human rights law . . .' (resolution annexed to UN Doc E/CN.4/Sub.2/1987/22–*Report of the Working Group on Indigenous Populations on its Fifth Session*).

[15] Galey, 'Indigenous Peoples'.

[16] The Working Group proposed that 1992 be designated as the International Year of the World's Indigenous Populations, 500 years after the 'discovery' by Columbus of the Americas. However, the proposal was blocked by Spain in the Human Rights Commission. Instead, the Sub-Commission proposed that the 'year' be rescheduled to 1993 to coincide with the end of the Second Decade on Racism: see *Rev. ICJ*, Nos. 40/1988, 24, and 41/1988, 26; Sanders, 'The UN Working Group on Indigenous Populations', *Human Rights Quarterly*, 11 (1989), 406.

[17] *Partial Revision*, Report VI(1), 1–2.

the partial revision took place at the seventy-fifth session of the International Labour Conference in 1988. Following that discussion, the International Labour Office prepared and communicated to the governments a report containing the proposed Convention based on the conclusions adopted.[18] Governments were requested to consult representative organizations of employers and workers and also urged to consult organizations representing indigenous and tribal peoples in their countries, if any. The following are major issues raised by the drafts.

Definition

The Working Group dealt with the definition of 'indigenous' in its second and third sessions. India and Bangladesh wanted to limit the definition to peoples in the Western Hemisphere and Australia. China, the USSR, India, and Bangladesh in effect deny that there are any indigenous peoples in their territories—a parallel to denials of the existence of minorities in Latin America.[19] In both cases, the denial is perhaps normative rather than cognitive, and the fear is that of investing groups with 'inappropriate' rights.[20] The Working Group has not adopted a formal definition,[21] but the current draft clearly envisages universal application.

The ILO revision proposes to retain both 'tribal' and 'indigenous', while deleting 'semi-tribal' and references to groups as in a less advanced stage than the population at large. A textual innovation is proposed in Article 1(2): 'Self-identification as indigenous or tribal shall be regarded as a fundamental criterion for determining the groups to which the provisions of this Convention apply.' Sweden observed: 'The subjective criterion . . . might be taken to be the sole criterion to be applied. It would be inadvisable for objective criteria . . . not to be also applicable.'[22]

---

[18] *Partial Revision*, Report IV(2A), 1–2.

[19] *Supra*, ch. 16. Succinct accounts of debates are provided by Barsh, 'Indigenous Peoples: An Emerging Object of International Law', 373–6; and Hannum, op. cit., 662–6. Bangladesh, e.g., maintained that 'indigenous' refers only to those countries where racially distinct people coming from overseas established colonies and subjugated the indigenous populations. The entire population of Bangladesh was autochthonous and all had coexisted prior to the fomentation of ethnic divisions by British administrators. The Indian position is discussed in Sinha, 'A Special Deal for Tribals in India: A Historical Appraisal', *Tribe*, No. 4 (1970), 1.

[20] See however, *supra*, ch. 39, n. 36.

[21] *Supra*, ch. 39, n. 58. See generally the Reports of the Working Group on Indigenous Populations, 2nd Session, UN Doc E/CN.4/Sub.2/1983/22; 3rd Session, UN Doc E/CN.4/Sub.2/19/84/20; 4th Session, UN Doc E/CN.4/Sub.2/1985/22 (the issue of definition resurfaced at the 4th Session).

[22] *Partial Revision*, Report IV(2A), 13. The International Labour Office commented: 'Self-identification would not appear to be the sole criterion applied to coverage of the Convention, as suggested by the Government of Sweden'—ibid. The UN Working Group has noted the importance of both 'subjective' and 'objective' factors in definition, UN Doc E/CN.4/Sub.2/1982/33, para. 42.

Self-Determination

Self-determination in International Law is a right of 'all peoples'.[23] Considerable interest therefore attaches to the choice of terminology in this area. The UN Working Group is styled as a group on indigenous populations; the ILO text to be revised is a convention on indigenous populations. None the less, the rights proposed in the Draft Declaration are the rights of indigenous peoples,[24] and the proposed ILO text is a convention concerning indigenous and tribal peoples in independent countries. Government observers at the Working Group have expressed reservations on the utilization of 'peoples', precisely because it might lead to assumptions about self-determination, secession, and separatism.[25] Observations by governments to the ILO have been forthright. Bolivia commented that there 'should be a specific clarification that "peoples" has no connotations relating to the political self-determination of peoples, as understood in contemporary international law and United Nations practice. The introduction of the term 'peoples' without this clarification would be outside the ILO's mandate.'[26] Canada proposed a specific qualifying clause: 'The use of the term "peoples" in this Convention does not imply the right to self-determination as that right is understood in international law.'[27] Canada added: 'Concern with the use of . . . "peoples" is related to the issue of self-determination as that term is understood in international law. This position is not meant to prejudice the attainment of greater levels of autonomy for indigenous populations at the national level.'[28] Critical observations on this issue were also made by Brazil, Chile, Ecuador, India, and the USA. A number of other States preferring 'peoples' to 'populations' stressed that the use of the former should not have effects outside the revised Convention.[29] The commentary by the International Labour Office made a similar point.[30] Gabon expressed a positive view of 'peoples' as the correct term, since it is 'more appropriate in the context of the Convention as the reference is to a social and cultural community which is distinct in its identity'.[31] Peru made a concurring observation: 'peoples' refers to ethnic identity and the right to maintain a territorial base.[32]

This is some way from claims of indigenous groups to self-determination. The Draft Declaration avoids reference to self-determination, preferring the

[23] *Supra*, ch. 1.
[24] The draft Preamble makes seven references to 'indigenous peoples'.
[25] Report on the 5th Session of the Working Group, UN Doc E/CN.4/Sub.2/1987/22, para. 56.
[26] *Partial Revision*, Report IV(2A), 8.
[27] Ibid. 8–9.
[28] Ibid. 9.
[29] Ibid. 8–11. The States in the latter category were Australia, Finland, and Norway.
[30] Ibid. 11–12.
[31] Ibid. 10.   [32] Ibid.

language of human rights, and prevention of genocide and ethnocide, stressing indigenous rights in the cultural sphere.[33]

Integration and Assimilation

The Draft Declaration is premised on the right to be different, strengthening indigenous cultures, ethno-development, self-management, protection against genocide and ethnocide, or 'any form of forced assimilation or integration . . .',[34] maintenance of traditional economic structures, participation at the State level, and cultural autonomy. The basis is that indigenous societies are in no way inferior, only different, and that cultural change must not be imposed on groups. Similar thinking informs the revision of Convention No. 107. The first three conclusions adopted by the Meeting of Experts convened to advise the Governing Body were: (1) the Convention's integrationist approach is inadequate and no longer reflects current thinking; (2) indigenous and tribal peoples should enjoy as much control as possible over their own economic, social, and cultural development; and (3) the right of these peoples to interact with the national society on an equal footing through their own institutions should be recognized.[35] The integrationist approach, according to the experts, manifested itself in two ways: all government programmes should, for the ultimate benefit of the groups, be directed towards their integration into national society; and in the inherent assumption that the indigenous groups were culturally inferior.[36] The approach

can also be described as 'paternalistic', with benevolent as well as harmful aspects. It is benevolent in its adoption of a protective attitude towards weaker elements of society. It is harmful . . . in the sense that it assumes that governments can and should take measures for the groups regardless of their wishes, since they are presumed to be incapable of expressing a valid opinion.[37]

The purpose of the revision is thus to change the orientation of the instrument, rather than engage in substantive revision of most of the articles. The new orientation was strongly challenged by Ecuador: 'This new basic orientation . . . gives rise to extremely dangerous situations which are conducive to the disintegration of many Member States . . . .'[38] None the

---

[33] Appendix 7 to the present work, UN Doc E/CN.4/Sub.2/1988/24. Much of the work that could be achieved by the use of the contentious term 'self-determination', particularly 'internal' self-determination, might be achieved by building from a foundation of rights more acceptable to States. The combination of individual and collective rights set out in the draft Declaration would achieve most of the aims of indigenous groups.

[34] Para. 5.
[35] *Partial Revision*, Report VI(1), 27.
[36] Ibid. 27–29.
[37] Ibid. 28.
[38] *Partial Revision*, Report VI(2), 9.

less, this approach is carried through consistently in the revision. The effect is most noticeable in Article 2, the fundamental policy article of the Convention. The proposed revision reads:

1. Governments shall have the responsibility for developing, with the participation of the peoples concerned, co-ordinated and systematic action to protect the rights of these peoples and to guarantee respect for their integrity. 2. Such action shall include measures for: (a) enabling members of these societies to benefit on an equal footing from the rights and opportunities which national laws and regulations grant to other members of the population; (b) promoting the full realisation of the social, economic and cultural rights of these peoples with respect for their social and cultural identity, their customs and traditions and their institutions; (c) assisting the members of the peoples concerned to raise their standard of living to that enjoyed by other members of the national community, in a manner compatible with their aspirations and ways of life.[39]

The article captures the essence of the revision which has not, it may be noted, met the full approval of indigenous organizations.[40]

Land Rights

The Draft Declaration proclaims the right of indigenous peoples to ownership and possession of the lands which they have traditionally occupied; 'Such lands may only be taken away from them with their free and informed consent as witnessed by a treaty or agreement.'[41] The draft also calls for the right to recognition of land tenure systems, the right to special measures to ensure control over surface resources, and the right

to reclaim land and surface resources or where this is not possible, to seek just and fair compensation for the same, when the property has been taken away without consent, in particular, if such deprival has been based on theories such as those relating to discovery, *terra nullius*, waste lands or idle lands. Compensation . . . may take the form of land or resources of quality and legal status at least equal to that of the property previously owned by them.[42]

The proposed rule for subsoil resources is for States to obtain the consent of the indigenous peopoles before permitting exploitation, and compensate for disturbance.

The changes in the ILO revision have necessitated a major redraft of Part

---

[39] *Partial Revision*, Report IV(2B).
[40] Report on the 5th Session of the Working Group on Indigenous Populations, (*supra*, n. 25), paras. 39–40. The criticisms refer mainly to the lack of indigenous participation in the revision process, the insufficient attention paid to the principle of self-determination, and the inadequacy of land rights provisions including the continued permission for States to remove indigenous peoples from their lands.
[41] Para. 12.
[42] Para. 15. For *terra nullius*, waste lands, etc., see notes *supra*, ch. 39.

II of the Convention. The major addition to Article 11 is a requirement that governments shall take necessary steps to identify the lands traditionally occupied, and to guarantee effective protection of the right of ownership. The revision affirms the right of the peoples to surface resources, including the right to participate in their management and conservation. The right is not extended to sub-surface resources; instead, governments are required, in a rather weak formulation, to 'seek to obtain' the agreement of peoples to exploitation, whose participation is to be secured 'wherever possible'. Any stronger version of this right was ruled out by the ILO on the grounds that it would prove incompatible with the legal systems of a number of countries.[43] States have been critical of the proposals. Australia observed that seeking the consent of peoples could amount to a veto power, and preferred 'consult with'.[44] Chile stated baldly: 'The requirement for consent is contrary to the principle of non-discrimination'.[45] India considered that it was unacceptable to extend ownership of land to control over natural resources.[46]

The draconian Article 12 is reformed to establish the basic principle that peoples shall not be removed from territories occupied without their free consent, and only as an exceptional measure. The list of situations where they can be removed is deleted. The second paragraph is revised to ensure that, when removal takes place, the new lands should not only be of equal quality to the old, but have equal legal status, an important improvement on the original text. This is therefore no absolute right to remain, but there is a qualified right to return, whenever possible, 'as soon as the grounds for removal cease to exist'. Australia observed that the temporary nature of relocation should be made more explicit, but India expressed the view that free and informed consent must be qualified with 'as far as possible'.[47] A new article would provide for penalties in cases of unauthorized intrusion on indigenous lands. These revisions may be welcomed, but they are some way from rights claimed by the groups, including 'The right to continue peacefully in the use, enjoyment and occupation of ancestral lands without unwanted intrusion, supervision or development',[48] and broad claims to resources.[49]

---

[43] *Partial Revision*, Report VI(1), 72.

[44] *Partial Revision*, Report IV(2A), 37.

[45] Ibid. 38.

[46] Ibid. 39.

[47] Ibid. 41–3.

[48] Four Directions Council, UN Docs. E/CN.4/Sub.2/AC.4/1984/NGO/1 and E/CN.4/Sub.2/1984/NGO/3.

[49] Indian Law Resource Center, UN Doc E/CN.4/Sub.2/AC.4/1982/R.1; World Council of Indigenous Peoples, UN Doc E/CN.4/Sub.2/AC.4/1983/5, 15. The text approved by the ILO is included as Appendix IX to the present volume — ILO Convention No. 169.

PART VII

Conclusions and Recommendations:
Lex Lata and *Lex Ferenda*

42. The Rights of Minorities and Their Members in Contemporary International Law

There is a measure of truth in Sieghart's remark that 'all human rights exist for the protection of minorities'.[1] 'Minorities' in this sense includes many groups besides ethnic, religious, and linguistic groups; human rights in general exist for the weak, the vulnerable, the dispossessed, the inarticulate. The strong have little need of human rights, at least in a democracy committed to majority rule, though, strictly speaking, in the letter of the international instruments encoding human rights, they are also beneficiaries: the premiss of these instruments is a universal premiss. Sieghart's statement need not, however, be interpreted in a formalistic sense: it means only that minorities, including those the subject of the present work, are the natural 'consumers' of human rights, in fact if not in form.

It follows that much of the protection accorded to ethnic, religious, and linguistic groups is indirect in character.[2] The indirect protection of groups means that in many relevant texts there is no mention of minorities. The basis for selecting materials in the present work is that they contain at least some reference to an ethnic, religious, or linguistic connection in the area of human rights. Indirect protection means also that international law hesitates to name groups as holders of rights, preferring to attribute rights to 'members' of groups.[3] The individualist frame of reference indicated by this last term is central to the conception of human rights. Departures from this are rare, though not unknown; the neglect of collective rights is only relative—the Genocide Convention, some important instruments in the field of racial discrimination,[4] and the Indigenous and Tribal Population Convention all make reference to collective rights expressly or by implication. However, the specific rule on minorities, Article 27 of the Covenant on Civil and Political Rights, contents itself with a reference to the rights of individuals (even if exercised communally), and it still appears to be the case, as evidenced by the responses of some States to Yugoslavia's draft Declaration on Minorities, that, at least where minorities are specifically mentioned in a text, any talk of group rights is anathema to many States.[5]

---

[1] Sieghart, *The Lawful Rights of Mankind*, 168 (Oxford: OUP, 1985).
[2] Ermacora, 'The Protection of Minorities before the United Nations'.
[3] As in Article 27 of the Covenant on Civil and Political Rights.
[4] The UNESCO Declaration on Race and Racial Prejudice.
[5] Part IV, *supra*, on the Right to Identity.

Taking a more specific meaning from Sieghart's remark, by confining it to ethnic, religious, and linguistic groups, it remains true that violations of the rights of man are as frequently associated with membership of such groups as with any other cause such as political affiliation.[6] There is sound practical sense in the common insertion of an anti-discrimination clause into instruments on human rights. The principle of equality and the attribution of rights to all human beings necessarily imply that there should exist no discrimination in the exercise of human rights, but it is profitable to make this clear by referring to non-discrimination on grounds of race, colour, religion, etc.[7] This serves not only as a specific instruction to States that the 'equal treatment of equals' and 'unequal treatment of unequals' demanded by the principle of equality does not imply that membership of a race or religion makes individuals inherently unequal in the law of the State, but also as a practical recognition that the 'ethnic' motive is a primary motive in denial of rights to human beings. Antagonisms based on race, religion, and language have not yet given way to antagonism between classes in the Marxist sense as the sole progenitors of conflict. In many areas of the world the two kinds of conflict may overlap: political opposition may have an ethnic dimension and ethnic self-consciousness may be expressed in apparently 'non-ethnic' political forms. It is often difficult to draw a line between the two concepts, the political and the ethnic, which sometimes has the effect of making subterfuges possible; the discussion of the Genocide Convention showed not only that States are reluctant to criminalize 'political genocide' but also that 'real' genocide may be justified as being 'merely' an exercise in the elimination of political opposition.[8]

The particular question of minorities intrudes itself in to the general issue of ethnic and religious conflict. International law, as noted above,[9] has sought throughout its history to regulate some of the negative consequences of the redrawing of political boundaries and of population movements, engaging itself by means of treaties governing the treatment of particular groups. The system of protection of minority groups under the League of Nations represents the most detailed and comprehensive attempt by the international community to regulate human rights by the method of specific treaties. But, unlike the limited number of contemporary examples of such treaties,[10] the League instruments did not function against a general international background of human rights law, so that gaps in the treaties left certain groups without protection against the law of the State. The present system of human rights, based largely on a range of multilateral treaties

---

[6] Generally, Moskowitz, *The Politics and Dynamics of Human Rights*; Thornberry, *Minorities and Human Rights Law*.

[7] Partsch, in Vasak and Alston (eds.), *The International Dimensions of Human Rights* (Paris: UNESCO, 1982), 61.

[8] *Supra*, The Right to Existence.

[9] *Supra*, Part I.

[10] Capotorti Report, Add. 2.

dealing with general human rights and more specific matters, represents a much more ambitious attempt to reform the human rights practices of States, replacing the previous focus on a limited number of troublesome cases.

The universal system to protect human rights implies a demotion of the 'classic' minorities question. The protection of minorities is now only a part of a larger system. It is, however, for the above reasons (importance of 'ethnic' motives in persecutions, etc.), a vital part of any system to protect human rights. The protection of minorities also tests the veracity of a universal system. Without a focus on vulnerable groups and a practical effort to ameliorate their position, 'universal' human rights can become merely vacuous, benefiting everyone in general but no one in particular. Protection of minorities is a 'hard case' for a legal system based on the State: humanitarian impulses may be dimmed if the groups whose human rights are to be protected offer a rival constituency to the State.[11]

In some ways it is remarkable that the institution of the protection of minorities survives, in view of the apparent threat posed to States by dissident groups perhaps wishing to secede.[12] Despite the anti-minorities rhetoric of some States, and the denial of their existence,[13] there has always been a *sotto voce* perception at the United Nations that minorities could not simply be wished away and that States, in their own interest and in the interests of international peace, needed to grapple realistically with problems of minorities on their territory. Initiatives there have tended to come from, primarily, the independent experts of the Sub-Commission on the Prevention of Discrimination and Protection of Minorities, rather than from the State dominated Commission on Human Rights and other State dominated United Nations bodies. However, the institution of the protection of minorities, in the sense of rules specifically directed at minorities and their members, survives only in a very attenuated form. Article 27 of the Covenant on Civil and Political Rights is a weak article, although an interpretation of it is offered in the present text which gives it more substance and meaning.[14] Its lack of specificity means that, even though it may impose positive obligations on States to support minority identity, the article leaves a wide discretion to States on the modalities of its application.[15] The effort to supplement the article by means of a Declaration on Minorities has made slow progress, and, on present evidence, the idea of a general convention on

---

[11] The rival constituency may be 'internal' in the sense of organized groups within the State claiming autonomy or secession; or 'external' in the case of a group such as the Kurds whose territory straddles a number of States: organized 'universal' religions provide striking examples of 'external' foci and loyalty beyond the State.

[12] For a specific study, see Buchheit, *Secession: The Legitimacy of Self-Determination* (New Haven: Yale UP, 1978). Also Kamanu, 'Secession and Self-Determination: an OAU Dilemma'. Also, *supra*, ch. 1.

[13] The Right to Identity, *supra*, Part IV.

[14] Ibid.

[15] Ibid.

minorities comparable to, say, the International Convention on the Elimination of All Forms of Racial Discrimination, seems distant. States, while offering in many cases generous treatment to minorities in their municipal law[16] are reluctant to extend their obligations *vis-à-vis* minorities into detailed rules of universal application. Other States are ungenerous in their treatment of minorities, both in the formal legal and constitutional sense of an absence of relevant laws, and in practice.[17] The broad international consensus required to produce a more positive revaluation of minorities to be codified in a treaty is not yet in existence.

There is, none the less, perceptible evidence of change which can only be beneficial for minorities. The mere fact that United Nations efforts on the Minorities Declaration are making progress, the promulgation of the Declaration on the Elimination of All Forms of Intolerance and Discrimination based on Religion, the movement represented by the UNESCO Declaration on Race in favour of the 'right to be different' and group rights, the establishment of the United Nations Working Group on Indigenous Populations, and the revision of ILO Convention 107, have all been commented upon.[18] A further important contribution to a possible *lex ferenda* is outlined in the following pages: an 'official' document representing primarily the views of governments, and therefore a possible signpost to future developments. This is subject to the *caveat* that States are prepared to include certain *desiderata* in a declaration which they might hesitate to commit themselves to in a treaty.

The World Conference on Racism and Racial Discrimination, 1983[19]

The Second World Conference to Combat Racism and Racial Discrimination makes a very positive statement on minorities. The Preamble to the Conference's Declaration, expressing the views of the 128 States represented at the Conference, recites the participants' recognition of the fact that continued vigilance is necessary to obviate measures which discriminate against 'persons belonging to national, ethnic and other minorities', and that 'United Nations initiatives in respect of the rights of persons belonging to minorities and indigenous populations merit the widest support'. While the general thrust of the Declaration is aimed, as the title of the Conference suggests, at racial discrimination, including above all the doctrine of apartheid, the Conference makes specific mention of minorities and cultural diversity at a number of points, alluding both to groups and individuals.

---

[16] Thornberry, *Minorities and Human Rights Law*.

[17] Ibid.; see also the many reports of the Minority Rights Group for evidence of law and practice that is frequently unflattering to States.

[18] *Supra*, ch. 41.

[19] A/CONF.119/26.

The operative part of the Declaration states that: 'All peoples and all human groups have contributed to the progress of civilisation and cultures which constitute the common heritage of humanity.'[20] Minorities are accorded a very positive valuation in operative paragraph 21 of the Declaration, instead of being regarded, as they have often been historically, as merely a source of instability:

Persons belonging to national, ethnic and other minorities can play a significant role in the promotion of international co-operation and understanding, and the national protection of [their] rights . . . in accordance with the International Convention on the Elimination of All Forms of Racial Discrimination, and the International Covenant on Civil and Political Rights, including its Article 27, is essential in order to enable them to fulfil this role. . . .

This paragraph also stresses that granting members of minorities the right to participate fully in the life of a country 'can contribute to the promotion of understanding, co-operation and harmonious relations between persons belonging to the different groups living in a country'. The Conference recognizes, further, that special protection of the rights of persons belonging to minority groups may be called for, 'in particular by the adoption of effective measures in favour of persons belonging to particularly disadvantaged minority groups'.[21] The Conference expresses its confidence that future action currently envisaged by the United Nations will 'appropriately enhance'[22] the protection of members of minorities. The paragraph concludes with what amounts to a warning against using the 'rights of minorities' in furtherance of the secessionist tendencies of groups: 'in promoting and guaranteeing the rights of persons belonging to minorities, there should be strict respect for the sovereignty, territorial integrity and political independence of the countries where they live and for non-interference in their internal affairs.'

Paragraph 22 of the Declaration expresses current concern with the rights of indigenous populations. There is an instructive difference between the language of paragraph 21 on minorities, and the paragraph on indigenous populations; whereas the former paragraph insists on the phraseology of the rights of 'persons belonging to' minorities, paragraph 22 refers to indigenous populations as whole groups or entities:

The rights of indigenous populations to maintain their traditional economic, social and cultural structures, to pursue their own economic, social and cultural development and to use and further develop their own language, their special relationship to their land and its natural resources should not be taken away from them; the need for consultation with indigenous populations as regards proposals which concern them should be fully observed.

The Conference also welcomes the establishment of the United Nations

---

[20] Para. 4.   [21] Para. 21.   [22] Ibid.

Working Group on Indigenous Populations. The participants at the Conference included most of the Latin American States with large indigenous populations, including Bolivia, Colombia, Brazil, and Peru, but Paraguay was not represented.[23]

The translation of the promises of the Declaration into practical action would be welcomed by indigenous groups. The document reflects in good measure the state of international and indigenous group opinion, marking the conceptual changes therein beyond the prescriptions of International Labour Organization Convention 107. The Declaration is complemented by a 'Programme of Action', which restates and elaborates the provisions of the Declaration. The main emphasis *vis-à-vis* minorities is the abolition of discrimination against members of such groups. There is a fuller account than in the Declaration of the necessity for minorities to 'express their characteristics freely and to develop their education, culture, language, traditions and customs'.[24] The 'transnational' effects of ethnic groups divided amongst two or more nations are confronted: members of minorities 'should be in a position to develop the necessary contacts inside and outside their country with due respect for the sovereignty, territorial integrity, the principle of non-interference by one State in the internal affairs of another State, and the political independence of the States concerned'.[25] States are exhorted to combat 'inter-group antagonism'[26] by adopting measures to promote mutual understanding between ethnic groups. Some consequences of the widespread blindness of States to the existence of ethnic and religious differences among their population are hinted at in a paragraph which states that 'where tension and friction exist [within States], their elimination cannot be achieved if the realities of political, economic, cultural, religious and linguistic differences between the various components of the society concerned are not taken into account'.[27] There is further recognition here, in the context of a document devoted to the elimination of racial discrimination, that there is a limit to the 'flattening' effect of anti-discriminatory measures in combating injustice to groups. Differences must be accounted for, and not ignored in realistic assessments of, and programmes for, the resolution of inter-group conflicts.

The Programme of Action for indigenous groups is more specific than for minorities. The achievement of justice for such groups may pose less of a threat to States than justice for minorities. While maximum demands, up to secession and self-determination, are made by some indigenous groups,[28] many groups require less, and perhaps not much more than the minimum forms of control and self-protection to safeguard their form of life. The participating States are prepared to accommodate a variety of demands of the more modest kind, and recognize, as the basic rights of indigenous

---

[23] For a list of participants, see pp. 4–5 of the document, *supra*, n. 19.
[24] Para. 32 of the Programme of Action.
[25] Ibid.   [26] Para. 33.   [27] Ibid.   [28] *Supra*, ch. 40.

groups, the following:[29] to call themselves by their proper name and to express freely their own identity; to have official status and representative organizations; to maintain a traditional way of life in the areas where they live, which should not affect their right to participate on an equal basis in the development of the State; to maintain and use their own language, 'wherever possible'; to enjoy freedom of religion or belief; to have access to land and its natural resources; and to 'structure, conduct and control their own educational systems'. The Programme further stresses the need for consultation of indigenous groups, self-management, special measures to remedy past discrimination, facilitation by States of links between groups, and support for the efforts of the United Nations. There is also a reference to the vulnerability of the populations to discrimination and violation of their human rights. While the concept of 'ethno-development' is not referred to as such, these proposals reflect much of its substance.

International Law and Policy

There is a plausible argument, evidenced by such documents and other 'unofficial' ones, that, in terms of the policies of States,[30] the emphasis on assimilation of minorities is not now as important as integration, and there is some movement towards recognition of cultural pluralism as a desirable goal. This is to be combined with 'strict respect' for the sovereignty and territorial integrity of States. Cultural pluralism implies a measure of differential treatment of minority groups to meet their particular circumstances and to ensure genuine equality in law with respect for different traditions. It needs to be said that there is only a trend or direction to favour such a policy. In any case, as Moskowitz rather pessimistically observes:

no country has yet evolved an internal order which stands for a true pluralism in which human values are subject only to the minimum restraint required by the public order. Everywhere where ethnic diversity clashes with the ideal of national homogeneity, only iron restraint and relentless probing from within and without can stay the hand of oppression which always reaches out to crush those of another race, another creed, or another language. More than a century and a half of effort to transfer the struggle of ethnic loyalties from the field of battle to the conscience of the citizen has had but little effect on the practices of Governments.[31]

In terms of general international law, however, the effort to implant human rights 'in the conscience of the citizen', or as a precursor, in the 'practices of governments' is much more recent and may yet bear fruit.

However, in terms of desirable State policies for minorities it is clear that,

---

[29] Para. 34 of the Programme of Action.
[30] *Supra*, ch. 1.
[31] 'The Politics and Dynamics of Human Rights', 125.

thus far, international law does not exhibit a consistent position. Some leading international instruments may be interpreted to favour a policy of, effectively, assimilation, even where the term 'integration' is used; others, such as the Covenant on Civil and Political Rights, are anti-assimilationist at least, but would effectively favour integration rather than cultural pluralism, unless they are interpreted along the lines set out above. The doctrine of apartheid has been indicated as a potent factor disfavouring any form of differential treatment of groups. Whilst it can be, and ought to be, distinguished from differential treatment *simpliciter* (as in Judge Tanaka's dissenting Opinion in the *South-West Africa Case* 1966),[32] it may be that as long as the spectre of apartheid continues to dominate the thinking of many States, the effort to distinguish the two concepts is unlikely to be made with sufficient force to legitimate differential treatment and protection of minorities through an international treaty.

The rights set out in the present text provide at least the minimum forms of protection. The protection of the basic group 'right to existence'[33] is secured mainly through the Genocide Convention. The notion of 'existence' is, however, not a very extensive one: 'cultural genocide', (protecting a group's identity) is, so far, merely a phrase which is not securely anchored in international criminal law; rather, it expresses itself in Article 27 of the International Covenant on Civil and Political Rights.[34] The importance of the criminalizing of attacks upon the most basic forms of physical existence of groups is not, however, to be underrated: genocide is a twentieth-century phenomenon as well as historical fact.[35] The international community as yet lacks the specific forms of adjudication and punishment of such offences, but even the symbolic or psychological effect of the basic prohibition is an advance on the earlier lack of one. The concept of 'genocide' is perhaps substitutable by 'violation of human rights', but its specific, potent quality as a concept is worth retaining, as is its specific focus on destruction of groups, which is as much a part of reality as the destruction of individuals.

The 'right to identity',[36] which is the second right of minorities, or their members, is sometimes regarded as constituting the whole of 'minority rights'. It remains the essential right under modern conditions of human rights and is a direct right for members of minority groups. It is secured by treaty rather than by customary law.[37] It is a right which reflects diversity in human nature, and might also be styled the 'right to be different'.[38] For reasons already described, it is a difficult right for States to concede. It is not truly a collective right under modern law, but, at most, effects a compromise between group rights and individual rights. Like genocide, it lacks any

---

[32] *Supra*, ch. 36.   [33] *Supra*, Part II.   [34] *Supra*, Part IV.

[35] Kuper, *Genocide. Its Political Use in the Twentieth Century*; Ruhashyankiko, *Study on the Question of the Prevention and Punishment of the Crime of Genocide*, UN Doc E/CN.4/Sub.2/416.

[36] *Supra*, Part IV.   [37] Ibid.

[38] Lerner, 'New Concepts in the UNESCO Declaration on Race and Racial Prejudice'.

specific form of remedy or sanction, appropriate to its character, since the destruction of the identity of a group is irreversible and 'damages' might be a misdirected form of compensation, unlike the case of violations of other human rights, where this compensation may be appropriate and just.[39] The irreversible quality of the damage inflicted by violating this right indicates its fundamental quality. As a human right it must not be regarded as a mere luxury, although in many States of the world, no doubt, it will not be ranked as highly as rights to the securing of basic forms of economic well-being, and will be related practically to the overall economic situation in a State. As one writer put it 'The effective political implementation of virtually all human rights consumes resources.'[40] Resource problems of developing countries may present a real difficulty here. This point was made at a seminar on the human rights of minorities at Ohrid, Yugoslavia in 1974:

The gap between the levels of economic development of various regions of the world constituted an essential element in the sharp differentiation between the situations of minorities in advanced industrial States and that of minorities in the developing countries. The promotion and protection of the latter could not be realized so long as various groups, because of their economic, social and cultural underdevelopment, could not enjoy even elementary human rights, such as the right to work or the right to culture . . . The highest priority had therefore to be given to the economic and social development of these countries. The achievement of the necessary progress in that direction was a pre-requisite for the promotion of the rights of minorities in the developing countries . . . It would, therefore, be a mistake to apply general concepts with respect to the rights of minorities without specifically relating them to the overall economic and social environment.[41]

Such a viewpoint is not unacceptable, provided that prerequisite is not taken to mean that minorities should not have their rights unless economic progress is adequate. This would represent a rather different claim from that which requires minority rights to be related to the overall social and political environment, an interpretation of the right to identity which is implicit in the analysis offered in the present work.

The right to identity needs also to be brought into balance with the right of the State to political independence and territorial integrity. This qualification also illuminates the need for better international efforts to secure the right, as well as the general human rights of members of minorities: the alternative to international protection may well be interference by a kin State of the minorities in the affairs of a host State, or attempts at secession by minority groups.[42] There is little room for such alternatives in an interna-

---

[39] Brownlie, in relation to the Dene Indians (*supra*, ch. 25).

[40] Donnelly, 'Cultural Relativism and Universal Human Rights', *Human Rights Quarterly*, 6 (1984), 400 at 408.

[41] *Seminar on the Protection of the Human Rights of National, Ethnic and Other Minorities*, ST/TAO/HR/49 (1974).

[42] Consult Sigler, *Minority Rights. A Comparative Analysis* for a development of models of minority protection.

tional community in which peace as well as justice is a primary requirement.[43]

Minority rights, it has been suggested, function at the limits of the international law of human rights by testing States in their humanitarian concerns. In a conceptual sense also, respect for diversity also tests the limits of the 'universal' concept of rights,[44] which derives largely from Western tradition, in particular the legalistic moral tradition of Natural Law.[45] The philosophical tendency of this approach is to generalize certain features of human beings into statements of universally applicable moral and legal rules. In practice, however, the Natural Law and Natural Rights tradition has represented a projection of 'Western' values into global prescriptions.

From such a perspective (a 'Western' perspective), O'Brien's very negative points against minority rights and cultures will be recalled.[46] Dilemmas about offensive customs are not, however, peculiar to 'minority rights'. The writer's critique is directed against aspects of whole cultures and religious systems which may or may not involve 'minorities'. There may be a problem in general, however, as to what lengths cultural 'authenticity' and 'identity' may be carried. The answer suggested in the present work is that minority rights need to be brought into balance with human rights or, more correctly, to be seen as part of human rights. Whatever respect must be paid to the rights of groups, the stance of modern international law is clear in according primacy to individual choice: respect for group rights does not justify 'group determinism', the overriding of individual choice by claims of the group.[47]

The third right outlined above is the right not to be discriminated against on grounds of race, religion, or language. This is conceived primarily as a right of individuals. This right is granted by a number of treaties, is a specific part of the 'law of the United Nations' and is probably reflected in customary international law.[48] There is little doubt that many States regard this right as fundamental. It must, however, be brought into harmony with the right to identity which has been neglected by comparison. The right not to be discriminated against is better understood as a complement to the right to identity rather than as a rival concept expressing a different philosophy—that of the homogeneous State, blind to the diversity of cultures within itself. For reasons given in the text,[49] the rule of non-discrimination is not a complete substitute for the right to an identity, but is an essential step in the protection of minorities.

[43] 'Nothing would be a more foolish footnote to man's demise than that his final destruction was occasioned by a war to ensure human rights': Franck and Rodley, 'After Bangladesh: The Law of Humanitarian Intervention by Military Force', 300.

[44] Donnelly (*supra*, n. 40).

[45] Midgley, *The Natural Law Tradition and the Theory of International Relations*; Finnis, *Natural Law and Natural Rights*.

[46] O'Brien (*Supra*, ch. 22, n. 30).

[47] For further elaboration, see Claydon, 'Internationally Uprooted People and the Transnational Protection of Minority Culture' *New York Law School Law Review*, 24 (1978), 125.

[48] *Supra*, chs. 35 ff.   [49] *Supra*, Part V.

The rights of indigenous populations may be seen as representing a legal institution *sui generis* or as a special, intense, and difficult area for application of the rights of minorities in general. Most indigenous populations conform in all respects with the Capotorti definition of minorities,[50] with the added ingredient of an economic and cultural gap between the indigenous group and the dominant group or groups in the State. Of all cases of the 'rights of minorities', a just resolution of the claims of such groups may require a special category of human rights rules, with considerably less emphasis on the rights of the individual, since many of these groups have little conception of individual rights, in land ownership or other legal institutions. Any ultimate resolution of such conceptual problems, if such is possible, should not detract from the urgent necessity to protect such groups in very basic terms, including protection from genocidal attack. Beyond this immediate question, it is ardently to be hoped that the formulation of international standards will proceed rapidly. To date international law has hardly grappled with the question of the rights of such groups: an unkind view of ILO Convention 107 is that it is as much of a contribution to the cultural destruction of such groups as it is to their salvation.[51]

In terms of the theory of international law, the opening section of the present work referred to the question of minorities as 'subjects of international law'. The International Court of Justice has observed that 'the subjects of law in any legal system are not necessarily identical in their nature or in the extent of their rights.'[52] Therefore, whatever status may be accorded to minorities in international law, it is clear that such attribution need not involve claims that minorities have rights and duties similar to those of States or international organizations. The phrase 'subject of international law' is not a very precise one, and is better rendered as: what rights, duties and procedural capacities are possessed by minorities in international law?[53] The following remarks are made on the basis of materials cited in the present work.

Formally speaking, minorities as such as holders of rights and duties are almost ignored in international law. The rights that exist are attributed to individuals with, as noted above, some recent leaning towards groups. In terms of petitions, some instruments such as the International Convention on the Elimination of All Forms of Racial Discrimination accept petitions from groups; others, such as the International Covenant on Civil and Political Rights, accept petitions from individuals. The reference to petitions in Article 14 of the former instrument does not, however, mention minorities as such, but only 'groups of individuals'.

---

[50] *Supra*, ch. 1.

[51] *Supra*, chs. 39–40.

[52] Reparations for Injuries Suffered in the Service of the United Nations, Advisory Opinion, *ICJ Reports* (1949), 174.

[53] Nørgaard, *supra*, ch. 3, n. 25; Sohn and Buergenthal, *International Protection of Human Rights*, ch. 1.

Under the League of Nations system, minorities as such had no special *locus standi* before the organs of the League. Even in the so-called 'Upper Silesian System', a special regime under its particular treaty,[54] while there was great liberality in the matter of *locus standi* before an international tribunal, representatives of minorities had no privileged place beyond the generality of individual petitioners. The majority of commentators in that period agreed that minorities were not subjects of international law.[55]

In terms of substance, however, the reality of the existence of minorities is difficult to ignore. Genocide makes little sense as a concept unless one regards it as the violation of a collective right (formally, the genocide law consists of a prohibition of certain acts to individuals rather than an affirmation of rights). The right to identity conceals the collective right behind the rights of individuals. The group is the 'unacknowledged presence' behind the individual rights. Collective rights are a substantive, if not a 'formal' aspect of the legal reality. The greater part of this reality is given over to individual rights. 'Minority rights' are substantive and indirect, not formal and direct.

De Lege Ferenda

The above picture of what international law offers to minorities may be contrasted with the minority 'demands' set out in the opening section of this work. From the point of view of minorities, and, it is submitted, international order as a whole, there are defects in the present level of protection. One defect is the largely indirect nature of the rules. The lack of a definition of minority incorporated expressly in an international instrument is also a fault. However, legal institutions may survive without express definition, and a definition is available to draw upon, following the work of Special Rapporteur Capotorti.[56] None the less, it should not be possible for States simply to deny the existence of groups on their territory with such facility. Capotorti's work has demonstrated that there are few States, if any, in the world that could, truthfully, be said to be homogeneous in an ethnic sense. The potential range of any minorities instrument is close to being universal. The minorities instrument *in statu nascendi* at the United Nations has not so far attempted a definition of minority.

A further point is the lack of any remedy which adequately reflects the nature of threats to minorities. The rights of petition are oriented towards individuals and hardly reflect a group dimension. The Economic and Social

---

[54] The Polish-German Convention relating to Upper Silesia 1922. See *Memorandum by the Secretary-General of the United Nations*, UN Doc E/CN.4/Sub.2/126 (1951); Sohn and Buergenthal, ibid. 267.

[55] Ermacora, *The Protection of Minorities before the United Nations*, 338.

[56] *Supra*, ch. 1.

Council Resolution 1503 procedure which, on the face of it, appears to be a suitable reflection of the group nature of human rights denials, does not have a particular focus on minorities. It has, in any case, proved to be a very limited procedure. International criminal law, which also might be expected to deal with gross violations of rights, exists so far only as a concept with no specific organs of implementation. Implementation of rights in general is often hampered by excessive respect for the 'domestic jurisdiction' of States and their sensitivity to criticism, though this weakness is an abiding one for the implementation of all human rights.

Any further provision in international law should make a very explicit prescription of the limits of minority rights in terms of the security and territorial integrity of the State. States have a legitimate interest in not allowing the grant of minority rights to generate further, expanded claims on behalf of minorities. It is surely the case that, in terms of ongoing historical processes, such claims will continue to be made, but States can hardly be expected to acquiesce in any international instrument which provides added impetus to such developments. Any future legal instrument on minorities should also make a positive statement on the value of minorities to the international community: the Second World Conference on Racism and Racial Discrimination has provided a model of such a statement.[57] Minorities require to be perceived as part of the solution to international disputes rather than the problem. Such a psychological development can only occur in the context of a strict rule of non-interference in the host States with respect for their political independence and territorial integrity.

Some further separation may have to be achieved and sustained between the question of indigenous groups and minorities. This process is already rather mature and works for the benefit of indigenous groups, since they are not perceived by the relevant States as a 'threat' of the same order as minorities in general.

It is debatable if all progress on the protection of minorities can be achieved at the universal level. In view of its historical associations with 'the minorities question', Europe is perhaps the only possible 'continental' starting-point for a regional instrument on minorities. It is much to be regretted that, to the extent that the European Convention on Human Rights is the most successful 'working' model of a human rights institution, its prescriptions do not contain a 'minorities' article.

In the real world, States are the main creators and bearers of rights and duties in international law. Enthusiasts for 'human rights' may occasionally overlook such a basic fact of existence. The ability of international law to contribute to a more humane, stable, and just order is limited by the nature of the system. Minority rights have provoked a peculiar resistance on the part of States, which continues to be deep-seated. 'Progressive transnational

---

[57] *Supra*, text following n. 19.

promotion' of human rights[58] needs to work on the State system. A modified international law of minorities must reflect a true consensus of State opinion. The development of suitable instruments on minorities may be expected only to generate such a consensus in the long term. The great experience of international law in dealing with the question of minorities is not to be neglected, but it requires new, more specific instruments. The translation of humanitarian prescriptions into legal form is only a first step in securing justice for minority groups and their members, but it would be grossly to underestimate the psychological force of laws if such a step were to be regarded as unimportant. International law may not be the most powerful force in international relations, but it is stitched into the fabric of international society and its concepts function as a standard, a symbol, and a hope for peace among nations and justice for human beings.

[58] Cassese, 'Progressive Transnational Promotion of Human Rights', in Ramcharan (ed.), *Human Rights Thirty Years After the Universal Declaration*, 249.

Appendix 1

The Polish Minorities Treaty

from *Protection of Linguistic, Racial and Religious Minorities by the League of Nations*, IB Minorities. 1927. I.B.2. (Geneva, August, 1927)

Extract from the Treaty between the United States of America, the British Empire, France, Italy, Japan and Poland

SIGNED AT VERSAILLES, June 28th, 1919

(In force as from January 10th, 1920)

The United States of America, The British Empire, France, Italy and Japan,

The Principal Allied and Associated Powers, on the one hand;
And POLAND, on the other hand;

Whereas the Allied and Associated Powers have by the success of their arms restored to the Polish nation the independence of which it had been unjustly deprived; and

Whereas by the proclamation of March 30, 1917, the Government of Russia assented to the re-establishment of an independent Polish State; and

Whereas the Polish State, which now in fact exercises sovereignty over those portions of the former Russian Empire which are inhabited by a majority of Poles, has already been recognised as a sovereign and independent State by the Principal Allied and Associated Powers; and

Whereas under the Treaty of Peace concluded with Germany by the Allied and Associated Powers, a Treaty of which Poland is a signatory, certain portions of the former German Empire will be incorporated in the territory of Poland; and

Whereas under the terms of the said Treaty of Peace, the boundaries of Poland not already laid down are to be subsequently determined by the Principal Allied and Associated Powers;

The United States of America, the British Empire, France, Italy and Japan, on the one hand, confirming their recognition of the Polish State, constituted within the said limits as a sovereign and independent member of the Family of Nations, and being anxious to ensure the execution of the provisions of Article 93 of the said Treaty of Peace with Germany;

Poland, on the other hand, desiring to conform her institutions to the principles of liberty and justice, and to give a sure guarantee to the inhabitants of the territory over which she has assumed sovereignty;

For this purpose the HIGH CONTRACTING PARTIES represented as follows:
[*Here follow the names of the plenipotentiaries.*]

After having exchanged their full powers, found in good and due form, have agreed as follows:

Chapter I

Article 1

Poland undertakes that the stipulations contained in Articles 2 to 8 of this Chapter shall be recognised as fundamental laws, and that no law, regulation or official action shall conflict or interfere with these stipulations, nor shall any law, regulation or official action prevail over them.

Article 2

Poland undertakes to assure full and complete protection of life and liberty to all inhabitants of Poland without distinction of birth, nationality, language, race or religion.

All inhabitants of Poland shall be entitled to the free exercise, whether public or private, of any creed, religion or belief, whose practices are not inconsistent with public order or public morals.

Article 3

Poland admits and declares to be Polish nationals *ipso facto* and without the requirement of any formality German, Austrian, Hungarian or Russian nationals habitually resident at the date of the coming into force of the present Treaty in territory which is or may be recognised as forming part of Poland, but subject to any provisions in the Treaties of Peace with Germany or Austria respectively relating to persons who became resident in such territory after a specified date.

Nevertheless, the persons referred to above who are over eighteen years of age will be entitled under the conditions contained in the said Treaties to opt for any other nationality which may be open to them. Option by a husband will cover his wife and option by parents will cover their children under eighteen years of age.

Persons who have exercised the above right to opt must, except where it is otherwise provided in the Treaty of Peace with Germany, transfer within the succeeding twelve months their place of residence to the State for which they have opted. They will be entitled to retain their immovable property in Polish territory. They may carry with them their movable property of every description. No export duties may be imposed upon them in connection with the removal of such property.

Article 4

Poland admits and declares to be Polish nationals *ipso facto* and without the requirement of any formality persons of German, Austrian, Hungarian or Russian nationality who were born in the said territory of parents habitually resident there, even if at the date of the coming into force of the present Treaty they are not themselves habitually resident there.

Nevertheless, within two years after the coming into force of the present Treaty, these persons may make a declaration before the competent Polish authorities in the country in which they are resident, stating that they abandon Polish nationality, and they will then cease to be considered as Polish nationals. In this connection a declaration by a husband will cover his wife, and a declaration by parents will cover their children under eighteen years of age.

Article 5

Poland undertakes to put no hindrance in the way of the exercise of the right which the persons concerned have, under the Treaties concluded or to be concluded by the Allied and Associated Powers with Germany, Austria, Hungary or Russia, to choose whether or not they will acquire Polish nationality.

Article 6

All persons born in Polish territory who are not born nationals of another State shall *ipso facto* become Polish nationals.

Article 7

All Polish nationals shall be equal before the law and shall enjoy the same civil and political rights without distinction as to race, language or religion.

Differences of religion, creed or confession shall not prejudice any Polish national in matters relating to the enjoyment of civil or political rights, as, for instance, admission to public employments, functions and honours, or the exercise of professions and industries.

No restriction shall be imposed on the free use by any Polish national of any language in private intercourse, in commerce, in religion, in the press or in publications of any kind, or at public meetings.

Notwithstanding any establishment by the Polish Government of an official language, adequate facilities shall be given to Polish nationals of non-Polish speech for the use of their language, either orally or in writing, before the courts.

Article 8

Polish nationals who belong to racial, religious or linguistic minorities shall enjoy the same treatment and security in law and in fact as the other Polish nationals. In particular, they shall have an equal right to establish, manage and control at their own expense charitable, religious and social institutions, schools and other educational establishments, with the right to use their own language and to exercise their religion freely therein.

Article 9

Poland will provide in the public educational system in towns and districts in which a considerable proportion of Polish nationals of other than Polish speech are residents adequate facilities for ensuring that in the primary schools the instruction shall be given to the children of such Polish nationals through the medium of their own language. This provision shall not prevent the Polish Government from making the teaching of the Polish language obligatory in the said schools.

In towns and districts where there is a considerable proportion of Polish nationals belonging to racial, religious or linguistic minorities, these minorities shall be assured an equitable share in the enjoyment and application of the sums which may be provided out of public funds under the State, municipal or other budget, for educational, religious or charitable purposes.

The provisions of this Article shall apply to Polish citizens of German speech only in that part of Poland which was German territory on August 1, 1914.

Article 10

Educational Committees appointed locally by the Jewish communities of Poland will, subject to the general control of the State, provide for the distribution of the proportional share of public funds allocated to Jewish schools in accordance with Article 9, and for the organisation and management of these schools.

The provisions of Article 9 concerning the use of languages in schools shall apply to these schools.

Article 11

Jews shall not be compelled to perform any act which constitutes a violation of their Sabbath, nor shall they be placed under any disability by reason of their refusal to attend courts of law or to perform any legal business on their Sabbath. This provision, however, shall not exempt Jews from such obligations as shall be imposed upon all other Polish citizens for the necessary purposes of military service, national defence or the preservation of public order.

Poland declares her intention to refrain from ordering or permitting elections, whether general or local, to be held on a Saturday, nor will registration for electoral or other purposes be compelled to be performed on a Saturday.

Article 12

Poland agrees that the stipulations in the foregoing Articles, so far as they affect persons belonging to racial, religious or linguistic minorities, constitute obligations of international concern and shall be placed under the guarantee of the League of Nations. They shall not be modified without the assent of a majority of the Council of the League of Nations. The United States, the British Empire, France, Italy and Japan hereby agree not to withhold their assent from any modification in these Articles which is in due form assented to by a majority of the Council of the League of Nations.

Poland agrees that any member of the Council of the League of Nations shall have the right to bring to the attention of the Council any infraction, or any danger of infraction, of any of these obligations, and that the Council may thereupon take such action and give such direction as it may deem proper and effective in the circumstances.

Poland further agrees that any difference of opinion as to questions of law or fact arising out of these Articles between the Polish Government and any one of the Principal Allied and Associated Powers or any other Power, a Member of the Council of the League of Nations, shall be held to be a dispute of an international character under Article 14 of the Covenant of the League of Nations. The Polish Government hereby consents that any such dispute shall, if the other party thereto demands, be referred to the permanent Court of International Justice. The decision of the Permanent Court shall be final and shall have the same force and effect as an award under Article 13 of the Covenant.

THE PRESENT TREATY, of which the French and English texts are both authentic, shall be ratified. It shall come into force at the same time as the Treaty of Peace with Germany.

The deposit of ratifications shall be made at Paris.

Powers of which the seat of the Government is outside Europe will be entitled merely to inform the Government of the French Republic through their diplomatic representative at Paris that their ratification has been given; in that case they must transmit the instrument of ratification as soon as possible.

A procès-verbal of the deposit of ratifications will be drawn up.

The French Government will transmit to all the signatory Powers a certified copy of the procès-verbal of the deposit of ratifications.

IN FAITH WHEREOF the above-named Plenipotentiaries have signed the present Treaty.

Done at Versailles, the twenty-eighth day of June, one thousand nine hundred and nineteen, in a single copy which will remain deposited in the archives of the French Republic, and of which authenticated copies will be transmitted to each of the Signatory Powers.

Appendix 2

Agreement between India and Pakistan 1950 concerning Minorities (Extract)

A.   The Governments of India and Pakistan solemnly agree that each shall ensure to the Minorities throughout its territory complete equality of citizenship, irrespective of religion, a full sense of security in respect of life, culture, property and personal honour, freedom of movement within each country and freedom of occupation, speech and worship, subject to law and morality. Members of the minorities shall have equal opportunity with members of the majority community to participate in the public life of their country, to hold political or other office, and to serve in their country's civil and armed forces. Both Governments declare these rights to be fundamental and undertake to enforce them effectively. It is the policy of both Governments that the enjoyment of these democratic rights shall be assured to all their nationals without distinction.

Both Governments wish to emphasize that the allegiance and loyalty of the minorities is to the State of which they are citizens, and that it is to the Government of their own State that they should look for the redress of their grievances.

Appendix 3

State Treaty of 15 May 1955 for the Re-establishment of an Independent and
Democratic Austria (Fed. Law Gazette No. 152/1955)

Articles 1−6. . .

Article 7

Rights of the Slovene and Croat Minorities

1. Austrian nationals of the Slovene and Croat minorities in Carinthia, Burgenland and Styria shall enjoy the same rights on equal terms as all other Austrian nationals, including the right to their own organisations, meetings and press in their own language.

2. They are entitled to elementary instruction in the Slovene or Croat language and to a proportional number of their own secondary schools; in this connection school curricula shall be reviewed and a section of the Inspectorate of Education shall be established for Slovene and Croat schools.

3. In the administrative and judicial districts of Carinthia, Burgenland and Styria, where there are Slovene, Croat or mixed populations, the Slovene or Croat language shall be accepted as an official language in addition to German. In such districts topographical terminology and inscriptions shall be in the Slovene or Croat language as well as in German.

4. Austrian nationals of the Slovene and Croat minorities in Carinthia, Burgenland and Styria shall participate in the cultural, administrative and judicial systems in these territories on equal terms with other Austrian nationals.

5. The activity of organisations whose aim is to deprive the Croat of Slovene population of their minority character or rights shall be prohibited.

Articles 8–38. . .

Appendix 4

UNESCO Declaration on Race and Racial Prejudice, 27 November 1978

Extracts

The General Conference of the United Nations Educational, Scientific and Cultural Organization, meeting in Paris at its twentieth session, on 27 November 1978 adopted unanimously and by acclamation the following Declaration:

Preamble

The General Conference of the United Nations Educational, Scientific and Cultural Organization, meeting at Paris at its twentieth session, from 24 October to 28 November 1978,

Whereas it is stated in the Preamble to the Constitution of Unesco, adopted on 16 November 1945, that the great and terrible war which has now ended was a war made possible by the denial of the democratic principles of the dignity, equality and mutual respect of men, and by the propagation, in their place, through ignorance and prejudice, of the doctrine of the inequality of men and races, and whereas, according to Article I of the said Constitution, the purpose of Unesco 'is to contribute to peace and security by promoting collaboration among the nations through education, science and culture in order to further universal respect for justice, for the rule of law and for the human rights and fundamental freedoms which are affirmed for the peoples of the world, without distinction of race, sex, language or religion, by the Charter of the United Nations',

Recognizing that, more than three decades after the founding of Unesco, these principles are just as significant as they were when they were embodied in its Constitution,

Mindful of the process of decolonization and other historical changes which have led most of the peoples formerly under foreign rule to recover their sovereignty, making the international community a universal and diversified whole and creating new opportunities of eradicating the scourge of racism and of putting an end to its odious manifestations in all aspects of social and political life, both nationally and internationally,

Convinced that the essential unity of the human race and consequently the fundamental equality of all human beings and all peoples, recognized in the loftiest expressions of philosophy, morality and religion, reflect an ideal towards which ethics and science are converging today,

Convinced that all peoples and all human groups, whatever their composition or ethnic origin, contribute according to their own genius to the progress of the civilizations and cultures which, in their plurality and as a result of their interpenetration, constitute the common heritage of mankind,

Confirming its attachment to the principles proclaimed in the United Nations Charter and the Universal Declaration of Human Rights and its determination to promote the implementation of the International Covenants on Human Rights as well as the Declaration on the Establishment of a New International Economic Order,

Determined also to promote the implementation of the United Nations Declaration and the International Convention on the Elimination of all Forms of Racial Discrimination,

Noting the International Convention on the Prevention and Punishment of the Crime of Genocide, the International Convention on the Suppression and Punishment of the Crime of Apartheid and the Convention on the Non-Applicability of Statutory Limitations to War Crimes and Crimes against Humanity,

Recalling also the international instruments already adopted by Unesco, including in particular the Convention and Recommendation against Discrimination in Education, the Recommendation concerning the Status of Teachers, the Declaration of the Principles of International Cultural Co-operation, the Recommendation concerning Education for International Understanding, Co-operation and Peace and Education relating to Human Rights and Fundamental Freedoms, the Recommendation on the Status of Scientific Researchers, and the Recommendation on participation by the people at large in cultural life and their contribution to it,

Bearing in mind the four statements on the race question adopted by experts convened by Unesco,

Reaffirming its desire to play a vigorous and constructive part in the implementation of the programme of the Decade for Action to Combat Racism and Racial Discrimination, as defined by the General Assembly of the United Nations at its twenty-eighth session,

Noting with the gravest concern that racism, racial discrimination, colonialism and apartheid continue to afflict the world in ever-changing forms, as a result both of the continuation of legislative provisions and government and administrative practices contrary to the principles of human rights and also of the continued existence of political and social structures, and of relationships and attitudes, characterized by injustice and contempt for human beings and leading to the exclusion, humiliation and exploitation, or to the forced assimilation, of the members of disadvantaged groups,

Expressing its indignation at these offences against human dignity, *deploring* the obstacles they place in the way of mutual understanding between peoples and *alarmed* at the danger of their seriously disturbing international peace and security,

Adopts and solemnly proclaims this Declaration on Race and Racial Prejudice:

Article 1

1. All human beings belong to a single species and are descended from a common stock. They are born equal in dignity and rights and all form an integral part of humanity.

2. All individuals and groups have the right to be different, to consider themselves as different and to be regarded as such. However, the diversity of life styles and the right to be different may not, in any circumstances, serve as a pretext for racial prejudice; they may not justify either in law or in fact any discriminatory practice whatsoever, nor provide a ground for the policy of apartheid, which is the extreme form of racism.

3. Identity of origin in no way affects the fact that human beings can and may live

differently, nor does it preclude the existence of differences based on cultural, environmental and historical diversity nor the right to maintain cultural identity.

4. All people of the world possess equal faculties for attaining the highest level in intellectual, technical, social, economic, cultural and political development.

5. The differences between the achievements of the different peoples are entirely attributable to geographical, historical, political, economic, social and cultural factors. Such differences can in no case serve as a pretext for any rank-ordered classification of nations for peoples.

Article 2

1. Any theory which involves the claim that racial or ethnic groups are inherently superior or inferior, thus implying that some would be entitled to dominate or eliminate others, presumed to be inferior, or which bases value judgements on racial differentiation, has no scientific foundation and is contrary to the moral and ethical principles of humanity.

2. Racism includes racist ideologies, prejudiced attitudes, discriminatory behaviour, structural arrangements and institutionalized practices resulting in racial inequality as well as the fallacious notion that discriminatory relations between groups are morally and scientifically justifiable; it is reflected in discriminatory provisions in legislation or regulations and discriminatory practices as well as in anti-social beliefs and acts; it hinders the development of its victims, perverts those who practice it, divides nations internally, impedes international co-operation and gives rise to political tensions between peoples; it is contrary to the fundamental principles of international law and, consequently, seriously disturbs international peace and security.

3. Racial prejudice, historically linked with inequalities in power, reinforced by economic and social differences between individuals and groups, and still seeking today to justify such inequalities, is totally without justification.

Article 3

Any distinction, exclusion, restriction or preference based on race, colour, ethnic or national origin or religious intolerance motivated by racist considerations, which destroys or compromises the sovereign equality of States and the right of peoples to self-determination, or which limits in an arbitrary or discriminatory manner the right of every human being and group to full development is incompatible with the requirements of an international order which is just and guarantees respect for human rights; the right to full development implies equal access to the means of personal and collective advancement and fulfillment in a climate of respect for the values of civilizations and cultures, both national and world-wide.

Article 4

1. Any restriction on the complete self-fulfilment of human beings and free communication between them which is based on racial or ethnic considerations is contrary to the principle of equality in dignity and rights; it cannot be admitted.

2. One of the most serious violations of this principle is represented by apartheid, which, like genocide, is a crime against humanity, and gravely disturbs international peace and security.

3. Other policies and practices of racial segregation and discrimination constitute

crimes against the conscience and dignity of mankind and may lead to political tensions and gravely endanger international peace and security.

Article 5

1. Culture, as a product of all human beings and a common heritage of mankind, and education in its broadest sense, offer men and women increasingly effective means of adaptation, enabling them not only to affirm that they are born equal in dignity and rights, but also to recognize that they should respect the right of all groups to their own cultural identity and the development of their distinctive cultural life within the national and international context, it being understood that it rests with each group to decide in complete freedom on the maintenance and, if appropriate, the adaptation or enrichment of the values which it regards as essential to its identity.

2. States, in accordance with their constitutional principles and procedures, as well as all other competent authorities and the entire teaching profession, have a responsibility to see that the educational resources of all countries are used to combat racism, more especially by ensuring that curricula and textbooks include scientific and ethical considerations concerning human unity and diversity and that no invidious distinctions are made with regard to any people; by training teachers to achieve these ends; by making the resources of the educational system available to all groups of the population without racial restriction or discrimination; and by taking appropriate steps to remedy the handicaps from which certain racial or ethnic groups suffer with regard to their level of education and standard of living and in particular to present such handicaps from being passed on to children.

3. The mass media and those who control or serve them, as well as all organized groups within national communities, are urged—with due regard to the principles embodied in the Universal Declaration of Human Rights, particularly the principle of freedom of expression—to promote understanding, tolerance and friendship among individuals and groups and to contribute to the eradication of racism, racial discrimination and racial prejudice, in particular by refraining from presenting a stereotyped, partial, unilateral or tendentious picture of individuals and of various human groups. Communication between racial and ethnic groups must be a reciprocal process, enabling them to express themselves and to be fully heard without let or hindrance. The mass media should therefore be freely receptive to ideas of individuals and groups which facilitate such communication.

Article 6

1. The State has prime responsibility for ensuring human rights and fundamental freedoms on an entirely equal footing in dignity and rights for all individuals and all groups.

2. So far as its competence extends and in accordance with its constitutional principles and procedures, the State should take all appropriate steps, *inter alia* by legislation, particularly in the spheres of education, culture and communication, to prevent, prohibit and eradicate racism, racist propaganda, racial segregation and apartheid and to encourage the dissemination of knowledge and the findings of appropriate research in natural and social sciences on the causes and prevention of racial prejudice and racist attitudes, with due regard to the principles embodied in

the Universal Declaration of Human Rights and in the International Covenant on Civil and Political Rights.

3. Since laws proscribing racial discrimination are not in themselves sufficient, it is also incumbent on States to supplement them by administrative machinery for the systematic investigation of instances of racial discrimination, by a comprehensive framework of legal remedies against acts of racial discrimination, by broadly based education and research programmes designed to combat racial prejudice and racial discrimination and by programmes of positive political, social, educational and cultural measures calculated to promote genuine mutual respect among groups. Where circumstances warrant, special programmes should be undertaken to promote the advancement of disadavantaged groups and, in the case of nationals, to ensure their effective participation in the decision-making processes of the community.

Article 7

In addition to political, economic and social measures, law is one of the principal means of ensuring equality in dignity and rights among individuals, and of curbing any propaganda, any form of organization or any practice which is based on ideas or theories referring to the alleged superiority of racial or ethnic groups or which seeks to justify or encourage racial hatred and discrimination in any form. States should adopt such legislation as is appropriate to this end and see that it is given effect and applied by all their services, with due regard to the principles embodied in the Universal Declaration of Human Rights. Such legislation should form part of a political, economic and social framework conducive to its implementation. Individuals and other legal entities, both public and private, must conform with such legislation and use all appropriate means to help the population as a whole to understand and apply it.

Article 8

1. Individuals, being entitled to an economic, social, cultural and legal order, on the national and international planes, such as to allow them to exercise all their capabilities on a basis of entire equality of rights and opportunities, have corresponding duties towards their fellows, towards the society in which they live and towards the international community. They are accordingly under an obligation to promote harmony among the peoples, to combat racism and racial prejudice and to assist by every means available to them in eradicating racial discrimination in all its forms.

2. In the field of racial prejudice and racist attitudes and practices, specialists in natural and social sciences and cultural studies, as well as scientific organizations and associations, are called upon to undertake objective research on a wide interdisciplinary basis; all States should encourage them to this end.

3. It is, in particular, incumbent upon such specialists to ensure, by all means available to them, that their research findings are not misinterpreted, and also that they assist the pubic in understanding such findings.

Article 9

1. The principle of the equality in dignity and rights of all human beings and all peoples, irrespective of race, colour and origin, is a generally accepted and

recognized principle of international law. Consequently any form of racial discrimination practised by a State constitutes a violation of international law giving rise to its international responsibility.

2. Special measures must be taken to ensure equality in dignity and rights for individuals and groups wherever necessary, while ensuring that they are not such as to appear racially discriminatory. In this respect, particular attention should be paid to racial or ethnic groups which are socially or economically disadvantaged, so as to afford them, on a completely equal footing and without discrimination or restriction, the protection of the laws and regulations and the advantages of the social measures in force, in particular in regard to housing, employment and health; to respect the authenticity of their culture and values; and to facilitate their social and occupational advancement, especially through education.

3. Population groups of foreign origin, particularly migrant workers and their families who contribute to the development of the host country, should benefit from appropriate measures designed to afford them security and respect for their dignity and cultural values and to facilitate their adaptation to the host environment and their professional advancement with a view to their subsequent reintegration in their country of origin and their contribution to its development; steps should be taken to make it possible for their children to be taught their mother tongue.

4. Existing disequilibria in international economic relations contribute to the exacerbation of racism and racial prejudice; all States should consequently endeavour to contribute to the restructuring of the international economy on a more equitable basis.

Article 10

International organizations, whether universal or regional, governmental or non-governmental, are called upon to co-operate and assist, so far as their respective fields of competence and means allow, in the full and complete implementation of the principles set out in this Declaration, thus contributing to the legitimate struggle of all men, born equal in dignity and rights, against the tyranny and oppression of racism, racial segregation, apartheid and genocide, so that all the peoples of the world may be forever delivered from these scourges.

Appendix 5

Commission on Human Rights, Thirty-fourth session, Item 21 of the agenda

Rights of Persons belonging to National, Ethnic, Religious and Linguistic Minorities

Draft Declaration proposed by Yugoslavia

The General Assembly,
Recognizing that one of the basic aims of the United Nations is to promote and enhance the respect for human rights and the fundamental freedoms for all, without distinction as to race, sex, language or religion,
Bearing in mind international instruments relating to human rights, including the rights of national, ethnic, linguistic or religious minorities, such as the International Covenant on Civil and Political Rights, the International Convention on the Elimination of All Forms of Racial Discrimination, the Convention of the United Nations Educational, Scientific and Cultural Organization against Discrimination in Education, the Convention of the International Labour Organisation concerning Discrimination in Respect of Employment and Occupation, as well as the instruments adopted at the regional level and concluded between individual States Members of the United Nations,
Considering that the friendly relations and co-operation among States in the spirit of the Declaration on Principles of International Law concerning Friendly Relations and Co-operation among States in accordance with the Charter of the United Nations, contribute to international peace and stability and to the creation of more favourable conditions for the realization and promotion of the right of national, ethnic, linguistic or religious minorities, and that the realization and promotion of the rights of minorities, in turn, contributes to friendship and co-operation among peoples and States.
Recognizing the need to ensure even more effective implementation of the existing instruments of international law relating to the rights of national, ethnic, linguistic or religious minorities,
Bearing in mind the work done so far within the United Nations system, in particular by the Commission on Human Rights and the Sub-Commission on the Prevention of Discrimination and Protection of Minorities, on securing and promoting the rights of minorities, and the need for further efforts aimed at ensuring and promoting the rights of national, ethnic, linguistic or religious minorities,
Proclaims this Declaration on the Rights of National, Ethnic, Linguistic or Religious Minorities:

Article 1

National, ethnic, linguistic or religious minorities (hereinafter: minorities) have the right to existence, to the respect for, and the promotion of, their own national, cultural, linguistic and other characteristics and to enjoyment of full equality in relation to the rest of the population, regardless of their number.

Article 2

1. Members of minorities shall enjoy all human rights and the fundamental freedoms without any discrimination as to national, ethnic or racial origin, language or religion.

2. Any propaganda or activity aimed at discriminating against minorities or threatening their right to equal expression and development of their own character-istics, is incompatible with the fundamental principles of the Charter of the United Nations and the Universal Declaration of Human Rights.

Article 3

For the purpose of realizing the conditions of full equality and all-round develop-ment of minorities, *as collectivities*, and members of minorities, it is essential to undertake measures which will enable them freely to express their characteristics, develop their culture, education, language, traditions and customs and to participate on an equitable basis in cultural, social, economic and political life of the country in which they live.

Article 4

1. In ensuring and promoting the rights of minorities strict respect for sovereignty, territorial integrity, political independence and non-interference in the internal affairs of countries in which minorities live, should be observed.

2. Respect for the aforementioned principles shall not prevent the fulfilment of international commitments of States Members of the United Nations in relation to the minorities. Member States should fulfil, in good faith, their international com-mitments assumed under the Charter of the United Nations and international instru-ments, and the commitments assumed under other treaties or agreements to which they are parties.

Article 5

1. The development of contacts and co-operation among States, the exchange of information and experiences on the achievements of minorities in cultural, educa-tional and other fields, creates favourable conditions for the promotion of the rights of minorities and for their general progress.

2. The States Members of the United Nations are invited to take the needs of minorities into account, in developing their co-operation with other states, especially in the fields of culture, education and related areas of particular importance for the minorities.

Appendix 6

CSCE in Europe: Concluding Document from the Vienna Conference
(4 November 1986–17 January 1989)

LMXXVIII (March 1989)

16. In order to ensure the freedom of the individual to profess and practise religion or belief the participating States will, *inter alia,*

16a ● take effective measures to prevent and eliminate discrimination against individuals or communities, on the grounds of religion or belief in the recognition, exercise and enjoyment of human rights and fundamental freedoms in all fields of civil, political, economic, social and cultural life, and ensure the effective equality between believers and non-believers;

16b ● foster a climate of mutual tolerance and respect between believers of different communities as well as between believers and non-believers;

16c ● grant upon their request to communities of believers, practising or prepared to practise their faith within the constitutional framework of their states, recognition of the status provided for them in their respective countries;

16d ● respect the right of religious communities to
　● establish and maintain freely accessible places of worship or assembly,
　● organize themselves according to their own hierarchical and institutional structure,
　● select, appoint and replace their personnel in accordance with their respective requirements and standards as well as with any freely accepted arrangement between them and their State,
　● solicit and receive voluntary financial and other contributions;

16e ● engage in consultations with religious faiths, institutions and organizations in order to achieve a better understanding of the requirements of religious freedom;

16f ● respect the right of everyone to give and receive religious education in the language of his choice, individually or in association with others;

16g ● in this context respect, *inter alia,* the liberty of parents to ensure the religious and moral education of their children in conformity with their own convictions;

16h ● allow the training of religious personnel in appropriate institutions;

16i ● respect the right of individual believers and communities of believers to acquire, possess, and use sacred books, religious publications in the language of their choice and other articles and materials related to the practice of religion or belief;

16j ● allow religious faiths, institutions and organizations to produce and import and disseminate religious publications and materials;

16k ● favorably consider the interest of religious communities in participating in public dialogue, *inter alia,* through mass media;

17. The participating States recognize that the exercise of the above-mentioned rights relating to the freedom of religion or belief may be subject only to such limitations as are provided by law and consistent with their obligations under international law and with their international commitments. They will ensure in their laws and regulations and in their application the full and effective implementation of the freedom of thought, conscience, religion or belief.

18. The participating States will exert sustained efforts to implement the provisions of the Final Act and of the Madrid Concluding Document pertaining to national minorities. They will take all the necessary legislative, administrative, judicial and other measures and apply the relevant international instruments by which they may be bound, to ensure the protection of human rights and fundamental freedoms of persons belonging to national minorities within their territory. They will refrain from any discrimination against such persons and contribute to the realization of their legitimate interests and aspirations in the field of human rights and fundamental freedoms.

19. They will protect and create conditions for the promotion of the ethnic, cultural, linguistic and religious identity of national minorities on their territory. They will respect the free exercise of rights by persons belonging to such minorities and ensure their full equality with others.

Appendix 7

Draft Universal Declaration on Indigenous Rights as Contained in Document
E/CN.4/Sub.2/1988/25

The General Assembly,

Considering indigenous peoples equal to all other human beings in dignity and rights in accordance with existing international standards while recognizing the right of all individuals and groups to be different, to consider themselves different and to be regarded as such,

Considering that all peoples and human groups have contributed to the progress of civilizations and cultures which constitute the common heritage of humankind,

Recognizing the need to promote and protect those rights and characteristics which stem from indigenous history, philosophy of life, traditions and social structures, especially as these are tied to the lands which the groups have traditionally occupied,

Concerned that many indigenous peoples have been unable to enjoy and assert their inalienable human rights and fundamental freedoms, frequently resulting in insufficient land and resources, poverty and deprivation, which in turn may lead to rebellion against all forms of oppression,

Convinced that all doctrines and practices of racial, ethnic or cultural superiority are legally wrong, morally condemnable and socially unjust,

Reaffirming that indigenous peoples in the exercise of their rights should be free from adverse distinction or discrimination of any kind,

Endorsing calls for the consolidation and strengthening of indigenous societies and their cultures and traditions through ethnodevelopment and comprehensive participation in and consultation about all other relevant development efforts,

Emphasizing the need for special attention to the rights and skills of indigenous women and children,

Believing that indigenous peoples should be free to manage their own affairs to the greatest possible extent, while enjoying equal rights with other citizens in the political, economic and social life of States,

Calling on States to comply with and effectively implement all international human rights instruments as they apply to indigenous peoples,

Acknowledging the need for minimum standards taking account of the diverse realities of indigenous peoples in all parts of the world,

Solemnly proclaims the following rights of indigenous peoples and calls upon all States to take prompt and effective measures for their implementation.

Part I

1. The right to the full and effective enjoyment of all fundamental rights and freedoms, as well as the observance of the corresponding responsibilities, which are universally recognized in the Charter of the United Nations and in existing international human rights instruments.

2. The right to be free and equal to all the other human beings in dignity and rights to be free from adverse distinction or discrimination of any kind.

Part II

3. The collective right to exist and to be protected against genocide, as well as the individual rights to life, physical integrity, liberty and security of person.

4. The collective right to maintain and develop their ethnic and cultural characteristics and identity, including the right of peoples and individuals to call themselves by their proper names.

5. The collective right to protection against ethnocide. This protection shall include, in particular, prevention of any act which has the aim or effect of depriving them of their ethnic characteristics or identity, of any form of forced assimilation or integration, of imposition of foreign life styles and of any propaganda directed against them.

6. The right to preserve their cultural identity and traditions and to pursue their own cultural development. The rights to the manifestations of their cultures, including archeological sites, artifacts, designs, technology and works of art, lie with the indigenous peoples or their members.

7. The duty of States to grant—within the resources available—the necessary assistance for the maintenance of their identity and their development.

8. The right to manifest, teach, practise and observe their own religious traditions and ceremonies, and to maintain, protect and have access to sacred sites and burial grounds for these purposes.

9. The right to maintain and use their own languages, including for administrative, judicial and other relevant purposes.

10. The right to all forms of education, including in particular the right of children to have access to education in their own languages, and to establish, structure, conduct and control their own educational systems and institutions.

11. The right to promote intercultural information and education, recognizing the dignity and diversity of their cultures, and the duty of States to take the necessary measures, among other sections of the national community, with the object of eliminating prejudices and of fostering understanding and good relations.

Part III

12. The right of ownership and possession of the lands which they have traditionally occupied. The lands may only be taken away from them with their free and informed consent as witnessed by a treaty or agreement.

13. The right to recognition of their own land-tenure systems for the protection and promotion of the use, enjoyment and occupancy of the land.

14. The right to special measures to ensure their control over surface resources pertaining to the territories they have traditionally occupied, including flora and fauna, waters and sea ice.

15. The right to reclaim land and surface resources or where this is not possible, to seek just and fair compensation for the same, when the property has been taken away from them without consent, in particular, if such deprival has been based on theories such as those related to discovery, *terra nullius*, waste lands or idle lands. Compensation, if the parties agree, may take the form of land or resources of quality and legal status at least equal to that of the property previously owned by them.

16. The right to protection against any action or course of conduct which may result in the destruction, deterioration or pollution of their land, air, water, sea ice, wildlife or other resources without free and informed consent of the indigenous peoples affected. The right to just and fair compensation for any such action or course of conduct.

17. The duty of States to seek and obtain their consent, through appropriate mechanisms, before undertaking or permitting any programmes for the exploration or exploitation of mineral and other subsoil resources pertaining to their traditional territories. Just and fair compensation should be provided for any such activities undertaken.

Part IV

18. The right to maintain within their areas of settlement their traditional economic structures and ways of life, to be secure in the enjoyment of their own traditional means of subsistence, and to engage freely in their traditional and other economic activities, including hunting, fresh- and salt-water fishing, herding, gathering, lumbering and cultivation, without adverse discrimination. In no case may an indigenous people be deprived of its means of subsistence. The right to just and fair compensation if they have been so deprived.

19. The right to special State measures for the immediate, effective and continuing improvement of their social and economic conditions, with their consent, that reflect their own priorities.

20. The right to determine, plan and implement all health, housing and other social and economic programmes affecting them, as far as possible through their own institutions.

Part V

21. The right to participate fully in the political, economic and social life of their State and to have their specific character duly reflected in the legal system and in political institutions, including proper regard to and recognition of indigenous laws and customs.

22. The right to participate fully at the State level, through representatives chosen by themselves, in decision-making about and implementation of all national and international matters which may affect their life and destiny.

23. The collective right to autonomy in matters relating to their own internal and local affairs, including education, information, culture, religion, health, housing, social welfare, traditional and other economic activities, land and resources administration and the environment, as well as internal taxation for financing these autonomous functions.

24. The right to decide upon the structures of their autonomous institutions, to select the membership of such institutions, and to determine the membership of the indigenous people concerned for these purposes.

25. The right to determine the responsibilities of individuals to their own community, consistent with universally recognized human rights and fundamental freedoms.

26. The right to traditional contacts and co-operation, including cultural and social exchanges and trade, with their own kith and kin across State boundaries in accordance with established laws and practices.

27. The duty of States to honour treaties and other agreements concluded with indigenous peoples.

Part VI

28. The individual and collective right to access to and prompt decision by mutually acceptable and fair procedures for resolving conflicts or disputes between States and indigenous peoples, groups or individuals. These procedures should include, as appropriate, negotations, mediation, national courts and international human rights review and complaints mechanisms.

Appendix 8

The 27 States Parties to ILO 107

Angola, Ghana, Guinea-Bissau, Malawi.

Egypt, Iraq, Syria, Tunisia.

Argentina, Bolivia, Brazil, Colombia, Costa Rica, Cuba, Ecuador, El Salv., Mex.,
Panama, Paraguay, Peru.

B'desh, India, Pakistan.

Belgium, Dom. Rep., Haiti, Portugal.

Appendix 9

The General Conference of the International Labour Organization,

Having been convened at Geneva by the Governing Body of the International Labour Office, and having met in its 76th Session on 7 June 1989, and

Noting the international standards contained in the Indigenous and Tribal Populations Convention and Recommendation, 1957, and

Recalling the terms of the Universal Declaration of Human Rights, the International Covenant on Economic, Social and Cultural Rights, the International Covenant on Civil and Political Rights, and the many international instruments on the prevention of discrimination, and

Considering that the developments which have taken place in international law since 1957, as well as developments in the situation of indigenous and tribal peoples in all regions of the world, have made it appropriate to adopt new international standards on the subject with a view to removing the assimilationist orientation of the earlier standards, and

Recognising the aspirations of these peoples to exercise control over their own institutions, ways of life and economic development and to maintain and develop their identities, languages and religions, within the framework of the States in which they live, and

Noting that in many parts of the world these peoples are unable to enjoy their fundamental human rights to the same degree as the rest of the population of the States within which they live, and that their laws, values, customs and perspectives have often been eroded, and

Calling attention to the distinctive contributions of indigenous and tribal peoples to the cultural diversity and social and ecological harmony of humankind and to international co-operation and understanding, and

Noting that the following provisions have been framed with the co-operation of the United Nations, the Food and Agriculture Organization of the United Nations, the United Nations Educational, Scientific and Cultural Organization and the World Health Organization, as well as of the Inter-American Indian Institute, at appropriate levels and in their respective fields, and that it is proposed to continue this co-operation in promoting and securing the application of these provisions, and

Having decided upon the adoption of certain proposals with regard to the partial revision of the Indigenous and Tribal Populations Convention, 1957 (No. 107), which is the fourth item on the agenda of the session, and

Having determined that these proposals shall take the form of an international Convention revising the Indigenous and Tribal Populations Convention, 1957; adopts this twenty-seventh day of June of the year one thousand nine hundred and eighty-nine the following Convention, which may be cited as the Indigenous and Tribal Peoples Convention, 1989:

Part I. General policy

Article 1

1. This Convention applies to:

(*a*) tribal peoples in independent countries whose social, cultural and economic conditions distinguish them from other sections of the national community, and whose status is regulated wholly or partially by their own customs or traditions or by special laws or regulations;

(*b*) peoples in independent countries who are regarded as indigenous on account of their descent from the populations which inhabited the country, or a geographical region to which the country belongs, at the time of conquest or colonization or the establishment of present state boundaries and who, irrespective of their legal status, retain some or all of their own social, economic, cultural and political institutions.

2. Self-identification as indigenous or tribal shall be regarded as a fundamental criterion for determining the groups to which the provisions of this Convention apply.

3. The use of the term "peoples" in this Convention shall not be construed as having any implications as regards the rights which may attach to the term under international law.

Article 2

1. Governments shall have the responsibility for developing, with the participation of the peoples concerned, co-ordinated and systematic action to protect the rights of these peoples and to guarantee respect for their integrity.

2. Such action shall include measures for:

(*a*) ensuring that members of these peoples benefit on an equal footing from the rights and opportunities which national laws and regulations grant to other members of the population;

(*b*) promoting the full realization of the social, economic and cultural rights of these peoples with respect for their social and cultural identity, their customs and traditions and their institutions;

(*c*) assisting the members of the peoples concerned to eliminate socio-economic gaps that may exist between indigenous and other members of the national community, in a manner compatible with their aspirations and ways of life.

Article 3

1. Indigenous and tribal peoples shall enjoy the full measure of human rights and fundamental freedoms without hindrance or discrimination. The provisions of the Convention shall be applied without discrimination to male and female members of these peoples.

2. No form of force or coercion shall be used in violation of the human rights and fundamental freedoms of the peoples concerned, including the rights contained in this Convention.

Article 4

1. Special measures shall be adopted as appropriate for safeguarding the persons, institutions, property, labour, cultures and environment of the peoples concerned.

2. Such special measures shall not be contrary to the freely-expressed wishes of the peoples concerned.

3. Enjoyment of the general rights of citizenship, without discrimination, shall not be prejudiced in any way by such special measures.

Article 5

In applying the provisions of this Convention:

(*a*) the social, cultural, religious and spiritual values and practices of these peoples shall be recognised and protected, and due account shall be taken of the nature of the problems which face them both as groups and as individuals;

(*b*) the integrity of the values, practices and institutions of these peoples shall be respected;

(*c*) policies aimed at mitigating the difficulties experienced by these peoples in facing new conditions of life and work shall be adopted, with the participation and co-operation of the peoples affected.

Article 6

1. In applying the provisions of this Convention, governments shall:

(*a*) consult the peoples concerned, through appropriate procedures and in particular through their representative institutions, whenever consideration is being given to legislative or administrative measures which may affect them directly;

(*b*) establish means by which these peoples can freely participate, to at least the same extent as other sectors of the population, at all levels of decision-making in elective institutions and administrative and other bodies responsible for policies and programmes which concern them;

(*c*) establish means for the full development of these peoples' own institutions and initiatives, and in appropriate cases provide the resources necessary for this purpose.

2. The consultations carried out in application of this Convention shall be undertaken, in good faith and in a form appropriate to the circumstances, with the objective of achieving agreement or consent to the proposed measures.

Article 7

1. The peoples concerned shall have the right to decide their own priorities for the process of development as it affects their lives, beliefs, institutions and spiritual well-being and the lands they occupy or otherwise use, and to exercise control, to the extent possible, over their own economic, social and cultural development. In addition, they shall participate in the formulation, implementation and evaluation of plans and programmes for national and regional development which may affect them directly.

2. The improvement of the conditions of life and work and levels of health and education of the peoples concerned, with their participation and co-operation, shall be a matter of priority in plans for the overall economic development of areas they inhabit. Special projects for development of the areas in question shall also be so designed as to promote such improvement.

3. Governments shall ensure that, whenever appropriate, studies are carried out, in co-operation with the peoples concerned, to assess the social, spiritual, cultural and environmental impact on them of planned development activities. The results of

these studies shall be considered as fundamental criteria for the implementation of these activities.

4. Governments shall take measures, in co-operation with the peoples concerned, to protect and preserve the environment of the territories they inhabit.

Article 8

1. In application of national laws and regulations to the peoples concerned, due regard shall be had to their customs or customary laws.

2. These peoples shall have the right to retain their own customs and institutions, where these are not incompatible with fundamental rights defined by the national legal system and with internationally recognised human rights. Procedures shall be established, whenever necessary, to resolve conflicts which may arise in the application of this principle.

3. The application of paragraphs 1 and 2 of this Article shall not prevent members of these peoples from exercising the rights granted to all citizens and from assuming the corresponding duties.

Article 9

1. To the extent compatible with the national legal system and internationally recognised human rights, the methods customarily practised by the peoples concerned for dealing with offences committed by their members shall be respected.

2. The customs of these peoples in regard to penal matters shall be taken into consideration by the authorities and courts dealing with such cases.

Article 10

1. In imposing penalties laid down by general law on members of these peoples account shall be taken of their economic, social and cultural characteristics.

2. Preference shall be given to methods of punishment other than confinement in prison.

Article 11

The exaction from members of the peoples concerned of compulsory personal services in any form, whether paid or unpaid, shall be prohibited and punishable by law, except in cases prescribed by law for all citizens.

Article 12

The peoples concerned shall be safeguarded against the abuse of their rights and shall be able to take legal proceedings, either individually or through their representative bodies, for the effective protection of these rights. Measures shall be taken to ensure that members of these peoples can understand and be understood in legal proceedings, where necessary through the provision of interpretation or by other effective means.

Part II. Land

Article 13

1. In applying the provisions of this Part of the Convention governments shall respect the special importance for the cultures and spiritual values of the peoples concerned of their relationship with the lands or territories, or both as applicable, which they occupy or otherwise use, and in particular the collective aspects of this relationship.

2. The use of the term "lands" in Articles 15 and 16 shall include the concept of territories, which covers the total environment of the areas which the peoples concerned occupy or otherwise use.

Article 14

1. The rights of ownership and possession of the peoples concerned over the lands which they traditionally occupy shall be recognised. In addition, measures shall be taken in appropriate cases to safeguard the right of the peoples concerned to use lands not exclusively occupied by them, but to which they have traditionally had access for their subsistence and traditional activities. Particular attention shall be paid to the situation of nomadic peoples and shifting cultivators in this respect.

2. Governments shall take steps as necessary to identify the lands which the peoples concerned traditionally occupy, and to guarantee effective protection of their rights of ownership and possession.

3. Adequate procedures shall be established within the national legal system to resolve land claims by the peoples concerned.

Article 15

1. The rights of the peoples concerned to the natural resources pertaining to their lands shall be specially safeguarded. These rights include the right of these peoples to participate in the use, management and conservation of these resources.

2. In cases in which the State retains the ownership of mineral or sub-surface resources or rights to other resources pertaining to lands, governments shall establish or maintain procedures through which they shall consult these peoples, with a view to ascertaining whether and to what degree their interests would be prejudiced, before undertaking or permitting any programmes for the exploration or exploitation of such resources pertaining to their lands. The peoples concerned shall wherever possible participate in the benefits of such activities, and shall receive fair compensation for any damages which they may sustain as a result of such activities.

Article 16

1. Subject to the following paragraphs of this Article, the peoples concerned shall not be removed from the lands which they occupy.

2. Where the relocation of these peoples is considered necessary as an exceptional measure, such relocation shall take place only with their free and informed consent. Where their consent cannot be obtained, such relocation shall take place only following appropriate procedures established by national laws and regulations, including public inquiries where appropriate, which provide the opportunity for effective representation of the peoples concerned.

3. Whenever possible, these peoples shall have the right to return to their traditional lands, as soon as the grounds for relocation cease to exist.

4. When such return is not possible, as determined by agreement or, in the absence of such agreement, through appropriate procedures, these peoples shall be provided in all possible cases with lands of quality and legal status at least equal to that of the lands previously occupied by them, suitable to provide for their present needs and future development. Where the peoples concerned express a preference for compensation in money or in kind, they shall be so compensated under appropriate guarantees.

5. Persons thus relocated shall be fully compensated for any resulting loss or injury.

Article 17

1. Procedures established by the peoples concerned for the transmission of land rights among members of these peoples shall be respected.

2. The peoples concerned shall be consulted whenever consideration is being given to their capacity to alienate their lands or otherwise transmit their rights outside their own community.

3. Persons not belonging to these peoples shall be prevented from taking advantage of their customs or of lack of understanding of the laws on the part of their members to secure the ownership, possession or use of land belonging to them.

Article 18

Adequate penalties shall be established by law for unauthorised intrusion upon, or use of, the lands of the peoples concerned, and governments shall take measures to prevent such offences.

Article 19

National agrarian programmes shall secure to the peoples concerned treatment equivalent to that accorded to other sectors of the population with regard to:

(*a*) the provision of more land for these peoples when they have not the area necessary for providing the essentials of a normal existence, or for any possible increase in their numbers;

(*b*) the provision of the means required to promote the development of the lands which these peoples already possess.

Part III. Recruitment and conditions of employment

Article 20

1. Governments shall, within the framework of national laws and regulations, and in co-operation with the peoples concerned, adopt special measures to ensure the effective protection with regard to recruitment and conditions of employment of workers belonging to these peoples, to the extent that they are not effectively protected by laws applicable to workers in general.

2. Governments shall do everything possible to prevent any discrimination between workers belonging to the peoples concerned and other workers, in particular as regards:

(*a*) admission to employment, including skilled employment, as well as measures for promotion and advancement;

(*b*) equal remuneration for work of equal value;

(*c*) medical and social assistance, occupational safety and health, all social security benefits and any other occupationally related benefits, and housing;

(*d*) the right of association and freedom for all lawful trade union activities, and the right to conclude collective agreements with employers or employers' organisations.

3. The measures taken shall include measures to ensure:

(*a*) that workers belonging to the peoples concerned, including seasonal, casual and migrant workers in agricultural and other employment, as well as those employed by labour contractors, enjoy the protection afforded by national law and practice to other such workers in the same sectors, and that they are fully informed of their rights under labour legislation and of the means of redress available to them;

(*b*) that workers belonging to these peoples are not subjected to working conditions hazardous to their health, in particular through exposure to pesticides or other toxic substances;

(*c*) that workers belonging to these peoples are not subjected to coercive recruitment systems, including bonded labour and other forms of debt servitude;

(*d*) that workers belonging to these peoples enjoy equal opportunities and equal treatment in employment for men and women, and protection from sexual harassment.

4. Particular attention shall be paid to the establishment of adequate labour inspection services in areas where workers belonging to the peoples concerned undertake wage employment, in order to ensure compliance with the provisions of this Part of this Convention.

Part IV. Vocational training, handicrafts and rural industries

Article 21

Members of the peoples concerned shall enjoy opportunities at least equal to those of other citizens in respect of vocational training measures.

Article 22

1. Measures shall be taken to promote the voluntary participation of members of the peoples concerned in vocational training programmes of general application.

2. Whenever existing programmes of vocational training of general application do not meet the special needs of the peoples concerned, governments shall, with the participation of these peoples, ensure the provision of special training programmes and facilities.

3. Any special training programmes shall be based on the economic environment, social and cultural conditions and practical needs of the peoples concerned. Any studies made in this connection shall be carried out in co-operation with these peoples, who shall be consulted on the organisation and operation of such programmes. Where feasible, these peoples shall progressively assume responsibility for the organisation and operation of such special training programmes, if they so decide.

Article 23

1. Handicrafts, rural and community-based industries, and subsistence economy and traditional activities of the peoples concerned, such as hunting, fishing, trapping and gathering, shall be recognised as important factors in the maintenance of their cultures and in their economic self-reliance and development. Governments shall, with the participation of these people and whenever appropriate, ensure that these activities are strengthened and promoted.

2. Upon the request of the peoples concerned, appropriate technical and financial assistance shall be provided wherever possible, taking into account the traditional technologies and cultural characteristics of these peoples, as well as the importance of sustainable and equitable development.

Part V. Social security and health

Article 24

Social security schemes shall be extended progressively to cover the peoples concerned, and applied without discrimination against them.

Article 25

1. Governments shall ensure that adequate health services are made available to the peoples concerned, or shall provide them with resources to allow them to design and deliver such services under their own responsibility and control, so that they may enjoy the highest attainable standard of physical and mental health.

2. Health services shall, to the extent possible, be community-based. These services shall be planned and administered in co-operation with the peoples concerned and take into account their economic, geographic, social and cultural conditions as well as their traditional preventive care, healing practices and medicines.

3. The health care system shall give preference to the training and employment of local community health workers, and focus on primary health care while maintaining strong links with other levels of health care services.

4. The provision of such health services shall be co-ordinated with other social, economic and cultural measures in the country.

Part VI. Education and means of communication

Article 26

Measures shall be taken to ensure that members of the peoples concerned have the opportunity to acquire education at all levels on at least an equal footing with the rest of the national community.

Article 27

1. Education programmes and services for the peoples concerned shall be developed and implemented in co-operation with them to address their special needs, and shall incorporate their histories, their knowledge and technologies, their value systems and their further social, economic and cultural aspirations.

2. The competent authority shall ensure the training of membes of these peoples and their involvement in the formulation and implementation of education programmes, with a view to the progressive transfer of responsibility for the conduct of these programmes to these peoples as appropriate.

3. In addition, governments shall recognise the right of these peoples to establish their own educational institutions and facilities, provided that such institutions meet minimum standards established by the competent authority in consultation with these peoples. Appropriate resources shall be provided for this purpose.

Article 28

1. Children belonging to the peoples concerned shall, wherever practicable, be taught to read and write in their own indigenous language or in the language most commonly used by the group to which they belong. When this is not practicable, the competent authorities shall undertake consultations with these peoples with a view to the adoption of measures to achieve this objective.

2. Adequate measures shall be taken to ensure that these peoples have the opportunity to attain fluency in the national language or in one of the official languages of the country.

3. Measures shall be taken to preserve and promote the development and practice of the indigenous languages of the peoples concerned.

Article 29

The imparting of general knowledge and skills that will help children belonging to the peoples concerned to participate fully and on an equal footing in their own community and in the national community shall be an aim of education for these peoples.

Article 30

1. Governments shall adopt measures appropriate to the traditions and cultures of the peoples concerned, to make known to them their rights and duties, especially in regard to labour, economic opportunities, education and health matters, social welfare and their rights deriving from this Convention.

2. If necessary, this shall be done by means of written translations and through the use of mass communications in the languages of these peoples.

Article 31

Educational measures shall be taken among all sections of the national community, and particularly among those that are in most direct contact with the peoples concerned, with the object of eliminating prejudices that they may harbour in respect of these peoples. To this end, efforts shall be made to ensure that history textbooks and other educational materials provide a fair, accurate and informative portrayal of the societies and cultures of these peoples.

Part VII. Contacts and co-operation across borders

Article 32

Governments shall take appropriate measures, including by means of international agreements, to facilitate contacts and co-operation between indigenous and tribal peoples across borders, including activities in the economic, social, cultural, spiritual and environmental fields.

Part VIII. Administration

Article 33

1. The governmental authority responsible for the matters covered in this Convention shall ensure that agencies or other appropriate mechanisms exist to administer the programmes affecting the peoples concerned, and shall ensure that they have the means necessary for the proper fulfilment of the functions assigned to them.

2. These programmes shall include:

(*a*) the planning, co-ordination, execution and evaluation, in co-operation with the peoples concerned, of the measures provided for in this Convention;

(*b*) the proposing of legislative and other measures to the competent authorities and supervision of the application of the measures taken, in co-operation with the peoples concerned.

Part IX. General provisions

Article 34

The nature and scope of the measures to be taken to give effect to this Convention shall be determined in a flexible manner, having regard to the conditions characteristic of each country.

Article 35

The application of the provisions of this Convention shall not adversely affect rights and benefits of the peoples concerned pursuant to other Conventions and Recommendations, international instruments, treaties, or national laws, awards, custom or agreements.

Part X. Final provisions

Article 36

This Convention revises the Indigenous and Tribal Populations Convention, 1957.

Omissis

List of Principal Works Consulted

Books

AKEHURST, M., *A Modern Introduction to International Law*, 6th edn. (London: George Allen and Unwin, 1987).

ALCOCK, A. E., *The History of the South Tyrol Question* (Geneva: Michael Joseph Ltd., 1970).

ALCOCK, A. E., TAYLOR, B. K., WELTON, J. M. (eds.), *The Future of Cultural Minorities* (London: Macmillan, 1979).

ALEXANDROWICZ, C. H., *An Introduction to the History of the Law of Nations in the East Indies* (Oxford: OUP, 1967).

——*The European–African Confrontation. A Study in Treaty-Making* (Leiden: Sitjhoff, 1973).

ARENS, R. (ed.), *Genocide in Paraguay* (Philadelphia: Temple University Press, 1976).

ASHWORTH, G. (ed.), *World Minorities*, 3 vols. (Sunbury: Quatermaine House Ltd., 1977, 1978, 1980).

AZCÁRATE, P. DE, *The League of Nations and National Minorities* (Washington: Carnegie Endowment for International Peace, 1945).

BAGLEY, I. H., *General Principles and Problems in the Protection of Minorities* (Geneva: Imprimeries populaires, 1950).

BALOGH, A. DE, *La Protection Internationale des Minorités* (Paris: Les editions internationales, 1930).

BANTON, R., *Which Relations are Racial Relations?* (London: Royal Anthropological Institute, 1988).

BARKER, SIR E. (ed.), *Social Contract: Essays by Locke, Hume, and Rousseau* (Oxford: OUP, 1951).

BARON, S. W., *Ethnic Minority Rights. Some Older and Newer Trends* (Oxford: OUP, 1985).

BARROS, J., *The Aaland Islands Question: Its Settlement by the League of Nations* (New Haven: Yale, 1968).

BASSIOUNI, M. C. and NANDA, V. P. (eds.), *A Treatise on International Criminal Law*, vol. i. (Illinois: Charles C. Thomas, 1973).

BENNETT, G., *Aboriginal Rights in International Law* (London: Royal Anthropological Institute, 1978).

BENTWICH, N. and MARTIN, A., *A Commentary on the Charter of the United Nations* (London: Routledge and Kegan Paul, 1950).

BISCHOFF, R., *Nazi Conquest Through German Culture* (Cambridge, Mass.: Harvard UP, 1942).

BLAUSTEIN, A. P. and FLANZ, G. H., *Constitutions of the Countries of the World* Dobbs Ferry: Oceana Publications, 1973–   ).

BROWNLIE, I., *Basic Documents on Human Rights*, 2nd edn. (Oxford: OUP, 1981).

——*Principles of Public International Law*, 3rd edn. (Oxford: OUP, 1979).

BUCHHEIT, L. C., *Secession: The Legitimacy of Self-Determination* (New Haven: Yale UP, 1978).

BUERGENTHAL, T. and HALL, J. (eds.), *Human Rights, International Law and the Helsinki Accord* (New York: Allanheld, 1977).

BULL, H. (ed.), *Intervention in World Politics* (Oxford: OUP, 1984).

CARATINI, R., *La Force des Faibles. Encyclopédie des Minorités* (Paris: Larousse, 1986).

CASSESE, A., *UN Law. Fundamental Rights: Two Topics in International Law* (Alphen aan den Rijn: Sijthoff and Noordhoff, 1979).

——*International Law in a Divided World* (Oxford: OUP, 1986).

CASTAÑEDA, J., *The Legal Effects of United Nations Resolutions* (New York: Columbia UP, 1969).

CLAUDE, I. L., *National Minorities: An International Problem* (Cambridge, Mass.: Harvard UP, 1955).

CRAWFORD, J. (ed.), *The Rights of Peoples* (Oxford: OUP, 1988).

——*The Creation of States in International Law* (Oxford: OUP, 1979).

CREASY, SIR E., *First Platform on International Law* (London: John van Voorst, 1876).

DAY, A. J. (ed.), *Border and Territorial Disputes* (Harlow: Longmans, 1982).

DINSTEIN, Y., *Models of Autonomy* (New Brunswick and London: Transaction Books, 1981).

DROST, P., *Human Rights as Legal Rights* (Leiden: Sijthoff, 1951).

——*The Crime of State*, 2 vols. (Leiden: Sijthoff, 1959).

EZEJIOFOR, G., *Protection of Human Rights Under the Law* (London: Butterworths, 1964).

FALK, R. A., KOLKO, G., and LIFTON, R. J., *Crimes of War* (New York: Vintage Books, 1971).

FAWCETT, SIR J., *The International Protection of Minorities*, Minority Rights Group Report No. 41 (London: Minority Rights Group, 1979).

——*The Application of the European Convention on Human Rights*, 2nd edn. (Oxford: OUP, 1987).

FEINBERG, N., *La Juridiction de la Cour Permanente de Justice dans le Système de la Protection Internationale des Minorités* (Paris: Rousseau, 1931).

FERENCZ, B., *An International Criminal Court: A Step Towards World Peace* (London: Oceana Publications, 1980).

FERRARIS, L. V., *Report on a Negotiation, Helsinki–Geneva–Helsinki, 1972–75* (Alphen aan den Rijn: Sijthoff and Noordhoff, 1979).

FINNIS, J., *Natural Law and Natural Rights* (Oxford: OUP, 1980).

FIORE, P., *Nouveau Droit International Public* (Paris: Durand et Lauriel, 1868).

FOUQUES-DUPARC, J., *La Protection des Minorités de Race, de Langue et de Religion* (Paris: Librairie Dalloz, 1922).

GANJI, M., *International Protection of Human Rights* (Geneva: Librairie E. Droz, 1962).

GLASER, S., *Droit International Pénal Conventionnel*, 2 vols. (Brussels: Emile Bruiylant, 1970 and 1978).

GOODRICH, L. M. and HAMBRO, E., *Charter of the United Nations Commentary and Documents*, 2nd edn. (London: Stevens and Sons, 1949).

GOODWIN-GILL, G. S., *International Law and the Movement of Persons Between States* (Oxford: OUP, 1978).

HACKWORTH, G. N., *Digest of International Law* (Washington: Govt. Printing Office, 1940–44).

HANNUM, H., *Guide to International Human Rights Practice* (London: Macmillan, 1984).

HARRIS, D. J., *Cases and Materials on International Law*, 3rd edn. (London: Sweet and Maxwell, 1983).

HEINZ, W. S., *Indigenous Populations, Ethnic Minorities and Human Rights* (Berlin: Quorum Verlag, 1988).

HENKIN, L. (ed.), *The International Bill of Rights. The Covenant on Civil and Political Rights* (New York: Columbia UP, 1981).

HURST, M. (ed.), *Key Treaties of the Great Powers 1814–1914* (Newton Abbot: David and Charles, 1972).

Independent Commission on International Humanitarian Issues, *Indigenous Peoples. A Global Quest for Justice* (London and New Jersey: Zed Books, 1987).

Institute of Marxism, *Leninism and the National Question* (Moscow: Progress Publishers, 1977).

International Commission of Jurists, *The Events in East Pakistan 1971: A Legal Study* (Geneva: 1972).

ISRAEL, F., *Major Peace Treaties of Modern History 1648–1967* (New York: Chelsea House, 1967).

Israel in Lebanon, *The Report of the International Commission to Enquire into Reported Violations of International Law by Israel during the Invasion of the Lebanon* (London: Ithaca Press, 1983).

JACOBS, F., *The European Convention on Human Rights* (Oxford: OUP, 1975).

JAULIN, R. (ed.), *L'Ethnocide à Travers les Amériques. Textes et Documents* (Paris: Librairie Arthème Fayard, 1972).

JOHNSON, H. S., *Self-Determination Within the Community of Nations* (Leiden: Sijthoff, 1967).

JOYCE, W. A. (ed.), *Human Rights: International Documents* (Alphen aan den Rijn, Sijthoff and Noordhoff, 1978).

KELSEN, H., *Principles of International Law* 2nd edn., (New York: Tucker, 1966).

KOHEN, A. and TAYLOR, J., *An Act of Genocide: Indonesia's Invasion of East Timor* (London: Tapol, 1979).

KUPER, L., *Genocide. Its Political Use in the Twentieth Century* (London: Penguin Books, 1981).

——*International Action Against Genocide*, Minority Rights Group Report No. 53 (Minority Rights Group, 1953).

——*The Prevention of Genocide* (New Haven: Yale UP, 1985).

LACQUEUR, W. and RUBIN, B. (eds.), *The Human Rights Reader* (New York and Scarborough, Ontario: Meridian, 1979).

LADOR-LEDERER, J. J., *International Group Protection. Aims and Methods in Human Rights* (Leiden: Sijthoff, 1968).

LAPONCE, J. A., *The Protection of Minorities* (Berkeley and Los Angeles: University of California Press, 1960).

LAUTERPACHT, H., *International Law and Human Rights* (London: Stevens and Sons, 1950).
——*Recognition in International Law* 2nd edn. (London: Cambridge UP, 1948).
LEIRIS, M., *Race and Culture* (Paris: UNESCO, 1958).
LEMKIN, R., *Axis Rule in Occupied Europe* (Washington: Carnegie Endowment for International Peace, 1944).
LERNER, N., *The UN Convention on the Elimination of All Forms of Racial Discrimination* 2nd edn. (Alphen aan den Rijn: Sijthoff and Noordhoff, 1980).
LILLICH, R. B. (ed.), *Humanitarian Intervention and the United Nations* (Charlottesville: University Press of Virginia, 1973).
LILLICH, R. B. and NEWMAN, F. C., *International Human Rights: Problems of Law and Policy* (Boston and Toronto: Little, Brown and Co., 1979).
LINDLEY, M. F., *The Acquisition and Government of Backward Territory in International Law* (New York: Negro Universities Press, 1969).
MACARTNEY, C. A., *National States and National Minorities* (London: OUP, 1934).
MACDONALD, R. ST. J. and JOHNSTON, D. M. (eds.), *The Structure and Process of International Law* (Dordrecht, Boston, Lancaster: M. Nijhoff, 1986).
MCDOUGAL, M. S., LASSWELL, H. D., and CHEN, LUNG-CHU, *Human Rights and World Public Order* (New Haven and London: Yale UP, 1980).
MCKEAN, W., *Equality and Discrimination under International Law* (Oxford: OUP, 1983).
MERON, T. (ed.), *Human Rights in International Law: Legal and Policy Issues* (Oxford: OUP, 1984).
——*Human Rights Law-Making in the United Nations: A Critique of Instruments and Processes* (Oxford: OUP, 1986).
MIDGLEY, E. B. F., *The Natural Law Tradition and the Theory of International Relations* (London: Paul Elek, 1975).
MILLER, D. H., *The Drafting of the Covenant* (New York: G. B. Putnam and Sons, 1928).
MODEEN, T., *The International Protection of National Minorities in Europe* (Åbo: Åbo Akademi, 1969).
MOORE, J. B., *A Digest of International Law* (Washington: Govt. Printing Office, 1906).
MOORE, J. N. (ed.), *Law and Civil War in the Modern World* (Baltimore: Johns Hopkins, 1971).
MOSKOWITZ, M., *The Politics and Dynamics of Human Rights* (New York: Oceana Publications, 1968).
MUELLER and WISE (eds.), *International Criminal Law* (London: Stevens & Sons, 1965).
NØRGAARD, C. A., *The Position of the Individual in International Law* (Copenhagen: Munksgaard, 1962).
NUSSBAUM, A., *A Concise History of the Law of Nations* (New York: 1961).
OPPENHEIM, L., *International Law: A Treatise*, vol. i, 7th edn. (London: 1958).
PARRY, C., *The Sources and Evidences of International Law* (Manchester: Manchester UP, 1965).
PHILLIMORE, R. J., *Commentaries upon International Law*, 2nd edn. (London: Butterworths, 1971).

PLAWSKI, S., *Étude des Principes Fondamentaux du Droit International Pénal* (Paris: Librairie générale de droit et de jurisprudence, 1972).

POMERANCE, M., *Self-Determination in Law and Practice. The New Doctrine at the United Nations* (The Hague: M. Nijhoff, 1982).

POPPER, K., *The Open Society and its Enemies* (London: Routledge and Kegan Paul, 1966).

RAMCHARAN, B. G. (ed.), *Human Rights Thirty Years After the Universal Declaration* (The Hague: M. Nijhoff, 1979).

RAWLS, J., *A Theory of Justice* (Cambridge, Mass.: Harvard University Press, 1971).

RIGO-SUREDA, A., *The Evolution of the Right of Self-Determination* (Leiden: Sijthoff, 1973).

ROBINSON, J., *Das minoritäten Problem und seine Literatur* (Berlin: W. de Gruyter and Co., 1928).

ROBINSON, J., *Were the Minorities Treaties a Failure?* (New York: Institute of Jewish Affairs, 1943).

ROBINSON, N., *The Genocide Convention. A Commentary* (New York: Institute of Jewish Affairs, 1960).

RONZITTI, N., *Rescuing Nationals Abroad Through Military Coercion and Intervention on Grounds of Humanity* (Dordrecht: M. Nijhoff, 1985).

ROUCEK, S., *The Working of the Minorities System under the League of Nations* (Prague: Orbis, 1929).

ROZAKIS, C. L., *The Concept of Jus Cogens in the Law of Treaties* (Amsterdam and Oxford: North Holland, 1976).

RUSSELL, R. B. and MUTHER, J. S., *A History of the United Nations Charter. The Role of the United States 1940–45* (Washington: Brookings Institution, 1958).

SALZBERG, J., *The United Nations Sub-Commission: A Functional Anaylsis* (Ann Arbor: University Microfilms International, 1973).

SHAW, M. N., *Title to Territory in Africa* (Oxford: OUP, 1986).

SIEGHART, P., *International Law of Human Rights* (Oxford: OUP, 1983).

——*The Lawful Rights of Mankind* (Oxford: OUP, 1985).

SIGLER, J. A., *Minority Rights: A Comparative Analysis* (London: Greenwood Press, 1983).

SIURUAINEN, E. AND AIKIO, P., *The Lapps in Finland* (Helsinki: Society for the Promotion of Lapp Culture, 1977).

SNOW, A. H., *The Question of Aborigines in the Law and Practice of Nations* (Northbrook, Illinois: Metro Books, 1972).

SOHN, L. and BUERGENTHAL, T., *International Protection of Human Rights* (Indianapolis, The Bobbs-Merrill Co., 1973).

STAVENHAGEN, R., *Derecho Indígena y Derechos Humanos en América Latina* (Mexico City: El Colegio de Mexico and Instituto Interamericano de Derechos Humanos, 1988).

TEMPERLEY, H. W. V., *A History of the Peace Conference of Paris* (1920–24, London: H. Prowde, Hodder and Stoughton, 6 vols., repr. 1969 OUP).

THORNBERRY, P., *Minorities and Human Rights Law*, Minority Rights Group Report No. 73. (London: Minority Rights Group, 1987).

TUNKIN, G. I., *Theory of International Law* Butler (trans.) (London: George Allen and Unwin, 1974).

TYLOR, SIR E., *Primitive Culture* (London: Murray, 1871).

UDINA, M., *Gli Accordi di Osimo* (Trieste: Edizione Lunt, 1979).

UNESCO, *Four Statements on the Race Question* (Paris: UNESCO, 1969).

VAN DYKE, V., *Human Rights. The United States and the World Community* (New York: OUP, 1970).

——*Human Rights. Ethnicity and Discrimination* (Westport, Conn, and London: Greenwood Press, 1985).

VAN HOOF, G. J. H., *Rethinking the Sources of International Law* (Deventer: Kluwer, 1983).

VAN LANGENHOVE, F., *The Question of Aborigines Before the United Nations: The Belgian Thesis* (Brussels: Royal Colonial Institute, 1954).

VASAK, K. and ALSTON, P., *The International Dimensions of Human Rights* (Paris: Greenwood Press and UNESCO, 1982).

VIERDAG, E. W., *The Concept of Discrimination in International Law—with Special Reference to Human Rights* (The Hague: M. Nijhoff, 1973).

WALTERS, F. P., *A History of the League of Nations* (London: OUP, 1952).

WEIS, P., *Nationality and Statelessness in International Law* (London: Stevens and Sons, 1956; 2nd edn., Alphen aan de Rijn: Sijthoff and Noordhoff, 1979).

WESTLAKE, J., *Chapters on the Principles of International Law* (Cambridge: CUP, 1984).

WHITEMAN, M., *Digest of International Law* (Washington: Dept. of State, 1963–65).

WINTGENS, H., *Der völkerrechtliche Schutz der nationalen, sprachlichen und religiösen Minderheiten. Handbuch des Volkerrechts*, 2 vols. (Stuttgart: W. Kohlhammer, 1930).

WIRSING, R., *Protection of Minorities. Comparative Perspectives* (New York: Pergamon Press, 1981).

Articles

AKEHURST, M. B., 'Custom as a Source of International Law', *BYIL*, 47 (1974–5), 1.

——'Equity and General Principles of Law', *ICLQ*, 25 (1976), 801.

——'The Hierarchy of the Sources of International Law', *BYIL*, 47 (1974–5), 273.

ALCOCK, A. E., 'A New Look at Protection of Minorities and the Principle of Equality of Human Rights', *Community Development Journal*, 12 (1977), 85.

ALEXANDROWICZ, C. H., 'Paulus Vladimiri and the Development of the Doctrine of Co-Existence of Christian and Non-Christian Countries', *BYIL*, 34 (1963), 441.

ALFREDSSON, G., 'International Law, International Organisations and Indigenous Peoples', *Journal of International Affairs*, 36 (1982), 113.

ALSTON, P., 'Conjuring Up New Human Rights: A Proposal for Quality Control', *AJIL*, 78 (1984), 607.

ARANGIO-RUIZ, G., 'The Normative Role of the General Assembly of the United Nations and the Declaration of Principles on Friendly Relations', *Rec. des Cours*, 137 (1972), 528.

BARSH, R. L., 'Indigenous Peoples: An Emerging Object of International Law', *AJIL*, 80 (1986), 369.

——'Revision of ILO Convention No. 107', *AJIL*, 81 (1987), 756.

BARTLETT, R. H., 'The Indian Act of Canada', *Buffalo Law Review*, 27 (1978), 581.

BASSIOUNI, M. C., 'International Law and the Holocaust', *California Western International Law Journal*, 9 (1979), 201.

BAYEFSKY, F., 'The Human Rights Committee and the Case of Sandra Lovelace', *Canadian Year Book of International Law*, 20 (1982), 244.

BEDAU, H. A., 'Genocide in Vietnam?', *Boston University Law Review*, 53 (1973), 574.

BEHUNIAK, T. E., 'The Law of Unilateral Humanitarian Intervention by Armed Force: A Legal Survey', *Military Law Review*, 79 (1978), 157.

BENNETT, G., 'The ILO Convention on Indigenous and Tribal Populations: The Resolution of a Problem of Vires', *BYIL*, 46 (1972–3), 382.

——'Developing Law of Aboriginal Rights', *Review of the International Commission of Jurists*, 22 (1979), 37.

BERMAN, H. R., 'The Concept of Aboriginal Rights in the Early Legal History of the United States', *Buffalo Law Review*, 27 (1978), 637.

——'The ILO and Indigenous Peoples: Revision of ILO Convention 107', *The Review of the International Commission of Jurists*, 41 (1988), 48.

BLAMONT, P., 'Human Rights and the ILO', *Howard Law Journal*, 11 (1965), 413.

BLEICHER, S., 'The Legal Significance of Re-Citation of General Assembly Resolutions', *AJIL*, 63 (1969), 444.

BLUM, Y. Z., 'Reflections on the Changing Content of Self-Determination', *Israel Law Review*, 10 (1975), 509.

BOWETT, D. W., 'Self-Determination and Political Rights in the Developing Countries', *Procs. ASIL 1966*, 129.

BRIDGE, J. W., 'The Case for an International Court of Criminal Justice and the Formulation of International Criminal Law', *ICLQ*, 13 (1964), 1255.

BROWNLIE, I., 'In Re the Mackenzie Valley Pipeline Inquiry', Unpublished opinion (March, 1976).

BRUEGEL, J. W., 'A Neglected Field, the Protection of Minorities', *RDH*, 4 (1971), 413.

CAGGIANO, G., 'Some Reflections on the Treaty of Osimo', *Italian Year Book of International Law*, 2 (1976), 248.

CAPOTORTI, F., 'The Protection of Minorities under Multilateral Agreements on Human Rights', *Italian Year Book of International Law*, 2 (1976), 3.

——'I Diritti dei Membri di Minoranze: Verso una Dichiarazione delle Nazione Unite?, *LXIV Rivista di Diritto Internazionale* (1981), 30.

CARNEGIE, A. R., 'Jurisdiction over Violations of the Laws and Customs of War', *BYIL*, 39 (1963), 402.

CHENG, B., 'United Nations Resolutions on Outer Space: "Instant" International Customary Law?', *Indian Journal of International Law*, 5 (1965), 23.

CLARK, R. S., 'The United Nations and Religious Freedom', *New York University Journal of International Law and Politics*, 11 (1978), 197.

CLAYDON, J., 'Internationally Uprooted People and the Transnational Protection of Minority Culture', *New York Law School Law Review*, 24 (1978), 125.

——'The Transnational Protection of Ethnic Minorities', *Canadian Year Book of International Law 1975*, 25.

COLEMAN, H. D., 'The Problem of Anti-Semitism under the International Convention on the Elimination of All Forms of Racial Discrimination', *Human Rights Journal*, 2 (1969), 609.

CUMMING, P. A. 'The Rights of Indigenous Peoples: A Comparative Analysis', *Procs. ASIL*, 68 (1974), 265.

DAES, E.-I. A., 'Protection of Minorities under the International Bill of Human Rights and the Genocide Convention', *Festschrift für Pan J. Zepos*, vol. ii (1973), 35.

D'AMATO, A., 'The Concept of Human Rights in International Law', *Columbia Law Review*, 82 (1982), 1110.

DE NOVA, R., 'The International Protection of National Minorities and Human Rights', *Harvard Law Journal*, 11 (1965), 275.

DE ZAYAS, A., 'International Law and Mass Population Transfers', *Harvard International Law Journal*, 16 (1975), 207.

DINSTEIN, Y., 'Collective Human Rights of Peoples and Minorities', *ICLQ*, 25 (1976), 102.

DUGARD, J., 'The Legal Effect of the United Nations Resolutions on Apartheid', *South African Law Journal*, 83 (1966), 44.

EGGLESTON, E., 'Prospects for United Nations Protection of the Human Rights of Indigenous Minorities', *Australian Yearbook of International Law*, 5 (1970–3), 68.

ERMACORA, F., 'The Protection of Minorities before the United Nations', *Rec. des Cours*, 182 (1983), 251.

FEINBERG, N., 'The Legal Validity of Undertakings Concerning Minorities and the Clausula Rebus Sic Stantibus', *Studies in Law, Scripta Hierosolymitana*, 5 (1958), 95.

FERENCZ, B., 'The Draft Code of Offences Against the Peace and Security of Mankind', *AJIL*, 75 (1981), 674.

FONTEYNE, J.-P. L. 'The Customary International Law Doctrine of Humanitarian Intervention: its Current Validity under the U.N. Charter', *California Western International Law Journal*, 4 (1974), 203.

FRANCK, T. and RODLEY, N., 'After Bangladesh: The Law of Humanitarian Intervention by Military Force', *AJIL*, 67 (1973), 275.

GALEY, M. E., 'Indigenous Peoples, International Consciousness-Raising and the Development of International Law on Human Rights', *RDH*, 8 (1975), 21.

GHANDHI, P. R., 'The Human Rights Committee and the Right of Individual Communication', *BYIL*, 57 (1986), 201.

GITTLEMAN, R., 'The African Charter on Human and Peoples' Rights: A Legal Analysis', *Virginia Journal of International Law*, 22 (1982), 667.

GOLDENBERG, S. L., 'Crimes Against Humanity 1945–1970', *Western Ontario Law Review*, 10 (1971), 1.

GORMLEY, P., 'The Emerging Protection of Human Rights by the ILO', *Alberta Law Review*, 30 (1966), 13.

GRAVEN, J., 'Les Crimes contre l'Humanité', *Recueil des Cours*, 76 (1950), I, 490.

GREEN, L. C., 'Canada's Indians, Federal Policy, International and Constitutional Law', *Ottawa Law Review*, 4 (1970), 101.

——'The Eichmann Case', *MLR*, 23 (1960), 507.

——'International Crimes and the Legal Process', *ICLQ*, 29 (1980), 567.

GROSS, L., 'Some Observations on the Draft Code of Offences Against the Peace and Security of Mankind', *Israel Yearbook on Human Rights*, 13 (1983), 9.

HANNUM, H., 'New Developments in Indigenous Rights', *Virginia Journal of International Law*, 28 (1988), 649.

HANNUM, H. and LILLICH, R., 'The Concept of Autonomy in International Law', *AJIL*, 74 (1980), 858.

HASSAN, F., 'The Doctrine of Incorporation: New Vistas for the Enforcement of International Human Rights', *Human Rights Quarterly*, 5, no. 1 (1983), 68.

HAUSER, R., 'International Protection of Minorities and the Right of Self-Determination', *Israel Yearbook on Human Rights*, 1 (1971), 92.

HAVER, P., 'The United Nations Sub-Commission on the Prevention of Discrimination and Protection of Minorities', *Columbia Journal of Transnational Law*, 21 (1982), 103.

HEYKING, A., BARON, 'The International Protection of Minorities – the Achilles Heel of the League of Nations', *Transactions of the Grotius Society* XIII (1927), 31.

HUDSON, M. O., 'Integrity of International Instruments', *AJIL*, 42 (1948), 105.

HUMPHREY, J. P., 'The Implementation of International Human Rights Law', *New York Law School Law Review*, 24 (1978), 31.

——'The UN Sub-Commission on Prevention of Discrimination and Protection of Minorities', *AJIL*, 62 (1968), 869.

HUSTON, J., 'Human Rights Enforcement Issues of the United Nations Conference on International Organisations', *Iowa Law Review*, 53 (1967), 272.

JOHNSON, D., 'The Effect of Resolutions of the General Assembly of the United Nations', *BYIL*, 32 (1955–6), 97.

JONES, M., 'National Minorities: A Case Study in International Protection', *Law and Contemporary Problems*, 14 (1949), 599.

KAMANU, O. S., 'Secession and Self-Determination: An OAU Dilemma', *Journal of Modern African Studies*, 12 (1974), 355.

KELLY, J. B., 'National Minorities in International Law', *Journal of International Law and Policy*, 3 (1973), 253.

KIWANUKA, R. N., 'The Meaning of "People" in the African Charter on Human and Peoples' Rights', *AJIL*, 82 (1988), 80.

KUNZ, J., 'The United Nations Convention on Genocide', *AJIL*, 43 (1949), 738.

——'The Present Status of the International Law for the Protection of Minorities', *AJIL*, 48 (1954), 282.

LADOR-LEDERER, J. J., 'The Eichmann Case Revisited', *Israel Yearbook on Human Rights*, 14 (1984), 54.

LANNUNG, H., 'The Rights of Minorities', *Mélanges offerts à Polys Modinos* (Paris: Editions A. Pedone, 1968), 181.

LAPIDOTH, R., 'Some Reflections on Autonomy', *Mélanges offerts à Paul Reuter* (Paris: Editions A. Pedone, 1981).

LASOK, D., 'The Eichmann Trial', *ICLQ*, 11 (1962), 355.

LAUREN, P. G., 'First Principles of Racial Equality: History and the Politics and Diplomacy of Human Rights Provisions in the United Nations Charter', *Human Rights Quarterly* 5, no. 1 (1983), 1.

LAUTERPRACHT, H., 'The Universal Declaration of Human Rights', *BYIL* 25 (1948), 354.

——'The Law of Nations and the Punishment of War Crimes', *BYIL* 21 (1944), 58.

LEBLANC, L. J., 'The United Nations, Genocide and Political Groups: Should the United States Propose an Amendment?', *Yale Journal of International Law*, 13 (1988), 268.

LEMKIN, R., 'Le Crime de Genocide', *Revue de Droit International de Sciences Diplomatiques, Politiques et Sociales*, 24 (1946), 213.

——'Genocide as a Crime under International Law', *AJIL*, 41 (1947), 145.

LERNER, N., 'New Concepts in the UNESCO Declaration on Race and Racial Prejudice', *Human Rights Quarterly*, 3, no. 1 (1981), 48.

——'Curbing Racial Discrimination–Fifteen Years CERD', *Israel Yearbook on Human Rights*, 13 (1983), 170.

LIEBHOLZ, G., 'Some Remarks on the Protection of Racial and Linguistic Minorities in Europe during the Nineteenth Century', *Internationales Recht und Diplomatie 1972*, 119.

LILLICH, R., 'Intervention to Protect Human Rights', *McGill Law Journal*, 15 (1969), 205.

MCDOUGAL, M. S., 'Freedom from Discrimination in Choice of Language and International Human Rights', *Southern Illinois University Law Journal 1976*, no. 1, 151.

MCDOUGAL, M. S., LASSWELL, H. D. and CHEN, LUNG-CHU, 'The Right to Religious Freedom and World Public Order', *Michigan Law Review*, 74 (1976), 765.

MCKEAN, W., 'The Meaning of Discrimination in International and Municipal Law', *BYIL*, 44 (1970), 177.

MARKS, S., 'UNESCO and Human Rights', *Texas International Law Journal*, 13 (1977), 35.

MERON, T., 'The Meaning and Reach of the International Convention on the Elimination of All Forms of Racial Discrimination', *AJIL*, 79 (1985), 283.

MODEEN, T., 'The International Protection of the National Identity of the Aaland Islands', *Scandinavian Studies in Law 1973*, 177.

MONACO, R., 'Minorités Nationales et la Protection Internationale des Droits de l'Homme', *René Cassin Amicorum Discipulorumque Liber* (Paris: Editions A. Pedone, 1969), 175.

NANDA, V. P., 'Self-determination in International Law: the Tragic Tale of Two Cities: Islamabad (West Pakistan) and Dacca (East Pakistan)', *AJIL*, 66 (1972), 321.

NEFF, S. C., 'An Evolving International Legal Norm of Religious Freedom: Problems and Prospects', *California Western International Law Journal*, 7 (1977), 543.

NIEC, H., 'Human Right to Culture', *Yearbook of AAA* (1974), 109.

PANTER-BRICK, S. K., 'The Right of Self-Determination: its Application to Nigeria', *International Affairs*, 44 (1968), 254.

PARTSCH, K. J., 'Elimination of Racial Discrimination in the Enjoyment of Civil and Political Rights', *Texas International Law Journal*, 14 (1979), 191.

PAUST, J. J. and BLAUSTEIN, A. P., 'War Crimes Jurisdiction and Due Process: The Bangladesh Experience', *Vanderbilt Journal of Transnational Law*, 11 (1978), 1.

REEBER, C., 'Linguistic Minorities and the Right to an Effective Education', *California Western International Law Journal*, 3 (1972), 112.

REISMAN, W. M., 'Responses to Crimes of Discrimination and Genocide', *Journal of International Law and Policy*, 1 (1971), 29.

RENOUF, A., 'The Present Force of the Minorities Treaties', *Canadian Bar Review 1950*, 804.

RICHARDSON, H. J., 'Self-Determination, International Law and the South African Bantustan Policy', *Columbia Journal of Transnational Law*, 17 (1978), 185.

ROBINSON, J., 'From Protection of Minorities to Promotion of Human Rights'. *Jewish Year Book of International Law 1948*, 115.

——'International Protection of Minorities: A Global View', *Israel Yearbook on Human Rights*, 1 (1971), 61.

RODLEY, N. S., 'Human Rights and Humanitarian Intervention: The Case Law of the World Court', *ICLQ*, 38 (1989), 321.

ROSTING, H., 'Protection of Minorities by the League of Nations', *AJIL*, 17 (1923), 641.

ROTH, S. J., 'Anti-Semitism and International Law', *Israel Yearbook on Human Righs*, 13 (1983), 208.

RUSSELL, H. S., 'The Helsinki Declaration: Brobdingnag or Lilliput?', *AJIL*, 70 (1976), 242.

SACERDOTI, G., 'New Developments in Group Consciousness and the International Protection of the Rights of Minorities', *Israel Yearbook on Human Rights*, 13 (1983), 116.

SANDERS, D., 'The UN Working Group on Indigenous Populations', *Human Rights Quarterly*, 11 (1989), 406.

SCHACHTER, O., 'The Twilight Existence of Non-Binding International Agreements', *AJIL*, 71 (1977), 296.

SCHEUNER, U., 'Conflict of Treaty Provisions with a "Peremptory" Norm of General International Law', *ZAORV*, 29 (1969), 28.

SCHWARZENBERGER, G., 'The Eichmann Judgment', *Current Legal Problems*, 15 (1962), 248.

——'The Problem of an International Criminal Law', *Current Legal Problems*, 3 (1950), 263.

SCHWELB, E., 'Crimes Against Humanity', *BYIL*, 23 (1946), 178.

——'International Court of Justice and the Human Rights Clauses of the United Nations Charter', *AJIL*, 66 (1972), 337.

——'Some Aspects of International Jus Cogens', *AJIL*, 61 (1967), 946.

——'The International Convention on the Elimination of All Forms of Racial Discrimination', *ICLQ*, 15 (1966), 996.

SHIHATA, I., 'The Treaty as a Law-Declaring and Custom-Making Instrument', *Revue Egyptienne de Droit International*, 22 (1966), 51.

SLOAN, F. B., 'The Binding Force of a "Recommendation" of the General Assembly in the United Nations', *BYIL*, 25 (1948), 1.

——'Human Rights, the United Nations and International Law', *Nordisk Tidsskrift for International Ret, Acta Scandinavica Juris Gentium*, 20 (1950), 30.

SOHN, L. B., 'Enforcing the Universal Declaration of Human Rights', *ICLQ*, 22 (1973), 161.

——'The Concept of Autonomy in International Law and the Practice of the United Nations', *Israel Law Review*, 15 (1980), 180.

——'The Universal Declaration of Human Rights: A Common Standard of Achievement', *Journal of the International Commission of Jurists*, 8 no. 2 (1967), 17.

SØRENSEN, M., 'The Quest for Equality', *International Conciliation*, 507 (March 1956), 291.

STAVENHAGEN, R., 'Indigenous Peoples, the State and the UN System: Claims, Issues and Proposals', *The Thatched Patio* 2, no. 3 (1989), 1.

SULLIVAN, D., 'Advancing the Freedom of Religion or Belief Through the UN Declaration on the Elimination of Religious Intolerance and Discrimination', *AJIL*, 82 (1988), 487.

SWEPSTON, L., 'The Indian in Latin America: Approaches to Administration, Integration and Protection', *Buffalo Law Review*, 27 (1978), 715.

THORNBERRY, P., 'Is there a Phoenix in the Ashes?—International Law and Minority Rights', *Texas International Law Journal*, 15 (1980), 421.

TOLLEY, H., 'The Concealed Crack in the Citadel: The United Nations Commission on Human Rights' Response to Confidential Communications', *Human Rights Quarterly*, 6, no. 4 (1980), 420.

TOUSSAINT, C. E., 'The Colonial Controversy in the United Nations', *Year Book of World Affairs 1956*, 177.

UMOZURIKE, U. O., 'The African Charter on Human and Peoples' Rights', *AJIL*, 77 (1983), 902.

VAN DIJK, P., 'The Final Act of Helsinki—Basis for a Pan-European System?', *Netherlands Year Book of International Law*, xi (1980), 97.

VAN DYKE, V., 'The Cultural Rights of Peoples', *Universal Human Rights*, 2, no. 2 (1980), 1.

——'Human Rights and the Rights of Groups', *American Journal of Political Science*, 18 (1974), 725.

——'The Individual, the State, and Ethnic Communities in Political Theory', *World Politics*, 23 (1966–7), 343.

VAN LANGENHOVE, F., 'Le Problème de la Protection des Populations Aborigènes aux Nations Unies', *Rec. des Cours*, 89 (1956), 321.

VERDOODT, A., 'Ethnic and Linguistic Minorities and the United Nations', *World Justice*, 11 (1969), 66.

VERDROSS, A., 'Jus Dispositivum and Jus Cogens in International Law', *AJIL*, 60 (1966), 55.

VIRALLY, M., 'Réflexions sur le "Jus Cogens" ', *AFDI* XII (1966), 5.

VUKAS, B., 'General International Law and the Protection of Minorities', *RDH*, 8 (1975), 41.

——'Le Projet de Declaration sur les Droits des Personnes Appartenant à des

Minorités Nationales, Ethniques, Religieuses et Linguistiques', *AFDI*, 23 (1979), 281.

ALDOCK, H., 'General Course in Public International Law', *Rec. des Cours*, 106 (1962), 1.

RIGHT, Q., 'National Courts and Human Rights—the Fujii Case', *AJIL*, 45 (1951), 62.

ᴣᴘᴇs, J. M., 'Les Problèmes Fondamentaux du Droit des Gens en Amérique', *Recueil des Cours*, 47 (1934), I, 5.

Index of States and Groups

Index